THE OXFORD HAND

PROCE
PHILOSOPHY AND
ORGANIZATION
STUDIES

THE OXFORD HANDBOOK OF

PROCESS

PHILOSOPHY

AND

ORGANIZATION

STUDIES

Edited by
JENNY HELIN,
TOR HERNES,
DANIEL HJORTH,
and
ROBIN HOLT

OXFORD
UNIVERSITY PRESS

Great Clarendon Street, Oxford, OX2 6DP,
United Kingdom

Oxford University Press is a department of the University of Oxford.
It furthers the University's objective of excellence in research, scholarship,
and education by publishing worldwide. Oxford is a registered trade mark of
Oxford University Press in the UK and in certain other countries

Published in the United States of America by Oxford University Press
198 Madison Avenue, New York, NY 10016, United States of America

British Library Cataloguing in Publication Data
Data available

Library of Congress Cataloging in Publication Data
Data available

ISBN 978-0-19-966935-6 (Hbk.)
ISBN 978-0-19-874653-9 (Pbk.)

Contents

List of Illustrations

About the Contributors

Kostas Amiridis, University of Lancaster, UK

Tore Bakken, BI Oslo, Norway

Jack Barbalet, Hong Kong Baptist University, China

Timon Beyes, Copenhagen Business School, Denmark

Christian Borch, Copenhagen Business School, Denmark

Robert Chia, University of Glasgow, UK

Robert Cooper, formerly University of Lancaster, UK

Bogdan Costea, University of Lancaster, UK

Ann L. Cunliffe, University of Bradford School of Management, UK

Matias Møl Dalsgaard, Copenhagen Business School, Denmark

Henrika Franck, Aalto University School of Business, Helsinki, Finland

Marius Gudmand-Høyer, Copenhagen Business School, Denmark

Wen Haiming, Renmin University, Beijing, China

Nancy Harding, University of Bradford, UK

Jenny Helin, University of Uppsala, Sweden

Tor Hernes, Copenhagen Business School, Denmark

Daniel Hjorth, Copenhagen Business School, Denmark

Robin Holt, Copenhagen Business School, Denmark

Heather Höpfl, formerly University of Essex, UK

Carien de Jonge, formerly Erasmus University, The Netherlands

Mihaela Kelemen, University of Keele, UK

Anders R. Kristensen, Copenhagen Business School, Denmark

Wendelin Kuepers, Karlshochschule, International University, Germany

Yuan Li, Renmin University, Beijing, China

Stephen Linstead, University of York, Leicester, UK

Nick Llewellyn, Warwick Business School, University of Warwick, UK

Thomas Lopdrup-Hjorth, Copenhagen Business School, Denmark

Philippe Lorino, ESSEC, France

John T. Luhman, Eastern New Mexico, USA

Saku Mantere, McGill University, Canada

Ajit Nayak, University of Exeter, UK

Richard P. Nielsen, Babson College, Boston, USA

Thomas C. Powell, University of Oxford, UK

Sverre Raffnsøe, Copenhagen Business School, Denmark

Robert Richardson, Cooper Union, New York, USA

Barbara Simpson, University of Strathclyde, UK

Bent Meier Sørensen, Copenhagen Business School, Denmark

Matt Statler, New York University, Stern, New York, USA

Chris Steyaert, University of St Gallen, Switzerland

Andrus Tool, University of Tartu, Estonia

Melissa Tyler, University of Essex, UK

Linh-Chi Vo, École de Management de Normandie, France

Elke Weik, University of Leicester, UK

Richard Weiskopf, University of Innsbruck, Austria

Gail Whiteman, University of Lancaster, UK

Hugh Willmott, Cass Business School, City University London and Cardiff Business School, University of Cardiff, UK

Mike Zundel, University of Liverpool, UK

CHAPTER 1

....

PROCESS IS HOW
PROCESS DOES

....

JENNY HELIN, TOR HERNES, DANIEL HJORTH, AND ROBIN HOLT

1.1 *SUR LE MOTIF*

....

PAUL CÉZANNE is painting Mount Sainte-Victoire, just to the east of his home in Aix in 1887. The closer he looks the less separated things become; the longer he is present the more querulous becomes the tree that edges the frame and the more hesitant the linear weave of walls and fields that pulls the frame into perspective. He has painted the mountain many times, each time anew, often leaving his canvasses *in situ* for weeks. He is not reproducing the mountain, but trying to reveal it, and in doing so increasingly contesting his own status as a separate, observing agent, looking anew, allowing Nature to come at him *sur le motif*. He is going after the nature of substance, of what 'is', but rather than outlines he is using modulations of tone that allow things to glow. Apparently fixed, isolated objects begin to burst through their edges, colours flow within one another as greens are pulled into more distant purples and pinks, which themselves are pulled back into occasional foreground details, hesitant to comply with the form-giving order to recede. In places he leaves the canvas bare, or stripped back, and these absences become as present as the carefully painted rock forms that rise and then fall into the Aur valley like a pendant human body. The mountain lies exposed to a distant sky and yet is brought right forward by the enveloping foreground play of leaves and branches whose bending, arching lines echo its purple ridge. An empty railway viaduct appears mid-distance, the headlong railroad of progress, the suggestion of yet further movement to come from within the trees and heat, the prospect of a mistral in linear steam.

Look at this painting, and no sooner do you rest on something than the eye is taken away anew, and more attentive you become to apparent order the less fixed is any individual element. Ehrenzweig (1967) calls the affect 'eye wander', the image feels right, not in detail, or likeness, but as an entire world inviting the viewer to come into the frame and be amid things. The haltering perspective of the image works in reverse to normal, it reaches out rather than closes off using a kind of reverse vanishing point whose pushing outwards implicates everything it touches. The image orchestrates tone, vibrancy, and substance into a coherent, arresting whole, and yet also upsets entirely the conceits of any neat organization of the world by allowing movement and insubstantiality equal voice amid a democracy of presence. Things are apparent, and then loosen. Cézanne's mountain is not 'a' mountain, but geology underway; it is both in the distance and before us, the colour of earth found in the colours of sunset; his building is not 'a' building but a generational residue of human toil and possession given architectural form and animated by feelings—perhaps envy, perhaps contentment; his leaf is not 'a' leaf but a seasonal placement of mute, breeze-blown life indifferent to the other lives it might shade and touch. There are patches everywhere, each gaining or losing form because of their being placed in communion with other patches, the whole an irreducible and irreconcilable rendition of a persistent concealing and revealing, showing us viewers as directly as is possible what it means for anything to be: an inexhaustible coming to presence of the world. In the words of Maurice Merleau-Ponty (1948/1964: 13), Cézanne wanted to show the sciences—human and natural—the primal condition of all nature by which any disciplinary perspective was made possible: '[H]e did not want to separate the stable things which we see and the shifting way in which they appear; he wanted to depict matter as it takes on form, the birth of order through spontaneous organization.'

Invited by such painting, we can step away from the image so as to describe, more in the language of the social science and humanities scholar, what Cézanne does. He does many things, but if we concentrate on this painting as a performance of process, in what sense is Cézanne helpful? The painting maintains its capacity to multiply and do many things for different viewers. There is no true painting, one that would correctly express the intentions of the painter, nor one that would generalize successfully a few rules about how it signifies a message or generates affect. However, there are several paintings that are true. As such a multiplicity the image resists becoming locked into the fixity of thingness, as it keeps open the endless capacity of seeing variation. The image conveys things without its being fixed into a whole-with-parts, and without the possibility of its being deconstructed into mute, causally implicated matter on the one hand, or metaphysically resonant meaning on the other. It is experienced as what Henri Bergson would call an intensive manifold, intuitively, and entire. Neither the painter nor the mountain act upon the world; both are implicated with one another, pulled along and mixed within the fluidity of fact. As such it is an expression of the world understood processually. Cézanne's biographer Alex Danchev suggests '[A]t the core of the Cézannian revolution is a decisive shift in the emphasis of observation, from the description of the thing apprehended to the process of apprehension itself' (2013: 338). It is such a decisive shift that also marks out the writers in this *Handbook*—process philosophers—for whom, in many different and vivid ways, there is little distinction to be had between experiencing, apprehending, understanding, and representing the ordering of things.

Process philosophy was originally a moniker for a small collection of philosophers including Alfred North Whitehead, Henri Bergson, and William James, and then extending back to Heraclitus. Yet it can be expanded to cover others interested in understanding and showing how the world is a world of organizing, how things swell, how life—including human lives—never reaches the settlement we presume or hope it might. In understanding the world processually, these writers work from within things, staying with them, suspicious of abstracting too far into hierarchies of being; they stick with things and the experience of things, rather than reaching into a more certain, stable, and invariant world of ideas. In this they reverse the usual relationship between ideas and life: instead of finding life wanting when set against immobile truths, values and ideals, they question the role of such divisions we are wont to impose on our understanding of life. Taking the world entire as they do, they do not draw such ready oppositional lines between the whole and the part, the pure and the tawdry, the essential and the apparent, all of which impute another, more perfect world.

Process thinking sticks with one world, this world, demanding what William James (1907: 55) calls 'an attitude of orientation—of looking away from first things, principles, categories supposed necessities; and of looking towards last things, fruits, consequences, facts'. These last things are all there 'is', and we are implicated in them entirely. Cézanne stays with last things, and it is both the 'things' (the actively indeterminate, reserve of surprises) and the 'staying' (belonging to in duration) that matters. The moment things are teased out of their 'thingness' is also when they leap into language and are on the route to some form of determination. So, staying with them is also to dwell in the indeterminate multiplicity that their potential becomings hold; being and becoming are entwined. Martin Heidegger, in his comments on Cézanne, describes this entwinement using the term presence. Cézanne's paintings are so good because they show both presence and what more cryptically Heidegger calls 'making present'. We viewers of paintings like Mont Sainte-Victoire typically see things present in their being: the empty, perhaps baleful railway viaduct, the smell of pines mingling with that of grass, the settlement of stone and earth. Yet attend to the painting and we might also see the making present: the horizon of disclosure by which all beings are revealed and concealed (Young, 2001: 156–7). Making present is particular to human forms of life (art, science) by which we experience and socially codify things, and yet which can only be experienced in the presence of things themselves. Cézanne's image of Mont Sainte-Victoire redounds with such awareness; the picture is no longer a representation, but an originating region where, from nothing, something emerges, and other things fall away into nothing. This is what Merleau-Ponty meant when he described it as showing the 'birth of order through spontaneous organization'. We glimpse what William James and Nishida called pure experience, a world unmediated by socially settled distinctions between object and subject. We begin to view the painting and right away we are met with a fragmentation of vision, the coming together of opposites (the near and far, the dark and light, the horizontal and vertical) spoken of in *Daodejing*, in whose paradoxical proximity comes a subtlety of understanding unavailable from a singular search for first things.

Staying with last things is thus a struggle with how experience of the world is socially coded. Cézanne is a painter and the mountain is part of the scenery which is to become the painter's motif. This is a set of relationships for which there are 'already constituted relations, contracted into bodies as habit' (Massumi, 2002: 82). Cézanne knows this, and struggles to overcome it. Overcome the platitudinous version of habituated meanings that saturate this situation and prevent the event of this mountain, here and now *for* Cézanne from being shown as being and becoming. How can he maintain his receptive power so that he can belong to the situation—the mountain, the scenery, the light, the canvas, the colours, his body and its capacities—and in the duration of this belonging, become *with* the event, the trace of which is the painting, that is then copied onto this book's cover, and many other places. Every belonging to a situation is a participation in a field of potential (all the multiplicities that the situation holds together via its many relationships) and the event (painting a picture, viewing it, reproducing it) is the release of this potential into a becoming. The whole multiplicity cannot be released into a creative becoming as bodies and their contexts provide conditions and limitations. There is an actual Mont Sainte-Victoire, which is the grounding component in the situation that includes Cézanne's body (and its capacities) and the scenery at large. But there is a virtual Mont Sainte-Victoire too, an idea, sense, affect that Cézanne wants to actualize as a painting. This is done as an intensive (passionate) process of receiving the situation so that one belongs to it, become with the event of 'painting it', and make this materialize on a canvas.

To us, this is a splendid example of process 'research': learning to see the world in its multiplicity, nurturing one's receptive capacity so one can abide with the world, belong to it or stay with it, and direct the forces of the event in an intensive process of becoming that creates by differentiating the quality of the new—an image of Mont Sainte-Victoire in this case. Using process philosophy in organization studies finds us similarly following intensive processes, provocations, a restless observation and curiosity that might, with diligence, be inspired as was the expressiveness of Cézanne. Going into organization we find what James called a whole 'blooming buzzing' condition. This is the basis from which the subjects, objects, norms, procedures, and judgements arise, all of them the separating abstractions of the researcher to which we are socially habituated in thought (with its representations and relations) and action (with its goals, and regimented movement). Process philosophy begins with undifferentiated unity existing prior to any individuation, even the individual—there is raw experience prior to an individuated conscious being, there is desire productive of subjects. Such a world of last things is not readily confined by the concepts and categories of language if, as process thinking suggests, we are to remain with, and attend to, experience as we find it. To the extent we can become part of the picture (an admittedly poor word to use referring to the painting), to the extent we belong to it, we also become *with* it. This, being part of life, staying with the things, maintaining an openness towards the multiplicity of things, we will try to describe using aspects of process.

1.2 THINKING PROCESS

On the basis of working with process philosophers and the chapters in this book, we have arrived at a way to think process that has crystallized into five aspects: temporality, wholeness, openness, force, and potentiality. Together our five aspects are an attempt to provide what could be described as themes in a musical score guiding the process of thinking and enquiring processually into process. As aspects, following Wittgenstein, they do not supplant one another, but can persist together, with one dawning and others being occluded, without thereby being lost. Not all writers devote themselves equally to all five aspects, yet all resonate in some way. Equally important, all five aspects touch on emerging concerns in organization studies. Temporality, dynamism, and experiences of time arise in longitudinal, sensemaking, discourse and historical studies, as well as in ethnographic, genealogical, and narrative analyses. Wholeness, or resisting dualisms, finds expression in studies of materiality and technology, of gender and identity, and of actor-network analysis. It also forms a concern for the entire gamut of studies concerned with language itself, such as communication, rhetoric, and performativity, all related in various ways under the elusive label of (post-)structuralist. Openness, understanding things in relation to 'the other', is of interest in ethics, institutional work studies and studies of human relations more generally, in policy communities, political economy, studies of new organizational forms, often related to innovation, entrepreneurship, and non-governmental organizations. Force, intensity, the enquiry after movement, is what concerns studies of creativity, innovation, and (again) entrepreneurship, operations management and supply chains, and governance, as well as power, resistance, and influence (such as governmentality studies) and gender and identity studies. Finally, potentiality, that which 'might become', is what grounds strategy studies and broader enquiry into the possibility of alternative economic and social settings (such as in social entrepreneurship).

Using the metaphor of (musical) score to describe this way of thinking and enquiring processually into process stresses the importance of music and dance for our understanding of process. For thinking process there is then a task presented to us, which Nigel Thrift describes as 'following being in its genesis, by accomplishing the genesis of thought in parallel with the object' (Thrift, 2007: 256) or 'ontogenesis' or, again, as 'the self-production of being in becoming' (Massumi, 2011: 84). Let us then move on to this score, held together by five aspects, which describes how we relate ourselves to the task of ontogenesis, i.e. what orients us when thinking process. Following this we will move on to propose how we can 'do process research'.

Temporality. The passing of time represents the perishability of the world, what Whitehead called the passage of nature. The perishability of the world is what creates its multiple possibilities of creating new forms. Bergson, Heidegger, Whitehead, and Mead all engage intensely with time, where vulgar or clock time, left to itself, constitutes a flattening and deadening of what they feel is a more primordial, lived, or qualitative time—what Bergson called duration. Duration, Deleuze says, is 'inseparable from the movement of its actualization' (1988: 42–3). Time, as duration, loosens the thingness of things as their becomings are revealed, while not depriving them of their right to thingness. The incessant shift between becoming and thingness is temporally conditioned, as presents turn into events to be modified with the passing of time. The great enigma is that of the present, which for Bergson is a non-numerical duration in which the world opens as an irreversible, intense manifold of experience whose multiplicity refuses the stabilizing embrace of intellectual definition. For Mead, on the other hand, the present is forever emergent, and does not exist as a stretch of time per se, while Whitehead sought to incorporate human experience of the present as a 'slab of duration', something akin perhaps to Heidegger's 'spans', though these are woven with an accompanying sense of mortality, a being-unto-death Peter Sloterdijk twists gracefully into a being-unto-life. Garfinkel, extending from phenomenology, associated the present with indeterminacy, which confers upon it creative agency and the possiblility of acquiring 'eventness' (Bakhtin). Processually minded writers, while being loath to take distinctions for granted, would open for understanding actors thrown into time, while seeking to incorporate how they establish their existence with the use of ordered time, such as schedules, clocks, and calendars. Being in time means that we are forever wedged between the absolute absences of what has been and what may become. Process thinking invites us to treat past and future as blank slates upon which the processual narrative is inscribed, slates which would be the same token signals that there is no continuity of future without continuity of past, nor is there change of future without a change of past.

Wholeness. The intimacy between the whole and the parts is a persistent theme in process philosophy, where the thrust of their thinking is how the one emerges from the many, or vice versa. Wholeness, for example, means we cannot think away society and focus on the individual, nor think away the individual and focus on society; a closeness that John Dewey describes as the sympathy between intention (individual) and habit (collective), the latter allowing the former space to become aware of what is of situational significance, the former endowing the latter with the possibility of transformation. It also means we cannot think away the body from the experience of thought (Merleau-Ponty), nor thoughts from extensions of the body. Actors and organizations are simultaneously consubstantial and empirically inseparable; they are understood in the light of how they produce each other, and themselves. Massumi (2002: 71) provides a condensed description of such wholeness: 'they might be seen as differential emergences from a shared realm of relationality that is one with becoming—and belonging'. Process thinking takes the world whole, connected, and permits connections between everything. Bergson expands on such by suggesting that such an insight that such connectivity is not spatial (a mathematical way of looking at the world folded out, map-like, into representations of things, parts of things, and possible relationships between them) but relational (space is in things rather than things being in space), whereby we have to appreciate the varied simultaneity of experience. In our own experience, for example, change occurs to us entirely, not in parts, and the change only makes sense in relation to a persistent awareness of (connection to) wholeness from which the possibility of change emerges. The whole alerts us to what is not sensed as being there; being absent, which does not mean that it is non-existent. Spinoza's ontology thinks *one* substance (God or Nature, used interchangeably) is all that exists, and everything else is connected as modes and attributes. How something becomes is always a question of how it is related and what forces are at play in such relations. Relationality indicates connective capacity, how in joining the world (rather than separating from it) we hazard an improvisation along what Deleuze calls lines of flight. There is always a potential for change maintained via such openness, which always makes relations and situations spill over, revealing the excessive creativity of life, far exceeding our intellectual capacity to represent it.

Openness. The openness of the world begins with awareness of one self as being open. The open self is emphasized by Mead as a continuous process of self-construction in a process of social accomplishment that realizes neither a fixed nor an essentialist being. In her analysis of Adolf Eichmann, Arendt showed how an elastic self, ready for different inscriptions, might under certain conditions lead to the monstrous and absurd, entreating us to be wary of such exposure. Bakhtin too emphasizes openness. Inspired by Dostoevsky's novels, he uses the notion of 'unfinalizability' to underline that closed, finalized accounts of our world are a reduction of that which is life-giving since 'nothing conclusive has yet taken place in the world, the ultimate word of the world and about the world has not yet been spoken' (Bakhtin, 1984: 166); ambiguity is continuously at play here. Since the world is open, ordering is a project that is 'always ongoing and ever unfinished; and it is always opposed to the essential messiness of the world' (Morson and Emerson, 1990: 139). That is why absolute order can never be an actual factum; it is an ideal and all kinds of abstract logics and theories by which the social world is neatly put in boxes is superficial. Concepts too, as Deleuze stressed, might be made more open, less assertive, more nomadic, without losing their capacity to transform what the poet T.E. Hulme (1936: 215) called the 'cindery' nature of direct experience into something graspable, ordered. Here abstractions illuminate by crystallizing experience, intensifying it through grammatical or aesthetic organization, rather than generalizing everything in a common denominator light of evening out. Concepts can be created and enlisted to provoke as much as to clarify. As people, things, and technologies share this openness, it is our capacity for duration, for sensing the 'span' or 'bloc' of becoming (as Bergson, Deleuze, Whitehead, and James all were concerned with) that will decide to what extent we can understand such phenomena processually. Openness brings us into encounters with absence. Typically we consider absence with aversion: a hole to be filled, a territory to be claimed and occupied, a wasteland to be made productive, a darkness to be lit, rather than go along with it, treating it as a provocative ally of analysis, like the use of the unmarked space in Spencer-Brown's mathematics of form. Perhaps this urge to complete, to find presence, finds its apotheosis in organization studies in the question of the human agent and agency, with what Sloterdijk calls the mania for identity, a preoccupation with how best to articulate and protect the agent as the bearer and measure of all things, all the while forgetting that it is an accompanying insubstantiality through which any self carries equal potential. This mania is so prevalent that even otherness itself becomes its own form of presence, as in De Beauvoir's analysis of women being given the largely servile ontological status of 'other'. Openness further points us into the aspect of force, which is ever only observable as effect, but which maintains its virtual reality while producing these effects. Kirkegaard's concept of freedom (openness) and the necessity to decide and shape the self provides an example of how openness calls for force.

Force. When we insist on staying with life, without resort to external start points such as 'structure' or 'desire' as the cause of change, we become alert to the dynamics of the social and self, but as creative forces. Dewey, for one, argued against the 'veil that shuts man off from nature', joining in Whitehead's (and Bergson's) plea to consider process as creative energy rather than interacting masses. Stability is reached in hierarchies, yet a hierarchy is always a contested relationship between dominating and dominant forces; forces are always relative to other forces, and their strength and accomplishments. Forces, Nietzsche teaches us, are either active or reactive, but never fully graspable if not related to what he calls a will to power, which can be either negative or affirmative. Reactive forces are adaptive and limiting; they separate active forces from what they can do, and deny active forces or turn against themselves. Active forces find their way to the limits of their consequences, and affirm their difference (Deleuze, 1983, reading Nietzsche). We understand organizational life not so much from positions, structural coordinates, or subjectivities. Instead, we follow how dominant and dominated forces shape subjectivities, how subjectification affects what can be said, by whom and when/where. Force is perhaps the monarch of all processual characteristics, that which gives vent when we dissolve the view of the organization as configured by positions, co-ordinates, and sovereign agents, or of our intellect configured solely as an organ of utility and measurement that begins and works towards immobile things such as concepts (like Kant's antinomies). Force allows our intuition in a capacity to work with force in all its sinuous play (Bergson, 1922: 32–9). Foucault, for example, spent much effort on describing and analysing forces operating in the social, normalizing the expectation that certain effects in behaviour would habitually be expected to 'be performed'—force, in this case, securing the predictability, and therefore control, of behaviour. His empirical archival work follows how dominant and dominated forces shape subjectivities, how subjectification affects what can be said, by whom, and when/where. Tarde, Dewey, Peirce, and De Beauvoir all worked similarly on how force is subjectivity, upending the idea that force is what emanates from the decision of a subject, bringing to questionability the very basic and beguiling idea that there is such a thing as a 'subject' to be found, once all the characteristics, habits, the lived effects of time, and attributes have been stripped back.

Potentiality. The concept of potential that qualifies process as the production of the new is for Whitehead (1929: 28) an awareness that '[T]he reality of the world exceeds that of objects, for the simple reason that where objects are, there has also been their becoming. And where becoming has been, there is already more to come. The being of an object is an abstraction from its becoming' (Massumi, 2011: 6). Thus potential is a curious melange of time and force, a 'felt moreness to ongoing experience', as Massumi

(2002: 141) puts it. Potential receives its most persistent and original airing in the work of Spinoza, who understood a body as dynamic composition of movements and rest. Not so much actual physical movement, but the capacity to enter into movement and rest, which he called its power to affect and be affected. Potentiality can also describe the virtual powers of becoming that characterize all life and into which we are thrown. This becoming carries no causal initiation or origin point, there is no sentient or even material agency starting something. Process thinking finds such an ontology of starting points upended by what Dewey calls one of complicit experience; we do not act upon the world, but through belonging to it. Here Bergson, again, is careful to note we maintain life's openness and recognize the multiplicity involved in experience; there is, he suggests, little difference between the real and possible where the former is a spooling off from precedent. Creation needs to be understood as actualization of the virtual, rather than as realization of the possible, without conflating the virtual with the unreal (Bergson, Deleuze). For the real would already be in the possible, and all of the possible cannot be realized, and realization is thus a limited copying of the possible, i.e. no creation. Actualization does not need to realize anything. The virtual is real, but lacks actuality, and this requires difference and creation—for it needs to establish a contextual-relational presence in an ongoing world, where forces and will to power already are at work. Gregory Bateson refers to this contextualized presence as ontogenesis, extending the biological term describing the maturing of an organism through its life cycle to cover the environmental conditions that require adaptive behaviours from organisms which in turn prosthetically reach out into the wider environment; a beaver's lodge being a classic example of how such ontogenesis broaches any distinction between being, environment, and presencing. Where human thought has gone awry, processually speaking, is in thinking their constructions, unlike those of the 'thoughtless' beavers, are designed through a unique capacity for reason by whose operations they presume themselves separate from the world, occupying a perspective from which to impose already elaborated plans (see Ingold, 2000: 175). Process thinking eschews such separatist metaphysics, instead finding human exposure to the wider environment akin to that of animals, feeling (in sensation, perception, action, and thought all as one), in a tentative, emergent, and relational way, life being what Bergson (1911/2002: 27) calls 'a current passing' through which all organisms move and flow. It is from such awareness that Thrift (2007) and Massumi (2002) also refer to ontogenesis, but here referring to a specifically human form of consciousness and thought as that which accompanies the genesis of being as the mode by which being dwells, to use Heidegger's term. In dwelling with the wider environment we not only learn to skilfully accommodate ourselves appropriately to the wider world of things (materials, skies, and even spirits), but we do so also in imagination. Here thought exposes itself to the unhomely, the strange, the different, that which is other than but which invites us to strive, to open up, and move along lines of flight. It is through this ontogenesis as the thought accompanying of our evolution of being that we become aware of our self-productive potential as that which makes being present in various possibilities of actualization.

We now go on to think with these five aspects of process philosophy as we elaborate on how we can engage in process research.

1.3 Doing Process Research

Process philosophy encourages us to follow the goings-on of organization, finding a world of swelling, falling away, erupting, and becalming without rest. The *techne* or craft of doing research becomes more like following, a going with things, rather than attempting to capture and fix them. To investigate organizational life is to use representational concepts whilst being attentive to how they can, in turn, use us, confining our vision with prescriptions of neatness that find us smoothing over the frayed and recalcitrant aspects of experience. We cannot but help use concepts, categories, words. Yet we might become wary of how in 'producing' knowledge we have had a tendency to reach after glass-smooth claims whose clarity and transparency resist falsification; knowledge and perfectibility become synonyms. Wittgenstein (1980: II: 289) finds this tendency to avoid the 'rough ground' a form of sublimation. This sublimation is experienced as exactitude (knowledge is refined through precision, typically manifest in an ascendency of numerical or algebraic symbols), exclusion (strong knowledge claims resist encroachment from rivals), and entailment (claims are set into logical sequences that themselves become institutionalized settings for further claims) (Hänfling, 2000: 122–4). In many ways process philosophy is method—the nature of being is revealed in the disclosive forms of life by which beings are both given vent and fall away. This though is a far cry from the typical appreciation of method taught, say, to social scientists. Here the doing of research implies an explicit use of method from which there are a raft of options to choose, each appropriate to an already specified task at hand. In this sense the 'doing' means following or building a way that in turn makes the search somehow apparent (transparent) to readers. Re-search entrusts methods' moulds, templates, and rules to secure repetitions that generate (statistically) consistent results. Things are identified, their elements parsed, and their context unfolded. Concepts like variables are employed to identify what these things are, categories like dependency used to represent possible relationships between them, and classes are used as generalities by which analysed variables find homes as being of a type. This all assumes a passive world of mass rather than energy, adaptation rather than creativity, and retention rather than protention. Passive in the sense of a world assumed amenable to measurement and so transparent, a world that can be confined to 'still life' nicely set up (as in a laboratory, or a case study) and looked upon with the enquiring, trained mind of an outside observer using neutral (and hence dispassionate, translatable) language. Values and perspectives come in of course, yet these are attended to honestly (limitations of research), and compensated for through techniques like triangulation.

There is no presumption that such analysis will ever reach the status of covering law, but nevertheless that some form of explanatory framing of organizational phenomena can be realized, affording proponents awareness of the organizational world unavailable to everyday common sense. The world is presented as what Bergson calls an extensive manifold, a region of things in relation to one another. This can be very complex, and changeable, rendered through narrative as much as strict propositional logic, whilst all the time researchers are being keyed into the demands of making apparent: the approach they took, the rationale for doing so, and the knowledge being produced.

1.3.1 What is the Way of Process Research then?

A processual way of relating to the world is revealed already here: *how* something becomes determines what it *is* (i.e. that it becomes). It therefore never 'is' in a fixed way. Its being is its becoming, as Nietzsche discovered and as emphasized by Whitehead. Method, from the Greek *meta* ('after') and *hodos* ('way, motion, travelling, journey') means to follow a way. There is both unity and distinction here. From the beginning Heraclitus noted that the way up and down are one and the same, indicating the whole-ness (connectivity) and dynamic multiplicity of the world and time. Then Nietzsche stressed that whilst he had his way, all others must follow theirs, recognizing that your thinking is part of the world and its becoming, that you are following things in life, that you want to actively participate in moving human life beyond its inherited boundaries, and all this requires a different gaze and the courage to make your way. Foucault, renew-ing the force of this message through his own method of genealogy, was careful in mak-ing his way through the accidents, turns, and events that provided for habituated and discursively reproduced concepts, styles of thinking, and talking, their force being regis-tered as true, normal, useful, or good... or not.

So to resist showing 'the' way of doing things, when we want to describe how process research can be done, we find ourselves on the verge of doing it. We are pulled by a per-formative urge to make with language, to keep life alive in language. We are thus not seeking to secure consistent repetition, but through imitation find difference—'Ah, now I can go on' said Wittgenstein, describing how we might follow rather than obey rules. We see no point in pressing an artificial *Stillleben* model upon the world and examine how we can make it fit. Here we can take inspiration from Cézanne who, forever assidu-ous in developing technical skill and attentiveness, and who remains in amid things *sur le motif*, paints movement and intensity presented entire (without pre-designed, stable elements). At its own ground process research is work that transforms this world to the extent that in studying we imprint the provisional world we experience in and on our bodies and make it part of the coming to be. There is little distinction to be made between researcher and researched in a relationship that belongs to the world, describ-ing it carefully and without reference to an external, objective, detached 'being'. We write *for* something—the missing world-to-come that we want this *Handbook* to have made incipient through its descriptions, examples, lives of writers.

More specifically, then, on the basis of the five aspects we have introduced in section 1.3, what would we emphasize as guides of conduct, building, and walking the roads of process research? Importantly, the aspects introduced would more specifically come to us here as forces. As we learn from Nietzsche, the qualities of forces are either active or reactive, and he urges us to become more active, an urge echoed by Simone de Beauvoir's political commitments, by Arne Naess and Gregory Bateson, who advocate an acknowledgment of nature made possible in activism, and equally forcefully, though more mathematically, by Spencer-Brown for whom all distinction begins with an action of splitting. These active qualities derive from the will to power, which itself is either negative or affirmative. If we relate affirmatively to the active becoming of life we will also increase our connective capacity to things in the world and thus acquire a capacity to see or listen to this life-in-process. Having become skilled in this sense, we would better know how to build our way, how to research processually, and by implication use research to change the world while describing it selectively in its richness. Like with the bee, we could use active forces to act upon forces, bend them, learn how to belong to the flower, how to become under the influence of nectar, how to form a temporary bloc of becoming with the daisy that has opened up, increased its interactive capacity. If we summarize, the following is how we would make our way, how we can engage in process research:

Belonging to and becoming with the world. Interactively staying open to one's involvement in the world and being part of the world's dynamics and spontaneity (Naess) while not losing sight of its materiality (Massumi, 2002). Process research trusts the concreteness of the world and recognizes the writer's involvement in it; it is entirely and utterly empirical. We are always already engaged with the world, our thinking participates in its becoming and our descriptions are part of how it changes. We have no access to a neutral outside position, from which we can observe the world and inform it how it properly needs to be corrected (as in un-reflexive so-called critical theory). It also means we recognize the power of examples, and that examples are contextual and personal (although not subjective) in the relational sense. Let's take this *Handbook* as an example. This is an example of process philosophy, but it has become what it is because of its context being shaped by organization studies' engagement with process thinking. What it is is a question of how it has become this specific process philosophy *Handbook*; a *Handbook* ready at hand for organization studies scholars in particular. It also means that although there are four bodies that have performed the subjectivity of editors in this process, and forty-eight authors, the *Handbook* cannot be understood as a subjective expression. Apart from it being intensely collective, there is also a desire for process philosophy and process thinking (in organization studies) that is productive as such. This desire has produced the subject position 'editor for a *Handbook on Process Philosophy and Organization Studies*' and we happen to be the four that have acted, and affirmed that subjectivity, as the authors the request for authorship. We can understand the becoming of the *Handbook* more processually to the extent that we belong, interactively, with life and follow its 'achieving being' as a thing, and how the subject position as editor is entangled with this process. This is a process that also and properly includes publishers, language editors, printers, contracts, supply chains, inks, grammar, and so on. The *experience* is thus never reducible to the objective truth about it. Beyond the objective truth or the experience objectified, there is (Massumi, 2002 reminds us) always the situation

(Dewey), the event (Whitehead), and the interaction of the elements or ingredients in the experience and the effect of their interaction (Merleau-Ponty). Truth, then, would be the realism of acknowledging this multiplication of things and experiences: the objective nature of it, the interaction of its ingredients, and the effect of that interaction. Being with that, staying with this multiplicity in its becoming, this is characteristic of doing process research.

The particular. If what something is is determined (contextually-relationally stabilized) by how it becomes, this means that each thing is a multiplicity of becomings relative to the connections it makes (and is potentially capable of). Small things matter if attended to. A flower is one thing to the human seeing, but another to a bee's seeing. The bee's seeing is produced by a particular desire that the flower can satisfy. In the connection with the bee, the flower becomes something in particular (e.g. a pollinator, a life-giver, a feast). In connection with the human, several other potential becomings could determine what the flower is, in the context of a particular relation (a symbol for love, a sign of summer, a weed) and interaction (looking at, picking, giving). The processual nature of things, the world, knowledge—the knowing subject will thus suggest we attend to the particular compositions of this multiplicity that is stabilized in a context of enquiry. The challenge, one again we suggest we can learn from Cézanne, is to increase our receptive capacity, to see more. All these particularities are experienced because of a studiously developed receptivity, a power to be affected by listening softly. Yet this focus on the particular must not be confused with 'methodological individualism' or 'the action frame of reference', for it is not a question of explaining the social by starting with individual action and intention. The particular is here about the power of the example as well as the (Wittgensteinian) aspect's capacity to change the way you see the world. One aspect in your field study story, when focused on, alters 'the whole' that the story is about. Laughter in a meeting, for example, reveals the relationship between a dominant and a dominated, and the whole room (as well as your study) changes. There is no priority given to the doer above the deed (Nietzsche). Where traditional research would focus on the actor to understand the deed, the process researcher is more interested in how the deed (including the said) arouses connections (Bakhtin), or conceals potential. There is an interest in following the deed, to see how following it changes the way we see the whole of which the deed is one part. The process writer would thus be interested in how the particular *now* generates its context, as well as how the context makes the particular achieve being in a specific way. If there is a guide, supplementing Nietzsche's urge that we build our own way in our study, it would be Foucault's (no doubt Nietzsche-inspired) genealogical tracing of how the particular has become what it is today, and, focusing on the particular, in the context of its emergence, studying how it generates its context where we presently find it.

Performativity. Studying the world processually acknowledges the performative nature of research. Research, in the non-representational sense, does not leave the world alone when describing and modelling it. It takes part as we imagine relationships and 'explanations' without regulating origins or objectives anchored as touchstones of truth. In the absence of such regulating structure (an ontological condition for positivist epistemology) we have discourse and play. Play, Thrift notes, 'is a process of performative experiment…in other words, about producing variation' (2007: 119). Experiencing the world via performativity makes us leave theory as representation behind. Non-representational theorizing is attentive to practices and how they play out in everyday life (and its productive sets of institutions, cultures, habits). It demands that experience and thought are seen as temporal and partly irreversible processes rooted in transformative action involving sociality and materiality (Peirce). This upgrades the importance of time and materiality and bodies and their durations, speeds/slowness, and movements. Research shapes practices (rather than representing them) and generates 'handles' through which we deal with, add to, and change the world. In addition, performativity makes us alert to affect and intensities as pre-individual forces that are productive of relations, settings, situations, and encounters. Affect enrols bodies in events and makes situations productive of subjectivities rather than subjectivities productive of situations. Desire for changing a situation sets up encounters with bodies, intensifies the social, and initiates subjectification processes. The performativity of time and space, the need to make room for the new, and the politics of such room-making would also become more central. Attending to performativity makes our imaginative theorizing more realistic in so far as the world becomes processually by multiplying in particular relationships (as noted earlier). A flower is not a flower, but becomes a 'flower' in particular relationships and contexts, generates variation relative to modes of engagement: a flower can be the access to someone loved, can be food for a bee, can be shelter for a bug, a remnant of a past life.

In terms of writing, where would this bring us? We're thinking of the more performative ways of writing: manifestos, poems, letters, and even diaries (cf. Richardson, 1997). These ways of writing are all personal, expressive, and, yes performative, oriented towards the particular and receptive to change as indicated by the details. You need to listen softly (as Nietzsche puts it in *Thus Spoke Zarathustra*) to receive these thoughts/words, so as to write the world while participating in it, rather than from an elevated or external position. Processual-performative writing would acknowledge that thinking and writing is part of the world, changes the world, and affects it. Thrift (2007) has then suggested we theorize the world in ways that maintain the push that keeps the world rolling over; an effective (or performative) rather than representational way of understanding the world. Lingis (1998) likewise suggests that we write from within, even impressionistically; from such first-person fragmentation he is then able to reformulate Socrates' dictum, arguing that 'the unlived life is not worth examining', and a lived life is a life of bodily movement, desire, difficulty, mundanity in which we start with life and stay there.

1.4 THIS VOLUME

What then can you expect in the continuation of this volume? The organizing logic of the *Handbook* is straightforward. Each chapter deals with the work of a specific writer and addresses their life and work, and how this could potentially be useful for working processually in organization studies. While it is common to structure a handbook like this thematically we found that too limiting for our purpose. Since we see process philosophy not as a specific theory to be used but rather a way of thinking, we rather wanted to spend time on how these active writers might make us see things anew. This way of organizing the *Handbook* has made it possible to enrich process thinking in organization and management studies primarily in two ways.

First, it shows the multitude of writers whose work can serve as a starting point for our work and thereby widen its philosophical grounding. While some of the figures included are the 'main suspects' such as Whitehead, Bergson, and James, there are yet others whom are not as often addressed from a process perspective such as Dilthey and Tarde. However, focusing on the processual gist of their work widens the philosophical heritage that we can make use of in our research. In reading about different writers it becomes clear how some of them resonate and build on each other while yet others are at odds. This is significant for making process research a vibrant research community where a multitude of research approaches are welcomed. Not structuring the *Handbook* thematically is thus an attempt to increase its virtual capacity for actual interconnections. We encourage you to read the *Handbook* in this way, as a set of texts that increases your capacity to connect and therefore multiply the thematic uses of the separate discussions.

Second, the departure from a specific writer gives us space to elaborate more in-depth with the work and not only scrape the surface, which is a way to deepen our understanding of the processual concepts available to us. To further the deepened understanding of a writer's work each chapter also addresses some of the background and context of the person, their ideas and actions, and their community. This cannot of course be compared with a biography, but at least puts some emphasis on the contextual surrounding of significance for going along with any particular writer. In addition, it emphasizes the importance of the relations and makes clear that what the relations do is something in addition to what the related parts do, which per se is an important aspect of processual thinking.

Contributors to the *Handbook* were invited to concentrate on three things: the (intellectual) background of the writer, their work with a focus on the processual gist of their ideas, and the potential contribution to organization studies research. Hence, we didn't ask for a complete review but rather a selective choice of that which is helpful for us doing process-based work. Most of the authors who have contributed in this book are from organization studies (broadly defined), since we thought they would be most suitable for relating to the current as well as prospective conversations on process thinking in our field. All the chapters but one are written about others, the exception being Robert Cooper's chapter on process thinking. This can be treated as both an afterword, and beginning. Cooper has been a transitional and transformational figure in organization studies, bringing process thinking to bear by exemplifying what it means to think processually. His chapter is his last such exemplification.

The point of the *Handbook* is not to philosophize over some themes or problems. The point is not to invite organization scholars to become philosophers in a text. The point is to have writer's thinking affect how we think process in the context of organization studies. This is what this *Handbook* does. This is how it is how it does.

REFERENCES

Bakhtin, M.M. (1984). *Problems of Dostoevsky's Poetics*, ed. and trans. C. Emerson (Manchester: Manchester University Press).

Bergson, H. (1907/1922). *Creative Evolution* (London: Macmillan).

—— (1911/2002). Perception of Change, in K. Ansell Pearson and J. Mullarkey (eds), *Henry Bergson: Key Writings* (New York: Continuum): 248–67.

Danchev, A. (2013). *Cézanne: A Life* (London: Profile Books).

Deleuze, G. (1983). *Nietzsche and Philosophy*, trans. Hugh Tomlinson (New York: Continuum, 2006).

Ehrenzweig, A. (1967). *The Hidden Order of Art* (Berkeley: University of California Press).

Hänfling, O. (2000). *Philosophy and Ordinary Language* (London: Routledge).

Hulme, T.E. (1936). *Speculations* (London: Keegan Paul).

Ingold, T. (2000). *The Perception of the Environment* (London: Routledge).

James, W. (1907). *What is Pragmatism?* (London: Longman's Green and Co.).

——(1996). *Essays in Radical Empiricism* (Lincoln: University of Nebraska Press).

Lingis, A. (1998). *The Imperative* (Bloomington: Indiana University Press).

Massumi, B. (2002). *Parables for the Virtual: Movement, Affect, Sensation* (Durham, NC: Duke University Press).

—— (2011). *Semblance and Event: Activist Philosophy and the Occurent Arts* (Cambridge, MA: MIT Press).

Merleau-Ponty, M. (1948/1964). Cezanne's Doubt, in his *Sense and Non-Sense*, trans. H.L. Dreyfus and P.A. Dreyfus (Evanston, IL: Northwestern University Press): 9–25.

Morson, G.S. and Emerson, C. (1990). *Mikhail Bakhtin: Creation of a Prosaics* (Stanford, CA: Stanford University Press).

Richardson, L. (1997). *Fields of Play. Constructing and Academic Life* (New Jersey: Rutgers University Press).

Thrift, N. (2007). *Non-Representational Theory: Space, Politics, Affect* (London: Routledge).

Whitehead, A.N. (1929). *Process and Reality* (New York: Macmillan).

——(1968). *Modes of Thought* (New York: Free Press).

Wittgenstein, L. (1980). *Remarks on the Philosophy of Psychology*, Volume 1, ed. G.E.M. Anscombe and G.H. von Wright, trans. G.E.M. Anscombe; Volume 2, ed. G.H. von Wright and H. Nyman, trans. C.G. Luckhardt and M.A.E. Aue (Oxford: Basil Blackwell).

Young, J. (2001). *Heidegger's Philosophy of Art* (Cambridge: Cambridge University Press).

CHAPTER 2

··

LAOZI'S *DAODEJING* (6TH CENTURY BC)

··

JACK BARBALET

2.1 INTRODUCTION

Daodejing, as it is written in the modern pinyin romanization of Chinese, or *Tao te ching* in the earlier Wade-Giles romanization, consists of 81 aphoristic and poetic chapters of what is known today as a mystical, religious, or philosophical text written by Laozi, or Lao Tzu in Wade-Giles romanization. In fact Laozi is a mythical figure and the *Daodejing* is a compilation of sayings relating to engagement in political and practical affairs in early China. It began to acquire extraneous meanings long after its original compilation in the fourth century BC.

Section 2.2 of this chapter discusses the text of *Daodejing*, its difficulties, origin, and purpose. As a handbook for aspirants to state rule, *Daodejing* is focused on a practical understanding of both action and process. The character of *Daodejing* as an exposition of process, and the work's treatment of the unfolding of process through paradox, is outlined in section 2.3. Moving from paradox to the mechanisms of process in imminence and latency, section 2.4 provides an exposition of the idea that something comes from nothing. Section 2.5 shows that while *Daodejing* is often seen as advocating a philosophy of non-action, there is instead an important understanding of a particular type of action within process that is given exposition in this text.

2.2 THE TEXT AND ITS USES

Daodejing is a work about which there is little agreement. It is a source of Chinese and East Asian reflective traditions, frequently translated into European languages and confusingly subject to diverse and starkly contrasting description and interpretation.

Earlier disagreements concerning the date of its first appearance and its authorship are now more or less settled; it existed in written form from approximately 300 BC with earlier oral transmission and is a compilation of sayings. *Daodejing* appears obscure and ambiguous without an understanding of its form, background, and purpose. It has acquired exotic meaning as more recent commentators have brought their own preoccupations to it, especially philosophical and religious.

While there are a number of problems surrounding *Daodejing*, none of them are fatal for its application in the type of thinking about social and allied processes outlined in this chapter. As *Daodejing* is the work of many hands, there is a possible problem of consistency and coherence in its point of view. Emerson (1995) indicates that *Daodejing* is a stratified text consisting of a number of historically sequential layers, each preoccupied with distinct themes. At the same time he shows that no theme is absent from any single layer and that there are continuities between them; any differences which can be identified might be understood as developments rather than disjunctive departures. While the text is without a single authorial purpose, there are nevertheless organizing principles unifying it, largely because *Daodejing* is a collection of sayings developed in and applied by a group, community, or college of moral-political thinkers and practioners. More will be said about this later.

Current scholarly discussion acknowledges three distinctive manifestations of *Daodejing*. There is a problem, then, in determining which one is authoritative. The so-called Wang Bi version has been the more or less consistently referred to since the third century AD. This text was collated by the post-Han dynasty scholar, Wang Bi, from 'as many as six different versions available to him' (Hansen, 1992: 400). During the late twentieth century archeological findings have provided two additional extant forms, known by the names of the location of the sites in which they were found as the Mawangdui and Guodian texts. These are each different in a number of ways from the traditionally accepted version and also from each other. There is no evidence, however, that one is a more original version of *Daodejing* than another (Hansen, 1992: 201–2). While it is possible to distinguish extant texts in philological and archeological terms (Hansen, 1992: 400–1), what must also be given proper attention is their influence on subsequent discussion and elaboration. In this sense the Wang Bi text remains the principal version.

Another problem, for those who do not read Old or Archaic Chinese in which *Daodejing* was written, is that of translation. But before translation there is the problem of Old Chinese itself, a language which was used until the third century BC. Grammatically Old Chinese lacks distinctions of case, person, or tense and does not distinguish between active and passive forms, or between singular and plural. It is a language without punctuation and has few connecting words. At best it is a written language that is terse and vague (Welch, 2003: 9–10). All modern Chinese renderings of *Daodejing* are translations from Old Chinese. English translations of (modern) Chinese translations of *Daodejing* are numerous and varyingly reliable. Many scholarly translations include commentaries which provide not only information about the text but also the translator's reasons for their presentation and interpretation, as in Lau (1963), which is used here. The problem of meaningful translation of *Daodejing* concerns not only linguistic reliability. Consider the notion of education and learning, and how it is treated in *Daodejing*.

When *Daodejing* refers to education, learning, and knowledge, it is typically to deride or challenge their value, as in chapter 20: 'Exterminate learning and there will no longer be worries.' The terms 'education' and 'learning' as they appear in translations of *Daodejing* are English words. The Chinese character for education, which in pinyin is *jiaoyu*, implies raising or nurturing, similar to the Latin root for education. But Chinese characters are pictograms, not words. The left side of the character *jiao* 'is made up of strokes showing the "influence" (of the master) over the "disciple" (or "son") and the right side of the character shows the master bearing a "rod" ' (Stafford, 1995: 6–8). Furthermore, the left side of *jiao* could easily be mistaken for (and is often written the same as) the character *xiao* (filial piety), which is very clearly comprised of the strokes for *lao*, old or senior, placed above the stokes for *zi*, son (descendants, seed). Embedded in both characters, *jiao* and *xiao*, is hierarchy and seniority and also transmission through the male not the female, as descendants and disciples. In the broader discussion from which Stafford's quotations are taken, he warns against overstating the significance of the embedded meaning of the Chinese characters in alerting us to the potential they possess. In understanding *Daodejing*'s negative assessment of education, however, the embedded meaning of the characters, which totally escapes an English translation of the text, is essential.

Interpretations of *Daodejing* and its uses in different contexts, historical and political as well as philosophical and religious, are extensive, diverse, and contradictory. This is not simply a question of the different emphasis of themes treated in the text, including those of the nature of *dao* (way), self and personhood, political rule, military technique, and so on. Rather, it is a problem of focus, of which passages or notions are treated as paradigmatic and therefore how related ideas are to be understood. The question of the selection, definition, and application of 'core' notions in *Daodejing* is also, then, an issue of the intellectual context into which the text is placed. *Daodejing* opens with the statement that 'The way [*dao*] that can be spoken of is not the constant way [*dao*]': Schwartz (1985: 186–254) takes this to mean that the experience of *dao* is ineffable and therefore mystical, whereas Hansen (1992: 196–230), who can find no evidence of a metaphysical *dao*, takes the statement to be part of a critique of the limitations of language as a social form. Indeed, it is possible to show, as one writer concludes, that 'not only are explicit references to mystical experience lacking in [*Daodejing*], but it does not seem that the earliest commentators even read the text as an attempt to express knowledge implicitly gained through such experience' (Csikszentmihalyi, 1999: 51). Another writer, however, after identifying what he believes are mystic practices reported in other texts of the period, especially the *Neiye*, finds evidence of mysticism in *Daodejing* by using these other texts as interpretive filters through which selected passages in *Daodejing* are understood (Roth, 1999) or, as LaFargue (1994: 181–91) has shown, misunderstood. Because *Daodejing* proceeds without reference to time, place, or personalities, it invites projection of its meaning through the prism of extraneous outlooks. Indeed,

commentary on the text is today dominated by philosophical and religious interpretation, a trend begun in China from the third century AD with the sinicization of
Buddhism, a missionary import from India.

It is now widely accepted that *Daodejing* has its origins in an oral tradition and that
the text comprises a more or less coherent collation of aphorisms compiled to capture
and preserve the ideas expressed in them. In pre-Han Chinese society it was not unusual
for a leading thinker to engage in the complementary activities of offering his services
of moral, administrative, and strategic advice to a political leader and also establish a
school or college of like-minded individuals. The advice emanating from such a voluntary association, or *shi*, expressed both the ideas of its leader, a respected master or
teacher, and also the form of self-cultivation practised in the *shi* which produced and
animated those ideas. Unlike the later schools of Chinese literati, these *shi* were infor-
mally organized and not subject to state control. It is important to appreciate that the
characteristic advice offered to political leaders functioned in terms of the methods of
self-cultivation developed within the particular *shi* rather than in clearly developed doctrines or philosophies. Different *shi* followed different *dao*. Rivalry between *shi* was not
conducted at the level of theoretical debate between philosophical thinkers but in devis-
ing and implementing alternate solutions to the problems of political rule and administration with which the *shi* leaders dealt.

Sociologically, members of *shi* stood between feudal lords and peasant farmers,
and may have included individuals from deposed aristocracies; it is likely that they
thought of themselves as a new nobility. *Daodejing* appears to be drawn from the sayings
developed within a particular Warring States (475–221 BC) *shi* (LaFargue, 1994: 91–4;
Needham, 1956: 63). The preoccupations of this *shi* are clearly expressed in the chapters of *Daodejing*. Government service, if not leadership, was preeminent among its
concerns as expressed in a number of chapters, including 10, 22, and 57. There is also a
clear concern with military affairs, from a particular point of view. Military solutions to
political problems are disfavoured: 'One who assists the ruler of men by means of the
way does not intimidate the empire by a show of arms...In the wake of a mighty army
bad harvests follow without fail' (chapter 30). But neither does *Daodejing* resile from the
use of arms, noting in chapter 69 that 'of the two sides raising arms against each other, it
is the one that is sorrow-stricken that wins'. While military arts are positively assessed,
as in chapter 68, military triumphalism is rejected, 'When victorious in war, one should
observe the rites of mourning' (chapter 31). In addition to the moral-political and military outlook of what might be called the *Laozi shi* there is also represented in *Daodejing*
its internal activities of teaching and learning the self-cultivation that supports its practical counsel. The teaching referred to in *Daodejing* is not so much by instruction as
example: 'the sage...practices the teaching that uses no words' (chapters 2 and 43); 'the
good man is the teacher the bad learns from' (chapter 27); 'One who knows does not
speak; one who speaks does not know' (chapter 56). The teaching and development of
self-cultivation, generative of the *Laozi shi's* distinctive approach to statecraft and rulership, is focused on self-knowledge (chapter 33), self-valuation (chapter 44), and virtue
through virility and harmony (chapter 55).

Given the concerns identified in the preceding paragraph it is not surprising that a good deal of *Daodejing* is directed to consideration of the best approach to action. It emphasizes the importance of timeliness and spontaneity, of avoiding precipitousness and interference with others; and especially the tactical advantages of knowing one's vulnerability to external forces, typically expressed in terms of self-effacement in pursuit of a goal or purpose. The background or framing supposition of these and related considerations is the constancy of change and especially the assumption of process. It is this dual focus on action and process that provides *Daodejing* with a unique quality of thought and its continuing relevance to readers from ages and places unconnected with its origins. The concerns of the discussion to follow are continuous with the questions of both action and process articulated in *Daodejing*. These questions are not brought to the text from outside of it but, as we shall see, are internal to it and integral to its sense and meaning. The significance given to action in *Daodejing* means that the understanding of process never lapses into metaphysical or mystical reflection. The significance given to process means that the understanding of action never lapses into voluntarism or methodological individualism.

2.3 LANGUAGE, PARADOX, AND PROCESS

In philosophical discussions of *Daodejing* much is made of the notion of *dao*, which literally means way or path. In such treatments *dao* is sometimes regarded as a creator force, among other things. In fact, the term is used in a variety of ways in *Daodejing*, each with a different specific meaning. In a well-known discussion, Fu (1973) identifies six senses in which the term *dao* can be understood, but in none of them does *dao* refer to 'an entity, substance, God, abstract notion, Hegelian *Weltgeist*, or anything hypostatized or conceptualized' (Fu, 1973: 369). The different meanings of the notion of *dao*, which vary with the context in which they are applied and the emphasis they receive, converge in referring to an identifiable approach or orientation to action. This approach or orientation is provided with a meaning and sense in terms of its particular application, *de*, or capacities.

The term *de* is sometimes translated as virtue, in the sense of 'by virtue of'. Waley makes the important point that the concept of *de* 'is bound up with the idea of potentiality' and that it refers to a 'latent power, a "virtue" inherent in something' (Waley, 1958: 31, 32). It has more recently been translated as 'efficacy' (Moeller, 2006: 42). The point to be made here is that *dao* is not a provisioning concept and *de* a dependent particular, as philosophers have generally treated them (Chan, 1963: 11; Fung, 1952: 180). Rather, the notions refer to qualities that are entirely interdependent: a journey or way can only be travelled through the efforts of movement taken by the traveller, out of which the journey is constituted. The traveller, at the same time, is guided by accepting a destination, by a timetable which includes how much time is available for the journey, by a sense of the terrain, and also by an understanding of what the journey is for, whether business, pleasure, exploration, or escape. These constraints on or guides to the traveller might be summarized as the journey. Each of these, traveller and journey, is a manifestation of the other (see Hall and Ames, 1998: 61–2).

Dao does not refer to an entity, then, and *dao* is never independent of the actions or practices of those who accept a particular approach to things. It is possible that *dao* may expressively be given a linguistic form, for emphasis, which refers to it as a 'thing'. Fu (1973: 371), on the other hand, regards such reference as an accidental and unfortunate consequence of the limitations of language: 'because Lao Tzu has to use the symbol "Tao" as a grammatical subject…he may immediately mislead his readers into interpreting him as supposing that there is a real subject corresponding to the grammatical one'. But the authors of *Daodejing* are arguably aware of this problem and, if they were understood properly, can be seen as applying it to make a particular point of their own. Chapter 1 opens with an apparent reference to *dao* as an entity: 'The way that can be spoken of is not the constant way'. This has been taken to be a statement of the ineffability of the *dao*, and this in turn is taken to indicate the mystical disposition of the text and those who wrote it, as noted earlier. But this is not the only possible reading of chapter 1 and it is highly likely that it is not the intended meaning.

After indicating that the *dao* that can be spoken of or named is not the 'constant' *dao*, the chapter goes on to say that 'The nameless was the beginning of heaven and earth; the named was the mother of myriad creatures.' This is presented as a dichotomy, with the 'nameless' or the constant *dao* responsible for heaven and earth, while the named or non-constant *dao* responsible for the manifest beings which occupy heaven and earth. Heaven here is not 'heaven' in the Christian and European sense but refers simply to the sky and what is in it; earth is the terrain inhabited by humans. Heaven, in Chinese *tian*, is nature as an emergent order of natural forces. Neither form of *dao* indicated in the passage just quoted is a creator but indicates rather a scope and level of understanding or a perspective. This is apparent in the following sentence: 'rid yourself of desires in order to observe [*dao's*] secrets; but always allow yourself to have desires in order to observe its manifestations'. This apparently contradictory demand, to be both rid of desires and to experience them, is attainable when 'rid yourself of desires' is understood as a call for spontaneity, in Chinese *ziran*, which is to locate oneself accommodatingly in the world and its processes rather than attempt to subject the world to one's own purpose. Indeed, the characteristic of the way of the *Daodejing*, its *dao*, is precisely to privilege spontaneity, *ziran*, to be natural rather than purposeful and willful. But this is not the negation of desire, through which the world and its limits are tangibly experienced. Again, there is interdependence, not opposition, between these different possibilities.

The chapter goes on to say: 'These two are the same but diverge in name as they issue forth.' Contrasting this statement with the opening statement of the same chapter, 'The way that can be spoken of is not the constant way', suggests that a major theme here is the limitation of language itself: that names fail to capture the sameness of things and coincidentally fail to capture the particularity of a given thing at a single time and place. Yet the power or force of language is the subject of chapter 2, which claims that to call something beautiful is at the same time to generate a contrasting sense of ugliness. This is not a defence of language but points to a problem of language which goes back to a leading idea in chapter 1: to name something gives it a putative sense of reality or being, to not name something leaves it without being. Internal to the awareness of the acute limitations or distorting power of language in these two chapters is also another paradox, a paradox of generation: what is not named is not known and in that sense does not exist, and named things thus may have efficacy and be responsible for effects.

Contrasting couples are indicated throughout *Daodejing*. The contrast between *dao* and *de* has already been mentioned and there are many others: sagacity is contrasted with ignorance (chapter 19), self-effacement with illustriousness (chapter 22), female with male (chapter 28), the submissive with the powerful (chapter 43), and so on. In all of this there is an apparent preference for the lesser or lower element of the couple against the greater or higher element (chapters 36, 40, 76). Indeed, this may be regarded as a political orientation of *Daodejing*, emphasized by commentators from Needham (1956) to Moeller (2006) (see also Lau, 1963: xix; Schwartz, 1985: 203). But it would be erroneous to see the presentation of contrasting couples as primarily signalling an abiding preference for one side of the couple over the other side. This is because the contrasting couples do not necessarily indicate enduring relationships. It is frequently mentioned in *Daodejing* that there is no constancy in things themselves or in the relations between them. The easy becomes difficult, the weak become strong, each state or condition is necessarily temporary and yields to a different and frequently contrasting state or condition (chapters 2, 63, 64, 76).

The last point of the previous paragraph must be emphasized, namely that what endures is change and transformation rather than discrete states or conditions. While change, transformation, and process are predicates of nature, and *dao* models itself on nature (chapter 25), the experience of process, if not its mechanism, consists of contrasting couples or opposites (chapters 2, 56, 77), which is itself the way of nature (chapter 56). So while *Daodejing* seems to point to the moral virtue, social value, and strategic force of subordination over domination, a deeper reading reveals a more profound paradox, perhaps that the limitations of insufficiency may not be greater than the problems of abundance. This more prescient reading provides greater generality but it remains an incomplete appreciation of the approach to paradox in *Daodejing*, in which it is held that not only are the paradoxes through which process occurs never resolved, but that they continually develop and transmute.

The significance of paradox to process has been noted in organizational studies, but typically understood within a framework of management and as a means of drawing on plural sources for innovation (Bobko, 1985; Lewis, 2000; Quinn and Cameron, 1988; Sundaramurthy and Lewis, 2003). If this perspective in the management literature does have a Chinese source, as one commentator has argued (Chen, 2002), it is Confucian, not Daoist. In *Daodejing* paradox relates to process inherently and process is understood to occur through a paradoxical generation of paradox. It is possible to distinguish a number of distinct forms of paradox in *Daodejing*.

One form of paradox is in the interdependency of opposite elements in which one requires the other for its meaning or purpose. The social definition of one value in terms of another, opposite value, on which it therefore relies for its meaning, has been indicated earlier in the case of the social construction of beauty, which also applies to goodness, that both generates and relies upon a correlative construction of their opposites, respectively ugliness and badness (chapter 2). Another instance of such a paradox of opposite factors interdependently formed is in the mutual formation of certain social structural elements: 'the superior must have the inferior as root; the high must have the low as base' (chapter 39). The process implicit in these paradoxes is internal to the relations between the elements of the couple, one defining the other. It is also possible that there be a process extrinsic to a paradox of interdependency, such as strengthening something in order to weaken it (chapter 36). This is arguably a special case of a frequently mentioned possibility in *Daodejing*, namely that in order to achieve a purpose, one may apparently move away from one's goal, in overcoming an adversary one may be strategically compliant; in neither case is the goal forsaken or ultimate strength absent, but it is insightfully observed that in bending one may become straight (chapter 22). There is an additional aspect of paradox in these latter instances, namely that something paradoxically gives access to its opposite. Indeed, this may be seen as a distinct form of paradox.

One thing paradoxically giving access to its opposite can take different forms. In one of them, unintended consequences, which are broadly appreciated and not confined to *Daodejing*, acquire a paradoxical form. A thing may generate its opposite as a consequence of its mere operation rather than its extended development in a given social context. In this case the consequences are not merely unintended but are paradoxical because they are negative outcomes of an ostensibly positive phenomenon, which must therefore be re-evaluated once its consequences are known. In chapter 18, for example, it is indicated that 'when cleverness emerges there is great hypocrisy', and in chapter 57 that 'the better known the laws and edicts the more thieves and robbers there are'. Cleverness and law might typically be regarded as things that are to be valued in their own right; but when they are contextualized in terms of their unanticipated societal consequences, which are not only unintended but the opposite of that which might be intended by their corresponding element in the couple, then an irresolvable paradox is revealed that requires a reconsideration of the original evaluation of the first element of the couple. A much more general and potent form of this paradox is expressed in the idea that nothing produces something and something comes from nothing (chapters 2 and 40), to which we now turn.

2.4 ABSENCE, IMMINENCE, AND LATENCY

The idea that something comes from nothing is mentioned a number of times in *Daodejing*. Emptiness is seen not as a void but rather as a source of potentiality. While the idea that something comes from nothing might be counter-intuitive, it is nevertheless operationally quite familiar. A common experience of academic life is to have a thought concerning the nature of a fact or the significance of a connection between ideas. For something to come of such a thought a typical strategy is to commit to giving a conference paper and thereby to a definite deadline with a resulting experience of something coming from nothing. Indeed, it is possible to show that the latent function of conferences is to provide the context and stimulus for such a process of generation in the development of an idea into a presentation and possibly a publication (Gross and Fleming, 2011). The concept of a latent function, mentioned here, is developed by Merton (1968) to refer to functions of institutions that are neither recognized nor intended. In Merton's sense, such functions are latent because they are hidden within the institution, though their effects or consequences may be felt by incumbents even though not understood by them in this sense. Another sociological writer, who did not share Merton's functionalism, also has a use for the notion of latency in stating a theory of conflict in which latent interests connect social structure and role incumbents: latent interests, according to Dahrendorf (1969: 178), are 'undercurrents of the behavior of [a role incumbent or "player"] which are predetermined for him for the duration of his incumbency of a role, and which are independent of his conscious orientations'. In these accounts is the idea that social relationships are somehow implicit in a given set of institutional or social structural conditions (Lockwood, 1992: 407).

While sociology does provide conceptual space to the notion of latency, something hidden in something else which enhances a social process but nevertheless appears to be not there, it is seldom discussed and not developed beyond the instances already noted here. The treatment of latency in Merton and Dahrendorf can be distinguished in so far as the latency of one is hidden in its form but not its effect, whereas for the other it is hidden in its effect but not in its structural form. The difference can be made clearer by distinguishing between latency and an associated term, imminence, in terms of their relationship with action. Imminence implies that something has a force behind it, independently of the actor who may be subject to it, whereas latency suggests that the actor's efforts may be instrumental in the realization of something not yet present. Such a distinction reveals something about both functionalism and action theory. From the point of view of action theory, functionalism is seen as static and conservative. It is ironic, therefore, that it is functionalism which offers conceptual space to latency, something that comes from nothing through the efforts of action. Action theory, on the other hand, which has nothing to say about imminence because it operates at the level of agency rather than process, has little to add to an understanding of latency as it typically focuses on the environment of action as providing resources for action. This means that the processes in the environment outside of the immediate concerns of the actor are beyond the theoretical grasp of action theory. *Daodejing*, on the other hand, sees action not in terms of the agent's interests, as in action theory or a sociological theory of power, but within a framework of interconnectedness and sensitivity to the dynamics of an actor's situation: here, then, there is significant intellectual space for both imminence and latency.

Discussion of nothing or emptiness in *Daodejing* includes treatment of latency and imminence as one of four distinct themes, the other three being the functionality of emptiness, emptiness as a goal or purpose to be achieved, and finally emptiness as an epistemic theme relating to those things that appear indistinct. The last of these, in which *dao* is treated as possibly 'indistinct and shadowy' (chapters 14 and 21) is the least interesting for the purpose of this chapter and does not require further discussion. The idea of emptiness as a goal or purpose is indicated in a number of chapters in the *Daodejing*. In chapter 16 it is stated that the sage or aspirant to leadership does his 'utmost to attain emptiness'. This should not be taken literally but rather as an injunction to adapt to the natural forms and forces of life. In chapter 15 *dao* is likened to various forms of vacuity, as in chapter 4, 'vacant like a valley', and being 'not full'; the meaning of these statements is in the idea that these states are phases in a process, a process of being 'newly made'. The idea of emptiness in this sense is associated with the idea of imminence and latency, of something new and emergent, which shall be discussed more fully later. Being empty, then, is to imitate the way of nature, to be spontaneous, draw benefit from one's surroundings and, rather than being narrowly self-centred, self-interested, or willful, it is possible to 'act from knowledge of the constant [process of nature and] one's actions will lead to impartiality [or accommodation]' (chapter 16). Emptiness as a goal, then, means that in choosing between options, the one that offers more potential possibilities rather than present richness is the one to be preferred.

This leads us to consideration of emptiness as latency and imminence. The idea that something comes from nothing (chapter 2) is connected in *Daodejing* with a consideration of the potent nature of emptiness (chapters 4 and 6). The generative relationship between nothing and something is emblematic of process itself, that things are in constructive relationships with other things and the properties of those things, and that the relationships themselves, like the subjects of these relationships, are never constant and unchanging. It is repeated a number of times in *Daodejing* that emptiness is in the nature of *dao*, the suggestion being that emptiness is not a void but a source of potentiality: 'the way is empty but use will not drain it' (chapter 4). The typically paradoxical form of this statement indicates that emptiness or nothing is something and that that something is not only usable but use of it will not deplete it or make it empty. In process some things are imminent and latent at one time only to become manifest at another; and process is ongoing. From the perspective of political affairs and other practical considerations, this means that 'Difficult things in the world must needs have their beginnings in the easy; big things…in the small' (chapter 63). Here is the idea of qualitative as well as quantitative change in process.

The relational basis of change is commonplace in all the social sciences today. The likelihood of risk and its consequences are widely discussed and consideration of uncertainty as a condition of all behaviour subject to an emergent and therefore unknown and unknowable future is axiomatic across the social sciences. And yet there remains an assumption in all of them of projection, repetition, and recurrence, encouraged by statistical and other methods of research founded on the certainty of past and currently present conditions. Unambiguous appreciations of the non-ergodic nature of the social world are few and far between (but see Elias, 1978: 114–16 and North, 2005: 19–21). In *Daodejing*, however, the assumption of non-recurrence is frequently suggested. There is caution against rigid categories, or categories at all (chapter 1), fluidity is unavoidable, and boundaries always ambiguous (chapters 28, 32, 34, 42). Process is unending and it is therefore difficult to even determine the conclusion of any single episode. This latter issue has currency in Chinese thought in the story of 'the old man of the passes who lost a horse', preserved in the second-century compilation of political wisdom and reflective anecdote, the *Huainanzi*. Each episode of the story reverses the assessment or valuation of the preceding episode: the old man has the misfortune of losing a horse, but then the good fortune of the horse returning with a number of other horses; in attempting to ride the horses, the old man's son has the misfortune of falling and becoming lame, but then has the good fortune to be rejected for service in fighting neighbouring barbarians. There is no point at which it might be said that this is the conclusion, each episode is a reversal of the preceding one through the manifestation of imminent and latent properties, and these processes are continuous (chapters 22, 25, 28, 40, 45, 58, 63, 64, 74, 77).

Another theme concerning emptiness in *Daodejing* that deserves to be highlighted is its functionality. In chapter 11 this is expressed in terms of a physical metaphor: 'Thirty spokes share one hub. Adopt the nothing therein . . . and you will have the use of the cart.' It is the emptiness of the hub that permits an axle to be inserted that makes a wheel. The chapter goes on to describe the kneading of clay so that it surrounds emptiness and hence is a vessel, the function of which is in the empty space that may then be filled (see also chapters 22, 28, 67). Here the relation between nothing and something is not serially through time but in coterminous interaction, in a synchronic rather than diachronic mode. Again, the idea is applicable to the social realm and not unknown in social science, in which it is not fanciful to say that a situation or process may be understood in terms of what is not present. Barrington Moore (1969: 20–9) explains the historical rise of democracy in England in terms of the absence of a peasantry. This type of account should not be confused with explanations of why something does not occur, as in Weber's (1964) discussion of the absence of capitalism in traditional China (Hamilton, 1984). Whereas in Weber capitalism is simply absent and without efficacy, in Moore the absence of a peasantry is an emptiness contributing to a particular political configuration of English political institutions, it is a factor in the process. The functionality of absence or emptiness, then, is in its enablement of other things to emerge. In this sense absence is neither a limitation or constraint nor the implicit potential that is found in growth and development. The functionality of emptiness expresses what has been called *Daodejing*'s 'active negativism' (Chang, 1981: 3–4), the vitality of the intangible in contributing to operations internal to process.

The functionality of emptiness refers to a natural property of things, a property inherent in their nature. In *Daodejing* much prominence is given to the idea that process itself has predominant functional aspects so that if things are left to run their course and not suffer interference by the action of rulers then the outcome shall be positive. In statecraft, the best ruler has the quality of emptiness, he is 'a shadowy presence' (chapter 17). This is because nature is 'like a bellows' in the sense that it is 'empty without being exhausted: the more it works the more comes out' (chapter 5). In these circumstances proactive rulership will be counterproductive (chapters 48, 57, 63, 64) and it is best not to act for then 'nothing is left undone' (chapter 37); submissive passivity achieves manifold outcomes (chapters 43, 78). It is necessary, then, to consider the treatment of action and the power of action in *Daodejing*.

2.5 ACTION, CONTEXT, AND PROCESS

A concept of power in *Daodejing* operates in terms of a paradoxical strategy described in chapter 36 as 'subtle discernment', namely that the 'submissive and weak will overcome the hard and the strong'. It is expressed metaphorically in chapter 78: 'In the world there is nothing more submissive and weak than water. Yet for attacking that which is hard and strong nothing can surpass it' (see also chapters 36, 43, 61, 66). The paradox of power, then, is that the weaker party is paradoxically more powerful than the stronger. Thus there is strategic advantage in avoiding confrontation (chapters 69 and 73), in using persuasion rather than force, and in leading by following (chapter 66). When discussing paradox earlier in this chapter it was shown that formulations such as these are primarily methodological: the paradoxical dyads are not to be understood as enduring relations of actual beings; each condition is necessarily temporary and gives way to a different and contrasting condition. In discussing the appropriate orientation to action of those engaged in practical affairs, including aspirants to political leadership, *Daodejing* emphasizes a form of 'subtle discernment'. The paradox of strategy emphasizes withdrawal, disengagement, non-assertiveness, and possibly self-effacement. A concept covering these prospects is *wuwei*, usually translated as 'non-action'. *Wuwei* is not an absence of action, however, but a particular type of action informed by practices indicated in our earlier discussion of emptiness.

Action is typically understood in terms of an actor's intentions to achieve a future outcome they desire. This seems to be the obverse of *wuwei*. Chapter 2 says that sages give benefit but 'exact no gratitude', accomplish tasks 'yet lay claim to no merit'. As well as constituting action that does not direct the relations it facilitates, *wuwei*, according to chapter 63, is action that is timely and therefore understands the sequences of the events it nurtures: 'difficult things…have their beginnings in the easy; big things…in the small'. This theme is continued in chapter 64, but the perspective shifts from process to the correlative restraint on the actor; those who do things ruin them and those who grasp things lose them, but because the sage 'does nothing [coercively he] never ruins anything; and, because he does not lay hold of anything, loses nothing'. In these statements *wuwei* is action that is appropriate to the inherent dynamic of what is acted on, subordinating the actor's extraneous and self-centred purposes in order to realize the full potential of events as they unfold. It is in subordination to this larger process that individuals ultimately realize their purposes: chapter 7 asks 'Is it not because he is without thought of self that he is able to accomplish his private ends?'

The idea of *wuwei* as being commensurate with the nature of the thing towards which the action is directed means that if the nature of something is understood, then action towards it can be both appropriate and timely—neither premature nor too late, as in chapter 64: 'deal with a situation before symptoms develop...Keep a thing in order before disorder sets in.' This acknowledgement of a dynamic dimension and unfolding of events in process, which means that things become other than they were and will become other than they are, is a source of paradox that *Daodejing* addresses and exemplifies throughout, as we have seen. There is a further element of *wuwei* as a form of action, which is *wuwei* as example to others, teaching that uses no words, that goes beyond what can be said (chapters 2 and 43). This practice of teaching implies that another person's action can be achieved by example. Not only does this indicate a particular form of power, it expresses an idea of rulership frequently indicated in *Daodejing*, namely that government or organization is a context in which the spontaneity of others is efficacious, as in chapter 57. The educative role of *wuwei*, action that is effective in the example it provides to another, can be seen to have efficacy in at least two senses. Action as example is conduct of one that animates another; also, action as example means that the different positions or roles in any given situation participate together in the realization of an outcome. Both of these understandings of action presuppose interconnectedness in the world and in agency, through which *wuwei* is realized.

This account indicates a number of elements of action identified in *Daodejing*. Three themes in particular emerge. First, the thing or event acted upon is never regarded as inert, passive, or without its own agentic capacity; second, no actor is independent of other actors and non-actors, but is interconnected with them in various ways; third, things are subordinate to the processes through which they have manifestation, and these processes are dynamic and things in them are ever becoming different. These background ideas inform the notion of *wuwei* as non-interfering action which accommodates to social processes, as non-wilful action directed to realizing the potential of events and others, and as action that animates others to act on their own behalf. In all of these *wuwei* is not self-assertive but self-effacing or 'weak'. Thus the concept of *wuwei* implies an approach to action and power that is not only quite different from standard mainstream treatments but that arguably offers a broader grasp of the issues raised by action and power. *Wuwei*, as effortless or non-coercive action, intervenes in events in a manner that does not confront or operate in tension with them but rather accommodates to them. This requires that *wuwei* as action cannot be described principally in terms of the actor's intentions or capacities but in terms of the thing acted upon and the processes to which it is subjected: synchronicity through action as *wuwei* replaces the notion of causality in power. This requires that those who practise *wuwei* are aware of the relationships that constitute the objects of their concern more than they are of their own interests.

2.6 CONCLUSION

In consideration of process a conclusion is necessarily arbitrary. Indeed, one of the attributes of the sage who practises *wuwei*, which further indicates the distinctiveness of *wuwei* as a type of action rather than non-action, is knowing not simply when but how to stop (chapters 9, 17, 30, 32, 44). This is a major consideration for any outlook which emphasizes process rather than outcomes. It is also a major concern to anyone engaged in affairs of state, or the heart. Whereas the western outlook is typically animated by principles directed to moving forward, *Daodejing* emphasizes the advantage of standing still. For this reason, Welch (2003: 164–5) regards it as advocating 'the power of negative thinking'. What it actually does is place action, as *wuwei*, in the centre of process.

References

Bobko, P. (1985). Removing Assumptions of Bipolarity: Towards Variation and Circularity, *Academy of Management Review 10*(1): 99–108.

Chan, W.-t. (1963). The Philosophy of Tao, in *The Way of Lao Tzu (Tao-Te Ching)*, trans. with Introductory Essays, Comments, and Notes by W.-t. Chan (Indianapolis, IN: The Bobbs-Merrill Company): 3–34.

Chang, A.I.T. (1981). *The Tao of Architecture* (Princeton, NJ: Princeton University Press).

Chen, M.-J. (2002). Transcending Paradox: The Chinese 'Middle Way' Perspective, *Asia Pacific Journal of Management 19*: 179–99.

Csikszentmihalyi, M. (1999). Mysticism and Apophatic Discourse in the *Laozi*, in M. Csikszentmihalyi and P.J. Ivanhoe (eds), *Religious and Philosophical Aspects of the* Laozi (Albany, NY: SUNY Press): 33–58.

Dahrendorf, R. (1969). *Class and Class Conflict in Industrial Society* (London: Routledge and Kegan Paul).

Elias, N. (1978). *What is Sociology?* (New York: Columbia University Press).

Emerson, J. (1995). A Stratification of Lao Tzu, *Journal of Chinese Religions 23*: 1–27.

Fu, C. W.-h. (1973). Lao-Tzu's Conception of Tao, *Inquiry 16*: 367–94.

Fung, Y.-l. (1952). *A History of Chinese Philosophy*, Volume I, trans. D. Bodde (Princeton, NJ: Princeton University Press).

Gross, N. and Fleming, C. (2011). Academic Conferences and the Making of Philosophical Knowledge, in C. Camic, N. Gross, and M. Lamont (eds), *Social Knowledge in Making* (Chicago: University of Chicago Press): 151–79.

Hall, D.L. and Ames, R.T. (1998). *Thinking from the Han: Self, Truth, and Transcendence in Chinese and Western Culture* (Albany, NY: SUNY Press).

Hamilton, G.G. (1984). Patriarchalism in Imperial China and Western Europe, *Theory and Society 13*(3): 393–425.

Hansen, C. (1992). *A Daoist Theory of Chinese Thought: A Philosophical Interpretation* (New York: Oxford University Press).

LaFargue, M. (1994). *Tao and Method: A Reasoned Approach to Tao Te Ching* (Albany, NY: SUNY Press).

Lau, D.C. (1963). *Lao Tzu: Tao Te Ching*, trans. with an Introduction by D.C. Lau (London: Penguin).

Lewis, M.W. (2000). Exploring Paradox: Toward a More Comprehensive Guide, *Academy of Management Review 25*(4): 760–76.

Lockwood, D. (1992). *Solidarity and Schism* (Oxford: Oxford University Press).

Merton, R. (1968). *Social Theory and Social Structure* (New York: Free Press).

Moeller, H.-G. (2006). *The Philosophy of Daodejing* (New York: Columbia University Press).

Moore, B. (1969). *Social Origins of Dictatorship and Democracy* (London: Peregrine Books).

Needham, J. (1956). *Science and Civilization in China*, Volume 2 (Cambridge: Cambridge University Press).

North, D.C. (2005). *Understanding the Process of Economic Change* (Princeton, NJ: Princeton University Press).

Quinn, R.E. and Cameron, K.S. (eds) (1988). *Paradox and Transformation: Toward a Theory of Change in Organization and Management* (Cambridge, MA: Ballinger).

Roth, H.D. (1999). The *Laozi* in the Context of Early Daoist Mystical Praxis, in M. Csikszentmihalyi and P.J. Ivanhoe (eds), *Religious and Philosophical Aspects of the* Laozi (Albany, NY: SUNY Press): 59–96.

Schwartz, B.I. (1985). *The World of Thought in Ancient China* (Cambridge, MA: Belknap Press).

Stafford, C. (1995). *The Roads of Chinese Childhood* (Cambridge: Cambridge University Press).

Sundaramurthy, C. and Lewis, M. (2003). Control and Collaboration: Paradoxes of Governance, *Academy of Management Review* 28(3): 397–415.

Waley, A. (1958). *The Way and Its Power: Lao Tzu's Tao Tê Ching and Its Place in Chinese Thought* (New York: Grove Press).

Weber, M. (1964). *The Religion of China: Confucianism and Taoism* (New York: The Free Press).

Welch, H. (2003). *Taoism: The Parting of the Way* (Boston: Beacon Press).

CHAPTER 3

....

HERACLITUS (540–480 BC)

....

AJIT NAYAK

Heraclitus' thought is neither inaccessible nor inconsistent, but intrinsically engimatic and intricate. Not by neglecting it, but by facing this fact can we succeed in making sense of it.

(Dilcher, 1995: 7)

What I understand is excellent, and I think the rest is also. But it takes a Delian diver to get to the bottom of it.

(Kahn, 1979: 95)

It is a hard road, filled with darkness and gloom; but if an initiate leads you on the way, it becomes brighter than the radiance of the sun.

(Kahn, 1979: 95)

3.1 INTRODUCTION

THIS CHAPTER offers an overview of Heraclitus' philosophy and its inspirations for process thinking in organization studies. The main aim is to enable organizational scholars to move beyond merely acknowledging Heraclitus as the founding father of process thinking. The central argument put forward here is that thinking with Heraclitus offers insights into thinking beyond conventional categories and concepts and unsettles our views on organization. His enigmatic and intricate fragments invite us to dive deeper into our organization of thought and understand organization as a generic process. One of the greatest pleasures of reading Heraclitus is that there are only rough beginnings and becomings; no endings and ends. What initially confronts the reader are puzzlement, disillusionment, and unexpected turns. Yet, this obscure style of writing has a subtle and hidden power to animate thought. Rather than passively consuming what Heraclitus has to say, the reader is asked to endure puzzles and wordplay that turns back on itself to become, to paraphrase one of the opening quotes, radiant as the sun. The negative feelings of puzzlement and disillusionment unexpectedly turn into a positive force, one that points to what lies beyond one's thought. For organizational scholars burdened with the anxiety of establishing definitive meaning, assigning clarity to words, and developing inert concepts, Heraclitus' fragments pose insurmountable challenges. The fragments will appear to be incoherent, incomplete, and contradictory. For organizational scholars sympathetic to the linguistic turn and those who take their cues from post-structural thinking, Heraclitus offers refreshing insights into process, movement, and infusing words with life.

I divide the chapter into three main sections. In section 3.2 I provide an overview of Heraclitus' life. In section 3.3 I discuss Heraclitus' writings. I discuss the challenges facing Heraclitus scholars and provide a background understanding for a way of reading Heraclitus that takes linguistic density and resonance seriously. I examine Heraclitus' fragments thematically to elaborate on their meanings and connections. In section 3.4 I discuss the challenges facing organizational scholars in reading and engaging with Heraclitus.

3.2 LIFE

Our main source of Heraclitus' life, as with several early Greek philosophers, is Diogenes Laertius' *Lives of Eminent Philosophers* (Laertius, 1925) in which he states that Heraclitus 'flourished in the 69th Olympiad' (504–500 BCE) and died at the age of 60. Diogenes Laertius provides several personal details and interesting and amusing anecdotes about Heraclitus' life and death which confirm his reputation as 'The Obscure' and the 'The Dark Philosopher'. Diogenes Laertius states that Heraclitus was born to the ruling family in Ephesus, which is on the west coast of modern-day Turkey. Heraclitus is said to have given up his right to rule to his brother, preferred to spend time playing games with children rather than manage the affairs of a kingdom, and despised his fellow Ephesians. Diogenes Laertius' anecdote about Heraclitus' death also paints an interesting portrait of the man. Having isolated himself from others, Heraclitus wandered the mountains and lived on a diet of grass and herbs. However, this gave him dropsy and he returned to the city. Rather than seeking cure from the doctors, he posed a riddle: 'whether they were competent to create a drought after heavy rain. They could make nothing of this, whereupon he buried himself in a cowshed, expecting that the noxious damp humour would be drawn out of him by the warmth of the manure' (Laertius, 1925: 411). Diogenes Laertius offers three versions of Heraclitus' death: 'Being thus stretched and prone [in dung], he died the next day and was buried in the market-place' or 'being unable to tear off the dung, he remained as he was and, being unrecognizable when so transformed, he was devoured by dogs' or 'he was cured of the dropsy and died of another disease' (Laertius, 1925: 413).

Rather than a factual biography of Heraclitus' life and death, Diogenes Laertius employs a biographical method which interprets the life of the philosopher through his philosophy (Chitwood, 2004). In other words, what we know about Heraclitus' life through Diogenes Laertius may have been imagined and interpreted through his philosophical writings, rather than accurately represent his life history. As Chitwood states:

> [F]or biographers such as Diogenes Laertius, philosophical works were also, and sometimes even primarily, read as autobiography. Philosophy ... was seen as a collection of personal or autobiographical statements, to which the biographer responds in

kind. For example, in the course of his philosophical work, Heraclitus compares men to apes and children. The biographer, interpreting these remarks as personal rather than philosophical convictions, saw an ugly misanthropy at work and perhaps even one that applied to him personally. The biographers' reaction to Heraclitus and to his work was, in fact, generally unfavorable and manifests itself in an unusually hostile biography; hence Heraclitus' refusal to rule becomes another example of the philosopher's misanthropy. (Chitwood, 2004: 3)

Thus, anecdotes about Heraclitus' life and death may be a result of turning Heraclitus' philosophy, as interpreted by Diogenes Laertius, into his biography. Furthermore, one can be sure that Diogenes Laertius had no personal knowledge of Heraclitus' life since he wrote his text around 500 years after Heraclitus' death. Notwithstanding the accuracy of Heraclitus' life, the anecdotes confirm his status as an eminent philosopher of his time and act as an interesting beginning to understanding Heraclitus' philosophy.

3.3 WORK

Heraclitus of Ephesus was in his prime, i.e. in his forties, around 504–501 BCE. He is supposed to have written a book around 490 BCE, entitled *On Nature*. However, we are not sure whether he did indeed write a book or whether what we have is a collection of sayings that have been recorded by others. All we have are fragments reconstructed from references to Heraclitus in the writings of various philosophers through the ages. One of the main issues confronting Heraclitean scholars is distinguishing between Heraclitus' own words from interpretations and misinterpretations by philosophers. As Dilcher reminds us:

> The ground on which we walk is often thinner and more fragile than would be desirable. If we do not want to risk taking later inadvertent reworkings for the original thought, we constantly have to keep in mind the whole history of ancient thought through which medium we are compelled to grasp Heraclitus. (Dilcher, 1995: 7)

Heracliteans are indebted to two Greek philosophers, Theophrastus and Cleanthes, who are important intermediaries in preserving, translating, and distorting, in equal measure, Heraclitus' philosophy. Theophrastus, who succeeded Aristotle as the head of the Lyceum, wrote *The Opinions of the Natural Philosophers*, in which he interpreted Heraclitus' work in terms of explanations and causes about things in nature. Cleanthes, successor to Zeno, the founder of the Stoic school of thought, on the other hand was guided by Stoic philosophy in his interpretation of Heraclitus. He associated and interpreted Heraclitus' sayings within the Stoic philosophy of the cosmic whole. In contrast to the Aristotelian dislike of vague, confusing, and indeterminate phrasings, the Stoic interpretations were also more sympathetic and partial to Heraclitus' style of writing which is poetic and allusive rather than clear and conclusive.

Modern Heraclitean scholarship is indebted to Hermann Diels, who compiled *The Fragments of the Presocratics* (Diels, 1903; Freeman, 1946, 1948) in which he collected 139 fragments attributed to Heraclitus. Rather than find a way of organizing these fragments thematically, or because of the insurmountable challenge of definitively identifying Heraclitus' themes, he chose to order the fragments in alphabetical order of the name of the author citing Heraclitus. Diels' ordering of the fragments provides a referencing system that is followed by all Heracliteans.[1] Departing from Diels' ordering and recognizing that an arbitrary ordering suggests that Heraclitus did not offer a thesis, recent Heracliteans have attempted to develop themes that bring together these fragments. Chief among them[2] are Burnet (1930), Kirk (1954), Guthrie (1962), Marcovich (1967), and Kahn (1979). It is the last's arrangement[3] and exposition that this chapter draws on. As Kahn states:

> Heraclitus' discourse as a whole was as carefully and artistically composed as are the preserved parts, and that the formal ordering of the whole was as much an element in its total meaning as in the case of any lyric poem from the same period. The true parallel for an understanding of Heraclitus' style is … Pindar and Aeschylus. The extant fragments reveal a command of word order, imagery, and studied ambiguity as effective as that to be found in any work of these two poets. I think we can best imagine the structure of Heraclitus' work on the analogy of the great choral odes, with their fluid but carefully articulated movement from image to aphorism, from myth to riddle to contemporary allusion … The literary effect he aimed at may be compared to that of Aeschylus' *Oresteia*: the solemn and dramatic unfolding of a great truth, step by step, where the sense of what has gone before is continually enriched by its echo in what follows. (Kahn, 1979: 7)

Kahn (1979) argues that there are two key complementary ideas in preparing to understand the fragments. Firstly, we assume that each fragment has linguistic density. By this we mean that 'multiplicity of ideas are expressed in a single word or phrase' (Kahn, 1979: 89). What at first glance may seem to be scattered ideas gather together divergent and discordant connections. As Dilcher remarks:

> We have first to concentrate with meticulous patience on single statements and even single words. Heraclitus' philosophy is, for certain reasons, so tersely phrased that no cursory reading will yield an adequate idea. It is vital to penetrate the deeper layers behind the surface meaning. Often the shadings and overtones of particular expressions need to be scrutinized in order to determine their scope. (Dilcher, 1995: 8)

One can begin to appreciate the significance of Heraclitus' 'terse phrasing' in understanding his opening words: 'this *logos* here being forever men ever fail to comprehend' (I, D. 1).[4] On the one hand the opening words 'this *logos* here' is a standard way of expressing 'what you are about to read'. However, the use of 'forever' is ambiguous. It could mean 'this *logos* is forever' or it could mean 'men forever fail to comprehend'. Kahn argues that ambiguities such as these are deliberately used by Heraclitus to hint and to suggest rather than to state explicitly. They force the reader to go back and forth over the same words and uncover hidden depths. As Kahn (1979: 95) argues, 'it is important to leave open the possibility that the difficulty of deciding between them is itself the intended effect... the relation between the surface meaning and the *hyponoia* or "deeper sense" is itself unstable and complex'.

Secondly, we assume that there is resonance between the fragments. By resonance we mean 'a relationship between fragments by which a single verbal theme or image is echoed from one text to another in such a way that the meaning of each is enriched when they are understood together' (Kahn, 1979: 89). Throughout the fragments there are strong and weak echoes that move thought from one fragment to another. The effect of resonance is that of proleptic introduction and gradual and circuitous development, similar in style to Aeschylus' *Oresteia*:

> In its early occurrences the image is elliptical and enigmatic. It is a *griphos* or riddle whose solution is strung out over the course of the individual drama or the entire trilogy. Significance increases with repetition; the image gains in clarity as the action moves to a climax. Prolepsis and gradual development of recurrent imagery, along with the corollary, movement from enigmatic utterance to clear statement, from riddle to solution, dominate the structure of the *Oresteia*. (Lebeck, 1971: 1)

However, unlike the *Oresteia*, with Heraclitus' fragments we are left in suspense about the climax. Each time we move from one fragment to the next in a different order, we are encouraged to hear faint echoes of words and images brought back from earlier fragments we passed over. For example, Heraclitus' use of *logos* has echoes of several meanings as it appears in various fragments: 'sayings, speech, discourse, statement, report; account, explanation, reason, principle; esteem, reputation; collection, enumeration, ratio, proportion' (Kahn, 1979: 29). We are also presented with echoes of well-known saying and stories that Heraclitus engaged with. For example, the fragment 'Most men do not think things in the way that they encounter them, nor do they recognize what they experience, but believe their own opinions' (IV, D. 17) alludes to Archilochus' use of 'in the way that', and at the same time overturns his meaning. As Kahn elaborates:

> in a fragment of Archilochus (68 Diehl): 'The heart (*thymos*) of mortal men, Glaucos son of Leptines, becomes such as the day which Zeus brings upon them, and their thoughts (*phroneusin*) are such as the deeds (*ergmata*) that they encounter (*enkyreosin*)', that is, their thought is determined by their situation. The first clause of [Heraclitus' fragment] IV contains, in two verbs and its comparative structure (*toiauta...hokoia* 'in the way that' or 'such...as') a clear echo of Archilochus' own words. But Heraclitus echoes Archilochus only to deny what the latter affirms. (Kahn, 1979: 103)

Such subtle allusion to well-known stories and sayings resonate throughout Heraclitus' fragments.

Once we accept that the Heraclitus' text was ordered, rather than being a collection of sayings, and we accept linguistic density and resonance, we can begin to connect with the 'hidden unity' of all things being one. We are encouraged to move beyond the task of looking for clarity by thematically arranging the fragments towards a more powerful and hidden unity they signify: 'from all things one, and from one thing all' (CXXIV, D. 10). This requires the reader not to just passively read the fragments, but to match Heraclitus' stylistic device of allusion and riddle by complicating one's engagement with the fragments. We must be 'prepared to regard ambiguity not as a blemish to be eliminated but as a meaningful stylistic device to be accepted and understood' (Kahn, 1979: 93). There is no doubt that on reading Heraclitus we are faced with his reputation as 'The Obscure' and 'The Riddler'. One important implication from this is Heraclitus' deliberate attempt to engage the readers of his text, and draw them into actively participating in comprehending and forever bringing his ideas to life. We are faced with fragments that are loosely coupled together by assemblage of ideas, imagery, wordplay, and riddles. There are no clear divisions and dividing lines between themes. We are confronted with 'the solemn and dramatic unfolding of a great truth, step by step, where the sense of what has gone before is continually modified and enriched by its echo in what follows' (Kahn, 1964: 190). Some texts precede what is to come, and some texts proceed from what has already been intimated.

3.3.1 Everything Flows

As they step into the same rivers, other and still other waters flow upon them.
(L, D. 12)
One cannot step twice into the same river, nor can one grasp any mortal substance in a stable condition, but it scatters and again gathers; it forms (endures) and dissolves, and approaches and departs.

(LI, D. 91)

That his ideas were widely read, discussed, and influenced all Greek philosophers is attested to by Plato and Aristotle. We owe Heraclitus' famous statements, 'you cannot step into the same river twice' and 'everything flows', to Plato. In *Cratylus* Plato states:

Heraclitus says somewhere that 'everything gives way and nothing stands fast', and, likening the things that are to the flowing of a river, he says that 'you cannot step into the same river twice'. (*Cratylus*, 402a)

Similarly, Aristotle also refers to Heraclitus' 'everything flows' philosophy:

They held that in general everything is in a state of becoming and flux, and nothing is stable. (*On the Heavens*, 298b29)
And in fact some thinkers maintain not that some things are in motion and some not, but all things are in motion always, though this escapes our senses. (*Physics*, 253b9)

Whilst the popularity of 'everything flows' is undeniable, since the fragments, particularly 'one cannot step twice into the same river', are interpretations by others, there is sufficient doubt in Heraclitean scholarship to ascertain what Heraclitus meant to signify. There is agreement that fragment L, D. 12 is in Heraclitus' own words. The more popular 'one cannot step into the same river twice', part of fragment LI, D. 91, is not his own words, but the tone of scatters and gathers, forms and dissolves, and approaches and departs in the same fragment is more in keeping with Heraclitus' mode of expression. It is this we turn to first.

3.3.2 Opposition, Transformation, and Hidden Unity

The themes of hidden unity, opposites, and transformation dominate Heraclitus' fragments. These themes find their popular expression is the pairing of Heraclitus with Democritus: one the weeping philosopher and the other the laughing philosopher. Although they were not contemporaries, the pairing of these opposites captured an interesting theme in understanding the human condition and were popularized as subjects of several paintings in the Renaissance era.

One common interpretation of this opposition is the recognition that life is both tragic and comic at the same time. Lutz (1954) draws on a poem in the *Greek Anthology* to illustrate the juxtapositioning of the two philosophers:

> Weep for life, Heraclitus, much more than when thou dids't live, for life is now more pitiable. Laugh now, Democritus, at life, far more than before; the life of all is now more laughable. (*Greek Anthology III.* 9.148, quoted in Lutz, 1954: 309)

Lutz also points to Lucian's satirical look at philosophers in her *Philosophies for Sale*, where Zeus auctions various philosophers. Unsuccessful in selling them separately, they are put for auction together as a 'buy one get one free' offer. Baffled by their contrasting views on life, they attract no bids and remain unsold.

> The god: day and night, winter and summer, war and peace, satiety and hunger. It alters, as when mingled with perfumes, it gets named according to the pleasure of each one. (CXXIII, D. 67)
> Cold warms up, warm cools off, moist parches, dry dampens. (XLIX, D. 126)
> A man is found foolish by a god, as a child by a man. (LVII, D. 79)
> The same is there: living and dead, and the waking and the sleeping, and young and old. For these transposed are those, and those transposed again are these. (Fr. XCIII)
> The sea is the purest and foulest water: for fish drinkable and life-sustaining; for men undrinkable and deadly. (LXX, D. 61)
> It is not better for human beings to get all they want. It is disease that has made health sweet and good, hunger satiety, weariness rest. (LXVII, D. 110–11)
> The way up and down is one and the same. (CIII, D. 60)

The opposition between weeping and laughing alludes to Heraclitus' use of opposites in various fragments. Perhaps the 'bow and the lyre' fragment is the second most popularized of Heraclitus' fragments. Along with several other fragments, Heraclitus points to the unity of opposites using subtle variations on the theme. Firstly, Heraclitus refers to succession, change, and regularity by pairing day/night, winter/summer, war/peace, living/dead, hot/cold, moist/dry, living/dead, waking/sleeping, young/old. In several of these pairings, one pair succeeds the other. For example, day turns into night and back again with regularity. Some suggest one pair overcoming the other, for example, hunger overcome by satiety. Others still suggest disruption and restoration, for example, we are disrupted from our sleep. In all these we perceive the contrast between the pairings and we name them according to 'the pleasures of each one'. Each pairing is distinctly different but will change, alter, and succeed into the other and back again. Secondly, 'the pleasures of each one' hints at the relative experience of opposites. For example, the sea is both pure and foul, for fish and men respectively and man is foolish to god, as a child is to man. Hence, there is no essential difference between the opposites. Thirdly, Heraclitus shows how the opposites, although at first reading can be divided into positive (health, satiety, rest) and negative (disease, hunger, weariness), are in fact such that the negative makes a positive contribution. In other words, by getting what we want, we would be denied the contrast by which we can appreciate the 'sweet and the good'. This positive contribution of the negative term provides the unity between opposites.

The most subtle unity of opposites posed by Heraclitus is between the way up and down being the same. This pairing contains echoes of relative experience of direction, but has 'the way' as common without reference to anyone in particular. Here we keep the relativity, i.e. whether the way is up or down depends on your direction of travel, but lose the positive/negative connotation. We can say that the way differs from itself by agreeing with itself. It differs from itself because the way is either going one way or the other, but it agrees with itself because it combines both directions.

Heraclitus hits an even more subtle note in his theme of unity, transformation, and opposition in the following fragment:

> They do not comprehend how a thing agrees at variance with itself: <it is> an attunement (or fitting together, harmonie) turning back <on itself>, like that of the bow and the lyre. (LXXVIII, D. 51)

The use of *harmonie* contains echoes of several connections to how the unity of opposites fits together. Firstly, there is a physical fitting together of parts. The bow and the string physically fit together, are in tension and opposition, i.e. pulling in different directions, and yet appear to be stable and unchanging. It may also signal the use of the bow, as the archer pulls in opposite directions to fire an arrow, and how pulling in opposite directions fits together. Secondly, *harmonie* intimates the unity or agreement or coalition of hostile opponents. Here Heraclitus alludes to the imagery of *Harmonie*. As Kahn states *Harmonie* is used:

> figuratively, for 'agreements' or 'compacts' between hostile men (*Iliad*, XXII.255, and hence for the personified power of 'Reconciliation', the child of Ares and Aphrodite

in Hesiod (*Theogony*, 937). So Empedocles could employ *Harmonie* as another name for *Philotes* of Aphrodite, his counterpart to Strife or Conflict, the principle of proportion and agreement which creates a harmonious unity out of potentially hostile powers. (Kahn, 1979: 196)

Thirdly, *harmonie* indicates a pattern of musical attunement, one that is achieved by striking different notes together on the lyre. Unlike the unifying tension of opposition of the bow, the tension of the strings of the lyre is not uniform but varies to produce different notes and produce music. The three variations indicate the combination of *harmonie* as technical, political, and artistic unity of opposition: crafting materials by joining them together, political coalition by bringing together warring factions, and the art of composing beautiful music.

> Graspings: wholes and not wholes, convergent divergent, consonant dissonant, from all things one, and from one thing all. (CXXIV, D. 10)
> The hidden attunement is better than the obvious one. (LXXX, D. 54)

For Heraclitus, opposites form both a unity and a plurality. However, he arrives at this unity and plurality obliquely, rather than directly. As the fragment 'the hidden attunement is better than the obvious one' states, 'the immediate "surface" meaning is often less significant than the latent intention carried by allusion, enigma, and resonance' (Kahn, 1979: 203). Kahn argues that this fragment is 'one of the shortest and most beautifully designed of the fragments' (Kahn, 1979: 202), demonstrating how the negative term, non-apparent and not obvious, i.e. the hidden, rings true. Furthermore, as the term 'graspings' (*syllapsies*) indicates, we need to take his words together. If we separate out the sounds, i.e. each syllable, we lose our ability to understand and grasp.

In summary, we return to Heraclitus' river fragment and his depiction as the weeping philosopher which popularly represents his philosophy:

> As they step into the same rivers, others and still other waters flow upon them. (L, D. 12)

Heraclitus' use of '*potamoisin toisin autoisin embainousin*' (As they step into the same rivers) 'suggests the incessant movement of the river water by the rhythm and assonance of the four words ending in—*oisin* or *ousin*, reinforced by the more explicit repetition in "other and other waters"…represents the oncoming waters from upstream' (Kahn, 1979: 167). Unity, transformation, and opposition are also suggested in contrast between Heraclitus and Democritus. Whereas most paintings depict Heraclitus and Democritus separately, a painting by Rembrandt is more puzzling. As Lutz (1954) argues, one way to interpret this painting is to see the laughing Rembrandt-Democritus who is plainly visible, painting the sad, hidden, and dark Rembrandt-Heraclitus. This interpretation echoes Heraclitus' suggestion of going in search of knowledge.

3.3.2.1 *Undoing, Knowing, Being Wise*

> Not comprehending, they hear like the deaf. The saying bears witness to them: absent while present. (II, D. 34)
>
> Although the account (*logos*) is shared most men live as though their thinking (phronesis) were a private possession. (III, D. 2)
>
> Most men do not think things in the way that they encounter them, nor do they recognize what they experience, but believe their own opinions. (IV, D. 17)
>
> Not knowing how to listen, neither can they speak. (XVII, D. 19)
>
> It belongs to all men to know themselves and think well. (XXIX, D. 116)
>
> Speaking with understanding they must hold fast to what is shared by all, as a city holds to its law, and even more firmly. For all human laws are nourished by a divine one. It prevails as it will and suffices for all and is more than enough. (XXX, D. 114)

Knowledge, for Heraclitus, is 'absent while present'. In his customary way, Heraclitus firstly undoes what we commonly consider to be knowledge before signalling what he means by knowing. Knowledge is not private possession or private understanding, but is shared by all in its absent presence. This common knowledge is common because it is the generic process of organizing rather than knowledge about specific things. We do not recognize or understand the generic process of organizing, but believe our own opinions. Hence, our common condition is characterized negatively as being deaf to our shared account despite being experienced by all.

> Whatever comes from sight, hearing, learning from experience: this I prefer. (XIV, D. 55)
>
> Eyes and ears are poor witnesses for men if their souls (psychai) do not understand the language (literally, 'if they have barbarian souls'). (XVI, D. 107)
>
> Much learning does not teach understanding. For it would have taught Hesiod and Pythagoras, and also Xenophanes and Hecataeus. (XVIII, D. 40)
>
> The teacher of most is Hesiod. It is him they know as knowing most, who did not recognize day and night: they are one. (XIX, D. 57)
>
> Men are deceived in the recognition of what is obvious, like Homer who was wisest of all the Greeks. For he was deceived by boys killing lice, who said: what we see and catch we leave behind; what we neither see nor catch, we carry away. (XXII, D. 56)

Not knowing and not being able to understand one's experience hints at the need to reflect and 'know thyself'. Heraclitus is also critical of 'much learning' which can still lead to not seeing what is commonplace, especially if one relies upon experts, such as Hesiod, rather than preferring to reflect on one's own experience. This reflection of what one's eyes and ears witness is complemented by being able to understand language. This language can elude the most learned of them all, such as Hesiod and Homer. The example of day/night aims to illustrate how, although Hesiod knows the distinction between day and night, he fails to recognize the unity of opposites. As Kahn (1979: 109) elaborates, 'Hesiod had conceived Night (*Nyx*) in the manner of early mythic thought, as a positive force which blots out the light of day and the vision of men, as death blots out human life'. By stating this well-established opposition between night and day as being one and the same, Heraclitus affirms the unity of, in our terms, the 24 hours. In attacking the expert knowledge of Homer, Heraclitus refers to the riddle that is supposed to have led to his death. The answer to the riddle—what we see and catch we leave behind; what we don't see we take with us—was known to children, but Homer was blind to this and is supposed to have died of grief in not being able to solve it.

> The lord whose oracle is in Delphi neither declares nor conceals but gives a sign. (XXXIII, D. 93)
> It belongs to all men to know (ginoskein) themselves and think well (sophronein, keep their thinking sound). (XXIX, D. 116)
> Thinking well (sophronein) is the greatest excellence and wisdom: to act and speak what is true, perceiving things according to their nature (physis). (XXXII, D. 112)

Having described knowing as being absent in its presence in shared experience, and having attacked experts of the day for not knowing (the day/night unity) and not seeing (what children can see), Heraclitus 'neither declares nor conceals' but points towards wisdom. We are made aware that wisdom is not private and it is not possession of facts. We are also reminded that men should keep their 'thinking sound' and 'know themselves'. Fragment XXXII, D. 112—'Thinking well is the greatest excellence and wisdom: to act and speak what is true, perceiving things according to their nature'—points to several ways of understanding 'thinking well'. Firstly, 'thinking well' is a unity of excellence or courage (*arête*) and good judgement or discretion (*sophie*). This combination, however, is not one that is personal or private but directed towards what belongs to all and is shared. Secondly, 'thinking well' is a unity of acting, speaking, and perceiving what is true. Thus, thinking well is a unity of doings, sayings, and seeings what is true. The understanding of this fragment turns on the meaning of 'true' (*alethes*). In keeping with Heraclitus' flux and becoming in unity, *alethes* has echoes of unconcealment and opening. In other words, 'true' is uncovered, recovered, and discovered in how we do, say, and see things in their openness. As Kahn summarizes:

> What is distinctive here is the meaning of self-knowledge as recognition of one's true or hidden self, and the connection of this with knowledge of a universal *logos* which distinguishes things 'according to their nature'. (Kahn, 1979: 122)

By referring to the universal *logos* we are left with the question of what this *logos* means which we must learn to speak well, listen well, and understand. Although this *logos* is common to all, the path to uncovering it has many unexpected turnings.

3.3.2.2 Logos

> Although this account (*logos*) holds forever, men ever fail to comprehend, both before hearing it and once they have heard. Although all things come to pass in accordance with this account (*logos*), men are like the untried when they try such words and works as I set forth, distinguishing each according to its nature and telling

how it is. But other men are oblivious of what they do awake, just as they are forgetful of what they do asleep. (I, D. 1)

   Although the account (*logos*) is shared, most men live as though their thinking (phronesis) were a private possession. (III, D. 2)

As stated earlier, Heraclitus' use of *logos* has echoes of several meanings: 'sayings, speech, discourse, statement, report; account, explanation, reason, principle; esteem, reputation; collection, enumeration, ratio, proportion' (Kahn, 1979: 29). The meanings associated with 'collection' signal *logos* as joining or gathering. One can see the resonance of this in the verb, *legein*, to gather. Heraclitus' gathering together of words and thoughts to speak in this book is one such gathering. However, as Kahn states:

   Perhaps no other Greek author—or none except Aeschylus—has so systematically exploited the possibilities of ambiguity and allusiveness that are implicit in all human speech. The characteristic expression of this ambiguity is in word-play, of which the fragments are full. (Kahn, 1964: 193)

Heracliteans widely agree that fragment I, D. 1 are the first lines of his book. In this, the reader is introduced to the *logos* as being 'forever'. We are asked to listen to the *logos*, not to Heraclitus: 'It is wise, listening not to me but to the report, to agree that all things are one' (XXXVI, D. 50). The opening fragment continues to connect the forever *logos* to failing to comprehend, not only once we have heard it, but also before we have heard it. This suggests that the *logos* is ever-present and available for comprehension but Heraclitus expects his words and works to fall on deaf ears as men fail to uncover what they experience. He signals the tension and unity between universal and available *logos* and our inability to grasp it. However, there is no 'it-ness' of the *logos* to grasp. In the second fragment quoted earlier, Heraclitus replaces 'forever' with 'shared' or 'common' to describe *logos*. If it was separate, it would be available for private possession. Heraclitus warns against such an interpretation. While 'forever' may draw the reader into thinking that the *logos* stands apart from, is objective, and exists independently, 'shared' and 'common' guards against imposing a subjective–objective divide by emphasizing that the *logos* is part of, constitutive, and relational. In other words, the *logos* joins and separates simultaneously. It is constitutive of what is shared and common, and it is forever. This ceaseless unity of opposites reveals the hidden nature of things. As Heraclitus states, 'Nature loves to hide' (X, D. 123). And it is in 'thinking well' about the movement of joining and separating (the bow and the lyre) that we recognize the hidden unity of all.

3.4 Resonance

Heraclitus rightly occupies a prominent place in process thinking. Within organization studies, his river fragments and 'everything flows' are cited often to develop a processual approach. However, there is little or no attempt to engage with any of his other frag-ments. There are good reasons why organizational theorists might eschew engag-ing with Heraclitus' fragments, chief among them being his infamous epitaph as 'The Obscure'. However, rescuing him from obscurity requires us to engage with his style of writing which 'neither declares nor conceals, but gives a sign' (XXXIII, D. 93). His generic way of thinking echoes and resonates across various fragments, working against the tendency to move from rough beginnings to determinate ends. Rather than reach an end point, Heraclitus encourages thought to join, gather, connect, share, discover, and invent what is common to all.

Organization studies is replete with binary oppositions such as internal–external, power–resistance, stability–change, agency–structure, tacit–explicit, noun–verb. Key among them is the ontological and epistemological distinction between entity and pro-cess (Thompson, 2011), where Parmenides represents the entitative view and Heraclitus the process view. However, the challenge for organizational scholars is to move beyond fixing Heraclitus' views to process thinking in opposition to entitative thinking. Heraclitus' emphasis on 'shared', 'joining', and 'common' invite a deeper appreciation of process, as one that moves beyond binary oppositions.

Fundamental to moving beyond binary oppositions is to recognize that Heraclitean process is not an ontological worldview or a principle that transcends. It does not belong prior to our understanding of the world. Instead it participates in the world. It is the interdependence and joining of the opposites that reveals Heraclitean thinking. Each pairing and joining reveals the hidden truth that belongs and constitutes both pairs. The hidden connection prefers to hide, but the task of Heraclitean thinking is to uncover the seemingly separate and demonstrate how they seam together. For example, consider 'One must realize that war is shared and Conflict is Justice' (LXXXII, D. 80). By saying war is shared or common, and conflict is justice, Heraclitus brings together terms that would not normally be paired. Heraclitus asks us to think about the hidden connec-tion, one that would not reveal itself. The challenge is to understand how the opposition 'agrees at variance with itself' (LXXVII, D. 51). In order to understand the pairings of war–shared and conflict–justice, we are looking for how one term uncovers the hidden meaning of the other and vice versa. The pairing, war–shared, is better uncovered by the term 'community', rather than shared (Schindler, 2003). By binding war and community together, Heraclitus reveals a hidden connection between the two that is essential for both. Consider 'community is war'. Community is not the common and shared unity, but hides war, difference, and conflict within it. Community exists and is constituted by holding differences together.

> Speaking more metaphysically, we might say that the movement that generates com-munity cannot be simply a movement towards oneness, because such movement, were it to find ideal completion, would result in a difference-excluding-identical unity. Instead, the movement must follow two relatively opposed directions simul-taneously; it must move at precisely one and the same time towards unity and away from unity. (Schindler, 2003: 429)

Thus, community is war. War participates in community. Just as war completes our understanding of community, so does community our understanding of war. What does it mean to say, war is community? One way of understanding this is that war is not war if it is not shared by the opposing parties. If the tension between the two warring factions is not symmetrical, we do not have war, but a complete annihilation of one by the other. War is truly war between worthy opponents, ones that are united in the war, but at the same time are opposed to each other. Hence, 'war is not simply violence but the ritualized struggle that paradoxically generates solidarity, its identification with community reveals what is most profound about war' (Schindler, 2003: 430–1).

The challenge that Heraclitus poses for organizational scholars is to move beyond binary oppositions. The movement beyond is not one that singles out one element, entity, and then the other, process. It is to recognize how the pairing works in tension and opposition as one. The opposition is not static, but one that actively constitutes both terms. Each term is relational, that is, they relate to each other as the hidden force that energizes and animates them.

3.5 Conclusion

If this chapter has succeeded in provoking the reader to deepen their understanding of Heraclitus' two famous sayings—'everything flows' and 'you cannot step into the same river twice'—and to move beyond these saying and connect with his ambiguous style and his generic process of organization, then it would ill have served its intention. Heraclitus' fragments are neither an exposition of a meaning nor a summary of a message. Heraclitus' philosophy indeed does provoke us to think beyond. Its provocation lies in bringing together the opposites by exploring hidden depths and latent connections. Unlike attempts to disprove, falsify, and discard, Heraclitean philosophy asks us to enquire into new meanings without the loss of the tension and opposition that joins and separates in the same movement. The Heraclitean way is to gather together scattered and disperse ideas. Heraclitus' writings are also important in reassessing our modern arrogance in mastering our world. Knowledge, progress, power, and control hides the subtle yet always present truth that 'as a man, he will not be wise, but only a lover-of-wisdom, a *philosophos*. It is to this ardent search for insight into the divine unity of all things that the words of Heraclitus would summon the reader. It is such *philosophia* which constitutes for him true piety' (Kahn, 1964: 203).

What animates Heraclitus' fragments is not particular things, but a generic process of organizing that joins and separates at the same time. The challenge for organizational scholars is to move from thinking about organizations to the organization of thought (Chia, 1997). This implies taking language seriously and recognizing the capacity of language to reveal and obscure at the same time. Heraclitus masterfully exploits the ambiguity and connectivity between words through linguistic density, and at the same time alludes to and resonates with broader themes. Yet it is not so much the words and broader themes that he conveys, but the hidden movement within. As Kahn summarizes, 'It is language itself which, by its dual capacity to reveal and obscure, provides the natural "sign" for the multifarious and largely latent connections between things' (Kahn, 1964: 193). Surprisingly, what Heraclitus achieves through his fragments is to convey his ideas by affirming what would be perceived as contradictory and illogical connections. His fragments are not an oeuvre; he does not build monumental theories densely argued over hundreds of pages. Instead, his paradoxical style deliberately avoids the monumental in favour of odd placing of words that are meant to catch the corner of the reader's eye, inviting them to savour different connections and discover new ones. Heraclitus' fragments provide us with the 'raw materials or rough beginnings of creative play' (Cooper, 2001: 330). Heraclitus' writings are indeed strange. Yet, is it not more interesting for thought to wander into the strange than to establish itself in the obvious?

Notes

1. In this chapter the Diels reference is shown as D. [number].
2. There are several notable non-English Heracliteans. However, without first-hand engagement with their texts, their contributions have not been included here.
3. Kahn offers a new numbering system, using Roman numerals. He also provides a table to cross-reference his numbering with Diels' numbering. This adds another layer of complexity to reading Heraclitus by asking the reader to go back and forth between the numbering systems to uncover their meanings. All references to Heraclitus' fragments in this chapter are referenced using both, Kahn's Roman numerals and Diels' ordering.
4. Amidst all the debate surrounding the ordering of Heraclitus' fragments, there appears to be agreement that this fragment is the first.

References

Burnet, J. (1930). *Early Greek Philosophy*, 4th edn (London: Adam and Charles Black).
Chia, R. (1997). Essai: Thirty Years On: From Organizational Structures to the Organization of Thought, *Organization Studies* 18(4): 685–707.
Chitwood, A. (2004). *Death by Philosophy* (Ann Harbor, MI: University of Michigan Press).
Cooper, R. (2001). Un-Timely Mediations: Questing Thought. *Ephemera* 1(4): 321–47.
Diels, H.A. (1903). *De Fragmente der Vorsokratiker* (Berlin: Weidmannsche Buchhandlung).
Dilcher, R. (1995). *Studies in Heraclitus* (Hildesheim: Georg Olms AG).
Freeman, K. (1946). *The Pre-Socratic Philosophers* (Oxford: Basil Blackwell).
——(1948). *Ancilla to the Pre-Socratic Philosophers* (Oxford: Basil Blackwell).
Guthrie, W.K.C. (1962). *A History of Greek Philosophy* (Cambridge: Cambridge University Press).
Kahn, C.H. (1964). A New Look at Heraclitus, *American Philosophical Quarterly* 1(3): 189–203.
——(1979). *The Art and Thought of Heraclitus* (Cambridge: Cambridge University Press).
Kirk, G.S. (1954). *Heraclitus: The Cosmic Fragments* (Cambridge: Cambridge Univeristy Press).

Laertius, D. (1925). *Lives of Eminent Philosophers,* trans. R.D. Hicks (London: William Heinemann).

Lebeck, A. (1971). *The Oresteia: A Study in Language and Structure* (Cambridge, MA: Harvard University Press).

Lutz, C.E. (1954). Demotritus and Heraclitus, *The Classical Journal 49*(7): 309–14.

Marcovich, M. (1967). *Heraclitus* (Merida, Venezuela: The Los Andes University Press).

Schindler, D.C. (2003). The Community of the One and the Many: Heraclitus on Reason, *Inquiry 46*(4): 413–48.

Thompson, M. (2011). Ontological Shift or Ontological Drift? Reality Claims, Epistemological Frameworks, and Theory Generation in Organization Studies, *Academy of Management Review 36*(4): 754–73.

CHAPTER 4

···

CONFUCIUS (551–479 BC)

···

YUAN LI AND WEN HAIMING

4.1 INTRODUCTION

KONGZI, OR Confucius (孔 子, 551–479 BC), the founder of Confucian philosophy, is one of the most influential philosophers in Chinese history. He was born in the Spring and Autumn Period (about 770–475 BC) in the state of Lu (today's Shandong province). He was a descendant of a noble family associated with the royal house of the Shang Dynasty (1600–1046 BC). In spite of his noble birth, he lived a penurious childhood because his father passed away when he was 3 and his mother died when he was 17. As an orphan he had to face the whole world alone. When Confucius reached adulthood, he became an educator and politician; he wanted to serve in high office in the hope that he could restore the ancient morality set by the founders of the Zhou Dynasty (1046–256 BC). He held various important positions. When he was 52, he served as acting prime minister in the position of minister of justice. However, he failed to realize his political ideal in his own state, and thereafter travelled from state to state, trying to find a more congenial home for his teachings, but never again had the opportunity to carry out his political reforms. Failing to make progress in the political arena, in his old age Confucius returned to the state of Lu, where he engaged deeply in education. Throughout his teaching career, he took on nearly 3,000 disciples, 72 of whom became quite accomplished and famous. Besides teaching, Confucius catalogued and ordered the poems, history, rituals, and music of the Zhou Dynasty. These documents later became classics and important teaching materials for personal cultivation. As a system of humanist culture and a live force in the Chinese people, Confucianism has exerted a far-reaching influence on generations of Chinese in almost all areas, including politics, education, values, and etiquette.

Generally, the Confucianism represented in the *Analects* and the *Four Books*[1] is an uplifting spirituality full of sagacity and magnificence, both necessary components for a community cultivating its communal spirituality. Confucius had a great understanding of the ancient ritual system and classics. He taught his disciples ancient classics and these were passed from generation to generation. We can discover some inspiration for modern organizational management in Confucian teachings and the perspective of processual thinking.

4.2 Processual Nature and the *Dao* of Leadership

In the *Analects*, Confucius does not say much about nature; he was more concerned with the nature of human beings. But while Confucius was a keen and careful observer of human affairs, he also had a deep understanding of the human condition. Once Confucius stood on a riverbank and said, 'The passage of time is just like the flow of waters, which goes on day or night!'[2] When Confucius talks about flowing water it is normally understood as time, which is changing at the moment of now. However, it is not just time that is changing but also everything in the world is changing ontologically, which Chinese philosophers understand as the 'ontological original state of *dao*'.[3] The Confucian attitude towards changing times is to be optimistic about the ever-changing things in the world and project a positive value on it.

Confucius felt that existence flowed continuously, just as Heraclitus (540–480 BC) considered everything to be in constant flux and movement, claiming that we cannot step twice into the same river. Confucius noticed that nature (*tian* 天) gives no explicit orders, but the four seasons march on and myriad things (*wanwu* 万物) flourish.[4] *Tian* is the creator of *wanwu*, but *tian* is not independent of what is created and ordered; rather, *wanwu* constitutes *tian*. There is no apparent distinction between the order itself and what orders it. In addition to an impersonal process and an emergent order, *tian* can also be understood as a transmitted living culture, according to Confucianism. It seems to symbolize a cumulative and continuing cultural legacy focused in the spirits of ancestors or some culturally significant human beings (Ames and Rosemont, 1998: 47). The analogy between *tian* and the sage or noble man is often mentioned in Confucian classics. The spirit of *tian* is very much present in the routines, regularities, and generative process of nature and in the social order of the human community. Any decay and disorder in the human world will symbiotically be reflected in *wanwu* and *tian*. Human beings and *tian* are actually integrated.

Confucius tends to avoid discussion of metaphysical or mystical questions. He maintains a respectful detachment from the unknown realm of gods and spirits.[5] Confucius shuns questions beyond empirical understanding and carefully keeps his discussion within the boundary of immediate experience. For example, he once commented that if one cannot serve the living people, how could one serve the spirit of the dead? If one cannot understand life, why should one think much about death?[6] *Tian* is closely related to another word—*ming* (命), which is often translated as 'fate' or 'destiny'. *Ming* is the mandate of *tian*, and it is what is ordained. *Ming* mostly refers to the so-called proper vocation of man or the enduring life task which *tian* has imposed on man. However, unlike western 'fate' or 'destiny', Chinese *ming* does not mean that one's fate is completely fixed or predetermined. It is not a power totally independent of and external to human beings and it is based on the continuity of the nature–human (*tian-ren* 天人) relationship. People can affect their circumstances through choosing how to respond to the emergent possibilities. In spite of his reticence to discuss mystical questions, Confucius is quite interested in *ming*. He insists that *ming* is a necessary condition for becoming a *junzi* (君子 exemplary person): 'A person who does not understand *ming* cannot become a *junzi*.'[7] To Confucius, *ming* refers to a *junzi*'s personal mandate to fulfil his moral-political vocation: a *junzi* or *shengren* (圣人 sage) has established an inherent relationship with *tian*, and therefore he can understand his *ming* and take his social responsibility to fulfil his *ming*.

Dao (道 the way-making) is of great importance in Confucius' thinking, and it appears nearly a hundred times in the *Analects*. For Daoism, *dao* is the source of all being and it manifests itself everywhere, while for Confucius the *dao* is primarily the *dao* of humans as it manifests itself in the realm of human life. 'The *dao* of Wen and Wu[8] has not fallen to the ground. It exists in people. Those of superior quality have grasped its essentials and the inferior have grasped a bit of it. Everyone has something of Wen and Wu's *dao* in him.'[9] In this way, the Confucian *dao* cannot be separated from the people: people are not only the heirs and propagators, but also creators of *dao*. The *dao* emerges throughout human activities: '*Junzi* works at the roots. Only when the roots are firmly set will the *dao* grow. Filial piety and brotherly obedience are the roots of humanity.'[10] Although Confucius frequently describes the *dao* as something precious received from preceding generations, he makes no assertion that people can realize *dao* by following in the footprints of their predecessors. Confucius says: 'It is the human being that can broaden the *dao*, not the *dao* that broadens the human.'[11] Human beings can broaden, extend, and continue the *dao* actively and creatively. Thus, we see that Confucius has a real preoccupation with human society, and Confucius' *tian* is basically about the human world. For Confucius, human beings are the participants in an open-ended, value-creative process. Humans are creative and active, though they also depend on cultural accumulation and the attendant enrichment of possibilities.

The Confucian *dao* is not a transcendental or a priori power, and it is historically composite and cumulative through the dynamic interaction process between human beings and their circumstances. The *dao* is 'determined by the exchange between an emerging humanity and a changing world', and it is 'a process of world making unified by the basic coherence of all humans' ongoing achievements in the areas of the various cultural interests' (Hall and Ames, 1987: 230). Therefore, *dao* is a continuous process of human civilization which is inherited and transformed by succeeding generations. *Dao* manifests itself in every era of human history, because 'each present perspective is a function of all past events, and is the ground of all future possibilities' (Hall and Ames, 1987: 231). The past casts the present and the future, and the present and the future can also recast and revise the past through succeeding perspectives of human experience and their changing ways of interpretation.

Thus, according to Confucius' teaching, the *dao* can be inherited, transmitted, broadened, extended, and created by people, since it is determined through the process of interaction between people and changing circumstances. Therefore, the *dao* of Confucian organizational management is not isolated and fixed; instead, it is in constant transformation as a result of human activities. Management of each organization always exhibits its own peculiarities because of its employees' uniqueness, particular cultural environment, and some other factors. Also the current *dao* of management in an organization receives great influence from past management practices, which will also affect and predict the future management style.

For Confucians, it is necessary to understand the *dao* of nature in order to apply it to human societies or organizations. The *dao*, as a basic pattern of the moving universe and of human society, is basically the same though it is present in every individual. The human hierarchical society is an imitation of the natural sequence where the heavens are high and the earth is low. This organization of natural phenomena cannot be denied. The *Great Commentary* of the *Book of Changes* was traditionally taken as the writing of Confucius himself, and the idea that the running pattern of human organization should follow the natural pattern has been one of the core values for Confucian organization throughout history. In this sense, a harmonious and moral society can be built and maintained through recognizing natural hierarchy and the central leadership role of moral persons (*junzi*).

4.2.1 The Process of Human Organizations and Self-Cultivation

Ren (仁 benevolence or humanity) and *li* (礼 ritual propriety) are two cardinal virtues in Confucianism. For Confucius, *ren* is an extensive love of human beings, and through the cultivation of the '*dao*, it enables a moral person to express concern for both the physical and moral well-being of others. The etymological meaning of *ren* is 'man in society', as the character *ren* (仁) is composed of two parts: a standing man on the left and *er* (二 number two) on the right. From the Confucian point of view, a person cannot become truly human without the reciprocal affection of other people. As Tu Wei-ming puts it, 'One's ability to relate to others in a meaningful way, such as in the spirit of filiality, brotherhood, or friendship, reflects one's level of self-cultivation' (Tu, 1972: 188). Tu insists that *ren* should be understood from the perspective of the newly discovered Guodian archaeological finds, where *ren* is composed of two components: the upper human body (*shen* 身) and the lower mind-heart (*xin* 心). One can realize oneself by making great efforts to harmonize one's relationships with others, rather than by detaching oneself from the world of human relations.

However, unlike Mozi's (墨子) idea of universal love, and the love for everyone including one's enemy in Christianity, Confucian love is graded according to the proximity and distance of various relationships. For Confucians, to deny the graded relationship is to obstruct the path of humanity and righteousness and even destroy the harmony of human organizations. From the Confucian perspective, an individual can be humane as long as they are in relationship to other human beings in a society, and *ren* can only be defined and realized through relationships and interactions with others. Thus, *ren* should be understood in the processual interaction of human organizations, where *li* (rite/ritual propriety) indicates a pattern of behaviour that is the foundation of human virtue. *Li* is manifested in a variety of rituals relating to personal conduct, social relations, political organizations, religious behaviour, and so forth. For Herbert Fingarette (1998), virtue (*de* 德) is realized in concrete human acts, acts in a pattern with certain features, which are represented by *li*. A virtuous leader should fully understand the code of *li* and behave according to *li* in a group. He should expand it into an organizational culture, in order to cultivate a moral atmosphere in an organization, in which members interact in an appropriate way through internalizing *li* as their moral code.

As Fingarette puts it: 'Men become truly human as their raw impulse is shaped by li. Li is the specifically humanizing form of the dynamic relationship of man-to-man' (Fingarette, 1998: 7). *Li* is the inherent requirement of morality, and as a code of conduct it is manifested in moral behaviour. As a comprehensive virtue, *ren* gives meaning to *li*. Correspondingly, *li* is an externalization of *ren* in a concrete social situation. As for the relationship between *li* and *de*, Confucius says, 'if you govern them (the common people) with decrees and regulate them with punishments, they will evade them, but will have no sense of shame. If you lead with virtue (*de*) and regulate them with rules of propriety (*li*), people will have a sense of shame and abide by the rules.'[12]

Just as human relatedness is central to the actualization of the ideal of *ren*, relating oneself to others is the underlying structure of *li*. As Tu Wei-ming points out, a person's authentic being can be fully manifested 'if and only if the individual enters into human–relatedness in the spirit of reciprocity' (Tu, 1972: 197). For Tu, *li* could be understood as the movement of self-transformation, through which man becomes more 'humane' in relationships (Tu, 1972: 197). For Confucius, one could not become a *junzi* or a sage without going through the process of ritualization or humanization. The humanization of *li* is best shown in a dialogue in the *Analects*. Yan Hui, Confucius' disciple, enquired about humanity (*ren*) and Confucius replied: 'Through self-discipline and observing ritual propriety (*li*)'. Confucius further explained that the specific character of *ren* should include: 'do not look at anything that violates *li*; do not listen to anything that violates *li*; do not speak about anything that violates *li*; do not do anything that violates *li*'.[13] Confucius proclaims that one must see, listen, speak, and behave according to *li*, and *li* should not be perceived as fixed and isolated rituals that are being imposed upon people without their inner moral consent. A person could not become virtuous by uncritically submitting themselves to the restrictions of society. In the *Analects*, Confucius used '*xiang yuan*' (乡愿) to denote a type of person who follows the conventions with no inner conviction and assumes the appearance of virtue. He says: '*xiang yuan* is virtue under false pretences'.[14] *Li* is embedded and manifested in a particular social context, and it varies according to different situations. Confucius himself did not stick to any fixed and dogmatic external restrictions. There were four things he abstained from entirely: 'he never holds arbitrary opinion; he had no dogmatism; he was not inflex-ible; he was not self-absorbed'.[15] For him, a person's self-realization should go through a dynamic and flexible process, which is manifested in the context of human relations.

In short, Confucians view society as a community of interrelated responsibilities. To achieve a moral, just, and harmonious society, the principle of *li* also recommends that an individual should do what is proper to fulfil his position (Romar, 2002). This requires a leader of an organization to well understand their role, tasks, and position in the pro-cess of management and rectify their mind and heart to apply the proper attitudes and knowledge to fulfil their role. That is, instead of behaving according to *li* like common people, leaders must set themselves higher moral standards and measure their moral behaviour with regard to their role as superiors and know how their actions will impact those around them.

4.2.2 Processual Learning: Self-Cultivation and Educating Others

Confucius advocates a view of processual learning. On the one hand, one should cul-tivate oneself throughout one's lifetime, and on the other, educating others is always processual. Confucius describes his spiritual autobiography in six stages: 'At fifteen my heart-and-mind were set upon learning; at thirty I took my stance; at forty I was no longer doubtful; at fifty I realized the decree of *tian* (*tianming* 天命); at sixty my ear was attuned; at seventy I could give my heart-and-mind free rein without overstepping the boundaries'.[16] Through continuous learning and self-cultivation, one can gradu-ally brighten the eyes, attune the ears, and refine the mind, and consequently reach the heart-and-mind's (*xin* 心) freedom. Confucian virtues such as *ren* (humanity or benevolence 仁), *li* (ritual propriety 礼), *shu* (altruism 恕), and so forth are not given at birth, but must be achieved through learning and practice. Learning is the way in which human beings guide themselves into effective being (Grange, 2005). For Confucius, the enrichment of life through learning and refinement is an end in itself, and therefore learning is not a means to secure a livelihood. Rather, it is a way of life. Life is an inces-sant process of learning.

Confucius himself cherishes enthusiasm for learning, and describes his efforts as 'eager to learn': 'There are, in a town of ten households, bound to be people who are better than I am in loyalty (*zhong* 忠) and trustworthiness (*xin* 信), but there will be no one who can compare with me in the love of learning'.[17] If self-sacrifice is the key to the Christian message, then learning is the vital ingredient of the Confucian message (Dawson, 1981: 10). A piece of jade cannot become an object of art without elaborate chiselling, and a person cannot refine and realize oneself without constant learning. The dynamics of thinking in Confucianism can be explicated as a constant interplay between learning (*xue* 学) and reflecting (*si* 思) (Hall and Ames, 1987). Confucius' learn-ing is an unmediated process of 'becoming aware' rather than a 'conceptually mediated knowledge' of an objective world (Hall and Ames, 1987: 44). Becoming a learned person requires engaging in both teaching and studying, which are indispensable in the process of learning.

The objective of the learning process is the transmission of human culture. Confucius says: 'The Zhou Dynasty looked back to the Xia and Shang Dynasties. Such a wealth of culture! I follow the Zhou.'[18] Confucius regarded traditional culture highly, and he took the transmission and revival of the cultural legacy as his foremost mission. Learning stands for the acquisition and transmission of the meaning invested in the cultural tradition. To Confucius, although learning defers to the excellence of one's cultural legacy, this is not to deny innovation and change. What Confucius suggests is that one must be creative to take full advantage of traditional culture, both in using it as a foundation to realize one's own possibilities, and in adapting it for one's own place, time, and situation. It is indispensable for one to acquire the ancient cultural legacy, but it is equally vital for one to take a further step in creatively applying what has been learned in new circumstances. Confucius says: 'he who can recite the three hundred Songs (*shi* 诗), when charged with state affairs, does not know how to handle them; when dispatched as envoy to other states, cannot respond on his own—though he knows so many, of what use is it?'[19]

As Hall and Ames point out, learning for Confucius is not a process of reasoning, but is essentially performative, as it is an activity that aims at practical results. 'Thus, in place of any activity that merely assesses an objective set of facts and/or values, thinking for Confucius is *actualizing* or *realizing* the meaningfulness of the world' (Hall and Ames, 1987: 44). In the *Focusing the Familiar* (*Zhongyong* 中庸), knowledge is formed in three ways: some are born with knowledge; some acquire knowledge by learning; and some acquire knowledge after a painful feeling of their ignorance.[20] Confucius believes that most people, including himself, are not born with knowledge, and he seems not as enthusiastic about pure contemplation and reasoning as the way to reach knowledge as his western counterparts. 'I am not born with knowledge. Rather, loving antiquity, I am earnest in seeking it out.'[21] For him, the purpose of learning is to perfect oneself morally and socially and to contribute to the whole goodness of the society. Practice is a necessary part of the learning process if one intends to acquire and develop knowledge.

Confucius proposed one thing that is essential for organizations and individuals yet is missed by the 'Learning Organization' proponents, namely the joy of learning. In the *Analects*, Confucius says at the very beginning: 'Having studied, to then repeatedly practice what you have learned—is this not a source of joy?'[22] Learning is not a task that is imposed by external forces, and it also should not be simply for the purpose of obtaining material benefits. Since the 1990 publication of Peter Senge's *The Fifth Discipline*, many managers have attempted to promote learning at their organizations. It is believed that learning organizations promote continuous improvement (Levine, 2001) and innovation (Ramus and Steger, 2000), and also foster community building (Digenti, 1998). Confucius predates Senge's Learning Organization by about 2,500 years. According Confucius, learning is an inner need of people, and it is the purpose of life itself. Organizational performance and profit should not be the sole target of organizational learning. The ultimate target should be that every individual continually receives improvement both physically and spiritually, and experiences the real joy of learning.

4.3 PROCESSUAL LEADERSHIP WITH MORAL FORCE: SITUATION-GUIDED ART

Confucian leadership is a situation-guided art of ruling through moral force, not only guiding people to behave in a proper way, but also trying to help them develop a good sense of morality so that they can regulate their minds according to appropriate ritual. It is common that a leader wants people to behave appropriately according to the requirements of particular situations, but to help people understand their circumstances and then let them actively choose certain patterns of behaviours is the special art of the Confucians. In short, for a Confucian leader it is not enough just to make people behave well; the leader must also help people think well, and in this way an organization would be led in a Confucian manner.

Confucius himself pays much attention to organizational leadership, and particularly emphasizes it in Book II of his *Analects*. The first three lines of Book II are particularly meaningful in laying out Confucius' own views on organizational leadership, and this section will mainly focus on an analysis of Confucian leadership based on them.

4.3.1 The Power of Leading People's Minds with Forceful Moral Propensity

The general topic of Book II of the *Analects* is 'the art of ruling, leading, or governing' (*weizheng* 為政). The first line of the book says, 'Governing with excellence (*de* 德) can be compared to being with the North Star: the North Star dwells in its place, and the multitude of stars pay it tribute'[23] (Ames and Rosemont, 1998: 76). The location of the North Star is unique, and is like the place of the emperor or leader. The centrality of a leader, or the place (*suo* 所), is particularly important for a leader to exemplify their *de* (virtue), normally taken as a set of moral behaviours that are good enough for common people to follow. However, the *de* also forms a particular political situation with a forceful propensity to inspire people to behave well according to good examples. Arthur Waley translates the *de* as 'moral force',[24] indicating that leading with *de* is leading with moral force, which always comes from the highest position, and is based on either military or political force. Therefore, 'using *de*' is to create a morally forceful propensity that others feel they should follow. The virtue, in this sense, is a systematic mode of thinking and behaving that a leader presents in construing a moral situation. This virtue in situation influences his people to follow willingly and actively.

For Confucius, the art of how to lead or rule rests in one most important factor: a central leader led by *de*, whom all people will naturally follow. It is not an art of using anything outside oneself, and the decisive factor is the place of a leader and their virtues or excellences, and whether they can effectively create a moral force based on them. What Confucius tries to argue is that using the moral force in a technical way is far from enough, and he requires the leaders to have a kind of virtue which helps them to rule properly. The virtue in this sense is the art of using power properly.

We argue that Confucian leadership is a situation-guided art because a Confucian leader needs to create a kind of situation in which their people will follow. This kind of situation is firstly political, because people are set into a particular situation without choice and then only later realize the moral situation that their leaders have set up. The leader should be authoritative, so that people will want to follow what they have done and said. People should have a sense of the force of the political situation, so that they can accommodate their behaviours properly to what the situation demands. Therefore, the power of leading does not come from certain kinds of principle or law, but from the people's sensibility and civility to adjust their minds and behaviours appropriately. People's sensibility secures their understanding of the leader's moral example, and people's civility makes sure they have the ability to choose and behave according to what they have comprehended.

The virtue of *de* is not just a combination of personal virtuous characteristics, but is an inner power of thinking and behaving. Leaders reside in their unique places and influence people through their words and deeds. Thus, they can shape their context with the members in their organizations. A Confucian leader does not force people to do and say right things, but cultivates people to think and do things in the right way. People do not follow great leaders passively, like being threatened or compelled to do things against their wills, but they are inspired by their leader's great moral capacity and consider following such moral words and deeds to be the best choice they could have in the organization they are situated in.

A leader's words and deeds form their *de* and help them shape the context with those being led. Thereby the leader is distinguished as better and more powerful than other people. A leader's *de* can surely influence their context and, by expressing their *de*, they are able to cultivate and transform their people to be virtuous or noble persons. In this way, a person's inner virtue is powerful because the *de* will extend to those being led and change their thoughts and behaviours accordingly. It is the 'place' of the North Star from which the power of commanding comes. In other words, without the highest central place, it is hard to command other stars. The authority of leading or commanding comes from occupying a powerful position.

The Confucian idea of 'rectifying the names' (*zhengming* 正名, *Analects* 13.3) can help an organizer guide people into proper places and functions. If people all think properly according to their positions and roles, then the world is well organized. The Confucian ideal of social management is to 'set an example yourself for those in office, pardon minor offenses, and promote those with superior character and ability'[25] (Ames and Rosemont, 1998: 161). Confucius wants people to follow a sequence of justice and putting people with various talents into different places. Thus, Confucian justice can be rendered as assigning people to function in places according to their ability and roles.

4.3.2 Leading People to Thinking Properly

The second line of Book II relates to Confucius' editing of the *Book of Songs/Poetry* and says, 'Although the Songs are three hundred in number, they can be covered in one expression: " 'Go vigorously without swerving" '[26] (Ames and Rosemont, 1998: 76). It seems to be about Confucius' editing of the *Book of Songs/Poetry* down from 3,000 verses to 300. However, most historical commentators indicate that this line is actually related to the education of the common people, because Confucius advocates that rituals and music are the two most powerful ways to cultivate people. Rituals help people behave well and follow some kind of code, and music helps people release their emotions and adjust their feelings. According to the historical commentaries on this second line, the function of music is not only to adjust people's feelings, but also to help them think in a proper way. A great leader not only needs to cultivate people to behave well, but also try to guide them to think properly. In this second line, it seems a leader knows how to guide people onto a right track, where dirty or evil thinking is far away. The situation between the leaders and the ruled will guide people to a non-coercive but forceful propensity, so that people know how to behave and how to adjust their ways of handling things. Most importantly, this helps people think and behave properly.

Thus, a Confucian leader actually focuses on the pattern of people's thinking, and guides people to act properly according to their way of thinking. Max Weber claimed that Confucianism is an ethic of 'unconditional affirmation of and adjustment to the world' (Weber, 1968: 229), but Xingzhong Yao does not agree with him. Yao argues that 'Confucian education is designed to penetrate the inner world of a learner, based on the conviction that cultivation of inner virtues is more important than adjustment of external behavior' (Yao, 2000: 281–2). A leader's virtue is to exemplify their proper way of handling situations and guide people to think properly. In order to prevent oneself from thinking of and doing evil, one needs to know the limits of improper ways of thinking. As for an organizational leader, one needs to promote those people who can behave better than other people, and try to avoid or suppress those who are evil and do not follow the rituals.

For Confucius, simply controlling one's behaviour is far from enough, since according to him a person not only needs to control their mind but also needs to regulate the activity of mind into the realm of 'no evil'. This is famously expressed in Confucius' claim, also in Book II, about the realm he reached when he was 70 and how he could give his heart-mind 'free rein without overstepping the boundaries' (Ames and Rosemont, 1998: 76). Hagop Sarkissian points out that tracing charitable or deplorable behaviours back to a person's character has been rendered problematic by compelling experimental data compiled throughout the 1970s and 1980s. This leads him to favour situationalism, which claims that morally significant behaviour is influenced by situational factors to a far greater extent than we normally suppose (Sarkissian, 2010: 2–3). A great Confucian leader is a master of adjusting people's thinking, their intentions, and wills, so that they will know things from good to evil, and choose to behave in ways that are good rather than evil. Thus, any evil thinking and doing will be stopped from being actualized or realized.

4.3.3 Guide Organization by Morality

The third line of Book II says, 'Lead the people with administrative injunctions (*zheng* 政) and keep them orderly with penal law (*xing* 刑), and they will avoid punishments but will be without a sense of shame. Lead them with excellence (*de* 德) and keep them orderly through observing ritual propriety (*li* 禮) and they will develop a sense of shame, and moreover, will order themselves'[27] (Ames and Rosemont, 1998: 76). This indicates that, for Confucius, people do shameful deeds simply because they cannot control their own desires, but whether one has the sense of shame is very important for an organization since people might behave well if they have a strong sense of shame. However, it is hard to rule or guide if people do not have a good sense of shame. Confucius believes that if one is able to control one's desires, then one should be able to 'regulate, control, or bring (*ge*) into proper degree'. 'To be free from (*mian*)' is that one will stop oneself from doing wrong things because of the sense of shame, not because one is afraid of getting caught. Confucius thinks that fear is not enough, and that one can avoid doing something that one feels improper for oneself and the situation. Together with the second line, which says that people should autonomously control their thinking and feelings, what Confucius is trying to emphasize is that it is not enough for a person just to control their thinking and feelings; they also need to actively regulate their deeds so that they can be morally good people. This way can be called a Confucian way of ruling and leading.

Most interpretations of Confucian leadership which discuss the third line of Book II highlight that it is based on the leadership of virtues, which means that a leader's virtue is decisive in judging what type of leadership it is. It suggests that common people might have freedom to follow the leader or not. However, this is not Confucius' point. What Confucius emphasizes is that common people should develop a sense of shame and thus actively cultivate themselves. However, this kind of cultivation is not based on free choice, nor is it based on the spontaneous development of one's nature. People choose to follow their leader because they acknowledge their leadership, and consider following the leader as the best way of living under the leadership. Thus, the leader's virtue provides a guiding principle for people to follow, and people seem to self-cultivate themselves with a great sense of community and the circumstances.

It is clear that the debate over governing a society by law or by morality existed long before Confucius' time. Later legalists like Han Fei argued that a society should be governed by deterrents (*qi* 齊, to 'regulate, bring into line') but, for Confucius, people under this kind of leadership would try to avoid punishment, and thus become cunning. While avoiding overt crime, they nonetheless do not develop any sense of shame. The sense of shame is acquired passively, based on the experience of other people's judgements about one's own behaviours. It is an experience known through being taught or through communications. Once one knows that some behaviours are shameful, one will try to avoid them. In this way, the self-awareness of shame becomes an active power of directing one's behaviours into a proper way.

There are two different ways to govern people: the first one is more legalist and works on the level of the common people, while the second one is more Confucian and works on people with higher moral standards. Confucius clearly does not deny the legalist approach to governing, but emphasizes that it is not enough to bring a state into proper order just by applying laws. Confucius believes that an organization leader should pay attention to people's thinking properly, and guide them to avoid shameful misdoings. Along these lines, Confucian leadership might be more effective in cultivating and governing the elite than common people. For leading an organization, it seems the Confucian way is more useful when functioning with middle-level and above managers. Still, Confucian leaders would not deny that it might be more effective to organize the lower, uneducated people through a stricter sense of rules.

Confucian leaders apply the art of leading to guide most people with good moral sensibilities, while leaving those with little sense of morality to naturally follow the examples that leaders set up for them. For an organization, a Confucian leader creates a moral propensity among the group and helps people cultivate themselves according to this propensity. As family and relationships are always discussed in relation to Confucian leadership, a good Confucian organizer knows how to create a morally harmonious community so that no one will be isolated from it.

4.3.4 The Art of Leading Appropriately: *Zhongyong* 中庸

As the metaphors of family and community suggest, Confucius does not provide the basis for a 'general theory of being' or a 'universal science of principles' (Hall and Ames, 1987: 248). He offers a situation-guided art: a leadership that focuses on leading a community as a flowing entity, keeping focus on the mean between extremes, or as Ames and Hall translate it, 'focusing the familiar'. In an organization, every member is mutually interdependent, and therefore people should be guided through a kind of way of mediation, which is not just the middle point between two extremes, but a proper way of handling changing situations.

The idea of *Zhongyong* (中庸) as a key concept of Confucianism first appeared in the *Analects* where Confucius said: 'The constant *zhongyong* as *de* (virtue) is sublime indeed! The people have been unable to practice it for a long time.'[28] *Zhongyong* was translated into English by James Legge as 'the Doctrine of Mean'. Ames and Hall translate one line in the *Zhongyong* which is very similar to the *Analects* 6.29: The Master said, 'Focusing (*zhong* 中) the familiar affairs of the day is a task of the highest order. It is rare among the common people to be able to sustain it for long' (Ames and Hall, 2001: 90). It is not easy for a person to reach the state of *Zhongyong* and common people could reach it just for a short time and not sustain it for long. However, for a Confucian organization leader, it is very important to cultivate oneself and reach the realm of *Zhongyong* so that one can maintain a balanced and harmonious state, and thus bring balance and harmony to their organizations.

Zhongyong suggests the virtues of balance, moderation, and appropriateness (Li, 2004; Liu, 2009). *Zhongyong* is also a situation in which every proposition and viewpoint can coexist without any bias or prejudice. It is the original status of thinking before philosophy breaks away from it. Every proposition has its limitations in certain situations, so one should always keep an attitude to 'return' to a neutral and plain position, which has infinite potential. The one who has this moderate attitude can see everything as it is without illusion and preconception, and thus can get rid of any burdens derived from one's knowledge and experience. It is necessary for an organization leader to cultivate their ability to control desires and emotions, since once the leader's desires and emotions have been brought into equilibrium the focus and harmonious state can be reached. However, the ideal state is to reach a grand harmony in which everyone knows how to practise the art of focusing the familiar; then, the world will be harmonized and the *Dao* of humanity will prevail (Li, 2004: 177).

For Aristotle, the notion of human virtues is intimately connected with the ethical mean, and for each virtue there is an appropriate mean located between the two extremes of defect and excess. Aristotle defines virtue as a 'purposive disposition, lying in a mean that is relative to us and determined by a rational principle' (Aristotle, 1976: 101). The Aristotelian 'mean' seeks for the equity of human beings so as to obtain the real morality, and people's ethical choices are disciplined by habits and rational deliberation. In contrast, *Zhongyong* advocates 'optimizing the creative possibilities of the ever changing circumstances in which the human experience takes place' (Ames and Hall, 2001: 8). *Zhongyong* is a shifting equilibrium and it underlies this optimizing process by experiencing the flow of all kinds of events and embracing various possibilities. This kind of organization-leading art is typically processual.

In order to achieve *Zhongyong*, leaders must adjust their actions so as to be appropriate to specific times and situations. One of the differences between a *junzi* (君子) and a petty man (*xiaoren*小人), according to Confucius, is that a gentleman practises well-timed centrality while the petty man has no concern for others and the world and is biased towards the extremes.[29] Thus, practising *Zhongyong* avoids extremes and appropriately regards the timing and situation. Moreover, rather than simply taking a fixed, absolute middle way all the time, it is a dynamic exercise; it is an integration of all kinds of strengths into a harmonious interaction (Li, 2004: 184). As Confucius says, 'The *junzi* is harmonious but not conformable; the petty man is conformable but not harmonious.'[30] The Confucian harmony is not merely to go along with the flow without contention or unprincipled compromise; rather, it stresses timely and appropriate actions. *Zhongyong* strongly opposes the radically extreme and reckless destruction of social relations and natural laws. It requires a leader to reach equilibrium in conflicting and complicated situations, without amoral compromise. A leader should always be flexible in their behaviour according to timing and situation, but firm in their basic moral principles.

4.4 Conclusion

Confucianism sheds some light on modern organization leadership from a processual perspective. The cosmological foundation of Confucianism is the *dao* and its processual nature. Confucian leaders, such as sages and exemplary persons, apply the *dao* of nature in their art of leadership. Self-cultivation is one of the Confucian core values because people living in a processual organization need to cultivate themselves to be able to deal with changing situations. Thus, learning to be a better person and educating the common people are two sides of improving the capacity to accommodate changing situations.

Notes

1. The *Analects* (*Lunyu* 论语) is a record of Confucius' words and deeds and was written by his disciples and second-generation disciples, and it is a collection of brief dialogues and gnomic utterances. Since the time of Zhu Xi (朱熹, 1130–1200 AD), the *Analects* and three other classics, *Mencius* (Mengzi 孟子), *The Great Learning* (Daxue 大学), and *The Focusing the Familiar* (Zhongyong 中庸), have been known as the *Four Books* (sishu 四书), which served as authorized books for civil service examinations in ancient China for over six hundred years. These four Confucian classics are regarded as the 'soul' of Chinese traditional culture (Brooks and Brooks, 1998; Cai and Yu, 1998; Li, 1998: 18; Lau, 1979; Leys, 1997; Lin, 2009; Tu, 2008; Van Norden, 2008).
2. From *Analects* 9.17: '子在川上，曰：逝者如斯夫！不舍昼夜。'
3. 朱熹《集注》: '天地之化，往者过，来者续: 无一息之停，乃道体之本然也。'
4. See *Analects* 17.19: '天何言哉。四时行焉: 百物生焉。天何言哉!'
5. See *Analects* 6.22: '敬鬼神而远之'
6. See *Analects* 11.12: '季路问事鬼神。子曰：未能事人，焉能事鬼? 曰：敢问死。曰：未知生，焉知死? '
7. From *Analects* 20.3: '不知命，无以为君子也。'
8. King Wen and King Wu were ancient sage kings; they were greatly admired by Confucius.
9. ' 文武之道，未坠于地，在人。贤者识其大者，不贤者识其小者，莫不有文武之道焉。'
10. From *Analects* 1.2: '君子务本，本立而道生。孝弟也者，其为人之本与。'
11. From *Analects* 15.29: '子曰：人能弘道，非道弘人。'
12. From *Analects* 2.3: '子曰：道之以政，齐之以刑，民免而无耻;道之以德，齐之以礼，有耻且格。'
13. From *Analects* 12.1: ' 颜渊问仁。子曰：克己复礼为仁。...子曰：非礼勿视，非礼勿听，非礼勿言，非礼勿动。'
14. From *Analects* 17.13: '子曰：乡原，德之贼也。'

15. From *Analects* 9.4: '子绝四：毋意，毋必，毋固，毋我。'

16. From *Analects* 2.4: '子曰：吾十有五而志于学，三十而立，四十而不惑，五十而知天命，六十而耳顺，七十而从心所欲，不逾矩。'

17. From *Analects* 5.28: '子曰：十室之邑，必有忠信如丘者焉，不如丘之好学也。'

18. From *Analects* 3.14: '子曰：周监于二代，郁郁乎文哉！吾从周。'

19. From *Analects* 13.5: '子曰：颂《诗》三百，授之以政，不达；使于四方，不能专对；虽多，亦奚以为？'

20. From Ames and Hall, 2001: '或生而知之，或学而知之，或困而知之。'

21. From *Analects* 7.20: '子曰：我非生而知之者，好古，敏以求之者也。'

22. From *Analects* 1.1: '子曰：学而时习之，不亦说乎？'

23. From *Analects* 2.1: '子曰：为政以德,譬如北辰,居其所而众星共之。'

24. Waley considers *de* to be 'a force or power closely akin to what we call character and frequently contrasted with *li*, "physical force"'. And he maintains that the normal translation of 'virtue' 'can only end by misleading the reader, who even if forewarned will be certain to interpret the word in its ordinary sense (virtue as opposed to vice) and not in the much rarer sense corresponding to the Latin *virtus*' (Waley, 1938: 33).

25. From *Analects* 13.2: '子曰：先有司，赦小过，举贤才。'

26. From *Analects* 2.2: '子曰：《诗》三百，一言以蔽之，曰："思无邪"。'

27. From *Analects* 2.2: '子曰：道之以政，齐之以刑，民免而无耻；道之以德，齐之以礼，有耻且格。'

28. From *Analects* 6.29: '子曰：中庸之为德也，其至矣乎！民鲜久矣。'

29. From Zhong Yong (Ames and Hall, 2001), chapter 2: '仲尼曰：君子中庸，小人反中庸. 君子之中庸也，君子而时中；小人之中庸也，小人而无忌惮也'.

30. From *Analects* 13.23: '子曰：君子和而不同，小人同而不和。'

REFERENCES

Ames, R.T. and Hall. D.L. (2001). *Focusing the Familiar: A Translation and Philosophical Interpretation of the Zhongyong* (Hawaii: University of Hawai'i Press).

—— and Rosemont, H. (1998). *The Analects of Confucius: A Philosophical Translation* (New York: Ballantine Books).

Aristotle. (1976). *The Nicomachean Ethics*, trans. J.A.K. Thomson (Harmondsworth: Penguin).

Brooks, E.B. and Brooks, A.T. (1998). *The Original Analects: Sayings of Confucius and His Successors* (New York: Columbia University Press).

Cai, J.J. and Yu, E. (1998). *The Analects of Confucius* (America-rom Publishing Company).

Dawson, R. (1981). *Confucius* (Oxford: Oxford University Press).

Digenti, D. (1998). Toward an Understanding of the Learning Community, *Organizational Development Journal* 16(2): 91–6.

Fingarette, H. (1998). *Confucius: The Secular as Sacred* (Prospect Heights, IL: Waveland Press).

Grange, J. (2005). Process Thought and Confucian Values, in W.-y. Xie, Z.-h. Wang, and G.E. Derfer (eds), *Whitehead and China: Relevance and Relationship* (Lancaster: Ontos Verlag): 69–76.

Hall, D.L. and Ames, R.T. (1987). *Thinking through Confucius* (Albany: State University of New York Press).

Lau, D.C. (1979). *The Analects of Confucius* (Harmonsworth: Penguin Books).

Levine, L. (2001). Integrating Knowledge and Process in a Learning Organization, *Information Systems Management*, Winter: 21–32.

Leys, S. (1997). *The Analects of Confucius* (New York and London: W.W. Norton & Company).

Li, C.Y. (2004). Zhongyong as Grand Harmony—An Alternative Reading to Ames and Hall's *Focusing the Familiar, Dao: Journal of Comparative Philosophy* 3(2): 173–88.

Li, Z.-H. (1998). *Reread the Analects Today* (He Fei: Anhui Literature and Art Publishing House).

Lin, Y.-T. (2009). *The Wisdom of Confucius* (Beijing: Foreign Language Teaching and Research Press).

Liu, H. (2009). *Chinese Business: Landscapes and Strategies* (London: Routledge).

Ramus, C.A. and Steger, U. (2000). The Roles of Supervisory Support Behaviors and Environmental Policy in Employee 'Ecoinitiatives' at Leading-Edge European Companies, *Academy of Management Journal* 43(4): 605–26.

Romar, E.J. (2002). Virtue is Good Business: Confucianism as a Practical Business Ethics, *Journal of Business Ethics* 38(1/2): 119–31.

Senge, P. (1990). *The Fifth Discipline* (New York: Doubleday).

Sarkissian, H. (2010). Minor Tweaks, Major Payoffs: The Problems and Promise of Situationism in Moral Philosophy, *Philosopher's Imprint* 10(9): 1–15.

Tu, W.-M. (1972). Li as a Process of Humanization, *Philosophy East and West* 22(2): 187–201.

——(2008). *An Insight of Chung-yung,* trans. D. Dezhi (Beijing: People's Press).

Van Norden, B.W. (trans.) (2008). *Mencius: With Selections from Traditional Commentaries* (Indianapolis/Cambridge: Hackett Publishing Company).

Waley, A. (trans.) (1938). *The Analects of Confucius* (London: George Allen & Unwin Ltd).

Weber, M. (1968). *The Religion of China: Confucianism and Taoism* (New York: Free Press).

Yao, X. (2000). *An Introduction to Confucianism* (Cambridge: Cambridge University Press).

CHAPTER 5

ZHUANGZI (369 BC)

YUAN LI AND WEN HAIMING

The utmost persons are selfless,
The holy person has no merit,
The sage is nameless.

(Zhuang Zi, *Wandering at Ease*)[1]

5.1 INTRODUCTION

ZHUANG ZI (or Chuang-Tzu, 庄子 c.369–286 BC) was a Daoist thinker from the state of Song (encompassing parts of modern-day Shandong and Henan provinces) with influence during his time, and the work named after him contains his wisdom regarding political and social management. In China, philosophical Daoism is also called 'Lao-Zhuang (老庄)' philosophy, and this directly refers to the two most influential Daoist texts, the *Daodejing* 道德经 by Lao Dan (Lao Zi) and the *Zhuangzi* 庄子 by Zhuang Zi. The messages expressed in the *Daodejing* and the *Zhuangzi* are largely similar; however, while the latter focuses on personal spirituality and freedom, the former is more concerned with social and political practices (for example, rule by non-assertive action, *wuwei* 无为而治). Zhuang Zi is not just an annotator and a follower of Lao Zi, since he creatively uses Lao Zi's view as an expressive tool for his own ideas (Wu, The Hundred Schools of Thought, flourished during the Warring States period (475–221 BC), which was indeed the most vital era in the development of Chinese thought). Nearly all of these schools emerged in response to political disruption and social chaos, suggesting various solutions to cure the political illnesses of the day. Zhuang Zi made his living weaving straw sandals before becoming a low-ranking official. His answers differ from most other thinkers of his time, and the main theme of his answers is freeing oneself from the world.

Though in economic distress for much of his life, this great philosopher convinced many to be resigned to the disposition of nature and to stay free of worldly concerns.

Zhuangzi is full of luscious figurative language and snappy stories laden with inspiration as well as connotation, and it has been regarded as one of the greatest philosophical books in the history of China. It has even been deemed 'one of the most entertaining as well as one of the profoundest books in the world' (Waley, 1939: 163). Yet both in the East and in the West, Lao Zi and Confucius attract far greater attention than Zhuang Zi. Perhaps because he is too playful, his stories seem to verge on the grotesque and go far beyond the realm of the familiar. As a philosophical text, the book *Zhuangzi* is mainly a discourse about personal realization, and it also concerns social and political order.

Zhuang Zi is truly a master of language and sophisticated argument, aphorism, lyrical prose, anecdote, and gnomic verse (Graham, 1989: 199), and he employs every resource of rhetoric in his writing to persuade people to free themselves from any artificial bondage, encouraging people to keep aloof from politics and earthly obsessions, which he sees as shackles to a free and authentic mind. He urges people to understand that human beings interact and are interdependent on the prevailing environment, and he goes on to advocate 'wandering' through life as part of the universal process of nature. This bears a striking similarity to Whitehead's thought, which holds that the universe is an infinite, open, dynamic process of becoming, full of diversity and creativity (Whitehead, 1925, 1947). However, whereas Whitehead dedicated himself to reconstructing speculative metaphysical philosophy, Zhuang Zi's main concern was that people live more freely.

5.2 FREE AND SPONTANEOUS WANDERING

> Within yourself, no fixed position,
> Things as they take shape disclose themselves.
> Moving, be like water,
> Still, be like a mirror,
> Respond like an echo.
>
> (Zhuang Zi, *Tian Xia*)[2]

From Zhuang Zi's perspective, we should all find enjoyment in a free and spontaneous way of wandering. Basically, any organization (gathering) is normally regarded as a burden, but it is also impossible to get rid of the burden of being in a particular organization, since as long as we have a physical body, some level of organization exists. Thus, Zhuang Zi advocates free and spontaneous wandering, going past a spiritual liberation. Zhuang Zi employs a metaphor of a totally free and easy journey, using the word *you* (wandering 游) to refer to the way in which the free-minded person wanders through the world, enjoying its delights without ever being attached to any one part of it (Watson, 1968: 6). For Zhuang Zi, real freedom is a state of 'no reliance' (*wudai* 无待), which means depending on nothing whatsoever and freeing oneself from man-made restrictions and obligations. Thus one can 'wander through the boundless' because there is 'nothing else to depend on'.[3] The way to realize 'no reliance' is through 'sitting and forgetting' (*zuowang* 坐忘). Yan Hui, a disciple of Confucius, once said to Confucius that he improved himself through sitting and forgetting everything: 'I let my limbs and body drop away, drive out perception and intellect, cast off form, and go along with the universal thoroughfare. And this is what I mean by *zuowang*.'[4] This is a state of not relying on anything else, in which people feel their physical existence to be not as important as spiritual fulfillment.

In Zhuang Zi's opinion, the world is in the process of continuous and spontaneous transformation, and so demarcations between one state/form and another, which is to say solid distinctions between self and other, are not necessary. Human beings have continually stunted and maimed their spontaneous aptitudes by habitually distinguishing between alternatives and reasoning in instrumental, cost-benefit terms. Zhuang Zi expresses this belief in the well-known parable of the Butterfly Dream.[5] One day Zhuang Zi dreamt he had become one of these happy, fluttering insects. But when he woke up, he wondered whether he was Zhuang Zi who dreamed of being a butterfly or a butterfly who dreamed of being Zhuang Zi. Here the philosopher illustrates the treacherous boundary between illusion and reality as well as that occurring between 'myself' and 'other' existence. He thus suggests that in order to cope spontaneously and freely with the vicissitudes of life, and to understand the intricacies of the external world, one should respond to the prevailing situation with an immediacy akin to an echo following a sound or shadow drawing after a shape, rather than treating it in a static and isolated manner.

For Zhuang Zi, 'the fundamental error is to suppose that life presents us with issues which must be formulated in words so that we can envisage alternatives' (Graham, 1981: 6) and judge them rationally. Those dexterous and skilful people, such as the butcher, carpenter, wheelwright, swimmer, and even the engraver, do not precede each move by weighing rationally the arguments for different alternatives. Rather their respective skills have become part of them, such that they simply act instinctively and spontaneously, achieving success. They are described by Zhuang Zi as 'artists'. In the story of 'Cook Ding Cutting an Ox',[6] Cook Ding gives his attention to the whole situation, letting its focus roam freely, so that he forgets himself in his absorption in the object, whereby the trained hand reacts spontaneously with a confidence and precision merely by following the *Dao*, which proves impossible to anyone who is applying man-made rules and theories. Cook Ding takes the ox as a whole and goes along with the natural structure of the ox. When his knife enters the ox's body, it moves freely in the spaces between the joints, finding a pleasure in entering a world of nothingness. Zhuang Zi believes that people should develop spontaneous and natural energies instead of using the heart-mind to think, name, categorize, and conceive ends and principles of action.

With the abandonment of the engrained 'machine-like' way of thinking and rule-bound way of life, one's attention roams without restriction over the endlessly changing panorama, and responses spring directly from one's natural energies (Graham, 1981: 8). 'The way to wander free and easy is to transform oneself to be no form, and to exist as if there is no self' (Wen, 2012: 49). Thus one can be free like the edge of Cook Ding's knife in the body of an ox.

Confucian philosophy is generally characterized by its emphasis on moral precepts, virtues, regulative education, and worldliness, and it has been a doctrine embraced by state officials in China for over 2,000 years. Daoist philosophy, on the other hand, has been frequently characterized in terms of passivity, spirituality, femininity, otherworldliness, anarchy, and quietism, and has been favoured by artists, recluses, and mystics (Ames, 1998b: 5). In fact, the Daoist attitude is frequently misunderstood as merely passive, submissive, and anarchic, so it is necessary to further mention Daoism's central concept of *wuwei*. Although like *wuwei*, anarchy also refers to activity performed in the absence of coercively determinative constrains, the difference lies in that while anarchy describes the fundamentally dualistic relationship between a particular thing and a determinative principle, *wuwei* describes an interdependent relationship that exists between two particulars (Ames, 1998b: 7). In terms of governance, Daoist *wuwei* is a non-intentional and non-interfering approach on the part of authorities. It is action in perfect harmony with the dynamism of the whole world; it is action that seems both spontaneous and effortless, as it is in perfect accordance with our place in the world and with our nature. *Wuwei* is a completely free state, because there is no coercion and no violence, 'it is not "conditional" or "limited" by our own individual needs and desires, or even by our own theories and ideas' (Merton, 1965: 28). It is an effortless and natural approach following simply from the *Dao*, and standing in opposition to artificial regulation, punishment, and intervention.

Zhuang Zi's *wuwei* thinking can be seen in his basic concepts of *wuwo* (no self 无我), *wudai* (no reliance 无待), *wugong* (no merit 无功), and *wuming* (no name 无名) (Yu, 2009). The secret of the *Dao*, according to Zhuang Zi, is not the accumulation of virtue as taught by Confucianism, but *wuwei*, which is not concerned with predesigned plans or deliberately organized endeavours and is not intent upon results. Though shunning politics, Zhuang Zi advised the rulers of his time to take up non-assertive action or acting without effort (*wuwei*): 'Emptiness, stillness, purity, silence, and *wuwei* are the substance of the *Dao* and its power, therefore the emperor, the ruler, the sage rest therein. In the emptiness they attain fullness; in fullness they grasp the patterns of things. Empty they are still;... still, they rest in *wuwei*; being *wuwei*, then those charged with affairs fulfill their responsibilities.'[7] He calls for those in power to respect the nature of mankind, and let nature follow its course. Changes should be absorbed by people gradually and in silence instead of being brought about by coercion. He counselled that artificial and arbitrary interference would do more harm than good. As plants will flourish if they grow according to natural laws, so too will a nation achieve order and peace if it is simply let be.

5.3 THE WHOLENESS, EQUALITY, RELATEDNESS AND RELATIVITY OF *WANWU*

> Master Dong-guo asked Zhuang Zi, 'This thing called the Dao—where does it exist?'
> Zhuang Zi said, 'There is no place it does not exist.'
> Dong-guo said, 'Please be more specific.'
> 'It is in the ant.'
> 'As low a thing as that?'
> 'It is in the wild grass.'
> 'But that is lower still!'
> 'It is in the tiles and shards.'
> 'How can it be so low?'
> 'It is in the piss and shit.'
>
> (Zhuang Zi, *Zhi Bei You*)[8]

Similar to how Whitehead establishes his cosmology by taking it as a continuous process, Zhuang Zi's free and easy wandering way of life needs to be based on a cosmological perspective where the myriad things in the world exist in a kind of wholeness. *Dao* exists together with the existence of the wholeness of everything, and it cannot be viewed as a separate, independent entity. This continuous *Dao* moves in the wholeness of things, which is normally called Heaven and Earth (*tiandi* 天地), a collective name for all things in the world (*wanwu* 万物). Everything follows *Dao* as a matter of natural course. In Zhuang Zi's story, the ability of the bird Peng to fly high, of the cicada to fly low, of the Chun tree to live long, and of the morning mushroom to remain short— all these are abilities from nature, i.e. from *dao*, not abilities from purposeful action (Jochim, 1998b: 57). Zhuang Zi believes that the myriad of things, *wanwu*, be they vast or small, long-lived or short-lived, are equal in value. All things are what they are, and they follow their spontaneous 'thusness'. Each thing is self-contained, and self-preserving, and each requires freedom to develop its own inner tendencies (Coutinho, 2004: 60). To wander freely is to allow the myriad of *wanwu* to be what they are. Nothing is better than anything else; things only differ in kind.

Also, if an individual thing is viewed as being a perspective on *Dao*, which entails *wanwu* being integral with itself, any distinction will fall apart: 'If you look at things in terms of how they differ, the gap between liver and gall is as great as the distance from the state of Chu to the state of Yue; if you look at them in terms of their sameness, everything is continuous.'[9] *Dao* is the abstract category embracing the totality of *wanwu*'s nature. 'It comes out from no source; it goes back in through no aperture. It has reality yet no place where it resides; it has duration yet no beginning or end.'[10] Just as Zhuang Zi said, *Dao* is in the ant, in the wild grass, in the tile, and even in the excrement, thus the *Dao* is in the world and everywhere, rather than being something that transcends the world. The cycles of the seasons, the howling winds, the rampant floods, the giant soaring birds, and the small darting fish, and even the conventionally ugly and painful things are presentations of the grand *Dao*. *Dao* does not 'exhaust itself in what is great, nor does it absent itself from what is small. Therefore, the myriad things are realized in it. The *Dao* is so broad that there is nothing it fails to accommodate, so deep that it is unfathomable.'[11] *Dao* is the whole (Feng, 1964).

An important topic for Zhuang Zi is the 'usefulness of uselessness'. Conventionally, the possession of qualities or talents is thought to be useful, and usefulness is what people are typically keen on, while uselessness is often ignored or disparaged. However, Zhuang Zi claims that, 'All men know the uses of the usefulness, but no one knows the uses of the uselessness.'[12] 'Uselessness' is the key for the preservation of human life, and conversely, usefulness frequently brings injury and grief to the possessor. An inferior timber is 'useless for anything, [which] is why it has been able to grow so old and giant'.[13] Because of its uselessness and ugliness, the tree is able to preserve its life and experience its own natural development, such that its virtue lies precisely in its uselessness. *Zhuangzi* includes a series of stories about mutilated criminals, cripples, and freaks who would be disliked and rejected by communities in which conventional values dominate. According to Zhuang Zi, if these men can accept catastrophe as their destiny, and care nothing for the disparaging judgement of others, all while remaining inwardly unrestricted by conventional values and recognizing that it would be safer to conform to them in the future, they would be nearer to the *Dao* than Confucius (Graham, 1989: 24).

The consummate human being in *Zhuangzi* is the '*zhenren*' ('Authentic Person' or 'True Man' 真人),[14] who transcends artificial restraints and acts according to the *Dao* (道) rather than moral principles. The realization of this human ideal itself is the elegant and harmonious process of nature. Zhuang Zi claims that 'there must be the Authentic Person before there can be authentic knowledge',[15] and denies a pre-existing and objective type of knowledge. The world could not be known without the knower, and knowledge is always acquired within an experience rather than in an isolated existence. The 'knowers' and their worlds are in a transformative process of wholeness, and knowledge is actively created during this process.

'No-self (*wuwo* 无我)', or no sense of self is the solution Zhuang Zi offers to the predicament where it is extremely difficult for people to escape social intercourse or transcend all interests. Zhuang Zi suggests that people regard themselves as part of the world, rather than establishing a 'self' that exists in opposition to the world. This is quite akin to Ricoeur's idea of 'self'. For Ricoeur (1992), there is a genuine mutual relationship between self and others, and the self is never a fixed entity, and never a self-sufficient *cogito*; rather, the self is a living, growing, changing, and responding 'becoming' which is in the process of interpreting and reinterpreting itself and its world. Similarly, Zhuang Zi says, 'Without an Other there is no Self; without Self, an Other would have nothing to take hold of.'[16] Self and Other are mutually dependent. Therefore, 'No thing is not "other," no thing is not "self." If you treat yourself too as "other" they do not appear, if you know of yourself you know of them.'[17] Zhuang Zi therefore claims: 'heaven and the earth live together with me, and the myriad things and I are one'.[18] By taking oneself and the events which befall oneself as part of the transformation of things, and not as something special to invest ego concerns, one could be free of oneself and obtain the *Dao*.

There is a story in *Zhuangzi* about a swimmer who could navigate turbulent waters that even fish and turtles avoided. The swimmer's explanation described his knack for staying afloat in the water, saying: 'I have no way. I began with what I was used to, grew up with my nature, and matured in what is destined for me. I enter with the inflow, and emerge with the outflow, following along the way the water goes and never thinking about myself. That is how I can stay afloat.'[19] By becoming coextensive with the nature of water, this swimmer is able to cross the flow easily, and by becoming coextensive with the nature of the ox, the Cook Ding is able to intimately know its lines and grains without distraction. The absence of a discrete self makes these skilful people follow the *Dao* of their environments, and the environment correspondingly makes them potent in a mutually nourished process. Human beings are 'interdependent with the world in which they reside, simultaneously shaping and being shaped by it' (Ames, 1998a: 227).

However, this concept of 'no-self' does not refer in an overly simplistic fashion to a totally independent ego-self. Rather, it is a process of assimilating a sense of self within numerous relations throughout the whole world. 'We begin as an inchoate, incipient focus of relationships, and have the opportunity to cultivate and extend these intrinsic relations, transforming them into a situated and relationally constituted "self"' (Ames, 1998a: 220). A story tells of Zhuang Zi arguing with Hui Zi about how he could know how fish enjoy themselves in the river;[20] Zhuang Zi's experience with the fish entails continuity between his world and that of the fish. Zhuang Zi's 'Happiness' is a fluid, holistic, and emergent situation without a discrete agent, and therefore there is no self-based happiness, but rather the happiness of a whole situation.

Zhuang Zi's ideas of *zhenren* (True Persons) and 'no-self' are normally taken as ways of living over and against the control of human organizations. However, it is also valuable to recognize Zhuang Zi's view towards liberating people from the alienation of human organization and societal bondage. Zhuang Zi proposes liberation of human beings from the organizer's power of forcing people to be their slaves. In other words, it is also important for the leaders of a group to empathize with the people within their organizations, and to enable them, as much as possible, to be free and attain happiness.

5.4 LIFE IS A PROCESS

I received life because the time had come, and to lose it because the order of things passes on; be content with the time and settled on the course, and sadness and joy cannot find a way in. In ancient times this was called the 'freeing of the bound'.

(Zhuang Zi, *Da Zong Shi*)[21]

It is common for Chinese people to understand their leaders as taking on a leadership role not only in everyday business, but in acting as personal exemplars as well. In contrast with the Confucian ideal of the *junzi*, the exemplary or superior person who usually behaves morally, Zhuang Zi favours leaders becoming *zhenren*, authentic people. Zhuang Zi's Authentic Person is able to realize an integration and continuity with the process of natural change as whole and model conduct on the rhythm and cadence of the process, thereby achieving genuine freedom. For example, the Authentic Person is free and easy, whether in life or in death, whether healthy or ill, whether in honour or in disgrace, due to having surpassed all distinctions and finding freedom from any single form of existence.

> The True Man of ancient times knew nothing of loving life, knew nothing of hating death. He emerged without delight; he went back in without a fuss. He came briskly, he went briskly, and that was all. He did not forget where he began; he did not try to find out where he would end. He received something and took pleasure in it; he forgot about it and handed it back again. This is what I call not using the mind to repel the Way, not using man to help out Heaven. This is what I call the True Man.[22]

Tian (Heaven 天) is an important concept to Chinese thinkers. In Confucianism, *tian* is somewhat like a supreme power operating independently of human will. Human way-making is related to the decree of *tian*—one's success or failure, wealth or poverty, life or death, could be related to *tian*. The way to narrow the gap between man and *tian*, for Confucians, is through cultivating humanity towards morally good conduct. For Zhuang Zi, there is no need to obey *tian*, and one should live life as generated by *tian*, and spontaneously follow the process of life without vainly attempting to force intentions onto the process. To wit, 'when attending and responding, in ways which we can never fully express in language or justify by reasons, our behaviour belongs with the birth, growth, decay and death of the body among the spontaneous process generated by Heaven' (Graham, 1981: 16).

The most unusual and rhapsodic expression from Zhuang Zi concerns death. He is neither an optimist nor a pessimist. He regards joy and sorrow, birth and death, and the like as alternating and inseparable like day and night. Living and dying mutually give rise to each other, and so each is the potential source of dissolution for the other. When Zhuang Zi's wife died, he was found thumping a pot and singing. He said: 'in the mist of the jumble of wonder and mystery a change took place and she had a spirit. Another change and she had a body. Another change and she was born. Now there's been another change and she's dead. It is just like a progression of the four seasons, spring, summer, fall, winter.'[23] On his deathbed, he even laughed at his disciples for preferring to have him decently buried and eaten by worms and ants rather than leaving his body in the open to be eaten by crows.[24]

Nature emerges with the slow and persistent revolutions of heaven and earth; and the process of birth, growth, development, and decay is the result of the passing of time. Zeno observes that the absolute continuity of time does not allow for such things as discrete atemporal moments; Zhuang Zi's cosmology is in constant change. He holds that 'the sun at noon is the sun setting; the thing born is the thing dying'.[25] Things become what they are, not through an infinite series of imperceptible or dramatic changes and transformations but rather they come into and go out of existence as mere stages of larger organic processes, which take place along a continuum of transformation, where the temporal boundaries are regions of connections instead of points of separation. Just as Zhuang Zi says:

> In seeds there are germs. In the water they become filaments, on the edges of the water they become algae. If they sprout in elevated places they become plantain. If the plantains get rich soil, they turn into Wuzu Plants. The roots of Wuzu turn into maggots and their leaves turn into butterflies. Before long the butterflies are transformed and turn into insects . . . after a thousand days, the insects become birds called Dried Leftover Bones . . . Green Peace animals produce leopards and leopards produce horses and horses produce men. Men in time return again to enter the wellsprings of nature. So the myriad things all come out from the wellsprings and all reenter the wellsprings.[26]

The stages of the formation of things are described temporally. 'There is a beginning', writes Zhuang Zi, observing that 'there is not yet beginning to be a beginning. There is not yet beginning to be not yet beginning to be a beginning.'[27] At first, it is not just that there are no things, but that things have 'not yet begun to be' in the state of being just about to become, which is to say in the process of becoming. Similarly, there is no absolute origin in Whitehead, no *creatio ex nihilo*, no single beginning of a timeline. For Whitehead, the beginning is always happening, here, now, and it erupts out of the potentiality of 'not yet beginning'. Zhuang Zi continues, 'There is being. There is nonbeing. There is a not yet beginning to be nonbeing. There is a not yet beginning to be a not yet beginning to be nonbeing.'[28] By highlighting the processes of transformation between becoming and unbecoming, and being and non-being, Zhuang Zi deconstructs both linear temporality and substance ontology just as Whitehead later does, where for him becoming dissolves essences (Keller, 2005: 40–1).

5.5 ORGANIZATIONAL IMPLICATIONS OF *ZHUANGZI*

In organizational management, there is a tendency to impose deliberate forethought, purposeful design, established rules, or even the manager's personal proclivities onto every aspect of management. Coercively determinative constraints dictated without awareness of the clumsiness of those actions on employees, managers, and the elements of organization's internal and external environments not only deprive environing particulars of their possibilities, but further impoverish the organization's potential as a whole. Freedom in management can be achieved through *wuwei*, a productively creative relatedness. The role of the managers of an organization is not to 'make', 'control', or 'block' dogmatically, but to 'let' things happen and change naturally. Excess regulations, rules, instructions, surveillance, or any other organizational initiatives would arbitrarily snuff out the natural or spontaneous 'flow' of organizational activities and development, and the organization in question would no longer be an enterprise promoting the healthy development of people.

At the individual level, Zhuang Zi is not advocating that people should retreat from an active human existence into inertia. In fact, he suggests that people enjoy their life through non-assertive action and not through seeking things, which means following the flow of life. Zhuang Zi found that what the people honour are wealth, eminence, long life, and fame, and that people seek their happiness in rich food, easy life, fine clothes, and so forth, while looking down on poverty, early death, and infamy. He thinks it is stupid to define and bind happiness like this, as it tends to situate happiness in certain situation and only seek it there. But the freedom and happiness within *Dao* is to be found everywhere, 'perfect happiness knows no happiness',[29] such that if one obtains joy in freedom, the joy is unconditional.

Zhuang Zi invites people to participate in the flow throughout their lives, like fish swimming in water, rather than joining in a well-planned life that is intermittently punctuated by enjoyable moments of flow. In this flow, people are so involved in what they are doing that nothing seems to matter, and 'the experience itself is so enjoyable that people will do it even at great cost, for the sheer sake of doing it' (Csikszentmihalyi, 1990: 4). The experience of flow is 'autotelic'—it is intrinsically rewarding rather than tied to any external goal or benefit (Jochim, 1998: 63). While clear goals are important in organizational management practices, when operation begins in earnest, goal consciousness disappears amidst the flow. 'Concern for the self' is gone, and effortless involvement produces the real joy for members of the organization.

The Authentic Person or *zhenren*'s activity is characterized by efficacy, flexibility, and frictionlessness, which can be seen in the excellence of the collaboration with the natural and social environments. However, Zhuang Zi's free and easy wandering cannot only be attained by the sage or the *zhenren*; it can be reached by common people in the most humble jobs of daily life through spontaneous action in one's environment and through a unified view to one's life, manifesting in the perfection of skills (like with Cook Ding). Thus, every member in the organization, no matter in what position, can be an expert in their own field and find genuine joy in work as it is. Moreover, Zhuang Zi's uselessness is only apparent uselessness, for it appears to be so in order to be different from a conventional point of view. The art is to discover a usefulness that 'goes beyond the limitations of conventional usage' (Coutinho, 2004: 74). Zhuang Zi brings a fresh consciousness to managerial thinking where even the most trivial tasks, the most ordinary and untalented employee, and the most ridiculous ideas and suggestions, which is to say all these seemingly useless details, could be vital factors that rescue, sustain, strengthen, or destroy the organization. Therefore, it is risky for an organization to neglect the usefulness of uselessness.

In Zhuang Zi's stories, he repeatedly mentions the theme of vastness. For instance, there are the giant birds and fish, creatures that live for thousands of years, and he uses these to try to make people notice the limitations of the routine and the commonplace. What we are familiar with and believe in may just be the sky to a cicada, and we never know what the sky looks like in the eyes of the giant bird Peng. Our mastery and familiarity with the daily grind is far from enough to enable us to deal with the differences and irregularities that go unanticipated by us. The unprecedented complexity of managing organizations in modern society gives increasing credence to the view that 'scientific theories' and 'right answers' are not always a panacea for all ills, and that the regular and universal tends to be narrow and shallow if it remains blindly proud of its self and unable to vary in different situations. So Zhuang Zi exhorts us to go roaming beyond the restrictions that tie us down. These restrictions include not only the inertia and inflexible ways of management, but also the instrumental and short-term profit/performance-oriented considerations.

Vastness thereby implies on the one hand that an organization should release itself from the shackles of social convention and construction that constrain its choices and development, and on the other, that it should broaden its considerations, regarding itself as a part of the vast *wanwu*, rather than setting a boundary between itself and others. Rather than aiming at profit maximization and performance optimization, the *wuwei* approach takes efficiency and effectiveness as by-products or spontaneous consequences (Suen et al., 2007).

Leaders of an organization should be flexible in both mind and action. According to Zhuang Zi, things are prone to change gradually and even dramatically, and situations change in the blink of an eye. Familiar things can turn unfamiliar and peculiar in the meandering paths of transformation. 'The unity or continuity of things, then, is not a bland indistinguishability, but a holistic interconnectedness of developmental, organic pathways' (Coutinho, 2004: 171). What something was, what it is, and what it becomes are not marked by separate, sudden, and radical displacements, but occur in a continuous process of evolution. Zhuang Zi insistently cautions people to avoid imposing inflexible boundaries, which set limits and make artificial constraints on the possible and the impossible, the true and the false, self and others, and so forth. One could wander at ease beyond the plethora of disintegrative dualisms, not through escaping the real world, but by coming to realize the mutually entailing identity of oneself and one's world. While an analytic attitude demands a rational resolution and tries to force inconsistent situations into an allegedly perfect framework, the Daoist attitude when facing complexity and paradox in management points to the benefit of reconciling ourselves with the paradox and identifying with the changes, so that we do not fear anything beyond convention, logic, and reason. When one finds identity with the whole process, there will be an imperturbable calm, and knowledge, like second nature, of when to bend and when to stand firm. Contrary to instrumentally rational action in which thought precedes and orients action, flexible actions are spontaneous responses to situations. Spontaneous actions are not led by pre-established goals and are not shackled by pre-existing rules and theories; they are based on instinct or even on the unconscious, focusing on the process rather than on the end. Management of an organization is itself a fluid process with penumbral transformation. Although management theories seem to require fixity, simplicity, and stability in order to be understood universally, it is impossible for a manager to apply consistently certain management theories or measures to an organization at any stage of its development, to say nothing of applying a given theory or measure on organizations in a social context.

The Daoists, especially Zhuang Zi, never intended to offer any systematically fixed principles, rules, disciplines, or standards for social and political governance in ancient China. Nowadays, there is a clear predominance of explicitly Confucian values, which vigorously promote moral cultivation, appropriate social protocols, systems, and state-imposed control. Nevertheless, Daoist thinking, particularly that of Zhuang Zi' with its emphases on *wuwei*, wholeness, the equality of *wanwu*, relatedness, relativism, pluralism, process and so forth, is what organizations urgently need in the bewildering complexity of today's globalized world. Instead of any grand, instrumental, systematical theories, these notions only offer clues that lead us in entering the shadows of our understanding where we ordinarily do not dwell, in discovering a precious wisdom that was once buried beneath the machinery of rationality, in freeing us from conventional restrictions, and enabling us to live effortlessly with inconsistency, paradox, emergency, and unpredictability. Those who dream of developing fixed and universal principles or models for organizational management by turning to Daoist thinking, are doomed to fail to reach the *Dao*, since *Dao* is unnamable, indescribable, and ultimately ungraspable.

NOTES

1. From *Zhuang Zi:· Wandering at Ease* (*Xiao Yao You*) (庄子·逍遥游): '至人无己, 神人无功, 圣人无名'.
2. From *Zhuang Zi:·Tian Xia* (庄子· 天下): '在己无居, 行物自著.其动若水, 其静若镜, 其应若响', translated by Graham (1981).
3. From *Zhuang Zi· Xiao Yao You* (庄子·逍遥游): '以游无穷者,彼且恶乎待哉!'
4. From *Zhuang Zi·Da Zhong Shi* (庄子·大宗师): '颜回曰: "堕肢体, 黜聪明, 离形去知, 同于大通, 此谓坐忘"'.
5. See *Zhuang Zi· Qi Wu Lun* (庄子·齐物论).
6. See *Zhuang Zi Yang Sheng Zhu* (庄子: 养生主).
7. From *Zhuang Zi: Tian Dao* (庄子:天道): '夫虚静恬淡寂寞无为者,天地之平而道德之至. 故帝王圣人休焉.   体则虚,   虚则实,   实则伦矣.   虚则静,...静则无为.   无为也, 则任事者责矣'.
8. From *Zhuang Zi: Zhi Bei You* (庄子: 知北游): '东郭子问于庄子曰: "所谓道, 恶乎在?" 庄子曰: "无所不在." 东郭子曰: "期而后可." 庄子曰: "在蝼蚁." 曰: "何其下邪?"曰: "在梯稗" 曰 "何其愈下邪?" 曰"在瓦甓". 曰: "何其愈甚邪?" 曰: "在屎溺"'.
9. From *Zhuang Zi: De Chong Fu* (庄子: 德充符): '自其异者视之, 肝胆楚越也; 自其同者视之,万物皆一也'.
10. From *Zhuang Zi: Geng Sang Chu* (庄子: 庚桑楚): '出无本, 入无窍. 有时而无乎处, 有长而无乎本剽'.

11. From *Zhuang Zi: Tian Dao* (庄子: 天道): '于大不终, 于小不遗. 故万物备, 广广乎其无不容也, 渊乎其不可测也', translated by Mair (1994).

12. From *Zhuang Zi: Ren Jian Shi* (庄子: 人间世): '人皆知有用之用, 而莫知无用之用也'.

13. From *Zhuang Zi: Ren Jian Shi*: '是不材之木也. 无所可用, 故能若是之寿'.

14. Taoists sometimes use the term 'sage' (*shengren* 圣人) for the consummate human being.

15. From *Zhuang Zi: Da Zong Shi* (庄子·大宗师): '且有真人而后有真知'.

16. From *Zhuang Zi: Qi Wu Lun* (庄子: 齐物论): '非彼无我, 非我无所取'.

17. From *Zhuang Zi: Qi Wu Lun* (庄子: 齐物论): '物无非彼, 无无非是. 自彼则不见, 自知则知之'.

18. From *Zhuang Zi: Qi Wu Lun* (庄子: 齐物论): '天地与我并生, 而万物与我为一'.

19. See *Zhuang Zi: Da Sheng* (庄子: 达生).

20. See *Zhuang Zi: Qiu Shui* (庄子: 秋水).

21. From *Zhuang Zi: Da Zhong Shi* (庄子: 大宗师): '且夫得者, 时也, 失者, 顺也; 安时而处顺, 哀乐不能入也. 此古之所谓县解也'.

22. From *Zhuang Zi: Da Zhong Shi* (庄子: 大宗师): '古之真人, 不知说生, 不知恶死; 其出不䜣, 其入不距; 翛然而往, 翛然而来而已矣. 不忘其所始, 不求其所终; 受而喜之, 忘而复之, 是之谓不以心捐道, 不以人助天. 是之谓真人', translated by Watson (1968).

23. From *Zhuang Zi: Zhi Le* (庄子: 至乐): '杂乎芒芴之间, 变而有气, 气变而有形, 形变而有生. 今又变而之死. 是相与为春秋冬夏四时行也', translated by Watson (1968).

24. See *Zhuang Zi: Lie Yu Kou* (庄子: 列御寇).

25. From *Zhuang Zi: Tian Xia* (庄子: 天下): '日方中方睨, 物方生方死'.

26. See *Zhuang Zi: Zhi Le* (庄子: 至乐).

27. From *Zhuang Zi: Qi Wu Lun* (庄子: 齐物论): '有始也者, 有未始有始也者, 有未始有夫未始有始也者'.

28. From *Zhuang Zi: Qi Wu Lun* (庄子: 齐物论): '有有也者, 有无也者, 有未始有无也者, 有未始有夫未始有无也者'.

29. From *Zhuang Zi: Zhi Le* (庄子: 至乐): '至乐无乐'.

References

Ames, R.T. (1998a). Knowing in the Zhuangzi: From Here, on the Bridge, over the River Hao, in R.T. Ames (ed.), *Wandering at Ease in the Zhuangzi* (Albany: State University of New York Press): 219–30.

—— (ed.) (1998b). *Wandering at Ease in the Zhuangzi* (Albany: State University of New York Press).

Coutinho, S. (2004). *Zhuangzi and Early Chinese Philosophy: Vagueness, Transformation and Paradox* (Burlington: Ashgate Publishing Company).

Csikszentmihalyi, M. (1990). *Flow: The Psychology of Optimal Experience* (New York: Harper and Row).

Feng, Y.-L. (1964). *Chuang-Tzu* (New York: Paragon Book Reprint Corp).

Graham, A.C. (1981). *Chuang-Tzu: The Seven Inner Chapters and other Writings from the Book Chuang-Tzu* (London: George Allen & Unwin).

—— (1989). *Disputers of the Tao: Philosophical Argument in Ancient China* (Peru, IL: Open Court).

Jochim, C. (1998). Just Say No to 'No Self' in Zhuangzi, in R.T. Ames (ed.), *Wandering at Ease in the Zhuangzi* (Albany: State University of New York Press): 35–74.

Keller, C. (2005). The Tao of Postmodernity: Process, Deconstruction, and Postcolonial theory, in W.-y. Xie, Z.-h. Wang, and G.E. Derfer (eds), *Whitehead and China: Relevance and Relationship* (Lancaster: Ontos Verlag): 39–68.

Mair, V.H. (1994). *Wandering on the Way: Early Daoist Tales and Parables of Chuang Tzu* (New York: Bantam Books).

Merton, T. (1965). *The Way of Chuang Tzu* (Toronto: Penguin Books Canada, Ltd).

Ricoeur, P. (1992). *Oneself as Another* (Chicago: The University of Chicago Press).

Suen, H., Cheung, S.-O., and Mondejar, R. (2007). Managing Ethical Behavior in Construction Organizations in Asia: How do the Teachings of Confucianism, Daoism and Buddhism and Globalization Influence Ethics Management?, *International Journal of Project Management* 25: 257–65.

Waley, A. (1939). *Three Ways of Thought in Ancient China* (London: George Allen & Unwin Ltd).

Watson. B. (1968). *The Complete Works of Chuang Tzu* (New York: Columbia University Press).

Wen, H.-M. (2012). *Chinese Philosophy* (Cambridge: Cambridge University Press).

Whitehead, A.N. (1925). *Science and the Modern World* (New York: Free Press).

——(1947). *Essays in Science and Philosophy* (New York: Philosophical Library).

Yu, S.-S. (2009). Three Expositions of Zhuangzi's Philosophy of Management (in Chinese), *Journal of Higher Education Management* 3(5): 55–61.

CHAPTER 6

....

BARUCH SPINOZA (1632–1677)

....

DANIEL HJORTH AND ROBIN HOLT

6.1 Life and Place

....

Spinoza, dead for quite some time, is seldom read in organization studies, and only occasionally figures in discussions on process philosophy or process thinking. He was a serious scholar in the full sense of the word, looking at you from old portraits with his somewhat sad, sympathetic, and curious eyes etched brightly with his life's dictum: 'Not to laugh, not to lament, not to curse, but to understand.' He was a Renaissance figure, his Latin tracts were littered with intense and considered expressions that set alight this already bright period of discovery and debate as ideas bounced in among such figures as Hobbes, Pascale, Descartes, and Leibniz. Amsterdam, his birthplace, was a city steeped in such free thinking, momentarily a place of social, commercial, and philosophical experiment into which he found himself thrown as the middle son of a Spanish-Jewish family forced to leave the Iberian peninsula as a result of the Portuguese inquisition. It was a liberal city cast under the pragmatic eye of the Republican Government run by the de Witt's. Rembrandt was painting his self-deprecating, self-examining portraits and quietly luminescent images of 'slobbish' ordinary life only one block away from Spinoza's family home, religious control was being loosened, allowing the city's 'Portuguese Nation' (*La Nação*) to flourish with spiritual and commercial vibrancy (Nadler, 2003), and the voices of Hobbes, Pascale, and Descartes might be heard in lively conversation.

Already of mongrel birth, he readily begins to mix and challenge his religion. Raised through Jewish learning, then apprenticed into his family's trading business, before, at the impressionable age of 23 in 1656, he finds himself the subject of *herem*, an excommunication, probably for heresy; if young Baruch was questioning the immanent presence of an interventionist figure called God he was ripping the fabric by which his community was bound to one another. He had been seduced by the rationalistic (and Christian) thinking of Descartes, entranced by the purported individuality and separability of the human mind. The allure lasted long enough to sustain his own separation (changing his name to Benedictus and associating with a group of open-minded Christians), before the influence of Descartes and then Christianity also dissipated into a more pantheistic vision of a world of endlessly circuiting determinations of self-similar substance. Spinoza too dissipates, leaving Amsterdam to rove around the Netherlands, ending up in The Hague, from which low-lying capital he witnesses the first signs of religious intolerance and state-sponsored repression flowing over the civic weal, an irrepressible tide that his *Theological-Political Treatise* (1670) and then, posthumously, his opus magnum the *Ethics*, could do little to abate.

Receptions of his work have been varied. His books made it to the 'forbidden reading list' of the Catholic Church (always a sign of quality), and were championed by Enlightenment thinkers like Bayle for their rationalist calm, yet we have Samuel Taylor Coleridge suggesting Spinoza's writing was the closest any mortal had come to apprehending God. It was the quality of such apprehension that got Spinoza in hot water; at the time of their expression his pantheistic assertions were incendiary. Spinoza's God was all pervasive—so far so orthodox—but Spinoza meant it literally. Up until Spinoza, omnipotence had been a kind of grammatical gesture towards the unknown, a willingness to cede to an overwhelming, otherworldly force. Spinoza argued otherwise, declaiming God was all there was. It was not a God as universal animating spirit; it was literally equivalence between God and all Nature. This equivalence unhinges any reader careful enough to realize that with such complete omnipotence comes an equally complete lack of divine distinction. We cannot find God as a separate being or entity. We cannot then revere God as some kind of providential force, nor is there a resolving end point to life, distinct from life. Nature/God is all there is, and it is its own self-causing, determining a flow of forces to which all bodies are inevitably in thrall as endless and inevitably partial expressions of this unity. Heaven was brought down to earth, and earth elevated to heaven.

It is with this open, bodily-governed, and specific configuration of ethics that we find Spinoza becoming a most apposite thinker of organization and process. Spinoza's thinking resists the tendency to focus on individual agents in their status as subjects, or on structures as determining constraints, instead finding both agency and structure as the active or passive modulation of nature, each affecting and being affected by all others, coming together as assemblages also capable of affecting and being affected. Through all this Spinoza becomes a philosopher of joyful life, wanting to help us understand—as modulations of Nature—how we can increase our capacity to act.

6.2 WORLD

Spinoza's sense of the world is, to steal a phrase of Wittgenstein's, a simple one, but not easy to grasp. He works from three basic terms: substance, mode, and attribute.

Substance is '[W]hat is in itself and is conceived through itself, i.e., that whose concept does not require the concept of another thing, from which it must be formed' (Spinoza, 2006: I, definition 3). Modes are '[T]he affections of a substance; that is, that which is in something else and is conceived through something else' (Spinoza, 2006: I, §5). Attributes are '[W]hat the intellect perceives of substance, as constituting its essence' (Spinoza, 2006: I, §4). From this trinity he builds an entire appreciation of the world. Touching all in such a world is God. Yet it is a God whose infinite nature means it carries no distinctiveness, it has no anthropological sympathy, indeed it is not at all interested in the world as such, or humans in particular; rather, it is the world. Spinoza's God, being omnipresent, carries infinite attributes and hence infinite substance; all things are modes or modifications—of God. As substance is defined as that which is conceived in itself, and no two substances can carry the same attribute (essence), then God, being infinite, is all there is. God is Nature; Nature is God. Even in lascivious seventeenth-century Amsterdam such a literal equivalence is startling in its implication. God cannot exist beyond Nature, there is no transcendent place from which to whimsically and angrily intervene, and without providence there is little room for the superstitions of a priestly class. Nor is there room for an inner enclave called the mind from whose ghostly battlements human beings might claim some form of sovereign independence from a world in decaying flux. This is where Spinoza dissolves the questions posed by Descartes: 'How does the mental interact with the physical? How does mind sit within and govern the body?' Descartes' *Principles*, published in 1644, seemed to want to reduce things to quantity, *res extensia*; all things were modifications of extended substance that could be explained by covering laws. The exceptions were mind, and then God (a separate, uncreated substance); these were immaterial and resisted mathematics. Spinoza's Nature brings together the experiences of the mind, body, and God that Descartes had been so attentive in taking apart. He does not partake of Cartesian dualism and transcendence, but develops a univocity: there is only one substance (God or Nature; as active power) (Viljanen, 2007: 404) and substance is only its expressions, i.e. we are all part of an infinite plurality of Nature.

With our God and ourselves firmly caught in the soil, with the soil, as Nature, Spinoza's unified Nature is absent of the salving purpose by which the world (and our place in it) is either held to account, or lost to us (hell also carries comforts). Without ultimate purpose we are left adrift trying to apprehend Nature, to understand its attributes. Those infinite attributes of Nature to which we humans are privy are extension and thought. Modes of extension are material bodies, and are apprehended generally by laws such as those cohering around shape (geometry) and movement (physics). Modes of thought are ideas and are apprehended generally by laws of consistency (logic) and pattern (psychology). Both extension and thought are also apprehended in the particular modes of finite expression configured in everyday experience, events of movement, or argument.

Spinoza envisages these attributes of extension and thought as entirely distinct. There is no interaction between these expressions (as body and mind were separate attributes); one we call action, the other ideas, and both are expressions of Nature's determining, productive force. Action and ideas exist in parallel, thus each mode of extension con-figured through causal laws has an equivalent mode of thought governed by laws of pattern. The metaphysical poet John Donne, a near contemporary of Spinoza, acknowl-edges this when writing about love: 'Love's mysteries in soules doe grow/ But yet the body is his booke'; act and idea cohere, entirely independently, as parallel expressions of love, but the body is first in this communion: 'For soule into the soule may flow/ Though it to body first repaire' (Donne, 'The Ecstasy', 1635: 46). The body is always quicker than the mind. It registers potential before we acknowledge it; the skin changes its chemical balance, the eye reacts to light. Our thinking is parallel to this affect that the body pro-duces. Knowledge and feeling flow their own ways, yet each remains intimate with one another: 'all that is action in the body is also action in the mind, and all that is passion in the mind is also passion in the body' (Deleuze, 1988: 88; Spinoza, 2006: II, §12). The individual mind, constituted by what is primary in the mode of thinking—an idea—is the idea of the corresponding body (Deleuze, 1988: 86); the body and mind admit of no hierarchy, they are parallel.

So for Spinoza we human beings are modifications of Nature, able to apprehend such (including ourselves) through action and thought, but never at a distance. There can be no contemplating observation of the world; not even God is offered such a life-denying position. This carries interesting epistemological and ethical implication. To know about the world, Spinoza recognizes we begin with particular modes, appreciating the world as specific, and the significance of things attests to immediacy in our interests, yet with wisdom we learn to connect things, to appreciate the unity of things; what the religions have called God. Thus Spinoza's hope is that we ascend from particular knowl-edge of material and mental life through to awareness of generalities, and then towards a synthesis of the two, a direct appreciation of the whole unmediated by concepts. It is in the relation of the particular to the general mode that Nature is experienced as some-thing immanent, a rolling, irresistible, productive, determining force that we, as reason-able beings, are able to apprehend calmly, unaccompanied by the theatrical thunder and fire-smiting invective of a metaphysical intervention. Yet in this immanence Spinoza acknowledges what we might call an epistemology of striving. Disappointed by the inadequacy of concepts, urging ourselves beyond our pauce perspectives, we experience an intellect yearning and stretching at awareness, enticed by the irreducible otherness that lays the other side of silence. To be a human being is to want to be elsewhere, driven by a passion to urge oneself somewhere; this is the grounding of intellect and really of the human condition. Intellectually, we are not, then, defined by reason, but by the pas-sion to become, to drive, to will; as partial modifications of the whole, our intellect finds us striving towards the whole. This restlessness is what defines us, it is our essence; we will never be complete.

We can witness such an epistemology of striving by going back to John Donne. Donne, like Spinoza, is riven with concern for how mind and body relate: 'I am a litle world made cunningly/ Of elements and an Angelike sprite/ But black sinne hath betrayed to endlesse night/ My worlds both parts, and (oh) both parts must die' (1633/2005: 7). Mind and body are separate entire, yet both must die, but because of sin, or being different expressions of the same Nature and finitude? These vexing questions are compounded in Donne's realization that we begin with and rarely escape the world; like Spinoza, Donne is aware that knowledge begins from a condition often full with passionate unruliness and an untutored gamut of emotion. Start to think about an experience like love, say, and right away we are plunged in to a maelstrom of uncertainty. Donne, like Spinoza, is metaphysical in the going along with, and then beyond, sense of *meta* (ideas accompanying body), and begins with the ordinary experience of love: its mutuality, acts of sexual congress, desire. From these particulars of feeling he strives to write outwards, scattering his imagination abroad, reaching for general answers, yet always with uneasiness, aware of frailties of language and body alike. Donne was expressing how enlightenment comes only darkly, and only then by working through, not above, the world

Intimate with this epistemology of striving comes an equalizing of the body and mind that has huge ethical resonance. Recall that Spinoza does not partake in the Cartesian philosophy of dualism and transcendence, but develops a univocity: there is only one substance (God or Nature, as active power) and substance is only its expressions, i.e. we are all part of an infinite pluralism without any hierarchy of beings or possibility of sustained distinction. Being is nothing more than becoming in all its difference (Deleuze, 1992; Duffy, 2004; Nail, 2008; Viljanen, 2007). Deleuze argues that this mobility and immanence finds Spinoza questioning the viability of morality, if by the moral we mean a total standard that provides the basis for judgement from the outside according to transcendent values of good and evil (a question of obligation). This he contrasts with ethics, which is situational and pragmatic, and seeks to answer the question 'what a body can do' in relation to the ways of existing it is experiencing (a question of power, *potentia*) (see Deleuze, 1995: 100). Where, traditionally, morality was about fixed standards of the good, Spinoza probed the moving struggle by which the idea of good was made sense of as possibility. Massumi puts it like this: 'It means assessing what kind of potential they [actions] tap into and express. [...] The ethical value of an action is what it brings out in the situation, for its transformation, how it breaks sociality open. Ethics is about how we inhabit uncertainty together' (2003: 7). Deleuze relies on Nietzsche here, though whereas Nietzsche discusses 'good and bad' (rather than good and evil) as judged from a particular style of life (Nietzsche used noble and slave styles; the noble 'creates values as a positive affirmation of self', whereas the 'slave's values are created in response to what is determined to be other than his nature', Schrift, 2006: 188), Deleuze reframes this in a Spinozist way, talking instead of active and reactive forces. And here ethics concerns the body as much as thought, each entirely separate expressions of the same Natural condition of immanence.

Ethics, being a condition of handling uncertainty, takes us back into epistemology. Spinoza's ethics urge us to reach after that which is most conducive to our flourishing in particular situations set within the long-standing habits of human converse into which one is thrown. There is a pragmatic ethics here, one that is both discerning (knowledge) and feeling (sensitivity) to what situations demand of us as we stumble upon them. Hearing our condition (rather than imposing a morality upon it), finds us striving to reach into the cracks, to listen intently as to what matters and might matter, in attempted sympathy with others. In *Middlemarch* the novelist George Eliot—credited with the first completed English translation of Spinoza's *Ethics*—is acutely aware of the quotidian demands of such an ethics and epistemology of striving. A moving force in the narrative (there are no real central characters), Dorothea Brooke yields to an infectious enthusiasm and capacity for social and cultural improvements amid the backwater townsfolk of Middlemarch. She brings others 'on' in her struggle to initiate civic projects, mend lives, improve manners, whilst all the while falling short of an accurate reading of those with whom she lives, most disastrously in her yearning for the stilted Edward Casaubon. Eliot shows how we often misread others, indeed nearly always finding their character playing out differently to how we had read them, and so always attempting to find sympathy with the world on the basis of feeling as much as knowledge. On marrying Casaubon her feeling for him tarnishes with each page: 'the large vistas and wide fresh air which she has dreamed of finding in her husband's mind were replaced by anterooms and winding passages which seemed to lead nowhither' (Eliot, 1965: 145). She realizes how she had been caught in thrall to her own metaphors, misjudging Casaubon's loftiness for profundity, his pedantry for probity. She creates Casaubon as an amalgam of abstract conceptions gilded by desire; she read the signs with excited feeling, completing the blanks of her perception with imagined perfections (Hillis Miller, 2001: 71). Confronted with this fraility of awareness, however, Dorothea persists, always striving beyond felt ignorance. Experiencing the increasingly bloodless Casaubon finds Dorothea diminished, frustrated, yet retaining the potential for feeling, to which she can give vent when—with the death of Casaubon—she finds communion with the artist Will Ladislaw. There is no fickleness here, nor resentment, but a commitment to finding joy in the wake of disappointment. Eliot finds in Spinoza awareness that we will never know what is 'other', nor even know ourselves fully, prey as we are to the smooth attraction of imagined states and enticing metaphors. What matters is that despite the impossibility of complete knowledge (Byatt, 2007) we sustain our capacity to strive after awareness; that we find potential amid the ruins of our ignorance and disappointment; that we have the force to fling out passion anew. Dorothea emerges as Dorothea because of such force; her identity is not fixed first and then brought to events. She is shaped and shaping in the company of others as others, all the while exposing herself in her ignorance against which she strives, without ever finding a stable vanishing point. Despite failure we should not stop urging some form of completed clarity into our life, what Dorothea experiences as an 'enthusiastic acceptance of untried duty', holding forth the prospect of a world to be filled with beneficent activity and emotion, but whose effects can never be known. Her social schemes, for example, use the prospect of improvement to open up the lives of others, gently, and perhaps unpredictably, and never without qualification (see Miller, 2001: 78). The town too improves, materially and as a civic space. By the end of the novel we reach an encomium to an ethical and epistemological strength of which she has become a striving and catalysing aspect:

> Her full nature, like that river of which Cyrus broke the strength, spent itself in channels which had no great name on the earth. But the effect of her being on those

around her was incalculably diffusive: for the growing good of the world is partly dependent on unhistoric acts; and that things are not so ill with you and me as they might have been, is half owing to the number who lived faithfully a hidden life, and rest in unvisited tombs. (Eliot, 1965: 894)

Spinoza would see such an ending as joyful, and Deleuze as a performative, by which acts and speech Dorothea has been able to strive from within the modulations of everyday life, without resentment. She practises a passion of the mind as well as body. This passion is as quiet as it is intense, as errant as it is well tuned, as playful as it is serious, and all the while in such a span of life she give event to the possibilities of ordinary life free from the conceits and surface brilliance of perfection. Spinoza's concept describing Dorothea's experience was *conatus*.

6.3 *CONATUS*

Spinoza would recognize in writers like Eliot and Donne a complex expression of what is in every person: a capacity, an intensity of forces, and a striving to maintain existence in experiencing interplay of finite (particular) and infinite (general) modes—a striving after modes that Spinoza calls *conatus*. If we understand something adequately, Spinoza suggests, as Donne does love, or Elliot the more rounded requirements of effective community life, our capacity to act increases accordingly and we experience joy. If we do not understand, our capacity to act diminishes. However here our power to be affected is raised and this means our connective capacity—our openness—is greater. If we then encounter an individual whose force or acts are conflicting with ours, preventing us from becoming active, we experience sadness—a decreased capacity to act. A body's capacity—and this is a perspective shared by both Nietzsche and Spinoza—would then answer to how composite it is, how complex its composition is. Complexity increases a body's connective capacity and thus its affective capacity and thus, potentially, its capacity to become active, or become passive (Spindler, 2009), as when Dorothea's misguided and hence sad affection for Casaubon finds her then more open to the potentially joyful advances of Ladislaw. A more complex composition exposes us to greater possible affect, which means more chances to persist, meaning greater *conatus*. *Conatus* thus describes a body/mind's engagement as well as its readiness to try, attempt, and experiment. *Conatus* is affirmative determination, a striving to come into and maintain one's capacity to be affected (Deleuze, 1992: 215–16; Macherey and Ruddick, 2011: 171). This is personified in Dorothea; a mannered striving in which life is enhanced, as both feeling and intellect, without one being privileged, nor presuming that either reaches any form of bedrock.

Spinoza argues that affections that a mode experiences determine its *conatus*. *Conatus* determined by affections we actually experience is called desire and is as such accompanied by consciousness. Desire is thus a question of passion (affections that are results from external modes/bodies), but also a question of our power to act (Deleuze,

1992: 220). A desire, born from joyful passion, determines us to do things, and thus to attempt to preserve our power (in the set of relations in which we have become the mode that we are). This informs our understanding of individuation or becoming a subject, as a dynamics of *conatus*. Spinoza's *conatus* is closely evoked by Nietzsche's will to power here (Spindler, 2009), not least because both are based on a recuperated status of the body in philosophy. Will to power describes what one is capable of, and *conatus* is will to maximize one's existence. Under the guise of *conatus*, or will, what we have come to refer to as consciousness is an awareness of the passage from greater to lesser, or lesser to greater, capacity to act. This is thus as much a state of the body as it is a movement in thought. We can be more or less conscious, more or less affected by our idea of an idea, our awareness of our capacity.

This capacity is both our will to power and our capacity for exposure, to be affected: 'an existing mode has, for its parts, an essence that is identical to a degree of power; as such it has an ability to be affected, a capacity to be affected in a very great number of ways' (Deleuze, 1992: 218). Not in an infinite number of ways, for this is reserved for God/Nature, and we humans are only ever striving. Affections that can be explained by the nature of the affected body are an action (based on adequate ideas and active feelings), and in this sense reserved for God/Nature. Affections that cannot be explained without taking the influence from another body into account are passions (inadequate ideas and passive feelings). We mortals, however, exist inevitably by being affected by other modes/bodies, and so our affections 'are at the outset, and tend to remain, passions' (Deleuze, 1992: 219). Thus our capacity to engage in active affections seems to present a challenge of folding the external, the outer forces—what we become affected by through our power to be affected, our passion—into inner, active affections; a force that enables determination to overcome resistance, habit, traces, made investments, and tradition.

This folding brings us back to another, more chaotic expression of Dorothea's striving. She feels duped by her investment in Casaubon, scared by her imaginative excess that believed his mind intense and spiritually hungry, only to find Casaubon had long since quitted any abandonment to feeling, having once tried and found the stream 'an exceedingly shallow rill' (Elliot, 1965: 62). Dorothea had not been aware of Casaubon's inability to feel, trussed up as he was in the isolation of his self-confirming edifice. She had been seduced by an image made rigid by a spoiling pride, and her realization of this steals across her like a slow, irrisitible mist. She becomes aware of this as a quotidian tragedy occurring as the scales fall away from our eyes. The disappointment is inevitable, and if it were not, if we had a capacity to know all, that would be worse still:

> If we had a keen vision and feeling for all ordinary human life, it would be like hearing the grass grow and the squirrel's heart beat, and we should die of that roar which lies on the other side of silence. As it is the quickest of us walk about well-wadded with stupidity. (Eliot, 1965: 226)

If we could see through silence we would encounter the chaos (ungoverned occurrence), condemned like Cassandra to know everything but never be heard above the roar of ineradicable happening. Metaphor, words, provide wadding, their smoothing distortions shielding us from the oceanic swell, a tragedy that Nietzsche was to later play out in the interweaving of Apollo and Dionysius. The silence lends us stabilizing order (cf. James), but with Spinoza it also affords us a capacity to simply leap without knowledge, to say 'yes' ungirded by truth claims, allowing us to feel and relish passion, exposing us to the possibility of joy.

If we recall Spinoza talks about modes as what is in something else and conceived through something else. The mode is the modification of the substance—Nature/God. We are all modes in the sense of modifications of substance. This is precisely why subjectification can happen—there is no subject to start with. It is a result of individuation, which Spinoza would describe in terms of a modification of substance. Modifications of Spinoza's body/mind include movement/rest and imagination/will, and it is a body's/mind's capacity for being affected and to affect that defines it. For Massumi, 'there is no subject separate from the event. There is only the event as subject to its occurring to itself. The event itself is a subjective self-creation: the how-now of this singular self-enjoyment of change taking place' (2011: 8).

Thus in asking after the subject we ask: What affects does a body/mind have? What increases or decreases its power of acting? What power to be affected does it hold? These are the questions replacing the usual: 'What is the subject?' or 'What constitutes the subject?' They are questions of modes, of affections. Modes are relationally, dynamic powers to act and be affected. Deleuze, later on, discussing Foucault, is venturing—using Spinoza—to reinvent the concept of subject and uses a somewhat peculiar phrasing of subjectification to describe what is happening in terms of 'a magnetic or electrical field' (1995: 92). He goes on:

> We're no longer in the domain of codified rules of knowledge (relations between forms) [cf. morality or the sphere of obligations as discussed earlier], and constraining rules of power (the relation of force to other forces), but in one of rules that are in some sense optional (self-relation): the best thing is to exert power over yourself.... That's what subjectification is about: bringing a curve into the line, making it turn back on itself, or making force impinge on itself.... It's idiotic to say Foucault discovers or reintroduces a hidden subject after having rejected it. There's no subject, but a production of subjectivity: subjectivity has to be produced, when its time arrives, precisely because there is no subject. (Deleuze, 1995: 113–14)

To think of such a production through *conatus* we use the admittedly ugly term 'actorship'; the 'eventness' of the event (of agency) where modification of substance is experienced as a 'self-enjoyment of change taking place'. However, it is chosen to emphasize the becoming-active of a body, what we traditionally describe as 'acquiring agency'. Actorship suggests a body's/mind's capacity for being affected (and to affect), undergoing modifications, experienced as change underway: subjectification always immanent to a certain power to act, an increase or decrease, a stronger or weaker *conatus*. Massumi likens it to a passing present, 'understood not as a point in metric time but rather as a qualitative duration—a dynamic mutual inclusion of phases of process in each other, composing a "span" of becoming' (2011: 9). This resonates with Deleuze and Guattari's (1988: 238) comment: 'a becoming lacks a subject distinct from itself; [but also that] it has no term, since its term in turn exists only as taken up in another becoming of which it is the subject, and which coexists, forms a block, with the first'. This becoming of subject would be a striving to come into existence; and once existence is granted by the relations into which it has entered, *conatus* is also the effort to maintain a capacity for being affected (Deleuze, 1992). The time of *conatus*, attached to previous affections and tending towards the next, is the span. In terms of an image, Deleuze uses the span of a bee, when in the bloc of becoming that is formed with the flower, is characterized by the simultaneous 'becoming pollinator' and 'becoming feeder' that is created in this relationship. It is, Spinoza would say, two bodies that affect each other in such a way that the productive capacities of both increase: there is joy, more life. Dorothea likewise, in the bloc of becoming formed in the civic and material space of Middlemarch and with the likes of Casaubon and Ladlislaw, experiences a span in becoming cultural pollinator and feeder of love and affection; the productive capacities of all increase, potentially. This 'bloc of becoming' involves 'more life' for her and the community, albeit quiet life (unhistorical, in places unnoticed even, in channels with no great name, her tomb unvisited).

Subjects are subjectified through affect and being affected, a change in intensity, a passage from one experiential state of a body/mind to another. The passage results in an increase or a decrease in that body's capacity to act. An affecting body and an affected body form a state—a state of affection refers to the passage towards greater or lesser power to act of a body/mind in parallel. Having become active or having become passive in a set of relationships with other affecting bodies is a question of a state—*affectio*. Becoming active or becoming passive is a question of passing, increasing/decreasing of capacity—*affectus*. Now we're back at agency, or actorship as we call it. Affect is not a personal feeling (emotion). It is pre-personal, supra-personal, and sub-personal. It is 'the effectuation of a power' of relations to the collective, which 'throws the self into upheaval and makes it reel' (Deleuze and Guattari, 1988: 240). Affect is a collective-relational change in intensity, a passage of becoming active or becoming passive, through which the capacity to act increases or decreases accordingly.

Spinoza, trying to clarify what he means by such a condition, writes in his *Ethics*: 'if a number of individuals to concur in one action that together they are all in the cause of one effect, I consider them all, to that extent as one singular thing' (Spinoza, 2006: II, definition 7). He describes a body similarly; in Deleuze's words: '[I]n the first place, a body, however small it may be, is composed of an infinite number of particles; it is the relations of motion and rest, of speeds and slownesses between particles, that define a body, the individuality of a body. Secondly, a body affects other bodies, or is affected by other bodies; it is this capacity for affecting and being affected that also defines a body in its individuality' (Deleuze, 1988: 123; cf. Spinoza, 2006: II, definition 1, proposition 12, 13). A body can thus be an assemblage of particular human bodies, forming an assemblage, and is individuated or subjectified on the basis of its movements and capacity for affecting and being affected (Spinoza, 2006, definition of body in part II). Dorothea and Middlemarch are such. She is an individual who persistently finds herself in gradual actions with others who have patterned and connecting effects, which Eliot holds together in skilful metaphor. Her actorship is a becoming active and passive in communion with others set in place itself always shifting. 'March', in English, is a term for the edge, or liminal, an in-between border, the middle of which is found as nothing other than an effectuation of power in which characters reel in their actorship.

The opening, so far, has been an exercise of intensifying our relationship with Spinoza's concepts. This prepares us for the rest of the chapter—to make readers become active as processual thinkers. The relationship we seek to establish with the reader would then somehow form a bloc of becoming, an effectuation of a power which seeks to increase our capacity to act as processual thinkers. Following the previous sections we seek to move on by working with the philosophy of Spinoza in a further discussion of agency and organizations. This includes a particular focus on affect, *conatus*, and subjectification. The movement following will include a discussion of how organization studies scholars can use Spinoza's processual philosophy.

6.4 Actorship and Organization

Our reading has Deleuze sitting on Spinoza's back. Not only is the encounter with Deleuze–Spinoza contextualized by post-structuralism and Deleuze's philosophy of becoming (in particular), it is also nurtured by an interest in how, given the dropping of the self-grounded (Cartesian) subject, we can describe processes of becoming a subject, how subjectivities achieve being as modifications of Nature, answering to body's/mind's affective capacities. We have attended primarily to Spinoza's concepts of affect and affective capacity as rendered in an epistemology of striving and an ethics of coping, in order to better appreciate how humans discover identity in settings of recognition into which they are folded and refolded. This is the condition of organization woven with affect, subjectification, and event without any sense of a supporting or grounding condition by which we might anchor truth claims; the unit of analysis shifts to the composition of affective relations in actorship. Actorship evokes the relational character of our power to be affected and affect, and thus our *conatus*, our will to capability. It draws on the nature of the actor's act in the theatre play. Agency in such a context is about intensity, becoming active, collectively achieved in the round, and within an audience. An individual body/mind is always already part of a multitude of reciprocal relationships. Agency is thus always a question of affective relationships to collectives, of belonging as basis for becoming (Massumi, 2002). For Spinoza, these collectives are not a result of preformed individuals then coming together; instead, bodies are always in a multitude of relations, in which individuation happens as event. The actor and audience become subjects as they submit themselves to the demands and discipline of an organized setting by which they are recognized, or acknowledged. The resultant individual (properly named 'dividual', as Deleuze has stressed) is always attached to previous affections (states, capacities) and tending towards the next, finding themselves in spans, like Dorothea or Donne, with life pulling them hither and thither as they strive to place themselves and in so making their place present, reach beyond it. Such a body's power to be affected, its openness or receptivity, and its power to affect, to act, its spontaneity—this is a question of passion.

We humans are born, passionate, in relationships that affect with passive feelings and inadequate ideas. This passionate state, however, is still one in which our power to act is alive. Passions can increase our capacity for being affected, and a composite composition increases our capacity for being affected, but keeps us separate from what we can do. Actorship is a task of bending forces back upon the individuated expression of an attribute of a substance, a modulation of the modes of expression allowing the affirmation of self through available styles to become something that affects as well as being affected by. The process of rehearsal, of training, or preparation, when actors seek what kind of act they can and need to do in order for the play to become what it should, is a dynamic process of building actorship. The power of the actor is both a 'will to capability' (potential, active-actual power) and intensity, allowing a body to become subjectified into a specific subject position to which belong certain socially constituted capacities (joy or sadness). Deleuze, explaining the concept of power in Spinoza, writes: '[A]ll power is inseparable from a capacity for being affected, and this capacity for being affected is constantly and necessarily filled by affections that realize it' (1988: 97). Affections are the relationally constituted states of a body, its images of other bodies, how it imagines itself and its relations on the basis of the corporeal traces of what previously has happened to it. Dorothea is nearly all preparation and preparedness; her willingness to experiment, to practise at life, sustains her in her becoming and being affected by events in Middlemarch. Likewise the power of the bee as a life-enhancing body will thus increase when it flies into a field of flowers in full blossom. A bee with greater capacity for being affected by the flower—for example with greater capacity to register the scent a flower emits—also has greater power as pollinator/eater (cf. Nietzsche); and Dorothea, with greater capacity for hearing the artistic yearning of Ladislaw, has imaginative power to further belong in yet others' lives.

We have previously said that affirmative acts are part of a process of moving beyond oneself in order to become other. We suggest actorship helps here, grasping a dynamic between the actor and the text in which there is not a one-to-one relationship between actors and the strictures of the play (the text, the stage) but a field of potentials that relations between bodies in assemblages give rise to. Here 'subjectivity does not presuppose identity but is produced in a process of individuation, which is always already collective or "populated"' (Deleuze, 1998: 9, in Semetsky, 2004: 325). Just as there are endless versions of A Doll's House or Hamlet, there are of course endless versions of transmutative organizational actorships. Reactive forces and negative will to power limit such a field of potentials. When a mode is affected with passive feelings and its power to be affected is negative, i.e. separating it from what it can do, its power to act (will to power) is diminished and this decrease is, in Spinoza's terms, 'sadness'. This is how formal organizational structures (procedures, roles, hierarchies, standards, goals) work. Within such structures agency is understood as a form of countervailing struggle or acceptance from a separate subject. Research on leadership, institutions, and entrepreneurship tradition-ally follows such consciousness (the cognitive or psychological), which expresses the relation of forces to the ones that dominate them, and in this sense is primarily focused on the reactive, and how through adept response such subjects might enhance or widen their knowledge in order to better realize already known goals. This makes sense in a Cartesian philosophy where mind and body are distinct and perception of objects in the world is the basis for understanding them.

Under Spinoza the phenomena of organization and subject are very different. Subjectivity is never singular (a subject) but is always only the speed/slowness of a mode as constituted by its affections and power to be affected. Any subject would then always be a result of suppressed multiplicity (subject and structure are expressions of one and the same) which occurs as an intensity manifesting the potential of the body (the lat-ter being a composition of active and reactive forces). This potential of the body—its power—is a capacity to multiply and intensify affective connections—something related to its complex composition. This power to affect and be affected is, in human beings, experienced as a striving towards what is not present but might become so, a striving that is both action and imagination (parallelism), a striving that is evoked by the term *conatus*—'the effort to experience joy, to increase the power of acting, to imagine and find that which is a cause of joy' (Deleuze, 1988: 101).

In such a Spinozian philosophy, affect comes in and the formation of ideas—created by bodies affecting each other—becomes a natural focus. Studying entrepreneurship, for example, would find researchers investigating the active imagination and creation of opportunities and transmuting forces oriented towards building 'blocs of becoming' in relationships with other bodies. Spinozian entrepreneurship studies would be focused on what bodies—including teams, groups, organizations—can do, what active forces there are, and how to affirm them so as to differentiate and create new value (increasing joy). There would be awareness of the subject as an imprisoning image. The idea of an 'experiencing one' that grounds all experience, a 'doubting one' that thinks and therefore secures the thinking subject as what cannot be doubted, is an idea that throws us back upon the transcendence and totalization that Spinoza was so adamant we should avoid. The effects of such a reliance are a debilitating negativity based on judging life with refer-ence to values exterior to it; a negativity that characters like Dorothea and writers like Eliot and Donne resist in their active, creative willingness to eschew the etiolated com-fort of vanishing points. To invoke such isolated subjects corresponds to a will to control that only survives in so far as it avoids life in favour of ideas. In the stead of such terms, a Spinozan organization studies would acknowledge a flow of disordered experiences to which we experientially respond by creating a concept of an experiencing subject, which in turn—according to the tendency (nihilistic) to prioritize reactive forces—sug-gests we can control this flow. It would reveal how difference is not grounded in identity, as the idea of transcendence suggests. Rather, the identity of the subject is abstracted from difference. Spinoza's thinking dissolves the tendency to think in terms of negative (outside) forces because, for Spinoza, bodies are understood relationally, as transitions between movement and rest, as intensive capacities or powers to be affected and affect, as a composition of active and reactive forces. The affected body is then of a different reality from the one at rest; the acting one different from the passive one; hence our use of the terms 'actor' and 'actorship', which releases our capacity to think the subject in more relational-processual terms. In relationship to others that increase your capacity to act, i.e. add 'joy', in Spinoza's terms, a body gets represented as someone that is capable of certain acts. When such a capacity is endowed with character, it becomes an actor, i.e. a body–mind capacity with qualities, history, desires, life (Latour, 1996). Each mind-and-body composition is a degree of power corresponding to a capacity for being affected and to affect. Affections are actions and passions, where the former are a power to act and the latter a power to be acted upon. Affirmation is—as we saw in describing intensity earlier—Nietzsche's concept for embracing life's capacity for variation and capability to overcome itself, to become new. Thus 'entrepreneur', as an actor, is a concept we can use to describe this particular subjectivity that fills the function of going beyond oneself in order to affirmatively transmute or create new value, resources, businesses, or industrial logics. Entrepreneur is then an intensified body–mind capacity that has become an actor in relation to a script focused on beginning a venture.

We might then extend such a study to that of institutional entrepreneurs understood as responses to the negativity characteristic of inevitable technologies of control. These technologies (admissions procedures, legal regulations, qualifications, routines) seek to separate bodies'/minds' capabilities from what they can do. The observed dilemma of lukewarm support for change in organizations indicates the general problem with such reactive/passive forces. 'When reactive force separates active force from what it can do, the latter also becomes reactive' (Deleuze, 1988: 64). This is the reason behind the magnetic force of the status quo in organizations, legitimized with reference to fixed (external) measurements in the form of made investments and costs, with well-established habits represented as efficiencies. Those benefiting from the existing organizational order will make any striving for joy—increased creative capacity—difficult as they have costs and efficiency on their side. Reflecting on this, we see how networking is important in order to get new things done in and through organizations. Being dominated by affects contrary to your own nature, sadness will be the result: as active forces are separated from what they can do and bodies' creative capacity diminishes. This can be balanced by actively building networks in whose relations 'joy' is more intensely incipient (cf. Johannisson, 1987). Thus Spinoza shows how sadness—separating bodies from what they can do, and diminishing their productive capacity—can be understood as the effect of control and homogeneity: chance, becoming, and life are denied. In a homogenous sociality only one productive power can be sustained, and only in so far as it is built on consensus. Creativity, as has been shown numerous times in studies thereof (e.g. Amabile, 1996, 1998; Austin and Devin, 2003; Hargadon and Bechky, 2006), benefits from heterogeneity. An organizational capacity for creativity, as a corporate body, would then depend on its composition, its complexity, its willingness to act into the void, to leap regardless of unknowable consequences, to say yes on the grounds of untried duty. Spinoza would support such organizational creativity as built on heterogeneity, and its immanent creative potential. Such 'joy' as might emerge depends on tolerating multiple centres of power, chance, and life's openness. In this Spinoza provides a far richer philosophical basis than the still-preponderant Cartesian one for explaining the emergence of 'open innovation' systems (Chesbrough, 2003), 'crowd-sourcing' organizational forms (Brabham, 2008), and the formation of ensemble creativity. There is a preponderance of organizational forms dominated by sadness, where a dominant homogeneity is securing control, efficient adjustment and homage to costs, and economic traces. Spinoza exposes us to different modes of organization, where there is no form (order) that aligns homogeneity, and no subject that secures predictive behaviour (and thus control). This is the organization of motion and rest, intensity, and individuating affective states of actorship. This is the organization of creation, and, this, a becoming of organizing.

References

Amabile, T. (1996). *Creativity in Context* (Boulder, CO: Westview Press).

——(1998). How to Kill Creativity, *Harvard Business Review*, September/October: 77–87.

Austin, R.D. and Devin, L. (2003). *Artful Making: What Managers Need to Know About How Artists Work* (Upper Saddle River, NJ: Financial Times Prentice Hall).

Brabham, D.C. (2008). Crowdsourcing as a Model for Problem Solving, *The International Journal of Research into New Media Technologies* 14(1): 75–90.

Byatt, A.S. (2007). Wit and Wisdom. *The Guardian*, 4 August.

Chesbrough, H.W. (2003). *Open Innovation* (Cambridge, MA: Harvard University Press).

Czarniawska, B. and Wolff, R. (1991). Leaders, Managers, Entrepreneurs: On and off the organizational stage, *Organization Studies* 12(4): 529–46.

Deleuze, G. (1988). *Spinoza—Practical Philosophy* (San Francisco: City Lights Books).

——(1992). *Expressionism in Philosophy: Spinoza* (New York: Zone Books).

——(1995). *Negotiations* (New York: Columbia University Press).

—— and Guattari, F. (1988). *A Thousand Plateaus*, trans. Brian Massumi (Minneapolis: University of Minnesota Press).

Donne, J. (1633/2005). The Holy Sonnets from *The Variorum Edition of the Poetry of John Donne*, 7, 1 (Bloomington: Indiana University Press).

—— (1635). *Poëms with Elegies* (London: John Marriot).

Duffy, S. (2004). 'The Logic of Expression in Deleuze's Expressionism in Philosophy: Spinoza: A Strategy of Engagement', *International Journal of Philosophical Studies*, 12(1): 47–60.

Elliot, G. (1871–2/1965). *Middlemarch* (Harmondsworth: Penguin).

Hargadon, A.B. and Bechky, B.A. (2006). When Collections of Creatives Become Creative Collectives: A Field Study of Problem Solving at Work, *Organization Science* 17: 484–500.

Hillis Miller, J. (2001). *Others* (Princeton: Princeton University Press).

Johannisson, B. (1987). Anarchists and Organizers: Entrepreneurs in a Network Perspective, *International Studies of Management and Organization* 17(1): 49–63.

Latour, B. (1996). *Aramis, or, The Love of Technology* (Cambridge, MA: Harvard University Press).

Macherey, P. and Ruddick, S.M. (2011). *Hegel or Spinoza* (Minneapolis: The University of Minnesota Press).

Massumi, B. (2002). *Parables for the Virtual—Movement, Affect, Sensation* (Durham and London: Duke University Press).

—— (2003). Navigating Movements, *21C* 2, <http://www.21cmagazine.com/>

—— (2011). *Semblance and Event—Activist Philosophy and the Occurrent Arts* (Cambridge, MA: MIT Press).

Nadler, S. (2003). *Rembrandt's Jews* (Chicago: University of Chicago Press).

Nail, T. (2008). Expression, Immanence and Constructivism: 'Spinozism' and Gilles Deleuze, *Deleuze Studies* 2(2): 201–19.

Schrift, A.D. (2006). Deleuze becoming Nietzsche becoming Spinoza becoming Deleuze, *Philosophy Today*, supplement, 50: 187–94.

Semetsky, I. (2004). The Complexity of Individuation, *International Journal of Applied Psychoanalytic Studies* 1(4): 324–46.

Spindler, F. (2009). *Spinoza: Multitud, Affect, Kraft* (Munkedal: Glänta Produktion).

Spinoza, B. (1677/2006). *The Ethics* (Teddington: The Echo Library).

Viljanen, V. (2007). Field Metaphysics, Power, and Individuation in Spinoza, *Canadian Journal of Philosophy* 37(3): 393–418.

CHAPTER 7

GOTTFRIED WILHELM LEIBNIZ (1646–1716)

ELKE WEIK

7.1 LIFE AND WORKS

Perhaps never has a man read as much, studied as much, meditated more, and written more than Leibniz.

(Denis Diderot, cited in Look, 2008)

GOTTFRIED WILHELM Leibniz enters the world of process philosophy with a fanfare. 'The principal standard bearer of process theory in modern philosophy was Leibniz', declares Rescher (1996: 12). The seventeenth-century philosopher from Germany has known many eponyms, the word 'genius' figuring most prominently among them. In retrospect, he was the last to embody mastery of philosophy as well as every scientific discipline. Apart from his philosophical contributions, to which this chapter is devoted, he invented the infinitesimal calculus and binary numbers, mathematical and logical forms of notation still in use (Leibniz-Forschungsstelle, 2012). All this was done, as we would say today, in his spare time while travelling in coaches through Europe in the service of various masters. His 'work time' was devoted to politics, and for most of his adult life he served as what Rescher (1979: 4) calls a 'minister-without-portfolio in charge of historico-legal, cultural, and scientific affairs', combining the work of a Privy Counsellor and diplomat with the more practical concerns of engineering a solution to rid the ducal silver mines of water, or designing the waterworks for the Palace in Hanover. In contrast to a modern reader, Leibniz seems never to have seen any contradiction in this (although he, understandably, felt the restrictions of a 24-hour day quite keenly and often complained about them). On the contrary, he permanently translated knowledge won in one area to the others, deeply convinced that the world of theory and the world of praxis, the world of nature and the world of morals, the divine and the human world, all formed one perfect system.

This last word introduces the big leitmotif in Leibniz's thinking. Not only does he believe there is such a thing as a system of the world and that a universal science can be developed to analyse it, he also presents us in his work with one of the most elaborate and consistent systems in occidental philosophy. Rescher (1979) considers it to be without flaws (the only problem being that a modern audience cannot accept its premises); the great Leibniz exegete Loemker likens it to a Leviathan. Unfortunately, it also stands out in occidental philosophy as the system most unsystematically exposed. In his lifetime, Leibniz only wrote two books and nine essays. The rest of his oeuvre consists of 50,000 independent pieces, among them 15,000 letters he exchanged with 1,100 addressees, archived in the ducal archives of Hanover and the Academy of the Sciences in Berlin. Of these—as of summer 2012—less than 50 per cent have been edited.[1] In these letters, Leibniz, whose irenic temperament has often been commented upon, always adapts his argument to the level of knowledge of his correspondent, which leaves us with documents written in three different languages (German, French, and Latin) and in many different styles featuring many different concepts. Moreover, quite naturally, he modified and elaborated his thoughts over the years. In terms of exegesis, it is a nightmare. Bertrand Russell (1995: 572), who seems to have felt personally affronted by this careless manner of exposition and even suspected Leibniz of deliberately hiding his system, writes: 'He did work on mathematical logic which would have been enormously important if he had published it; he would, in that case, have been the founder of mathematical logic, which would have become known a century and a half sooner than it did in fact'—despite the grumpy overtones, no mean verdict from a star contributor to the field.

In terms of writing a handbook chapter about Leibniz, this situation is not the stuff of dreams, either. For this reason, I will rely more than usual on secondary authors who have studied the unpublished works: Broad (1975), Cassirer (1962), Loemker (1956, 1973), Rescher (1979, 1981, 1996), and Russell (1951, 1995). A useful quick guide to Leibniz's philosophy is Look (2008).

Before we move on to his philosophy proper, let me briefly put Leibniz's life and work into context. Gottfried Wilhelm Leibniz was born in Leipzig in 1646. When the child was 2 years old, the Thirty Years' War came to a conclusion. It had ravaged the continent, most severely the former Holy Roman Empire at its centre, and reduced its population by an estimated quarter. The experience of this war, fought over religious as well as proto-nationalist differences, left a deep impression on the philosophers of the time. It created the desire to find a means of settling disputes decisively, irrevocably, and to the benefit of all parties. Leibniz's dream, like that of many of his contemporaries, was to overcome religious and political divisions. Russell (1995: 572 f.) quotes him as writing: 'If controversies were to arise, there would be no more need of disputations between two philosophers than between two accountants. For it would suffice to take their pencils in their hands, to sit down to their slates, and to say to each other (with a friend as witness, if they liked): Let us calculate.'

Leibniz studied philosophy and law in what were, at the time, the philosophical backwaters of Europe. Paris was the continental hub of the new thinking, with Descartes having died only 20 years earlier. Leibniz's education, nevertheless, provided him with two skills he would make heavy use of: one was a sound foundation in ancient and scholastic philosophy, the other the ability to teach himself at breathtaking speed. His first employment was with the Elector of Mainz, who sent him on a mission to Paris—perhaps the most decisive journey of his life. Leibniz stayed in Paris from 1672 to 1676, where he met, among many others, Malebranche and Huygens and studied unpublished manuscripts of Descartes and Pascal. Arriving as an autodidact in mathematics, he presented the world four years later with the infinitesimal calculus. At the same time, he started sharpening the contours of his own philosophy vis-à-vis the Cartesians. From Paris, he made a trip to London in 1673, where he was made a member of the Royal Society. On his way back to Mainz in 1676, he travelled via Amsterdam to meet Spinoza shortly before the latter's death. He corresponded, among many others, with Hobbes, Locke, and Newton as well as Boyle, Mariotte, and Jakob and Johann Bernoulli.

When the Elector of Mainz died, Leibniz entered the service of the Dukes of Hanover. He served three dukes, among them George, the later King of Great Britain, whose accession he helped negotiate. Leibniz died in 1716 leaving a staggering legacy, the importance of which only became clear in the nineteenth and twentieth centuries. In physics, he proposed the law of the conservation of energy and developed a dynamics based on it. He saw, 200 years before Einstein, that energy was the essence of matter and that time and space were relative to it. In mathematics he developed the differential and infinitesimal calculus as well as binary numbers and saw that the latter could form a basis for calculating machines. His input into logic, though for many years unpublished, led Frege to say: 'Leibniz threw out such a profusion of seeds of ideas that in this respect he is virtually in a class of his own' (Frege, cited in Look, 2008). His philosophy stands at the beginning of process metaphysics in the modern age.

7.2 METAPHYSICS: A SYSTEMATIC SKETCH

7.2.1 Substances

Here it is, the Evil Word for process theory. I must start the metaphysics part with the admission that the standard bearer of modern process philosophy doubles as one of the greatest substance philosophers of all times. Substances—his 'monads' that we will discuss in more depth later on—are the beginning, middle, and end of Leibniz's metaphysics. They are what he inherits from his classical and scholastic education; they are what his contemporaries, most notably Descartes, build their systems on. Leibniz, however, gives them a dynamic twist. He has studied the ancient philosophers well enough to see that it has been done before, and he is genius enough to fuse his mathematical and physical discoveries with the old notion. What he arrives at is a basic building block of reality—a substance—that is not a thing but a process or dynamic principle. In what follows, I will say more about substances; at this moment may it suffice to sketch them as uncorporeal spirits that develop autonomously in accordance with their own inborn programme or entelechy.

7.2.2 Basic Principles

Nothing gives more convincing testimony to the systematicity of Leibniz's thought than the fact that different exegetes declare different principles in Leibniz's works to be the basic ones, and still manage each time to reconstruct his system from these different starting points. In this sense, one may pick from the following (ordered according to their simplicity):[2]

The *principle of non-contradiction* goes back to Aristotle, who states that a proposition cannot be true and false at the same time and in the same respect. Thus, either 'A is b' or 'A is non-b' must be true at a certain time.

The *principle of the best* holds that God always acts for the best. This follows from the fact that God is perfect and that anything sub-optimal lacks something (in comparison to the optimum) and is thus not perfect.

I should hasten to add at this point—because we will come back to God a couple of times—that Leibniz, like most occidental philosophers, is a thoroughly unreligious person. (The folk in Hanover, in fact, nicknamed him 'believe-in-nothing' and distrusted him for it.) God, to him, is not a Judeo-Christian anthropomorphization but a logical and metaphysical principle expressing utmost perfection, omniscience, and omnipotence. In most cases where this chapter will refer to Him, it does not hurt to picture Him as the ultimate supercomputer—Leibniz, who came up with binary numbers and spent much of his money building calculation machines, would have approved.

The *principle of the identity of indiscernibles* states that no two substances can have an identical set of attributes. They must at least have one attribute to distinguish them; otherwise they are not two substances but one.

While these first three principles agree with common sense and basic logic, the fourth principle is less intuitive.

The *predicate in notion* (*praedicatum inest subiecto*) principle assumes that everything that can be said (predicated) of a substance is already contained in the name of that substance (the subject). For example, the fact that Leibniz died in 1716 is contained in the notion of Leibniz, as is him meeting the Duchess of Hanover in the Palace Gardens at two o'clock on the 23rd of August 1680. Everything, in other words, that Leibniz ever did or was is contained in his notion. This implies that all propositions about him are analytical. The same applies to persons or things currently living or even to persons or things yet to be born: everything they will ever do or be is already implied in their notion. This would, one may object, only be true if we knew everything about that person, which is impossible, especially with regard to the future. True, concedes Leibniz, but there is one mind who knows it all: the perfect, omniscient mind, God. To Him every proposition is a priori true or false. To human beings, things are not as clear, and so many propositions about individuals have a synthetic character within our limited understanding. [3]

7.2.3 Conclusions Drawn from the Principles: God and the World

The ultimate building blocks, as we have seen, are substances. Substances have attributes. Some of these attributes, like colour or age, refer to the substance alone, while others, like family status or profession, refer to other substances. Because of the latter, substances are related among each other. Now, if we take the principle of non-contradiction into account, we can see that, as God created the world, She could not create substances that stood in a contradictory relationship to each other (for even omnipotence cannot overcome contradiction). She could not, for example, make Adam the father of Cain and make Noah the father of the same Cain. This implies that a decision for one particular substance limits the options of the available other substances. In this sense, there are 'sets' of substances—Leibniz calls them 'compossible substances'—of which either set A or set B can be realized. Which set did God choose? God, being perfect, chose the best. This is Leibniz's *doctrine of the best of all possible worlds*, which, as we see, does not claim that this world is perfect but only claims that it is the best among the available choices. This world is also in harmony, not because it contains violins or a particular aesthetic value, but because it does not contain contradictions. And since this harmony was created at the beginning of the world, it is called a *pre-established harmony*.

Still, Leibniz's contemporaries (and many afterwards) found it difficult to believe that a world that contains so much suffering should be better than, say, a world that only contained a single rose. In other words, what was God's criterion for determining the best? Leibniz argues that it is maximization of existence. Among worlds that may be equally good, God will choose the one with the most creatures in it. This is the *principle of plenitude*. While the argument is not the strongest in logical terms, Leibniz clung to it because his and others' discoveries in physics (for example, Fermat's optics or the Brychystochrone curve; see Rescher [1979] for details) all seemed to indicate that nature followed minimization and maximization principles. In this spirit, Leibniz often uses the example of water forming spherical droplets that contain the biggest volume within the smallest surface area. He says: 'The ways of God are those most simple and uniform... [being] the most productive in relation to the simplicity of ways and means' (Leibniz, cited in Rescher, 1979: 29).

The world of monads forms a continuum because monads only differ from each other in their point of view (see section 7.2.4) and these differences can be infinitesimal. Hence its derivatives, the physical and psychological world, form a continuum, too. This implies that they contain infinite actualizations. As human beings have finite minds, they cannot grasp this infinitude. So to them it becomes *contingence*. If we, for example, knew everything about Caesar (as God did in that particular moment), we would have been able to predict that he would cross the Rubicon. If we knew everything about a radioactive atom, we would be able to predict whether it will decay at a particular moment. Since we do not, these events appear contingent to us. The same goes for freedom of will. Very much like modern neurobiologists, Leibniz argues that every one of our actions is predetermined by the entelechy of our monad, but since we do not know what this entelechy entails, we are, for all practical purposes, free in our actions. As Rescher (1979) rightly maintains, Leibniz is probably nowhere in his metaphysics more indebted to mathematics than in the concept of infinity. It is what bridges the gap between divine omniscience and human contingency in both the physical and the moral world. Or, to quote Leibniz: 'In truth there are two labyrinths in the human mind, one concerning the compositions of the continuum, the other concerning the nature of freedom. And both of these spring from exactly the same source—the infinite' (Leibniz, cited in Rescher, 1979: 43).

There is no difference in principle between the world of physics and the world of psychology. Both are construed in parallel, one following the laws of efficient causation, the other the laws of teleology. This is so because metaphysically speaking they go back to the same form of causation. In the predicate in notion principle, we have seen that the subject contains all its predicates. Metaphysically speaking, the subject, which is the substance or monad, is indeed the reason for its predicates because it takes on or sheds attributes in accordance with its own drive or force. It is, hence, not only true to say that Caesar crossed the Rubicon but that Caesar was the reason why Caesar crossed the Rubicon, meaning that something in Caesar (his dispositions, preferences, or skills) drove him to cross that river. The same is true for physical events. The reason for the eruption of Mount Vesuvius in 79 AD is Mount Vesuvius.

A further epistemological consequence of the predicate in notion principle is the distinction between *truths of reason* and *truths of fact*. Truth, to Leibniz, is the absence of contradiction. This is a quite harmless proposition if read in purely logical terms. In Leibniz's metaphysical terms, however, it forms a far more powerful statement. If we remember that God created the world without contradictions, then this implies that a true proposition refers to a fact of the world, or vice versa, that a false proposition refers to a non-existing set-up of the world. For example, the proposition that London is the capital of France is wrong for two reasons. First, it contradicts the fact that Paris is the capital of France and that each country can only have one capital. Second, it contradicts the principle that only a French town can be the capital of France. In this sense, Leibniz is one of the precursors of a coherence theory of truth.

Now, one may object, how does somebody from the proverbial Texas know whether London is a French town or Paris already claims to be the capital of France? This is where truths of reason differ from truths of fact. For truths of reason (analytical, mathematical, logical truths), a finite analysis of subject and predicate will show whether or not they contain a contradiction. For truths of fact, i.e. claims about the physical or psychological world, we again face infinity and would have to conduct an infinite analysis of the infinite predicates of an individual substance to come to a conclusion. This is something beyond human capability. Hence, Leibniz argues, we have to content ourselves with the (empirical) analysis of phenomena and devise concepts and notations to approximate the infinite, as we do in mathematics. This, however, is not as humble as it sounds. Leibniz was convinced that physical as well as psychological events were connected by *laws*. These laws were created by God in accordance with Her initial decision to create the best of all possible worlds. Since human beings can optimize too, they can discover these laws.

More particularly, as physics and psychology strive for maximization or minimization, mathematical curve sketching can give us the ideal states they are striving for. These physical and psychological laws also allow human beings, who are unable to list the infinite number of real occurrences, to nevertheless come up with the law that encompasses them. This works in the same way as the finite expression 'f(x)' refers to an infinite number of values. It applies even on a metaphysical plane, for if a monad is a substance developing in accordance with an internal programme or law, then there should be a function to capture the temporal sequence of states the monad develops into. We can, thus, see that Leibniz's scientific programme is indeed quite ambitious. He would, nevertheless, hold that science can only reach reality through abstractions, whereas the true building blocks of reality are individualizations. As with irrational numbers (Leibniz's example), we may come up with a finite notation and some form of approximization, but we can never grasp the fully individualized realization.

This shortcoming, one may note, is of an ontological, not an epistemological nature. In contrast to Kant, Leibniz was not worried about our ability to perceive empirical phenomena. He held that we are able to gain knowledge of the properties of things, for example the melting point of gold or its hardness, and discover lawful relations between them.

7.2.4 The Monads

It is now time to discuss the most famous (or infamous) elements of Leibniz's metaphysics. The word 'monad' derives from Greek 'monas', which means unity. The term had been used in classical and medieval philosophy (among others, by Plato to denote ideas), but nowadays is almost exclusively reserved for Leibniz's conception (Lötzsch, 1984). His monads are, in many respects, Platonic *ideas*. This means they are uncorporeal, spiritual, and eternal. As a consequence of this, they are indivisible (because only extended bodies can be divided). Since they do not consist of parts, they cannot change because change involves a shedding of old parts and the acquisition of new ones. For the same reason, they cannot become or perish but remain eternally. Eternity, however, should not be equated with rest. Ideas also strive for perfection, which includes striving to exist.[4] They are therefore active. It might be helpful, for clarification purposes, to add some negative characteristics to this list. Ideas are not thoughts or mental contents (rather, they make thoughts possible). Nor are they signs (because signs are arbitrary while ideas are real).

Monads have two functions: *appetition* (drive, which Leibniz calls 'conatus') and *perception*. Appetition is a movement from one state to the next—this is all a monad can 'do'. The states differ from each other by the different perceptions the monad has of other monads. Each monad is a unifying principle as it synthesizes the perceptions of all other monads (the 'many') into its own unique point of view (the 'one'). The principle of the identity of indiscernibles ensures that there are never two identical points of view. True to an idealist position, Leibniz thus makes the 'I' of each substance the basic unifying principle. This has two important consequences. One is the characterization of *being as unity*, or as Leibniz (cited in Look, 2008) states: 'that what is not truly *one* being is not truly one *being* either'. The second is that Leibniz goes beyond Descartes' '*cogito ergo sum*' to say that I am not only certain of my thinking but also, at the same time, of my thoughts, which are hence as foundational as the thinking process (Cassirer, 1994: 357). The unity of the self is constituted at the same time as the unity of the object. The act of co-constitution leads Leibniz to a *subject–object relation* that differs very much from the Cartesian one.

Both appetition and perception characterize monads as *forces* rather than things. The driving force behind the monad is of a *teleological* nature (Aristotle would call it an entelechy) as it strives for self-realization. Everything, including efficient causation, is ultimately derived from this teleological force. Since it is a primordial force, it cannot be affected (i.e. overcome) by other, lesser forces. This is the reason why Leibniz cannot allow efficient causality to have an impact on monads: it would mean that efficient causality is stronger than a monad's appetition while at the same time being derived from it, which is contradictory. In Leibniz's time, Ham and van Leeuwenhoek discovered spermatozoa under the—recently invented—microscope (Loemker, 1956: 62). This served as a confirmation of his view that an innate programme existed that controlled the whole future development of a monad.

Monads, as we have seen, are *living mirrors* in that they perceive every other monad. These perceptions, however, cannot impact upon the appetition of the monad, for example by diverting it from its initial intentions. In this sense, monads are *windowless*' i.e. immune to external influences. They will single-mindedly follow their innate 'programme'. This has important implications for efficient *causality*, namely that there is no such thing on a metaphysical plane. Monads do not interact with one another in any causal sense (see above). What we perceive to be efficient causality is a phenomenon, which means it is real but not independent because it can be reduced to something more basic and more real—the teleology of the monads.

What, then, happens when a billiard ball bumps into another? Leibniz's answer is: nothing. The monads behind the balls—we'll talk about monads and bodies in a moment—go their own, separate ways devised at the dawn of time. God, in His perfection, has managed to actualize a monad A (corresponding to the first ball) that is in point p at time t and another monad B (corresponding to the second ball) that rolls off p at t. So, what we perceive to be interaction is in reality just coincidence—but a perfectly planned coincidence. This perfectly planned coincidence is part of the pre-established harmony, and gives us a glimpse of how super a supercomputer Leibniz thought God to be.

Efficient causality is hence 'only' a phenomenon. Leibniz, however, calls it a *well-founded phenomenon (phenomenon bene fundatum)*. This distinguishes it from mere phenomena or illusions. A well-founded phenomenon derives in a regular fashion from the monads that it consists of, whereas a mere phenomenon exists only in the eyes of the observer. A well-founded phenomenon exists but does not have the same degree of reality as a monad.

In the same way that efficient causality is a well-founded phenomenon, *time and space* (as well as relations[5]) are well-founded phenomena. In modern language, we would say that Leibniz conceptualizes time and space as relative. Against Newton, he argues that they are not empty receptacles to be filled with objects, but that we derive these notions from the way the monads are ordered. This follows from the principle of the identity of indiscernibles: if two otherwise identical substances only differ in their spatial (or temporal) location, they must be different substances. This implies that their spatial (or temporal) location is an (internal) attribute of theirs, not an independent 'thing'. The manner in which contemporary monads are ordered relative to each other gives us the notion of space, while their successive order gives us the notion of time. Time and space are thus derivatives and indeed particular to our own world.

Most *physical bodies* that we observe are well-founded phenomena. They are unified or even structured aggregates of monads. They are not, however, 'things' in the sense of 'individuals'. This is because their unity is not firm enough for individuation. They appear to be units—hence we call them 'phenomena'. Every physical body is made up of an infinite number of monads. All these monads have, as we have seen, perceptions; this is Leibniz's *panpsychism*. Perceptions can vary on a continuum between clear and confused. Monads perceiving things more clearly can come to dominate other monads and form an organism. Thus, liver cell monads are more confused than liver monads, who are in turn more confused than human body monads. Stone monads are, quite literally, dead confused.

The interaction between the monads and their respective bodies has been a persistent problem, the 'mind–body problem'—unsolved as up to date—ever since Descartes separated the two realms. Although Leibniz does not follow him in this separation and takes bodies to be derivatives of spirit, the problem remains because once created bodies are different 'things' to monads. He solves the problem in a similar way as he solves the problem of causal interaction, viz. through pre-established harmony. God, again, arranges intentions and body movements in such a perfect way that my arm will rise shortly after I have taken the decision to raise it. Defending his argument against the Cartesian as well as the Occasionalist view, Leibniz uses his famous *metaphor of the clockmaker*. This runs as follows: imagine two clock pendula swinging in harmony. If this harmonic movement is supposed to continue forever, the clockmaker has three options. First, he could watch the two clocks and interfere if their movements become asynchronic. This represents the Occasionalist solution to the mind–body problem in which God intervenes every time to make causation happen. Secondly, the clockmaker could connect the two pendula through some mechanistic device, for example a bolt. This is the Cartesian solution of the pineal gland translating intentions into corporeal impulses. But, thirdly, a truly perfect clockmaker would have no need to resort to such unprofessional behaviour and would construct the clocks from the beginning well enough to perform the task. They would then also be the best of all possible clocks. This is, of course, Leibniz's solution of pre-established harmony.

7.3 LEIBNIZ: QUESTIONS AND ANSWERS

7.3.1 What Were the Philosophical Problems of the Time that Leibniz Directed His Philosophy At?

The second half of the seventeenth century and the turn to the eighteenth were so extremely productive that it is difficult to focus on just a few ideas. Descartes, however, was probably the man of the hour, even for Leibniz, who was born around the time Descartes died. The other big names, both from Leibniz's and from our own perspective, were Spinoza, Hobbes, and Newton. Since this chapter is mainly concerned with Leibniz's metaphysics, I will focus on his responses to Descartes and Spinoza.

With regard to Cartesianism, Leibniz addressed primarily the following problems:

D1. The assumption that matter is a substance and equiprimordial to spirit. Leibniz thought this wrong because matter is extended and can thus be divided. Something that can be divided further cannot form an ultimate part in a system because it is made up of smaller parts itself. Moreover, the assumption of identical ultimate parts violates the principle of the identity of indiscernibles.

D2. Extension, the prime attribute of matter, cannot provide the idea of force. If force is not introduced at the beginning, it cannot be introduced later because it cannot be conceived of as derivative of matter.

D3. A separation of mind and matter creates the mind–body problem as the two seem to interact. The pineal gland is no proper solution to this because it is itself corporeal.

D4. A separation of mind and matter also creates two independent realms of morals and nature. This is problematic because it 'frees' morals from natural laws and withdraws the possibility of a science of morals (read 'science' in the positive connotations of the seventeenth century).

Spinoza, who also devoted much of his philosophy to these problems, is in many of his proposed solutions quite close to Leibniz. 'Spinoza would be right if it were not for the monads', Leibniz remarks at one point (Broad, 1975: 3). He, however, disputed the following parts of Spinoza's system:

S1. Spinoza holds that spirit and matter are not substances themselves, but attributes of the one divine substance. Leibniz rejects this notion, first, on definitional grounds claiming that Spinoza defines the term 'attribute' as constituting the essence of the substance (Spinoza, 1982: Def. 4). This, however, is what other authors, including Leibniz, would call a 'substance'. What Spinoza hence calls 'attributes' are in fact substances, and the apparent difference vanishes. Second, Leibniz argues against the idea that there is only one substance. This would imply, he holds, that an individual human mind is only a state or experience in God's mind—an assumption that seems weird to him.

S2. Everything that happens in the world is determined because nothing happens without a lawful cause. This implies that there is no contingency or human freedom. As we have seen, Leibniz comes very close to drawing the same conclusion from the same premises. He, however, then brings in infinity to argue that perfect determination only exists for the omniscient mind, while limited human minds experience contingency.

7.3.2 How did Leibniz Solve Them?

The purely *spiritual* nature of the monads solves D1. Leibniz saw quite clearly that it is comparatively easy to derive matter from spirit (through perception) but that the opposite does not work as well. The fact that monads are *active* and thus are *prime forces* solves D2. Leibniz hence inverts Descartes' ideas and derives matter from force instead of vice versa. Again, it is easier to conceptualize rest as a special case of motion or resistance as a special form of force than to create motion out of rest, or force out of resistance. Since matter is a derivative of the monads, the two are not perfectly separate (D3 and D4). Although Leibniz often talks about physics in purely mechanistic or dynamic terms and without referring to monads, at the end of the day (i.e. metaphysically speaking), monadic *teleology* overrides physical causality since the latter is derived from the former. When he talks non-metaphysically about the world of well-founded phenomena (D4), Leibniz stresses the *parallel construction of mind and matter*, morals and nature. They both follow, *mutatis mutandis*, the same laws. This is because God used the same principle (of the best) to create them. The interaction between mind and body (D3) is ultimately reducible to an interaction between monads, i.e. an interaction of spirits, and as such follows a pre-established harmony. The interaction between monads already implies that monads are *finite* substances. They have been created by God at a certain point in time but continue *independently* on their trajectory from then on. This independence negates the possibility that they are states of another substance (S1). It also shows that Leibniz takes the act of creation seriously and takes a middle stance between the uncreated attributes Spinoza proposes (S1) and the permanent recreation Descartes assumes. With regard to this creation, Leibniz also takes pains to show that God had a choice in creating (or not) particular monads (S2), and that She made this choice not in an arbitrary way, as Descartes would assume, but with a view to creating the best of all possible options. According to Leibniz, She acted out of love and indeed deserves praise for Her decisions.

7.3.3 What is Processual about this?

Everything. If the ultimate building blocks of the world are forces, than everything is process. It is as simple as it is revolutionary. Leibniz's big achievement, however, is not to have sparked a revolution and broken with tradition, as Descartes did, but to have modified a core term of occidental philosophy in a way that still allows him to stand on the shoulders of giants but turn his gaze in a very different direction.

7.3.4 Why did He Call the Monads Substances?

Given what we know about the man behind the philosophy—his boyhood and education, his irenic temperament—Leibniz was no revolutionary. He firmly believed in progress but in a progress that built on the existing foundations rather than demolishing them. In this sense, it seems quite natural that he starts with what is there, modifying and developing it, instead of coming up with entirely new concepts. Moreover, the concept of substance in Leibniz's time, as opposed to our own, was still alive, varied, modified, and debated. A processual substance was a valid option, and Leibniz took it. Using the old term also saved him a lot of time in explaining things. To the philosophers of his time, the term immediately signalled a number of properties, such as activity, self-sufficiency, primordiality. One important term in this regard was matter. In classical and scholastic substance philosophy, drawing on Aristotle (1993a, 1993b), matter is a technical term that is defined very differently from what we today understand matter to be. For Aristotle, matter (*hylê*) is not something material but a principle. This principle guarantees continuity in the process of becoming (Weik, 2011), i.e. ensures that we can still speak of the same object (or use the same grammatical subject) although the object changes. For example, we need matter to meaningfully express that a bucket of water has turned into ice (instead of saying that the water has gone and been replaced by the ice). In this sense, matter relates the different stages of a process and guarantees continuity between them. Matter, however, is not an active principle in the sense of causing things to change. Leibniz retains this concept. This means monads have matter in the sense of possessing a passive aspect. Moreover, it is this passive aspect—in the guise of resistance and solidity—that we derive the phenomenon of matter in the modern sense from. (Note that Leibniz saw clearly, against Descartes, that resistance is a force.) This allows him to keep his metaphysical system simple—a force with active and passive aspects—and focused on force and process rather than on an extended, material atom. (Atoms would also have violated the principle of the identity of indiscernibles for they would form an infinite number of identical substances.)

7.3.5 What Toads have Modern Readers to Swallow?

As Rescher (1979: 1) remarks, Leibniz's system is admirably consistent given its complexity, but its premises no longer appeal to the modern reader. Probably the two biggest toads one has to swallow in order to digest the system are the fact that monads are windowless, i.e. will not be influenced by any force external to them, as well as his idea of contingency and freedom, which do not exist metaphysically (because to an omniscient mind everything is determined) but only for practical purposes (because human minds are too limited to grasp the determination). Panpsychism also tends to be rather unpopular although modern authors have yet to come up with a better answer to the mind–body problem.

7.3.6 Which Philosophers did He Influence?

Leibniz himself, given his non-academic career, had no pupils. His philosophy was, however, taken up by Christian Wolff, who modified it—i.e. took the interesting bits out—and turned it into the standard philosophy taught at German universities in the eighteenth century. Wolff's school more or less died with him towards the end of the eighteenth century. In some respects, Leibniz paved the way for Kant. Kant (1977: 814) himself saw this quite clearly when he commends Leibniz for holding that concepts have to be brought forth by an activity of the imagination (*Vorstellungskraft*), not from the outside. Leibniz also linked time and space to the study of phenomena rather than the study of monads. This foreshadows Kant's (1989) use of time and space as properties of the phenomena, not the *Dinge an sich*.

With regard to process philosophy, Whitehead seems to be the philosopher most strongly influenced by Leibniz, although in *Process and Reality* (Whitehead, 1985), he seems more interested in stating the differences between his Actual Occasions and Leibniz's monads than acknowledging his indebtedness to the German philosopher. Still, unity through perception, panpsychism, the relativity of the point of view, the derivativeness of time from non-temporal building blocks, the concept of harmony, and, last but not least, the 'windowlessness' of Actual Occasions during concrescence show this indebtedness, to me, quite clearly. Peirce has taken Leibniz's notions of existence, possibility, and harmony and reinterpreted them as chance, logic, and love (Loemker, 1956: 101).

7.3.7 Which Organization Studies Authors Use Leibniz Today?

While interest in Leibniz continues in philosophy, mathematics, and logic, organization studies have focused more on Descartes (mostly in a critical way) and Kant. Often, Leibniz merely figures as a person of historical interest or precursor, for example as a proponent of rationalism (Becker and Niehaves, 2007), apperceptions (Packard and Chen, 2005), *petits perceptions* (Helfenstein and Saariluoma, 2006), or most popularly the question of why evil can exist in a world created by a benevolent God (theodicy) (Dubnick and Justice, 2006; Kayes, 2006; Morgan and Wilkinson, 2001). More substantial arguments are taken into account by Harré (2004) who, not surprisingly, invokes him as crown witness for the idea of two grammars or languages of description. Other elaborated arguments draw on the ability of Leibniz's system to bridge the individual–collective divide by construing individuals as bundles of relations (Pedersen, 2008) or, in a similar vein, to redefine 'essence' in relational terms (Barnham, 2009). Further discussions concern the ontological status of mathematical and computer models (Churchman, 1970) or the idealist critique of reality claims made by the natural sciences (Clark, 2000).

To my knowledge, the only major theorist to draw on Leibniz's metaphysics is Bourdieu. He borrows three central themes of his social theory from the German philosopher. The first is Leibniz's theory of non-causation, the second the notion of the monad as an active and productive ultimate building block, and the third the ontological priority of relationality. The theory of non-causation plays an important role in the way Bourdieu construes the interplay of agency and structure (Weik, 2010). While many sociologists assume that structure and agency can causally influence each other (much like Descartes assumed that matter and mind could influence each other), Bourdieu introduces a mediated relationship between the two. His concept of habitus holds that the social structure in t_1 cannot influence the (adult) agent as the agent's dispositions have been formed at an earlier time, viz. during socialization. In a comparatively stable society, the fit between the agent and the structure is not caused by mutual adaptations in the present, but by their match created in the past (or, from the point of view of the present, pre-established). As the operative force creating this pre-established harmony, Bourdieu uses history, which might be regarded as a secularized version of Leibniz's God. Bourdieu's construction is, of course, less strict than Leibniz's—he would deny the possibility of optimization and allow the modification of structures and agents—but the general theoretical construction is the same. The concept of the habitus, second, also owes much to Leibniz's monads because Bourdieu (1984, 1990, 1992) construes it as a generative mechanism, i.e. an active force. In rejection of the critics who consider the habitus to be an inflexible blueprint for the agent's behaviour (e.g. Jenkins, 1992; King, 2000), Bourdieu likens it to a programme that produces behaviour in accordance with certain rules but also dependent on the input from the environment. In this sense, the habitus is truly creative, just like the monad is. And just like Leibniz does with force, Bourdieu introduces activity and creativity at this first stage because he realizes that it cannot be derived from anything at a later stage. If we, for example, assume that agents are products of structures, then there is no way to explain how agents can be creative in their behaviour. The priority of relationality, finally, is a very prominent topic in Bourdieu's work (Bourdieu and Wacquant, 1996). Again, he goes further than Leibniz in maintaining that agents can take events and structures into account and change their course accordingly, but the basic theoretical construction remains the same: whether we look at an individual habitus or the field, one point of view always mirrors the rest of the world in its own, unique way.

7.3.8 What may Organization Studies Take from Him?

Loemker (1956: 1) takes the explosion of the fourth atomic bomb at Bikini on 1st July 1946—the 300th birthday of Leibniz—as doubly significant for the legacy of the German philosopher: He was the first to hold that energy was the essence of matter, and he was also the last to oppose 'the divorce between truth and action, and between power and its moral controls'. To Leibniz, the world is a system of interrelated entities without gaps or principal divides. We may use two distinct 'grammars' (in Harré's sense) to talk about it, but we should never think we are talking about distinct things.

Talking about mind and body within this unified system, Leibniz refers to a principle that later scholars will call 'supersession', i.e. the process of higher entities taking control over the functioning of lower entities. Susanne Langer (1967) and Roger Sperry (1980) among others, have, used this notion to talk about the mind–body problem in recent decades. Supersession, as well as the related problem of emergence, also plays a significant role in complexity theory (Hodgson, 2000; Holland, 1998; Lichtenstein, 2000). In the same vein, variety and order—the one and the many—is a persistent theme in Leibniz. Very much like complexity theorists (Goodwin, 1997; McKelvey, 2004) today, he assumes that God (Nature) follows limitational considerations with regard to variety and order, i.e. creates that form of order that will allow the greatest variety of phenomena.

To organizational process theorists, finally, he has bequeathed the notion of substance. Loemker (1973: 53) sees quite clearly that, although the category has been banished from modern process philosophy, its functions must still somehow be served (see also Weik, 2011). What preserves the continuum of a process? How can self-determination embrace external (causal) influences? What is the relation between self-determination and freedom? How do universals emerge from the process? Leibniz's answer, as we have seen, was to make use of 2,000 years of (substance) philosophy, taking what he could use. If modern authors, in contrast, prefer not to stand on the shoulders of giants, they have to come up with pretty long ladders.

Notes

1. The edition of the Leibniz papers started in 1901, but effectively came to a standstill during the wars and the ensuing German separation (the German Academy being located in East Berlin). It was restarted in 1985 (Leibniz-Akademie, 2012).
2. There are two more, the principles of continuity and of sufficient reason, but they are not necessary for the aspects of Leibniz's metaphysics that I am reconstructing in this chapter.
3. Broad (1975) would add that human definitions of a thing or person also differ from God's notions in that they only contain a comparatively small number of predicates. For example, we may define Elizabeth I as the English queen who reigned during 1533–1603. In consequence, the proposition that Elizabeth I was the daughter of Henry VIII is synthetic because the predicate is not contained in the original definition.

4. Note that being does not imply existence. Existence presupposes actualization. There may be monads that 'are' but have not been actualized, i.e. do not exist.

5. For an in-depth discussion of relations, see Rescher (1981).

REFERENCES

Aristotle. (1993a). *Metaphysics*, in A. Mortimer (ed.), *Great Books of the Western World* (Chicago: Encyclopedia Britannica): 499–626.

—— (1993b). *Physics*, in A. Mortimer (ed.), *Great Books of the Western World* (Chicago: Encyclopedia Britannica): 259–355.

Barnham, C. (2009). Essence, *International Journal of Market Research* 51(5): 593–610.

Becker, J. and Niehaves, B. (2007). Epistemological Perspectives on IS Research: A Framework for Analysing and Systematizing Epistemological Assumptions, *Information Systems Journal* 17(2): 197–214.

Bourdieu, P. (1984). *Distinction* (Cambridge, MA: Harvard University Press).

—— (1990). *The Logic of Practice* (Stanford, CA: Stanford University Press).

—— (1992). *Die verborgenen Mechanismen der Macht* (Hamburg: VSA).

—— and Wacquant, L. (1996). *An Invitation to Reflexive Sociology* (Cambridge: Polity Press).

Broad, C.D. (1975). *Leibniz. An Introduction* (Cambridge: Cambridge University Press).

Cassirer, E. (1962). *Leibniz' System in seinen wissenschaftlichen Grundlagen* (Hildesheim: Georg Olms Verlag).

—— (1994). *Philosophie der symbolischen Formen, 3 Bände* (Darmstadt: Wissenschaftliche Buchgesellschaft).

Churchman, C.W. (1970). Operations Research as a Profession, *Management Science* 17(2): B37–B53.

Clark, S.R.L. (2000). Have Biologists Wrapped up Philosophy?, *Inquiry* 43(2): 143–65.

Dubnick, M.J. and Justice, J.B. (2006). Accountability and the Evil of Administrative Ethics, *Administration & Society* 38(2): 236–67.

Goodwin, B. (1997). *How the Leopard Changed its Spots: Evolution of Complexity* (London: Phoenix).

Harré, R. (2004). Discursive Psychology and the Boundaries of Sense, *Organization Studies* 25(8): 1435–53.

Helfenstein, S. and Saariluoma, P. (2006). Mental Contents in Transfer, *Psychological Research* 70(4): 293–303.

Hodgson, G. (2000). The Concept of Emergence in Social Science: Its History and Importance, *Emergence* 2(4): 65–77.

Holland, J. (1998). *Emergence. From Chaos to Order* (Oxford: Oxford University Press).

Jenkins, R. (1992). *Pierre Bourdieu* (London: Routledge).

Kant, I. (1977). Versuch den Begriff der negativen Größe in die Weltweisheit einzuführen, in W. Weischedel (ed.), *Immanuel Kant: Werke in zwölf Bänden*, Band 2 (Frankfurt/Main: Suhrkamp): 779–824.

—— (1989). *Kritik der reinen Vernunft* (Frankfurt/Main: Suhrkamp).

Kayes, D. (2006). Organizational Corruption as Theodicy, *Journal of Business Ethics* 67(1): 51–62.

King, A. (2000). Thinking With Bourdieu Against Bourdieu: A 'Practical' Critique of the Habitus, *Sociological Theory* 18(3): 417–33.

Langer, S. (1967). *An Essay on Human Feeling* (Baltimore, MD: Johns Hopkins Press).

Leibniz-Akademie. (2012). *Leibniz-Edition* (Potsdam, Germany).

Leibniz-Forschungsstelle. (2012). *Leibniz-Archiv* (Hanover, Germany).

Lichtenstein, B. (2000). Emergence as a Process of Self-Organizing, *Journal of Organizational Change Management* 13(6): 526–44.

Loemker, L. (1956). Introduction, in L. Loemker (ed.), *Gottfried Wilhelm Leibniz. Philosophical Papers and Letters* (Chicago: University of Chicago Press): 1–101.

—— (1973). On Substance and Process in Leibniz, in I. Leclerc (ed.), *The Philosophy of Leibniz and the Modern World* (Nashville, TN: Vanderbilt University Press): 52–77.

Look, B. (2008). Gottfried Wilhelm Leibniz, in E.N. Zalta (ed.), *The Stanford Encyclopedia of Philosophy*, <http://plato.stanford.edu/entries/leibniz/>

Lötzsch, F. (1984). Monade, Monas, in J. Ritter and K. Gründer (eds), *Historisches Wörterbuch der Philosophie* (Darmstadt: Wissenschaftliche Buchgesellschaft): 114–17.

McKelvey, B. (2004). Complexity Science as Order-Creation Science: New Theory, New Method, *E:CO* 6(4): 2–27.

Morgan, D. and Wilkinson, I. (2001). The Problem of Suffering and the Sociological Task of Theodicy, *European Journal of Social Theory* 4(2): 199–214.

Packard, N. and Chen, C. (2005). From Medieval Mnemonics to a Social Construction of Memory: Thoughts on Some Early European Conceptualizations of Memory, Morality, and Consciousness, *American Behavioral Scientist* 48(10): 1297–319.

Pedersen, M. (2008). Tune In, Break Down, and Reboot—New Machines for Coping with the Stress of Commitment, *Culture & Organization* 14(2): 171–85.

Rescher, N. (1979). *Leibniz. An Introduction to his Philosophy* (Oxford: Blackwell).

—— (1981). *Leibniz's Metaphysics of Nature* (Dordrecht: D. Reidel).

—— (1996). *Process Metaphysics* (New York: State University of New York Press).

Russell, B. (1951). *A Critical Exposition of the Philosophy of Leibniz* (London: George Allen & Unwin).

—— (1995). *History of Western Philosophy* (London: Routledge).

Sperry, R. (1980). Mind–Brain Interaction: Mentalism, Yes; Dualism, No, *Neuroscience* 5(2): 195–206.

Spinoza, B. (1982). *Ethik* (Leipzig: Reclam).

Weik, E. (2010). Bourdieu and Leibniz. Mediated Dualisms, *The Sociological Review* 58(3): 486–96.

—— (2011). In Deep Waters: Process Theory between Scylla and Charybdis, *Organization* 18(5): 655–72.

Whitehead, A.N. (1985). *Process and Reality* (New York: Free Press).

CHAPTER 8

···

SØREN KIERKEGAARD
(1813–1855)

···

SVERRE RAFFNSØE, MATIAS MØL DALSGAARD,
AND MARIUS GUDMAND-HØYER

8.1 INTRODUCTION

THE DANISH philosopher of existence and theologian Søren Kierkegaard (1813–1855) draws attention to the human self, and in particular to human existence, choice, will, commitment and responsibility, subjective truth, and meaning as ineradicable concrete dimensions of reality. He thus opened a fruitful field of investigation that has challenged philosophy, psychology, theology, literary criticism, fiction, the humanities, social sciences, social political thought, institutions, and organizations in inspiring and prolific ways (Stewart, 2009, 2011a, 2011b, 2011c).

Moreover, Kierkegaard has also managed to influence the approach to studying human beings; he points out that the critical dimension of the human existential self can only be inadequately elucidated and tends to be eradicated within traditional science, philosophy, and scholarship. This is because the latter endeavours aim at 'becoming objective' by giving an unbiased and general account of reality and being (Kierkegaard, 1992, 1997b: 4). Instead, the processual, finite, and existentially engaged human self must be conceived as an ineradicable critical 'subjective' condition of possibility for the world to become a relevant object of interest for the human being (Styhre, 2004: 9). 'What is?' and 'What is the case?' may be questions and issues of first-rate importance for science, organizations, the philosophical traditions, and in daily life. Even so, the questions 'What becomes?' and 'What may become?' may play an important part in these contexts too. According to Kierkegaard, however, the existential dimension remains the decisive point: how is it that what is, what becomes, and even what may become, concerns me or us at all? How can it come to concern a human self that is still in becoming?

Kierkegaard's insistence that the subjective human self in becoming constitutes an unavoidable and irreducible condition for human life in the world is fraught with consequences. Accordingly, it not only implies a rejection of traditional western ('substance') metaphysics and science, in so far as this tradition begins from the intuition that being and the true object of knowledge should be thought of as static and immutable. In addition, Kierkegaard's focus on subjective becoming also finds expression in an open critique of process philosophy, in so far as this—with Hegelianism—takes to court the history of western metaphysics as 'the tendency towards substance', only to make the case for understanding the processual character of the world in terms of a self-unfolding dialectics of mediation, aiming at conflict resolution (see Chapter 14, this volume). For Kierkegaard, a process philosophy that takes the form of mediation is bound to misconceive and hence eradicate the character of subjective becoming.

Towards the end of his life, Kierkegaard's reticence with regard to processes of mediation came to the fore in a damning criticism of organized religion, in particular the religious institutions of his time and the well-established representatives of the church. Still, Kierkegaard's anticlerical campaign also expresses a general reservation with regard to the ability of societal institutions and organizations to contain and express human subjectivity. In this way, Kierkegaard's focus on subjective becoming—process thinking, critique of institutions, advocacy for the subjective element and all its inherent difficulties—still presents a challenge that organizations and organization studies must respond to.

This challenge may have become even more pertinent and acute as today's organizations are based not only on human creativity, but also on human self-dependence: the entrepreneurial self and self-management. In one sense this opens modern organizations to a Kierkegaardian understanding of the human being. In another sense, however, the tendency poses a real threat to the Kierkegaardian human being to the extent that the inclination is often followed by attempts at instrumentalizing and objectifying the human dimension that—according to Kierkegaard—by very definition are beyond instrumentalization or objectification.

In order to explore these general issues and review Kierkegaard's relevance for process philosophy in an organizational setting, the present introduction to his thought and selected writings proceeds in three main sections. Section 8.2 discusses important facets of the background for Kierkegaard's philosophy. After a few notes on biographical matters, attention is drawn to Kierkegaard's consummation of the Lutheran-Protestant tradition, which forms an imperative and irreducible theological tenet in his entire work. This heritage also plays a decisive role in Kierkegaard's lifelong existential critique of Hegelian philosophy, which we therefore outline subsequently with special regard to the confrontation between subjective existence and traditional philosophical systems. Section 8.2 ends with a short overview of Kierkegaard's influence on later thinkers with close affinity to process philosophy.

Section 8.3 concentrates on what we consider to be the most significant contributions to existential and process philosophy developed in Kierkegaard's thought. We discuss some of the most well known texts in Kierkegaard's oeuvre, such as *Either/Or* (1843), *Fear and Trembling* (1843), *Concluding Unscientific Postscript* (1846), and particularly to *The Sickness Unto Death* (1849); these contributions entail an analysis of the human self that is radically and fundamentally processual. Kierkegaard makes an important contribution to process philosophy, as his analysis of the human self demonstrates how the relationship that it establishes to itself adds yet another irreducible process of becoming to any pre-existing process. Following on from this discussion, section 8.4 examines the purport of Kierkegaard's (addition to) process philosophy for organizational studies and organizational practice.

8.2 BACKGROUND

8.2.1 Inheritance: Biographical Notes

Kierkegaard is a figure of transition. In European thought and in Danish intellectual life he established a bridge—a broken one, maybe—between pre-modern and modern thought and living, between Christian and atheist existence, between metaphysics and post-metaphysics. The philosophical battles and alliances in his authorship are of a complex and often surprising nature. By considering the religious and intellectual background of Kierkegaard some of the complexities and surprises might gain a certain, clarifying perspective.

Søren Aabye Kierkegaard was born in 1813 as the youngest of seven siblings. His mother, Ane Sørendatter Lund (1768–1834), seems to have played a relatively minor role in his intellectual formation, whereas his father, Michael Pedersen Kierkegaard (1756–1834), may have had a considerable impact on his religious and intellectual life and formation. Michael Kierkegaard, who originally came from poor circumstances in western Denmark, achieved great riches in the early nineteenth century through the wool trade and real estate in Copenhagen. The family's wealth gave Kierkegaard financial independence, first as a gifted student of theology, later as a famous writer, almost exclusively within the perimeter of the capital city. An even more important inheritance from the father, however, seems to have been the affinity for pietistic 'Christianity of the heart'—which was most probably mixed with a great portion of religious doubt. As a child, Kierkegaard would go with his father to the Herrnhutian *brødremenighed* ('congregation of brothers') (Garff, 2000). This Christian movement emerged around the German Earl Nikolaus Ludwig von Zinzendorff (1700–1760) in the eighteenth century, who strongly emphasized an emotional relationship with Jesus rather than orthodox teachings or dogma. In Kierkegaard's later authorship, which was concerned with existence or religious living, he would remain faithful to this pietistic position in so far as he would consider and analyse the existential, processual *modus* of the individual human being rather than the orthodox *factum* of Christian theology or dogma.

Looking back on his authorship, Kierkegaard stated that his work evolved around one question: how to become Christian (Kierkegaard, 2009: 14). It was never the *what* of Christianity, but always the *how* of living as a Christian that was the question. It was against this backdrop that Kierkegaard developed a highly modern, processual, and subject-oriented philosophy of existence and, in the process, identified a number of religious, existential, and intellectual enemies as well. In Hegel, Kierkegaard saw the most outstanding proponent of the rationalist position. Likewise, Kierkegaard would systematically attack the notion of a state church or state Christianity. Rationalized or organized Christianity might not be bad in itself—Kierkegaard was politically conservative and had no intentions of reforming the church as such (Kierkegaard, 2010 14: 111)—but he would consistently oppose a notion of Christianity that defines the essence of Christianity in terms of Christian institutions or visible works or ethics. The essence of Christianity was the life of the heart. Subjectivity or the will was the place of true Christian or existential reform, not outward institutions or politics.

8.2.2 Heritage: The Consummation of Lutheran-Protestant Theology

Kierkegaard's existential and critical challenge was not totally unprecedented, but can be seen as a culmination and a radicalization of a long-standing tradition in western thought. The heritage from Lutheran-Protestant theology plays a decisive role with regard to both the existential and organizational dimensions of Kierkegaard's philosophy.

The Lutheran break with the Catholic Church and with the notion of the good works in the sixteenth century was based on a theology that not only viewed the specific historical life and organization of the church as problematic. Any earthly organization of religious life and divine justification and salvation is inherently problematic to this theology. The human being is *fallen*, sin is *the human condition* and starting point for any consideration of the opportunities of the human being vis-à-vis God. The notion of sin is radical. Due to its fallen nature, the human being is by definition self-centred. All attempts to achieve justification before God will be driven by self-centredness and vanity, indeed Luther tellingly introduces his famous lectures on the Romans with the statements: 'The sum and substance of this letter is: to pull down, to pluck up, and to destroy all wisdom and righteousness of the flesh (i.e. of whatever importance there may be in the sight of men and even in our own eyes), no matter how heartily and sincerely they may be practiced, and to implant, establish, and make large the reality of sin (however unconscious we may be of its existence)' (Luther, 2006: 3). This condition renders any earthly organization of justification, i.e. a church institution, highly problematic. The soteriological authority of the church is thus abandoned in the Lutheran theology and substituted with the notion of universal priesthood. Earthly organizations cannot be organizations of salvation or justification.

This situation leads to the doctrine of two kingdoms—the spiritual and the worldly (Luther, 1995: 33). The fact that the human being is incapable of justifying itself before

God, i.e. in the spiritual kingdom, in no way entails the view that this kingdom is of limited importance. On the contrary, this is where the essential evaluation of the human being takes place; only it is beyond human control (Dalsgaard, 2012: 79 ff). Earthly organizations and institutions are not institutions of salvation—humanly created institutions are worldly institutions and thus neutral in terms of salvation and justification matters. Human freedom vis-à-vis institutions is thus granted in this tradition by a spiritual dimension, a dimension which is *the* determining dimension in soteriological matters, by definition evading earthly authorities.

Kierkegaard's thought develops against this backdrop. Radical individual freedom manifesting itself as ongoing conflict or tension between institutional and individual life, and the challenges of a sinful will (the non-unified, non-purified will) are essential elements to Kierkegaard's philosophy of existence. This background in radical Lutheran theology shows itself in Kierkegaard's critique of the established religious ethos of his time (Kierkegaard, 1987).

To Kierkegaard, this ethos was an example of institutionalized Christianity, and thus an example of a perverted Christianity. No true Christianity could exist without individual risk and tension. Most famously this standpoint is developed in *Fear and Trembling* (1843, in Kierkegaard, 1983), where Kierkegaard describes the faith of Abraham, willing to risk the sacrifice of his own son at the call of God with disregard for what common sense tells him. Kierkegaard, late in his career, attacked the Danish state church for not professing true Christianity (*The Moment*, 1855, in Kierkegaard, 1998).

8.2.3 Setting: Kierkegaard's Negativity versus Hegelian Systems

Kierkegaard's critique of traditional Christendom, in so far as it turned the task of becoming Christian into a matter of being a citizen in a Christian state, was to a large extent directed at the popular Hegelianism of his time. Kierkegaard attacked Hegel's notions of a world historical system. It has been pointed out that Kierkegaard's critique was rather directed at the vulgarized and prevailing Hegelianism of nineteenth-century Denmark than at Hegel himself (Stewart, 2003). But in this critique we find some of Kierkegaard's key arguments against 'systems', and thus, in a certain sense, also against institutions and organizations.

The world historical perspective in the Hegelian system claims that Christianity throughout history has taken itself to higher and higher levels of refinement (Hodgson, 2005: 85–99). Not only has Christianity become more refined over time, it has been instrumental to a spiritual progress, which has shaped the objective world order. This Hegelian point of view leads to the idea that the world as such has become Christian over time. This ultimately means that being born in a 'Christian state' guarantees one's being Christian.

It is of no existential help to be told that 'the world has become Christian' when one, as an individual human being, finds it hard to maintain one's own faith in a good and merciful God. This idea that the world and not the individual human being is or can be Christian is absurd to Kierkegaard. World historical systems will not save the individual faith or existence. Kierkegaard's conception of human life as process is absolutely central to his critique of Hegelian ideas about world historical systems. Since human life only exists in becoming, and since Christianity simply and solely takes place in and with the individual person, it cannot, from a processual viewpoint, be meaningful to say that Christianity exists objectively as a system or as a world history. Either the individual is in a movement towards faith or away from faith. This is where Christianity has its existence—or not. The process of individual existence, of *being here and now*, is the process of Christianity, which is also why Christianity cannot meaningfully exist as an objective system independent from individual subjectivity. The critique of the Hegelian systems, both in general and with particular reference to the processual nature of Christianity, is most elaborately carried out in Kierkegaard's major work, *Concluding Unscientific Postscript* (1846), a work that establishes and performs a sophisticated critique of 'the system' and a Hegelian science of life (Kierkegaard, 1992).

8.2.4 Legacy: Influence on Later Process Philosophy

Although Heidegger explicitly stressed how this influence should never be understood as a blind appropriation (McCarthy, 2011: 97), Kierkegaard's assertion of the dimension of human, subjective, and finite existence can still be regarded as a significant philosophical contribution to Heidegger's existential analysis (Dreyfus, 1991). This early influence is particularly evident in the process philosophy carried out in *Being and Time*, where Heidegger affirms not only the fundamental temporality of existence, but also that the understanding of being on the part of human existence (*Seinsverständnis*) is what makes the occurrence of Being possible (Heidegger, 1927).

A perhaps more important influence on process philosophy is found in the early works of Deleuze. Kierkegaard, with Nietzsche, explicitly serves as a main source of inspiration for Deleuze in his doctoral dissertation *Difference and Repetition*, when the latter strives to conceive movement (*'le movement'*) in a manner that enables him to move beyond the Hegelian conception of it (Deleuze, 1981). In a negative sense, what makes Kierkegaard an important precursor to Deleuze is his stern opposition to 'false movement', to an objectified, 'logical', and 'abstract' motion conceived as 'mediation' (Deleuze, 1981: 16). In a more positive sense, it is Kierkegaard's persistent endeavour to 'set metaphysics in motion, in activity', be it traditional or even processual metaphysics (Deleuze, 1981: 16). To Kierkegaard it is no longer sufficient to depict, represent, or even reflect movement. It becomes imperative to let it take action directly, to put it into effect, and to set it to work so effectively that it 'reaches the soul' and affects it (Deleuze, 1981: 17). Only by staging and rehearsing a succession of various personae that supplant and repeat each other can Kierkegaard make room for and address an ineradicable subjective moment in becoming that cannot be presupposed, but must be recreated on a continuous basis. As such, his 'theatre of repetition' (Deleuze, 1981: 19) distinguishes itself from a 'representational theatre' dear to traditional thought, be this processual or not, as the former repeatedly focuses on and rehearses a dynamic performance to affect the spirit of the audience directly in indelible ways. In this way, Kierkegaard's *Repetition* (Kierkegaard, 1997b) rehearses and manages to express 'singularity against generality', 'the remarkable against the ordinary', 'the moment against the variations', 'and an eternity against the permanent' (Deleuze, 1981: 9). Thus, Kierkegaard's subjective repetition forms an addition that questions the generality of objective law, to make room for another 'more profound and artistic reality' (Deleuze, 1981: 9).

Summing up Kierkegaard's legacy in a short passage, Sloterdijk has recently acknowledged Kierkegaard's addendum to the western tradition as a contribution of fundamental significance:

> 'In this choice 'as for the first time' Kierkegaard discovers the heartbeat of the existential time directed towards the future. With him the possibility of the essentially new appears—that is not only valid due to its resemblance to eternal models. In this way, one can claim that the radical thought of modernity—floating in experiments—begins with Kierkegaard. He was the first to enter the age of doubt, of suspicion and of creative decision. (Sloterdijk, 2009: 101, authors' translation).

8.3 CONTRIBUTIONS

8.3.1 The Human Self in Becoming

Kierkegaard most systematically articulated the active processual, practical, and first-person character of human existence in *The Sickness Unto Death* (1849) (Kierkegaard, 1980). Published under the pseudonym of Anti-Climacus and subtitled *A Christian Psychological Exposition for Upbuilding and Awakening*, it is an outstanding work and one that Kierkegaard considered among the most important in his oeuvre. For these reasons, Kierkegaard's thorough analysis of the human self in becoming is examined here more closely.

In a dense and somewhat enigmatic opening passage, Kierkegaard declares that a human being is not a particular finite or determined 'thing' that has a specific character or nature, but an existence characterized by *spirituality*—a self that *exists in relation to itself*. Regarding the perpetual *relating itself to itself* as the very being of the human self, Kierkegaard could therefore reinterpret the notion of spirituality in more secular terms: the human self has its very being in its constant *relating itself to itself*. 'A human being is spirit. But what is spirit? Spirit is the self. But what is the self? The self is a relation that relates itself to itself or is the relation's relating itself to itself in the relation; the self is not the relation but is the relation's relating itself to itself' (Kierkegaard, 1980; 13; Kierkegaard et al., 1963: 73).

Drawing heavily on idealist terminology, Kierkegaard further implies that a human being is a 'synthesis of the infinite and the finite, of the temporal and the eternal, of freedom and necessity, in short a synthesis'. Since 'a synthesis is a relation between two', this means that the human self is a relationship that resides within and establishes a relation between these opposites (Kierkegaard, 1980: 13; Kierkegaard et al., 1963: 73). However, as Kierkegaard repeatedly criticized the popular Hegelian concepts of mediation, the term 'synthesis' seems to be used mockingly here or in an abstruse sense (Stewart, 2003). In Kierkegaard, no true synthesis or mediation between the thesis and the antithesis is ever achieved. On the contrary, he stresses that 'in the relation between two, the relation is the third', but here only present in the form of 'a negative unity'. In the actual world, the ends never meet to form a coherent whole; and 'considered in this way', as a relationship and synthesis in the Hegelian sense, 'man is not yet a self' (Kierkegaard, 1980: 9).

Still, and by contrast, the relation may also form 'a positive third', provided that 'the relation relates itself to itself'. According to Kierkegaard, it is this relationship that 'is the self' (Kierkegaard, 1980: 13; Kierkegaard et al., 1963: 13, 73). Consequently, the human self is present, not in a given static relation or tension between opposites, but in the 'relation's relating', or in the establishment of an active relationship to the relation or tension. Here Kierkegaard varies a theme dear to processual philosophy in general—that passage takes priority over position. This inspired Deleuze in Kierkegaard (cf. Deleuze, 1981: 9–18).

A person establishes itself in a positive sense, only to the extent that the person is able to assume responsibility for being both body and mind, to relate actively to this condition, and to establish a particular relationship between body and mind. A human being can only be spiritual and soulful to the extent that it establishes and expresses its own specific relationship between body and mind. In this sense, and restricted to this sense, the human being can only be itself by itself—by becoming itself in relating to itself.

It is important to understand that when Kierkegaard defines the self as a relation, it is not only to be conceived as a relation between body and soul. Body-soul is only one expression of the relation. As noted, relations come across on multiple dimensions: as finite–infinite, temporal–eternal, necessity–freedom, and so on (Kierkegaard, 1980). The human is caught between the finite and the infinite, and between necessity and freedom in the sense that real life circumstances are always necessary and limited. Experienced from within the concrete 'existential situation' (cf. Tillich, 1944: 63; Yalom, 1980: 1), there are finite and necessary dimensions of life that cannot merely be changed, but must be dealt with accordingly. At the same time, however, dealing with the necessary and finite is always already a task of freedom, of the infinite in so far as it opens up a vast space for a never-ending choosing of actions. Over and over again there will be an encounter between necessity and a human freedom that is no less radical and open towards the future than the one that is found in Kierkegaard's definition of 'anxiety' as 'freedom's actuality as the possibility of possibility' (1997d: 166, 42; 1997c: 13).

It is in this manner, and with absolutely no aspirations as to any easiness pertaining to human freedom and choice, that Kierkegaard articulates an eradicable element of subjective becoming. For Kierkegaard anxiety comes to represent the radical experiential expression of freedom as a finite infinity, ever inhabiting each and every given existential situation of the human self. With no possible mediation or synthesis, it confronts the self in the most radical way with the virtual process of possibility inherent in every necessity, which—if taken seriously or recognized as such—is impossible not to take into account when dealing with human existence.

8.3.2 The Willing Self

According to Kierkegaard, a human being faces the task of becoming itself over and over again. The self does not only relate itself to itself on special occasions or under exceptional circumstances. As long as the self exists, the task is always and incessantly there. Importantly, however, this relationship is not a mere descriptive fact about the self, even in the form of an ongoing process that can be taken for granted and consequently be presupposed and relied upon. On the contrary, the self-relation is given to the human self as an assignment to be confronted and as a challenge that the self must measure up to in any given context or relation.

As a consequence, becoming a self is not primarily a matter of *knowledge*. Knowing oneself does not necessarily help a human being become a self and is indeed insufficient in or by itself. Against this common presupposition, Kierkegaard stresses the *volitional* and the *practical* rather than the *cognitive* or *theoretical* element of self-relation (Glenn, 1997: 11). Against the backdrop of the cognition, affection, and conation triad provided by the tradition of faculty psychology (Hilgard, 1980; Kant, 2006), Kierkegaard is certainly counted among those who in the nineteenth century strongly emphasized the importance of the affective dimension in human existence in preference to the cognitive faculties (Stan, 2011). For Kierkegaard, there is no person without a self-relation; there is no self-relation without a will; and the character of one's self-relation becomes a result of how one wills (see Chapter 13, this volume). Either one wills to be oneself, or one does not will to be oneself. There is a will at play in every action of the self. Most often this volition is a will not to be, or to take the full responsibility for what one is, or has become. There is a latent opposition to oneself in the human being. Also, this opposition is exactly a position of the will, a not-willing what one has been handed. Kierkegaard agrees with Nietzsche that man's spiritual health is frail (Nietzsche, 1974: §382). It needs to be reconquered as one continually loses and regains one's own being as a human self.

Kierkegaard's concept of not willing to be oneself is termed 'despair' (Cappelørn, Deuser, and Søren Kierkegaard Research Centre, 1996: 15–32 and 33–60; Beabout, 1991). *The Sickness Unto Death* contains a detailed analysis of how despair plays out in different versions of not being willing to be oneself. Despair, generally defined as a 'complete loss or absence of hope' (*Oxford English Dictionary*), must, according to Kierkegaard's account, be understood as the experience of a lack of ability on the part of the human being to pull itself together, emphatically as well as existentially. As is evident from the Danish and German equivalents to despair, *'fortvivlelse'* and *'Ver-zweiflung'*, the human experiences a state of 'two-ness' or dispersion, whereby he or she falls apart, thus becoming a 'di-vidual' and consequently not a coherent self.

Despair is thus a rejection of the will to become a self, by the human self, even as it is an indication of a possible superior existence. Kierkegaard distinguishes between two conceptions of despair. In the first case, despair is the will not to will oneself—what one wants is not to be a self and have a self-relation. In the second case, despair is the despair of despairingly willing to be oneself—it is the will to construct an artificial and better self (Dalsgaard, 2012).

Even though every human being is thus relational, the relationship to the relation and hence the character of the relation is not given in advance. Every self-relation has its own particular character, since one's will is always implied in one's relating to oneself. When relating itself to its self, a human being faces, over and over, the challenge of how to establish itself in the form of a singular self (Harré, 1998). Manifesting itself in despair, the dysfunctional mode of the will is a common mode of the will. To become and remain a human being, one must fashion oneself in the form of a unique human being over and over again.

8.4 RECEPTION AND IMPACT

8.4.1 Freedom, Process, and Responsibility as Contests for the System

Being one of the key originators of existential philosophy, Kierkegaard represents a challenge to the understanding of individual human life (Stewart, 2011a), which in turn represents a challenge to organizational thought (Abramson, 2011; Baxter and Rarick, 1989; Drucker, 1949; Styhre, 2004; Weick, 1999a;). In Kierkegaard's account, authentic human life transgresses any system or organization. This is because freedom is at the core of the human being. Becoming truly human is a matter of becoming responsible for one's life—in freedom. It should be noted, though, that Kierkegaard's notion of human freedom is highly complex. Freedom is not an empty concept, and it does not involve any claim that the human being is free to meaningfully choose whatever it desires. Human life is limited, or as outlined previously, it always takes place exactly between the limited and the unlimited, between necessity and freedom.

Human resistance to the system or organization is not only related to the negativity of human freedom in Kierkegaard's thought. As Kierkegaard's philosophy of existence is a philosophy of *process* and *becoming*, the human being only exists in becoming, being a relation that relates itself to itself and the world. Most importantly, this existential becoming emerges and must be recognized as a first-person act and experience in time: as *a first-person process,* which is therefore categorically different from the systems or organizations that the individual human is (also) part of. When Kierkegaard vehemently criticized Hegelian notions of the system, it was to stress that the individual human being's existence is the life of a first-person in time, and therefore it is of less importance what world historical, religious, cultural, or economical system this individual is considered a part of in an abstract *third-person perspective*.

From this perspective, Kierkegaard possibly only offers an approach to a critique of systems and organizations, rather than positive theories of organization building or management. If one seeks guidance on how to organize human life—religiously, culturally, or economically—there is only limited help to be found in Kierkegaard's thought. Considered more carefully, however, Kierkegaard's line of thinking might be able to inform organizational theory and practice. The notion of the human in Kierkegaard's thought can, at least indirectly, both challenge and inform modern management of organizations. Kierkegaard makes the highly important point that a human life, conceived as a self-dependent mode or process of existence, forms an irreducible field that organizational theory and practice must address, even though its subjective and dynamic nature is difficult—or perhaps even impossible—to chart and include.

8.4.2 The Singular Self and the Human Dimension in the Organization

In the face of a more traditional strategic approach to management and to organizations, Kierkegaard's philosophy thus presents a note of caution. The fact that the people who make up an organization are themselves singular human self-relations introduces an irreducible, existential dimension into the organization. This does not merely imply that it is problematic to conceive the organization simply as a social entity that has a collective goal and is linked to an external environment (March, 1965). It seems insufficient even to perceive the organization as an entity that is constantly reorganizing (Stacey, 2005; Fullan, 2001), or should be reorganized according to certain collective processes (Cameron and Green, 2004; Connor and Lake, 1988).

From Kierkegaard's perspective, the organization should also be regarded as a context into which humans repeatedly enter and come to existence as singular selves. With the human self, an ongoing process of subjective becoming enters the organization that exceeds and goes beyond organizational aims and processes, and in fact points beyond any given human attempt to organize. Among issues that appear pertinent for the human self are: human will, commitment, and choice—as well as the avoidance of exposure; responsibility (or the ability to give an account of yourself and for others), and the refusal of responsibility; anxiety, existential isolation, and meaninglessness; personal well-being and life fulfilment (cf. Yalom, 1980).

Insisting on the radical freedom of the individual, or the schism between what belongs to the worldly kingdom and what belongs to the spiritual kingdom, any effort to include, mediate, and satisfy the existential dimension within the larger totality of the organization would not only have a totalizing effect, but also a totalitarian character. It risks reinterpreting an earthly organization as a sanctuary and a place of salvation, to the possible detriment of those included as well as those who would not fit in. From

this viewpoint, even well-intentioned efforts to bring the existential dimension to fulfilment within the organization would risk blurring lines of demarcation that should be
retained: the boundary between the person and the organization, no less than between
the personal and the professional identity.

The potential critique pertaining to Kierkegaard's lines of thought could be further analysed on different levels. On the level of interpersonal management, the critique would
relate to the respect of singular freedom. How does a manager or employee properly meet
another employee? If the essence of the other person were freedom, many of the common
practices of interpersonal management in vogue today would be challenged. This regards
modes of management and the use of management tools where the 'unknownness' of the
other person, *qua* the other person's freedom, is not taken into account. If there is only
room for appreciation of predefined features of the employee, which will often be the case
in the context of an organization (Bushe, 2011), then the appreciation is not of the other
person's freedom, but of predefined models for personality instead.

In sum, the existential dimension introduces an irreducible 'external' and foreign element that exerts a decisive influence even inside the organization and its organizational
processes.

8.4.3 The Externality of the Self within the Organization

When carried to its logical conclusion, Kierkegaard's existential approach affects the way
organizations can be conceived theoretically and in practice. The existence of an irreducible existential dimension in becoming shakes the 'classical picture' of the organization as a 'social entity' that can be represented fairly objectively (cf. e.g. Cartwright, 1965,
1–47: 1). It challenges the received characterization of the organization as something that
is organized, stable over time, and 'predictable' (Cartwright, 1965), with relatively clear
delineations between an 'in-here' and an 'out-there', as well as between recognizable elements (Weber, 1966). Indeed, this is often supported by the conviction that what should
primarily be studied and managed are the internal orders and regulations of the organization (Donham, 1922, 1–10).

This handed-down picture of the organization as a 'thing-in-itself' (Hernes, 2008: 2–4,
14), having 'properties like that of physical objects' (Czarniawska, 2008: 7) that can and
should be objectively represented, is difficult to maintain in the face of Kierkegaard's
philosophy.

Kierkegaard tracks a plane of freedom that affects the spatiality of the organization and necessitates understanding the organization as 'a process of formation' in
which various irreducible elements emerge and co-evolve as they relate to each other
(Hernes, 2008).

Hence, with Kierkegaard's tracking of a plane of radical freedom, the picture of
an existing, relatively clear-cut, static distinction between the inside and outside of
an organization seems difficult to maintain. Since the existence of an independent

existential element introduces an irreducible outside within the organization, any process or practice of organizing is always already the temporary result of a relationship between what appears to be an inside and an outside of an organization as a given entity.

In these ways, Kierkegaard anticipates insights that have since gained crucial importance for post-structuralist thought in general and have in particular shaped approaches to organizational theorists inspired by post-structuralism. When simultaneously developing central strands of Foucault's and his own thought, Deleuze thus stresses 'the relationship to oneself' as it takes the form of an 'an independence' (Deleuze, 1986: 127, 107). On the one hand, this independent relationship of the self to the self affects the layers of the organization. The inwardness of the self expresses itself in the form of a deflection or recurvature of the existing forces in the organization that makes them re-emerge in a new form and direction (Deleuze, 1986: 128). On the other hand, with this element of an independent 'subjectivity', characterized as 'Foucault's fundamental idea' (Deleuze, 1986: 109), the organization also enters into relationship with an outside (Deleuze, 1986: 127), which is folded into and becomes an essential irreducible part of the organization. According to Deleuze and Foucault, the existence of the self as an independent curvature fundamentally affects how one can conceive the spatial construction of the organization (Hernes, 2008). As 'every inside-space', with the intervention of the independent self, is 'in contact with the outside-space, independent of distance and on the limits of a "living"' (Deleuze, 1986: 126), it seems insufficient to picture the organization as the effect of a simple 'strategy of entanglement' (Deleuze, 1986: 119), or of various interlacing intentionalities in three-dimensional Euclidean space. Instead, 'any organization (differentiation and integration)' presupposes 'the primary topological structure of an absolute outside and inside that encourages relative intermediary exteriorities and interiorities' (Deleuze, 1986: 126). Accordingly, the spatial construction of the organization can only be rendered intelligible along the lines of a generalized topological space, in which objects twist and bend, stretch and shrink as layers and distances are folded in, become interior, and converted into new relations. Within this topological space indicated by a self in becoming, what is not fully present gains crucial importance for the organization (Raffnsøe, 2013). This is not to be conceived as the possible (Staunæs, 2011), but as the virtual: as that which effects and is felt through its effects. 'It is more apparitional than empirical' (Massumi, 2002: 135).

8.4.4 The Human Turn in Organizational Life

Kierkegaard did not only exert a decisive influence on western theory and thought. In many ways, his assertion of the crucial importance of the human existential dimension has triumphed on its way to ubiquitous presence—and maybe even to a ruinous victory—in modern organizational practice. In modern organizations and corporations, in fact, human activity and human existence appear to have become present everywhere as an explicitly or at least implicitly recognized and unavoidable condition for management and organizational activity.

This tendency is apparent in many major forms of present management technologies, such as performance management, coaching, auditing, or even lean production (Raffnsøe, 2010). They all presuppose that employees can be treated as independent humans who are self-dependent and have the ability to assume responsibility for themselves and the task they must perform—even as they try to provide and promote the conditions for their very being. Performance and development reviews in which employees prove totally incapable of keeping tabs on and developing themselves would not make any sense.

It has thus become insufficient for organizational contexts to discuss human beings as given entities, as a part that may or may not exist, and may or may not be of relevance for the organization. Instead, the crucial point is that, *in so far as* one makes use of current forms of managerial and organizational techniques, one has always already *to some degree* begun to presuppose human existence and the human self as a *general condition of possibility* for management, organizational life, and modern work. The human self, and its ability to relate independently to itself, forms an integral part of modern organizational life, without which it would not be possible. The same tendency towards the inclusion of human existence has left a decisive mark on the development of management theory since the beginning of the twentieth century (Raffnsøe and Johnsen, 2014, forthcoming). Up till this day, the human factor has proven increasingly decisive for value creation in organizational life and within management theory, as testified by a number of prolific writes in the field (Drucker, 2008, 2007: 139–69 Mayo, 1933; McGregor, 1960).

With the introduction of the human self and its relationship to itself as an unavoidable condition for management and organizational activity, Kierkegaard's analysis of human existence therefore also gains significance for modern work life and organizational life in a more direct sense. Still, this transition raises the question how to reformulate his investigation and invocation of the human self, as the subjective element has become an explicit and privileged object for management and organizational undertakings, and not something that should first and foremost be safeguarded from the already given alienation of systems and institutions.

Even though this transformation and turn towards the human self would have been difficult to imagine without Kierkegaard's contributions, it is important to note that his conception of self also differs radically from the human self that has proliferated since then. Distancing itself from an approach to the human self that focuses on 'expected behavior' and 'obedience to authority' (Milgram, 2010), the humanistic psychology originating most markedly in the United States has, for example, primarily emphasized certain definable qualities that make a human being human, including 'human capacities and potentialities', 'growth', 'self-actualization', and 'ego-transcendence' (Sutich, cited in Bugental, 1964). Accordingly, the focus has been on enhancing management's ability to develop these capacities in organizational life. In diametrical opposition to this inflated self, Kierkegaard underlines the non-manageable limitations and tragic dimensions of human existence. Whereas humanistic psychology and modern managerial life speak at great length about the development of human potential and of peak experiences, Kierkegaard draws our attention to a different kind of challenge: contingency, human limitations, basic isolation, and the anxiety and despair they provoke. In contrast to a display of self-expression and self-transgression, Kierkegaard stresses inwardness and repetition.

As human existence is assigned the central role at the workplace and employed actively as a self, the workplace is in a sense 'humanized'. However, this place of labour is not necessarily a warm and all-embracing location that is open to the full variety of human existence. Rather, people are relentlessly challenged to go beyond themselves, to become all that they can be, as it were. They must constantly relate and enter into a process, in which they always find themselves 'at their limit', on the verge of becoming themselves, constantly challenged to transgress their hitherto unsurpassed maximum to find themselves anew (Raffnsøe, 2011). While human existence in modern organizational life is presumed to be in becoming, the process of becoming is required to follow a Hegelian logic of sublation. With regard to this logic of sublation, Kierkegaard's conception of the self remains radically untimely, especially when the self and its management have been expressly included in modern organizational life. Inwardness, loneliness, inner authenticity, despair, and a search for non-worldly meaning remain requirements and challenges that are not easily managed or sublated; and the ways they are dealt with form a critical acid test for management and organization thought.

Despite the fact that organization and management studies have failed to see Kierkegaard's relevance so far, with a few notable exceptions (Drucker, 1949; Styhre, 2004: 9; Weick, 1999a, 1999b), his thought could present an obvious inspiration and challenge for future studies. In an autobiographical note, Kierkegaard compared himself to a number of his succesful contemporaries. They were all benefactors of the age who had made a name for themselves by making life easier and more systematic, be it at a practical, organizational, or even spiritual level. He set a different goal for himself: 'You must do something but inasmuch as with your limited capacities it will be impossible to make anything easier than it has become, you must, with the same humanitarian enthusiasm, as the others, undertake to make something harder' (Kierkegaard, 2002: 171).

References

Abramson, N.R. (2011). Kierkegaardian Confessions: The Relationship between Moral Reasoning and Failure to be Promoted, *Journal of Business Ethics* 98(2): 199–216.

Baxter, G. and Rarick, C. (1989). The Manager as Kierkegaard's 'Knight of Faith': Linking Ethical Thought and Action, *Journal of Business Ethics* 5(1): 399–406.

Beabout, G. (1991). Existential Despair in Kierkegaard, *Philosophy and Theology* 6(2): 167–74.

Bugental, J. (1964). The Third Force in Psychology, *Journal of Humanistic Psychology* 4: 19–26.

Bushe, G.R. (2011). Appreciative Inquiry: Theory and Critique, in D. Boje, B. Burnes, and J. Hassard (eds), *The Routledge Companion To Organizational Change* (Oxford: Routledge): 87–103.

Cameron, E. and Green, M. (2004). *Making Sense of Change Management: A Complete Guide to the Models, Tools & Techniques of Organizational Change* (London: Kogan Page).

Cappelørn, N.J., Deuser, H., and Søren Kierkegaard Research Centre. (1996). *Kierkegaard Studies: Yearbook 1996* (Berlin: Walter de Gruyter).

Cartwright, D. (1965). Influence, Leadership, Control, in March, J.G. (ed.), *Handbook of Organizations* (Chicago: Rand McNally): 1–47.

Connor, P.E. and Lake, L.K. (1988). *Managing Organizational Change* (New York: Praeger).

Czarniawska, B. (2008). *A Theory of Organising* (Cheltenham: Edward Elgar Publishing).

Dalsgaard, M.M. (2012). *Det protestantiske selv: kravet om autenticitet i Kierkegaards tænkning* (Denmark: Anis).

Deleuze, G. (1981). *Différence et répétition* (Paris: Presses Universitaires de France).

——(1986). *Foucault* (Paris: Editions de Minuit).

Donham, W.B. (1922). Essential Groundwork for a Broad Executive Theory, *Harvard Business Review* 1(1): 1–10.

Dreyfus, H.L. (1991). *Being-in-the-World: A Commentary on Heidegger's* Being and Time, *Division I* (Cambridge, MA: MIT Press).

Drucker, P.F. (1949). *The Unfashionable Kierkegaard* (Tennessee: Sewanee).

——(2007). *Management Challenges for the 21st Century* (Oxford: Butterworth-Heinemann).

——(2008). *Managing Oneself* (Cambridge, MA: Harvard Business Press).

Fullan, M. (2001). *Leading in a Culture of Change* (San Francisco: Jossey-Bass).

Garff, J. (2000). *SAK Søren Aabye Kierkegaard: En Biografi* (Copenhagen: Gads Forlag).

Glenn, J.D. (1997). The Human Telos in Kierkegaard's Concluding Unscientific Postscript, in R.L. Perkins (ed.), *International Kierkegaard Commentary Volume 12* (Macon: Mercer University Press): 247–62.

Harré, R. (1998). *The Singular Self: An Introduction to the Psychology of Personhood* (London and Thousand Oaks, CA: Sage Publications).

Heidegger, M. (1927). *Sein und Zeit* (Tübingen: Niemeyer).

Hernes, T. (2008). *Understanding Organization as Process: Theory for a Tangled World* (London and New York: Routledge).

Hilgard, E.R. (1980). The Trilogy of Mind: Cognition, Affection, and Conation, *Journal of the History of the Behavioral Sciences* 16(2): 107–17.

Hodgson, P.C. (2005). *Hegel and Christian Theology. A Reading of the Lectures on the Philosophy of Religion* (Oxford: Oxford University Press).

Kant, I. (2006). *Anthropology from a Pragmatic Point of View*, ed. R.B. Louden, with an introduction by M. Kuehn (Cambridge: Cambridge University Press).

Kierkegaard, S. (1962). *Samlede Værker, Bind 5: Frygt og Bæven. Gjentagelsen. Forord*, ed. A.B. Drachmann, J.L. Heiberg, H.O. Lange, and P. Rohde (Copenhagen: Gyldendal).

——(1980). *The Sickness unto Death: A Christian Psychological Exposition for Upbuilding and Awakening*, ed. and trans. H.V. Hong and E.H. Hong (Princeton: Princeton University Press).

—— (1983). *Fear and Trembling; Repetition*, ed. and trans. H.V. Hong and E.H. Hong (Princeton: Princeton University Press).

——(1987). *Either/Or, Part 1. Volume 3 of Kierkegaard's Writings*, ed. and trans. H.V. Hong and E.H. Hong (Princeton: Princeton University Press).

——(1992). *Concluding Unscientific Postscript to Philosophical Fragments*, ed. and trans. H.V. Hong and E.H. Hong (Princeton: Princeton University Press).

——(1995). *Works of Love*, ed. and trans. H.V. Hong and E.H. Hong (Princeton: Princeton University Press).

——(1997a). *Enten-Eller, Første Del og Anden Del* (EE1, EE2), in *Søren Kierkegaards Skrifter 1–28*, Volumes 2–3 (Copenhagen: Gads Forlag).

—— (1997b). *Frygt og Bæven* (FB), in *Søren Kierkegaards Skrifter 1–28*, Volume 4 (Copenhagen: Gads Forlag).

—— (1997c). *Gjentagelsen* (G), in *Søren Kierkegaards Skrifter 1–28*, Volume 4 (Copenhagen: Gads Forlag).

—— (1997d). *Begrebet Angest* (*BA*), in *Søren Kierkegaards Skrifter 1–28*, Volume 4 (Copenhagen: Gads Forlag).

—— (1998). *The Moment and Late Writings*, ed. and trans. H.V. Hong and E.H. Hong (Princeton: Princeton University Press).

——(2002). *Afsluttende uvidenskabeligt Efterskrift til de philosophiske Smuler* (AE), in *Søren Kierkegaards Skrifter 1–28*, Volume 7 (Copenhagen: Gads Forlag).

—— (2004). *Kjerlighedens Gjerninger* (KG), in *Søren Kierkegaards Skrifter 1–28*, Volume 9 (Copenhagen: Gads Forlag).

—— (2006). *Sygdom til Døden* (SD), in *Søren Kierkegaards Skrifter 1–28*, Volume 11 (Copenhagen: Gads Forlag).

——(2009). *Øieblikket*, No. 1-10 (Oi1-Oi10), in *Søren Kierkegaards Skrifter 1–28*, Volume 13 (Copenhagen: Gads Forlag).

—— (2010). *Foranlediget ved en Yttring af Dr. Rudelbach mig betræffende* (YDR), in *Søren Kierkegaards Skrifter 1–28*, Volume 14 (Copenhagen: Gads Forlag).

—— Drachmann, A.B., Heiberg, J.L., Lange, H.O., and Rohde, P.P. (1963). *Tvende ethisk-religieuse smaa-afhandlinger. Sygdommen til døden* (Copenhagen: Gyldendal).

Luther, M. (2006). *Luther: Lecture on Romans*, ed. and trans. W. Pauck (Louisville: Westminster John Knox Press).

—— (1995). *Von der Freiheit eines Christenmenschen* (Munich: Gütersloher Verlagshaus).

March, J.G. (1965). *Handbook of Organisations* (Chicago: Rand McNally).

Massumi, B. (2002). *Parables for the Virtual: Movement, Affect, Sensation* (Durham: Duke University Press).

Mayo, E. (1933). *The Human Problems of an Industrial Civilization* (New York: Macmillan).

McCarthy, V. (2011). Martin Heidegger: Kierkegaard's Influence Hidden and in Full View, in J. Stewart (ed.), *Kierkegaard and Existentialism. Kierkegaard Research: Sources, Reception and Resources*, Volume 9 (Farnham: Ashgate): 95–126.

McGregor, D. (1960). *The Human Side of Enterprise* (New York: McGraw-Hill).

Milgram, S. (2010). *Obedience to Authority: An Experimental View* (London: Pinter & Martin).

Nietzsche, F. (1974). *The Gay Science: With a prelude in rhymes and an appendix of songs*. Trans. with commentary by Walter Kaufmann (New York: Random).

Raffnsøe, S. (2010). The Obligation of Self-Management: The Social Bonds of Freedom, in J. Petersen and H. Tronier (eds), *Villum Foundation and Velux Foundation; The Annual Report* (Søborg: Villum Foundation & Velux Foundation): 56–63.

—— (2011). The Five Obstructions: Experiencing the Human Side of Enterprise, *Ephemera* 11(2): 176–88.

—— (2013). Beyond Rule, Trust and Power as Capacities, *Journal of Political Power* 6(2): 241–60.

—— and Johnsen, R. (forthcoming 2014). Den humane vending inden for ledelse, organisation og værdiskabelse, in S. Raffnsøe, M. Gudmand-Høyer, M. Raffnsøe-Møller and D.V. Holm (eds), *Den humane Vending* (Aarhus: Aarhus Universitetsforlag).

Sloterdijk, P. (2009). *Philosophische Temperamente: Von Platon bis Foucault* (München: Diederichs).

Stacey, R.D. (2005). *Experiencing Emergence in Organizations: Local Interaction and the Emergence of Global Pattern* (London and New York: Routledge).

Stan, L. (2011). Michel Henry. The Goodness of Living Affectivity, in J. Stewart (ed.), *Kierkegaard and Existentialism. Kierkegaard Research: Sources, Reception and Resources,* Volume 9 (Farnham: Ashgate, 2011): 127–54.

Staunæs, D. (2011). Governing the potentials of life itself? Interrogating the promises in affective educational leadership, *Journal of Educational Administration and History* 43(3): 227–47.

Stewart, J. (2003). *Kierkegaard's Relation to Hegel Reconsidered* (Cambridge: Cambridge University Press).

—— (ed.) (2009). *Kierkegaard's International Reception* (Farnham, England; Burlington, VT: Ashgate).

—— (ed.) (2011a). *Kierkegaard and Existentialism. Kierkegaard Research: Sources, Reception and Resources,* Volume 9 (Farnham, Surrey; Burlington, VT: Ashgate).

—— (ed.) (2011b). *Kierkegaard's Influence on the Social Sciences,* Volume 13 (Farnham, Surrey, England; Burlington, VT: Ashgate).

—— (ed.) (2011c). *Kierkegaard's Influence on Social Political Thought. Kierkegaard Research: Sources, Reception and Resources,* Volume 14 (Farnham, Surrey, England; Burlington, VT: Ashgate).

Styhre, A. (2004). Thinking Driven by Doubt and Passion: Kierkegaard and Reflexivity in Organization Studies, *Philosophy of Management* 4(2): 9–18.

Tillich, P. (1944). Existential Philosophy, *Journal of the History of Ideas* 5(1): 44–70.

Weber, M. (1966). *The Theory of Social and Economic Organization* (New York: Free Press).

Weick, K.E. (1999a). *Sensemaking in Organizations* (Thousand Oaks, CA: Sage).

—— (1999b). *That's Moving Theories that Matter* (Thousand Oaks, CA: Sage).

Yalom, I.D. (1980). *Existential Psychotherapy* (New York: Basic).

CHAPTER 9

....

WILHELM DILTHEY
(1833−1911)

....

ANDRUS TOOL

9.1 LIFE AND HISTORICAL BACKGROUND

....

COMING FROM a pastor's family, Dilthey began his university studies in the field of theology, first in Heidelberg in 1852, but mostly at the University of Berlin. In the course of his studies, however, his interest shifted from theology to philosophy and history. His coming to history was largely influenced by the representatives of the so-called Historical School who were teaching at the University of Berlin at the time—Leopold von Ranke (1795–1886), Theodor Mommsen (1817–1903), and others. But unlike most of German historians, Dilthey also took seriously the alternative to the Historical School—H. Th. Buckle's positivistic conception of history. The discrepancies between the Historical School and the positivistic interpretations of history (Dilthey, 1989: 48–9) were a reason why, starting as early as 1860, he gradually developed a plan to treat systematically the philosophical assumptions on which the historical human sciences were based (De Mul, 2004: 14).

From 1867–1869, Dilthey was a professor at Basel University, and from 1869–1871 at Kiel University. During this period he worked on his first major publication, the biography of F.D.E. Schleiermacher, a Protestant theologian and philosopher. The first volume of this work was published in 1870. According to his own words, he kept coming up against the fundamental philosophical questions during this historical-biographical work, as a result of which he realized that, in order to continue his research, he would have to first form his own philosophical position in detail (Dilthey, 1989: 52). He worked on this from 1871–1882, while a professor at the University of Breslau. This led to the publication of the first volume of Dilthey's main work, *Introduction to the Human Sciences* (Dilthey, 1989: 47–240). While still in print, this work had a major role in Dilthey being invited in 1882 to occupy the prestigious chair of the Professor of Philosophy in Berlin, earlier held by Hegel.

Dilthey struggled to finish the second volume of the work, but many manuscripts of this work have been published posthumously (Dilthey, 1989: 243–501). His endeavours to finish his main work grew more intense in the 1890s when he published several studies in which he elaborated the themes of the second volume of the *Introduction*. The central work of this period became his *Ideas for a Descriptive and Analytic Psychology*, which appeared in 1894 (Dilthey, 2010: 115–207). His work on the philosophy of human sciences was interrupted because of the publication of a destructive review by Hermann Ebbinghaus, a prominent representative of mainstream psychology. In the following years his research focused on the history of European culture.

Dilthey returned to the philosophy of human sciences during the last decade of his life, influenced by Edmund Husserl's *Logical Investigations*, which appeared in 1900–1901. Dilthey believed that Husserl was thinking along the same lines as he did in elaborating his concept of psychology. In this period Dilthey aimed to create the theory of the interpretation of cultural objectifications. The most important publication on this topic is his comprehensive work entitled *The Formation of the Historical World in the Human Sciences* (Dilthey, 2002: 101–209).

The most influential part of Dilthey's heritage has been his treatment of the specific nature of human sciences in relation to natural sciences. In connection with the latter, Dilthey initiated a debate on the topic of the relationship between understanding and explanation in scientific knowledge, and whether beside sciences which proceed similarly to the natural sciences, there is room for 'interpretative' (*verstehende*) social science. In addition to his own school, he also exerted influence on the fundamental ontology of Martin Heidegger (see De Mul, 2004: 296–325), the philosophical anthropology of Helmuth Plessner (Hilt, 2011: 35–57), and the philosophical hermeneutics of Hans-Georg Gadamer (see De Mul, 2004: 325–37).

9.2 PHILOSOPHICAL VIEWS

The formation of Dilthey's views took place in an age when the grandiose systems of German idealism that had prevailed in the European intellectual world during the first half of the nineteenth century lost their credibility. German philosophers, wishing to find a way out of the identity crisis of philosophy and to reshape it, were first and foremost trying to demonstrate that philosophy had its positive function to fulfil within the conceptual framework set by the special sciences. Dilthey's interest focused on the humanities and social sciences, the generic name of which in German culture became the human sciences, *Geisteswissenschaften*. In his lifetime these sciences were still in the process of formation and were fighting for acknowledgement as a legitimate part of the scientific world. Dilthey was one of the first philosophers to distinguish the specific features of the forms of knowledge acquired by the human sciences.

In its endeavours to elaborate the epistemology of scientific knowledge, German philosophy relied on the philosophical legacy of Immanuel Kant. 'Back to Kant' became the catchword for a number of diverse philosophical quests in the second half of the nineteenth century in Germany. Dilthey, too, was influenced by this movement, as the ambitious name that he gave to his epistemological aspirations testifies—he set out to create 'the critique of historical reason', i.e. to complete in the philosophy of human sciences something analogous to what he thought Kant had achieved within the framework of his critique of reason in elaborating the epistemological foundations of natural sciences. This, however, involved critically reviewing Kant's premises.

Dilthey's philosophical analysis proceeds from one fundamental principle:

> The highest principle of philosophy is the principle of phenomenality. According to it, everything that is there-for-me is subject to the most general condition that it is a fact of my consciousness. All external things too are given to me only as connections of facts or events of the consciousness; an object, a thing, is there only for and in consciousness. (Dilthey, 2010: 8)

According to the principle of phenomenality, all facts that exist for us ultimately exist only as facts in our consciousness, which are the ultimate data, which do not allow any further analysis (Dilthey, 1989: 246).

With the principle of phenomenality Dilthey, of course, did not claim to have come up with something new. Rather, he deliberately adopted the point of departure of the modern subject-philosophy. He took the originality of his position, rather, to consist in setting the sphere of the facts of consciousness as a whole to be the basis of knowledge, whereas the hitherto existing philosophy—including Kant—had reduced this sphere solely to its cognitive aspect, thus revealing 'intellectual narrow-mindedness'. He asserted that the different kinds of facts of consciousness—the cognitive, volitional, as well as emotional—are connected with the continuity of consciousness as one integral whole, and if one wishes, in the footsteps of Kant, to find out the conditions of the possibility of scientific knowledge, one has to analyse psychic life as a totality formed of those different components.

Philosophy should describe the different ways in which the facts of consciousness are given to us. Dilthey concedes that it does not, normally, occur to us that the external things are formed out of the facts of consciousness. This we discover by consciously attending to a specific mode of awareness that Dilthey called *Innewerden*—reflexive awareness. In reflexive awareness the content of consciousness is not distinguished from the act of consciousness, nor is the content represented as being opposed to the subject as an object placed in front of him (Dilthey, 1989: 250).

The facts of consciousness organize themselves in such a manner that one can see a gradation emerge according to the degree the content separates itself from the subject and is opposed to it. The more distinct the self-awareness of the one who experiences the world becomes, the more objectified their picture of the outer world will become, and vice versa.[1] In this process, Dilthey singled out the processually charged states of urge, will, and emotion, and not the static forms of representation such as sensations, perceptions, and cognitive processes that 'intellectualistic' theories prioritized. It is first and foremost the volitional and emotional states an agent experiences when their actions, which spring from a willful impulse, come up against an outer obstacle. He considered this to be the starting point for the process in the course of which 'I' and the outer world will differentiate from and oppose one another. While experiencing this resistance against which our volitional impulses clash, an image of the outer world is formed in us as something alien to and non-correspondent with our expectations, a force that hinders and pressurizes us. While experiencing this over and over again in the case of new phenomena, our experience of the external world becomes ever more 'condensed'. The peak of the 'condensation' of the outer world for us results in natural sciences, an image of the outer objects as a regularly connected integral whole (for the most thorough treatment of this see Dilthey, 2010: 8–57).

It should be pointed out, especially from the point of view of process philosophy, that this conception entails an assumption, according to which it is the flow of the facts of consciousness that is given primacy, while the permanence of the phenomena should be treated as something secondary and derivative. Dilthey was of the opinion that such congealed objectivation, thinghood (*Dinglichkeit*), is characteristic of that segment of reality examined by natural science.

In claiming that objectivation is a result of gradual development, Dilthey refused to grant something that the predominant epistemology assumed, namely that the way of conceiving the nature of reality upon which the natural sciences rely on is a non-derivative mode of awareness. Once this is denied, one should, of course, ask further questions. First, one should enquire into the nature of the primordial way of comprehending reality and, second, how the conception of reality, accepted by natural sciences, has evolved. What is the position of the research practice of human sciences in this context? According to Dilthey, it is precisely the recognition of primordial awareness of reality that enables the human sciences to achieve adequate self-comprehension and to define their status in relation to natural sciences, as well as to explain the conditions of apprehension that set limits to natural sciences.

Dilthey marked the totality and the development of these modes of awareness with the term 'life' or 'life-nexus' (*Lebenszusammenhang*), by which he means self-assertion, which consists of acts of the 'I' and reactions of the natural and social world, and the experience resultant from this. Consciousness should be described as a nexus of life in this particular sense. The event of counter-effecting between action and reaction that takes place at a definite moment of time is marked by the term 'lived experience' (*Erlebnis*). This is an internally segmented whole, the structure of which always contains the connection between cognitive, emotional, and volitional processes (Dilthey, 1989: 330).

In characterizing the reality of life in general terms, Dilthey emphasizes that, on the one hand, we are all familiar with it through our daily experience, while on the other hand, it is impossible to explain it conclusively, since it is never given to us as a finished totality. Dilthey is convinced that the necessity for such a comprehensive conception can never disappear, since it lies in human nature. However, he has to concede that this necessity can only ever be satisfied with the help of separate and separating sciences, which deal with detached aspects of life, abstracting their field of research from the integral reality of life.

> The stream of life never stands still for observation, but courses ceaselessly toward the ocean. We can neither grasp nor express it as it is, but we fix its partial contents. We break up what is flowing into firm discrete parts. From a reality whose complicated character we inadequately designate as complexity, many-sidedness, multiplicity, we select individual aspects as partial contents. (Dilthey, 1989: 282)

Starting from these assumptions about ontology, it has to be demonstrated that philosophical and scientific cognition and, above all, cognition in human sciences could justifiably claim to represent reality correctly. In order to achieve this goal, one has to assume the fundamental knowledge of the facts of consciousness, i.e. the nexus of life which, according to Dilthey, we possess at the level of reflexive awareness. Dilthey believed that it was with such reflexive awareness of the facts of consciousness that we humans realized our most certain state, since in this mode of awareness the contents of the act of awareness and the act itself are not separated from one another.

Reflexive awareness, by concentrating attention on some aspects of itself, changes into perception, the latter, in turn, becoming the basis for experience, one type of which is scientific and philosophical cognition. Dilthey divides perceptions into two very different types—inner perception and outer perception, depending on content, i.e. whether this content relates to oneself ('me') or the world. Whereas the content of the outer perception is the objectified outer world, the 'me', functions for the inner perception as an entirely different realm:

> In fact, whatever Heraclitus says about the stream of reality has complete validity concerning psychic life. In the presence of heightened attention, we find no constant state of consciousness, no constant inner fact. Every colour is perceived with fluctuating attention, and its emotional tint changes. What is fixed is merely a quality contained in this fact, in this perception, which has been favored by attention. It is only a partial content of this fact, of this perception, not the whole. Therefore, any psychology that bases its explanation on fixed elements or atoms of psychic life, as it were, is without foundation. (Dilthey, 1989: 370)

The followers of Kant, too, would have no objections to this. Dilthey, however, went further:

> Our ego-consciousness is also no exception to this general fundamental property of psychic states, for the ego is ordinarily not given to me separate from processes. The individual process contains only a reflexive awareness that it belongs to the same consciousness as other psychic processes. The individual psychic process dwells in this element, in the sea of reflexive awareness, an immediate knowledge of being contained together with all my other psychic processes in an ego, a self, or more precisely, a substantial 'me'. And precisely this 'me', this reflexive awareness of the element where all this takes place, is the most changeable of all that is changeable. (Dilthey, 1989: 370–1)

On the one hand, perception is immediate knowledge, yet on the other hand Dilthey concedes that, on the level of perception, knowledge is not yet conceptualized. In order to create the epistemological basis for scientific knowledge, one has to demonstrate that the knowledge about the inner reality which, according to him, we possess on the level of the reflexive awareness and perception, could be shaped into conceptual cognition without losing the certainty provided by perception that we supposedly possess on the primary level of knowledge.

Dilthey believed that in order to achieve this goal, one has to demonstrate that forms of thinking arise from the reality of life and the immediate knowledge that we possess of this reality. If this is so, the forms of thinking are not an alien supplement to perception and reality from the outside, as Kant and his followers saw it, but instead a structure that has immanently evolved from these (Dilthey, 2010: 124–5). 'The question which we all must address to philosophy cannot be answered by the assumption of a rigid epistemological *a priori*, but rather only by a developmental history proceeding from the totality of our being' (Dilthey, 1989: 51). For Dilthey, conceptual thinking is a function of the process of life. Conceptual thinking amplifies the awareness that a human being as a life unit possesses of the articulation of the nexus of life. This amplification is necessarily supported by categories of thinking, whose role is to contribute to our endeavours to understand the structure of the connections and relations of the life process. The categorical instrumentarium of human sciences should be able to represent the processual and historical development, essential to the reality segments that these sciences study (Dilthey, 1989: 414–18, 2010: 58–114). Dilthey saw a substantial hindrance to this endeavour in the fact that his contemporary culture of science tended to deflect human sciences towards taking over the categories successfully used in the natural sciences. These categories were created for the purpose of explaining the natural world. Dilthey was convinced, however, that the structure of the reality of the natural world was, in the relevant respect, opposed to the structure of the reality that was researched by the human sciences.

Since the scientific cognition of the natural world can only function by relying on the outer perception, it is accompanied by certain limitations which arise from the ontological characteristics of the objects perceived that way. According to Dilthey, one has to admit that we can perceive these objects not as they are in themselves but merely as appearances. The outer perception presents objects to us as isolated from one another in time and space; the inner connections that may exist between them are not given to us. In these conditions experience can only be realized if the discursive thinking complements that which has been given in perception with that which is not given there—the connections between objects. 'An explanative science is one that subsumes a phenomenal domain to a causal system by means of a limited number of univocally determined elements that are the constituents of that system' (Dilthey, 2010: 115). But since neither these elements nor the system have been given to us in the outer perception, it is impossible to directly verify the hypotheses of explanative sciences. A natural scientific explanation consists of constructing hypotheses about the respective connections which are indirectly verified by means of observation data. However, the intersubjective accessibility of the objects of outer experience, the relatively great durability and measurability enables, by means of observation, experiment, and measuring, to verify the research results. This is why there is extensive consensus about the validity of the natural sciences.

Until his late work, Dilthey (2010: 214–25) was of the opinion that cognition in human sciences involves a complex of processes within which, by means of discursive and reflective thinking, the inner and outer perceptions are connected, so that by means of this the facts of the human world are better understood and the conceptual cognition of the inner world that we possess expands. This type of experience possesses significant advantages over the outer experience that depends on the ontological characteristics of the reality segment, conceived in the inner perception. The main such advantage consists in the circumstance that the inner facts are given to us in perception not as appearances, like the objects of natural science, but instead as they are in themselves, so that we have been given, and can also directly experience, the inner connections between the facts of mental life. Dilthey thought that this allowed one to contend that the inner experience has no need to complement that which has been perceived for the purpose of associating the facts with hypothetical connection constructions, and that instead human sciences are capable of immediately and certainly analysing and describing the connection given in perception, without having any principled epistemological boundaries.

9.3 Theory of Human Sciences

In his main work, *Introduction to the Human Sciences*, Dilthey proceeded from the premise that, while researching human sciences, the scholar is directly given in his self-consciousness the primary elements of the object of his study, society, since he himself is one of such primary elements and therefore familiar with them, whereas natural scientists must identify the primary elements of the object they study via hypothetical inference. 'Nature is alien to us. It is a mere exterior for us without any inner life. Society is our world. We sympathetically experience the interplay of social condition with the power of our total being. From within we are aware of the state and forces in all their restlessness that constitute the social system' (Dilthey, 1989: 88).

According to Dilthey's analysis, society is formed from life units, i.e. psychophysical individuals. It is for this reason that the study of life units is the most fundamental of the human sciences. Accordingly, in the theory presented in Dilthey's main work, the basis of the system of human sciences was to be psychology (1989: 80).

Dilthey stresses that a research like this is based on abstraction:

> The object of psychology is … always merely the individual who has been singled out from the living context of socio-historical reality. Only through a process of abstraction can psychology establish the universal characteristics which individual psychic beings develop in this socio-historical context. Neither in experience nor through inference can psychology find man as he is apart from interactions with society—man as prior to society, as it were. (Dilthey, 1989: 82)

Dilthey discarded the conception of the relationship between the individual and society, the mistake of which is 'to isolate individuals and then to connect them mechanistically as the method of constructing society' (Dilthey, 1989: 82). On the other hand, he rejected the contrary approach as well, which treated the individual as the non-autonomous part of society, e.g. as being analoguous to a relationship in which one part of the organism relates to the organism as a whole (Dilthey, 1989: 83).

Such a fundamental science of psychology avoids one-sidedness and aims to develop general propositions, the subject of which is the individual life unit and the predicates of which are all those assertions about it that can be productive for understanding society and history (Dilthey, 1989: 84). These so-called first-order truths constitute the basis of further formation of the human sciences. However, Dilthey stresses that such a psychology 'can be a foundational human science only if it stays within the limits of a descriptive discipline that establishes facts and uniformities among facts.... only in this way can the particular human science obtain a foundation which is itself secure; at present even the best psychological accounts build one hypothesis upon another' (Dithey, 1989: 84). He developed this conception further in his later work, *Ideas Concerning a Descriptive and Analytic Psychology*.

As a next step it was necessary, with the support of the first-order truths, to elaborate the second-order theories, which were to deal with the interactions between individuals. He classified these as short-term and long-term interactions, stressing that only the latter had hitherto really been scientifically treated. He singled out three types of sciences that concern themselves with these interactions: (1) ethnology or comparative anthropology (Dilthey, 1989: 91–3); (2) the sciences of the cultural systems (Dilthey, 1989: 99–114); and (3) the sciences of the external organization of society (Dilthey, 1989: 114–36).

Unlike in his late work, here Dilthey assumes that the scientific study of social-historical reality has the aim of establishing the dependencies between the psychic or psychophysical elements that exist in the agents who act together in long-term interaction systems. These sciences, examining cultural systems and the external organization of society, deal with facts that are different in kind from the facts researched by psychology. Dilthey refers to them as the second-order psychic facts. The existence of second-order psychic facts justifies the existence of the second-order theories. Thus the scientific study of the social-historical reality does not consist, according to Dilthey, in simply reducing the elements and connections of this reality to the individual-psychological data or theories. Nevertheless, in his main work, he expressed the conviction that the second stage of knowledge in human sciences is, in a way that needs further epistemological concretization, based on the 'first-order truths' (Dilthey, 1989: 92, 95, 97–8, 118, 163–4).

The systems of culture are, for Dilthey, language, religion, art, philosophy, science, education, sociability, economic life, law, and political activities. 'They arise...when a purpose grounded in some aspect of human nature—which for that reason is enduring—relates psychic acts in different individuals to join them into a purposive system' (Dilthey, 1989: 94). Individuals join these purposive systems of their own free will in order to achieve in collaboration with others the aims that arise from human nature but which cannot be individually achieved (Dilthey, 1989: 94, 104). A cultural system is not a system that defines a culture, 'but an organization for the furtherance of certain ends that may either be part of a specific culture or transcend it' (Makkreel and Rodi, 1989: 16).

As examples of the forms of the external organization of society, he mentions families, communities, associations, churches, and states. They arise 'when enduring causes bind the wills of many into a single whole, whether theses causes be rooted in the natural articulation of social life or in the purposes which drive human nature' (Dilthey, 1989: 94). Dilthey directs attention to second-order psychic facts which are fundamental to the external organization of society. 'A feeling of community, a sense of being-for-oneself (a phenomenon for which we have no proper word), power, dependence, freedom, compulsion,—these are the kinds of second-order psychic and psychophysical facts the conceptual and propositional knowledge of which underlies the study of the external organization of society'. These psychic facts 'supply the external organization of society with the lifeblood which flows through even its finest veins. All group relationships are, psychologically viewed, derived from these facts' (Dilthey, 1989: 118).

Several authors have pointed out that the criteria previously mentioned cannot be applied to forms of cultural system or external organization to the same extent, and that the univocal classification of the latter to one or another class of interaction by them is not possible (see, for example Johach, 1974: 67; Makkreel, 1992: 65). As to the forms of interaction, though, Dilthey emphasizes that they are abstractions; in social life these forms are always intertwined (Dilthey, 1989: 102). At the same time, the notion of a cultural system can be considered more abstract than the notion of the external organization of society (Makkreel and Rodi, 1989: 17). Historically, cultural systems have always depended on the external organization of society, which has to an extent institutionalized their functioning (Dilthey, 1989: 98, 102, 104). According to Dilthey, it is a law of the historical life in the sphere of the external organization of society that the totality of the inner purposiveness of human life has been differentiated only gradually into particular cultural systems, and these cultural systems have only gradually attained their independence and individual development (Dilthey, 1989: 123).

Given that the types of interaction under discussion exist intertwined with one another, one can assert that the two classes of the social science that deal with them form the basis of one theory of culture (Lessing, 2011: 52). First and foremost, it is important to note that, within the context of culture, as with the connection between the systems and organizations of society, culture is rooted in human nature (Dilthey, 1989: 94, 97–8). The unity and relative stability of human nature supposedly make culture treatable in introspective terms. At the same time, human nature expresses itself through the diversity of individuals, which also causes the diversity of systems and organizations. Secondly, Dilthey points out that systems and organizations have a longer lifetime than the individuals who sustain them. For the individual, these represent an objectivity that does not depend on them, something that they have to conform with. Thirdly, Dilthey stresses that a particular individual is, as a rule, active in several different systems and organizations, thus representing the point of intersection of a plurality of such systems and organizations (Dilthey, 1989: 101, 115). At the same time, Dilthey is convinced that there will always be a sphere in the nature of an individual that is autonomous in relation to all systems or organizations in which that individual participates (Dilthey, 1989: 122, 131). This sphere is a foundation from which individuals can also be innovative with regard to systems and organizations—in each generation the content and richness of human nature flows into these systems and organizations (Dilthey, 1989: 101).

While treating in very general terms the external organization of society in the first, introductory book of his main work, Dilthey analyses the external organization of society with help from the notion association (*Verband*), which he defines as 'a lasting volitional unity of several persons, grounded in a purposive system' (Dilthey, 1989: 120). He stresses that the reality which is formed by associations represents a historical phenomenon: 'For this reality can be understood only in its historical context, and its fundamental law shows us that human group-life was not formed through a process of construction or synthesis, but was developed and differentiated from the unity of the family bond' (Dilthey, 1989: 123). He asserts that the external organization of society develops in manifold modifications of forms. 'This development manifests a powerful originality and unpredictability, flexibility and adaptability' (Dilthey, 1989: 124). But he also admits that 'the most fundamental and pervasive distinction in all human group-life is that between these associations and those others which are constituted by a definite act of voluntary agreement for a consciously set and limited purpose, and which therefore naturally belong to a later stage of group-life among all nations' (Dilthey, 1989: 124–5). The approach of human sciences to this immense richness of forms of all the external organizations that have been created in human history should be comparative. 'In all these forms it is the relation between purpose, function, and structure that yields its formative law and that is thus the point of departure for the comparative method' (Dilthey, 1989: 125).

9.4 LATER WORK

In the last decade of his life Dilthey modified his theory of human sciences to an extent. The change is especially conspicuous in his *The Formation of Historical World in the Human Sciences* and in his manuscripts, in which he deleveped further the themes of that work (Dilthey, 2002: 101–311). These changes are connected mainly with three notions—the objectification of life, the objective spirit, and the productive nexus.

In *The Formation of Historical World in the Human Sciences*, Dilthey asserts the narrow limits of an introspective method and emphasizes as characteristic of human sciences the understanding of the manifestations of life, especially the expressions of lived experience (Dilthey, 2002: 108). He now describes the understanding in human sciences as the interpretation of the meanings of life expressions. The meanings and senses (*Sinn*), i.e. the webs of meaning, are not reducible to psychic processes, although they cannot exist apart from the human mind (Dilthey, 2002: 106–7). Thus he no longer assigns to descriptive psychology the special status of the most fundamental science among other human sciences; it too has to proceed hermeneutically as other human sciences do (Makkreel, 1992: 302). 'These sciences are founded upon...a nexus of lived experience, expression, and understanding' (Dilthey, 2002: 109).

In the texts of this period, Dilthey called the complex of the manifestation of life and expressions of lived experience the objectification of life. He does not take the objectification of life any longer to be secondary and external to inner experience, as it seemed to be the case in his earlier work, but instead as the essential phase on the way to experience and accomplishment on the path of life. It is only by way of objectification that the meanings concealed in lived experiences evolve—they become 'articulated' and 'explicated'. While referring to the essential unity of the lived experience, life, and expression, Dilthey now conceived of the objectification also as a counterbalance to the subjectivity of lived experience. He emphasized that it was through such objectification that the structures of meanings concealed in lived experience would become scientifically treatable, since objectification is in principle accessible to everybody and it enables intersubjective research and the controlling of its results: 'The scope of the human sciences is identical with that of understanding, and understanding...has its unified material in the objectification of life' (Dilthey, 2002: 170).

Dilthey assumes that the understanding of the objectification of life is a many-layered phenomenon, the deepest layer of which is a further ontological aspect of the life process itself, in addition to lived experience and its expression. He emphasized especially that, on the most elementary level, understanding depends on another ontological aspect of the life process, namely the objective spirit. He characterized the latter as 'the manifold forms in which a communality existing among individuals has objectified itself in the world of the senses. In this objective spirit, the past is a continuously enduring present for us. Its scope extends from lifestyles and forms of social intercourse to the system of purposes that society has created for itself' (Dilthey, 2002: 229). However, an important characteristic of the social life process is that the depository of the objective spirit grows and the webs of meaning become ever more complex, although at the same time a certain part of the meaning is also forgotten. This historical legacy is the environment of the development, communication, and socialization of individuals.

> The individual always experiences, thinks, and acts in a sphere of communality, and only in such a sphere does he understand. Everything that has been understood carries, as it were, the mark of familiarity derived from such common features. We live in this atmosphere; it surrounds us constantly; we are immersed in it. We are at home everywhere in this historical and understood world; we understand the sense and meaning of it all; we ourselves are woven into this common sphere. (Dilthey, 2002: 168–9)

According to this characterization, one could identify the objective spirit with culture, although Dilthey himself does not do this. Unlike the contemporary cultural theorists, Dilthey does not think that cultural differences can create severe difficulties of understanding, and optimistically assumes that the entire sphere of objective spirit is in principle understandable (Dilthey, 2002: 169; Lessing, 2011: 139–40).

Such an elementary form of understanding is also the starting point for the interpretation of the forms of culture that takes place in human sciences. In the latter, the objectifications which are in everyday life understood through their regular cultural meanings are connected into increasingly more diverse and extensive horizons of meaning. This enables understanding to rise to the level of understanding objectifications as unique individualities. This process emerges from the necessities of life itself and the human sciences are characterized by a continuous feedback with life (Dilthey, 2002: 228–41). In Dilthey's view, this makes it harder to offer generally valid interpretations, but does not make it impossible (Dilthey, 2002: 159–60).

At the same time, Dilthey admitted that the permanent fixing of the manifestations of life is accompanied by certain difficulties in understanding the underlying dynamic life processes. It enables the undertaking of intersubjective research but brings along the danger that the understanding that has been made possible this way may lose sight of the processual nature characteristic of this world. The objectification of life is characterized by thinghood, whereas the spirit is characterized, first and foremost, by mobility, the historical changeability. In order to avoid the danger that the objective spirit could, to an unjustifiable extent, be fixed in his treatment, and in order to characterize more closely the structural versatility inherent to objective spirit, Dilthey introduced into his philosophy of the human sciences the concept of productive nexus (*Wirkungszusammenhang*).[2] The productive nexus is a connection that unites the apprehension of the existing situation, the determination of its value, the setting of the purpose that arises from both of these, and the production of goods that proceeds from this purpose.

> This productive nexus of the world of human spirit is distinguished from the causal nexus of nature by the fact that, in accordance with the structure of psychic life, it produces values and realizes purposes; and this occurs not occasionally, not here and there; rather, it lies in the very structure of human spirit to establish a productive system that generates values and realizes purposes on the basis of objective apprehension. (Dilthey, 2002: 175)

He saw in this notion the main means by which to open the structure and dynamics of the objective spirit—objective spirit, as he saw it, was describable as a sphere that is formed in the productive nexuses and their networks, which evolves in the bosom of different human associations. The carriers of these productive systems are individuals and systems in which they cooperate.

> This cooperation is determined by the fact that, in order to realize values, individuals subject themselves to rules and set themselves purposes. All these modes of cooperation manifest a life-concern connected to the human essence and that links individuals with each other—a core, as it were, that cannot be grasped psychologically but is revealed in every such system of relations among human beings. (Dilthey, 2002: 176)

Dilthey now interprets the culture systems and forms of external organization of society as such productive nexuses. While describing the relations between productive systems, Dilthey emphasized that on the one hand they influence one another but, on the other hand, each productive system (e.g. a particular individual or an organization) is characterized by a relatively closed horizon and by being centred on itself. The degree of such openness/reclusion varies as to different productive systems. Thus, according to Dilthey, large productive systems like nations and epochs are characterized by a much closer horizon compared to smaller ones. If the exterior influences are accepted at all, then these are assimilated into the immanent structures of meanings that constitute the given productive system. Each part of these totalities has its own significance through its relation to the totality. Such a relatively closed totality develops, first and foremost, due to its internal contradictions (Dilthey, 2002: 176–7, 187). Makkreel and Rodi indicate that by introducing the notion of productive nexus, Dilthey complements and corrects his conception of the human world as a complex of purposive systems: 'A productive nexus or system may be purposive without fulfilling a determinate purpose. It is to be conceived as producing objectifications that express human values as well as purposes—leaving open the extent to which specific goals are achieved' (Makkreel and Rodi, 2002: 6).

In Dilthey's view, the human sciences treat the facts in the human world inasmuch as these possess meaning through being linked to the totality of some productive system. These productive systems entwine with one another and form larger webs of meaning. Thus, one has to aim to understand both the parts of a single productive system in relation to it as a totality, and also the relationships between different productive systems. Dilthey hoped that the recognition of this mutual dependence in understanding the productive systems would, in the human sciences, contribute significantly to reaching generally valid results (Dilthey, 2002: 159–60).

9.5 Conclusions

Dilthey proceeded from the conviction that the manner in which the contemporary natural sciences comprehended empirical factuality—namely in the form of congealed objectivity—is not how reality actually encounters a human being. This congealed objectivity is the result of the objectivation process of the naturally processual reality. He stressed the fact that we are able to understand, in the case of the socio-historical reality, the inner forces of such objectification processes in the human life. The inner side of social objectivity is the creativity characteristic of human beings—the incessant production of understandings of reality, value orientations, and goals, and their connection in ever new forms of practice. Dilthey did not put these very general ideas into a more concrete form. However, ideas similar to those of Dilthey have opened up a way for comprehending the culture of the organization and its dynamics (see, e.g. Schein, 1985, and Hatch, 1993, 2000, 2004).

NOTES

1. R.A. Makkreel and F. Rodi note that Dilthey anticipates George Herbert Mead, who, incidentally, attended Dilthey's lectures on ethics and the history of philosophy in 1890 and 1891 (Makkreel and Rodi, 1989: 29; see also Joas, 1985: 19–20, 218).
2. H.-G. Gadamer's notion of effective history (*Wirkungsgeschichte*) is closely related to Dilthey's concept of the productive nexus (*Wirkungszusammenhang*) (De Mul, 2004: 331–2).

REFERENCES

De Mul, J. (2004). *The Tragedy of Finitude. Dilthey's Hermeneutics of Life* (New Haven and London: Yale University Press).

Dilthey, W. (1989). *Selected Works. Volume I: Introduction to the Human Sciences* (Princeton: Princeton University Press).

——(2002). *Selected Works. Volume III: The Formation of the Historical World in the Human Sciences* (Princeton: Princeton University Press).

——(2010). *Selected Works. Volume II: Understanding the Human World* (Princeton: Princeton University Press).

Hatch, M.J. (1993). The Dynamics of Organizational Culture, *Academy of Management Review* 18(4): 657–63.

——(2000). The Cultural Dynamics of Organizing and Change, in N. Ashkanasy, C. Wilderom, and M. Peterson (eds), *Handbook of Organizational Culture and Climate* (Thousand Oaks, CA: Sage): 245–60.

——(2004). Dynamics in Organizational Culture, in M.S. Poole and A. Van de Ven (eds), *Handbook of Organizational Change and Innovation* (Oxford: Oxford University Press): 190–211.

Hilt, A. (2011). An Ethos of Human Inscrutability and Eccentricity: From Dilthey's Critique of Historical Reason to Plessner's Philosophical Anthropology, in H.-U. Lessing, R. A. Makkreel, and R. Pozzo (eds), *Recent Contributions to Dilthey's Philosophy of the Human Sciences* (Stuttgart-Bad Cannstatt: frommann-holzboog Verlag): 35–57.

Joas, H. (1985). *G.H. Mead: A Contemporary Re-Examination of His Thought* (Cambridge, MA: MIT Press).

Johach, H. (1974). *Handelnder Mensch und objektiver Geist. Zur Theorie der Geistes- und Sozialwissenschaften bei Wilhelm Dilthey* (Meisenheim am Glan: Verlag Anton Hain).

Lessing, H.-U. (2011). *Wilhelm Dilthey. Eine Einführung* (Cologne: Böhlau Verlag).

Makkreel, R.A. (1992). *Dilthey: Philosopher of the Human Studies* (Princeton: Princeton University Press).

——and Rodi, F. (1989). Introduction to Volume I, in *Dilthey, Wilhelm. Selected Works. Volume I: Introduction to the Human Sciences* (Princeton: Princeton University Press): 3–43.

—— (2002). Introduction to Volume III. In *Dilthey, Wilhelm. Selected Works. Volume III: Introduction to the Human Sciences* (Princeton: Princeton University Press): 1–20.

Schein, E. (1985). *Organizational Culture and Leadership* (San Francisco: Jossey-Bass).

....

CHAPTER 10

CHARLES SANDERS PEIRCE (1839–1914)

....

PHILIPPE LORINO

10.1 INTRODUCTION

....

'GROUND ARMS!' This utterance is a sign with an apparently straightforward meaning: the officer wants the soldiers to ground arms (Peirce, 1998: 499). But this sign means more than the soldiers' expected move. The officer's tone is confident: the order also signifies his belief that, in this society, soldiers obey officers. Meaning is thus mediated: the semiotic link between the utterance and its expected practical effect requires another link, between the utterance and the belief in military obedience. If soldiers were not supposed to obey orders, the officer's words could hardly represent the officer's expectation that the soldiers will ground arms. This is the basis of Peirce's theory of sign: there is no meaning without a sign pointing to another sign (mediation), and thus no meaning which does not generate signs from signs, in long teleological chains deployed over time in a certain direction (semiosis). Meaning is a move from X to Y, and semiosis is the arrow of meaning moving across time, space, and society.

The father of pragmatism, Charles Sanders Peirce, is also the father of semiotics; he even invented the word. This is not a chance combination. Peirce's theory of sign plays a key role in pragmatist philosophy. The triadic view of meaning must have been particularly topical in the early twentieth century, since similar views were developed in German philosophy by Ernst Cassirer (1923/1955) (theory of symbolic forms) and in Russian psychology by Vygotsky (1986) (semiotic mediation of activity). In Peirce's view, 'the woof and warp of all thought is symbols' (Peirce, 1931–1958: 2.220), 'every thought is a sign' (Peirce, 1991: 49), and so is every act. His theory of sign thus serves as a foundation for the theory of thought and action. The process of thinking appears as a chain of signs, the recursive process of generating meaning from meaning that Peirce called 'semiosis'. The dynamics of thought and action is thus analytically rooted in the intimate mechanism of meaning, in the same way as the complex carbon chains which form the base of life result from the elementary structure of the carbon atom. The triadic sign has a property—mediation—which enables it to form long chains of interconnecting signs, the catenation of thought.

Breaking with a long-standing western view of meaning as a mirror image, Peirce views meaning as the process of *mean-ing*, or even the active process of '*mak-ing* something mean'. Thus he stresses that thought is a temporal and irreversible process; it is dialogical—meaning being always addressed to another party, mediated by signs which are simultaneously social and material, and rooted in transformative action through the process of inquiry. Peirce's theory of semiosis should be a major contribution to organization studies inspired by process, practice, dialogism, discursive performativity, and sociomateriality issues. Yet in comparison with their influence in philosophy, psychology, linguistics, semiotics, literary criticism, and computer science, his ideas have so far been surprisingly absent from organization studies. Apart from stylistic difficulties, more imaginary than real, this absence may result from the simplistic reduction of his work to pure logics, ignoring his stature as a major epistemologist focusing on the social construction of meaning.

This chapter begins by presenting a brief biography of Charles Sanders Peirce and a summary of his intellectual influence. It then introduces the key concepts of Peircean semiotics—mediation and semiosis—and their process orientation. Last it analyses the major contribution these concepts can make to process-oriented organization studies.

10.2 BIOGRAPHY AND INFLUENCES

Charles Sanders Peirce was born in 1839 in Cambridge, Massachusetts, and he died in 1914 in Pennsylvania. From his father, a professor of mathematics at Harvard University, he received an early intellectual education. He was astonishingly precocious, beginning an in-depth study of logic at 13 and an extensive study of philosophy at 16. He graduated from Harvard in 1859 and received the bachelor of science degree in chemistry in 1863. He was a very independent and original thinker, theorizing about logic, language, communication, knowledge, science, meaning, and signs. However, he could never get tenure in the academic world. He was employed by the US Coast and Geodetic Survey for 32 years, from 1859 to 1891, carrying out geodetic investigations. He made measurements of the earth's gravitational field using pendula that he had himself designed. He practised chemistry as an expert and consultant. From 1879 to 1884, he also taught logic in the Department of Mathematics at Johns Hopkins University. He lost his main job at the US Coast and Geodetic Survey in 1891 because of budget restrictions and spent his last years in poverty. He wrote from 1857 until 1914 texts which were partly published (12,000 pages) and partly unpublished (80,000 pages of manuscripts).

His writings have been difficult to collect and edit and, for a long time, their organization was unclear and made their reading difficult. Nevertheless he exercised a deep, direct or indirect, influence in many intellectual areas. First he was recognized by his pragmatist peers as their pioneering predecessor. He had a long and fruitful correspondence with William James, who identified his early papers as the first source of the pragmatist doctrine. John Dewey was his student at Johns Hopkins University and often referred to him in his works, particularly in his efforts to theorize inquiry and community. Though he does not quote Peirce explicitly, Mead's (1934) conceptualization of the Self shows such striking convergences with Peirce's dialogical view of the mind that an indirect influence through Dewey seems probable. C.I. Lewis (1929), the last of the 'classical pragmatists', based his anti-positivist argument on Peirce's definition of meaning as that which makes a testable difference in experience. Peirce's influence on philosophers, expectable in the case of new pragmatists such as Rorty (1979) and Joas (1996), extends far beyond the pragmatist movement. It is acknowledged by Russell and Whitehead, for whom 'the effective founders of the American Renaissance are Charles Peirce and William James' (1936 letter to Hartshorne, published in Kline, 1989: 198). Quine credits several of his ideas to him (1951). Putnam bases his approach to reality and truth on the discussion of Peirce's views (1992). Popper considers him as one of the greatest philosophers and models his concept of 'finite falsifiability' on Peirce's idea of 'finite and fallible' thought. More recently Deleuze (1986, 1989) uses Peirce's semiotics in his critical work about cinema, calling him a 'surprising philosopher whom I find most extraordinary'. Habermas (1971) makes Peirce's concepts of inquiry and community a focus of his theory of communicative action.

Apart from philosophy, there are three specific areas where Peirce's influence is particularly significant. Firstly his semiotic theory appears as one of the major references in modern linguistics, semiotics, and philosophy of language, with such prominent scholars as Roman Jakobson and Umberto Eco acknowledging their debt to him in most of their works. Secondly his theories of sign and abduction are frequent references in cognitive sciences, knowledge engineering (Steiner, 2013; Cavaleri, 2004), and information systems (Ross, 2010). Thirdly Lacan's discovery of Peirce's triadic model paved the way for a stream of psychoanalysis focused on the triad 'symbolic, imaginary, and real': 'A man named Charles Sanders Peirce built a logic which, due to his focusing on relations, is triadic. I follow exactly the same track' (Lacan, quoted by Balat, 2000: 8). By contrast, Peirce's ideas have so far had a surprisingly limited influence on management and organization studies. They have occasionally been used in marketing, to analyse consumer behaviour (Ogilvie and Mizerski, 2011), or in the sociology of financial markets, to analyse the pragmatics of pricing and valuation (Muniesa, 2007). On the other hand, Peirce's concept of abduction—the narrative art of making new hypotheses—has been more extensively used by organization scholars, either to develop narrative approaches to organizational theory (Czarniawska, 1999a, 1999b), or as the 'logic of discovery' to discuss research methods, particularly for theory-building (Alvesson and Kärreman, 2007; Alvesson and Skoldberg, 2000; Hansen, 2008; Locke et al., 2008; Van Maanen, Sørensen, and Mitchell, 2007). It is also worth mentioning that the researchers who developed the communicational paradigm of organizing (Cooren et al., 2006) resorted to Peirce's theory of thirdness to develop a relational view of agency (Robichaud, 2006; Taylor and Van Every, 2011).

The limited impact of Peirce's ideas in management and organization studies may result from the strong influence of representational frameworks and the view of organizations as information processors (Simon, 1957, 1996), often criticized but still dominant. Peirce's reputation of obscurity may also deter some organization scholars from reading and using his works. It is rather unjustified since his style is accurate and complex, yet clear. For some time the huge amount of unorganized writings raised real access difficulties. This is no longer the case, thanks to the careful edition of selected texts by competent editors, in particular at Indiana University-Purdue University (Peirce Edition Project: Peirce 1992, 1998). Peirce can now be considered as a fairly accessible author.

10.3 PEIRCE'S THEORY OF MEDIATION AND SEMIOSIS: THE PROCESS OF MEANING

10.3.1 Meaning is Mediated

10.3.1.1 The Category of Thirdness

In his theory of sign, Peirce (1931–1958) distinguishes two categories of relationships between 'characters'. One is 'secondness', or the 'brute' action–reaction couple, with no interpretive mediation: ' "Secondness" = brute action of one substance on another, regardless of law or of any third subject' (Peirce, 1931–1958: 5.469). For example, an object falls into water, and there are circular waves: the connection between the falling object and the waves belongs to the secondness category. The other concept is 'thirdness', which implies a third element. If a word, or more generally a generic meaning, is given to a situation, e.g. if the waves on the surface of the water are designated as 'waves', using a word, this is thirdness. When I cut logs for next winter, there is no fire yet, but I (along with others) am imagining the fire in the hearth: this anticipation in the action in progress (cutting logs) and this projection into the future is required for the situation—in this example, my efforts to cut logs—to make meaning. The piece of wood is made to mean 'log' well before it is actually used as a log, by a specific meaning-making perspective (winter will require fire, fire requires logs...).

Peirce illustrates the importance of the 'thirdness' category with the example of a gift:

> Any mentality involves thirdness. Analyze for instance the relation involved in 'A gives B to C'. Now what is 'giving'? It does not consist [in] A's putting B away from him and C's subsequently taking B up. It is not necessary that any material transfer should take place. It consists in A's making C the possessor according to *Law*. There must be some kind of law before there can be any kind of giving. In A's putting away B, there is no thirdness. In C's taking B, there is no thirdness. But if you say that these two acts constitute a single operation, you transcend the mere brute fact, you introduce a mental element. (Peirce, 1931–1958: 1.26)

The concept ('law') of 'giving' is not observable per se (what people are 'visibly doing' is just A putting B away and C taking B up), but is a key component of the situation.

10.3.1.2 *The Triadic Sign: The Dynamics of Meaning*

Saussure (1913/1983) defined a sign as a 'signifier' (sound–image) / 'signified' (concept) dyad, linked by an arbitrary convention. He 'depicted it as static and inert, for signifiers were, in his view, fixed, not free, with respect to the linguistic community that uses [them]' (Emirbayer and Maynard, 2011: 229). Therefore, in the dyadic view, the practical situation plays hardly any role in meaning-making. The meaning of a sign is considered to proceed exclusively from its relationship with other signs within a socially established syntactic system. This leads to structuralist theories, which tend to be deconstructive, flat, and immanent (the structure endogenously determines its own evolution). Peirce proposed an alternative triadic theory of interpretation (Peirce, 1931–1958; Eco, 1988, 1992), in which a sign is not a representation X of Y, but a thing B ('representamen' in Peirce's terms) 'which stands to somebody for something ("object") *in some respect*' ('interpretant') (Peirce, 1931–1958: 2.228, my emphasis). The sign, then, relates an object O not to *one* signifier A, in a static correspondence, but to *two* representations, 'B represents O in respect of A'. This opens the sign to the world and sets meaning in motion: 'A *makes* O mean B', in a *move* from O-A to O-B. For example, if I say that this object in front of me is 'a table', my statement generates a meaning because the word 'table'—associated with this object here and now—evokes the social concept of 'table'—equally associated with this object. By using the word, I evoke the concept; by mentally evoking the concept, I call up the word, for example in a conversation, and the word–concept pair enables me to understand and use this singular object as what our society calls 'a table'. The triadic dimension is primal and cannot be split into dyads:

> A Sign, or *Representamen*, is a First which stands in such a genuine triadic relation to a Second, called its Object, as to be capable of determining a Third, called its Interpretant, to assume the same triadic relation to its Object in which it stands itself to the same Object. The triadic relation is genuine, that is, its three members are bound together by it in a way that does not consist in any complexus of dyadic relations. (Peirce, 1998: 272–3)

The meaning of the sign is not deterministic, but contingent: 'We constantly predict what is to be. Now what is to be can never become wholly past. In general, we may say that *meanings* are inexhaustible' (Peirce, 1931–1958: 1.343); 'no agglomeration of actual happenings can ever completely fill up the meaning of a "*would be*"' (Peirce, 1998: 402). Peirce often takes the example of technological devices (weathercock, thermometer, thermostat, weaving loom). When some user makes meaning of such a device, for example watches a weathercock to know the direction of the wind (Peirce, 1998: 406), the device can be considered as a triadic sign: to give the direction of the wind, it must be read as an expression of the general law that governs the relationship of a plane object with the wind, provided it can veer freely. The observer may check that the device is not jammed by rust, which would modify the meaning: the meaning is contingent because it is situated. If the device triggers automatic moves, for example when a thermometer regulates a heating system, it is no longer a triadic sign and contingency disappears.

10.3.1.3 *The Concept of Mediation*

On the one hand, the sign is singular and situated. For Peirce, the meaning of a sign does not lie in its syntactic relationship to other signs but is indexical, i.e. involves the social, situated, and oriented context of its use. Its interpretation requires 'collateral observation', widening observation from the sign itself to the utterance *situation*: 'the whole burden of the Sign must be ascertained, not by closer examination of the utterance, but by collateral observation of the utterer' (Peirce, 1998: 406), for example the utterer's position, gestures, mimics, looks. The same sentence, e.g. 'this is extraordinary!', uttered by someone reading a paper or someone looking out of the window may have a completely different meaning (Peirce, 1998: 406).

On the other hand, the interpretant has the nature of a generic law—for example, the social conventions corresponding to the 'gift' notion. It escapes the singularity of one particular subject and situation: 'the general has the nature of a sign' (Peirce, 1998: 341).

As a result, signs have two faces and simultaneously belong to situated experience and to generic classes of meaning abstracted from the situation. That is what is meant by 'mediation': it is the constitutive characteristic of a sign to belong simultaneously to a concrete and unique situation and to socially constructed classes of meaning, 'to convey an *idea* about a *thing*' (Peirce, 1998: 4); 'in addition to denoting objects, every sign signifies characters. We have a direct knowledge of real objects in every experiential reaction ... These are directly *hic et nunc*. But we extend the category and speak of numberless real objects with which we are not in direct reaction' (Peirce, 1998: 304). For example, the words of a language have generic meanings and a contextual sense. But Peirce's concept of sign is much broader than linguistic categories and extends to anything interpreted (Eco, 1988; Peirce, 1991: 28): concepts, objects, tools, images, mimics, acts, colours, persons, and so on. In this approach, mediation is not a contingent addition to action or thought, bound to improve its effectiveness, but an intrinsic property of *any* meaning process.

The 'interpretant' is the third element, what the sign triggers about its object. Peirce distinguishes three dimensions of interpretant: emotional, when the sign triggers an emotion; energetic, when it triggers an effort; logical, when it triggers ideas (Peirce, 1998: 409). This classification shows his constant desire to avoid any dualist separation between reasoning and emotion: 'in all cases, (the interpretant) includes feelings' (Peirce, 1998: 409). The word 'logical' should not be misunderstood. Imagination plays an important role in the 'logical' interpretant, to undertake 'experimentation in the inner world' (Peirce, 1998: 418) and to mentally test a proposition (Peirce, 1998: 432) by imagining its consequences.

10.3.1.4 *Mediation, Temporality, and Addressivity*

Semiotic mediation instantiates past and future, other spatial and social places, and the views of others in the production of meaning here and now. It is the key to temporality and sociality: whenever something is recognizable, this recognition links it with past experience, possible futures, distant places, recognition by others, and social communication.

Orientation towards the *future* is a key characteristic of triadic signs: 'thirdness is that which is what it is by virtue of imparting a quality to reactions *in the future*' (Peirce, 1931–1958: 1.343); 'if a prediction has a tendency to be fulfilled, it must be that future events have a tendency to conform to a general rule. A rule to which future events have a tendency to conform is *ipso facto* an important element in the happening of those events. This mode of being..., I call a Thirdness' (Peirce, 1931–1958: 1.26). Orientation towards the future (winter ⇒ fire ⇒ 'this piece of wood is a log') is coherent with the contingent nature of the sign, since possible futures are multiple.

The triadic sign also involves the *past*. Its interpretant is based on social experience. The notion of interpretant is closely linked to the pragmatist concept of 'habit', defined as the experience-based disposition to act or think in a given way under certain circumstances. A habit links activity in a singular context, here and now, with an experienced way of doing something, a social and generic 'how to do' (Taylor and Van Every, 2011: 23).

The sign is thus a move from the past to the future, from antecedent to successor, not only in logical terms, but also in temporal terms: 'the first is agent, the second patient, the third is the action by which the former influences the latter. Between the beginning as first, and the end as last, comes *the process which leads from first to last*' (Peirce, 1992: 250) (my emphasis). With semiotic mediation, meaning is a historical process.

Peirce also focuses on the social addressivity of signs: 'A sign addresses somebody, that is, creates in the mind of that person an equivalent sign, or perhaps a more developed sign' (Peirce, 1931–1958: 2.228). Peirce had the intuition that the sign is intrinsically dialogical: 'Signs mostly function each between two minds, of which one is the agent that utters the sign, while the other is the patient mind that interprets the sign' (Peirce, 1998: 403). Fusing the temporal and dialogical dimensions ('yesterday' speaks to 'tomorrow'), he extends the notion of dialogue to dialogues between two temporal states of the same mind: 'Even the imaginary signs called thoughts convey ideas from the mind of yesterday to the mind of tomorrow' (Peirce, 1998: 402). Thus he anticipates ideas about the ever-experiencing and social/dialogical Self that Mead will later develop (Mead, 1934). For Emirbayer and Maynard (2011: 228), 'with this focus on addressivity, Peirce made the theme of fundamental sociality one of the key ideas of the pragmatist tradition'.

10.3.1.5 *Meaning is Anchored in Practical Experience*

Thought is not a neutral process of giving names to things, but an ongoing process of transformation, handling things in order to keep experience going. Transformation is not necessarily material and visible—the transformation of habits can take place before concrete action itself visibly changes. But unlike Descartes' subject withdrawing from the world into the splendid ivory tower of her/his meditations, Peirce's man, even the survivor of a shipwreck on a desert island, is immersed in the acting turmoil of the world. Meaning is action and action is meaning: 'When a person *means* to do anything he is in some state in consequence of which the brute reactions between things will be molded [in] to conformity to the form to which the man's mind is itself molded. Not only will meaning always, in the long run, mold reactions to itself, but it is *only in doing so that its own being consists*' (Peirce, 1931–1958: 1.343) (my emphasis). Meaning is rooted in the transformation of practice. Hence Peirce's famous 'pragmatist maxim': 'a conception, that is, the rational purport of a word or other expression, lies exclusively in its conceivable bearing upon the conduct of life' (Peirce, 1998: 332).

Furthermore, Peirce stresses the materiality of signs: 'Since a sign is not identical with the thing signified, but differs from the latter in some respects, it must plainly have some characters which belong to it in itself, and have nothing to do with its representative function. These I call the material qualities of the sign' (Peirce, 1931–1958: 5.287). Here again is the dual nature of the Sign, as both a social representation and a material object: 'If a Sign is to have any active mode of being, it must be physically instantiated' (Queiroz and El Hani, 2006: 97). Signs are materially involved in the situation.

10.3.1.6 Peircian Mediation as an Anti-Dualist Framework

For Peirce, sign and mediation are neither psychological nor subjectivist concepts: 'Peirce is quite distant from any subjectivism' (Robichaud, 2006: 110). Long before Actor Network Theory (ANT), Peirce questions the subject/object dissymmetry: 'Thought is not necessarily connected with a brain. It appears in the work of bees, of crystals, and throughout the purely physical world; and one can no more deny that it is really there, than that the colors, the shapes, etc., of objects are really there. Not only is thought in the organic world, but it develops there' (Peirce, 1931–1958: 4.551). Peirce does not focus on the person's intention, but on the *form* to which the person's intention ('man's mind'), the actual act ('molded reactions'), and representations all conform, the *meaning* of the act rather than the *intention* of the acting subject, what makes the sign recognizable by the Self and Others, something eminently social. To distance himself from subjectivist approaches, he introduces the notion of 'quasi-minds', meaning-making instances which are not psychological subjects, criticizing the psychologist deviation of logic as 'unsound and insecure' (Peirce, 1998: 412). For Peirce 'we never bestow meaning on signs by acts of sheer will or intention or "stipulative" fiat...Man proposes, but the sign disposes' (Ransdell, 1992: 2–3).

The subject/object dualism is so ingrained in management and organization studies that it is not easy to really be rid of it. Even Robichaud (2006), an incisive reader of Peirce, occasionally refers the theory of thirdness to 'consciousness' and 'individual cognition' (2006: 108). He describes Peirce's triad in the gift example (A gives B to C) as the given object B + the donor subject A + the donee subject C. Rather than an *intersubjective* relationship between two individual subjects (donor and donee), mediated by the given object, Peirce describes an *intertextual* relationship between the project to change the ownership of B (be this project individual, collective, or institutional) and some perceptible sign of this giving, e.g. a physical gesture (holding out the object), a speech, the signature of a legal act, and so on. What he characterizes then as 'third' or 'interpretant' is not the given object B, but the social concept of gift, what he calls a 'law' and makes the giving action socially recognizable.

Peirce also rejects the formalist view of classical logic and the western inclination to abstraction. He focuses on 'knowing' as a situated process:

> Considered as a purely logical idea, mediation is only a general idea, a concept which is objectively inserted between two other concepts. (With Peirce) we must move from an abstract idea to *mediation as an action*. We must distinguish, for example, in a geometric demonstration, between an intermediate equality which allows us to assert the equality of two extremes, and *mediating in action*, the construction which allows us to observe those equalities. (Chenu, 1984: 81, my emphasis and translation)

While logical inferences express static classifications ('Socrates is a man...' = Socrates belongs to the class of men), pragmatist mediation opens new action possibilities. In the relationships 'cut wood = log', 'log = fire', 'fire = heating in winter', the sign '=' does not reflect syntactic equivalences or inclusions ('log' belongs to the general class of 'fuel for the fireplace', etc.), but *active* constructions of the future in a situated process: 'cutting logs for future fire' makes 'wood' mean 'logs'; it makes 'logs' mean 'fire', it makes 'fire' mean 'heating in winter'..., each step moving thought from one place to another, and from one period to another, in a kind of journey.

Mediation is not then a structuralist function, such as an abstract discursive operator in the development of a text. In the case of narrative practices, for example, Peirce's perspective would discard any separation between the narrative and the narrating process. Umberto Eco (1985), a follower of Peirce's theory of sign, analyses the 'active reception' of a text or a discourse by the reader or the listener and the co-production of sense by the official author and the receiver in the receiving situation.

Unlike Bergson, who unilaterally stresses the reductionist nature of language, for Peirce signs are intrinsically ambivalent. Admittedly they reduce the infinite potentiality of reality by adopting a specific meaning perspective, but at the same time they open new territories to action and thought. They close some doors to open others. For example, the act of segmenting the spectrum of light to named colours impoverishes the endless diversity of physical reality (the continuum of wave lengths), but it makes 'colours' a topic for discussion, literary texts, or technical descriptions. It does not achieve a structural ordering of the world, but it responds to practical necessities, for example Van Gogh's strong desire to describe his last paintings in his letters to his brother.

10.3.2 The Semiosis Process

10.3.2.1 Definition of Semiosis: Reality in Process

Semiosis is primarily the action of a triadic sign: 'By semiosis, I mean an action which involves a cooperation of three subjects, such as a sign, its object, and its interpretant, this tri-relative influence not being in any way resolvable into actions between pairs' (Peirce, 1998: 411). But through mediation, the triadic sign opens onto a new triad—the interpretant of the first triad triggering a new triad—and the recursive catenation of signs in a cascade of meaning-making moves, the *semiosis* process (Eco, 1988, 1992; Peirce, 1931–1958: 5.484): 'It is of the essential nature of a symbol that it determines an interpretant, which is itself a symbol' (Peirce, 1998: 322). The semiosis process is opposed to automatic determination, for example Pavlovian reflexes. It is the very process of thought, embedded in a process of action, and vice versa. At one time in his life, Peirce saw this process as endless: 'A symbol produces an endless series of interpretants' (Peirce, 1998: 323), but later he envisioned semiosis as leading to an 'ultimate logical interpretant', namely a change in habits—i.e. a change in the predispositions to act in certain ways under certain conditions, a learning move. Actually it does not make much difference: semiosis leads to changes in habits, new habits are translated into situated action, and action may at any time lead to an unexpected situation which triggers a new semiosis. Experience is continuous but *punctuated by events*.

Semiosis thrives on making indeterminate or vague things more and more determinate in a given direction, tending towards a limit without ever reaching it. Peirce is visibly inspired by the mathematical notion of 'series': a series of values which come closer and closer to a limit but never reach it. This limit is what he defines as 'reality'. It exists, it cannot be reached, but it can be approached in an endless convergence: 'every endless series must logically have a limit ... *Reality can only be regarded as the limit of the endless series of symbols*' (Peirce, 1998: 323, my emphasis). He borrows the concept of 'entelechy' from Aristotle to name this view of 'reality' as a limit: 'The very entelechy of being lies in being representable' (Peirce, 1998: 324), i.e. being involved in semiosis. Therefore Peirce could be called a '*processual realist*', a realist for whom reality exists as an ongoing process: 'Peirce's term for the actualizing event of interpretation is "entelechy". Reality, for Peirce, is not something already given, a positum, that waits passively for signs to come and represent it. Signs, rather, take part in the realization of the real ... *Reality therefore is an unfinished project*' (Bracken, 2007: 109, my emphasis), 'a kind of tendency' (Hausman, 1999: 290).

10.3.2.2 *Semiosis, a Teleological Process*

Semiosis is purposeful: signs can generate meanings only with regard to some purpose (Peirce, 1998: 393, 498). The process is *progress*, in a spatial, not an axiological sense, *towards* something: 'Peirce's conviction that evolution includes teleological direction is crucial to a view of evolution that does not stop with a restricted Darwinian view and recognizes that evolution does occur not simply as process as such, but as progress' (Hausman, 1999: 298). Therefore the process of semiosis is teleological—'the entire process will *tend toward* some unitary and unifying interpretant' (Ransdell, 1992: 10)—and directional: it is neither a random process nor a reversible move, it goes *from* A *to* B. Nevertheless we are far from cognitive means-ends models. Semiosis does not target precise and invariant goals. Its teleological orientation is immanent. It can re-purpose itself at any time: 'This is the basis for characterizing *semiosis processes as autonomous* or self-governing' (Ransdell, 1992: 6, my emphasis). When stating that semiosis is teleological, 'the type of teleology involved is tendential rather than intentional' (Ransdell, 1992: 16).

Thus the process of semiosis is neither random nor deterministic. The future of semiosis is plural and conditional: 'The species of future tense of the logical interpretant is that of the conditional mood, the "would-be"' (Peirce, 1998: 410). Each new sign 'binds time together', unifies what was plural, but at the same time makes new pluralities emerge (Peirce, 1991: 185).

10.3.2.3 *Semiosis, The Thread of a Melody*

The semiosis process is therefore not a linear succession of signs and the simple addition of fragments of meaning, but an *emergent* shape. Its meaning emerges from the temporal deployment of the process over time, like a melody:

> In a piece of music there are the separate notes and there is the air. A single tone may be prolonged for an hour or a day, and it exists as perfectly in each second of that time as in the whole taken together; so that, as long as it is sounding, it might be present to a sense from which everything in the past was as completely absent as the future itself. But it is different with the air, the performance of which occupies a certain time, during the portions of which only portions of it are played. It consists in an orderliness in the succession of sounds which strike the ear at different times; and to perceive it there must be some continuity of consciousness which makes the events of a lapse of time present to us. We certainly only perceive the air by hearing the separate notes; yet we cannot be said to directly hear it, for we hear only what is present at the instant, and *an orderliness of succession cannot exist in an instant*. These two sorts of objects, what we are *immediately* conscious of and what we are *mediately* conscious of, are found in all consciousness. Some elements (the sensations) are completely present at every instant so long as they last, while others (like thought) are actions having beginning, middle, and end, and consist in a congruence in the succession of sensations which flow through the mind...Thought is a thread of melody running through the succession of our sensations. (Peirce, 1992: 128–9)

The semiosis process thus is a 'thread of melody', which sets each moment of thought within a shape which emerges, deploys and evolves over time—as in a musical performance, each new tone finds its expected or unexpected place in an emerging melody.

10.4 CONTRIBUTIONS OF SEMIOSIS THEORY TO ORGANIZATION STUDIES

Peirce's thought can make a highly valuable contribution to process organization studies, strengthening their theoretical bases and opening up new avenues for research. In particular—this list is not intended to be exhaustive—it can help to: clarify the concept of process in the field of organization research; recover the central role and theoretical complexity of practices in organizing, often forgotten in organization studies; overcome the 'repetition versus change, continuity versus novelty' dichotomy; and deepen the analysis of time and historicity, dialogism and sociality, mediation and sociomateriality in organizing processes.

10.4.1 Clarification of the Process Concept

A key point for process organization studies is of course clarification of how it understands the 'process' concept. Are organizing processes deterministic or contingent, controlled by one or several subjects or autonomous, teleological, or autopoïetic?

Process-oriented organization research stresses the meaning-making dimension of organizing: the continuity of the organizing process is 'located in the meaning that actors attach to their actions' (Hernes, 2010: 176). An organizing process can thus be considered as a semiosis. In the light of Peirce's theory, this semiosis would be classified as contingent rather than deterministic. As soon as there is a triad, there is contingency, since A is connected to B *contingently* to C (Peirce, 1931–1958: 1.26), and possible futures are multiple. Organizing processes would also be viewed as autonomous rather than subjective: they do not conform to a subjective intentionality, but involve some unpredictable transformations. Last, following the distinction between secondness (e.g. automatic regulation) and thirdness (semiosis), organizing processes would appear 'allopoïetic' (pursuit of 'something else', with a structural opening to the environment) rather than 'autopoïetic' (self-generating their own specifications, with a structural and organizational closure): for example, a hospital practice does not evolve only to preserve its own existence, but to heal patients, and this opening to the partly unknown world can at any moment disrupt habits.

10.4.2 Overcoming Dualism: The Organizing Process as a Semiotic Recursion

Since it is situated, action faces unpredictable and unexpected events: 'Experience invariably teaches by means of *surprises*' (Peirce, 1998: 194). Surprises disrupt habits and trigger inquiries to adapt or redesign them. Inquiries combine three modes of thinking. Firstly, abduction—hypothesis construction: the 'only process by which a new element can be introduced into thought' (Peirce, 1998: 224)—tries to restore intelligibility by finding some acceptable hypothesis, i.e. some plausible narrative account of the disruptive situation. Then deduction—the strictly logical mode of reasoning—translates the hypothesis into testable propositions. Last, induction develops an experimentation protocol to test the propositions empirically (Peirce, 1998: 441–2), applying, for example, statistical rules for sampling, representativeness, and so on. The inquiry leads to new habits, which are not an 'absolute truth' (Peirce, 1998: 419) but fallible schemes of meaning involved in future experience and exposed to new potential disruptions.

Peirce agrees with Bergson (1946) that intuition, narratives, and metaphor play a key role in thinking. Like Bergson, he rejects the idea that intuition can be cognitive and views intuition and cognition as two different ways of thinking. But, unlike Bergson, Peirce does not oppose intuition to cognition as antagonistic processes. Rather, he sees them as different moments in the same inquiry process: '[for Peirce], intuitions can become cognitive and thus contribute to discursive, conceptual, cognitive experience' (Hausman, 1999: 295). In his theory of abduction and inquiry, Peirce describes a process which starts with a surprising experience, continues with the intuitive and narrative construction of a hypothesis, and then proceeds to logical reasoning and experimental testing. Here again, he avoids dualism by rejecting the intuition–cognition opposition.

Semiosis is the basic material of which the movement of inquiring and learning is made. It is a recursive process, combining habitual meaning-making and inquiries which recreate habits when they are disrupted. Habits establish a conditional future, a 'would-be', an expectation, a setting for new inquiries, and inquiries generate new habits. There can be no inquiry without habits, and no habit without inquiries (Dewey, 1938/1980); no association without dissociation; no continuity without discontinuity; no routine without change: 'there must be a *continuity* of *changeable* qualities' (Peirce, 1992: 323) (my emphasis). Habit disruption, inquiry, novelty, do not break the flow of thought and experience; on the contrary, the inquiry is a narrative process (Lorino et al., 2011; Lorino and Tricard, 2012) in which abduction attempts to re-weave the threads of experience through a plausible narrative. With the concept of abduction, Peirce bridges the gap between aesthetic judgement, intuitive 'flashes', narrative imagination, and logical reasoning. In economics and organization studies the theory of abduction has been used to analyse innovation processes (Nooteboom, 1999), narrative practices (Boje, 2001), and research methods (Alvesson and Kärreman, 2007; Alvesson and Skoldberg, 2000; Czarniawska, 1999a, 1999b; Hansen, 2007; Locke et al., 2008; Van Maanen et al., 2007).

The organizing process is precisely made of the 'shuttle which weaves together the woof and the warp of the fabric under construction in the semiosis' (Ransdell, 1992: 15), the woof of the habit and the warp of the inquiry. The essence of semiosis is the permanent *unification* of the disconnected elements of experience, 'synthetic consciousness binding time together' (Peirce, 1991: 185). Peirce defines 'synechism' as the basic continuity of the semiosis process, continuity of experience, continuity between mind and matter, between past and future, between repetition and change. 'Continuity' does not mean 'conservation': the process of semiosis allows the reciprocal transformation of situations through habits and transformation of habits through situated experience, in the same way as a language allows conversational practices and at the same time evolves through its conversational uses. Eco (1985: 56) summarizes Peirce's recursive view: 'The semiosis dies and rises from its ashes constantly...The repeated action which responds to a given sign in turn becomes a new sign...and starts a new interpreting process'. Mead (1934: 181) adopts this recursive view between activity ('gesture' and 'attitude') and sign ('symbol'), reflecting Peirce's semiosis concept: 'Through gestures responses are called out in our own attitudes, and as soon as they are called out they evoke, in turn, other attitudes. What was the meaning now becomes a symbol which has another meaning.'

10.4.3 Recovery of Practice, in its Complexity

As some authors have observed (Barley and Kunda, 2001), organization theories have tended to de-emphasize activity and practice as research objects. Recent developments in organization studies try to 'bring practice back in'. But practice-based organization studies do not always provide clear definitions of action and practice. Peirce can help to fill this gap. 'The whole function of thought is to produce habits of action' (Peirce, 1992: 131). Peirce criticizes the western intellectual tradition of identifying thought with abstract concepts and separating it from real-life experience:

> Peirce argued that 'Doubt' or confusions arising in experience are what occasion thought in the first place and that, in turn, the results of thought must always be subjected to the pragmatic test: 'Consider what effects, which might conceivably have practical bearings, we conceive the object of our conception to have. Then, our conception of these effects is the whole of our conception of the object' (Peirce, 1992: 132). (Emirbayer and Maynard, 2011: 225)

This does not make him an empiricist: 'If pragmaticism really made Doing to be the Be-all and the End-all of life, that would be its death. For to say that we live for the mere sake of action, as action, regardless of the thought it carries out, would be to say that there is no such thing as rational purport' (Peirce, 1998: 341).

To distance himself from simplistic empiricism, Peirce carefully makes the distinction between situated action—he speaks of 'effort', or 'action', or 'energetic interpretant'—and practice as an experience-based, socially constructed disposition, which he calls 'habit' or the 'ultimate logical interpretant'. Schatzki (2002, 2005) also makes a clear differentiation between 'activity', a situated occurrence, and 'practice', the 'social site' of activity, meaning by 'site' a field of possibilities which orientates activity without determining it. However, Schatzki basically sees the relationship between activity and practice as an *inclusion* relationship: 'human activities are inherently *part of* social practices' (2005: 468), while Peirce views this relationship as a semiotic mediation: any situated action is the sign of a habit, and a habit is the sign of concrete experience. It is not a 'vertical' relationship between general (practice) and particular (activity), between an archetype and a particular instantiation, but rather a 'horizontal', recursive relationship between action moulding habit and habit moulding action, the ongoing endeavour to build meaningful experience through multiple semiotic mediations: 'Living thought does not consist in including within categories' (Merleau-Ponty, 1945/2010: 810).

10.4.4 Semiosis and Historicity

The meaning of a sign depends on past signs and anticipates coming signs, in a process characterized by its non-reversible directionality:

> One of the most marked features about the law of mind is that it makes time to have a definite direction of flow from past to future. The relation of past to future is, in

reference to the law of mind, different from the relation of future to past. This makes one of the great contrasts between the law of mind and the law of physical force, where there is no more distinction between the two opposite directions in time than between moving northward and moving southward. (Peirce, 1992: 323)

This distinction between reversible 'time in physical force', compared with space, and irreversible time in mind, is strikingly similar to Bergson's analysis of time.

Mediation continuously instantiates past and future as past-in-present and future-in-present and makes history an active component of the present situation. The history of organizing processes is not a static archive but a permanent generative work. Semiosis designs multiple futures and, at the same time, reinvents the past. Not only is 'past experience projected upon possible futures' (Hernes and Maitlis, 2010: 29; Wiebe, 2010), but, conversely, the possible futures are projected upon the past to reshape it.

10.4.5 Dialogical Self and Sociality

Taylor and Van Every (2011) view Peirce's theory of thirdness as strictly individualistic and instantiates Peirce's abstract logical concepts of firstness and secondness as designation of subject (secondness) acting on object(firstness): 'Peircian presentation of thirdness has a missing dimension: it involves only one actor (a "second") relating to one object (a "first"). People accept to be the firstness to the secondness of someone else' (Taylor and Van Every, 2011: 34). Thirdness is then assimilated to a cognitive representation of action: 'a kind of cognitive map that people use to guide their actions' (Taylor and Van Every, 2011: 35). However, it seems difficult to justify such a subjectivist and representational reading of Peirce, whose theory of thirdness appears as a radical argument *against* subject–object dualism. He repeatedly stressed the dialogical nature of thought, based on the addressivity of signs: 'A sign may be defined as a medium for the *communication* of a form. It is necessary that there should be two, if not three, quasi-minds' (Peirce, 1998: 544, note 22); 'a sign addresses somebody' (Peirce, 1931–1958: 2.228); 'all thinking is necessarily a sort of dialogue' (Peirce, 1977: 195); 'it cannot be too often repeated that all thought is dialogue' (Peirce, 1905: 56, quoted in Colapietro, 1989: xiv). He makes clear, as Bakhtin (1981, 1984) does, that, by 'dialogue', he does not mean interaction between psychological subjects, but between meaning-making entities ('quasi-minds'): 'signs require at least two Quasi-minds. Accordingly, it is not merely a fact of human Psychology, but a necessity of Logic, that every logical evolution of thought should be dialogic' (Peirce, 1931–1958: 4.551).

This debate between subjectivist and dialogical views is not simply an academic dispute about Peirce's ideas. It directly questions the nature of organizations, as shared representations or as dialogical processes. Subjectivism and the view of thirdness as a mental representation embodied in human subjects unavoidably raise the question: 'how is it possible that actors act together and share the sense of situations?', leading to the answer: 'collective action is possible because mental representations are *shared*'.

In this representationalist view, organization then appears as a set of shared representations (Simon, 1996), a figure of *commonality* (Taylor and Van Every, 2011). In the dialogical view, organizing appears as the continuous process of making sense of situations through dialogical interactions. Meaning does not have to be shared, just the opposite: if meanings are shared, there is no fuel for dialogue. Meaning rather appears as an emerging and never completely achieved pattern. It allows to overcome such dichotomies as 'individual–collective', 'individual–organizational', or 'microlevel–macrolevel'. Semiosis describes 'collective' and 'social' as permanent dialogical dynamics rather than 'macro-structures' which subsume the 'microlevel' of activity.

Like Mead (1934), Vygotsky (1986), and Bakhtin (1981), Peirce observes that, even in the case of lonely meditation, thought has a dialogic nature, because the Self is intrinsically dialogic. The 'I' addresses the 'me': 'Meditation is dialogue. "I says to myself, says I" is the vernacular account of it' (Peirce, 1979: 258–9). This dialogue is also a dialogue between today's and tomorrow's Self, 'every reasoning appealing to the self of the near following moment of time for assent' (Peirce, 1998: 429). The Self is social and inhabited by multiple identities and voices, since, for Peirce, 'the dialogical self is "multi-voiced" (Hermans, 2001)' (Raggatt, 2010: 400).

Thus the thinker is not an 'individual': '[it is] all-important to remember that a person is not absolutely an individual. His thoughts are "what he is saying to himself", that is, is saying to that other self that is just coming into life in the flow of time' (Peirce, 1998: 338). The interpretant is not psychological but social. The sign is a kind of 'forum' where multiple 'quasi-minds' meet, agree on meaning, and produce habits together. As a result, dialogical semiosis paves the way for sociality and gives birth to communities of interpreters (Peirce, 1992: 54–5): 'In such a community, dialogue can proceed in respect to the interpretation and adjudication of competing truth-claims, and a "settlement of opinion" can ultimately be brought about as "the result of investigation carried sufficiently far"…That communitarian dimension anticipated ethnomethodology's thrust into the empirical sphere of actual social relations' (Emirbayer and Maynard, 2011: 228–9).

10.4.6 Beyond the 'Sociomateriality' Syncretism, Sociomateriality as Semiotic Mediation

For the last 20 years, social studies of science, and more recently organization studies, have questioned the traditional separation between social phenomena and material/technological artefacts. These critiques have led to new accounts of organizational processes in terms of 'constitutive entanglement of sociality and materiality' (Barad, 2003), 'sociality with objects' (Knorr-Cetina, 1997), or sociomateriality (Orlikowski, 2007). Such expressions express the desire to reassemble what was unduly separated (social and material), but actually keep sociality and materiality as categories. While fusing 'sociality' and 'materiality' into 'sociomateriality' is a useful deconstructive phase in the critique of dualism, it is necessary to go further. How can we overcome the social–material dichotomy and find other analytical concepts to open the 'black box' of 'sociomateriality'? What exactly happens when so-called 'materiality' is engaged in so-called 'social' practices? Can we free ourselves from the dual categories of 'social' and 'material'?

Peirce stresses the indissolubly social and material nature of semiotic mediation in human activity. All his work is a critique of the separation between the 'material' and the 'social'. The sign is intrinsically material *and* social—like a written or uttered discourse. In the triadic sign, all three elements (object, representation, interpretant) are social *and* material, and they involve, not subjective issues of intentionality, but issues of social/ cultural meaning. This concept of mediation thus opens up an avenue for 'sociomateriality' studies to analyse material arrangements as semiotic mediations of organized activity. 'Material objects' are inseparably linked with 'social habits'. The actual use of a material device results from structural constraints and abilities, cultural habits (habitual uses), and situated inquiries to adapt habits in concrete situations. The 'material' device is *used* if it *means* something. It is not perceived as a static set of objective attributes, which are potentially endless, but as a set of emergent meanings, close to Gibson's (1986) and Norman's (1990) 'affordances' or Actor Network Theory 'inscriptions' (Akrich, 2006: 163): action possibilities.

Semiotic mediations, both in their symbolic and material dimensions, produce practical effects. Peirce stresses the performativity of signs, for example words and principles: 'Words do produce physical effects. It is madness to deny it' (Peirce, 1998: 184); 'general principles are really operative in nature' (Peirce, 1991: 244); 'the power of representations to cause real facts' (1931–1958: 2.322). Those practical effects can be predicted 'only to a limited extent, owing to our typically incomplete understanding of what the generative powers of a given sign actually are' (Ransdell, 1992: 2).

Peirce's insistence on the materiality and autonomous performativity of signs led him to give much attention to scientific tooling, in particular metrological devices, as a key component of scientific inquiries. For years he did his best to develop invariable standards of length (Lenzen, 1965), pioneering the idea of adopting a standard of length based on the length of a light wave. He also developed graphical heuristics—'existential graphs'—to represent schemes of reasoning in debatable ways. He gave much consideration to statistical methods that he viewed as the quintessence of inductive reasoning (Peirce, 1931–1958: 2.268) and a key tool for inquiries. It is interesting to report here an example of intellectual journey: the migration of pragmatist ideas, from philosophy to mathematics, then to graphical tooling, and to manufacturing practices (Mauléon and Bergman, 2009). The philosopher C.I. Lewis (1929), a follower of Peirce, stressed the importance of empirical and inductive verification. Shewhart (1939), referring to Lewis, theorized quality control in manufacturing as a semiosis, analysed the regularity and irregularity of manufacturing processes, developed their statistical control, and designed control cards including the graphical transcription of physical measurements (control curves). One of the pioneers of total quality control, Deming (1994), disciple of Shewhart and reader of Lewis, focused on managerial quality inquiries ('Deming wheel') involving control cards as material mediations. Since then manufacturing engineers often use control curves as taken-for-granted manifestations of scientific truth, ignoring their underlying theories. Thus thirdness disappeared and was replaced by secondness, with the automatic reading of graphical records.

Like Peirce, Actor Network Theory (ANT) questions the intrinsic relevance of the 'sociality' and 'materiality' categories, but it does not adopt Peirce's distinction between thirdness and secondness. For example, Latour (1993: 25–32) studies the case of the safety belt in a car that cannot be started until the driver fastens it. He observes that the belt displays a type of agency in opposing the human actor's agency. In Peirce's terms, this is an obvious example of 'secondness', brute action–reaction: the belt locks the starting system through automatic regulation. Latour reads the sociomaterial situation as a sequence of A-B, B-C dyads (driver/belt, belt/engine, driver/engine), in which the coupling of the belt and the starting system is a mechanical effect. This leads to such questions as: 'shall I fasten the belt or try to start the engine in spite of the unfastened belt?', 'do I put up with this constraint?', 'does fastening the belt become an unconscious habit?' But if we go a step further, broaden the boundaries of the situation in a thirdness perspective, and include the designer of the device in the situation, we can instil thirdness and semiosis into the situation. The connection between the safety belt and the engine expresses such interpretants as: 'the belt makes driving safer', 'now drivers have a tendency not to fasten it', 'but it is technically possible to use automated coupling' . . . By reintroducing a form of 'telos', i.e. finality, purpose, projection *towards* some image of the future, into the situation (Robichaud, 2006; Taylor and Van Every, 2011), we can read it as a (driver's gesture/designer's representation/engine reactions) triad, which expresses a certain view of driver psychology and safety. This can then raise other questions, such as: 'is this an effective strategy to improve safety?' The belt is a quasi-mind which voices the designer's past interpretants. It can generate immediate local actions, but also mediate distant actions, such as modifying the design of the device, viewed as a sign and not only as a non-human actant.

10.4.7 Research as a Dialogical and Mediated Inquiry

Is there a 'Peircian method' in organization research? What would a field study based on his ideas look like? As any form of knowledge construction, organization research is an inquiry, i.e. a close combination of narrative imagination, logical thinking, and experimental action. Since action is meaning and meaning is action, the research inquiry is an active transformation of the situation. Knowledge building requires an active involvement and a dialogical relationship between the researcher and field actors. Such dialogical inquiries (Lorino et al., 2011) are very far from 'neutral observation' and 'accurate descriptions' by researchers-outsiders who should hunt any 'subjective bias'. It looks like an 'observing participation' rather than a 'participant observation'. The epistemological and methodological debate about 'objectivity versus subjectivity', according to Peirce, is meaningless.

It does not mean that researchers' subjectivity can freely blossom. Beyond the opinions of participants, the conclusions of the inquiry are always conditional and must be validated. Validation, however, is not a correspondence validation: it does not consist in controlling the correspondence between models and reality. It is a praxis validation: it consists in evaluating the practical effects of the research inquiry. Do new habits (possibly purely conceptual habits) allow the felicitous continuation of experience?

Complete inquiries, with all their phases (abductive hypothesizing, deductive reasoning, inductive testing), are often long and complex social processes. Research projects, for lack of time and resources, cannot always achieve the complete inquiring process. They can be limited to a few phases of the inquiry: concept and theory-building in response to disruptive situations (abduction), theoretical development of a hypothesis to translate it into testable propositions (deduction), experimental verification (induction). But whatever the phase in which research takes place, in Peirce's view, researchers' inquiries should always respond to doubts and can only be validated through experimentation and social judgment.

10.5 CONCLUSION: THE ARROW OF SEMIOSIS

Organization research has used Peirce's ideas sparingly: abduction applied to organizational innovation or research methodology, thirdness applied to communicational/intersubjective agency, semiotics applied to social signs like prices. But organization studies are still often influenced by structural categories and classifying approaches, for example hierarchical inclusions of sub-species within species, signifier–signified dyads, or 'action–thought', 'real–symbolic', 'intentional–unintentional', 'individual–collective', or 'micro–macro level' dichotomies. Peirce proposes a challenging view of meaning as a process (the semiosis) always in the making, a process that is historical, dialogical, and teleological. This process is not only purposeful, but also purposing: it continuously adapts or recreates the purpose of action. The semiosis crosses and links situations, fields of knowledge, space, and time, in an ever-moving attempt to make sense of and narrate the story of living experience in progress. The basic component of meaning is triadic, which means not only that objects, languages, tools, and institutions are engaged in situated meaning-making and mediate it, but also that situated action mediates the ongoing transformation of languages, tools, and institutions. The pragmatist theory of sign and meaning can thus articulate different aspects of process approaches to organizations, such as practices, mediation, dialogism, discursivity, sociomateriality, performativity, and sense-making, by founding them upon the theory of semiosis: mean-*ing* as a process. Peirce's analyses can make a significant contribution to clarifying concepts, avoiding dualisms, overcoming unsolvable dilemmas, and thus consolidating the theoretical foundations of process organization studies.

References

Akrich, M. (2006). La description des objets techniques, in M. Akrich, M. Callon, and B. Latour (eds), *Sociologie de la traduction. Textes fondateurs* (Paris: Presses des Mines de Paris): 159–78. English translation: The Description of Technical Objects, in W.E. Bijker and J. Law (eds), *Shaping Technology / Building Society* (Cambridge, MA: MIT Press, 1992): 205–24.

Alvesson, M. and Kärreman, D. (2007). Constructing Mystery: Empirical Matters in Theory Development, *Academy of Management Review* 32(4): 1265–81.

——and Skoldberg, K. (2000). *Reflexive Methodology* (London: Sage).

Bakhtin, M. (1981). *The Dialogic Imagination. Four Essays*, ed. M. Holquist (Austin: University of Texas Press).

——(1984). *Problems of Dostoevsky's Poetics*, ed. and trans. C. Emerson (Minneapolis: University of Minnesota Press).

Balat, M. (2000). *Des Fondements Sémiotiques de la Psychanalyse. Peirce après Freud et Lacan* (Paris: L'Harmattan).

Barad, K. (2003). Posthumanist Performativity: Toward an Understanding of How Matter Comes to Matter, *Signs: Journal of Women in Culture and Society* 28(3): 801–31.

Barley, S.R. and Kunda, G. (2001). Bringing Work Back In, *Organization Science* 12(1): 76–95.

Bergson, H. (1946). *The Creative Mind*, trans. M.L. Andison (New York: Philosophical Library).

Boje, D. (2001). *Narrative Methods for Organizational and Communication Research* (London: Sage).

Bracken, C. (2007). *Magical Criticism: The Recourse of Savage Philosophy* (Chicago: University of Chicago Press).

Cassirer, E. (1923/1955). *Philosophy of Symbolic Forms, Volume I: Language* (New Haven: Yale University Press).

Cavaleri, S. (2004). Principles for Designing Pragmatic Knowledge Management Systems, *Learning Organization* 11(4/5): 312–21.

Chenu, J. (1984). Essai introductif, in C.S. Peirce, *Textes anticartésiens* (Paris: Aubier): 11–170.

Colapietro, V.M. (1989). *Peirce's Approach to the Self. A Semiotic Perspective on Human Subjectivity* (Albany: State University of New York Press).

Cooren, F., Taylor, J.R., and Van Every, E.J. (2006). *Communication as Organizing* (Mahwah, NJ: Lawrence Erlbaum).

Czarniawska, B. (1999a). Management She Wrote: Organization Studies and Detective Stories, *Culture and Organization* 5(1): 13–41.

——(1999b). *Writing Management: Organization Theory as a Literary Genre* (Oxford: Oxford University Press).

Deleuze, G. (1986). *Cinema 1: The Movement Image*, trans. H. Tomlinson and B. Habberjam (Minneapolis: University of Minnesota Press).

—— (1989). *Cinema 2: The Time Image*, trans. H. Tomlinson and R. Galeta (Minneapolis: University of Minnesota Press).

Deming, W.E. (1994). *The New Economics for Industry, Government, Education*, 2nd edn (Cambridge, MA: MIT Press).

Dewey, J. (1938/1980). *Logic: The Theory of Inquiry* (New York: Holt, reprinted 1980 New York: Irvington Publishers).

Eco, U. (1985). *Lector In Fabula* (Paris: Grasset and Fasquelle).

——(1988). *Le signe* (Brussels: Editions Labor).

—— (1992). *Interpretation and Overinterpretation*, ed. S. Collini (Cambridge: Cambridge University Press).

Emirbayer, M. and Maynard, D.W. (2011). Pragmatism and Ethnomethodology, *Qualitative Sociology 34*: 221–61.

Gibson, J.J. (1986). *The Ecological Approach to Visual Perception* (Hillsdale, NJ: Lawrence Erlbaum Associates).

Habermas, J. (1971). *Knowledge and Human Interests*, trans. J.J. Shapiro (Boston: Beacon).

Hansen, H. (2008). Abduction, in D. Barry and H. Hansen (eds), *The Sage Handbook of the New and Emerging in Management and Organization* (London: Sage Publications): 454–63.

Hausman, C.R. (1999). Bergson, Peirce, and Reflective Intuition, *Process Studies 28*(3–4): 289–300.

Hermans, H.J.M. (2001). The Dialogical Self: Toward a Theory of Personal and Cultural Positioning, *Culture and Psychology 7*: 243–81.

Hernes, T. (2010). Actor-Network Theory, Callon's Scallops, and Process-Based Organization Studies, in T. Hernes and S. Maitlis (eds), *Process, Sensemaking and Organizing* (Oxford: Oxford University Press): 161–84.

——and Maitlis, S. (2010). *Process, Sensemaking, and Organizing* (Oxford: Oxford University Press).

Joas, H. (1996). *The Creativity of Action* (Cambridge: Polity Press).

Kline, G.L. (ed.) (1989). *Alfred North Whitehead. Essays on His Philosophy* (Lanham, MD: University Press of America).

Knorr-Cetina, K. (1997). Sociality With Objects. Social Relations in Postsocial Knowledge Society, *Theory, Culture and Society 14*(4): 1–30.

Latour, B. (1993). *Petites leçons de sociologie des sciences* (Paris: La Découverte).

Lenzen, V.F. (1965). The Contributions of Charles S. Peirce to Metrology, *Proceedings of the American Philosophical Society 109*(1): 29–46.

Lewis, C.I. (1929). *Mind and the World Order: Outline of a Theory of Knowledge* (New York: Dover).

Locke, K., Golden-Biddle, K., and Feldman, M.S. (2008). Making Doubt Generative: Rethinking the Role of Doubt in the Research Process, *Organization Science 19*(6): 907–18.

Lorino, P. and Tricard, B. (2012). The Bakhtinian Theory of Chronotope (Time-Space Frame) Applied to the Organizing Process, in M. Schultz, S. Maguire, A. Langley, and H. Tsoukas (eds), *Perspectives on Process Organization Studies, Volume 2: Constructing Identity in and around Organizations* (Oxford: Oxford University Press): 201–34.

—— and Clot, Y. (2011). Research Methods for Non-Representational Approaches to Organizational Complexity: The Dialogical Mediated Inquiry, *Organization Studies 32*(6): 769–801.

Mauléon, C. and Bergman, B. (2009). Exploring the Epistemological Origins of Shewhart's and Deming's Theory of Quality. Influences from C.I. Lewis' Conceptualistic Pragmatism, *International Journal of Quality and Service Sciences 1*(2): 160–71.

Mead, G.H. (1934). *Mind, Self and Society from the Standpoint of a Social Behaviourist* (Chicago: University of Chicago Press).

Merleau-Ponty, M. (1945/2010). *Phénoménologie de la perception*, in M. Merleau-Ponty, *Œuvres*, ed. C. Lefort (Paris: Quarto-Gallimard, 2010): 655–1167. English translation: *Phenomenology of Perception* (London and Henley: Routledge and Kegan Paul Ltd, 1962/1978).

Muniesa, F. (2007). Market technologies and the pragmatics of price, *Economy and Society* 36(3): 377–95.

Nooteboom, B. (1999). Innovation, Learning, and Industrial Organisation, *Cambridge Journal of Economics* 23(2): 127–50.

Norman, D.A. (1990). *The Design of Everyday Things* (New York: Doubleday).

Ogilvie, M. and Mizerski, K. (2011). Using Semiotics in Consumer Research to Understand Everyday Phenomena, *International Journal of Market Research* 53(5): 651–68.

Orlikowski, W.J. (2007). Sociomaterial Practices: Exploring Technology at Work, *Organization Studies* 28(09): 1435–48.

Peirce, C.S. (1931–1958). *The Collected Papers of Charles Sanders Peirce*, ed. C. Hartshorne and P. Weiss (Volumes 1–6), A. Burks (Volumes 7–8) (Cambridge, MA: Harvard University Press). For Peirce's *The Collected Papers*, this chapter adopts the tradition of referring to parts/sub-parts rather than to page numbers.

—— (1977). *Semiotic and Significs: The Correspondence Between Charles S. Peirce and Victoria Lady Welby.* Ed. Charles S. Hardwick & J. Cook (1977) Bloomington, IN: Indiana University Press.

—— (1979). *Charles Sanders Peirce: Contributions to the Nation. Part Three: 1901–1908*, ed. K.L. Ketner and J.E. Cook (Lubbock: Texas Tech Press).

—— (1991). *Peirce on Signs*, ed. J. Hoopes (Chapel Hill, NC: University of North Carolina Press).

—— (1992). *The Essential Peirce, volume 1*, ed. N. Houser and C. Kloesel (Bloomington: Indiana University Press).

—— (1998). *The Essential Peirce, volume 2*, Peirce Edition Project (Bloomington: Indiana University Press).

Putnam, H. (1990). *Realism with a Human Face* (Cambridge, MA: Harvard University Press).

—— (1992). *Renewing Philosophy* (Cambridge, MA: Harvard University Press).

Queiroz, J. and El-Hani, C.N. (2006). Semiosis as an Emergent Process, *Transactions of the Charles S. Peirce Society: A Quarterly Journal in American Philosophy* 42(1): 78–116.

Quine, W.V.O. (1951). Two Dogmas of Empiricism, *The Philosophical Review* 60: 20–43. Reprinted in his *From a Logical Point of View* (Cambridge, MA: Harvard University Press, 1953; second revised edition, 1980): 20–46.

Raggatt, P.T.F. (2010). The Dialogical Self and Thirdness: A Semiotic Approach to Positioning Using Dialogical Triads, *Theory and Psychology* 20(3): 400–19.

Ransdell, J. (1992). Teleology and the Autonomy of the Semiosis Process, in M. Balat and J. Deledalle-Rhodes (eds), *Signs of Humanity / L'homme et ses signes, vol. 1* (Berlin: Mouton de Gruyter), <http://www.cspeirce.com/menu/library/aboutcsp/ransdell/autonomy.htm>. Referenced numbers are not pages but paragraphs.

Robichaud, D. (2006). Steps Toward a Relational View of Agency, in F. Cooren, J.R. Taylor, and E.J. Van Every, *Communication as Organizing* (Mahwah, NJ: Lawrence Erlbaum): 101–14.

Rorty, R. (1979). *Philosophy and the Mirror of Nature* (Princeton: Princeton University Press).

Ross, J.M. (2010). Informatics Creativity: A Role for Abductive Reasoning?, *Communications of the ACM* 53(2): 144–8.

Saussure, F. de. (1913/1983). *Course in General Linguistics*, ed. C. Bally and A. Sechehaye, trans. R. Harris (La Salle, IL: Open Court). First published in French: *Cours de linguistique générale* (Paris: Payot, 1913).

Schatzki, T.R. (2002). *The Site of the Social. A Philosophical Account of the Constitution of Social Life and Change* (University Park: The Pennsylvania State University Press).

—— (2005). Peripheral Vision: The Sites of Organizations, *Organization Studies* 26(3): 465–84.

Shewhart, W.A. (1939). *Statistical Method from the Viewpoint of Quality Control* (Washington, DC: Dover Publications).

Simon, H.A. (1957). *Administrative Behavior: A Study of Decision-Making Processes in Administrative Organization*, 2nd edn (New York: Macmillan).

——(1996). *The Sciences of the Artificial* (Cambridge, MA: The MIT Press).

Steiner, P. (2013). C.S. Peirce and Artificial Intelligence: Historical Heritage and (New) Theoretical Stakes, in V. Müller (ed.), *Philosophy and Theory of Artificial Intelligence*. Series: Studies in Applied Philosophy, Epistemology and Rational Ethics, Volume 5 (Berlin: Springer): 265–76.

Taylor, J.R. and Van Every, E.J. (2011). *The Situated Organization. Case Studies in the Pragmatics of Organization Research* (New York: Routledge).

Van Maanen, J., Sørensen, J.B., and Mitchell, T.R. (2007). The Interplay between Theory and Method, *Academy of Management Review* 32(4): 1145–54.

Vygotsky, L.S. (1986). *Thought and Language* (Cambridge, MA: The MIT Press).

Wiebe, E. (2010). Temporal Sensemaking: Managers' Use of Time to Frame Organizational Change, in T. Hernes and S. Maitlis (eds), *Process, Sensemaking and Organizing* (Oxford: Oxford University Press): 213–41.

CHAPTER 11

....

WILLIAM JAMES (1842–1910)

....

THOMAS C. POWELL

11.1 INTRODUCTION

....

MORE THAN 100 years after his death, William James remains America's greatest psychologist and philosopher. *Principles of Psychology* (1890a, 1890b) was the most influential
psychology textbook of its time; James' vivid account of the mind's 'stream of consciousness' inspired generations of psychologists, philosophers, and social scientists; his 'radical empiricism' laid the foundation for twentieth-century American epistemology;
and his pragmatism remains at the forefront of philosophical debate in the twenty-first
century. During James' lifetime, his ideas were debated and admired by an impressive
cross-section of European intelligentsia, including Ernst Mach, Henri Bergson, Alfred
North Whitehead, Bertrand Russell, Sigmund Freud, Edmund Husserl, and Ludwig
Wittgenstein. According to American philosopher John McDermott, 'William James is
to classic American philosophy as Plato was to Greek and Roman philosophy, an originating and inspirational fountainhead' (quoted in Richardson, 2006: xiv).

James' work influenced three major streams of social research—process philosophy,
phenomenology, and functionalism—and each of these left a deep imprint on management studies. As process philosopher, James influenced Whitehead and gave birth to a
new philosophy of change; as phenomenologist, James influenced Husserl and Schutz,
and foreshadowed a constructionist view of social relations; as functionalist, James
altered the course of twentieth-century empirical philosophy through his influence on
Russell and Wittgenstein, and introduced experimental, cognitive, and evolutionary
psychology to America. These were some of the impacts of his *first* book, *Principles of
Psychology*, long before his major works on pragmatism, religious experience, radical
empiricism, pluralism, education, and metaphysics.

William James' thought resists easy abridgement or summation. His work emanates
from a deeply held belief that all enquiry, whether in science, literature, or metaphysics,
is a fundamentally *human* enterprise, a narrative told by humans about how it feels to

be human. James regarded the stream of consciousness as a window to the way things are, and the task of the philosopher-psychologist as reporting what happens there as truly and completely as possible. A true report must include chaos as well as order, flow as well as constancy, discord as well as harmony. Everything in human consciousness *counts*, whether we understand it or not, whether we can measure it or not, whether we like it or not. Our explanations are accountable to experience and not to the concepts we devise to explain it; and if the concepts fail, then perhaps we have learned an even bigger lesson: that human experience is not the kind of thing that goes into a theory. As an educational theorist wrote: 'For James, the universe was not a system, hence needed no system to portray it' (Weber, 1960: 247).

William James believed in pluralism and change, and his evocative language inspired the imagery of process philosophy: the 'blooming, buzzing confusion' of a baby's consciousness; the 'aurora borealis' of change; the 'flights and perchings' of the stream of thought; life as a 'snowflake caught in the warm hand'. But James believed in many other things too, and it is James' *many-otherness* that gave his process philosophy its expansive character. He mixed process philosophy with brain science, art, hard empiricism, and religious sentiments, and he took intellectual risks in combining them and driving them to the limits of contradiction. Perhaps his greatest legacy was putting into practice what he told his student Gertrude Stein: 'Keep your mind open' (Stein, 1933: 87).

James' philosophical pluralism was matched, to an unusual degree, by the pluralism of his life. Section 11.2 gives an account of James' family upbringing and intellectual development. Section 11.2.1 discusses the origins and content of *Principles of Psychology*, and shows how *Principles* set the stage for James' later contributions to philosophy and psychology. Sections 11.3–11.5 review James' contributions to three branches of social research—process philosophy, interpretivism, and functionalism—and discuss their impacts on research in management studies.

11.2 WILLIAM JAMES

William James was born in New York City on January 11, 1842, in the Astor House, then the most famous hotel in America. A few days later, his parents moved him to their new brownstone in an elegant neighbourhood near Washington Square, a neighbourhood his younger brother, the novelist Henry James, later described as 'the ideal of quiet and genteel retirement'. The house at 21 Washington Place was demolished in James' lifetime—'amputated' is how his brother Henry put it—and the property is now part of New York University.

William's father, Henry James, Sr., inherited a fortune from his father and then established himself as a writer and lecturer on theology, aesthetics, and moral philosophy. Henry was lively, cultivated, and well connected, and, according to poet James Russell Lowell, 'the best talker in America' (Richardson, 2006: 26). Under the influence of mystic Emanuel Swedenborg, and inspired by Emerson, Thoreau, Carlyle, Tennyson,

Thackeray, and John Stuart Mill, all of whom he knew personally, Henry, Sr. expostulated on nearly every subject and preached his own eccentric brand of natural mysticism.

When William was three months old, the family home was visited by Ralph Waldo Emerson, already a legendary figure in America, who was mourning the death of his five-year-old son Waldo. According to a James biographer, Emerson 'gave his blessing to the babe, in what might be regarded as a prophetic event for the future philosopher of Pragmatism' (Allen, 1967: 13).

Henry James, Sr. had a large tolerance for disruption. When William was a year old, his father sold the house on Washington Place, moved the family to London, then to Paris, then back to London, and then back to New York, where they took a home near Union Square. William studied first with private tutors, then in a succession of academies in Paris, London, Geneva, Bonn, Boulogne-sur-Mer, and Newport, Rhode Island. In England, the family lived for a while at Frogmore Cottage, in the grounds of Windsor Castle, and then at 3 Berkeley Square in London, where William was tutored by the man who later taught Robert Louis Stevenson.

Unlike his brother Henry, who devoted himself to writing, William 'got his plans into a tangle and talked one moment of doing one thing and the next of doing another' (Allen, 1967: 208). As a teenager, he studied painting with Cogniet in Paris, and with William Morris Hunt in Rhode Island; but he enjoyed experimental science, conducting home experiments with batteries and dangerous chemicals in a dining room full of wires, microscopes, beakers, and bunsen burners. William's friends considered him warm, well adjusted, and happy, and his father said 'I never knew a child of so much principle' (Allen, 1967: 45); but William suffered from vague illnesses and severe bouts of depression, and his brother remembered his 'boldly disinterested absorption of curious drugs' (Allen, 1967: 48). William's health problems and sedentary pursuits—reading, writing, experimenting, painting—suited him for a life of monastic scholarship; but he loved the outdoors and postponed medical school for an expedition down the Amazon, collecting specimens with zoologist Louis Aggasiz.

After taking a degree in anatomy from Harvard, William spent 18 months in Germany, ostensibly for his health, but reading obsessively in philosophy, psychology, and European literature, and taking physiology labs and coursework in leading German universities. He read the poetry of Goethe and Schiller, and the philosophy of Kant, Hegel, and Schopenhauer. He suffered a near-suicidal bout of depression, and while in Germany his thoughts turned increasingly to psychology. Lab work in experimental physiology had convinced him that not all mental disorders have a physiological basis, and he took solace from the writings of French philosopher Charles Renouvier, who emphasized belief and freedom of choice.

Returning to Harvard, James finished his graduate studies and received a medical degree in 1871. The following year, at age 30, he was appointed to teach physiology at Harvard. The next year, he agreed to lead the department of physiology, but only on condition that he be allowed to 'fight it out in the line of mental science' (Allen, 1967: 181). Soon, James had established the first psychology lab in America, admitted the first doctoral student in psychology (G. Stanley Hall, later a prominent American psychologist), and taught a new graduate course called 'The Relations between Physiology and Psychology'. Psychology as an academic discipline had come to America, and the lecture notes for James' new course became *Principles of Psychology*.

11.2.1 *Principles of Psychology* (1890)

The period 1878 to 1890—when James was writing *Principles of Psychology*—was not so different from today. The latest thing in psychology was the connection between human behaviour and the brain. Empirical research was becoming more experimental and the latest theory was evolutionary psychology (Darwin's *On the Origin of Species* had appeared in 1859).

But psychology was still in its infancy. Scientists knew little about the limits of human sensation—for example, bandwidths of audible perception or skin sensitivities to pressure—and little about human memory, attention, or learning. They knew almost nothing about abnormal psychology or neuroses: Sigmund Freud was 14 years younger than James, and still a medical student. Psychology offered boundless opportunities for advance, but sat uneasily between philosophy and physiology.

Into these conditions came William James, a philosopher who was well trained in the brain and nervous system, had logged hundreds of hours in physiology labs in America and Europe, and was well acquainted with the work of German psycho-physiologists like Fechner, Wundt, and von Helmholtz. He was fully conversant with Darwin's theory, which had been debated by eminent scientists at the James dinner table long before James went to Harvard.

James could see where nineteenth-century psychology was going, and was wary. Whereas Wundt separated the elements of consciousness into discrete sensations, James preferred the 'functionalist' view of a holistic, purposive, and evolving human organism adapting to the conditions of life. James was also losing patience with experimentalism. He had done his share of lab research but did not want psychology to follow the pattern of chemistry. Among other things, James hoped to attract artists, writers, and philosophers to psychology—people with the creative and critical skills to portray human consciousness in the full—and did not welcome the prospect of training lab technicians.

James was equal parts psychologist and philosopher. *Principles of Psychology* reflected his belief that psychology (and every other science) should know where it stood in relation to classic problems in philosophy of science—for example, problems of determinism and free will, mind and materialism, realism and nominalism, and the problem of induction. James did not expect psychologists to *solve* these problems, but he expected appreciation and debate, on the premise that psychologists stood a better chance of gaining scientific legitimacy if they knew the foundations of their knowledge claims.

These three concerns—building a functionalist psychology, taking psychology beyond the lab, and dealing openly with philosophical problems in psychology—became the defining features of *Principles of Psychology*. The book was 1,400 pages long, in two volumes and 28 chapters. It contained many passages on cognitive psychology: sensation, perception, attention, memory, learning, and the structure and functions of the brain. However, its truly enduring contributions rest with its chapters on belief, the stream of thought, philosophy of mind, the relation of mind to external objects, the problem of determinism, and problems of tautology and contradiction. These chapters foreshadowed nearly every major theme in James' later works.

At its core, *Principles of Psychology* is an extended essay on what it is like to be human—based largely on what it was like to be William James. Everything we know about James the person—his rootlessness, his depression, his absorption in literature and the arts, his personal warmth, the influences of Renouvier, Emerson, Goethe, Mill, and his father—can be found there. For James, the subject of psychology was the whole of human consciousness, and he was unwilling to relinquish any tool that might help him take hold of his subject, including laboratory data, myths, thought experiments, and personal introspection. Gertrude Stein recalled James saying, 'Never reject anything.... If you reject anything, that is the beginning of the end as an intellectual' (quoted in Richardson, 2006: 317).

More specifically, *Principles* was concerned with what it *feels* like to be human. James sometimes used the term 'feel' as a marker for all mental states, including sensation, perception, thought, and emotions (see James, 1890a: 185). But elsewhere, he turned things around, treating every mental state as a feeling or 'quale' to be discovered by looking inward—exploring, for example, what it *feels* like to be rational (see James, 1879). James knew the arguments against psychological introspection (James, 1890a: 185–2), and accepted them; but denied that the problem of introspection could be laid at the doorstep of psychology: '*introspection is difficult and fallible; and...the difficulty is simply that of all observation of whatever kind*' (James, 1890a: 191) (all italics in James's quotes are in the originals).

James observed human consciousness like an anthropologist, taking nothing for granted and with an eye for the non-obvious. Many of his observations took the form of analogies or thought experiments, and others came as comments on phenomena in the unexplored crevices of consciousness, or phenomena wholly *absent*. For example: 'Suppose we try to recall a forgotten name. The state of our consciousness is peculiar. There is a gap therein; but no mere gap. It is a gap that is intensely active. A sort of wraith of the name is in it, beckoning us in a given direction, making us at moments tingle with the sense of our closeness, and then letting us sink back without the longed-for term' (James, 1890a: 251).

James drew most of his observations from everyday life. How does it feel to taste food the second time compared to the first? What happens between seeing dust particles on your sleeve and brushing them away? Why do I wake up with my memories instead of yours? What is the feeling of drunkenness? (Drinking makes things 'seem more utterly what they are, more "utterly utter" than when we are sober' (James, 1890b: 284); later, he described drunkenness as 'the great exciter of the "Yes" function' (James, 1892: 387)). To some readers, this way of thinking anticipates Wittgenstein or Deleuze—or Thomas Nagel when he asked what it is like to be a bat. But James pioneered the style, and was among the first to doubt seriously whether people can empathize with anything truly *other*, including other people (James, 1899).

James did not view consciousness as comprised of discrete elements to be examined apart from their contexts. In James' psychological accounting, everything a person feels—passions, sentiments, beliefs, reasonings, sufferings, delusions—is part of experience and therefore *included*. James felt that psychologists should spend less time simplifying and reducing, and more time raising their observational and literary powers to the task of explaining what is there.

If everything in human experience is fair game for the psychologist, then the corollary is: *and that's all there is*. Whatever lies beyond human experience is outside the psychological wall. We do not know what goes on there, or if anything goes on at all, and so the psychologist has to let it go. Peoples' beliefs and feelings about this 'domain' may enter into human experience, and these beliefs and feelings make excellent material for the psychologist—as in James' *The Varieties of Religious Experience* (1902). As for their substance, the empiricist James believed (anticipating Husserl's 'phenomenological reduction' and the positivism of Wittgenstein's *Tractatus*) that the only scientifically respectable view was to remain silent.

On publication, *Principles of Psychology* was praised by most of James' contemporaries, but the reception among experimentalists was subdued. Wilhelm Wundt wrote a concise review that must have amused James both for its insight and irony: 'It is literature, it is beautiful, but it is not psychology.' Some of James' colleagues preferred the functionalist chapters without the philosophical commentary, and two years later James published *Psychology: The Briefer Course* (1892). In the new book, most of the chapters that made *Principles* so memorable—the chapter on belief and all the chapters on philosophy—were removed, and the remaining chapters were rewritten to emphasize experimental psychology. The book was a big success, but in a letter to his publisher, James wrote:

> By adding some twaddle about the senses, by leaving out all polemics and history, all bibliography and experimental details, all metaphysical subtleties and digressions, all quotations, all humour and pathos, all *interest* in short...I have produced a...pedagogic classic which will enrich both you and me, if not the student's mind. (James and James, 1920: 314)

11.3 JAMES AS PROCESS PHILOSOPHER

James' thought has been called 'the most original and insightful in the field of process philosophy since the time of Heraclitus' (Lachs and Talisse, 2008: 617). James' colleague George Santayana summarized the significance of *Principles of Psychology* as follows:

> He saw that experience, as we endure it, is not a mosaic of distinct impressions, nor the expression of separate hostile faculties, such as reason and the passions, or sense

and the categories; it is rather a flow of mental discourse, like a dream, in which all divisions and units are vague and shifting, and the whole is continually merging together and drifting apart. (Quoted from Allen, 1967: 326)

In *Principles*, James wrote: 'Consciousness, from our natal day, is of a teeming multiplicity of objects and relations, and what we call simple sensations are results of discriminative attention, often pushed to a very high degree' (James, 1890a: 224). Then: 'whilst we think, our brain changes, and...like the aurora borealis, its whole equilibrium shifts with every pulse of change....It is out of the question, then, that any total brain-state should identically recur' (James, 1890a: 234).

Going beyond brain processes, the rhythms of change in our subjective experience rise and fall, and the 'wonderful stream of our consciousness...seems to be made of an alternation of flights and perchings' (James, 1890a: 243). James wrote:

> Let anyone try to cut a thought across the middle and get a look at its section, and he will see how difficult the introspective observation of the transitive tracts is....As a snowflake crystal caught in the warm hand is no longer a crystal but a drop, so, instead of catching the feeling of relation moving to its term, we find we have caught some substantive thing, usually the last word we were pronouncing, statically taken, and with its function, tendency, and particular meaning in the sentence quite evaporated. The attempt at introspective analysis in these cases is like seizing a spinning top to catch its motion, or trying to turn up the gas quickly enough to see how the darkness looks. (James, 1890a: 244)

James believed that much of human psychology—habits, attention, language, memory, time perception, space perception—evolved as adaptations to the radical flux of pure experience. But we should not mistake the adaptations for the experience. In the chapter on time perception, James wrote:

> To remember a thing as past, it is necessary that the notion of 'past' be one of our 'ideas.'...many things come to be thought by us as past, not because of any intrinsic quality of their own, but rather because they are associated with other things which for us signify pastness. But how do these things get their pastness? What is the original of our experience of pastness, from when we get the meaning of the term?...These lingerings of old objects, these incomings of new, are the germs of memory and expectation, the retrospective and the prospective sense of time. They give that continuity to consciousness without which it could not be called a stream. (James, 1890a: 606–7)

Scholars in organization and management have used similar language to describe the radical flux of organizational life. For example, Chia wrote:

> Reality is always *heterogeneous* and *becoming*, and hence seemingly concrete things such as 'individual' actors and their identities, 'organizations' and their attributes and 'institutions' and their cultures, are nothing more than temporarily stabilized event

clusters: momentary outcomes or effects of historical processes. Like the metaphor of the melody...reality is indiscriminate, fluxing, and ceaselessly becoming... Order, form, pattern, identity, predictability and organization are abstractions drawn from this 'primordial soup' of undifferentiated flux. (Chia, 2002: 866)

James' process philosophy came as a reaction to opposing ontologies, which he labelled the 'sensationalist' and 'intellectualist' views. Sensationalists dealt with change by reducing phenomena to discrete and static sensory chunks and denying their continuity and relations: 'sensations...juxtaposed like dominoes in a game, but really separate, everything else verbal illusion' (James, 1890a: 245). Intellectualists, however, acknowledged change, but treated it abstractly rather than empirically, something 'on an entirely different plane, by an *actus purus* of Thought, Intellect, or Reason, all written with capitals and considered to mean something unutterably superior to any fact of sensibility whatever' (James, 1890a: 245).

In such a debate, James might be called a contextualist. He wrote:

Consciousness...does not appear to itself chopped up in bits. Such words as 'chain' or 'train' do not describe it fitly as it presents itself in the first instance. It is nothing jointed; it flows. A 'river' or a 'stream' are the metaphors by which it is most naturally described. *In talking of it hereafter, let us call it the stream of thought, of consciousness, or of subjective life.* (James, 1890a: 239)

James acknowledged that experience contains contrasts, as when a thunderclap breaks the evening silence, but denied that such contrasts signal any discreteness in thought itself: 'The transition between the thought of one object and the thought of another is no more a break in the *thought* than a joint in the bamboo is a break in the wood. It is a part of *consciousness* as much as the joint is a part of the *bamboo*' (1890a: 240).

Organizational contextualists have waged similar wars with sensationalists and intellectualists in business schools. Theories of organization often subordinate process to structure, and change to stability, as if flux were a discrete property rather than woven into the fabric of events. Economists and institutional theorists often treat change as a succession of static equilibria or a form of industry classification on the spectrum of environmental volatility; and empirical researchers often follow the 'sensational' method of abstracting sub-elements of organizational or management experience, naming them as concepts, stabilizing them in time and space, and submitting them to measurement.

In a study of organization culture in a British boarding school, Pettigrew (1979: 570) wrote, 'The longitudinal-processual approach to the study of organizations recognizes that an organization or any other social system may profitably be explored as a continuing system with a past, a present, and a future.' More recently, Pettigrew summarized his processual view as follows:

The overriding intellectual purpose of my work has been to catch reality in flight. My interest is in the dynamic quality of human conduct in organizational

settings. . . . I have tried to make time for time, not only to reveal the temporal character of human conduct, but also to expose the relationship between human behaviour
and the changing and multiple levels of contexts in which it is embedded. . . . This is
achieved partly by locating present behaviour in its historical antecedents, but also
by analysing individual, group, and organization behaviour in their sectoral, cultural, economic, social, and political contexts. (2012: 1305)

To what extent is process thinking in management indebted to James? More than a
century after James' death, the trail can be hard to follow. Many organizational process
scholars have cited James (e.g. Carlsen, 2006; Tsoukas and Chia, 2002; Weick, 2001),
and others have cited thinkers such as Whitehead or Dewey, who drew inspiration from
James. But in other cases, the links are more tenuous. For example, Pettigrew (1985)
ascribed his contextualism not to James but to Stephen Pepper's book *World Hypotheses*
(1942). Professor Pettigrew kindly lent me his copy of *World Hypotheses*, in which
I found one chapter—'Contextualism'—marked in yellow highlighter. As it happens,
this chapter also contained a long passage on William James' theory of 'fusion' (from
Principles), which states that when many objects reach the sense impressions simultaneously—such as musical tones—they fuse psychologically into a new and indivisible
whole. Although Pettigrew did not draw consciously on James, much of James' influence
today is of this type, having been filtered through several generations of scholarship.

James' standing in relation to other process philosophers—such as Bergson, Mach,
Whitehead, and Wittgenstein—is worth noting, if only to suggest further channels
of James' influence. Bergson was 17 years younger than James and little known when
Principles was published in 1890. Bergson cited James in his early publications and
their influence became mutual in due course. In 1903, James and Bergson began writing to each other, and in 1905 and 1908 they met in Paris. Bergson greatly admired
James' work—'the only philosopher who, Bergson felt, moved in a similar direction'
(Kolakowski, 1985: 10)—and James paid tribute to Bergson by devoting an Oxford lecture to his ideas, later published in *A Pluralistic Universe* (1909).

James met Ernst Mach in the 1880s during his European travels, by which time Mach
was already an eminent physicist and, according to James, 'genius of all trades' (Allen,
1967: 248). The two established instant rapport and were regular correspondents until
James' death. Mach's *The Science of Mechanics* (1883) shaped James' thinking on radical
empiricism, and James was the main psychological influence on Mach's phenomenology of sensory experience in *Analysis of Sensations* (1914), which cited *Principles* more
than a dozen times.

Alfred North Whitehead was 19 years younger than James and a fellow at Trinity
College, Cambridge, when *Principles* was published in 1890. Whitehead regarded
James not only as a founder of process philosophy (see Whitehead, 1925: 10, 1929: vii;
Price and Whitehead, 1954), but as the first philosopher since Descartes to advance the
rationalist–empiricist debate, and the greatest philosopher ever in bringing the flux of
complex experience under the command of language. Whitehead said, 'In western literature there are four great thinkers, whose services to civilized thought rest largely on
their achievements in philosophical assemblage; though each of them made important

contributions to the structure of philosophic system. These men are Plato, Aristotle, Leibniz, and William James' (quoted in Richardson, 2006: xiv).

Ludwig Wittgenstein may have heard about James from Bertrand Russell. Russell regarded James as an innovator in empirical philosophy, who 'would, on this ground alone, deserve a high place among philosophers' (Russell, 1946: 840). Wittgenstein, however, gravitated to James' moral insights in *The Varieties of Religious Experience* and his ideas on language and perception in *Principles*. Certainly, the transformation in Wittgenstein's thought between the *Tractatus* (1922) and *Philosophical Investigations* (1958b) drew heavily on James' *Principles*. The opening section of *The Brown Book* (1958a) mentioned only two people: St Augustine and William James, and *Philosophical Investigations* mentioned James four times, more than anyone except Augustine (Goodman, 2002). Cooper et al. (1970) found more than 50 parallel passages between *Principles* and Wittgenstein's *Investigations* and *Zettel*, and former Wittgenstein students told of his admiration for *Principles*, which he apparently intended to use as a philosophy text in future lectures (Passmore, 1957: 428). According to Jackman (2004: 4), 'Wittgenstein was actively engaged with James' book for at least a decade. At one point the two volumes of the *Principles* made up the entirety of his philosophical library.'

Wittgenstein used James' *Principles* as sounding board, counterpoint, jumping-off place for a new philosophy of language, and exemplar of experimental thinking. In section 610 of *Investigations*, he wrote: 'Describe the aroma of coffee.—Why can't it be done?... James: "Our vocabulary is inadequate."' Wittgenstein also admired James as a philosopher and a person, perhaps based on conversations with Russell or others who knew him. When a student told Wittgenstein about his reading of *The Varieties of Religious Experience*, and that James was 'such a human person', Wittgenstein replied: 'That is what makes him such a good philosopher; he was a real human being' (Drury, 1981: 121).

11.4 James as Phenomenologist

In chapter 21 of *Principles*, James described the 'sense of reality' as a problem in propositional logic, distinguishing *belief* apart from the *object of belief*, the former a 'psychic attitude' toward the latter: 'In every proposition... four elements are to be distinguished, the subject, the predicate, and their relation (of whatever sort it be)—these form the object of belief—and finally the psychic attitude in which our mind stands toward the proposition taken as a whole—and this is the belief itself' (James, 1890b: 287).

One hears echoes of Franz Brentano, and indeed James had read *Psychologie*, in which Brentano wrote:

> Every object comes into consciousness in a twofold way, as simply thought of (*vorgestellt*) and as admitted (*anerkannt*).... We must insist that, as soon as the object of a thought becomes the object of an assenting or rejecting judgment, our consciousness

steps into an entirely new relation towards it. It is then twice present in conscious-ness, as thought of, and as held for real or denied. (Quoted in James, 1890b: 286)

But Brentano did not view judgements as affirming the truth or falsity of psychologi-cal objects. Psychological phenomena speak for themselves, and the only judgements we can make about them are existential—they exist or do not exist. Phenomena are prior to syntax and the propositional calculus, which are entangled in the accidents and distor-tions of language. There is no proposition 'I believe p', but only 'p exists', or simply, 'p'.

James felt that Brentano made too strong a claim for the reality of mental phenomena and the efficacy of mental introspection. He wrote:

> Even the writers who insist upon the absolute veracity of our immediate inner comprehension of a conscious state have to contrast with this the fallibility of our memory or observation of it.... If to have feelings or thoughts in their immediacy were enough, babies in the cradle world would be psychologists, and infallible ones. (James, 1890a: 189)

Then:

> We find ourselves in continual error and uncertainty so soon as we are called on to name and class, and not merely to feel. Who can be sure of the exact order of his feel-ings when they are excessively rapid? Who can be sure, in his sensible perception of a chair, how much comes from the eye and how much is supplied out of the previous knowledge of the mind? (1890a: 191)

James' views aligned more closely with those of Brentano's student Edmund Husserl. Husserl was 17 years younger than James, and *Logical Investigations* was published in 1900, ten years after James' *Principles*. Husserl's next major work in phenomenology appeared in 1913, three years after James' death.

Husserl's mature phenomenology, like Brentano's, was concerned with establishing a rigorous basis for human enquiry. Husserl held that human enquiry is fundamentally psychological, subjective, and *intentional*, in the Brentanian sense; that is, concerned with relations between judgements and objects. Genuine truth-seekers must undergo a kind of personal transformation, in which they shed the distortions—biases, habits, beliefs, prior assumptions—through which they perceive the everyday world. Only by suspending the 'natural attitude'—Husserl's 'phenomenological reduction', or *epoche*—can enquirers free themselves from naive ontological commitments and gain access to the raw phenomena of mental experience.

Husserl's diaries record that he first read James' *Principles* in a psychology class in 1891–1892, and again in 1894 on the recommendation of Carl Stumpf, a fellow student of Brentano's who had befriended James during his visits to Germany. According to Edie (1970: 488), 'Husserl's library, preserved at Louvain, includes most of James' major works and two reprints which James sent to Husserl.' Moreover, Husserl's personal copy of *Principles* contained 'marks and marginal notes which indicate that they were read intensively'. Ferrarello (2009: 2) wrote: 'Husserl... admired the audacity and originality of Jamesian analysis.... At that time (1894) he had planned to publish a series of articles in the *Philosophishe Monatshefte*, but he published only the first and decided to wait to see what James had done, before publishing the others.'

Husserl's phenomenology diverged from Brentano's on precisely the points that Husserl had emphasized in his reading of James. For example, it was James who formulated intentionality as 'an active and selective achievement of consciousness rather than a merely passive or static directedness to objects' (Edie, 1970: 494), which then became a central feature of Husserl's phenomenology. According to Edie (1970: 494), 'it is these very additions to Brentano's minimal conception of intentionality which figure in the passages of the *Principles* most carefully studied by Husserl'. Based on his review, Edie (1970: 485–6) wrote: 'Husserl's recognition of a debt to James is thus completely explicit; he calls him "a daring and original man," an "excellent investigator," unshackled by any tradition, a "genius," and states in his diary that James' influence was important for his own work.' Edie concluded: 'In many cases James preceded and certainly developed what were to become essential phenomenological themes prior to, and independently of, the work of European phenomenologists' (Edie, 1970: 485–6).

The path from James and Husserl to organizational phenomenology branched in several directions, the most influential being the social phenomenology of Alfred Schutz. Schutz's social theory was explicitly indebted to Husserl, who wrote approvingly of *Phenomenology of the Social World* (1932). But Schutz also drew influence from chapter 21 of James' *Principles*, especially its description of the 'sub-universes' of reality, such as the universe of sense impressions, the universe of science, and the universe of religious beliefs. James argued that what is real in one universe may be unreal in another—as a winged horse is real in the world of myth but not in the world of science—and that much philosophical confusion stems from misunderstandings of context: '*whatever excites and stimulates our interest is real;* whenever an object so appeals to us that we turn to it, accept it, fill our mind with it, or practically take account of it, so far it is real for us, and we believe it' (James, 1890b: 295).

Schutz saw these passages as the phenomenological bridge between psychology and social experience. The crucial turn was converting James' mental 'sub-universe' into a 'province of meaning', which people create and share in the social world. Schutz wrote:

> James' genius has touched on one of the most important philosophical questions. Intentionally restricting his inquiry to the psychological aspect of the problem he has refrained from embarking upon an investigation of the many implications involved.... In order to free this important insight from its psychologistic setting we prefer to speak... of finite provinces of meaning upon each of which we may bestow the accent of reality. We speak of provinces of meaning and not of sub-universes because it is the meaning of our experiences and not the ontological structure of the objects which constitutes reality. (1945: 533–4)

Schutz's insight had far-reaching consequences in social research. Thomas Luckmann was a student of Schutz's, and both *The Social Construction of Reality* (Berger and

Luckmann, 1966) and *The Structures of the Life World* (Schutz and Luckmann, 1973) were grounded in the turn from 'sub-universes of reality' to 'provinces of meaning'. Harold Garfinkel read Schutz's work during his doctoral studies at Harvard, met him when Schutz immigrated to America, and cited Schutz's work extensively in *Studies in Ethnomethodology* (1967). Indeed, Garfinkel's debt to Schutz—especially Schutz's emphasis on multiple realities and the minutae of everyday life—falls precisely where Schutz was most indebted to James.

George Herbert Mead noted the following passage in *Principles*: 'Properly speaking, a man has as many social selves as there are individuals who recognize him and carry an image of him in their mind....Many a youth who is demure enough before his parents and teachers, swears and swaggers among his "tough" young friends' (James, 1890a: 294). Mead, who tutored James' children while studying for his doctorate at Harvard (Richardson, 2006), combined James' 'social self' with his own thoughts on language, gesture, and symbolism, to fashion a theory of social interaction that became the foundation for symbolic interactionism. When Herbert Blumer (1969) defined the theory and empirical method of symbolic interactionism, it was under the influence of Mead, his mentor and colleague, and William James.

Perhaps the most prolific of empirical symbolic interactionists was Erving Goffman, a student of Blumer's at Chicago. Goffman drew influence from all the main figures in interpretivism, including Schutz, Mead, and James. Goffman's *Presentation of Self in Everyday Life* was premised on James' 'social self' (1959: 57), and *Frame Analysis* (1974) began:

> I try to follow a tradition established by William James in the famous chapter 'The Perception of Reality,'...Instead of asking what reality is, he gave matters a subversive phenomenological twist, italicizing the following question: *Under what circumstances do we think things are real?* The important thing about reality, he implied, is our sense of realness in contrast to our feeling that some things lack this quality. One can then ask under what conditions such a feeling is generated, and this question speaks to a small, manageable problem having to do with the camera and not what the camera takes pictures of. (1974: 2)

In phenomenology as in process philosophy, James' influence on management scholars may not be limited to those who read or cite his works. A management scholar who *has* read and cited James is Karl Weick. On Weick's list of the 55 'Important Resources for Organizational Sensemaking', the first is James' *Principles of Psychology* (Weick, 1995: 65–9). Weick's 'sensemaking' brought many elements of James' *Principles* to organizational analysis, including selective attention, the distinction between perception and conception, and the notion of extractive reasoning. Extractive reasoning occurs when an experienced mind makes sense of a whole situation by seizing on its most information-bearing detail. James gave the following example:

> A layman present at a shipwreck, a battle or a fire is helpless. Discrimination has been so little awakened in him by experience that his consciousness leaves no single point of the complex situation accented and standing out for him to begin to act upon. But

the sailor, the fireman, and the general know directly at what corner to take up the business. They 'see into the situation'—that is, they analyze it—with their first glance. (James, 1890b: 344; see Weick, 1995: 49–50)

Principles also served as the psychological foundation for Weick's concept of enactment. Here, Weick emphasized James' views on freedom of choice, as expressed in *Principles* and later essays (e.g. James, 1895). Weick wrote:

[James] asked the question, 'Is life worth living?'... His answer was, you can make either yes or no valid. If you assume life is not worth living and act accordingly, then you will be absolutely right and suicide will be the only plausible alternative. And if you believe that life is worth living, then that belief can validate itself. The issue turns on faith or the lack thereof, because it sets self-fulfilling action in motion. (1995: 38)

11.5 JAMES AS FUNCTIONALIST

James is often cited as a founder of the functionalist school of social thought. For example, Burrell and Morgan (1979) gave him a 'strong claim' to be considered among the founding fathers of functionalist sociology, along with Comte, Spenser, Durkheim, and Pareto.

James' functionalism can be derived from his own statements, especially in *Briefer Course*: 'Mental life is primarily teleological' (James, 1892: 4), and 'Mind and world...have been evolved together and in consequence are something of a mutual fit' (James, 1892: 4). On the other hand, one is never quite safe classifying James with an '—ism'—and he was, at best, a *nuanced* functionalist. For example, his acceptance of the correspondence between mind states and brain states can be interpreted *ironically*; that is, as a barely-disguised attempt to show the absurdities of materialism when driven to its limits: 'I shall therefore assume without scruple at the outset that the uniform correlation of brain-states with mind-states is a law of nature. The interpretation of the law in detail will best show where its difficulties lie' (James, 1892: 6).

Still, social scientists have read James' *Principles* as pure functionalism, and have brought to the social world its insights on perception, memory, attention, habit, and emotion. A good example of this is Herbert Simon, who read *Principles* as a student at the University of Chicago and used it as the psychological foundation for the concept of bounded rationality. As a student at Chicago, Simon was deeply impressed with Graham Wallas' *Human Nature in Politics* (1920), which used James' *Principles* to show the importance of impulse, instinct, emotions, and non-rational inference in politics. Indeed, Simon's behaviouralism (not *behaviourism*) closely paralleled Wallas' challenges to rationality in politics, and Simon later paid tribute to Wallas:

A central theme for Graham Wallas in *Human Nature in Politics* was the interplay of the rational and nonrational components of human behavior in politics. That, of course, was also a central theme for Harold Lasswell... But while Lasswell's psychological apparatus comes largely from Freud, Wallas acknowledges as his principal mentor William James. Although Lasswell was concerned with borderline and not-so-borderline pathology, Wallas was interested in the ubiquitous workings of instinct, ignorance, and emotion in normal behavior. Wallas, like his mentor William James, is the more closely attuned to the contemporary orientation in psychology. (Simon, 1985: 295)

Simon argued that American psychology had abandoned its obligations to explain human behaviour, and that psychology needed to recover the behavioural richness of James' *Principles*:

On the American side of the Atlantic Ocean, there was a great gap in research on human thinking from the time of William James almost down to World War II. American psychology was dominated by behaviorism, the stimulus-response connection (S arrow R), the nonsense syllable, and the rat. Cognitive processes—what went on between the ears after the stimulus was received and before the response was given—were hardly mentioned, and the word *mind* was reserved for philosophers, not to be uttered by respectable psychologists. (Simon, 1991: 190)

Simon's reaction against behaviourist psychology was evident in *Administrative Behavior* (1947), in which he cited James' *Principles* and Edward Tolman's *Purposive Behavior in Animals and Men* (1932), a functionalist psychology of goal-seeking and decision-making. In a footnote to the chapter on 'The Psychology of Administrative Decisions', Simon attributed his views on choice and goal-seeking to Tolman, and his views on cognition—human energies, memory, habit, impulse, selective attention, and emotion—to James' *Principles* and Dewey's *Human Nature and Conduct* (1930), which borrowed from James (see also Simon, 1991: 190).

Simon was also among the large group of social theorists, functionalist and otherwise, who drew influence from James' pragmatism. James absorbed a kind of pragmatism from meetings of the Cambridge 'metaphysical club' in the 1870s (Menand, 2001), especially from C.S. Peirce, who wrote: 'Consider what effects, which might conceivably have practical bearings, we might conceive the object of our conception to have. Then our conception of these effects is the whole of our conception of the object' (Peirce, 1878: 31). But in *Principles*, James' pragmatism took a surprising turn. Whereas Peirce was uncompromisingly scientific, and his pragmatism a precursor of logical positivism, James ranged over a broader field and sought philosophical justification for believing *anything at all*. James wondered how it was possible in a world of plausible psychology—with emotions, impulses, biases, flagging energies, and flawed sense perceptions—to attach the word 'true' or 'false' to *any* proposition. And if we cannot know whether a proposition is true, what is the foundation of scientific enquiry?

James believed that people attend largely to their own sub-worlds of perception: the general in the field attends to plans and instincts, the scientist attends to replicable observations, the priest attends to the authority of scripture. He was unimpressed by special pleadings for the veracity of science: 'The theory will be most generally believed which, besides offering us objects able to account satisfactorily for our sensible experience, also offers those which are interesting, those which appeal most urgently to our aesthetic, emotional, and active needs' (James, 1890b: 312). Then:

> no system which should not be rich, simple, and harmonious would have a chance of being chosen for belief, if rich, simple, harmonious systems were also there.... But as his abilities to 'do' lie wholly in the line of his natural propensities; as he enjoys reaction with such emotions as fortitude, hope, rapture, admiration, earnestness, and the like; and as he very unwillingly reacts with fear, disgust, despair, or doubt,—a philosophy which should legitimate only emotions of the latter sort would be sure to leave the mind a prey to discontent and craving. It is far too little recognized how entirely the intellect is made up of practical interests. (James, 1890b: 315)

James brought these ideas to fruition in *Pragmatism* (James, 1907), but the seeds of pragmatism were sown in *Principles*. In business schools today, functionally-oriented scholars in disciplines such as strategic management invoke pragmatism to establish the foundations of phenomena such as resource replication (Baden-Fuller and Winter, 2007) and competitive advantage (Powell, 2001, 2002, 2003); and phenomenologists and ethnographers invoke Jamesian pragmatism in support of interpretivism (Weick, 2012), strategy-as-practice (Johnson et al., 2007), and feminist studies (Rumens and Keleman, 2010; Scott et al., 2010). Indeed, many organizational scholars know James through pragmatism alone, or through his influence on John Dewey, and there is a lamentable tendency towards caricature and misunderstanding. In general, Jamesian pragmatism is most usefully employed as a psychologically-tractable philosophy of science, and not as a pretext for promoting 'common sense', 'practicality', or 'doing *instead* of thinking', ideas towards which the whole of James' life and thought stand as a kind of refutation.

11.6 Concluding Thoughts

William James pioneered process philosophy, and *Principles of Psychology* contains plenty of process philosophy. It also contains phenomenology, brain science, and cognitive psychology—and some pragmatism, ontology, religion, moral philosophy, and self-help. The distinctive character of James' process philosophy comes not only from the philosophy itself, but from the spark of opposing ideas clashing in close proximity.

People say of Alfred Marshall's *Principles of Economics* that 'All is contained in Marshall', and the same can be said of James' *Principles of Psychology*. James had a narrative flair that revelled in bringing arguments enthusiastically to the reader, and then carrying them to the brink of contradiction. James' godfather advised people to avoid foolish consistencies—'the hobgoblin of little minds, adored by little statesmen and philosophers and divines' (Emerson, 1841: 152)—and James took him seriously. He had a large capacity for 'negative capability' and took comfort in knowing that pluralism and self-contradiction were features held in common with poets and bibles and life itself.

No system comes out of James' work, and he said in Oxford near the end of his life that an 'incompletely unified appearance is the only form that reality may yet have achieved' (James, 1909: 44). Any true narrative of reality must itself be complicated and inconclusive—though it need not be dull nor devoid of drama. As Jacques Barzun wrote of *Principles of Psychology*, 'It is an American masterpiece, quite like Moby Dick, that ought to be read from beginning to end at least once by every person professing to be educated' (quoted in Goodman, 2002: 1).

References

Allen, G.W. (1967). *William James: A Biography* (New York: Viking Press).

Baden-Fuller, C. and Winter, S. (2007). Replicating Organizational Knowledge: Principles or Templates? SSRN Working Paper, SSRN ID 1118013.

Berger, P. and Luckmann, T. (1966). *The Social Construction of Reality* (New York: Doubleday).

Blumer, H. (1969). *Symbolic Interactionism: Perspective and Method* (Englewood Cliffs, NJ: Prentice-Hall).

Burrell, G. and Morgan, G. (1979). *Sociological Paradigms and Organisational Analysis* (Portsmouth, NH: Heinemann).

Carlsen, A. (2006). Organizational Becoming as Dialogic Imagination of Practice: The Case of the Indomitable Gauls, *Organization Science* 17(1): 132–49.

Chia, R. (2002). Essai: Time, Duration and Simultaneity: Rethinking Process and Change in Organizational Analysis, *Organization Studies* 23: 863–8.

Cooper, C., Geach, P., Potts, T., and White, R. (1970). *A Wittgenstein Workbook* (Oxford: Blackwell).

Dewey, J. (1930). *Human Nature and Conduct* (New York: Modern Library).

Drury, M.O'C. (1981). Conversations with Wittgenstein, in R. Rhees (ed.), *Ludwig Wittgenstein: Personal Recollections* (Oxford: Basil Blackwell): 112–89.

Edie, J.M. (1970). William James and Phenomenology, *The Review of Metaphysics* 23(3): 481–526.

Emerson, R.W. (1841). Self-Reliance, reprinted in B. Atkinson (ed.), *The Complete Essays and Other Writings of Ralph Waldo Emerson* (New York: Modern Library, 1940): 145–69.

Ferrarello, S. (2009). On the Rationality of Will in James and Husserl, *European Journal of Pragmatism and American Philosophy* 1(1): 1–12.

Garfinkel, H. (1967). *Studies in Ethnomethodology* (Englewood Cliffs, NJ: Prentice-Hall).

Goffman, E. (1959). *Presentation of Self in Everyday Life* (New York: Doubleday Anchor).

——(1974). *Frame Analysis* (New York: Harper & Row).

Goodman, R. (2002). *Wittgenstein and William James* (Cambridge: Cambridge University Press).

Husserl, E. (1900–1901). *Logical Investigations* (New York: Humanities Press, 1970).

——(1913). *Ideas: General Introduction to Pure Phenomenology* (New York: Collier, 1962).

Jackman, H. (2004). Wittgenstein and James's Stream of Thought, presented at the 2004 Meeting of the Society for the Advancement of American Philosophy, March 2004, <http://www.yorku.ca/hjackman/papers/WittJames.pdf>

James, W. (1879). The Sentiment of Rationality, *Mind* 4: 1–22.

——(1890a). *The Principles of Psychology*, Volume I (New York: Henry Holt and Company).

——(1890b). *The Principles of Psychology*, Volume II (New York: Henry Holt and Company).

—— (1892). *Psychology: The Briefer Course* (New York: Henry Holt and Company).

—— (1895). Is Life Worth Living?, *International Journal of Ethics* 6: 1–24.

—— (1899). On a Certain Blindness in Human Beings, in W. James, *Talks to Teachers on Psychology and to Students on Some of Life's Ideals* (New York: Henry Holt and Company): 3–46.

—— (1902). *The Varieties of Religious Experience: A Study in Human Nature* (London: Longmans, Green and Co., 1935).

—— (1907). *Pragmatism: A New Name for Some Old Ways of Thinking* (New York: Longmans, Green and Co., 1928).

—— (1909). *A Pluralistic Universe* (London: Longmans, Green and Co., 1932).

—— and James, H. (1920). *The Letters of William James: Volume 1* (Boston: Atlantic Monthly Press).

Johnson, G., Langley, A., Melin, L., and Whittington, R. (2007). *Strategy as Practice: Research Directions and Resources* (Cambridge: Cambridge University Press).

Kolakowski, L. (1985). *Bergson* (Oxford: Oxford University Press).

Lachs J. and Talisse, R.B. (2008). *American Philosophy: An Encyclopedia* (New York: Routledge).

Mach, E. (1883). *The Science of Mechanics* (London: Open Court).

—— (1914). *The Analysis of Sensations* (London: Open Court).

Menand, L. (2001). *The Metaphysical Club: A Story of Ideas in America* (New York: Farrar, Straus, and Giroux).

Passmore, J. (1957). *A Hundred Years of Philosophy* (London: Gerald Duckworth and Co.).

Peirce, C.S. (1878). How to Make our Ideas Clear, *Popular Science Monthly* 12: 286–302, reprinted in J. Buchler (ed.), *Philosophical Writings of Peirce* (New York: Dover, 1955): 23–41.

Pepper, S.C. (1942). *World Hypotheses: A Study in Evidence* (Berkeley: University of California Press, 1970).

Pettigrew, A.M. (1979). On Studying Organizational Cultures, *Administrative Science Quarterly* 24(4): 570–81.

—— (1985). Contextualist Research and the Study of Organizational Change Processes, in E. Mumford, R. Hirschheim, G. Fitzgerald, and A.T. Wood-Harper (eds), *Research Methods in Information Systems* (Amsterdam: North-Holland): 53–78.

—— (2012). Context and Action in the Transformation of the Firm: A Reprise, *Journal of Management Studies* 49(7): 1304–28.

Powell, T.C. (2001). Competitive Advantage: Logical and Philosophical Considerations, *Strategic Management Journal* 22(9): 875–88.

—— (2002). The Philosophy of Strategy, *Strategic Management Journal*, 23(9): 873–80.

—— (2003). Strategy without Ontology, *Strategic Management Journal*, 24(3): 285–91.

Price, L. and Whitehead, A.N. (1954). *Dialogues of Alfred North Whitehead* (Boston: Little, Brown and Co.).

Richardson, R.D. (2006). *William James: In the Maelstrom of American Modernism* (Boston: Houghton Mifflin).

Rumens, N. and Kelemen, M. (2010). American Pragmatism and Feminism: Fresh Opportunities for Sociological Inquiry, *Contemporary Pragmatism* 7(1): 129–48.

Russell, B. (1946). *History of Western Philosophy* (London: George Allen and Unwin).

Schutz, A. (1932). *The Phenomenology of the Social World*, trans. G. Walsh and F. Lehnert (Evanston, IL: Northwestern University, 1967).

—— (1945). On Multiple Realities, *Philosophy and Phenomenological Research* 5(4): 533–76.

—— and Luckmann, T. (1973). *The Structures of the Life World: Volume One* (Evanston, IL: Northwestern University).

Scott, L., Dolan, C., Johnstone-Louis, M.J., Sugden, K., and Wu, M. (2010). Enterprise and Inequality: A Study of Avon in South Africa, *Entrepreneurship Theory and Practice* 36(3): 543–68.

Simon, H.A. (1947). *Administrative Behavior*, 2nd edn (New York: Free Press).

——(1985). Human Nature in Politics: The Dialogue of Psychology with Political Science, *The American Political Science Review* 79(2): 293–304.

——(1991). *Models of My Life* (New York: Harper Basic).

Stein, G. (1933). *The Autobiography of Alice B. Toklas* (London: Penguin, 1966).

Tolman, E. (1932). *Purposive Behavior in Animals and Men* (New York: Appleton-Century).

Tsoukas, H. and Chia, R. (2002). On Organizational Becoming: Rethinking Organizational Change, *Organization Science* 13(5): 567–82.

Wallas, G. (1920). *Human Nature in Politics*, 3rd edn (London: Constable and Co.).

Weber, C.O. (1960). *Basic Philosophies of Education* (New York: Holt, Rinehart, and Winston).

Weick, K.E. (1995). *Sensemaking in Organizations* (Thousand Oaks, CA: Sage Publications).

——(2001). *Making Sense of the Organization* (Oxford: Blackwell).

—— (2012). Organized Sensemaking: A Commentary on Processes of Interpretive Work, *Human Relations* 65(1): 141–53.

Whitehead, A.N. (1925). *Science and the Modern World* (New York: Macmillan).

——(1929). *Process and Reality* (London: Cambridge University Press).

Wittgenstein, L. (1922). *Tractatus Logico-Philosophicus*, trans. B. McGuinness and D. Pears (London: Routledge).

——(1958a). *Preliminary Studies for the 'Philosophical Investigations' Generally Known as The Blue and Brown Books* (Oxford: Basil Blackwell).

——(1958b). *Philosophical Investigations* (Oxford: Basil Blackwell).

——(1967). *Zettel* (Oxford: Basil Blackwell).

CHAPTER 12

GABRIEL TARDE (1843–1904)

CHRISTIAN BORCH

12.1 INTRODUCTION

ONE OF the concepts that have figured centrally in discussions of the financial crisis of 2007–2008 is that of contagion (for an interesting analysis, see Peckham, 2013). The sub-prime crisis began in the United States, but soon spread, as if by a contagious-imitative force, to Europe and elsewhere, generating a worldwide crisis as a result of this process. Mobilizing a vocabulary of contagious imitation to understand the financial crisis invites discussion of how to conceive of imitative processes. Here the work of the French criminologist and sociologist Gabriel Tarde (1843–1904) may prove helpful, as contagion and especially imitation were key concepts in his theoretical architecture.

Since the late 1990s Tarde's work has experienced a veritable renaissance in social theory. Not only have important parts of his oeuvre been republished with extensive commentaries in France (e.g. Tarde, 1999a, 1999b), a still-growing international reception has transpired, buttressed by translations of Tarde into English and German (a few examples include Borch, 2005; Borch and Stäheli, 2009b; Candea, 2010; Latour, 2002; Toews, 2003). Interestingly, much of the new reception tries to render itself—if only for a moment—contemporaneous with Tarde in that it readdresses the debate about the proper understanding of sociology that Tarde engaged in with Émile Durkheim at the turn of the nineteenth century. This restaging of the Tarde–Durkheim debate plays a central role, not least in Bruno Latour's 'discovery' of Tarde. Latour in effect argues that the central benefit of a return to Tarde lies in the possibility of rethinking the nature of the social, and in following a different path from the one that much sociology pursued in the footsteps of Durkheim (Latour, 2002, 2005).

While the bulk of the new reception approaches Tarde in an affirmative manner, arguing that his theorizing provides a fresh and stimulating alternative to predominant conceptions of the social, some criticism has surfaced as well. Most notably, Laurent Mucchielli (2000) has, not without some right, characterized all the fuss about Tarde and the elevation of him as *the* new sociologist as 'Tardomania'. Among other things, Mucchielli tries to balance the claim, advanced among others by Latour, that Tarde was long forgotten in social theory, an alleged oblivion that justifies the notion of a contemporary 'resurgence' or 'renaissance' of his work. More importantly, perhaps, Mucchielli is sceptical about the current attempts to revive Tarde, as represented by Latour but also by Deleuzian scholars, since this (and here Mucchielli follows Durkheim) supposedly entails a return to a lack of proper methodology and rational explanatory logic.

While I do think that Tarde has much to offer to contemporary theorizing, both of a sociological and of a more organizational bent, I also believe that Mucchielli has a point in critically examining how Tarde is currently being received, or, perhaps better (re-)constructed. Indeed, I shall argue in this chapter that, as is the case with any author, there are different ways to read Tarde, and the ones currently in vogue may disclose some analytical potential also available in Tarde's writings. Consequently, in this chapter I shall try to delineate an interpretation of Tarde which differs somewhat from the one especially championed by Latour, and demonstrate some of its implications for thinking about processes and organizations, and more precisely modes of organizing. The latter distinction between organizations and organizing is important in the present context since—despite Tarde's current popularity—there are hardly any studies that apply Tarde to the organizational domain in a more classical sense. Also, Tarde himself did not single out organizations as a particular object of study or as a particular domain of the social, such as for example Niklas Luhmann did when designating organizations as a specific form of social systems (Luhmann, 2000). This does not preclude an application of Tarde's thinking to organizations, but as I shall come back to, Tarde's contribution to contemporary organization theory may lie more in understanding imitative processes that cross-cut the boundaries of formal organizations—and operate instead on the level of organizing, including how various modes of organizing are orchestrated in order to achieve specific effects.

The chapter has three sections. In section 12.2, I present some of Tarde's key ideas, along with biographical details and information about the intellectual climate he worked in. This includes a brief account of Durkheim's critique of Tarde. Section 12.3 discusses Tarde's theorizing via the recent Delezuian and Latourian interpretations. The Deleuzian reading, in particular, ties Tarde to process philosophical discussions. In section 12.4, I suggest my alternative reading, which revolves around Tarde's key notion of imitation. In this section I also apply my reading of Tarde to the field of organization and organizing, and return to the discussion of imitative economic dynamics. Section 12.5 concludes.

12.2 TARDE, IMITATION, AND EARLY FRENCH SOCIOLOGY

Gabriel Tarde's entry in the French academic system came at a late stage of his life and was, to begin with, of a more criminological than sociological nature. Tarde had worked for a number of years as a legal magistrate in Sarlat, in the Perigord Noir region, and capitalized on his knowledge about the penal field in a series of writings on criminological and penal matters in the 1880s and early 1890s. One of his key points was that in order to understand and deal with crime one had to see it in its wider imitative context: criminal activity rarely occurs as an isolated event, but is usually inspired by and an imitation of previous criminal acts—just as it may itself spark future imitative processes. One problem that attracted Tarde's special attention was that of criminal crowds, i.e. crowds of people going amok in the streets and committing all sorts of violent acts (e.g. Tarde, 1892, 1893). According to Tarde, such crowd events are characterized by particularly intense moments of imitation, not of previous acts, but of the hypnotic suggestion emanating from the crowd's leader. Indeed, Tarde wrote in his *Penal Philosophy* (1890), 'in an excited crowd...imitation is absolutely unconscious and blind and contrary to the habitual character of the person who is subjected to it, it is a phenomenon of momentary insanity which lessens responsibility or eliminates it' (1968: 302, n. 1).[1]

Gradually, Tarde's interests shifted from criminological problems to more sociological ones, but the focus on imitation was retained and would soon become his central sociological claim to fame. One of the first major formulations of his sociological programme appeared in his book *Laws of Imitation*, which was published in 1890 and in a second edition in 1895. In this book, Tarde fleshed out the idea that imitation should be placed centre stage in the understanding of society. Criminal activity and crowd eruptions might be instances of imitation, but it would be a mistake to take their apparently deviant nature as a sign that imitation was reserved for the abnormal domain. Quite the contrary, Tarde argued, imitation constitutes the very essence of society and the social. As he put it in a one-liner that was to summarize his sociological thought, '[s]ociety is imitation and imitation is a kind of somnambulism' (1962: 87, italics in the original). This definition implies at least four things.

First, imitation entails a recognition of that which is being imitated, be it a person, a gesture, a fashion, or whatever. By imitating something we pay respect to the object of imitation. Second, society is made up of innumerable rays of imitation. This is partly an ontological claim, asserting that the social plane is nothing but imitation, and partly an analytical claim, stating that in order to study social phenomena, one should resort neither to methodological individualism nor to structuralism. To study society and the social means rather to trace, in a meticulous manner, imitations and imitative processes (Barry, 2010). The ontological dimension basically refers to the idea that the social is relationally constituted. Of course, relational understandings of the social can also be found in the work of many other theorists, including Mikhail Bakhtin, George Herbert Mead, and Charles Sanders Peirce (see, respectively, Chapters 21, 12, and 10, this volume). And yet Tarde's conception differs from these since it entails, third, that societal imitation plays out in a more general context the same dynamics which, according to Tarde, can be identified in crowds. Indeed, Tarde's theory proposes that society is based on a non-conscious and irrational (or non-rational) foundation (Borch, 2012; Mazzarella, 2010). This is the essential message conveyed by the final part of Tarde's definition of society as imitation. Since, for Tarde, imitation is a matter of somnambulism or sleepwalking, the role of hypnosis assumes a most central place in Tarde's conception of the social (something clearly at odds with Mead's work; see Leys, 1993). While the notions of somnambulism and hypnotic suggestion might appear strangely awkward in a twenty-first-century setting, things were quite different in 1895 when Tarde published the second edition of *Laws of Imitation*. Thus, in that edition he noted a range of contemporaneous works, especially within psychiatry (Tarde particularly drew on the work of the famous French professor Hippolyte Bernheim), which had demonstrated the scholarly relevance and merits of categories such as somnambulism, suggestion, and hypnosis; to an extent, indeed, that '[n]othing could be commoner than [the idea of universal social suggestion] at present' (1962: 76, n. 1). Tarde even proposed to think of 'the social man as a veritable somnambulist' (1962: 76) and argued that:

> The social like the hypnotic state is only a form of dream, a dream of command and a dream of action. Both the somnambulist and the social man are possessed by the illusion that their ideas, all of which have been suggested to them, are spontaneous. (1962: 77)

Put differently, there lies at the heart of Tarde's theory a resonance with Spinoza's idea of the power to be affected as well as with the idea of a power to affect (see Chapter 6, this volume). The somnambulist is constantly affected, the hypnotizer affecting.

Fourth, Tarde's conception of society as a web of suggestive imitations implies a profoundly *processual* view on the social. This is clear not only from the fact that Tarde often made use of a processual vocabulary to describe his thinking (referring to notions such as waves, rhythms, diffusion, etc.). More importantly, perhaps, Tarde was aware that using the hypnotizer–hypnotized configuration as emblematic of the social was only adequate if supplemented by a processual dynamic that would allow for a successive or trickle-down effect of the influence emanating from the hypnotizer. In Tarde's words:

> Suppose a somnambulist should imitate his medium to the point of becoming a medium himself and magnetising a third person, who, in turn, would imitate him, and so on, indefinitely. Is not social life this very thing? Terraces of consecutive and connected magnetisations are the rule. (1962: 84)

It may be argued that Tarde's imitative conception of society raises questions such as what triggers imitation and what is being imitated? Tarde answered the former question by referring to *prestige*. The reason why one person is able to hypnotize another is that he or she is looked upon with a glowing admiration that the hypnotized would like to radiate on him or her. 'The magnetiser does not need to lie or terrorise to secure the blind belief and the passive obedience of his magnetised subject. He has prestige—that tells the story' (1962: 78).

To answer the second question—what is actually being imitated?—recourse is needed to Tarde's distinction between imitation and invention. Thus, imitations are essentially imitations of inventions, i.e. of novel ideas. However, producing a new

idea is not only difficult, according to Tarde; often when we consider ourselves original, we really only imitate, he stressed. More importantly, in the present context,
whereas imitation is described by Tarde as the key building block of the social, invention transcends the social and hence operates beyond the imitative realm. Almost
resonating with a Nietzschean positive will to power (see Chapter 13, this volume),
Tarde declared that '[t]o innovate, to discover...the individual must escape, for
the time being, from his social surroundings. Such unusual audacity makes him
super-social rather than social' (1962: 87–8). This does not entail a pure disconnection of imitation and invention. The point is just that inventions only become social
when imitated. As long as an idea 'remains locked up in the head of its creator, [it]
has no social value' (1899: 166). It is only when an invention becomes part of the imitative web that it enters the social plane. This relation between invention and imitation is only part of the story, though. Tarde stressed that although many imitations
are imitations of some invention, imitative processes also assume a self-propagating
dynamics, meaning that often an imitation is just as much an imitation of other imitations as it is an imitation of some original invention. As Tarde put it, 'three-quarters
of the time we obey a man because we see him obeyed by others' (1969: 314, 1989: 123;
see also Borch, 2005: 85). Further, it should be noted that Tarde did not claim that
such imitative processes are pure in the sense that the imitations remain precisely the
same over time. Indeed, minor changes in the imitative patterns will most likely take
place as they trickle down.

Tarde built a comprehensive sociological programme around these key notions, but
his work did not go uncontested. Not least, Durkheim challenged the conceptual and
analytical foundation of Tarde's sociology. This is not the place for an in-depth account
or analysis of Durkheim's critique (see for this purpose, Borch, 2012: 64–70). I shall
merely give a rough sketch of the critical comments Tarde encountered. The central aim
of Durkheim's programme was to establish sociology as a distinctive discipline, devoted
to examining the causalities and laws relating to the *sui generis* realm of 'social facts'
which are '*capable of exercising over the individual an external constraint*' (Durkheim,
1982: 59, italics in the original). Durkheim asserted that Tarde's sociology, with its focus
on imitation, did not allow for a study of such social facts and therefore did not qualify
as a proper sociological programme. This was due partly to the allegation that Tarde's
sociology amounted to a psychologism in poor disguise (unable to move from the individual to the extra-individual level of social facts), partly to the claim that Tarde mistook
cause and effect when studying imitation:

> imitation does not always express, indeed never expresses, what is essential and
> characteristic in the social fact. Doubtless every social fact is imitated and has...a
> tendency to become generalised, but this is because it is social, i.e. obligatory. Its
> capacity for expansion is not the cause but the consequence of its sociological char-
> acter.... Moreover, one may speculate whether the term 'imitation' is indeed appro-
> priate to designate a proliferation which occurs through some coercive influence.
> (Durkheim, 1982: 59, n. 3)

Durkheim repeated this critique in a subsequent discussion of the notions of contagion and imitation underpinning Tarde's somnambulistic conception of society:

> We no longer believe that zoological species are only individual variations heredi-tarily transmitted; it is equally inadmissible that a social fact is merely a generalized individual fact. But most untenable of all is the idea that this generalization may be due to some blind contagion or other. We should even be amazed at the continuing necessity of discussing an [sic] hypothesis which, aside from the serious objections it suggests, has never even begun to receive experimental proof. For it has never been shown that imitation can account for a definite order of social facts and, even less, that it alone can account for them. The proposition has merely been stated as an aph-orism, resting on vaguely metaphysical considerations. But sociology can only claim to be treated as a science when those who pursue it are forbidden to dogmatize in this fashion, so patently eluding the regular requirements of proof. (Durkheim, 1951: 142)

Put differently, in Durkheim's view, Tarde's sociological programme did not merit as academic, founded as it allegedly was on aphorisms and metaphysics. Needless to say, Tarde could not recognize this picture of his work as essentially unscientific, and he returned Durkheim's critique by arguing that it was Durkheim who conflated *explanan-dum* and *explanans* (Latour, 2002: 125).

Although Durkheim's dismissal of Tarde's work as basically unscientific may appear out of place, it was nevertheless highly consequential. Thus, Durkheim's gradual ascend-ance to power in the French sociological landscape at the turn of the nineteenth century entailed a concurrent marginalization of Tarde's programme, despite the fact that Tarde became chair in modern philosophy at the Collège de France in 1900.

12.3 THE TARDE REVIVAL—AND BEYOND

Durkheim's critique of Tarde forms the target in the two most important attempts to revive Tarde in a contemporary theoretical setting, namely those put forward by Deleuze and Latour. Granted, in Deleuze's work, there is no extensive systematic discus-sion of Tarde, who does appear, though, in a few scattered contexts. And yet an impor-tant Tardean influence can and has been identified in Deleuze's work, not least by Éric Alliez who has pointed out that Deleuze's *Difference and Repetition*, as the title suggests, was consonant with Tarde's emphasis on imitation and the transformations that take place through imitative processes (Alliez, 2004: 50).

The exchange between Tarde and Durkheim is addressed explicitly by Deleuze on more occasions. In a footnote in *Difference and Repetition*, for example, Deleuze defends Tarde against one of Durkheim's central allegations, namely that Tarde's thinking amounts to a psychologism (1994: 314, n. 3). This, Deleuze asserts, is a misunderstanding of the kind of microsociological programme Tarde instituted. In Deleuze's words, quot-ing Tarde from the latter's *Social Laws* (Tarde, 1899):

It is completely wrong to reduce Tarde's sociology to a psychologism or even an interpsychology. Tarde criticizes Durkheim for assuming what must be explained— namely, 'the similarity of thousands of men'. For the alternative—impersonal givens or the Ideas of great men—he substitutes the little ideas of little men, the little inventions and interferences between imitative currents. *What Tarde inaugurates is a microsociology,* which is not necessarily concerned with what happens between individuals but with what happens within a single individual: for example, hesitation understood as 'infinitesimal social opposition', or invention as 'infinitesimal social adaptation'. (1994: 314, n. 3, italics in the original)

The point of citing Deleuze at length here is that the quote addresses a number of key issues in Tarde's work. The first regards the relation between sociology and psychology. Contrary to what Deleuze intimates in the quote, Tarde did actually speak of his sociological programme as an 'interpsychology' (e.g. Tarde, 1903), in contrast to what he labelled intrapsychology. While this difference may not be as easy to sustain as Tarde seems to suggest, the central point to note is that Tarde's interest lies in analysing how ideas travel imitatively between individuals, and thereby form and connect the latter in an interpsychological manner. Importantly, as Deleuze stresses, these imitative transfers need not *necessarily* or exclusively play out between individuals, but may also take place *within a single individual*, where opposing rays of imitation may lead to hesitation: which imitative current to follow?

It is in analysing this link between the external rays of imitation and the internal hesitation that may arise when confronted with them that, according to Deleuze, Tarde's sociology emerges as a particular kind of microsociology: Tarde demonstrates that even thoughts that appear to be highly individual (micro) are actually formed by imitative, i.e. social, currents. It should be clear that this notion of microsociology is not to be conflated with, say, a more interactionist conception of microsociology à la Erving Goffman. Tarde's sociology is not primarily concerned with the micro dynamics between co-present individuals. Indeed, Tarde's theorizing actually cross-cuts traditional micro–macro distinctions. Deleuze recognizes this when stating, together with Felix Guattari, that 'microimitation does seem to occur between two individuals. But at the same time, and at a deeper level, it has to do not with an individual but with a flow or a wave. *Imitation is the propagation of a flow*' (Deleuze and Guattari, 1987: 219, italics in the original; see also Sampson, 2012: 8). Consequently, the 'Deleuzian Tarde', as it were, entails a minute analysis of how flows of imitation circulate and engender (individual and collective) desires. Relatedly, Deleuze's reading makes clear that Tarde's sociology does not place individuals first or centre stage. Rather, Tarde appears to be a post-structuralist theorist *avant la lettre*, in that he recasts individuals as containers of imitative rays (for a discussion of post-structuralism and Tarde, see also Moebius, 2004). Or, in the words of Ruth Leys:

By dissolving the boundaries between self and other, the theory of imitation-suggestion embodied a highly plastic notion of the human subject that radically called into question the unity and identity of the self. Put another way, it made the notion of individuality itself problematic. (Leys, 1993: 281)

Bruno Latour, too, focuses on how Tarde's work may help to reconceive the micro and macro levels. Thus, in one of Latour's key texts on Tarde (Latour, 2002), the latter is praised not least because he offers a way out of what in Latour's view is a micro–macro deadlock. Indeed, Latour highlights Tarde as the hitherto unrecognized 'forefather' of Actor Network Theory (ANT), who similar to his later ANT heirs argued partly 'that the nature/society divide is irrelevant for understanding the world of human interactions', and partly 'that the micro/macro distinction stifles any attempt at understanding how society is generated' (Latour, 2002: 118).

Latour focuses on Tarde's monadology, which is inspired by Leibniz, but also differs from the latter's monadology in that, for example, there is no God in Tarde's account (for a discussion of Tarde and Leibniz, see Lorenc, 2012: 77–80; see also Chapter 7, this volume). According to Latour, Tarde's monadology dismissed the nature–society divide because it (1) operates with a generalized notion of society, not confined to societies of human beings, but including as well stars, solar systems, and so on, as societal assemblages (Latour, 2002: 120; Tarde, 2012: 28); and (2) argues that all of these societies are made up of monads or, in Latour's terms, 'agencies, each of them endowed with faith and desire, and actively promoting one's total version of the world' (Latour, 2002: 119). It is also this monadological outlook which made Tarde dismiss the micro–macro distinction, according to Latour. Thus, for Tarde, the macro is nothing but the temporary (and necessarily fragile) stabilization of one monad's goals. In Latour's words, '[t]he big, the whole, the great, is not superior to the monad, it is only a simpler, more standardized version of *one monad's goals which it has reached in making parts of its view shared by the others*' (2002: 122, italics in the original). For Latour, Tarde's monadology is not simply a means through which to readdress central sociological debates and issues; it also offers a valuable analytical platform. For example, Latour has argued that new digital methods, obviously not available to Tarde himself, can be fruitfully employed to study monads in a contemporary setting, and in ways that allegedly avoid the pitfalls of the nature–society and micro–macro divides (see Latour et al., 2012).

As in the case of Deleuze, Latour's reading also revisits the Tarde–Durkheim debate and defends the Tardean position against Durkheim's critiques. And similar to Deleuze, Latour flatly rejects the accusation of an inherent psychologism in Tarde's work. For example, Latour claims that 'no sociology was ever further from psychology than Tarde's' (2002: 127). While interesting and influential, Latour's reading of Tarde invites critical comments on precisely this point. As I shall argue later, it is incorrect to say that no psychological influence is detectable in Tarde sociology—at least this assertion is true only if key dimensions of Tarde's sociological programme are disregarded. And this is indeed the problem with Latour's reading: it focuses almost exclusively on Tarde's monadology, and Tarde's entire imitative programme is more or less ignored.

To illustrate, Latour's influential 2002 article on Tarde does not refer to the latter's central sociological text, *The Laws of Imitation*. Indeed, the notion of imitation is only mentioned in passing in this article by Latour. To be sure, this is not the case in some of Latour's subsequent discussions of Tarde. For example, Latour and Lépinay's *The Science of Passionate Interests* offers an introduction to Tarde's *Psychologie économique*

(1902), in which the notion of imitation is granted a greater role, although the authors still attribute the monadology a more central importance in Tarde's theorizing (Latour and Lépinay, 2009). Similarly, in Latour et al. (2012) emphasis is on Tarde's monadology, whereas Tarde's key sociological notion of imitation is hardly mentioned. This obviously would not be a problem if the monadology were entirely consonant with Tarde's sociology of imitations. While Latour suggests that the two do in fact correspond to one another (Latour et al., 2012: 20), I will argue that they do not.

I will contest the central status ascribed to the monadology on two grounds. First, Tarde's essay on monadology—recently translated into English as *Monadology and Sociology* (Tarde, 2012)—was first published as a journal article in 1893 and subsequently reprinted in a collection of essays in 1895. In other words, it appeared three years after Tarde had published the first edition of *Laws of Imitation*, the second edition of which, as mentioned earlier, came out in 1895. While this suggests that the imitation theory was developed prior to the monadology, it does of course neither entail that the two are disconnected nor that they are opposed to each other. However, in one of the few places where Tarde explicitly brings together the monadology and his general sociological programme, he appears to regard the latter, i.e. the theory of imitation, as more significant than the monadology. In Tarde's own words, his general sociology represents the 'more solid and more positive arguments' as compared to the more 'metaphysical theory' of the monads (Tarde, 1899: 211).

What I am arguing here is not that the monadology does not play any role in Tarde's general sociological theorizing; it is certainly important to take it into account if one wants to understand how Tarde conceives of imitative rays and their desire to conquer the world (Tarde, 2012: 60). My point is simply that the link between the monadology and the imitation sociology is rather more complex and ambiguous than, for example, Latour's reading suggests (see also Borch and Stäheli, 2009a; Merz-Benz, 2009). More specifically, and this is the second aspect of my critique of the centrality attributed to the monadology, by focusing mainly on Tarde's theorizing on monads, the entire psychological edifice of his work (too) easily escapes attention. Thus, the emphasis on the monadology neglects (at least in Latour's reading) the somnambulistic layer of Tarde's imitation theory, i.e. the central reference to the domain of hypnotism, suggestion, and somnambulism as the key features of the social. A similar point has been made by Lisa Blackman (2007) and Tony D. Sampson (2012: 42). For example, Blackman writes that 'Latour's recent re-readings of Tarde which champion Tarde as a "thinker of networks"…cover over the importance of the psychological matter which made Tarde's formulations intelligible' (2007: 577). This 'psychological matter' refers precisely to the repertoire of hypnotism, suggestion, and somnambulism.

One may use this critical point as a springboard to revisit, once again, the Tarde–Durkheim debate. Thus, the problem with Durkheim's accusation of Tarde's alleged psychologism is not that it completely misses the target, as Deleuze and Latour claim. Rather the problem is that Durkheim entirely disregarded the possibility that fruitful analytical venues might be opened up precisely by combining insights from psychology and sociology.[2] In other words, it is the policing of the boundaries of the sociological discipline—and the exclusion of psychological input—which is truly problematic in Durkheim's position. As I shall try to demonstrate in section 12.4, it is indeed possible to distil a fruitful analytical programme from Tarde's thinking which revolves around, and links imitation processes to, the repertoire of hypnosis, suggestion, and somnambulism. This would not only allow for a fuller application of his rich theorizing, but also bring to the fore (better than a narrow focus on his monadology) the processual gist of Tarde's work, which is valuable for understanding contemporary organizations and organizing processes.

12.4 ORGANIZING IMITATION-SUGGESTION: A TARDEAN ANALYTICS OF POWER

In spite of the recent wave of interest in Tarde's work, there have been hardly any attempts to connect it to organization studies (a link also not provided explicitly by Tarde himself). There are a few exceptions to that picture, namely Barbara Czarniawska, Kristin Sahlin-Andersson, and Guje Sevón (Czarniawska, 2004; Sahlin-Andersson and Sevón, 2003). For example, Czarniawska has employed a Tardean framework to analyse how city politicians, administrators, and managers engage in imitative processes when they are 'looking at their counterparts in other cities' in order to brand their own city as profitably as possible (Czarniawska, 2004: 122; see also 2009). On more theoretical grounds, both Czarniawska, and Sahlin-Andersson and Sevón have argued that Tarde's theorizing contributes to organization theory by providing an important correction to Paul DiMaggio and Walter Powell's work on institutional isomorphism. Whereas DiMaggio and Powell (1991) distinguish between coercive, normative, and mimetic forms of isomorphism, and argue (in Czarniawska's words) that mimetic isomorphism is 'a sign of uncertainty: people imitate only when they do not know how to conduct themselves', Czarniawska suggests that Tarde's work makes plain that 'this explanation certainly underestimates the pervasiveness of *mimesis*.... Imitation is not a residual category, but a pivotal explanatory concept for those who try to understand the phenomena of [the] contemporary world of organizations' (Czarniawska, 2004: 121, italics in the original; see also Borch, 2010; Sahlin-Andersson and Sevón, 2003). The question is now what it would entail to take seriously this urge to place imitation centre stage.

Not surprisingly, perhaps, different analytical avenues present themselves as ways to study imitation in an organizational context. One Tardean approach—the one followed especially by Czarniawska—is to map in a detailed manner how organizations as supra-individual entities imitate one another in their quest for identity (and alterity) and how inventions are produced along with the imitative processes. Such an analysis is likely to entail a loose or plastic conception of organizations in the sense that organizational boundaries are hard to sustain: imitative currents do not necessarily respect formal organizational boundaries, but may well contribute to dissolving organizational 'identity' (not dissimilar to how imitation processes put into question personal selves). This is not to say that no forms of organization are possible;[3] the point is rather that Tarde's emphasis on imitation tends to shift the attention from formal *organizations* to modes and processes of *organizing*.

This shift in attention has been made clear in recent analyses of financial crises, specifically the exuberant contagious patterns referred to at the beginning of this chapter. For example, Sampson has argued that Tarde's sociology of imitations—and especially of *crowd* imitations—offers a highly relevant means to understand the current networked economy and how its 'uncontained financial contagion' is linked to 'an immeasurable chaotic force of relation. This force arises from the mostly unconscious desires of a relatively small group of traders whose speculative transactions trigger the inflation of bubbles of market value and sentiment in the capitalist economy' (Sampson, 2012: 98). Put differently, Tarde provides important insights into the processes underpinning the modes of organizing characteristic of today's financial markets. That is, to understand how these markets operate, it would be argued from a Tardean perspective, emphasis is needed on the potential cascading of imitation processes and how they might produce highly unanticipated consequences.

Another approach to imitation is the one that follows in the footsteps of Latour's interpretation. While the Latourian approach would pay less explicit attention to imitation, it too would aim at mapping the coming into being of particular organizational actor networks which may well cross-cut formal organizational boundaries.

What the approaches mentioned so far have in common is that they present a Tardean perspective that understands organizational dynamics (whether in formal organizations or in modes of organizing) as *processes of connectivity*. Put differently, these approaches all suggest that Tarde's theorizing is valuable as an analytics of imitation that attends to how imitative dynamics are tightly interwoven and may unfold in unpredictable manners. And although Czarniawska in particular focuses on how organizations build their identities on the basis of imitation, what is not explicitly addressed in these takes on Tarde is how imitation may not simply spread out, but may be *deliberately orchestrated*. This, however, is captured by the final approach I wish to discuss here—and which resonates with interpretations of Tarde put forward by Sampson (2012) and Thrift (2008). This approach would not only place *power* centrally in the understanding of how imitation unfolds; as intimated earlier, it would also pay less attention to organizations proper and instead stress processes of organizing that take place also beyond a formal organizational domain. Studying such processes in terms of power is consistent, I shall argue, with Tarde's work, as his general sociology of imitation contains an inherent power perspective. In the following, I will first show how power is integral to imitation processes and then proceed by illustrating how such processes are being organized in contemporary economic and political life.

As mentioned earlier, imitation is defined by Tarde as a kind of somnambulism. This amounts to saying that the notion of imitation is modelled around the difference between hypnotizer and hypnotized where the latter imitates the former, not least because of his or her alleged prestige. And it amounts to saying that imitation is enmeshed in suggestive processes where people do not act in a conscious and deliberate fashion, but rather as sleepwalkers, i.e. in a state of semiconscious hypnosis. It makes sense, I will argue, to see this suggestive-hypnotic relation as a power game where the hypnotized is subjected to the power of the hypnotizer. This squares nicely with Tarde's own comments that imitation is 'the action at a distance of one mind upon another' and that hypnosis is the process through which 'a quasi-photographic reproduction of a cerebral image upon the sensitive plate of another brain' is effected (Tarde, 1962: xiv). To be sure, referring to this relation as one of power is not new. Most notably, perhaps, Sigmund Freud did precisely that when criticizing, in his famous 1921 essay 'Group Psychology and the Analysis of the Ego' (1989), the importance attributed to the notion of suggestion in classical crowd psychological work by Tarde and Gustave Le Bon. In 1889 Freud had visited Hippolyte Bernheim in France and seen him trying to treat his patients by means of hypnotic suggestion. On Freud's view this had revealed itself as a form of 'tyranny', with the doctor 'trying to subdue [the patients] with suggestions' (Freud, 1989: 28). In order to distance himself from the allegedly tyrannical suggestion framework, Freud advocated his notion of libido as one which, he argued, inaugurated an alternative explanatory horizon. Rather than following Freud's path, however, I wish to adhere to Tarde's proposition and examine the potentials of focusing on suggestion (a notion which Freud, in my view, dismissed too rapidly).

What, then, is achieved by analysing imitation as a hypnotic-suggestive process? First, on a very general level, it points to the possibility of understanding '[h]ow order can exist without knowledge', as Niklas Luhmann has put it, with explicit reference to Tarde (Luhmann, 1998: 98): the flows of semiconscious imitations occur without the imitators necessarily having any knowledge about being subdued to the suggestions. Second, whereas scholars such as Luhmann would place communication first when analysing organizations and the social, Tarde's perspective in effect points to the role of pre-communicative processes (see also Borch, 2013). That is, a Tardean focus on imitation points to how the hypnotic suggestion of imitation conditions communication (without this necessarily entailing any theoretical upgrading of the status of the body). Similar to how the hypnotizer moulds the desires of the hypnotized and thereby affects the latter's communicative preferences, imitation processes make certain communications more likely than others in that they mould the flow of desires in the social domain. While this reading to some extent echoes Deleuze's interpretation, Latour's reading of Tarde forecloses, or at least ignores, this kind of analytical insight into the power exercised through imitation.

Before illustrating how this may play out, it is crucial to make one point about the application of the hypnotizer–hypnotized model to understand social processes. Thus, while the model in its more medical adaptation suggests that we have to do with two individuals (doctor and patient), it makes sense I think—and here important inspiration can be derived from Latour—to expand the reference to the non-human field. Put differently, as I have argued elsewhere, I propose that suggestion be analysed as something that can emanate from humans and non-humans alike (Borch, 2007: 563–4). Such a point has also been established within the study of crowds, which was so important to Tarde: despite often focusing on how the leader may exercise a hypnotic power over the crowd he or she leads, it is noted within this field that crowds may also be hypnotized by images or objects (Le Bon, 1960: 102–3; see also Brennan, 2004: 54). Consequently, to take the full implications of the imitation framework means attending to how imitation-suggestion processes are propelled through both humans and non-humans.

To illustrate how all of this may play out, I wish to attend to Nigel Thrift's work on contemporary trajectories of capitalism and politics (for a similar type of analysis, see Sampson, 2012). Thrift draws explicitly on Tarde's theory of imitation but also relates it to findings within, for example, neurobiology. In the present context I am not so interested in how Tarde's thinking might be aligned with ideas from neurobiological research; rather, I wish to point to Thrift's observations of how Tardean imitation dynamics apparently become ever-more integral to the ways both profit and political support are engendered. Taking the economic realm first, Thrift describes this in terms of a 'political economy of propensity' (Thrift, 2008). This label refers to a transition in economic reasoning from means-end schemata to a logic of propensity, where propensity is understood 'as a disposition to behave in a certain way which is only partly in the control of the agent' (2008: 83), i.e. similar to what Tarde describes with his notion of semiconscious imitation-suggestion. For example, Thrift discusses the fields of sensory marketing and neuromarketing, arguing that careful corporate design and use of 'fragrance and sound produce more powerful reactions than brand logos', and where the underlying 'intent is...to operate in the semiconscious domain' (2008: 90, 91). Similarly, Thrift notes how 'hormonal swashes and how to influence them through the media' has long been a wet dream of business, which is now becoming technologically possible, and which aims to 'identify susceptible populations and to render them open to suggestion' (2008: 91). According to Thrift, these and analogous developments testify to the increasing predominance of a power paradigm which comes close to what Tarde analysed and which aims to:

> conform to propensity and support it, not to guide, but to 'second'...This is not, it needs to be stressed, either non-action or passivity. Rather, it is the work of aiding and abetting certain aspects of continual transformation, strategically bending process so that it 'ripens' in certain directions rather than others. (Thrift, 2008: 90)

Moreover, this is a form of power that seeks to instill desires and imitations through the design of non-human entities.

Thrift argues that similar power modalities which pivot around basic imitation-suggestion processes can be identified in contemporary political life. Of course, strategic attempts to mould and organize political processes in order to achieve specific purposes are not new, but novel technologies such as websites devoted to raising awareness of and gathering support for particular political issues

> have shown that it is possible to produce a politics of political imitation which is effective and can have real political bite....Its speed and imitative capacity allow it to

stimulate the kinds of expressive interchanges that populate everyday life and provide a political form which in some ways is as important as content. (Thrift, 2007: 253–4)

To summarize, Thrift's examples point to a central idea in Tarde's sociology of imitation, namely the urge to analyse how specific desires to imitate are produced. While Tarde focused on how imitation is often rooted in some form of (often *personal*) prestige, contemporary modes of organizing imitation processes tend to revolve around more sophisticated functional equivalents that increasingly assume non-human forms. Whatever means are employed to buttress these processes, and whether or not they take place within formal organizations or assume broader shapes, the attempt to mould imitative processes is essentially an attempt to exercise power—a power that is not too different from Deleuze's notion of control (see Deleuze, 1995).

12.5 CONCLUSION

This chapter has presented and discussed Tarde's sociology and its analytical potential for understanding organizational and organizing processes. In addition to outlining key concepts and concerns in Tarde's work, I have attended to the influential interpretations put forward by Deleuze and Latour. As I have argued, I particularly find Latour's reading of Tarde one-sided and have opted for placing Tarde's key notion of imitation at the centre of the reception of his work. Furthermore, I have tried to demonstrate that the fact that organization studies still have not really picked up on Tardean ideas does not preclude stimulating analytical applications in this field. As argued, the processual gist of Tarde's theorization has two dimensions. One relates to pure connectivity, i.e. the fact that imitative flows can be identified and analysed among people and organizations as well as, for example, in financial markets where contagious imitative dynamics can assume accidental forms. The other processual dimension of Tarde's thinking lies in how imitative dynamics might be designed or orchestrated. This perspective offers a sophisticated analytics of power (and desire) that has relevance both for the understanding of organizations proper and of broader modes of (political, economic, etc.) organizing. That is, Tarde's work can be used not only to analyse how imitative flows unfold but also to examine how such flows are embedded in all sorts of strategic and powerful attempts to mould desires and thereby achieve specific effects.

NOTES

1. For an in-depth discussion of Tarde's theorizing on crowds, which situates it in the context of his larger sociological work, see Borch (2012: ch. 2).
2. To see such potential materialized, one need only refer to the early Frankfurt School, whose members excelled in producing stimulating analyses on the basis of a blend of psychoanalysis and sociology.

3. For example, in his writings on economic psychology, Tarde notes that '[i]t is through the conscious or unconscious, assembled or dispersed, association of workers that the solidarity of labours manifests itself' (2007: 618, italics in the original).

REFERENCES

Alliez, E. (2004). The Difference and Repetition of Gabriel Tarde, *Distinktion* 9: 49–54.

Barry, A. (2010). Tarde's Method: Between Statistics and Experimentation', in M. Candea (ed.), *The Social after Gabriel Tarde: Debates and Assessments* (London and New York: Routledge): 177–90.

Blackman, L. (2007). Reinventing Psychological Matters: The Importance of the Suggestive Realm of Tarde's Ontology, *Economy and Society* 36(4): 574–96.

Borch, C. (2005). Urban Imitations: Tarde's Sociology Revisited, *Theory, Culture & Society* 22(3): 81–100.

—— (2007). Crowds and Economic Life: Bringing an Old Figure Back In, *Economy and Society* 36(4): 549–73.

—— (2010). Organizational Atmospheres: Foam, Affect and Architecture, *Organization* 17(2): 223–41.

—— (2012). *The Politics of Crowds: An Alternative History of Sociology* (Cambridge: Cambridge University Press).

—— (2013). Spatiality, Imitation, Immunization: Luhmann and Sloterdijk on the Social, in A. La Cour and A. Philippopoulos-Mihalopoulos (eds), *Luhmann Observed: Radical Theoretical Encounters* (Houndmills, Basingstoke: Palgrave Macmillan): 150–68.

—— and Stäheli, U. (2009a). Einleitung—Tardes Soziologie der Nachahmung und des Begehrens, in C. Borch and U. Stäheli (eds), *Soziologie der Nachahmung und des Begehrens. Materialien zu Gabriel Tarde* (Frankfurt am Main: Suhrkamp): 7–38.

—— (eds) (2009b). *Soziologie der Nachahmung und des Begehrens. Materialien zu Gabriel Tarde* (Frankfurt am Main: Suhrkamp).

Brennan, T. (2004). *The Transmission of Affect* (Ithaca and London: Cornell University Press).

Candea, M. (ed.) (2010). *The Social after Gabriel Tarde: Debates and Assessments* (London and New York: Routledge).

Czarniawska, B. (2004). Gabriel Tarde and Big City Management, *Distinktion* 4: 119–33.

—— (2009). Gabriel Tarde and Organization Theory, in P.S. Adler (ed.), *The Oxford Handbook of Sociology and Organization Studies* (Oxford: Oxford University Press): 246–67.

Deleuze, G. (1994). *Difference and Repetition* (London: The Athlone Press).

—— (1995). Postscript on Control Societies, in *Negotiations, 1972–1990* (New York: Columbia University Press): 177–82.

—— and Guattari, F. (1987). *A Thousand Plateaus: Capitalism and Schizophrenia* (Minneapolis and London: University of Minnesota Press).

DiMaggio, P.J. and Powell, W.W. (1991). The Iron Cage Revisited: Institutional Isomorphism and Collective Rationality in Organizational Fields, in P.J. DiMaggio and W.W. Powell (eds), *The New Institutionalism in Organizational Analysis* (Chicago and London: University of Chicago Press): 63–82.

Durkheim, E. (1951). *Suicide: A Study in Sociology* (New York: The Free Press).

—— (1982). *The Rules of Sociological Method. And Selected Texts on Sociology and Its Method* (London: Macmillan).

Freud, S. (1989). *Group Psychology and the Analysis of the Ego* (New York and London: W.W. Norton & Company).

Latour, B. (2002). Gabriel Tarde and the End of the Social, in P. Joyce (ed.), *The Social in Question. New Bearings in History and the Social Sciences* (London and New York: Routledge): 117–32.

——(2005). *Reassembling the Social: An Introduction to Actor-Network-Theory* (Oxford: Oxford University Press).

——Jensen, P., Venturini, T., Grauwin, S., and Boullier, D. (2012). 'The Whole is Always Smaller than Its Parts'—A Digital Test of Gabriel Tarde's Monads, *British Journal of Sociology* 63(4): 590–615.

——and Lépinay, V.A. (2009). *The Science of Passionate Interests: An Introduction to Gabriel Tarde's Economic Anthropology* (Chicago: Prickly Paradigm Press).

Le Bon, G. (1960). *The Crowd: A Study of the Popular Mind* (New York: The Viking Press).

Leys, R. (1993). Mead's Voices: Imitation as Foundation, or, The Struggle against Mimesis, *Critical Inquiry* 19(2): 277–307.

Lorenc, T. (2012). Afterwoord: Tarde's Pansocial Ontology, in G. Tarde, *Monadology and Sociology* (Melbourne: re.press): 71–95.

Luhmann, N. (1998). *Observations on Modernity* (Stanford, CA: Stanford University Press).

——(2000). *Organisation und Entscheidung* (Opladen: Westdeutscher Verlag).

Mazzarella, W. (2010). The Myth of the Multitude, or, Who's Afraid of the Crowd?, *Critical Inquiry* 36(4): 697–727.

Merz-Benz, P.-U. (2009). Die 'Formel' der Geschichte. Ferdinand Tönnies, Gabriel Tarde und die Frage einer Geometrie des sozialen Lebens, in C. Borch and U. Stäheli (eds), *Soziologie der Nachahmung und des Begehrens. Materialien zu Gabriel Tarde* (Frankfurt am Main: Suhrkamp): 180–225.

Moebius, S. (2004). Imitation, Repetition and Iterability: Poststructuralism and the 'Social Laws' of Gabrial Tarde, *Distinktion* 9: 55–69.

Mucchielli, L. (2000). Tardomania? Réflexions sur les usages contemporains de Tarde, *Revue d'Histoire des Sciences Humaines* 3: 161–84.

Peckham, R. (2013). Economies of Contagion: Financial Crisis and Pandemic, *Economy and Society* 42(2): 226–48.

Sahlin-Andersson, K. and G. Sevón (2003). Imitation and Identification as Performatives, in B. Czarniawska and G. Sevón (eds), *The Northern Lights: Organization Theory in Scandinavia* (Malmo: Liber): 249–65.

Sampson, T.D. (2012). *Virality: Contagion Theory in the Age of Networks* (Minneapolis: Minnesota University Press).

Tarde, G. (1892). Les crimes des foules, *Archives de l'Anthropologie Criminelle* 7: 353–86.

——(1893). Foules et sectes au point de vue criminal, *Revue des Deux Mondes* 332: 349–87.

——(1899). *Social Laws: An Outline of Sociology* (New York: The Macmillan Company).

——(1902). *Psychologie économique* (Paris: Félix Alcan).

——(1903). Inter-Psychology, the Inter-Play of Human Minds, *International Quarterly* 7: 59–84.

——(1962). *The Laws of Imitation* (Gloucester, MA: Peter Smith).

——(1968). *Penal Philosophy* (Montclair, NJ: Patterson Smith).

——(1969). *On Communication and Social Influence. Selected Papers,* ed. with an introduction by T.N. Clark (Chicago and London: University of Chicago Press).

——(1989). *L'opinion et la foule* (Paris: Presses Universitaires de France).

——(1999a). *L'opposition universelle. Essai d'une théorie des contraires* (Paris: Institut Synthélabo pour le progrès de la connaissance).

——(1999b). *La logique sociale* (Paris: Institut Synthélabo).

——(2007). Economic psychology, *Economy and Society 36*(4): 614–43.

——(2012). *Monadology and Sociology* (Melbourne: re.press).

Thrift, N. (2007). *Non-Representational Theory: Space, Politics, Affect* (London and New York: Routledge).

——(2008). Pass It On: Towards a Political Economy of Propensity, *Emotion, Space and Society 1*(2): 83–96.

Toews, D. (2003). The New Tarde: Sociology after the End of the Social, *Theory, Culture & Society 20*(5): 81–98.

CHAPTER 13

FRIEDRICH NIETZSCHE
(1844–1900)

ROBIN HOLT AND DANIEL HJORTH

Strange father! Your children will not let you down, they are coming across the earth with the footsteps of gods, rubbing their eyes: where am I?

(Södergran, 'Strange Father', 1918/1984)

13.1 LIFE AND PLACE

NIETZSCHE, THE great declassifier, the most open of open minds, has confined himself to his room in Turin. Having come down from the mountains to overwinter in lower climes, the city's shadowed alleyways and sharply lit squares are witnessing the final self-governing steps of this wanderer. His light, once tight and as straight as the arrowed hands of a clock pointing upwards towards noon, is no longer burning with high, yellow energy; like a setting sun, he is at the end of his day. His landlady has heard pounding above; she investigates. Peering through the keyhole she sees her tenant naked, dancing across the room, his feet bringing the floorboards into repetitive, primal life. Nietzsche, echoing his father, is down-going beneath the horizon of sanity. The landlady's peephole world radiates with a last bursting glow of enveloping energy, and then darkens as she withdraws her eye. The heavens have ceded to this pastor's son one last time, revealing his room a 'dance floor for divine accidents' upon which it is his wont to dance. His final statement has been the dance, that most forceful and affirmative of human expression; without voice he descends, wordless.

He began with words. Nietzsche's chosen profession was to work with language, a wordmonger and analyser, a student of definition, who found delight in words becoming increasingly elusive when subject to analysis. His enquiries into words began early, filtered through the self-consciously demanding and traditional regimens of a school at

Pforta, near Naumberg, Saxony. He started here aged 14, in 1858, adjusting to an almost monasterial regime: rise early, pray, start studying, break classes for prayer and 'reading', more classes, homework, meal, prayer, bed, and so on. Within this strictest of daily rhythms, school life has already staged this enquirer as 'an outsider': he is wanting to write his assignments about unknown romantic poets like Hölderlin rather than more established, stolid Prussians; he is riddled with enigmatic maladies of the head and stomach, ailments he will never outgrow; he is feverishly composing musical works, all of them heavy with ponderous precocity. For fellow students and masters this boy exudes a perpetually upsetting and upset distinctiveness. He scrapes into a scholarship at the University of Bonn as a theology student, rapidly loses his Christian faith, and converts to study philology under Professor Ritschl. Professor and student move to the University of Leipzig, in whose streets, at Antiquariat Rohn, Nietzsche finds a second-hand copy of Schopenhauer's *World as Will and Representation*. Smitten, his world jolts, and while philology now gives way, becoming a means for tackling philosophical problems, his love for literary forms stays, helping him overcome the limits of philosophical expression. The biggest philosophical problem is given by Schopenhauer: how to overcome the pessimism besetting us amid a life that is always wavering, always eluding, always reaching beyond our attempts to wrestle it into representative submission, always issuing us into conflict? The Presocratic Greek playwrights like Sophocles had already provided one response; recognizing life was versed in conflict they wrote tragedy. Tragedy took standard plots and frames. Typically the universal, undifferentiated, and often indifferent force of nature (represented by the oceanic murmurings of a chorus) forms the background against which individual characters struggle, noble enough, yet beset by the pranks and petty jealousies of the gods, humbled, governed by furies and by fate, ignorant of the real identity of those most close to them. Nietzsche makes exhaustive studies of these forms and their comprehension of the human condition. He is finding his way only to discover that making his way will now become his way.

His studiousness finds him taking up a professorial chair in classical philology at the University on Basel, at age 25 and without his habilitation, having been recommended by a seriously impressed Ritschl. For a decade from 1869 he teaches within this walled city, but is never domesticated, always circling. Though Prussian by birth, even enduring brief forays serving in the artillery (cut short by a riding accident), and as a medical orderly during the Franco–Prussian War, he has, prior to joining Basel's faculty, renounced his nationality, remaining officially stateless, an alien force, until his death.

At Basel he rekindles an earlier meeting with Richard Wagner, whose nearby residence at Tribschen provides domestic and intellectual inspiration. It is from here he refines and intensifies his thoughts on the profound problem of pessimism and the tragic. His response—*The Birth of Tragedy Out of the Spirit of Music*—appears in 1872, an encomium to Wagner's capacity to render the tragic human condition in myths that still enoble us with the possibility of creative genius tragic. Yet no sooner issued, this enthusiasm for Wagner's totalizing art is gradually resisted as an arrogant and politicized myth-making took organizational hold at Bayreuth. By 1876 (later published as *Human, All Too Human*, 1878), Nietzsche has refined his thoughts on tragedy, and broken regular contact with the

Wagner circle, whose stuffy, romantic nationalism made him nauseous. Wagner's art is becoming freighted with unifying myth and enfeebled with exhibitionism and cleverness. Now Nietzsche is looking to science, a form of splenetic positivism takes hold. Science shows us unfeeling, moving nature, its keen instruments reveal the plenitude of occurrence, and we garner a cool knowledge of a world entirely indifferent to its being observed. Being Nietzsche's, it is a science that resists any tendency to idealize, to look behind or beyond for deeper meanings. Science simply describes without the connivance of proof or the warrant of essences, instinctively distrustful of the convictions that 'confirmed' hypotheses can yield (1878a: §635). *The Dawn* (1881) and then *Gay Science* (1882) expatiate upon such a world in which this solitary wanderer was wont to take one perspective, then another, relentlessly, without the comforts of settlement, adopting what Deleuze (2006: 58) calls a totalizing criticism that reaches its apotheosis in the four parts of *Thus Spake Zarathustra* (1887/1888). Nietzsche never rests, save to find in rest a perspective upon wandering. The speed at which he moves is bewildering, leaving no stable dots behind, only lines. He has long since left the confines of academia, and stays in a migratory circuit of pensions and hotels, high in the Alps during summer and towards southern European coasts during autumn and winter. Amongst the mountains he finds his rhythm, and his deep, glowing fire gets him up on the high hillside, where the air is clear but demanding to breathe. There is a cold glow, a style of his, crafted in the mountains. His income is meagre. He is relying on the pension graciously procured by his colleagues at Basel, the occasional royalty from his increasingly difficult to place publications, on frequent parcels of socks and sausage sent by his mother living in Naumburg, and on self-prescribed opiates. He falls in love, finds it unrequited, and then falls more readily still for love itself, loving as a giving over, a spilling over of self-created gifts issued by a non-possessing poet. The words spill forth: *Beyond Good and Evil* (1886), *Genealogy of Morality* (1887), a crescendo of prose building through *Wagner Case* (1888), *Twilight of the Idols* (1888/1889), *Antichrist* (1888/1895), *Ecce Homo* (1888/1908) before the climax of a breakdown in Turin during which he pleads with a beaten and broken horse lying on the street to forgive the sins of the men by whom it, and the world, suffers. The remainder of his life, after the horse, after the naked dance, after the ranting letters in which he signs himself Christ, is a bed-ridden madness. His legacy is preserved within pockets of reverence set like small jewels against the large, blank backdrop of a largely indifferent European academy. His friends Peter Gast, Franz Overbeck, and Georg Brandes sparkle, and gradually, sporadically, their enthusiasim becomes infectious. Nietzsche lasts another eleven years, tended by his anti-semitic sister, who, after her brother's death in 1900, begins to spin twisted selections of his unpublished prose into astringent forms whose sharp glint sharpens the paranoia of credulous fascists like Mussolini. In his *History of Western Philosophy* Bertrand Russell affeared such emotional appeal, finding in Nietzsche's contemplations of strife nothing but 'the power phantasies of an invalid'. Yet in contrast the poets D.H Lawrence and Edith Södergran, the pair of them invalided by tuberculosis, find Nietzsche a profound source of vital, primal stimulus; as he also became in the anarchism of Emma Goldman and Errico Malatesta, the humanist Zionism of Martin Buber, the dissonant compositions of Alexander Scriabin, and the freeform, mystical writing of H.P.

Lovecraft. It was always thus with Nietzsche, the mal-appropriations, the recoil, the curiosity merging with fear, the courage-inducing leap. His are difficult pills, and taken properly there is no going back. Perhaps easier to half swallow, spit out, and steal back indoors to the homely, wicker-basket comforts of homily and morality. We thought we had come to Nietzsche to read, but find ourselves with vertigo and the abyss, working with blacksmith's fire, and with the cold blowing in from too clear air.

13.2 PHILOSOPHY

13.2.1 Tragedy

The title page of *The Birth of Tragedy* carries a woodcut of Prometheus. The tragic Prometheus is a figure breaching the world of humans and gods. He pleads with vengeful Zeus to lessen the confinements being imposed on humans in punishment for their hubris, but his boons go unheeded. Undaunted, Prometheus takes it upon himself to intervene in fate and assist humanity against Zeus. He steals fire from the forge of Hephaestus, metalworker and machinist to the gods, and gifts it to mortals, who might now warm themselves, eat well, and create, thereby wresting themselves slightly from godly imprimaturs. Angered by such temerity, Zeus ties Prometheus to rocks, exposed, an eagle pecks at his organs and carries pieces into the sky, only for the organ to re-grow, and for the cycle of pain and recovery to repeat itself, endlessly. Prometheus—this cunning, equivocal, pain-enduring immortal—is there at the outset of Nietzsche's thought encountering dismal repetition head on, forever renewing his potential, his life generating organs, despite them suffering constant attack and diminution. He is chained, confined to such patterns, but he burns undimmed in their return. Nearly all of Nietzsche's work can be read as an evocation and exemplification of Prometheus.

Guided by gifting Prometheus, *The Birth of Tragedy* finds human life grounded in an unendurable condition of being its own backdrop. To search for tragic truth is to endure this pain by fleeing from oneself. In fleeing we realize how these feelings stay with us, our shadows; ideas and decisions are largely impotent in the wake of these drives and passions (Sloterdijk, 1985: 12–14). It is this experience of fleeing and finding one's shadow still stubbornly in place that constitutes our freedom; the eagle leaves, then descends and pecks anew, and we endure and look again to flee. Rather than inducing pessimism, Nietzsche suggests struggle might be turned to good account by those able to experience it as a 'joyous combat', something dramatized as the inevitable entwining of two forces: the Apollonian and Dionysian. Apollo, the messenger god of language, logical distinctions, and equivalences, delights in flying above the world noticing and making comparisons between well-articulated forms. Dionysius wells up and overspills from below, revelling in the 'cruel abundance' and plenitude of an undifferentiated nature, the source of all force, will, and creativity. Tragedy comes forth as an entwining of Apollo and Dionysius, and for Nietzsche this was no more dramatically expressed than in Wagner's 'total art'. Wagner's is a distinct setting loose of the creative animus by which individuals revel and find opportunity in the inexhaustible, meaningless, stirring, and striving of all life. Wagner accepts necessity and fate, whilst tarrying with nature's surging force.

Nietzsche is not alone in making these arguments. This sense of tragedy—that we humans possess apparent meaning-making powers, yet find ourselves thwarted by a puzzling, moving world—undergirds others' work in this period. As well as Nietzsche we have Thomas Carlyle, Ralph Waldo Emerson, John Ruskin, Nicoli Tolstoj, William James, and Maurice Maeterlinck affirming variations on a 'philosophy of life' framed by acceptance of nature's irresistible force (Dilthey, 1907). Such affirmation, however, was difficult to sustain. William James found it especially difficult. As a young man he had experienced a profound and disturbing fear that among the objects of love and aspiration that ground our greatest energies lies an emptying void, a palling nothing, overwhelmed by 'the big, blooming, buzzing confusion' that was unalloyed, godless sensation. James had been reading Emerson and was entranced by the near mystical evocations of nature—the fluxing, shifting, yawing, chattering, inexhaustible rhythms and surfaces. Where Emerson was sanguine, James remained unsettled; the meaninglessness of brutal material momentum was too overwhelming to be tarried with for long. There is only so much 'life affirmation' it is healthy to take, indeed it is to be avoided as much as embraced. This avoidance began in the habits of language whose familiar terms and sounds provided bulwarks against the flow of an indifferent, feckless world. Like planks used to make walkways and gangways, the long-settled grammars form a group upon which we are able to walk in and amid the turbid restless mess of direct sensation. Such habit, however, needs caretakers, refurbishment, as it bears the slap, spray, and salt of the flux. Gangway building is endless, wrought with an 'anguished activism' (Thomas, 1993: 26) which, no matter how intense, forever finds foundations washing away.

Nietzsche knew this as well. He too had been reading Emerson during the same period as James, yet rather than being wary becomes excited in his encounter with this raw rendering of our human place amid seething nature. Emerson gives Nietzsche (1878b: §369) the idea of an 'over-soul', she who creates worlds before her and, finding all facts fugitive, suggests any value to be had from life is from being open to even the most inscrutable suggestion through wandering. Nietzsche plays with this idea of the 'over- soul', how it resists the (inevitable) urges of language to avoid strangeness with categorization and grammatical arrangement (Brobjer, 2008). Rather than construct gangways like James, Nietzsche wants to find in language a vessel, 'a sail' setting out on the current-riven sea, a place of wandering. The sea becomes a recurring motif: plangent, storm-tossed, bewitchingly calm, briny and scouring, chameleon in colour and brightness, intangible yet capable of unrestrained force, inscrutable, deep, uncontainable; it is everything. The sea forms a culminating frame in Nietzsche's writing when, in *Thus Spake Zarathustra*, we find Zarathustra sealing his philosophy in encomium to the sea:

> If I be fond of the sea and all that is sea like. And fondest of it when it angrily contradicts me. If the exploring delight be in me which impels sails to the undiscovered. If the seafarers' delight be in my delight. If ever my rejoicing calls out 'The shore has

vanished'. Now has fallen from me the last chain. The boundless roars around me. Far away sparkle for me space and time (1887/1888: III, Second Dance Song, §5)

The sea, with which Nietzsche 'shares secrets' (1888/1908: §65), becomes what Blumenberg would call a grounding metaphor; impossible to conceptualize, it reveals not only how language can loosen itself, but also how in our linguistic habits we are so often snared on rocks, stuck fast with concepts, immobile, thwarted by gangways. Zarathustra's metaphors of the sea redound with the echoes of a world underway, dancing, playful, forceful, elusive, circular, chosen to affirm our perishable hours: 'But of time and becoming the best similes shall speak. A praise shall they be, and a justification, of all impermanence.' Nietzsche's life is like the sea. Can we then really know Nietzsche? The sea is forceful, but without capacity to support our steps, we can only affirm its fluid quality and set sail.

13.2.2 Genealogy

Nietzsche shows how language secures, and he then enjoins we remain suspicious of all such securing: 'every word is a prejudice' (1878b: §55). Though inevitable, we can be careful with how words fix, notably conceptual language that lies heavy with theory, holding us down with its talk of 'above' and 'below' (1887/1888: III, The Seven Seals, §7). Take the concept 'I', that well-walked gangway upon whose walking we historically distinguish ourselves. We treat this 'I' as identifying, defining, and securing an apparently inviolable inner us. The 'I' becomes fixed, separated, and in its thrall come subaltern conceptual distinctions, notably 'the will', the intentional condition by which 'I' connects to the world through 'thought' and 'action'. And this humanly willed thought and action is found to have distinct qualities. The directed motion of human intention is made distinct from, for example, the instinctual patterns by which tireless bees gather pollen, or from the random, breeze-bound fall of dying leaves. In defining and knowing the 'I' like this—asserting its distinctiveness from bees and leaves—we feel secure, we discover what sustains us physically and emotionally, calling such 'our interests', and we look constantly to secure the companionship or submission of things in the service of such interests (how to get things like bees and leaves to do our bidding).

Yet as much as this knowledge secures us, it makes us insensate to the primordial condition Nietzsche termed Dionysian. We might be reminded, for example, that Homer talks of three Bee Women who, when replete with ambrosia and heady with Dionysian life, are willing to whisper to the god Apollo the secrets of divining, and when deprived of such unearthly food can speak only bitterness. These Bee Women fly at us from an ancient past. We check ourselves, knowing that bees are not like humans, discounting Homer as myth and distancing ourselves from the experience of such immortal ecstasy and frustration. We are no longer open to the loosening experience of such a myth. In steadily and more accurately defining the 'I' (soul, self, ego, reason, agency, intention) we push ourselves away from such worlds as are inhabited by Bee Women, searching for the security of stable representations in which there are bees, and then women, neither of whom commune with gods. In this way, we are always looking away from living to what lies above and beyond life, to what is fixed 'as' something. Such habit is inevitable in many ways, we are all of us organized by this language of subjects (that about which things are said) and predicates (that which is said of things); and as with the way we identify ourselves as an originating 'I', so with all things. Even where we experience something enigmatic, striking, and sublime, like a lightening bolt, we are all ready with such grammatical scaffolding of subjects and predicates; 'If I say: "lightening flashes" I have posited the flash once as an activity and a second time as an object: I have thus presupposed a being underlying an event, a being that is not identical to the event but rather remains, is, and does not become' (Nietzsche, 1887: §45).

Nietzsche is probing how the things 'lightning' and 'I' have come to be. How something has become, he points out, determines what it is. Here he begins to loosen our grammatical scaffolds, simply by bringing time in and showing that words, and things, have lived a life. To understand the truth of something we enquire after its background, its genealogy. Nietzsche offers us a genealogy of ourselves. He goes back to Greek tragedy. Here he finds a sense of primal individuation too terrible to bear, the sheer emptiness of an indifferent cosmos. The subject arises as a tragic experience of fleeing and hence finding distance from this profound truth, a distance enabled first by an Apollonian delight in the vision and clarity of serene representation and second in experiencing a Dionysian swell of intoxicating vitality and *deliré* that arises from a giving over of self to uncontrollable flows of desire. Sloterdijk (1985: 17–30) suggests Nietzsche's genealogical skill lies in showing us this necessary interplay between the neatness of a mannered and upright self and an abandonment to basic drives. We can witness this in the tragedies of ancient culture, how through the representations in art and words we become aware of orgiastic and chaotic drives almost hidden benath a beauty of form, like glimpses of lava through newly-formed rock. In ancient culture, Apollonian form is always the most apparent, we are always within language, hence the regimen of festivals and chorus and revelry by which ancient lives were organized in managed and occasional mis-rule. Nietzsche traces the power of emblems and symbols, the importance of the chorus in plays, the beauty of outline and sound, all of such being examples of the form-giving skill of Apollo in keeping in check what lies below. Thus is set in historical play an image of the human being as centaur, forever caught in the drama of twisting, interplay of knowledge (Apollonian form) and sensuality (Dionysian urge).

Moving through history Nietzsche then identifies how thought, especially the load-bearing thought of philosophy and religion and their obsessions with theory and dogma generated by contemplation (and not action), has gradually removed us from this tragic interplay between Apollo and Dionysius, we have wound our sense of self into a unified, unmusical abstraction whose clarity of form is in direct proportion with its removal the delight and difficulty of having lived. The self becomes configured in opposition to its surroundings, a thing amid other things; in its neat totality it loses its vibrancy. The upshot is with us still; as Sloterdijk (1985: 64) observes, modern experience still presents us with 'the vacillation of souls between isolation and consolidation, between the effort to separate and the desire to unify, between the hell of difference and that of identity'.

Thus genealogy also reveals how the organization of language into subjects and predicates separates us from one another. In his essay *Schopenhauer as Educator*, and then echoed later in *Twilight of the Idols*, Nietzsche laments the ensuing loss of community. We are living like atoms, always separated and concerned with realizing a consistency of subjective presence and hurrying after self-induced goals, the entire endeavour organized so as to perpetuate a culture weaned on settled accumulation, whether of facts or material wealth. Concern with economy and society becomes the extension of the dry academic virtues of predictability and durability into material and symbolic wealth production. The world becomes organized into problems and classes of problems, with solutions the viability of which is measured against timeless yardsticks, and all the while the musicality of foibles, the intensity of love, the inexplicable curlicues of whim, the spasm of disquiet, are set aside as weaknesses to be overcome by a pragmatic commitment to recover settled or established habit. Habit, the authority of history 'sedimented' in practice, is necessary to practically get ahead, yet we must be wary of resenting messiness, including our own human messiness: our drives and ill-tempered outbursts are averred from as regretful, our longing for strange beauty comes configured as a source of degeneration.

13.2.3 Ressentiment and the Last Man

Our resentment at experiencing a messy world has, overtime, generated a peculiar quality to the western mindset, for which Nietzsche reserves the concept *ressentiment*, a peculiar form of vengeful resentment begat by reason. The world always escapes us, confronting us with elusive experience the most dramatic of which is our own death, and we compensate by waging war on the world, all the while erecting conceptual walkways from whose artificial heights we hurl tablets asserting what 'is' and what 'shall be'. We need only look carefully, genealogically, at the emergence of such beseeching and besmirching tablets. Finding the world strange, humans feel guilt (public), even shame (private), at their impotence. And so humans turn upon themselves, creating a moral architecture of 'the good' by whose strictures comes the possibility of asserting blame (and hence the semblance of control). This is how humanity copes, by creating morality: 'Into the basis of things have reward and punishment been insinuated' (1887/1888: II, Of the Virtuous). Punishment bears the semblance of control, a taking back of initiative and a repressing of our feelings of impotence, yet its effects are entirely life denying. So arise the virtuous ones, those 'higher men' who are set against life. Zarathustra calls them tarantulas, spinning vengeful webs of stricture hidden behind concepts like justice. These tarantulas are clever, cold, hidden, preaching 'world malignment' as in their judgements life is continually measured up against yardsticks of the godly and good (1887/1888: On the Tarantulas, II).

This world-maligning morality arises in religion, especially the Christian religion with its 'thou shalts', indulgences, and excommunications. Belief is ours, we control it, and despite the otherworldly invective, it is grounded in temporal concern. And when god dies, when the system topples under its own contradiction and godhead gives way to humans in isolation? Well something remains: 'the empty place demands to be

occupied anew and to have the god now vanished from it replaced by something else'
(Heidegger, 1977: 69). This something else is happiness. Happiness is the new yardstick
used by the tarantulas, their urge to punish is now recalibrated and set against all those
denying the equality and utility of lives lived commodiously; the yardstick shifts from
righteous justice to bourgeois ideas of the 'just and just so'. Without the threat of god
these yardsticks are popularized as a pursuit of happiness, a uniform feeling of measured
pleasure favoured by 'grocers, cows, women and Englishmen', all of whom are taught to
clamour for a reasoned equality by whose brittle protection they might clamour some
more for the infinite variety of products to be made over to them as estimable posses-
sions. Happiness is freedom, and freedom is freedom to consume and feel pleasure.

The upshot is a hollowing out of culture, a banal surface dwelling of the fashionable
and their apes (1882: V), a self-satisfied establishing of universal states of invented happiness. Zarathustra calls this the condition of the last men, happy in their achievements,
no longer capable of despising themselves or experiencing a struggle to a goal, even;
they all want the same and those who insist on thinking differently, who aspire to overcome themselves by despising what they are so that they might become something different, well they end up in the madhouse. Happiness has been won, but at the cost of
making the world a small, calculable coherence of measured forces in which humans no
longer experience any struggle. This is the real devastation, less the presence of dogmas
than the complete absence of striving (cf. Spinoza's *conatus*). The last men are trussed up
in logics of calculated equality and utility. Happiness is then quality-managed, accred-
ited, and a certified form of comfort.

How then to break this happiness of the last man? We need to drop the ego satisfac-
tions of special status; we have to begin again by going back to experience, to the maelstrom of noise, smells, sights, and urges that befall us continually, ordinarily. This is the
world. Why not stay with meaningless experience? Staying with experience is the job of
hard science, as in 'hard to bear', 'hard to breathe', rather than objectively certain science.
Darwin is here, his carefully observed texts, devoid of flummery, describe life as random
mutation selected through environmental fit; a godless world. Nietzsche assumes a similar stance, throwing himself into raw experience. Where Darwin hesitates, reluctant,
like James, Nietzsche leaps, cheerfully. Science shows us our place in the world, aware of
ourselves in an infinite and exposing expanse:

> In great silence the sea pale and mute, the sky playing in dusk is mute, the ribbon of
> rock spilling into the sea is mute—this silence, this malice. 'Oh sea! Oh evening. You
> are terrible masters. You teach the human being to cease being human! Ought he to
> sacrifice himself to you? Ought he become as you are now, pale, shimmering, mute,
> prodigious, reposing above oneself?' (1881: §423)

To cease being human is to cease comforting ourselves with world-maligning ascetic
ideals or, worse still, with the cessation of willing that characterizes the last man, he who
is inert with happiness. The science of the last man is one of devastating industrious-
ness, a science of outputs, technological massiveness, and factual assertion in which all

ideals have been replaced by mechanically configured arrangements of means and ends designed to make life comfortable and meaningful thoughtlessly. Nietzsche's form of science is very different. There is no reality behind what appears, only this world, the natural, humourless world, to which we are subject as equally as all other things. In the *Genealogy of Morals*, Nietzsche thus writes: 'there is no such substratum, there is no "being" behind doing, working, becoming; "the doer" is the mere appendage to the action. The action is everything' (1887: §26). The real is there but no perspective can claim it entire, we simply experience the real by being in it and, importantly, by adding to it. We mistake the word 'perspective' if by such we mean some kind of restricted vantage point, or confined meaning. Perspectives are contrasts, upsetting received views (Deleuze, 2006: 58). Fact is tremulous; we grasp truth and its clarity is momentary. Heraclitus knew this. Heraclitus suggested lightning governed all things and left it at that; not wishing to harness the spectacle with logic, the flash opens up directly, dramatically, a hitherto dark world, an opening which is just as rapidly closed off, without comfort. Heraclitus' world is one of strife, passing away, contradictions; a world in whose affirmation we find only perspectives. Perspectives find a world lit strangely, not for convenience. There is no resolution, no dialectical closing, no restful grounding; there is just acting, a mobility between polarized tendencies like self and social, repose and agitation, satiety and hunger, intensity and torpor. Throughout such perspective, taking the only value that matters is the transmutation of all values, a constant forming and reforming without recourse to higher authorities or to the stable objects of thought, without transcendence, satisfied all the while that we can endure a meaningless world because in some small way we ourselves organize the world, add to it, make it change.

To evoke such a world writing changes, becomes more open, demanding the reader think, and so too the author. Hence Nietzsche experiments with aphorism, with dramatizing knowledge, unafraid of the literary and even poetic style, the experiment becomes a tale, never epic though, and always inevitably incomplete, apparent digressions sustain a narrative, spurs for other adventurers, sailing further. Nietzsche (1878b: § 53) learns how to play this 'infinite melody' with language. Nietzsche was impure as philosopher, writing like the Irishman Lawrence Sterne with a suppleness that elicited similar suppleness in his readers, inducing force and potentiality rather than stating truths. In such narrative form, aphorisms hit home without reliance on verification, without long-winded reasoning. Nietzsche's language, metaphoric, sharp, comes like gobs of wet jewelled insight, urgent and salty, like sea spray wetting one's face. Readers are not pandered to, there is no presumption of knowing and comforting them: 'He who knows the reader, does nothing further for the reader' (1887/1888: I, Of Reading and Writing). The writing strives by tarrying with calm and malicious things, ever wary of the claims being made: 'Is your vision subtle enough to know what is true?' and resists the 'shameful craving' for sublimating knowledge (1881: §424). The texts meander, and then suddenly hasten, they repeat and then jump, their meaning carried by contraries, their power coming as often in the slightness of phrase as in a poetic hitting home. They are devoid of chains of reasoning or comforting contexts, they are images, and we readers read as though moving from mountain top to mountain top, always having to complete the movement between phrases ourselves, in our action: moving in this landscape is tough as the air Nietzsche offers; albeit clear and intoxicating, it is also cold and demanding to breathe. We have, since Nietzsche, been challenged to produce with language rather than use language as a tool to get at the real. Nietzsche was in the full sense of the word untimely.

13.2.4 Eternal Return and Will to Power

We are carriers, not subjects of fate. Heraclitus is still with him: 'Man's character is his fate' (1883–1888: §121). It dawns on us we should distrust all claims to being, including claims of fate itself to have the world already written out. We are left with what is open, as we enact fate ourselves.

> Belief in what has being is only a consequence: the real *primum mobile* is disbelief in becoming, the low valuation of all that becomes. What kind of man reflects in this way? An unproductive, suffering kind weary of life. If we imagine the opposite kind of man, he would not need to believe in what has being; more, he would despise it as dead, tedious, indifferent. (1883–1888: §585 A)

For this 'opposite' kind of man all knowledge is nothing more than an attempt, beyond right and wrong, beyond good and evil, alive with error. And error is not a mistake but the residue of our struggle to make attempts at going beyond the evidence, at sailing out into the wide ocean, 'we adventurers and birds of passage', we free spirits (1881: §136; Young, 2010: 308–14), content simply to organize rather than sheath life with stabilizing meaning and order. In Nietzsche's writing, passage takes priority over position.

So how, then, do we organize and cohere as a life without reaching after and relying on fixing concepts? To begin in such artistic self-creation we might start with walking. To walk is to be pulled into nature, away from ego, and to feel and observe differently, directly. Walking is part of Nietzsche's method, as it was Darwin's too; to walk was to think. Darwin's walks were often confined to circuits of the grounds of his home at Downe in Kent. He would place a pile of stones at the start of his walk, and with each completion of the circuit would kick one away, the thornier the problem he was thinking upon, the more stones he had to kick away. Some days the pile got very small. Nietzsche's thought-through-walking proceeded less incrementally. For a start he had a bigger stone, a glacial remnant set by the lakeside of Silvaplana, near Sils Maria in the Swiss Alps. It was beside this 'pyramidical rock' that he ushered in, or has ushered into him, what becomes a culminating idea in his thought and so life: the 'eternal return'. The eternal return is what enables Nietzsche to dissolve the apparent tension between a determining, indifferent, cruel world and a language-bound being able to think about but not control such a world. The eternal return gives sustenance to his idea of positive will to power. The eternal return is a question he poses to himself by the rock. The eternal return is what serves as the selective principle—willing as creating. The eternal return is intimately related to becoming, or is becoming in the sense of the return of difference, or transmutation. Strictly speaking, then, only becoming (as difference) returns, which is why there is becoming. What, he asks of himself, would we do were all life consigned to repeat itself? Assume all actions—like all events—were repeated in an endless cycle. How would we cope? The answer comes with Zarathustra. He too experiences this question when convalescing from having overexerted himself in struggling to give expression to his will amid what he feels is so much negative willing. Tired, depleted, he is being tended by his companions, his animals. Exhausted he is open to them, and through them and their ministrations (rather than through his own thought) comes an expression of eternal return:

> 'O Zarathustra', said the animals then, 'all things themselves dance for such as think as we: they come and offer their hand and laugh and flee—and return. Everything goes, everything returns, eternally rolls the wheel of existence. Everything dies, everything blossoms anew; the year of existence runs on forever. Everything breaks, everything is joined anew; the same house of existence builds itself forever. Everything departs, everything meets again; the ring of existence is true to itself forever. Existence begins on every instant; the ball There rolls around every Here. The middle is everywhere. The path of eternity is crooked. (1887/1888: III, The Convalescent, §2)

Such awareness can confound us with the sheer pointlessness of living (which Zarathustra shows us we humans have, historically, compensated for by taking succour from otherworldly fictions). Mass production might be one such experience of repetition, working along endlessly repeating production lines. So might the endlessly stupid managerial instruction to innovate, to become oneself anew. Yet such confronting of what returns can also enliven us into a condition of profound responsibility, given whatever we do redounds with infinite presence. Albert Camus' myth of Sisyphus exemplifies such responsibility. It was not the responsibility of leaving great monuments, because these look to defy infinity, and so inevitably create *ressentiment*. Nor was it to throw oneself into the flux carelessly like a bobbing cork. Rather, enduring the eternal return has to be worked at as an aesthetic concern with the future, with opening up in encounters with what is, inevitably, closing off. Nietzsche suggests we do this through the enduring and mingling of contraries, by keeping chaos in oneself (1887/1888: Prologue, §5), by being able, like salt, to unite apparent oppositions (1887/1888: III, Seven Seals, §4) and living with contradiction.

This mingling begins by admitting what is simply the case. If 'eternally rolls the wheel of existence', with the house of existence 'building forever', we are unfinished, 'our nature has not yet been fixed' (1887/1888: III, The Convalescent, §2). This is the first job of being creative, realizing that no matter how consummate our fixing concepts we will always remain distant from ourselves, unfinished. We acknowledge our incompleteness and frailty, we accept the chaos of the world is all there is, that our will 'cannot break time and times' desire'. This is a source of 'solitary tribulation', an imprisonment in the world that with its inevitable passing finds the will having to acknowledge that each past moment is irreversible, beyond control (Safranski, 2002: 264–7). Rather than have this resentment become *ressentiment*, the second job, after having absorbed this straining of awareness of always being underway, is to wish it so. So to the observation that we are always and only an experiment, Nietzsche adds 'we are experiments; let us also want to be such' (1881: §453). How to live with ourselves in this distant state, becoming, forever surpassing and overcoming, a transition, 'Who wills into this "perhaps"?' asks Zarathustra, gazing outwards, exiled, sails set for the undiscovered. To want to be such, to abandon comforts and take up struggles, to accept the thawing wind that breaks the gangways by which we tread upon the world. Nietzsche, too. He didn't simply sit down and write his Zarathustra book, challenging the reader for the fun of it. Indeed, if anyone knows what it is to struggle in order to learn to know one's knowledge, it is he (Spindler, 2009; Spinks, 2003; Vattimo, 2002). It is from within this struggle that he arrives at the ideas of lightness, play, dance, and laughter; the affirmation of transience and destruction finds Nietzsche's bow (*bios,* also life) shooting its arrow beyond even that of Heraclitus. Heraclitus had disdain for those wanting to fix a restless world with identities and claims; he met many such metaphysicians and avoided them, becoming a recluse, a 'star without atmosphere' (1888/1908: III, §3). The will to power brooks no such avoidance or near saying; like Heraclitus, those with will to power take the world as 'a sea of forces flowing and rushing together', but then relish it, finding possibility in such Dionysian force:

> This my Dionysian world of the self-creating, the eternally self-destroying, this mystery world of the two-fold voluptuous delight, my 'beyond good and evil', without goal unless the joy of the circle be itself a goal; without will, unless a ring feels good will toward itself—do you want a *name* for this world? A *solution* for all its riddles? A *light* for you too, you best-concealed, strongest, most intrepid, most midnightly men? *This world is the will to power—and nothing besides.* And you yourselves are also this will to power—and nothing besides! (1883–1888: §1067)

The will to power is both perpetual experiment, and wanting it thus. Deleuze (2006: 101) summarizes this affirmation: 'life goes beyond the limits that knowledge fixes for it, but thought goes beyond the limits that life fixes for it. Thought ceases to be reaction, life ceases to be a reaction.' This places will to power as a transformative rather than repetitive force. Zarathustra experiences this will as a vision. He sees a shepherd writhing with a black serpent hanging from his mouth. The shepherd pulls at the serpent in vain. Zarathustra shouts 'Bite', at which the shepherd bites off and spits out the head. The vision is enigmatic, a symbolic evocation of eternal return in which it is not the linear repetition of events that is being spoken of, but an acceptance of the writhing, twisting, unfixed world into which one sinks one's teeth and spits (Connolly, 2011: 112–13). The world self-organizes and we bite: we break with a dominant order and introduce a new one, demanding new organization. Thus the shepherd becomes a chancer, able to bite and survive a world forever writhing. And we might read the vision further still. The shepherd bites the head of, the black snake of historical repetition that prevented him from speaking, stuffing him full with dogmatic analysis, with solid facts, burdening him like a camel sent out into the desert with the settling weight of being correct. He bites, like a lion that knows how to say 'no', and then Zarathustra hears laughter greater than any other laughter rolling off the shepherd's lips. To laugh is to affirm life, and the becoming of life, like the child that plays. What returns is not being, but returning itself, i.e. the being of becoming. Becoming is not becoming *something*. Becoming has not started and cannot finish. It is pure becoming, what human thinking and acting have found to be a maelstrom of pure movement. Returning is the being of that which becomes, accelerating the process (Deleuze, 2006: 48). The eternal return is an answer to the problem of time's passage, how the present moment can pass only since it already belongs to the past and what is yet to come. The eternal return is how we affirmatively can think becoming as the return of difference. '[W]e can only understand the eternal return as the expression of a principle which serves as an explanation of diversity and its reproduction, of difference and its repetition' (Deleuze, 2006: 49). The shepherd is no prophet declaiming what ought be so, nor is he an expert deducing what is so, but a riddle tamer able to use language carefully, bravely and not passively, sometimes quietly, other times aggressively, being expressive, spontaneous. The shepherd is aware of a world consistently confirming disappointment upon us, but refusing to allow this to become a source of *ressentiment*, all the while bending with currents, from which he is sustained creatively as he gives himself back into this moving world. The 'I' sets sail and becomes a Yea: *Ecce Mundus*.

13.3 STUDYING ORGANIZATION

Thus inspired by the shepherd, goaded by Zarathustra, we too, as researchers, might succumb to organizational fate on such terms. Heidegger (1958: 75–8) suggests that reading Nietzsche teaches us to attempt to listen rather than oppose or add to others' work. To add or oppose additively is to belittle the thought of others; rather in listening we create thought, and so add to the world. The challenge is also to stay with experience and not fall into popular thought that separates a 'being' (lightning) from doing ('flash'). As Peirce put it: 'If we know what the effects of force are, we are acquainted with every fact which is implied in saying that a force exists' (1992: 136). Thus research learns from Nietzsche's extolling the will to power, to be wary of resting too easily with any idea or doctrine, including his own: 'Take heed lest you get crushed by a statue' (1887/1888: I, On the Bestowing Virtue, §3); where we see values, he sees what is all too human. All values are mutable. We forget this. Alphonso Lingis (2004: 123) reminds us: 'In taking our ambitions, our values, our achievements seriously, we turn ourselves into idols, which we cannot help fearing will be covered in graffiti and pigeon shit.' Thus even Nietzsche is renewed.

Nietzsche is always asking us 'where is your way, here is mine?', challenging researchers to create anew a *hodos*, (which means not only 'way' but also 'motion') without reducing it (a descending thought) to standardized method, separating life from thinking. Researchers might more often give voice to passionate feeling (1881: §481), they might recognize how their own ego often restricts awareness (1881: §438), but all the while prepared to investigate flexibly:

> One person converses with things like a policeman, another as father confessor, a third as wanderer and curiosity seeker. Sometimes one wrings something from them through sympathy, sometimes through violent force; reverence for their mystery leads one person forward and eventually to insight, whereas another employs indiscretion and roguery in the explanation of secrets. (1881: §432)

This is disorienting advice. Yet set against prevailing calls for disinterested and neutral work such research can feel creative, arriving at unthought possibilities and perspectives by virtue of its abundance, a sense of giving out rather than a taking in (Connolly, 2011: 114–16). It is research as a form of affirmative will to power, a yea saying to events that resists the philosophical tendency to reach after a single class of opinions and instead listens 'to the soft voice of different situations in life' (1878a: §618). Listening to the soft voice of different situations, aware that it is 'the stillest words that guide the world'. The head of the serpent is bitten again and again, since it crawls, again and again, down our throats. Creation is affirmation that differs from negation. Negation opposes affirmation and is thus limited to crawling down the throat: to block, stop, reduce, and cut off the access to clean, fresh oxygen. Biting off the head (of the black snake of historical learning) is not to oppose history, but to differentiate, to affirm affirmation, and create possibility.

Creation emerges in bringing art into science. Nietzsche calls upon all beings to act in a form of enlightened self-interest, a creator first of oneself and thence beyond that, finding what we find and making of it what we might, not in passionless knowledge, but restless activity (cf. Spinoza). This self-knowledge is self-mastery of the body, one's feelings, drives, and their spilling over into wider forces of living. Never mastery as in control, but as in the blacksmith that knows how the hammer 'talks' with the iron, like the poet that lets herself become written in the process of writing, so as to form a style, and line to make and follow. These feelings of anger, jealousy, longing, love, passion, each of them quotidian surges, never amounting to a unity (1881: §119; cf. Spinoza), are how we belong with and organize the world creatively, recognizing in ourselves 'an animal whose nature has not yet been fixed'. Why ignore such in our studies?

We go back to Prometheus' organs re-growing, having been bitten anew by eagles; the cycle of creation in recreation; and in this there is no *ressentiment*. Nietzsche remains generous, Prometheus is with him to the last, as he, like Prometheus, seeks forgiveness for human sin by whispering apologies into a horse's ear as it lay beaten and flattened on the streets of Turin in those half-mad days marked by his last dance.

To be creative is to experiment with how to situate oneself in found conditions: now lose all authorities in your own down-going and go on, find yourselves (*Gleichnis*); to become what one could become is a question of deep passion, a dark glow, and the clearest, coldest air driving your sail on open seas.

References

Brobjer, T.H. (2008). *Nietzsche's Philosophical Context—An Intellectual Biography* (Champaign: The University of Illinois Press).

Connolly, W. (2011). *A World of Becoming* (Durham, NC: Duke University Press).

Deleuze, G. (2006). *Nietzsche & Philosophy*, trans. H. Tomlinson, with foreword by M. Hardt (New York: Columbia University Press).

Dilthey, W. (1907). *Das Wesen der Philosophie* (Stuttgart: M. Riedl).

Heidegger, M. (1958). *What is Philosophy?*, trans. W. Kluback and J.T. Wild (London: Vision).

—— (1977). *The Question Concerning Technology and Other Essays, trans.* W. Lovitt (New York: Harper and Row).

Lingis, A. (2004). *Trust* (Minnesota: Northwestern University Press).

Nietzsche, F. (1878a). *Human all Too Human. A Book for Free Spirits*, trans. and ed. G. Handwerk (Stanford, CA: Stanford University Press, 1997).

—— (1878b). *Human all Too Human II & Unpublished Notes*, trans. and ed. G. Handwerk (Stanford, CA: Stanford University Press, 2012).

—— (1881). *Dawn. Thoughts on the Presumptions of Morality*, trans. B. Smith (Stanford, CA: Stanford University Press, 2011).

——(1882). *The Gay Science*, tr. W. Kaufmann (New York: Random House, 1974).

——(1883–1888). *Will to Power. Notebooks 1883–1888*, trans. W. Kaufman and R.J. Hollingdale (New York: Vintage Books, 1968).

—— (1887). *On the Genealogy of Morality*, trans. C. Diethe, ed. K. Ansell-Pearson (Cambridge: Cambridge University Press, 2007, revised edition).

—— (1887/1888). *Thus Spoke Zarathustra*, trans. R.J. Hollingdale (Harmondsworth: Penguin, 1976).

—— (1888/1908). *Ecce Homo—How One Becomes What One Is*, trans. R.J. Hollingdale (London: Penguin Classics, 2005).

Peirce, C.S. (1992). *The Essential Peirce: Selected Philosophical Writings, Volume 1 (1867–1893)*, ed. N. Houser and C. Kloesel (Bloomington: Indiana University Press).

Safranski, R. (2002). *Nietzsche* (London: Granta).

Sloterdijk, P. (1985). *Der Zauberbaum. Die Entstehung der Psychoanalyse im Jahr 1785. Ein epischer Versuch zur Philosophie der Psychologie* (Frankfurt am Main: Suhrkamp).

Södergran, E. (1984). *Complete Poems*, trans. D. McDuff (Old Woking, Surrey: Bloodaxe Books).

Spindler, F. (2009). *Nietzsche—kropp, kunskap, konst* (Gothenburg: Glänta).

Spinks, L. (2003). *Friedrich Nietzsche* (London: Routledge).

Thomas, J. (1993). Figures of Habit in William James, *The New England Quarterly* 66(1): 3–26.

Vattimo, G. (2002). *Nietzsche: An Introduction* (Stanford, CA: Stanford University Press).

Young, J. (2010). *Frederich Nietzsche* (Cambridge: Cambridge University Press).

CHAPTER 14

....

HENRI BERGSON
(1859–1941)

....

STEPHEN LINSTEAD

14.1 BIOGRAPHY AND BACKGROUND

HENRI-LOUIS BERGSON, progenitor of modern process philosophy and the language of 'becoming', was born in Napoleon III's rapidly-transforming Paris on 18 October 1859, a month before Charles Darwin published *The Origin of Species* and the year in which Marx published his *Critique of Political Economy*, setting out his version of Hegelian historical materialism. Bergson was later to challenge both. Notable contemporaries were John Dewey (two days younger, d. 1952), and Alfred North Whitehead (four months younger, d. 1947). Cosmopolitan son of Michel, a Jewish Polish musician and an Irish Catholic mother, Catherine Levison, from Doncaster, England, Bergson grew up and was educated in Paris, although from 1863 to 1866 the family lived in Switzerland, returning to Paris in 1866. His parents moved to England in 1870, although Henri remained boarding at the Springer Institution in Paris, continuing his studies at the Lycée Condorcet. He was therefore witness to the terrible consequences of French defeat in the Franco–Prussian War, including the Siege of Paris, the Commune, and its eventual overthrow in 1871; during and after World War I he became politically active in promoting international peace. Academically he displayed equal gifts in science and the humanities, attending the prestigious École Normale Supérieure (ENS) a year below Émile Durkheim (1858–1917). He taught philosophy at *lycées* first in Angers and then, in 1883, in Clermont-Ferrand, where he also taught at the university. He returned to Paris in 1888, teaching successively at *lycées* including the Lycée le Grand and the Lycée Henri IV (1890–1898) for ten years. Between 1894 and 1898 he applied twice to the Sorbonne, being rejected as a result of Durkheim's opposition (Kolakowski, 1985: vii), and was appointed Maître de Conference (Reader) at ENS in 1898.

In 1889 he published *Time and Free Will: An Essay on the Immediate Data of Consciousness*, introducing a now-classic distinction between time as measured and time as experienced (*durée* or duration) and seven years later *Matter and Memory* appeared, arguably prefiguring, and confirmed by, brain science in the 1970s and 1980s (McNamara, 1996). His marriage in 1891 was to Louise Neuberger, whose second cousin, Marcel Proust, acted as best man. In 1895 he was appointed to the prestigious Collège de France, where in 1900 he became Chair of Ancient Philosophy. That year *Le Rire* or *Laughter: An Essay on the Meaning of the Comic* (1900), his ground-breaking study of humour, illustrated the challenging processual crossing of levels between the physical and the intellectual that energized his critique of the philosophical reliance on intellect alone and neglect of intuition—the combination of which was the foundation of his anti-Cartesian, non-dialectical dualistic philosophy. In 1901 he was elected to the Academie des Sciences Morales et Politiques, and the following year received the Legion d'Honneur. In 1907 he published his most famous work, *Creative Evolution*, introducing the idea of *élan vital* (vital or life spirit). For the next 20 years Bergson was perhaps the world's best known philosopher. This was a mixed blessing—in 1914 he was both elected to the elite Academie Française and had his works placed on the Roman Catholic Church's Holy Index of prohibited literature (the Church rejected the idea of evolution). He received the Nobel Prize for Literature in 1927.

During World War I he undertook diplomatic missions to Spain and the United States due to his international prestige, and this developed into a commitment to the post-war activities of the fledgling League of Nations. The International Commission for Intellectual Cooperation (which prefigured UNESCO) organized a debate with Einstein concerning the consequences of his theory of relativity for Bergson's concept of duration as originally given in *Time and Free Will*. *Duration and Simultaneity* (1921) arose from this. Einstein rejected the possibility of his multiple and potentially reversible times being reconciled with Bergson's singular irreversible time (understood as a multiplicity), and Bergson was regarded by many as simply having misunderstood Einstein's theories, particularly the mathematics. Although he made an important contribution to the understanding of the Riemann equations, a view of multiplicity on which Einstein had drawn (Lawlor and Moulard, 2013), unfortunately Bergson's position was negatively received and from this point his reputation began to dwindle. This in combination with age and ill-health reduced his scholarly productivity. His last major work, *The Two Sources of Morality and Religion*, did not appear until 1932, and although it offered a highly original account of ethics that influenced Lévinas, this was occluded by its religious and mystic aspects in its reception. Additionally two collections of essays were published—*Mind-Energy* in 1919 and *The Creative Mind* in 1938, although the latter includes older essays such as his 'Introduction to Metaphysics', which dates back to 1903. In this later work though, there is a pulling back from the metaphysics of his second period and a return to the style of his earlier work.

In 1940 the Pétain government of Nazi-occupied France offered Bergson the opportunity not to register as a Jew, partly because he was only half-Jewish but also because he was an eminent and internationally recognized public figure. Although in later life he had embraced his mother's Catholicism, Bergson felt it was important that, as a figure of note, he identified with 'those about to be persecuted'. Having been forced to stand in line on the streets for several hours in the cold and damp to register, the experience proved too much for the heroic octogenarian's fragile health and he died of bronchitis on 3 January 1941.

14.2 Bergsonian Connections and Contrasts

Bergson's lifetime encompassed the rise of modernism in all its forms—art, design, philosophy, literature, science, social science, urbanism, politics, mass production, consumption, communication, and transport—including some of the definitive discoveries that shaped the twentieth century (electricity, air travel, the automobile, international telecommunications) and some of its indelibly tarnishing human disasters. Darwin's evolutionary thought in biology impacted Herbert Spencer, who inspired Bergson's early work, which launched a response to Spencer's mechanistic approach and its essentially static treatment of time. This was also found in nineteenth-century science more generally, and was carried into the founding of the social sciences by Durkheim, who stood firmly in the tradition of Descartes in separating mind from body. This exclusion of the physical body, as an entity more suited to investigation by biologists, was part of Durkheim's rationale for the sociality of social science. Bergson, however, contested this dualism, seeing it more as an interconnected duality with the brain practically engaged with the immediate world and selecting the most useful memories for dealing with it.

Durkheim's damaging influence kept Bergson on the margins of the philosophical establishment and outside the official university system, giving lectures open to the public at the Collège de France. His emotionally appealing ideas were immensely popular, and were rapidly taken up and adopted piecemeal. Having no access to graduate or doctoral students, Bergson could develop no 'school' of rigorous interpreters, nor a unified programme of Bergsonism: Deleuze's book of this title is in this sense ironic. His ideas were so widely dispersed, even dissipated, that pinning down his often unacknowledged influence on others is perplexing. Furthermore, his view of philosophy was that it must be in constant change to keep up with the shifting multiplicities of its main object, life, as its attentions brought new aspects into focus. Consequently other thinkers from a variety of disciplines found it possible, for better or worse, to take up different aspects of his thought and put them to a variety of uses.

Bergson particularly influenced phenomenology (Schutz, Merleau-Ponty, and Lévinas, impacting on social constructionism and secular ethics); existentialism (through critical engagements of Heidegger and Sartre); process philosophy (notably Whitehead—see Rescher, 1996), and post-structuralism (in different ways by Foucault, Derrida, and Deleuze). His dialogues with American pragmatists Dewey and James also had influence that has re-emerged in the postmodern pragmatism of Rorty (see Bergson, 1900/1999; Griffin et al., 1993). In the arts his conceptualizations of time and multiplicity influenced Cubism; the music of Debussy; American novelists Dos Passos, Faulkner, and poet/novelist/critic Gertrude Stein; 'stream of consciousness' novelists including Woolf, Joyce, and Proust's *The Remembrance of Things Past*; and suffused the poetry of Valéry and T.S. Eliot (Le Brun, 1967). Even a 'minor' work, *Laughter*, was absorbed by both Sigmund Freud and Charlie Chaplin and was regarded by Koestler as being a major influence on his book *The Act of Creation*.

Such a variety of interpreters have taken up and developed different aspects of his thought through their own particular intellectual lens that Bergson became himself a multiplicity. Yet, this is exactly what his own philosophy predicted in arguing that the process of perception is not the *replication* of its object but an act of *replying to it*, in that representation as a translation of stimulating sense data always entails interest, selection, and creation (Linstead, 2002).

14.3 BERGSON'S KEY IDEAS

Bergson suggested in 1911 (1938/1992: 108–9) that most philosophies have at their heart one single important idea, which may be fairly simple to appreciate but is impossible for them to fully articulate. The philosopher then spends their career circling this idea, never quite expressing it, but in a series of near-misses creating elaborate symbolic systems that always fail to capture it. Throughout Bergson's work this actualizes as a mistrust of language that distinguishes him markedly from the analytic philosophers of his day, for whom logic simply needed to direct its energies towards perfecting its symbolic language rather than accepting its current limitations.

> This influence of language on sensation is deeper [more profound] than is usually thought [generally believed]…the rough and ready [brutal] word, which stores up the stable, common, and consequently impersonal element in the impressions of mankind, overwhelms [crushes] or at least covers over the delicate and fugitive [fleeting] impressions of our individual consciousness. (Bergson, 1889/1913: 131–2; translations in square parentheses from Guerlac, 2006: 73)

Bergson's use of language, and particularly metaphor, attempts to evoke the ambiguity of the real rather than abstract and clarify it: avoiding reductionism, though not without a precision of its own. Bergson's suspicion of symbolic systems may be considered proto-post-structuralist (he worked at the same time as Saussure and Peirce were developing semiology and semiotics, structuralism's precursors) but the critique of language did not become a fixation, as the linguistic turn in Heidegger, Wittgenstein, Derrida, and post-structuralism has been accused of doing.

14.3.1 Time

If Bergson does have just one central insight, then according to Kolakowski (1985: 2) it is that *time is real.* Bergson grew up in the early shadows of evolutionary theory and, whilst excited by its revolutionary rethinking of the nature of the human, he was increasingly frustrated by its mechanistic assumptions, its determinism, its lack of a sense of movement, its passive rather than active view of the organism (including the issue of freedom), and its lack of any dynamic consideration of time. For Bergson, the problem of time was not one of being, uniformity, stability, and permanence, but of becoming, change, and the future as the unfolding of novelty. Whilst arguing for the continuity of the flow of becoming and the irreversibility of time, he acknowledged the tension with novelty and discontinuity, and sought to understand this duality as a rhythm of connected and elastic expansions and contractions rather than as an oppositional dialectic. His philosophy is both intensive and *tensile.*

Bergson in *Time and Free Will* demonstrates that human freedom, or free will, is itself a reality that can be validated by a consideration of 'real time'—time as experienced rather than measured—which he terms *durée* or 'duration'. Still not free of the Cartesianism that dominated nineteenth-century thinking, Bergson accepts implicitly the distinction between inner and outer experience, but rejects the assumption that they both consist of similar, quantitative, homogeneous units. For Bergson, the time of consciousness (duration) is inner, and immediate, experience—qualitative, heterogeneous, and dynamic. A moment of duration can be tasted in the qualitative difference between a clock minute spent in a poolside lounger; a minute driving a car in a competitive race; a minute searching for painkillers when you have a migraine; a minute rising to the surface from a coral-reef scuba dive; a minute spent in a group scouring a field for clues after the discovery of a corpse; a minute's trading on the FTSE; a minute birdwatching; a minute between rounds in a boxing ring; a minute fumbling for one's gas mask in an air raid; a minute waiting for the end-of-shift factory hooter; or a minute watching your first child being born. None of these is experientially comparable: if you were doing one of them you would not mistake that feeling for any of the others, such is their *qualitative* difference though quantitatively identical.

In contrast, science emphasizes homogeneous space over heterogeneous time. Space is abstract, quantitative, and static. Its parts are identical and can be described mechanistically. *Spatialized time* is time stripped of its intrinsic heterogeneity, the time of the clock or diary that can be represented on dials, inscribed on pages, and captured in formulae where one moment 't' is much the same as any other (Bergson 1938/1992: 12–13). This spatializing of time is essential to deterministic approaches to experience, because it represents the unfolding of a hidden destiny that is always already predetermined in the present condition of the world. Creativity and freedom are not required or even allowed as life unfurls along its prescribed path according to the laws of nature.

But for Bergson duration is definitively creative. Every emerging instant is new, unique, and novel. Duration's diverse components are our memories, perceptions, and affections, but they are entangled with each other and cannot be easily distinguished. Past, present, and future as memory, experience, and anticipation form duration where the real and the virtual meet. Spatialized time, which is of course artificial, consists of segments (which may be infinitesimally small) that are self-contained: in themselves they preserve nothing of any previous even though identical segment, being ahistorical and memory-less. This type of artificially manufactured time is constructed, against the 'real' time we have identified as duration, for the purposes of practical action, enabling us to do things in the world, to organize, sequence, synchronize, or manipulate life. Duration is not measurable in this way, and hence cannot be predicted—it is full of exciting or terrifying potential. We can never be sure exactly how things will turn out and Bergson therefore argues that we need to learn to think backwards, to *movement as prior to space*. This is reality as process.

For Bergson the subject is not determined *by* external states, it *is* these states. It does not find itself in the predicament of having to choose between predetermined alternative choices: rather by its free action it creates these very choices. When reflecting on actual action these virtual alternatives emerge and appear as though they pre-existed action—as pre-formed possibilities—and were rejected by the consciously acting subject. The real therefore creates the possible in retrospect; the virtual is *more* than the possible. Real choices and real time are qualitative, heterogeneous, and irreversible—and because, as he argues, they are prior to possible choices and spatialized time, the world is emergent and unpredictable, and we experience freedom. The flow of duration is without beginnings or ends, and is just constant movement in the middle. Freedom then is not only processual: it is a triumph of quality over quantity, duration over artifice. Rather than being apprehended by unreflective *instinct*, or the abstract operations of *intellect*, duration is known through engaged *intuition*.

14.3.2 Memory, Materiality, and Embodiment

Bergson argued in 1911 (Bergson, 1938/1992: 107) that philosophy must be close to real life, and in *Matter and Memory* (1896) he developed the position that method (whether philosophical or other) must be developed in relation to its object—and if that object changes, so must the method. So even methodology was to be in process.

What makes duration possible, Bergson argued, is memory. Memory cumulates the past in its entirety, not selectively. Not a single element is lost. Every remembered moment carries within itself the entire preceding flow of the past. As such it is irreversible, and specifically unrepeatable. Although our bodies—and other material counterparts of our memories—may decay, we are still able to recall the memories themselves. Old war stories may indeed be more vivid than those of the recent past. From this Bergson proposes that memory is entirely independent of matter, and is in no way constituted by it, as it would be regarded in the reductionist point of view that regards memory, and even consciousness, to be merely an effect of the material brain.

From this reductionist perspective, memory is a less vivid variant of perception, consciousness being an unextended epiphenomenon of the extended material world that impresses itself upon it. The Cartesian gap between mind and world, and hence mind and body is, for Bergson, incomprehensible and results from this spatialization of experience into the extended and the unextended. He argues that mind is primarily memory, and accordingly the mind–body relationship needs to be understood *through* time (past and present).

How this works needs some explanation. Bergson's view of consciousness involves his idiosyncratic concept of an *image* which can exist without being perceived—it sits somewhere between idea and representation, feeling and concept. The body thus becomes a centre of *virtual actions* which require pure perception for us to know they are there, but need memory to give them significance and meaning, or *recognition*. When the body repeats a familiar action, Bergson calls this *habit* or *automatic memory*. *Image* or *pure memory* is virtual and non-active, imprinting everything that happens in every moment of our experienced subjectivity, but it acts as a resource to occasion action when connected to, and actualized by, perception. However, this memory is the memory that releases itself into dreaming when not suppressed by the action-orientation of wakeful and pragmatic automatic memory. *Actual memory* is what connects the other two types of memory strategically, and allows for spontaneity, creativity, and innovation, in *action*.

Although suspicious of symbols, Bergson illustrated this with the image of an inverted cone, the lower tip of the upturned cone penetrating a flowing timeline of action in the present. At its widest base point, now at the top, the cone represents pure memory, an undifferentiated cloud. The cone, however, can be rotated clockwise and anti-clockwise like the lens of a telescope or SLR camera, thus bringing different parts of the cloud into focus, like stars in the Milky Way, forming images. The operation of intelligence on this process of focusing and refocusing then contracts these virtualities into a concentrated form that can be practically applied in action in the real world (Linstead, 2002, 2005).

Bergson is often seen, wrongly, as opposing instinct and intellect, and being anti-intellectual. He is anti-intellectual*ist* in his views of representation and the symbolic, but that does not stop him using language evocatively, and neither does it prevent his considerable intellectual exertions. For Bergson these domains are connected and work together. Bergson's view of memory is that it works on different levels, with bodily perception on the lowest and most material plateau, and with intellect operating at the most abstract. Intuition is not to be confused with instinct, as it is not understood either as reflex, or as an instant epiphantic flash of insight that emerges from nowhere. It consists rather of an often hard-won sensitivity, the moment of actualization of a virtual potential that is the result of a real engagement with the world, rather than abstract speculation alone. Bergson is interested in the crossing of these levels and sees that happening in different ways. One direction, from the physical to the intellectual, is the irruption of laughter, that responds spontaneously to deliberate or accidental exposition of the presumptions of abstraction and the limits of mechanical constraints upon life. Another is when the subconscious insinuates its way, through dreams, to take advantage of the relaxation of the practical preoccupations of the brain and draw on the image-memory to create interventions into the reality of consciousness. Further, he looks at the intellectual effort required to achieve breakthrough moments of insight, the special conditions under which intuition can operate most profoundly. These creative dynamics do not just offer partial interpretations or images of reality (Bergson in Mullarkey, 1999: 86):

> The real whole might well be, we conceive, an indivisible continuity. The systems we cut out within it would, properly speaking, not be *parts* at all, they would be partial views of the whole. (Bergson, 1911/1998: 31; see also Ingold, 2011: 226)

14.3.3 Creative Evolution

Bergson does not think that an adequate account of evolution can be generated by viewing it as linear and mechanistic inner adaptation to change in external circumstances. When life unfolds 'beneath the symbols which conceal it' we discover that 'time is just the stuff it is made of... no stuff more resistant nor more substantial'. This means that

> Our duration is not merely one instant replacing another; if it were, there would never be anything but the present—no prolonging of the past into the actual, no evolution, no concrete duration. Duration is the continuous progress of the past which gnaws into the future and swells as it advances... it follows us at every instant; all that we have felt, thought and willed from our earliest infancy is there, leaning over the present which is about to join it, pressing against the portals of consciousness. (Bergson, 1907/1998: 4–5)

Change then is directionless, needs no plan, and is propelled by its own inward force (Bergson's image is of *fusée*, flare or rocket) towards a multiplicity of directions realized in practice by the operations of intelligence, intellect, and instinct, through memory (Bergson, 1938/1992: 130–58; Brown, 2006). This vital impetus, or *élan vital*, is the human creative drive but connects to the creative power of life itself. Here Bergson's familiarity with Spinoza is demonstrated in the corporeal strength of this basic drive, drawing on Spinoza's concept of the *conatus* (see, for example, Chapter 6, this volume, and Scott's (2009) chapter on Deleuze's interpretation of Spinoza's joyfully embodied approach). Whitehead apparently coined the term 'creativity' (Robinson, 2009: 223 and n. 1; Meyer, 2005) but, had it existed, Bergson might have usefully deployed it here. Rather than simply being a matter of evolution as conformance to the demands of an environment, this is a turning of life towards itself, an autopoietic move that invents itself, involuntarily, as it evolves in an internal and intensive movement of difference.

Bergson attempts to create a biologically extended philosophy that can account for the continuity of all living creatures—not just human life—and also for the discontinuity that the qualitative fact of evolution entails: creative evolution is another way of saying continuous discontinuity (Ansell Pearson, 2002: 71). Bergson argues that neither Darwinian mechanism (of adaptation to externalities) nor Lamarckian finalism (where evolution proceeds teleologically, directed by the organism towards a pre-given final state), can adequately account for novelty and change. This original common impulse drives creation in all living species—the *élan vital*. This germinal life-force is intransitive, the constant elaboration of novel forms rather than simple reproduction (Ansell Pearson, 1999: 157). Although this impetus is common, the incredible diversity that has resulted from evolution must be explained by a principle of divergence and differentiation. Bergson suggests that these successive evolutionary movements constitute *tendencies* that cluster in two main divergent forms: instinct and intelligence. Human knowledge results from intelligence, which is analytic, external, practical, and spatialized—and engages with the world through tools. It is thus more distanced from experience and duration than is instinct, although better able to reflect on it. Intuition and creative evolution (or involution) have no knowable end point, remaining always open (Williams, 1916).

Bergson recognizes that the vital principle does not reside in the organism itself but in genetic energy, and this allows for a non-organismic reading of evolution (Ansell Pearson, 1999: 159–63). Essentially, organisms are to be thought of as intensive sites of influence, assemblages of symbionts, parasites, chemical, and other reactions, with permeable and porous boundaries, that enfold their environment and radiate (and are irradiated by) vectors of transversal communication, with complex and multiple causal relations.

14.3.4 Ethics

In *The Two Sources of Morality and Religion* Bergson considers the tensions between two human tendencies. The first is towards accepting moral obligation, duty, and the security of socially cohesive community, supported by rigid rules demanding obedience, a 'closed' morality, and static religion. Such a society exclusively aims at its own survival, and often sets itself at war with other societies, being intolerant of difference. Considering the often cultish nature of corporate culture initiatives, it is interesting to note that Bergson identifies in this society the 'fabulation function', a particular operation of the imagination that creates 'voluntary hallucinations'. Myths of gods, and god-like founders, support cultural cohesion and discourage questioning of values.

Alternatively, 'open' morality and dynamic religion are concerned with creativity and progress, are inclusive and welcoming of others and peaceful in their objectives, aiming to create an 'open society'. They are fuelled by 'creative emotions' like 'the impetus of love' that spur us inwardly and intensively to prosocial action (Lawlor and Moulard, 2013). Creative emotions are not formulaic—emotion is unstable and disrupts the habitual socialized response of intelligence by creating its own representations. This extreme emotional creativity is close to both madness and mysticism, but it is a genuine experience that provokes action, not a categorical response that signals and occasions conformity.

For Bergson, dynamic religion is mystical, but this dynamism could be extended to other less mystical cultural formations. Organized and ordered doctrines—or

engineered corporate cultures—are always static, because they are essentially representational and seek to render action predictable by controlling the predicates of action.
But social collaborations where cultures develop without prescriptions or objectives
are at least potentially dynamic. Machine bureaucracy and linear rule by accountants
quickly extinguishes entrepreneurial dynamism as well as real social responsibility and,
as Bergson would have expected, the spatialized extensive response is to try to engineer
some representation or measure of 'enterprise' back in, organize its 'antecedents', and
engineer its increase somehow without ever understanding what 'it' might be outside its
abstract expression. Bergson's active and changing morality discovers itself in action, as
'action on the move creates its own route, creates to a great extent the conditions under
which it is to be fulfilled, and thus baffles all calculation' (Bergson, 1935/1977: 291).

Bergson here links to the Kierkegaard of *Either/Or* (Kierkegaard, 1992) in which
judgement, by which we can read ethics, is more than the (extensive) application of
codes or principles unbendingly from situation to situation: ethics and intuition are
inextricably linked, and without intuition there can be no judgement, as ethics must be
both intensive and open in relation to the other in each new and novel encounter, and
must entail dynamic moral action. Existential uncertainty, and the risk that one may be
wrong, is part of an open morality—with the perhaps unexpected conclusion that being
ethical can bring its own excitement, as in Kierkegaard (see Chapter 8, this volume).
Bergson influenced Lévinas' development of an ethics of becoming in *Otherwise than
Being* (1999), where the encounter with the other is not only the first ethical and relational demand but also first philosophy, but Bergson's open society presents a stronger
social dimension.

14.4 Bergson in Organization Studies

Bergson's creative evolution was identified as a paradigm for rebalancing the
structure-process relation in human organization by the late Robert Cooper (Cooper,
1976: 1000; Thanem, 2001: 350). In his book on deconstruction, Chia follows Cooper,
discussing Bergson's approach to metaphysics in arguing for intuitive knowing against
analytic knowing, and metaphysical enquiry as a 'form of rigorous inquiry which
attempts to dispense with symbols' (1996: 209–11). Bergson's attempts to go beyond
symbols involved the play of a great number of images that pre-echoed the mood of
deconstruction but not its method. Chia complements his metaphysical argument
with a requirement to get empirically and intuitively closer to the object, yet the decidedly intellectual discussion stops at the level of organizational analysis and neglects the
potentially supportive existence of new anthropology and deconstructive ethnography.
Bergson subsequently becomes part of a 'process mix' with James, Bateson, Whitehead,
Deleuze, and Derrida in Chia and King (1998) on how organizations structure novelty; Chia (1999) on non-Parmenidean change; and Tsoukas and Chia (2002: 570–2)
on organizational becoming, focusing on intuition and perception with an ironically

highly rational argument, displaying a distinct cognitivist bias in parts. Expressing their central research question as 'What must organization(s) be like if change is constitutive of reality?' Tsoukas and Chia (2002: 570) miss the point that neither change nor reality in Bergson is transitive, which is what makes a language of change problematic. Chia and Holt (2009: 112–18 ff), put intuition, perception, and duration to work in a gentle critique of the implicit documentary realism of research on strategy-as-practice.

Discussing strategic change, Letiche (2000) studies Bergson carefully and extensively and utilizes intuition, duration, and the *élan vital* in outlining 'phenomenal complexity theory'. This critiques the varieties of complexity theory where terms frequently have several acceptations, and the more general neglect of consciousness, which leaves the core concept of 'emergence' poorly understood.

Memory suffers similar neglect, even in Chia's (2002) short essay on time and duration, although it serves a crucial function in the mediation of multiplicities of order (which include structure), and multiplicities of organization (understood as the activity of life), and in any understanding of history and evolution. Brown (2006), whose work elsewhere in the psychology of memory has drawn extensively on Bergson, offers an extended discussion of Bergson's take on evolution, and a careful exposition of the 'organizational impetus', and its relation to structure, both real and mythologized. Life is organization, in so far as it is the impulse to organize, rather than 'the organized forms which it leaves behind, like shed skin' (Brown, 2006: 319).

Scott (2010: 83–106) offers the most extensive and close reading of Bergson to date in the field of organization studies. His project is a reading of Deleuze, outlining the development of a Deleuzian view of organization. This important treatment inevitably remains flawed by its dependence on Deleuze's text on Bergson (Guerlac, 2006: 176–95 outlines important differences) and, being written ten years before it was published, neglects recent advances in Bergsonian and Deleuzian scholarship. Nevertheless, it highlights important issues:

a) Bergson is a *non-dialectical thinker*. He struggled against the dominant Hegelianism of his time, dualisms that become oppositions and dialectical agonistics.
b) Bergson's *ontology is positive* but not positivist. It is affirmative, and I would add practical. Again this affirmative approach seeks to sidestep the need for dynamism to be found only in conflict as in Hegel, replacing it with the dynamism of heterogeneous multiplicity, rather than the homogeneous multiplicity of order (Scott, 2010: 102).
c) Organization is the *actualization of the virtual*, but is not quantitatively predetermined because memory and duration, consciousness and freedom are qualitative. Thus there is a difference between the realization of the possible (in which the real resembles one possibility delimited and selected from others) and the evolutionary process itself, where virtualities *become* creatively actualized (as with the actualization of DNA to organism, for example—see Deleuze, 1988: 97–9).

d) Organization is *unforeseeable, and improvisable,* and defies information processing or semiotic approaches to its definition. Organization and meaning are linked, and opposed to order and information (Scott, 2010: 92). Approaches to (strategic) foresight are flawed because if prediction is able to foretell a future, it is because a simple virtual has multiple actualizations. But Bergson argues that the virtual transforms itself through the process of its actualization, actively creating these terms, so that the actual cannot therefore be foreseen. Being is an actualization of becoming, expressed in a language that is invented or improvised as it goes along.

e) Organization is *grounded in difference but contains convergence,* through the principle of coexistence at the level of the virtual—that is, everything is connected. Humanity can cut across the planes and divisions that disrupt this coexistence at the level of actuality by the exercise of consciousness, intuition, and intellect that offers freedom—the creative triumph over mechanism.

Two organization studies journals have garnered contributions applying Bergson to problems in the field. *Organization* (9/1, 2002) featured contributions by Linstead, Calori, O'Shea, and Wood. Linstead distinguishes Bergson's qualitative and intensive approach from the more mechanical approaches to psychological and affective phenomena, such as motivation and emotion, found in mainstream organizational psychology, and driving the continual refinement of means to measure the object, arguing for organization theory to be seen as a process of continual refocusing (developed in Linstead, 2005). Calori (2002) offers a dynamic attempt to integrate Bergson with Merleau-Ponty's hyperdialectics, illustrating this with the extensive reflections of a successful CEO of an international family company (Salomon). O'Shea (2002) addresses the issue of new product development and innovation. The future is not to be known, but to be realized, which makes a significant difference to understanding innovation, which he illustrates through ethnographic fieldwork. Wood (2002) applies the concepts of creative involution (Williams, 1916) and transversal communication to critique dominant approaches to the organization of knowledge, developing a threefold process model of problematization, differentiation, and temporalization (see also Wood, 2003; Wood and Ferlie, 2003).

There has also been a special issue of *Culture and Organization* (9, 1, 2003). Here Linstead and Mullarkey (2003) argue that Bergson offers an embodied conception of culture through his views of intuition as situated within experience rather than about it; the importance of the body in social experience; and the importance of morality and religion in social life. Bergson's culture for them is socialized time actualized in experienced duration or *durée*—culture is always in motion, and does not need culture clash to drive change. But actual cultural expressions and formulations are not, which runs counter to functionalist and psychoanalytic views of culture. Culture grounded in experienced time and driven by the *élan vital* is in ceaseless motion— it is duration because it is *en-dured* as a multiplicity rather than as a unity. Styhre (2003) complements Wood's work on knowledge and the virtual; Watson (2003) discusses bodily entanglement and affect; Hatzenberger (2003) offers a utopian read-ing of the concept of 'open' society in Bergson's final work; and Power (2003) outlines the relation between freedom and sociability, and hence culture, in Bergson (see also Scott, 2010: 105).

14.5 BERGSON: WHY NOW AND WHAT NEXT FOR ORGANIZATION STUDIES?

Organization studies has tended to encounter Bergson largely through a rear-view mirror and through Deleuze, and although there is a significant if still relatively small body of work that encounters Bergson directly he is usually discussed partially, along-side James, Whitehead, and Deleuze. As we have seen, his work has been used in dis-cussing creativity, innovation, knowledge management, new product development, and change management and these efforts merit further application. But outside existing studies, what more is there to gain by approaching his work directly after, in most cases, more than a century? Here I identify three orienting beacons of relevance, significance, and impact and a few more speculative inspirational fireworks to initiate the process.

First beacon, *relevance*: Bergson's philosophy is one of *action, process, and move-ment*. In a world where organizational change is regarded as constant, Bergson offers a philosophy that makes change its basic principle and thinks it through ontologically, metaphysically, and methodologically—offering the radical principle (for organiza-tion studies) that the discipline needs to change (conceptually, empirically) along with immanent changes in its object or field of enquiry. His tensile understand-ing of the real as virtual multiplicity dissolves polarized discussions of realism and constructionism.

Second beacon, *significance*: Bergson reorients the simplistic divisions that still haunt organization and management research by a radical clarification of the dis-tinction between *quantitative and qualitative multiplicity* (with associated concepts of the extensive and intensive, focusing and refocusing, and immanence) in a way that exposes the flaws of seeing the latter in terms of the former, without dismiss-ing the former—rather placing it more accurately in terms of what it can and cannot be used to achieve. His methodological questioning of *how to think the new* offers responses relevant to everyday life as much as to new media and the new sciences (Hansen, 2004).

Third beacon, *impact*: anyone who has read literature, watched cinema, or seen art from the twentieth-century period of aesthetic modernism has, directly or indirectly, been impacted by Bergson. This is because Bergson's philosophy is a *practical* one and requires philosophy to *engage, and stay engaged, with life directly*—the kind of super-empiricism that animates process philosophy more generally. Bergson's intuitive style offers resources to underpin a non-psychologized turn to affect, as suggested by Thrift's (2007) summary of non-representational theory. It also opens out to the incorporation of an immanent aesthetics into new methodologies incorporating the humanities and arts into the practices of social enquiry (cf. Rancière, 2010; see also Linstead and Höpfl, 2000).

More specifically, we can identify some *fusées* that could usefully be launched:

First flare: Bergson is an *aporetic* (or problem-focused) thinker (During, 2004; Moore, 1996: 97–104)—that is, he thinks philosophy in terms of the history of its problems and in particular its false problems (which are generated by its regimes of self-reference). Organization studies is rarely if ever conceived of in this problematizing way (Wood, 2002). Within critical approaches problems that emerge as the result of applying pre-assigned positions would fall more within the consideration of dialectics than Bergson's teasing out of problematic relations within duration. Rasche (2011) devotes considerable discussion to a Derridean approach to aporetics, but completely neglects Bergson's influential contribution.

Second flare: Bergson's view of (non-sexual) desire, like that of Deleuze and Bataille, is of a differentiating force that proliferates rather than as a lack to be filled. This alternate non-Hegelian take on desire is one that organization studies has found it difficult to integrate critically, but which underpins very different orientations to a variety of social and organizational phenomena including motivation, knowledge, consumption, and identity (Brewis et al., 2006). Bergson is a key figure in the translation of a tendency running from Spinoza through Lyotard and Baudrillard but significantly contrasting with Lacan and recent appropriations of his work in organization studies. Any question of freedom, as Guerlac (2006: 105) observes, is also a broader question of desire, and this is where Bergson's ethics engages with both alterity and novelty.

Third flare: Bergson's concept of duration and the nature of time remains to be applied to most areas of organizational studies as temporalization (Wood, 2002), where time is still spatialized as this mirrors the practical needs of its production-oriented object field. This has enormous empirical potential, especially in studies of culture. Approaches to storytelling and narrative can be informed by his cinematic understanding of the fabulation function (where stories are actively completed by the audience, and may therefore be incomplete in their presentation—a feature of common-sense understanding that influenced Schutz and Garfinkel, who found empirical evidence for the basic process; Mullarkey, 2009).

Fourth flare: Bergson's approach to memory within temporality has implications for organization and management history, and the emerging field of organizational memory studies, and remains distinct from that of his interpreters like Sartre or Ricoeur (*contra* Cunliffe et al., 2004). Whilst organizational memory has previously been recognized as part of the construction of organizational knowledge, and considered from perspectives of information conservation, narrative construction, and discourse analysis, Bergson's distinctive 'rotating cone' of processual focusing, refocusing, contracting, and inserting of memory into action emphasizes the dynamics of memory over its representational aspects.

Fifth flare: Bergson challenges evolutionary approaches familiar in organization studies (though more in tune with recent developments in biological thinking). His non-determinist thought challenges evolutionary approaches in organization theory that follow neo-Darwinist, Lamarckian, or evolutionary psychological approaches. His understanding of the nature of a population, the multilevel dynamics of variation-selection-retention, isomorphism, transversal communication, and the transmission of affect differs productively from current understandings in population ecology, institutional theory, and critical realism.

Sixth flare: Bergson also challenges some recent descendants of social constructionism in organization studies that argue for non-polaristic relationality. These attempts to reconnect constructionism, language, dialectics and dialogics, and existentialism are fruitfully undermined by Bergson's non-dialectical approach. Similar approaches to relationality that see the construction of reality as occurring in the communicative space between subject and subject (Cunliffe, 2011) simply add a qualitative spin to spatialization through their construction of intersubjectivity.

Seventh flare: Bergson can renew concerns with writing organization that avoid some of the 'exhaustion' characteristics of post-structuralist treatments of text and discourse. His suspicion of representation and his discussion of writing prefigure Derrida, in particular, and yet do not limit the scope of his attention nor his deployment of metaphor. Here his subtle understanding of 'image' can be a fruitful alternative to emerging cognitivist treatments of metaphor in organization studies, and connects to approaches to non-representational theory (Thrift, 2007).

Eighth flare: Bergson enables a revisitation of the human in human organization. Bergson was pioneering in attempting to incorporate the latest advances in biology and psychology into a philosophy of the human and social sciences. Contemporary developments in physics (Prigogine, 1997; Prigogine and Stengers, 1984), biology (Ansell Pearson, 1999; Dawkins, 1983), and complexity have underlined the continuing relevance of his ideas, including that of the irreversibility of time, and there has been increasing discussion of his connection to the 'new' sciences in the past two decades (Papanicolaou and Gunter, 1987; cf. also Rose, 2013).

Ninth flare: Bergson offers a radical ethics of alterity, grounded in the corporeal and empirical, creatively fusing questions of freedom and desire. Bergson influenced Lévinas, whose work has been taken up in some of the more ethical corners of organization studies, but in his later work Bergson offers a broader and less phenomenological understanding of notions like obligation (Mullarkey, 1999). Further, he offers an alternative to the Heideggerian prioritization of language as the 'house of being', and the insistence that being is one rather than multiple—Heidegger's collective concept of 'gathering' is not a multiplicity, nor does such 'gathering' constitute a community. Bergson's 'open society' offers a way to think of the immanence of commonality, the inclusive but dynamic 'community to come', participating in an intuited relationality that discovers itself in action with the potential of outstripping its own concepts—like ethics and social responsibility.

Finally, Bergson, for all his influence on others and the comfortable temptation to read him through these interpretive refractions, deserves the kind of direct and intimate reading that his method urged on philosophy in engaging with life itself. He did, after all, win the Nobel Prize for literature, and his writing is its own reward. But for those nervous of taking this journey alone, Robinson (2009: 220–34) offers a brief but useful process glossary.

References

Ansell Pearson, K. (1999). Bergson and Creative Evolution/Involution: Exposing the Transcendental Illusion of Organismic Life, in J. Mullarkey (ed.), *The New Bergson* (Manchester: Manchester University Press): 146–67.

——(2002). *Philosophy and the Adventure of the Virtual: Bergson and the Time of Life* (London: Routledge).

Bergson, H. (1889/1910). *Time and Free Will: An Essay on the Immediate Data of Consciousness* (London: George Allen & Unwin).

——(1896/1991). *Matter and Memory* (New York: Zone Books).

——(1900/1999). *Laughter: An Essay on the Meaning of the Comic* (Los Angeles: Green Integer).

——(1903/1998). *An Introduction to Metaphysics* (Kila, MT: R.A. Kessinger Publishing).

——(1907/1998). *Creative Evolution* (Mineola, NY: Dover).

——(1921/1999). *Duration and Simultaneity, with Reference to Einstein's Theory* (Manchester: Clinamen Press).

——(1932/1977). *The Two Sources of Morality and Religion* (Notre Dame, IN: University of Notre Dame Press).

——(1938/1992). *The Creative Mind (La pensée et le mouvant: essays et conférences)* (New York: Citadel Press).

——(1999). A Letter from Bergson to John Dewey, trans. J. Mullarkey, in J. Mullarkey (ed.), *The New Bergson* (Manchester: Manchester University Press): 84–7.

Brewis, J., O'Shea, A., and Boje, D. (2006). *The Passion of Organizing* (Lund: Liber/CBS).

Brown, S.D. (2006). Bonga, Tromba and the Organizational Impetus: Evolution and Vitalism in Bergson, *Culture & Organization* 12(4): 307–19.

Calori, R. (2002). Organizational Development and the Ontology of Creative Dialectical Evolution, *Organization* 9(1): 127–50.

Chia, R. (1996). *Organizational Analysis as Deconstructive Practice* (Berlin: De Gruyter).

——(1999). A 'Rhizomic' Model of Organizational Change and Transformation: Perspective from a Metaphysics of Change, *British Journal of Management* 10: 209–27.

——and Holt, R. (2009). *Strategy Without Design* (Cambridge: Cambridge University Press).

——and King, I.W. (1998). The Organizational Structuring of Novelty, *Organization* 5(4): 461–78.

Cooper, R. (1976). The Open Field, *Human Relations* 29: 999–1017.

Cunliffe, A.L. (2011). Crafting Qualitative Research: Morgan and Smircich 30 Years On, *Organizational Research Methods* 14: 647–73.

——Luhman J.T., and Boje, D.M. (2004). Narrative Temporality: Implications for Organizational Research, *Organization Studies* 25(2): 261–86.

Dawkins, R. (1983). *The Extended Phenotype* (Oxford: Oxford University Press).

Deleuze, G. (1988). *Bergsonism*, trans. H. Tomlinson and B. Habberjam (New York: Zone Books).

During, E. (2004). A History of Problems: Bergson and the French Epistemological Tradition, *Journal of the British Society for Phenomenology* 35(1): 4–24.

Griffin, D.R., Cobb, J.B., Jr., Ford, M.P., and Gunter, P.A.Y. (1993). *Founders of Constructive Postmodern Philosophy: Peirce, James, Bergson, Whitehead and Hartshorne* (Albany, NY: SUNY Press).

Guerlac, S. (2006). *Thinking in Time: An Introduction to Henri Bergson* (Ithaca, NY: Cornell University Press).

Hansen, M.B. (2004). *New Philosophy for New Media* (Cambridge, MA: MIT Press).

Hatzenberger, A. (2003). Open Society and Bolos: A Utopian Reading of Bergson's 'Final Remarks', *Culture and Organization* 9(1): 43–58.

Ingold, T. (2011). *Being Alive: Essays on Movement, Knowledge and Description* (London: Routledge).

Kierkegaard, S. (1992). *Either/Or: A Fragment of Life* (London: Penguin).

Kolakowski, L. (1985). *Bergson* (Oxford: Oxford University Press).

Lawlor, L. and Moulard, V. (2013). Henri Bergson, in E.N. Zalta (ed.), *The Stanford Encyclopedia of Philosophy* (Spring Edition), <http://plato.stanford.edu/archives/spr2013/entries/bergson/>

Le Brun, P. (1967). T.S. Eliot and Henri Bergson, *The Review of English Studies* 18(71): 274–86.

Letiche, H. (2000). Phenomenal Complexity Theory as Informed by Bergson, *Journal of Organizational Change Management* 13(6): 545–57.

Levinas, E. (1999). *Otherwise than Being, or Beyond Essence* (Pittsburgh, PA: Duquesne University Press).

Linstead, S. (2002). Organization as Reply: Henri Bergson and Casual Organization Theory, *Organization* 9(1): 95–112.

——(2005). Refocusing Organization Theory, in S. Linstead and A. Linstead (eds), *Thinking Organization* (London: Routledge): 201–17.

——and Höpfl, H. (eds) (2000). *The Aesthetics of Organization* (London: Sage).

——and Mullarkey, J. (2003). Time, Creativity and Culture: Introducing Bergson, *Culture and Organization* 9(1): 3–13.

McNamara, P. (1996). Bergson's 'Matter and Memory' and Modern Selectionist Theories of Memory, *Brain and Cognition* 30: 215–31.

Moore, F.C.T. (1996). *Bergson: Thinking Backwards* (Cambridge: Cambridge University Press).

Mullarkey, J. (1999). *Bergson and Philosophy* (Edinburgh: Edinburgh University Press).

——(2009). *Refractions of Reality: Philosophy and the Moving Image* (London: Palgrave).

O'Shea, A. (2002). The (R)evolution of New Product Innovation, *Organization* 9(1): 113–25.

Papanicolaou, A.C. and Gunter, P.A.Y. (eds) (1987). *Bergson and Modern Thought: Towards a Unified Science* (Chur, Switzerland: Harwood Academic Press).

Power, C. (2003). Freedom and Sociability for Bergson, *Culture and Organization* 9(1): 59–71.

Prigogine, I. (1997). *The End of Certainty* (Glencoe, NY: The Free Press).

—— and Stengers, I. (1984). *Order out of Chaos: Man's New Dialogue with Nature* (London: Flamingo).

Rancière, J. (2010). *Dissensus: On Politics and Aesthetics*, ed. and trans. S. Corcoran (London: Continuum).

Rasche, A. (2011). Organizing Derrida Organizing: Deconstruction and Organization Theory, in H. Tsoukas and R. Chia (eds), *Philosophy and Organization Theory* (Research in the

Sociology of Organizations, Volume 32) (Bradford: Emerald Group Publishing Limited): 251–80.

Rescher, N. (1996). *Process Metaphysics: An Introduction to Process Philosophy* (Albany: State University of New York Press).

Robinson, K. (2009). *Deleuze, Whitehead, Bergson: Rhizomatic Connections* (Basingstoke: Palgrave Macmillan).

Rose, N. (2013). The Human Sciences in a Biological Age, *Theory, Culture & Society* 30(1): 3–34.

Scott, T. (2010). *Organization Philosophy: Gehlen, Foucault, Deleuze* (London: Palgrave Macmillan).

Styhre, A. (2003). Knowledge as a Virtual Asset: Bergson's Notion of Virtuality and Organizational Knowledge, *Culture and Organization* 9(1): 15–26.

Thanem, T. (2001). Processing the Body: A Comment on Cooper, *ephemera* 1(4): 348–66.

Thrift, N. (2007). *Non-Representational Theory: Space, Politics, Affect* (London: Routledge).

Tsoukas, H. and Chia, R. (2002). On Organizational Becoming: Rethinking Organizational Change. *Organization Science*, 13(5): 567–82.

Watson, S. (2003). Bodily Entanglement: Bergson and Thresholds in the Sociology of Affect, *Culture and Organization* 9(1): 27–41.

Williams, C.L. (1916). *Creative Involution* (New York: A.A. Knopf).

Wood, M. (2002). Mind the Gap? A Processual Reconsideration of Organizational Knowledge Innovation, *Organization* 9(1): 151–71.

——(2003). The Process of Organizing Knowledge: Exploring the In-Between, *Process Studies* 32(2): 225–43.

——and Ferlie, E. (2003). Journeying from Hippocrates with Bergson and Deleuze, *Organization Studies* 24(1): 47–68.

CHAPTER 15

JOHN DEWEY (1859–1952)

LINH-CHI VO AND MIHAELA KELEMEN

15.1 INTRODUCTION

JOHN DEWEY was born on 20 October 1859 in Burlington, Vermont. He graduated from the University of Vermont and then spent two years as a high school teacher in Oil City, Pennsylvania. He obtained a doctorate in philosophy from Johns Hopkins University where he met and studied with Charles Sanders Peirce. He then taught at the University of Michigan (1884–1894), University of Chicago (1894–1904), and Columbia University (1904–1930).

Dewey was renowned for being one of the most controversial philosophy professors of his generation. He published over 700 articles in 140 journals and wrote approximately 40 books in his lifetime. He wrote extensively on many different subjects including philosophy, psychology, political science, education, aesthetics, and the arts. His pragmatist philosophy was developed over a number of critically acclaimed books, including *Essays in Experimental Logic* (1916/1989), *Human Nature and Conduct* (1922/1983), and *Logic: The Theory of Inquiry* (1938/1991). In psychology, some of Dewey's major writings were *Psychology* (1887), where he attempted a synthesis between idealism and experimental science, and *The Reflex Arc Concept in Psychology* (1896), where he argued against the traditional stimulus-response understanding of the reflex arc, suggesting that one's response depends on how the situation is understood in light of previous experiences. His writings on education include *Democracy and Education* (1916/1980), *The School and Society* (1899), and *The Child and the Curriculum* (1902), which accentuated the interests of the child and the use of the classroom to cultivate the interaction between thought and experience. In politics, he wrote *Freedom and Culture* (1939), which looked at the roots of fascism. He published *A Common Faith* (1934) in aesthetics and *Art as Experience* (1934/1987) in art.

Along with Peirce and James, Dewey has been credited as one of the most prominent classic pragmatist thinkers and pioneers. Dewey first became interested in the work of William James in the 1890s whilst he was trying to free himself from the restraints of

Hegelian influences. He was also inspired by Charles Peirce's work. Drawing on these two thinkers, Dewey started defining his own theory of pragmatism, which took a distinguishable shape and is often referred to as 'instrumentalism' or 'experimentalism'.

15.2 DEWEY'S PRAGMATISM: THE MAIN TENETS

The pragmatist thinkers sought to bring about a sea change with their rejection of Cartesian dualism (Bernstein, 2010). Peirce's saying that 'knowledge is habit' encapsulates this pragmatic stance (Kilpinen, 2009). James also challenged the subject–object or consciousness–content distinction in his essay 'Does "Consciousness" Exist?' (James, 1904). Subsequently, Dewey clarified that such a dualistic scheme is not the inevitable or necessary point of departure for all philosophy (Biesta and Burbules, 2003). He said: 'What have been completely divided in philosophical discourse into man and world, inner and outer, self and not-self, subject and object, individual and social, private and public, etc., are in actuality parties in life-transactions' (Dewey and Bentley, 1949/1989: 248).

Pragmatist thinking also implies a processual orientation. Dewey saw reality as emergent and processual rather than static and formed by ready-made elements. For him, the world exhibits: 'an impressive and irresistible mixture of sufficiencies, tight completeness, order, recurrences which make possible prediction and control, and singularities, ambiguities, uncertain possibilities, processes going on to consequences yet indeterminate' (Dewey, 1925/1981: 47).

These two dimensions are configured in the central tenets of Dewey's philosophy, as presented in what follows.

15.2.1 Experience and the Transactional Relationship between Man and the Environment

Dewey's notion of experience is at the core of his philosophy (Elkjaer, 2004). He developed this notion throughout his long life (Dewey, 1917/2000, 1925/1981, 1934/1987, 1938/1988). In Dewey's view, experience should not be mistaken with the everyday understanding of the notion, i.e. as an inner, personal reservoir of earlier experiences (Miettinen, 2000). It is not merely the sense perceptions of passive spectators looking at the world, the 'veil that shuts man off from nature', but rather 'the dynamic participation, the continuing process of an organism's adjustment not simply to environing conditions but within a biological (physical) and cultural environment' (Dewey, 1925/1981: 9). Dewey (1916/1980: 146) stated that: 'when we experience something, we act upon it, we do something with it; and then we suffer and undergo the consequences. We do something to the thing and then it does something to us in return: such is the peculiar combination.' The value of experience results from the connection of these two sides. Experience occurs continuously, because the interaction of man and environing conditions is involved in the very process of living (Dewey, 1934/1987).

Thus, the relationship between man and the environment is not dualist but transactional. Dewey (1934/1987) believed that man does not live *in* an environment; he lives by means of an environment. Dewey (1905/1983: 158) claimed that 'things—anything, everything, in the ordinary or non-technical use of the term "thing"—are what they are experienced as'. Dewey's transactional approach implies that reality only reveals itself as a result of the activities—of the 'doings'—of the organism (Biesta and Burbules, 2003). The process of living is enacted by both the environment and the organism, because they are integrated (Dewey, 1938/1991). An animal does not have the same environment as a plant, and the environment of any fish differs from that of a bird. The difference does not only lie in the fact that a fish lives in the water and a bird in the air, it also resides in the special way in which water and air enter and are made to enter into their respective activities (Dewey, 1938/1991). This means that everyone's experience is equally real; their accounts turn out to be different only because they bring with them to the transaction different standpoints, backgrounds, histories, and purposes and intentions (Biesta and Burbules, 2003).

15.2.2 Continuity and Habit

The principle of continuity rests upon the notion of habit. Dewey, Peirce, and James share similar conceptions of habit (Kilpinen, 2009). Habits, for them, are not only patterns of action but should be understood as predispositions to act. 'The essence of habits is an acquired predisposition to ways or modes of response, not particular acts...Habit means special sensitiveness or accessibility to certain classes of stimuli, standing predilections and aversions, rather than bare recurrence of specific acts' (Dewey, 1922/1983: 32). All three authors emphasized mental and mechanic dimensions of habit. The pragmatist position is that intentionality (or rationality) without habituality is empty, whereas habituality without intentionality and rationality of course is blind (Kilpinen, 2009). 'Habits of mind' is an expression favoured by both Peirce and Dewey, while James mentioned 'the principle of parsimony in consciousness' (1950/1890: 2.497) to point out that 'the more of the details of our daily life we can hand over to the effortless custody of automatism, the more our higher powers will be set free for their own proper work' (1950/1890: 1.122). The notion of habit so understood goes deeper than the ordinary conception of a habit as a more or less fixed way of doing things. 'It covers the formation of attitudes, which are emotional and intellectual; it covers our basic sensitivities and ways of meeting and responding to all the conditions that we meet in living' (Dewey, 1938/1988: 19).

From this point of view, the principle of continuity means that every experience takes up something from previous experience and also provides man with possibilities to cope to some extent with what comes after (Dewey, 1938/1988). As man passes from one experience to another, he does not move to another world, but to a different part or aspect of the same world. What he has learned in earlier experiences becomes an instrument of understanding and dealing effectively in the future. The process goes on as long as life and learning continue (Dewey, 1938/1988).

15.2.3 Situation

Any normal experience, according to Dewey, is an interplay of two conditions: objective and internal conditions. Taken together, in their interaction, they form what we call a situation. It denotes the entire and unique character of all conditions under which and within which a human acts at a given time. The phrase 'objective conditions' covers what is done and the way in which it is done. For example, a situation includes not only the words but the tone of voice in which they are spoken, the materials with which an individual interacts such as equipment, books, apparatus, and toys, and importantly, the total social set-up of the situation (Dewey, 1938/1988). An individual's life is composed of a sequence of situations, in which any given situation is supplied with the consequences of past experience and loaded with new possibilities.

There are, for Dewey, at least four types of situations (Dewey, 1938/1991; Kennedy, 1959). First, there are situations in which there is a smooth, ongoing routine of activity. Man and the environment are in tune. This type of situation can be called 'determinate'. Second, when this harmony is disrupted, things are unsettled, and man is disoriented and confused; here, another type of situation ensues. The situation now is 'indeterminate'. A situation is indeterminate with respect to its issue. It may be confused with respect to the anticipated outcome; it may be obscure about what movement is needed to reach final consequences, it may be conflicting due to discordant responses being evoked. Third, if the indeterminate situation gives way to an attitude of doubt, the situation becomes 'problematic'. Fourth, if the confusion disappears and the doubt is resolved as a result of a problem-solving activity, the situation then becomes 'determinate'. A new equilibrium has been achieved, but this determinate situation is not the original one. Man is now a different being within the environment, which has also been changed to some extent due to his problem-solving activity.

15.2.4 Inquiry

Dewey explored in detail a particular type of experiencing called *inquiry*. The transformation of an indeterminate situation into a determinate one happens in the process of einquiry.

Inquiry is fuelled by the existence of doubt. Doubt arises when our normal ways of doing things are disrupted because of surprises or unusual events that are difficult to comprehend and deal with. Dewey (1938/1991) referred to such disruptions as indeterminate situations in which habits and routines are not enough to explain what is going on and to offer a way out. The indeterminate situation is itself not cognitive. It is simply a normal event. It is only when such a situation is identified as a problematic situation that inquiry begins and experience turns into the cognitive mode. As Dewey put it, 'to see that a situation requires inquiry is the initial step in inquiry' (1938/1991: 111). It is important to note that what is problematic is not outside and independent of the individual. What is clear or confusing for one person is not necessarily the same for another person. All depends upon the organism–environment transactional relationship (Dewey, 1938/1991).

Qualification of a situation as problematic does not carry inquiry far. It is just an initial step in the institution of a problem; finding out what the problems are is to be well along in inquiry (Dewey, 1938/1991). The first step toward finding out what actually is problematic about the indeterminate situation involves the identification of the constituents of the indeterminate situation. 'They are the conditions that must be reckoned with or taken account of in any relevant solution that is proposed' (Dewey, 1938/1991: 113). This process results in a proposal for action: the hypothesis, which articulates a relationship between actions and consequences on the basis of a hypothetical interpretation of what is problematic about the indeterminate situation. Whether the suggested hypothesis corresponds with the actual connections can only be found out by means of acting out with the suggested line of action. If the action indeed has the expected result, a determinate situation has been created and the process of inquiry comes to an end (Dewey, 1938/1991).

It should be noted that there is no absolute end to inquiry. Inquiry does not remove doubt by returning to a prior equilibrium, but by the transformation of the current situation into a new one. It institutes new environing conditions that occasion new problems. There is no final settlement, because every settlement introduces the conditions of some degree of a new unsettling (Dewey, 1938/1991). As special problems are resolved, new ones tend to emerge, and the cycle repeats itself (Biesta and Burbules, 2003).

15.3 Dewey's Pragmatism and Organization Studies

Dewey's philosophy has influenced different areas of organization studies. Much of what counts as knowledge, knowledge generated by academic research, learning and organizational learning, research methods, and organizational research methods have been influenced by Dewey's work.

15.3.1 Knowledge

One can distinguish two major perspectives about knowledge in the literature (Chiva and Alegre, 2005; Vera and Crossan, 2003). From one perspective (cf. Grant, 1996;

Nelson and Winter, 1982; Nonaka, 1994), knowledge is a collection of representations of reality; it exists prior to and independently from the knowing subject. It is possible to codify, store, and transmit knowledge between people, just like a commodity. This perspective posits that knowledge is universal and, hence, two cognitive systems should come up with the same representation of the same objects or situations. From the other perspective, knowledge is not in the head, nor does it exist as a commodity; it is socially constructed (cf. Spender, 1996), yet it is not seen as a static map of reality. Practice articulates knowledge in and about organizing as practical accomplishment, rather than as a transcendental account of decontextualized reality. This perspective understands knowledge as a process, referring to it as knowing (Cook and Brown, 1999; Gherardi, 2000).

Dewey questioned the opposition between contextually constructed knowledge and universal knowledge. Being strongly influenced by James, who also sought to bridge the divide between the epistemological atomism of the empiricists and the 'block universe' monism of the idealists (Bernstein, 2010), Dewey did not deny the importance of theorizing but equally he did not believe in generating universal understandings (1938/1991). Dewey acknowledged the context-dependent and personal nature of knowledge to the extent that he defined knowledge as being the outcome of inquiry, located in the transaction between man and the environment (Dewey, 1938/1991). Knowledge, in this account, is always contextual, because it is always related to the specific inquiry in which it was achieved. On the other hand, there is also generalized knowledge, such as the kind of knowledge that explains why turning a handle causes the door to open (Polkinghorne, 2000). It is the convergent and cumulative effect of continued inquiry that defines knowledge in its general meaning. However, for him theory does not offer us a factual way of looking at the world. Theory is simply another account of the world. For these reasons, Dewey preferred to use the expression *warranted assertion* to denote the conceptual outcome of inquiry, rather than knowledge (Biesta and Burbules, 2003).

Rejecting the dualism of constructed knowledge and universal knowledge, Dewey conceived of knowledge not as an ensemble of absolute truths and certainties but as a series of practical acts judged by their consequences. It is not permanent and immutable. It is not a description or photograph of an external reality, independent of who and what one is as a person (Fenstermacher and Sanger, 1998). Just like in science, the question of the advance of knowledge is the question of what to do (what experiments to perform), so the problem of practice is what we need to know, how to obtain that knowledge, and how to apply it. Dewey argued that it is an illusion to imagine that our thoughts are purely theoretical for we must always consider consequences, which hang upon our thoughts. Otherwise, there is no point in thinking. The ultimate ground for the quest of cognitive certainty is the need for practical certainty in the results of action. Some scientists may readily persuade themselves that they are devoted to intellectual certainty for its own sake. However, according to Dewey, they want this certainty because of its bearings on safeguarding what they desire and esteem.

15.3.2 Knowledge Generated by Academic Research

There has been a controversy regarding the practical utility of academic research, which is characterized by the opposition between 'relevance' and 'rigor' or the academic—practitioner gap (Aram and Salipante, 2003; Kelemen and Bansal, 2002). The topic has been the subject of a number of special issues in academic journals and the focus of three presidential addresses at the annual meetings of the Academy of Management (Hitt, 1998; Huff, 2000; Mowday, 1997). Knowledge generation and testing by academics and practitioners have canonically been seen as separate endeavours, despite the claim that academic knowledge often arises from the study of real-life organizational problems and issues (Jarzabkowski et al., 2010). Academics are usually concerned with the issue of methodological rigour. It involves the quest for universal laws and principles describing the nature of things by relying on sophisticated data collection and analysis methods (Gulati, 2007). Relevance, on the other hand, is the practitioners' primary interest. Academic knowledge becomes relevant for them when it is context-specific, providing concrete recommendations for action or plans of action (Palmer et al., 2009).

Dewey, however, argued against the distinction between relevant and rigorous academic knowledge (Dewey, 1916/1980). He used the criterion of usefulness as an alternative to rigour and relevance. Dewey would see organization studies as a vehicle to help people lead better lives. It would be characterized by a focus on the practical relevance of research as well as a desire to search for novel and innovative approaches that might help serve human purposes (Wicks and Freeman, 1998).

First, the chief value of theory for Dewey is that it can be a useful organizing device to help solve real-world problems. A pragmatist researcher is interested in knowing what difference a given knowledge will have in practice. The practicality of knowledge is an important criterion to differentiate between meaningful and non-meaningful knowledge (Dewey, 1931/1984). From this it follows that theories should be judged by their usefulness in solving problems. Dewey argued for a shift from 'knowing as an aesthetic enjoyment of the properties of nature as a world of divine art, to knowing as a means of secular control—this is a method of purposefully introducing changes which will alter the direction of the course of events' (Dewey, 1929/1984: 81). Also, for Dewey (1916/1980) the reference of knowledge is future or prospective, although its content is based on what has happened and what is finished. Knowledge has to furnish the means of understanding or give meaning to what is still going on and what is to be done.

Second, for Dewey, academic knowledge does not involve the quest for universal laws and principles of organizational behaviour. Using pragmatic logic, one would not expect a unifying theory. But Dewey argued that knowledge must be credible and reliable. This does not mean that one has to systematically collect empirical data and use multivariate statistical techniques in analysis. Dewey (1938/1991) believed that to ensure the reliability and credibility of knowledge, a philosophical theory of knowledge must not only maintain a reasonable degree of internal consistency but must respect some methods by which beliefs about the world are reached. Such methods must abandon the traditional separation of knowledge and action and instead install action at the heart of knowledge (Dewey, 1929/1984). Such a view requires constant and effective interaction of knowledge and action. Action, when directed by knowledge, is method and means, not an end.

15.3.3 Learning

Learning has been traditionally conceptualized as either the acquisition of a piece of knowledge or the development of situated identities based on participating in a community of practice. Seen this way, learning is either a way of knowing the world or a way of being in the world. Dewey proposed a different view. For Dewey, learning is inherent in the process of inquiry. Dewey coined the concept of inquiry to refer to the actual way in which one has experiences and becomes knowledgeable.

Dewey believed that background knowledge functions below the level of consciousness and language (Polkinghorne, 2000). Background knowledge is our practical or know-how knowledge, which enables us to perform most of life's tasks without reflecting on how to do them, to know how and have the competence to cope in most situations without having to consciously think about what to do. This knowledge usually functions tacitly in the background and out of conscious awareness.

Dewey distinguished between this everyday, practical knowing-how and theoretical knowing-that-and-why, as illustrated in his statement that:

> We walk and read aloud, we get off and on streetcars, we dress and undress, and do a thousand useful acts without thinking of them. We know something, namely, how to do them...If we choose to call [this] knowledge...then other things also called knowledge, knowledge of and about things, knowledge that things are thus and so, knowledge that involves reflection and conscious depreciation remains of the different sort. (1922/1983: 124)

Although the background knowledge usually functions smoothly and without deliberation to complete our daily tasks, there are times when it is unsuccessful. Dewey (1922/1983: 125) wrote: 'it is a commonplace that the more...efficient a habit the more unconsciously it operates. Only a hitch in its workings occasions emotion and provokes thought.' When a breakdown occurs in the functioning of the background, we move from our practical mode of engagement with the world to a mode of deliberation or reflection and learn to enlarge or deepen our practical know-how and background knowledge. Dewey stated: 'Knowledge arises because of the appearance of incompatible factors within the empirical situation' (Dewey, 1916/1989: 7).

Moreover, we need overt action to determine the worth and validity of our reflective considerations. Otherwise, we have, at most, a hypothesis about the problem and a hypothesis about its possible solution. This means that learning is the combination of reflection and action (Dewey, 1939/1991). Dewey's position is neither an anti-intellectual praise of action, nor an elevation of praxis over knowledge, but rather an affirmation of the inseparability of thought and action and an acknowledgement of the role of consequences in reflective deliberation. Ideas are neither copies of the world, nor representations linked to one another, but rather ingredients for rules and plans of action. From this it also follows that learning is not something that takes place inside the human mind (Biesta and Burbules, 2003), which is why Dewey discussed learning by using the term 'knowing', which 'consists of operations that give experienced objects a form in which the relations, upon which the onward course of events depends, are securely experienced' (Dewey, 1929/1984: 235).

15.3.4   Organizational Learning

According to Elkjaer (2004), there are two metaphors for organizational learning: acquisition and participation. The former sees individual learning as a model for organizational learning (cf. Cyert and March, 1963; Levitt and March, 1988) or as individual learning in an organizational context (cf. March and Olsen, 1975; Shrivastava, 1983). Organizational learning is perceived as the accumulation of individual acquisition of relevant knowledge (Huysman, 1999). The latter implies that individuals are social beings who together construct an understanding of what they have around them, and learn from social interaction within social systems such as organizations (Gherardi et al., 1998). According to this view, organizational learning becomes a cultural process (Cook and Yanow, 1996) and a social construction (Brown and Duguid, 1991) within communities of practice. These two metaphors correspond to the two views of knowledge as independent object and contextual process as presented earlier. Elkjaer (2004) proposed a third way of organizational learning, which combines both the acquisition and participation metaphors for learning, by relying on the pragmatist philosophy of Dewey.

We share Elkjaer's view and argue that Dewey's notion of a community of inquiry can serve as a transcending concept of organizational learning. By applying his notion of a community of inquiry to public administration, Shields (2003) suggested that it is the uncertainty of practice that triggers the need for inquiry. But there are no universal standards by which one could judge the outcome of inquiry: it is the actual community being affected and affecting the inquiry that will decide what 'counts' as useful.

According to Dewey, focusing on a problematic situation is essential for it helps a community to form around the issue requiring resolution. Members of a community of inquiry must bring a scientific attitude to the problematic situation, but this attitude does not only refer to science but also to common sense and practical intelligence. Finally and most crucially, communities of inquiry must be democratic. They must take into account values and ideals such as freedom, equality, and efficiency in pursuing their goals and objectives (Evans, 2000). The community of inquiry is a powerful concept, although not without its shortcomings, that sees truth and knowledge as social phenomena, marked by contextual contingency (Shields, 2003).

15.3.5 Research Methods: Experimentalism

As mentioned previously, there has been a heated debate in organization studies about whether one could bridge academic rigour and practical relevance (Aram and Salipante, 2003; Gulati, 2007). The quest for rigour tends to favour sophisticated data collection and analysis methods (Gulati, 2007) and include quantitative measures with multivariate statistical techniques. The relevance perspective requires context-specific and problem-focused investigations that make practitioners' interest the focal point of inquiry. Action research (Susman and Evered, 1978) and Mode 2 of knowledge production (Gibbons et al., 1994; Tranfield and Starkey, 1998) are examples of this approach.

Dewey's pragmatist experimentalism differs from these two approaches in that it provides a perspective that is new not only in detail but also in kind (Dewey, 1941). Here we would focus on an entirely different question: 'how the world works' (Watson, 2011). The guiding principle is that truth is not to do with getting a correct representation of reality but is an expression of an interest of the power to act in relation to an environment (Joas, 1993). Dewey preferred to characterize his philosophy as experimentalism or instrumentalism, but gradually pragmatism was used as a convenient label to refer to a group of thinkers, including Peirce, James, and Dewey (Bernstein, 2010). Experimentalism seeks both creation of generalized knowledge and testing in actual context; it fuses practices arising from empirical situations and those of academic pursuits.

Instead of accepting this world as providing the objects of knowledge, scientific inquiry treats it as offering the materials of problems (Dewey, 1938/1991). It is the day-to-day richness of reality and its inbuilt ambiguities that triggers the need for scientific inquiry (West, 1989). The first step of an experimental research, then, is to localize the problems that are driven by the environment experienced in our everyday life (Dewey, 1938/1991). The researcher executes certain experiments—which are operations of doing and making—that 'modify antecedently given existential conditions so that the results of the transformation are facts which are relevant in solution of a given problem' (Dewey, 1938/1991: 498). This experimental strategy is to clarify the problem, as well as observe and find solutions. In other words, one should develop hypotheses on the problem and its solution, execute the suggested actions, reflect on the results, draw conclusions, continue the cycle if the problem remains, and retain an open attitude towards unforeseen ideas (Biesta and Burbules, 2003). Dewey suggests: 'the social scientist should conduct experimental research not as laboratory experiments but as reactions, influences, changes—*on* the process and from *within* the process' (Dewey, 1938/1991: 180, emphasis added). Moreover, methods and products must be traced back to their origin in primary experience: the researcher needs to state when and where and why his actions took place, the needs and problems out of which they arise, and the conclusions must be brought back to the ordinary experience for verification (Dewey, 1917/2000).

An important element in Dewey's experimental methodology is democracy. In Dewey's ideal, experimental inquiry and democratic behaviour become fused (Gouinlock, 1990). This means a willingness to question, investigate, and learn, a determination to search for clarity in discourse and evidence in argument. There is also a readiness to hear and respect the views of others, to consider alternatives thoroughly and impartially, and to communicate in a like manner in return. The blind following of custom, authority, and impulse is not allowed.

Moreover, no claims for universality can be made (Aram and Salipante, 2003). All conclusions of inquiries, or knowledge, are continually renewed. They serve as inputs for future inquiries to generate newer knowledge. It can be seen that Dewey does not speak much about concepts in inquiry process. He often uses the terms of hypothesis, working hypothesis, and guiding idea instead of concept to stress that concepts are always tentative and have the nature of hypotheses (Miettinen, 2000). He said: 'The recorded scientific result is in effect a designation of a method to be followed and a prediction of what will be found when specified observations are set on foot' (Dewey, 1925/2000: 36).

Finally, in experimental methodology, scholars need to consider validity as utilization (Aram and Salipante, 2003). As the value of the constructed knowledge lies in its applicability, the test is the functionality, the instrumental use of what results from the experimental process.

15.3.6 Researching Organizations and Management

For Dewey and his fellow pragmatists, science is distinguished from all other methods of inquiry by its cooperative or public character (Shields, 2003). Dewey's work conceptualizes further the scientific method by suggesting that it is ultimately a technique for turning doubt into a resource to help pursue inquiry (Dewey, 1929/1984). Dewey applauded science for offering methods for solving problems and acquiring information about how the world works, but science was not regarded as the ultimate or the only way to know the world. According to Dewey, there may be other, equally valid, means of experience (such as common sense or art) and the activity of knowing through them could also enrich human understanding (Shields, 2003). While the universal quest for certainty is impossible and even destructive, the scientific method allows one to reach relatively settled mini-truths that speak to particular situations. Though neither Peirce nor Dewey privileged science, they both saw it as the most successful intellectual enterprise that could help bring individual situations together. The scientific model of inquiry upheld by the pragmatists sees knowledge as inextricably linked with experience and, as such, open to fallibilism and criticism.

The pragmatist's interest in what works and how and why it works (or does not) translates into a notion of knowledge, which is anti-foundational, directed towards problem solving using the data and the understandings available at the time. The researcher is permitted (indeed encouraged) to use indeterminate truth values in the attempt to handle situational indeterminacy. The quest for pragmatic certainty sensitizes the researcher to multiple realities, paradox, and ambiguity. Doubt, then, rather than certainty, is central to the methodological process.

According to Dewey's pragmatism, the problem of practice is related centrally to what humans need to know, how to obtain that knowledge, and how to apply it. The practice of management/leadership in organizations cannot therefore be separated from the practice of conceptualizing what needs to be done and the consequences this will have upon various individuals and groups. The doings of managers have been the subject of numerous empirical studies going back many decades.

Indeed, it is not just the leaders who have to cope with ambiguity by trying to understand what is going on in organizations: individuals at all levels in the organization have no choice but to make sense of these practical situations in order to ensure they can survive in a complex environment, with a view to achieving their own agendas and needs. It is precisely the ambiguous and progressive nature of experience that allows the possibility of responding to the environment in new ways as well as to evaluate the effectiveness of such responses.

Conceptualizing day-to-day organizational practices in particular ways (rather than others) allows for making choices that help organizational members, be they managers or otherwise, to survive according to their own wishes, understandings, and material resources in a world full of contingencies and unpredictability. To regard organizational practice as separate or removed from the process of conceptualization would deny any possibility for making moral choices and rejecting alternatives that are not deemed suitable by individuals and groups.

What can Dewey teach organization researchers? First of all, management is a problem of life: we all do management in various guises and are subject to it. For Dewey, it is the day-to-day experiential uncertainty that triggers any scientific inquiry. Problems of science are therefore no more than practical problems of life, and science cannot be viewed as superior to practice but as part of it. Secondly, management as practice is never straightforward and unproblematic for it involves groups of people who usually have different agendas and interests. One could easily argue that inquiry into the practice of management by those who contribute to its workings is a prerequisite and a necessity. The methodological steps suggested by Dewey could easily apply to how individuals and groups in organizations approach their day-to-day problems.

In accordance with pragmatism's theoretical cornerstone, the pragmatist researcher is most likely to adopt research practices that will allow them to solve a practical problem in an efficient way. Abstract concepts and theories are translated/understood with respect to practice. Pragmatist theorizing means an acknowledgement of the full dialectics between knowledge and action. Hence, proper knowledge is knowledgeable action and proper action is actable knowledge. Moreover, the practicalities of knowledge help establish the difference between meaningful and non-meaningful knowledge.

The pragmatist researcher concentrates on human actions. By studying actions, they can better grasp how individuals and groups render the world meaningful. The sayings and the doings of organizational actors are both regarded as actions and therefore worth studying. Moreover, actions are placed in their practical context in order to avoid atomistic descriptions of individual actions.

The focus is on both successful and unsuccessful actions for learning from failure; mistakes are as fruitful as learning from successes. Indeed, much can be learnt from the experiences of the multinational corporations which have failed to tap into the local cultures or from the experiences of senior managers who feel overwhelmed by the multiple, conflicting demands from below and above and go down with stress and burn out (Kunda, 1993). Moreover, the focus on action is not done for its own sake but to ensure that individual and communal problems are solved more effectively and according to the interests of all parties involved. Thus, the task of the pragmatist researcher is not only to outline and challenge the relationship between agency and structure but also to provide an account and an explanation of change. Why is it, for example, that some people seek change when others placed in the same context are content to accept existing arrangements (Archer, 2003)? Why is it that the Anglo-Saxon model is at times accepted and at times resisted by the local cultures?

It is worth noting that in recent years a large and varied set of scholars has been investigating 'recurring action patterns' (Cohen, 2007), which have been labelled 'routine' (Feldman and Pentland, 2003; Nelson and Winter, 1982), 'practices' (Gherardi, 2000), or 'collective mind' (Weick and Roberts, 1993). One of the root foundations of their work is the notion of routine as developed in Simon's *Administrative Behavior* (1945/1997), who was also influenced by the philosophy of Dewey (Cohen, 2007). However, Simon's conceptualization of routine differs from that of Dewey, although both viewed individuals as having three broad faculties: habitual, cognitive, and emotional. While Simon emphasized cognition at the expense of action, Dewey was most interested in habits because they 'shape and empower the other two faculties' (Cohen, 2007: 775). For him, habits are basic blocks of all our actions, being integral to how we think and act. Effective action, whether at an individual or collective level, is mediated by habits. When we cannot comprehend new situations and engage in emotional and cognitive work to do repair work, the outcome is a vast array of relatively effective and coherent new habits that allow us to function smoothly at an individual and collective level.

To return to Dewey, his focus on experience has the potential to lead to the identification and formulation of connections between individuals and social structures that bridge the Cartesian dualism of individual and society, micro and macro environment. Viewed in this way, pragmatism's concern for experience as a route to knowledge and theorizing strikes one as harbouring considerable promise for management researchers wishing to develop anti-oppressive/emancipatory forms of research.

15.4 CONCLUSION

Organization studies have not been impervious to the influence of American pragmatism, although it is reasonable to assert that its influence is rarely acknowledged. As discussed at the outset, our aim in the chapter has been to examine what Dewey's work can offer organization studies. In so doing, we join a growing number of writers for whom

American pragmatism is relevant to organization and management scholars concerned with understanding the dynamic processes and practices of organizational life (Elkjaer and Simpson, 2011). Such discussions are starting to gather momentum (Elkjaer, 2004; Evans, 2000; Jacobs, 2004; Simpson, 2009; Whetsell and Shields, 2011). As we see it, these contributions add to the vitality of the field of organization studies, which is not always curious and open in its scope, ambition, and concerns.

Ontological debates in organization and management studies have seen an increased polarization of structuralist positions, where organizational life is seen in terms of objective entities with clear attributes that can be quantified and classified according to some general model, on the one hand, and social constructivist perspectives where ideas and meanings are central to what constitutes organizational reality, on the other hand. According to Thompson (2011), the epistemological response to such ontological divides has been to adopt positions that embrace an objective and evolutionary perspective on organizations while at the same time acknowledging the role played by intersubjective factors. Such mid-range theories (Weick, 1989) build on the idea that general principles and abstractions are necessary, despite the fact that they cannot cope fully with the singularities and complexities of organizational life. As Thompson (2011) argues, mid-range theories also embrace the view that there is a continuum between entity and process forms of organizational reality and any ontological movements researchers make on this continuum will represent an epistemological trade-off that could have positive or negative consequences on the theory developed. Ontological shifts are associated with positive theory outcomes while ontological drifts are seen as leading to bad theorizing.

With this in mind, we suggest that Dewey's ideas provide a useful platform for making ontological shifts and preventing the occurrence of ontological drifts. Such drifts refer to reification, a process that happens when a social construct is turned into an objective phenomenon with an undeniable objective existence (e.g. markets, institutions). Ontological drifts can also lead to processification, a situation that may be encountered when the attributes of a process are relegated to an entity. Dewey's pragmatism encourages us to make two types of ontological shifts, which are crucial to developing theories that are both rigorous scientifically and relevant to the communities of practice affected. Abstraction takes place when the complexity of organizational processes is simplified and translated into an isolable entity whose characterization could be used to advantage. Conjunction is the situation where one shifts from an entity-driven view of the world to one that seeks to acknowledge the processual dimensions of a construct. These shifts are at the heart of pragmatist theories, the tension between them encouraging researchers to change mental gear and see the world in its multitude of potentialities, in order to arrive at a workable solution and an acceptable explanation.

It is widely accepted that managers and other practitioners from organizational worlds prefer static constructs, since they are more likely to be expressed in a transparent language and hence are easier to implement. However, the subtleties and complexities present in organizations require a more processual understanding and a treatment that, although it may not yield quick solutions and à la carte management recipes, will lead to real dialogue amongst the affected parties and ultimately to effective problem solving.

Dewey and his fellow pragmatist thinkers are not against scientific rigour per se but redefine it in ways that are more relevant to the world of practice. As Schultz (2010) reasoned, scientific rigour, in its most traditional sense, emphasizes standardization, quantitative methods, testing, and generalization and leads to well-crafted studies of minor issues that may not be important for practitioners. These studies, while methodologically complex and cleverly written up, tend to be just some kind of intellectual acrobatics that serves no purpose beyond academia. Academic careers are propelled by a drive to discover and institutionalize new concepts in order to achieve recognition from peers, rather than by the wish to engage with significant problems rooted in the practice of day-to-day life.

According to Schultz (2010: 275), 'the virtue of the pragmatist tradition has been its ability to address issues in organizations that matter to people and point to different ways of organizing'. This takes us back to a central question in organization studies: what is a good theory? As suggested earlier, Dewey's way of theorizing looks for the most plausible explanations to a problematic situation by using creativity and insight. Such insight could come from the anomalies present in the real world or from combining theories from different fields to come up with a workable answer to an existing problem. Creativity could be the result of deductive or inductive logic: what matters then, not least for organization studies scholars, is that the resultant explanation is useful to the community of practice affected by the issue at hand. This is the most appealing insight Dewey has to offer organization studies.

References

Aram, J. and Salipante, P. (2003). Bridging Scholarship in Management: Epistemological Reflections, *British Journal of Management* 14: 189–205

Archer, M. (2003). *Structure, Agency and the Internal Conversation* (Cambridge: Cambridge University Press).

Bernstein, R. (2010). *The Pragmatic Turn* (Cambridge: Polity Press).

Biesta, G. and Burbules, N. (2003). *Pragmatism and Education Research* (Michigan: Rowman and Littlefield publishers, Inc).

Blosch, M. (2001). Pragmatism and Organizational Knowledge Management, *Knowledge and Process Management* 8(1): 39–48.

Brown, J.S. and Duguid, P. (1991). Organizational Learning and Communities-of-Practice: Toward a Unified View of Working, Learning, and Innovation, *Organization Science* 2(1): 40–57.

Chiva, R. and Alegre, J. (2005). Organizational Learning and Organizational Knowledge: Towards the Integration of Two Approaches, *Management Learning* 36(1): 49–68.

Cohen, M. (2007). Reading Dewey: Reflections on the Study of Routine, *Organization Studies* 28: 773–86.

Cook, S. and Brown, J. (1999). Bridging Epistemologies: The Generative Dance between Organizational Knowledge and Organizational Knowing, *Organization Science* 10(4): 381–400.

——and Yanow, D. (1996). Culture and Organizational Learning, in M. Cohen and L. Sproull (eds), *Organizational Learning* (Thousand Oaks, CA: Sage Publications): 430 –59.

Cyert, R.M. and March, J.G. (1963). *A Behavioral Theory of the Firm* (Englewood Cliffs, NJ: Prentice-Hall).

Dewey, J. (1887). *Psychology* (New York: Harper).

——(1896). The Reflex Arc Concept in Psychology, *Psychological Review* 3: 357–70.

——(1897/1972). The Significance of the Problem of Knowledge, in J.A. Boydston (ed.), *The Early Works* (Carbondale: Southern Illinois University Press): 4–24.

——(1899). *The School and Society: Being Three Lectures by John Dewey, Supplemented by a Statement of the University Elementary School* (Chicago: University of Chicago Press).

——(1902). *The Child and the Curriculum* (Chicago: University of Chicago Press).

——(1905/1983). The Postulate of Immediate Empiricism, in J.A. Boydston (ed.), *Middle Works 1* (Carbondale and Edwardsville: Southern Illinois University Press): 158–83.

——(1915). The Logic of the Judgments of Practice, *Journal of Philosophy* 12: 505–23.

——(1916/1980). Democracy and Education, in J.A.Boydston (ed.), *Middle Works 9* (Carbondale and Edwardsville: Southern Illinois University Press): 1–370.

—— (1916/1989). Essays in Experimental Logic, in J.A. Boydston (ed.), *Later Works 16* (Carbondale and Edwardsville: Southern Illinois University Press).

——(1917/2000). The Need for a Recovery of Philosophy, in J. Stuhr (ed.), *Pragmatism and Classical American Philosophy: Essential Readings and Interpretive Essays,* 2nd edn (New York: Oxford University Press): 445–55.

—— (1920/1982). Reconstruction in Philosophy, in J.A. Boydston (ed.), *Middle Works 12* (Carbondale and Edwardsville: Southern Illinois University Press): 77–201.

—— (1922/1983). Human Nature and Conduct, in J.A. Boydston (ed.), *Middle Works 14* (Carbondale and Edwardsville: Southern Illinois University Press): 1–227.

——(1925/1981). Experience and Nature, in J.A. Boydston (ed.), *Later Works 1* (Carbondale and Edwardsville: Southern Illinois University Press): 1–326.

——(1925/2000).Experience and Philosophic Method, in J. Stuhr (ed.), *Pragmatism and Classical American Philosophy: Essential Readings and Interpretive Essays,* 2nd edn (New York: Oxford University Press): 460–70.

——(1929/1984). The Quest for Certainty, in J.A. Boydston (ed.), *Later Works 4* (Carbondale and Edwardsville: Southern Illinois University Press): 1–250.

——(1931/1984). Philosophy and Civilization, in J.A. Boydston (ed.), *Later Works 3* (Carbondale and Edwardsville: Southern Illinois University Press): 3–10.

——(1934). *A Common Faith* (New Haven: Yale University Press).

——(1934/1987). Art as Experience, in J.A Boydston (ed.), *Later Works 10* (Carbondale and Edwardsville: Southern Illinois University Press).

——(1938/1988). Experience and Education, in J.A. Boydston (ed.), *Later Works 13* (Carbondale and Edwardsville: Southern Illinois University Press): 1–61.

——(1938/1991). Logic: Theory of Inquiry, in J.A. Boydston (ed.), *Later Works 12* (Carbondale and Edwardsville: Southern Illinois University Press): 1–527.

——(1939). *Freedom and Culture* (New York: Putnam).

—— (1941). Propositions, Warranted Assertibility, and Truth, *The Journal of Philosophy* 38(7): 169–86.

——and Bentley, A. (1949/1989). Knowing and the Known, in J.A. Boydston (ed.), *Later Works 16* (Carbondale and Edwardsville: Southern Illinois University Press): 1–294.

——Hickman, L.A., and Alexander, T.M. (1998). *The Essential Dewey*, Volume 2: *Ethics, Logic, Psychology* (Bloomington and Indianapolis: Indiana University Press).

Donaldson, L. (1996). *For Positivist Organization Theory* (London: Sage).

Elkjaer, B. (2004). Organizational Learning: 'The Third Way', *Management Learning* 35(4): 419–34.

——and Simpson, B. (2011). Pragmatism: A Lived and Living Philosophy. What Can It Offer to Contemporary Organization Theory?, in H. Tsoukas and R. Chia (eds), *Philosophy and Organization Theory (Research in the Sociology of Organizations, Volume 32)* (London: Emerald Group Publishing Limited): 55–84.

Evans, K.G. (2000). Reclaiming John Dewey: Democracy, Inquiry, Pragmatism, and Public Management, *Administration & Society* 32(3): 308–28.

Feldman, M.S. and Pentland, B.T. (2003). Reconceptualizing Organizational Routines as a Source of Flexibility and Change, *Administrative Science Quarterly* 48(1): 94–121.

Fenstermacher, G.D. and Sanger, M. (1998). What is the Significance of John Dewey's Approach to the Problem of the Knowledge?, *Elementary School Journal* 98(5): 467–78.

Gherardi, S. (2000). Practice-Based Theorizing on Learning and Knowing in Organizations: An Introduction, *Organization* 7: 211–24.

——Nicolini, D., and Odella, F. (1998). Toward a Social Understanding of How People Learn in Organizations, *Management Learning* 29(3): 273–97.

Gibbons, M., Limoges, C., Nowotny, H., Schwartzman, S., Scott, P., and Trow, M. (1994). *The New Production of Knowledge: the Dynamics of Science and Research in Contemporary Societies* (London: Sage Publications).

Gouinlock, J. (1990). What is the Legacy of Instrumentalism? Rorty's Interpretation of Dewey, *Journal of the History of Philosophy* 28: 251–69.

Grant, R.M. (1996). Toward a Knowledge-Based Theory of the Firm, *Strategic Management Journal* 17: 109–22.

Guba, E.G. and Lincoln, Y.S. (1994). Competing Paradigms in Qualitative Research, in N. Denzin and Y.S. Lincoln (eds), *Handbook of Qualitative Research* (London: Sage): 105–17.

Gulati, R. (2007). Tentpoles, Tribalism, and Boundaryspanning: The Rigor-Relevance Debate in Management Research, *Academy of Management Journal* 50: 775–82.

Hambrick, D. (2007). The Field of Management's Devotion to Theory: Too Much of a Good Thing, *Academy of Management Journal* 50: 1346–52.

Hitt, M. (1998). Presidential Address: Twenty-First-Century Organizations: Business Firms, Business Schools, and the Academy, *Academy of Management Review* 23: 218–24.

Huff, A. (2000). Presidential Address: Changes in Organizational Knowledge Production, *Academy of Management Review* 25: 288–93.

Husserl, E. (1936/1970). *The Crisis of European Sciences and Transcendental Phenomenology* (Evanston, IL: Northwestern University Press).

Huysman, M. (1999). Balancing Biases: A Critical Review of the Literature on Organizational Learning, in M. Easterby-Smith, J. Burgoyne, and L. Araujo (eds), *Organizational Learning and the Learning Organization* (London: Sage Publications): 59–74.

Jacobs, D.C. (2004). A Pragmatist Approach to Integrity in Business Ethics, *Journal of Management Inquiry* 13: 215–23.

James, W. (1950/1890). *The Principles of Psychology*, Volumes 1 and 2 (New York: Dover).

—— (1904). Does 'Consciousness' Exist?, *Journal of Philosophy, Psychology, and Scientific Methods* 1: 477–91.

Jarzabkowski, P., Mohrman, S., and Scherer, A. (2010). Organization Studies as Applied Science: The Generation and Use of Academic Knowledge about Organizations Introduction to the Special Issue, *Organization Studies* 31: 1189–207.

Joas, H. (1993). *Pragmatism and Social Theory*, trans. J. Gaines et al. (Cambridge, MA: Harvard University Press).

Kelemen, M. and Bansal, T. (2002). The Conventions of Management Research and Their Relevance to Management Practice, *British Journal of Management* 13: 97–108.

Kennedy, G. (1959). Dewey's Concept of Experience: Determinate, Indeterminate, and Problematic, *The Journal of Philosophy* 56: 801–14.

Kilpinen, E. (2009). The Habitual Conception of Action and Social Theory, *Semiotica* 173: 99–128.

Kuhn, T.S. (1962). *The Structure of Scientific Revolutions* (Chicago: University of Chicago Press).

Kunda, G. (1993). *Engineering Culture: Control and Commitment in a High Tech Corporation* (Philadelphia, PA: Temple University Press).

Levitt, B. and March, J.G. (1988). Organizational Learning, *Annual Review of Sociology* 14: 319–40.

March, J. and Olsen, J. (1975). The Uncertainty of the Past: Organizational Learning under Ambiguity, *European Journal of Political Research* 3: 147–71.

Miettinen, R. (2000). The Concept of Experiential Learning and John Dewey's Theory of Reflective Thought and Action, *International Journal of Lifelong Education* 19: 54–72.

Mowday, R. (1997). Presidential Address: Reaffirming our Scholarly Values, *Academy of Management Review* 22: 335–45.

Nelson, R. and Winter, S. (1982). *An Evolutionary Theory of Economic Change* (Cambridge, MA: Harvard University Press).

Nonaka, I. (1994). A Dynamic Theory of Organizational Knowledge Creation, *Organization Science* 5(1): 14–37.

Palmer, D., Dick, B., and Freiburger, N. (2009). Rigor and Relevance in Organization Studies, *Journal of Management Inquiry* 18: 265–72.

Polkinghorne, D. (2000). Psychological Inquiry and the Pragmatic and Hermeneutic Traditions, *Theory and Psychology* 10(4): 453–79.

Scherer, A.G. and Steinmann, H. (1999). Some Remarks on the Problem of Incommensurability in Organization Studies, *Organization Studies* 20: 519–44.

Schultz, M. (2010). Reconciling Pragmatism and Scientific Rigour, *Journal of Management Inquiry* 19: 274–77.

Shields, P. (2003). The Community of Inquiry: Classical Pragmatism and Public Administration, *Administration and Society* 35(5): 510–38.

Shrivastava, P. (1983). A Typology of Organizational Learning Systems, *Journal of Management Studies* 20: 7–28.

Simon, H.A. (1945/1997). *Administrative Behavior*, 4th edn (New York: The Free Press).

Simpson, B. (2009). Pragmatism, Mead, and the Practice Turn, *Organization Studies* 30: 1329–47.

Spender, J. (1996). Making Knowledge the Basis of a Dynamic Theory of the Firm, *Strategic Management Journal* 17: 45–62.

Susman, G.I. and Evered, R.D. (1978). An Assessment of the Scientific Merits of Action Research, *Administrative Science Quarterly* 23: 582–603.

Thompson, M. (2011). Ontological Shift or Ontological Drift: Reality Claims, Epistemological Frameworks and Theory Generation in Organization Studies, *Academy of Management Review* 36: 754–73.

Tranfield, D. and Starkey, K. (1998). The Nature, Social Organization and Promotion of Management Research: Towards Policy, *British Journal of Management* 9(4): 341–53.

Tsoukas H. and Chia, R. (2002). On Organizational Becoming: Rethinking Organizational Change. *Organization Science* 13(5):567–82.

Vera, D. and Crossan, M. (2003). Organizational Learning and Knowledge Management: Toward an Integrative Framework, in M. Easterby-Smith and M. Lyles (eds), *The Blackwell Handbook of Organizational Learning and Knowledge Management* (Oxford: Blackwell): 122 –42.

Watson, T.J. (2011). Ethnography, Reality and Truth: The Vital Need for Students of 'How Things Work' in Organizations and Management, *Journal of Management Studies* 48(1): 202–17.

Weick, K. (1989). Theory Construction as Disciplined Imagination, *Academy of Management Review* 14: 516–31.

——and Roberts, K.H. (1993). Collective Mind in Organizations: Heedful Interrelating on Flight Decks, *Administrative Science Quarterly* 38(3): 357–81.

West, C. (1989). *The American Evasion of Philosophy* (Madison: The University of Wisconsin Press).

Whetsell, T.A. and Shields, P.M. (2011). Reconciling the Varieties of Pragmatism in Public Administration, *Administration & Society* 43: 474–83.

Wicks, A. and Freeman, R.E. (1998). Organization Studies and the New Pragmatism: Positivism, Anti-Positivism, and the Search for Ethics, *Organization Science* 9: 123–40.

CHAPTER 16

ALFRED NORTH WHITEHEAD (1861–1947)

TOR HERNES[1]

16.1 LIFE AND TIMES

WHITEHEAD WAS born in Ramsgate, England, in 1861. Having matriculated at Trinity College, Cambridge he became a fellow of Trinity College in 1884, teaching mathematics. While at Trinity Whitehead supervised the doctoral dissertation of Bertrand Russell, also to become a major philosopher and who later came to supervise parts of Ludwig Wittgenstein's early work on the problems of logic. Between 1900 and 1910 Whitehead and Russell collaborated on the first version of *Principia Mathematica*. Whitehead was forced to leave Cambridge University in 1910, partly due to his defence of a colleague who had been involved in an adulterous affair, partly due to his activism to grant women access to academia. Actually, he was also reaching the 25-year limit for senior lecturers. Despite having pioneered what is widely considered one of the most important works on mathematical logic in history, he had to move on to another institution for not having been promoted to professor. The years between 1910 and 1926 were spent at University College London and Imperial College London, where he taught physics and philosophy of science while engaging in questions on education, which was a topic that he wrote on until the 1930s. The beginning of World War I marked the end of his collaboration with Russell, who pursued a logical approach to philosophy. In 1924, then aged 63, Whitehead was invited to pursue his ideas and teach philosophy at Harvard University, where he worked until his retirement. He died in 1947.

Whitehead took a speculative orientation to philosophy, which means that he saw philosophy as a progressive enterprise of approximation of philosophical thought towards actuality (Ramal, 2003) and the living world (not to be confused with the social world). He leaned towards Platonism and what some writers have associated with 'panpsychism', whereby he refused to grant mind-like qualities to humans alone. This is not to say that he thought that physical objects could have minds, which is a mistaken criticism of Whitehead. What he allowed for was for the composite experience of entities to exhibit mind-like qualities at events, which is a point that will be pursued in more detail in this chapter. Such thinking was in stark contrast to Russell and other proponents of logical philosophy, oriented towards the capabilities of the human mind to perform ever-increasing clarity of understanding through language. It also makes Whitehead a thoroughly modern thinker by our contemporary standards, and especially in relation to organizational analysis, where heterogeneous and temporal views are gradually taking hold.

Whitehead counted among his influences not just those he could agree with but also those whom he could disagree with. He attributed to Aristotle, for example, the existence of categories, which enabled the distinction of entities into primary and secondary qualities, but which was also a trait of western philosophy that Whitehead argued vehemently against. Still, he saw it as a major achievement. Whitehead praised Plato, who was less sanguine about the power of categories than Aristole, for the fluidity of his forms of thought (1920, 1938), which made it possible to think about potentiality, life, and motion (1938: 69). Whitehead saw Leibniz and his idea of monads as a major achievement of philosophy (see Chapter 7, this volume, in which Elke Weik suggests how much Whitehead actually let himself be influenced by Leibniz's thinking). Finally, James, his predecessor at Harvard, was important in the eyes of Whitehead, owing largely to James' metaphysical stance, his pluralism, and his insistence on direct experience (or 'pure experience') as the basis for knowledge. Whitehead's style of introducing his novel, radical, and to many, controversial ideas, was non-dogmatic, gentle in style, highly respectful of other thinkers, and above all 'level-headed', as Weber (2003: 27) puts it. Although he wrote about Newton that 'His cosmology is very easy to understand and very hard to believe' (1933/1967: 131), he also wrote that 'We cannot overrate the debt of gratitude which we owe to these men' (1925a: 59).

An event that added momentum to Whitehead's philosophical work was the empirical validation of Einstein's theory of relativity in 1919 as well as the emerging quantum physics by Faraday, Planck, and Maxwell, which signalled the downfall of the Newtonian dominance in scientific thought. The refutation of the Newtonian view helped shape the development of Whitehead's philosophical ideas, as the contemporary developments in physics gave impetus to seeing nature as energy rather than inert masses. Most important of these developments was the collapse of the time–space distinction proven physically by Einstein.

An important contribution of Whitehead's philosophy is to insist on life and creativity across the human–nature divide, and one way to do this was to work consistently from the idea of concrete experience, which is a point at which he connected to American pragmatism, and especially the work of James, his predecessor at Harvard. He did, in fact, emphasize in a 1936 paper that 'William James and John Dewey will stand out as having infused philosophy with new life, and with a new relevance to the modern world' (quoted in Weber, 2002: 19). Working from concrete experience is also an aspect of his work that Dewey (1941), as well as Mead later, pointed out as novel and valuable.

Dewey, for one, praised Whitehead for combining nature and human experience into a common theoretical framework, which obviously meant that any dualism between living humans and dead objects had to be done away with (Sherburne, 1992). Where Whitehead was radical was in refusing to limit 'living' or 'life' to human experience. Instead, life is in the world, nature is a living whole and does not discriminate between the organic and the non-organic. As pointed out by Sherburne (2004), Whitehead firmly rejected notions from physics as a basis for philosophy, which treated things as 'dead matter', which is one reason why he referred to his philosophy as a 'philosophy of organism' (1925a: 80). Whitehead, instead, preferred biology, which deals with all levels of existence, from humans via amoebae and cells to atoms. Developments in biology as well as physics at the time helped him replace mass with energy. And, he argued further that there is no way that one can get from dead matter to the richness of human experience (Sherburne, 2004: 9).

Still, the creation of continuity and extension in a living world relies on the use of abstractions. In order to form understanding we abstract from concrete experience, which is why he wrote that, 'Perspective is the dead abstraction of mere fact from the living importance of things felt' (1938: 11). Yet, abstraction is necessary for knowledge, Whitehead wrote:

> You cannot think without abstractions; accordingly, it is of the utmost importance to be vigilant in critically revising your *modes* of abstraction. It is here that philosophy finds its niche as essential to the healthy progress of society. It is the critic of abstractions. (1925a: 59)

But rather than pose abstractions and living experience as two sides of a dualism, he preferred to see abstractions and living experience as feeding off each other. Moreover, this is how philosophy can meet science: by questioning the abstractions from which science builds its assumptions, bearing in mind that science cannot help but rely on abstractions for its survival. However, the journey between living experience and abstraction is a perilous one, because we remove that from the world that made abstraction possible in the first place. Hence he wrote that 'Abstraction from connectedness involves the omission of an essential factor in the fact considered' (1938: 9). For every fact considered there is, according to Whitehead, a suppression of the environment required for the existence of that fact, since making sense of the world is about the ongoing work of making finite facts from infinite ones. Such is the necessity of scientific work, and at the same time its peril, because in deriving abstractions from living occasions something is lost on the way. We might say that actualizing is done from actuality, thereby losing the creative force offered by potentiality. The most critical passage is on the journey back from abstractions to living, concrete reality, as abstraction may lead us away from the real complexity of nature (1938: 125). It is this journey that leads to what he famously called the 'fallacy of misplaced concreteness' (1929a: 2). Still, he suggested that, 'There can be no objection to this procedure, however, as long as we know what we are doing' (1938: 10).

16.2 CONNECTIONS AND CONTRASTS
WITH OTHERS

In his writings, Whitehead gave much space to commentaries of other philosophers while contrasting them with his own ideas. Newtonianism was to Whitehead an inevitable result of systematic evolution and the need inherited from Aristotle to work with categoreal entities. Whitehead's charge was that abstractions—the building blocks of categories—were not able to explain their own workings. Hence he argued that the combination of Newton's theory of nature and Hume's theory of experience yields a barren theoretical landscape (1938: 135) of dead facts, unable to account for its own reasons. Newton's work, he argued, had enabled factors and causal connections between factors to be studied. Missing, however, was any understanding of how those categories come into existence. This, by the way, may be described as a deficiency of the present state of organization studies, which suffers from a proliferation of abstractions without the processual explanations that come with them.

Whitehead's charge to philosophy as it had been practised for two millennia was that it had fallen prey to what he referred to as 'the bifurcation of nature', consisting on the one hand of nature, operating according to its own laws, and of mind on the other. 'Thus there would be two natures, one is the conjecture and the other is the dream' (1920: 30). The bifurcation of nature, therefore, means that the human mind only interacts with its own images of a world. A further implication is that there is a world 'out there' that operates by certain sets of laws, and a mental world 'in here' operating by a different set of laws. This view, propagated by Descartes, Kant, and others, was untenable for Whitehead, as it was for others, including Merleau-Ponty (Hamrick, 1999) and Dewey. Consequently, as pointed out by Weber (2003: 27), Whitehead evoked at length 'the death of the Cartesian Ego'. Whitehead also presented his process philosophy as the inversion of Kant's philosophy, which saw process as flowing from subjectivity towards apparent objectivity. Whitehead took the opposite stance, explaining process as moving from objectivity towards subjectivity (Sherburne, 1966: 152). In other words, the subject emerges from process, and not vice versa ('The traffic signals are the outcome of the traffic'; Whitehead, 1938: 31).

This thinking put him at odds with Russell, his collaborator during the writing of *Principia Mathematica*. Whereas Russell saw clarity as a necessity for knowledge, Whitehead saw it as a danger, bluntly calling 'idiotic' the idea that thought can be perfectly, or even adequately expresses in words, even suggesting that such ideas had done 'immeasurable harm' to philosophy (Price, 1954: 325). He said to Russell once, for example, 'You think the world is what it looks like in fine weather at noon day; I think it is what it seems like in the early morning when one first wakes from deep sleep.'

Although Whitehead wrote on a number of issues, including religion (aiding the emergence of 'process theology' in the United States), education, and working life, what is most central for process thinking and organization studies is the ways in which they provide novel ways to conceptualize experience, time, and endurance (or extension) in a world of ceaseless change. In *The Rehabilitation of Whitehead*, Lucas writes,

> The experience of elements of the past being selectively constituted into present episodic occasions, characterized either by varying degrees of novelty or by mere repetition of prior patterns of behavior, is simply the most general description that can be offered of the ceaseless, remorseless, and dynamic activity characterizing the nature of things. (Lucas, 1989: 147)

It is precisely in this ceaseless, remorseless, and dynamic world that endurance becomes an important focus of analysis. If we can only experience but a minute portion of the world and experience is evanescent, how can we account for endurance in the absence of transcendent structure? In Whitehead's thinking, endurance can only be explained by the extension and connecting of events. Mead (1936), who made repeated attempts to integrate Whitehead's thinking into his own evolving thought (Cook, 1979: 107), sided with Whitehead on his event-based notion of time (with the exception of Whitehead's idea of 'eternal objects', among other things). Where Whitehead differed significantly from Mead was on the role of the social. Whitehead would not, and could not, give exclusive privilege to the social in the making of the world, whereas Mead's (1934) focus was primarily socio-psychological. Mead wrote incisively on temporality (Mead, 1932), notably on the 'nature of the present', in which he engaged with Whitehead's notion of temporal spread. However, while Whitehead saw experience of temporality as emerging from what he referred to as 'the passage of nature' (1920: 55, 1938: 46), Mead searched for temporality as emanating from human experience (Mead, 1932) and remaining within the sphere of social interaction (Mead, 1934).

Among more recent and major philosophers to draw inspiration from Whitehead is Deleuze (2004), who displayed enthusiasm for Whitehead's ideas mainly on the way Whitehead provides a way out of categorical thought (a lineage from Plato) and opening for understanding that links abstractions to lived experience (an extension of James' thinking). Deleuze's discontent with categories is that, while they may be open in fact, they are not open in principle (2004: 257), whereas the notions employed by Whitehead relate not only to possible experience but to 'real experience', something that in Deleuze's opinion makes Whitehead's *Process and Reality* one of the greatest books of modern philosophy' (Deleuze, 2004: 257). To Deleuze, Whitehead's incisive question 'What is an event?' marks a convincing alternative to what Deleuze scathingly referred to as 'the (Aristotelian) attributive scheme, the great play of principles, the multiplications of categories, the conciliation of the universal and the individual example, and the transformation of the concept into a subject: an entire hubris' (Deleuze, 2006: 86). Whitehead's notion of events, which is a spatio-temporal duration that lasts long enough to make it an event, invites the question as to what conditions make an event possible. How can the many (events) become the one? This is where Deleuze draws a line from Leibniz to Whitehead by focusing on the becoming of 'the one' from the many.

16.3 Temporal Atomism—The 'Gist' of Whitehead's Work

Whitehead's efforts were directed towards explaining how order comes about in an open universe, while avoiding the idea of time and space as inherent qualities of nature. He drew inspiration from the Roman poet and philosopher Lucretius, who subscribed to a view of the world as streams of invisible particles (atoms), which come together to form substances such as trees, water, and humans. While siding with Heraclitus on the principle of movement, Lucretius rejected Heraclitus' view that the world is made of flow and transition of substances. For Lucretius movement takes place through the changing patterns of eternal particles rather than through the transformation of a-priori-defined substances. For Lucretius, there were no a priori directive forces of processes. Instead he subscribed to Epicurus' term 'clinamen', which denotes a swerve—the deviation of processes without any observable reason for change. Hence the formation of things may emerge spontaneously but, once set in motion, the formation attracts particles into its process. We can see here the beginnings of a view of process as stochastic, yet contingent; indeterminate, yet not accidental (Schatzki, 2010).

While subscribing to an atomistic view analogous to that of Lucretius ('Thus, the ultimate metaphysical truth is atomism'; Whitehead, 1929a: 35), Whitehead replaced physical articles with 'actual occasions' (1929a: 18) which are like 'point-flashes' of instantaneous duration in time, similar to James' 'drops of experience' (James, 1890/1977: 104). Actual occasions do not refer to human experience as such, but to the actual experience produced by the occasion. In other words, it is meant as a metaphysical and analytical construct to describe actual experience. It was obvious to Whitehead that nature does not offer a present of temporal extension; the passage of nature leaves nothing between past and future. A present of temporal duration is a creation of the mind, which is what he called a 'specious present', which is when the past is gone and the future is not yet. Whitehead also likened actual occasions to Leibniz's monads, except that while Leibniz's monads could change, actual occasions can only become, then to become 'immortalised' (1929a). In line with Lucretius, Whitehead's atomistic views aimed at explaining how the many become one, an idea he had pursued from James' writings as early as 1910 while a mathematician at Cambridge (Weber, 2003). However, there is no movement or actual change according to Whitehead's thinking, only the becoming of experience happening at actual occasions (synonymous with 'actual entities'). Actual occasions are analytically speaking like temporal knife-edges of no real duration in time, which can only become then to perish and become 'data' for new occasions. Note that actual occasions are an analytical construct that Whitehead used to build his extensive framework of describing processes and not occasions of human experience, which he thought had duration.

Whitehead's thinking shares the core atomist assumption that experience is made up of indivisible particles. Two factors should be kept in mind here. First, it is an *assumption* that the particles are indivisible. It had not been settled whether elementary particles in physics can be divided further; in fact, it is debatable whether we can apply the word 'division' here at all. Whitehead assumed that actual occasions were the basic building blocks of processes, without really taking a stand as to whether or not they can be divided. Second, materialist atomism was untenable to Whitehead, which is why he replaced physical particles with occasions of experience involving—but not exclusive of—physical entities. Unlike particles, occasions of experience do not move; they become, then to fade away. As Stengers (2008) points out, Whitehead's occasions are temporally atomic occasions aiming to become 'one' by achieving self-determination through satisfaction, which designates the 'final phase of becoming'. When the 'one' is achieved from the initial many, the occasion no longer experiences, but attains 'objective immortality'. Once it has become 'objectively immortal' it can be felt by other subsequent occasions. A major implication is that 'becoming' is an experience in time. Thus, when Whitehead (1929a: 254) wrote that 'apart from the experience of subjects there is nothing, nothing, nothing, bare nothingness', he referred to the subject as a process of attaining unity in front of the perishing of time while embodying the past of its many constituent experiences.

Whitehead's idea of atomism is by no means devoid of intentionality. An aim does not have to be a teleological kind of aim, but can be an evolving whole that is continuously sensed, and which provides processes of becoming with a sense of direction or rationale. Lucretius' view was based on probabilities of occurrence, where contingencies lead to the emergence of flows that possess their own attraction. Their attraction, or aims, is the form of process itself. Replacing Lucretius' atoms with events Whitehead sees the prehension between events as having a 'vector character' (1929a: 231), by which an event becomes agency for the unfolding of new events. Added to this is the important aspect of intensity of feeling, implying that higher intensity gives a feeling a stronger agency in shaping events. In an atomistic world, a stronger intensity of feeling makes it more probable that events reach out and connect under the influence of that feeling (Hernes, 2008). This is where Whitehead's thinking is truly innovative, by assuming that temporal occasions of experience actively constitute one another in the flow of time, and where the force of his complex theoretical scheme becomes apparent.

16.4 INFLUENCE IN ORGANIZATION STUDIES

To speak of influence is potentially misplaced in relation to Whitehead's thinking, partly because of his reluctance to give agency to any one entity or event, partly because he insists that influence does not take place from one point in time to a future point, but the other way around, as suggested in Maclachlan's (1992) reading of Whitehead. In fact, Whitehead pointed out himself that 'It is an exaggeration to attribute a general change in a climate of thought to any one piece of writing or to any one author' (1925a: 143). His statement is also consistent with his analytical view of causality taking place not in virtue of the activity of the cause, but through the activity of the effect. Following Whitehead, then, it cannot be the cause that is active, because at the crucial point in time, the activity of the cause is over and done with. What is active is not the past, but the present actuality, which is in process of becoming by evoking the 'causal' or 'influential' event (Hernes, forthcoming).

Nevertheless, an early writer in organization and management to whom we may attribute influence by Whitehead is Mary Parker Follett, although Whitehead's influence on her writings is difficult to assess, both in terms of impact and timing. It is possible that his thinking had an amplifying effect on ideas that she had been nurturing already. Parker Follett referred explicitly to Whitehead in some of her later writing, and there are indications that she attended lectures by Whitehead or read some of his writings before they were published. Be that as it may. Whereas Parker Follett has exerted unquestionable influence on the process understanding of organizational life, as a contemporary of Whitehead her thinking corresponded with his critique of tendencies in philosophy and science to condense living experience down to dead facts, for then to turn those dead facts into generating elements of understanding. Lorino and Mourey (2013) point out how Parker Follett criticized the way situations were investigated in social studies in her time: 'the fallacy which dissected experience and took the dead products, subject and object, and made them the generating elements' (Follett, 1924), thus criticizing a form of closure, 'the fallacy of ends' (Follett, 1919: 588), as it does not consider the potentialities of human actions, which are not given but always in the making and partially unpredictable (Lorino and Mourey, 2013).

Parker Follett was very probably the first theorist to apply Whitehead's ideas (although it would be wrong to assume that those ideas came from Whitehead alone) to organizational life. Follett (1941) took this philosophical trajectory to organizational life by seeing how means of formal organization are mere elements of processes; how attempts at formal organization emerge from flows and re-enter flow in turn:

> An order or command is a *step* in a process, a moment in a movement of interweaving experience. We should guard against thinking this step is a larger part of the overall process that it really is. There is all that leads to the order, all that comes afterwards—methods of administration, the watching and recording of results, what flows out of it to make further orders. (Follett, 1941: 149–50)

There was little room for Whiteheadian influence in what may be called early modern organization theory starting in the late 1950s, as Whitehead's thinking was scarcely referred to in philosophy at the time, and hardly at all in social science. The only 'Whitehead' referred to was actually his son, Thomas North Whitehead, who was actively involved with the Hawthorne experiments in the 1930s as collaborator of Elton Mayo. Although the Hawthorne experiments have wielded extensive influence on field management and organization, and Thomas North Whitehead published extensively from the experiments (T. North Whitehead, 1936, 1938), there is little evidence of his father's influence in his writings.

There are, nevertheless, indirect influences of Whitehead via influential writers in social science who are important for the development of processual strands in organization studies; two writers in particular deserve mention, Niklas Luhmann and Bruno Latour. Both writers recognize the radical thought of Whitehead's thinking as fundamental elements in their own work. Niklas Luhmann (1995), whose social systems theory rests largely on the idea of self-creation (autopoiesis) and correspondingly self-referencing, refers to Whitehead's notion of actual occasions ('drops of experience') as the theory that enables connectivity. Whitehead's notion of 'societies' applies to the connecting of actual occasions that belong together in such a way that they mutually express and feel wholeness, and together can reproduce themselves as wholes. Luhmann, who built his theory from systems as consisting of communicative events, relied on Whitehead's event-based theory. When, for example, Luhmann (1995: 36) asks the fundamental question, 'how does one get from one elemental event to the next?', he puts this down to connectivity rather than to repetition. The statement resonates with Whitehead's statement that 'Connectedness is of the essence of all things of all types' (1938: 9). Events constitute a major aspect in Luhmann's autopoiesis, notably through their role in creating the system's temporality. Events take place in time and they mark the difference between 'before' and 'after'. As with Whitehead's actual occasions, Luhmann's events exist in time, but have by themselves no extension in time; they are essentially evanescent phenomena. In Luhmann's organization theory (Luhmann, 2000), for example, decisions act as events marking the difference between before and after (Åkerstrøm, 2003).

Although Luhmann here begins to depart from Whitehead's framework, notably by conflating actual occasions and events, the nature of temporal units as regards connectedness, evanescence, and markers of past–future are common to them and form a novel basis for organizational theorizing. There is still considerable resistance, probably due to scepticism to the perceived systems aspect of his work. With more widespread understanding that Luhmann really addresses profoundly processual aspects of social life, and with a deeper appreciation of how his systemic thinking applies to a processual understanding of organizational life, Luhmann's work should gain greater momentum in organization studies, and with it Whitehead's voice may be heard more clearly.

Bruno Latour, who hails Whitehead as the greatest philosopher of the twentieth century, is one of the rare social science writers who bridges philosophy and organizational phenomena, whereas other writers affiliated with Actor Network Theory (ANT) have extended ideas of ANT to areas such as economic sociology (Callon, 1986, 1998) and organization studies (Law, 1994, 2004). While engaging in various empirical domains, Latour has been persistently excavating the philosophical foundations of ANT, in which he makes explicit reference to Whitehead's thinking. A central tenet is made visible in Latour's work by the sentence 'Neither nature nor mind is in command', a phrase he borrows from Isabelle Stengers' (2002) book on Whitehead. Latour argues against the realist notion that there is a wired nature 'out there' which gives context to what goes on 'in here'. He thus shares Whitehead's scepticism towards the 'subject–predicate' type of dualism, which according to Halewood

(2005) has led much of philosophy and science astray. This thinking is applied in Latour's analysis of Louis Pasteur's 'discovery' of lactic yeast, in which lactic yeast did not 'exist' as a living organism prior to Pasteur's research, but emerges as a fact through experimentation, as Pasteur proceeds through 'propositions', a term that Latour borrows from Whitehead. In a similar vein to Whitehead's tenet of working from non-entities, his analysis works from something that at the outset is not recognized as existing, to something that grows into a discovery and subsequently into a recognized entity—'the becoming of one'. Once Pasteur can prove the role of lactic yeast, it becomes an entity that subsequently enters the stream in biological and chemical research, enabling a trajectory of 'entification' (Hernes, 2008) of Pasteur and the Pasteur Institute.

As of yet there has been relatively little direct influence of Whitehead on works in organization studies, with the exception of Cooper (1976), Chia and King (1998), Chia (1999), Bakken and Hernes (2006), Cobb (2006), and Hernes (2008). Some works have argued for revising aspects of organizational theorizing in the light of Whitehead's thinking. Chia (1999) and Chia and King (1998) draw upon Whitehead to argue for an ontology of becoming in organization studies and suggest the relevance for thinking movement and novelty. Bakken and Hernes (2006) draw upon Whitehead in arguing for a re-examination of the verb–noun relationship in organizational analysis. Cobb (2006) offers an analysis of how Whitehead's event-based thinking may enable an understanding of community which is different from western substantialist and individualistic views of community. Hernes (2008) discusses more systematically the relevance of Whitehead's work for a process view of organization, relating central notions of Whitehead's to ideas in James March, Karl Weick, Bruno Latour, and Niklas Luhmann. As yet, however, no one has attempted a more full-scale development of organizational theory from Whitehead's philosophy. Hernes (forthcoming) draws inspiration from Whitehead in developing a temporal, event-based theory of organization.

16.5 THE BECOMING OF EVENTS: TOWARDS AN EVENT-BASED ORGANIZATION THEORY?

The advantage of Whitehead's approach lies in boiling down organization to spatio-temporal experiences, which leaves us with the potentially exciting (but also onerous) journey of assembling these experiences into the more extensive temporal-socio-material phenomenon that we can recognize as organizations. Still, developing an event-based theory of organization could enable the overcoming of a number of dualisms inherent in traditional organizational theorizing, such as micro–macro, organization–environment, subject–object, and change–stability. Events, seen as spatio-temporal experiences of things (such as concepts, material objects, humans, social groups, etc.), maintain the fluidity required for process theorizing while not letting go of the existence of entities, however transient they appear.

Events, however, have been little explored as units of analysis in organization studies and, when they have, they have not been systematically considered as elements of a process theory of organization but as 'marker events'. Theorizing of events that is of interest for organization studies may be found, for example, in Schatzki (2010), who theorizes activity timespaces from Heidegger's notion of events as chronotopes. Also Bakhtin's notion of events (see Chapter 21, this volume) would help provide a foundation for event-based organizational theorizing.

A fuller event-based understanding of organization consistent with Whitehead's philosophy would involve seeing organizations as 'societies' of events that interconnect in such a way that they reproduce their mutual wholeness. The mutual wholeness created by the connecting of events might be seen as momentary actualizing of the organization, whereas its becoming would lie in the work of connecting events. Hence, based on the idea of how 'the many become one', events would be seen as the many contributing to their mutual wholeness, i.e. the organization. Herein would lie Whitehead's notion of 'creative advance', by which potentialities of process (the work of connecting) are actualized, which is 'when many become one and are increased by one' (1929a: 21), i.e. the many events create a wholeness which forms the basis for the emergence of new events. This would be in line with Whitehead's atomism, which expresses not just the indeterminacy and creativity of processes but also their contingencies. In fact, Whitehead's theoretical scheme was characterized by the urge to assume that all events, whether they involved humans or not, should be granted mind-like properties in order to account for the potentiality of process. For example, 1925a: 72 he writes that an event has anticipation. Here lies an important contribution to process philosophy and organizational analysis in that it brings to light the agency associated with events, as opposed to agency attached to physical entities, such as human actors.

In what follows I suggest three aspects of events that may help lay foundations for an event-based organization theory inspired by Whitehead's philosophy.

16.5.1 Events as Spatio-Temporal Durations

As discussed earlier, in Whitehead's view an event is a nexus of actual occasions. Whereas actual occasions (drops of experience) have no real duration in time, events exhibit extension in time and space (1929a: 73). The extension accorded to events is expressed in Whitehead's expression 'slab of nature' (1920: 53), which has both temporal and spatial connotations. For example, as he illustrates with reference to a molecule (1929a: 124), a molecule is a historic route of actual occasions, but such a route is an 'event'. The molecule as event exhibits both spatiality and duration which, Whitehead argues, is intrinsic to physical objects and derivative from the ways in which they are interconnected (1925b: 4). Thus the step from actual occasions to events is also marked by the step from one entity to multiple entities. Whereas an actual occasion marks the experience of one physical entity, an event involves multiple physical entities over time and in space. In fact, what we perceive as physical entities are also made up of event complexes.

Whitehead's dictum of process, 'how an entity becomes constitutes what that entity is' (1929a: 23), applies to such a view. 'The entity' in question is not a material thing per se, but the composite experience that involves entities. The resulting experience of entities takes place in time, endures over time, and may be called an 'event'. A running shoe, for example, in the company of which many people have experienced joyful as well as painful events, represents a trajectory of numerous past encounters between rubber, tissue, machines, plans, and humans. The material in some shoes is (or at least used to be) extracted from recycled materials, which had their histories in turn. As well as being a manifestation of past experiences between different types of entities, the shoe articulates possible future trajectories of connecting to events, which exhibit their own experiences, enabling them to prehend back and forth in time to other events. Some shoes, for example, come with sensors, enabling them to connect to the runner's ambitions, as well as to the internet or to mobile phones, which again create connecting experiences between runners, who again form communities. From this can be seen that to see the shoe as a simple object is a radical reductionism of what it represents. Actually, the shoe, although to many it seems the concrete manifestation of the processes that made it, is, in Whitehead's terms, an abstraction that takes part in the process of experiencing. To be an abstraction, in Whitehead's thinking, is to be abstracted from connectedness ('No fact is merely itself'; Whitehead, 1920: 13), hence the shoe (just like a plan, a person, or an organizational unit) is an abstraction from the concrete experiences that went into making it, and which derive from it. Every act of running is an experience, both for the runner and for the shoe, and the composite experience of the two entities in the making makes an event that connects to other events, both back and forth in time.

It is this spatio-temporal experience that constitutes an event as an experiencing entity. The experience, however, is not a human experience per se, but a composite experience *of* the event, directed towards other (past, contemporary, and future) events. While agreeing with Bergson on the notion of duration as passage, Whitehead would conceive of the passage of nature as the passing of durations into one another. The 'becoming of the world' is seen as experiences of duration that pass into each other, and where substantial entities are present, as Stengers (2008) points out, as means to 'vectorize' concrete experience. In other words, physical objects form part of the process of experiencing, but they are not things that do the experiencing. Instead, experience is seen as emerging from durations (such as a one-hour meeting) of collective experiencing of that event together with other, related events.

16.5.2 The Forming of Events through Mirroring

Given Whitehead's dominant notion of time and space as 'passage of nature', he was concerned with explaining continuity, which could only be put down to connectedness.

'Connectedness is', he wrote, 'the essence of all things of all kinds' and 'It is of the essence of types, that they be connected' (1938: 9). In the world everything is basically connected to everything else. 'No fact is merely itself' (1920: 13). Bearing in mind that facts are residues of experiential events, by implication no event can merely be itself, but creates itself relationally with other events, including past, simultaneous, and future events. This is what is important for 'the becoming of continuity' (1929a: 35). Importantly, however, events mirror themselves with past events, contemporary events, and future events. 'Mirroring' is not to be seen as synonymous with becoming identical, but conveys a symmetry of mutual creation. Thus events are nothing in themselves, nor are they causes of other events. However, they may include other events, but are not parts of other events.

In saying that events mirror themselves, Whitehead expresses relationality between events whereby they mutually create each other. Importantly and following from Whitehead's atomist stance, whereby he would not adhere to a serial conception of time (1929a: 35), a view he shared with James (1890: 607) (who denounced what he called a 'string of bead-like sensations and images'), events are not serially connected. Wholes (or complexes) of events may instead be seen as taking the form of 'manifolds' (1920: 86) or 'neighbourhoods' of events. It is in such manifolds that events can 'anticipate' or 'feel' other, past, contemporary, or future events ('antecedents-to-be' as formulated by Wallack, 1980: 167).

Events are not to be seen as closed, insulated entities connecting like billiard balls. As Field (1983) notes in his discussion of Whitehead's 'epochal' theory of time, durational entities with Whitehead are internally related. Whitehead speaks of this internal relatedness as 'prehension', by which each durational unit prehends those units which have gone before, and is prehended by subsequent units (Field, 1983: 270). Thus, as Field notes, even though the units are discrete, they are not insulated from one another, and the qualities of one unit pervade the constitution of those units which succeed it. In a meeting between colleagues, for example, other events are prehended as part of the discussion; they are brought into the present meeting and constituted by the dialogue that goes on in the meeting, and conversely, the meeting (and consequently its participants and agenda) is constituted by the same operation. In this way, mirroring becomes a process of mutual constitution, characterized by connectedness rather than by sameness.

16.5.3 The Open Structures of Events

To Whitehead, 'nature is a structure of events and each event has its position in this structure and its own peculiar character or quality' (1920: 166). At the same time, events are not discrete entities, but entities whose duration can extend to overlap or interpenetrate. According to Hamrick (1999), what Merleau-Ponty, for example, found valuable in Whitehead's view of nature was his rejection of the 'simple location' of allegedly discrete quanta of matter existing only in external relations with each other 'in favour of overlapping, encroaching, non-serial relations between instances of process' (Merleau Ponty, 1995: 157, in Hamrick, 1999). It is also worth repeating

Deleuze's discontent with closed categories and his embracing of Whitehead's notion of events as constituting each other through inner experience, and not through external relations.

Importantly, event structures are open and ever-changing, ever-renewed complexes of events, which remain open to the emergence of novelty while regenerating themselves. The wholeness of structures of events enables them to infuse events and bring new events into the manifold. Importantly, events and their interconnectedness in structures of events are subject to continuous reinterpretation in the present event, at which the configuration will change with the passing of time. For example, what at one point in time was seen as a singular occurrence may at another point in time be seen as an epoch. Conversely, what took place over time at some point in time may be experienced as a singular event at another point in time. The French Revolution, for example, was not a 'revolution' at the time of the storming of the Bastille in Paris in July 1789, but more a singular incident. As the various events accumulated to overturn the king and install a new political order, it came to be seen as a 'revolution' and the taking of the Bastille gained a huge symbolic value, although at the time it was actually of limited military and political value (Sewell, 1996). The events were significant in justifying actions that eventually led to reform, but the extensive reforms that came to be known as the French Revolution were not foreseen at that stage. The event of the French Revolution takes part in a structure of events of political change in history, and as such it is kept alive, although as an event is belongs to the past. Current and future political events become part of a structure of political change by creating themselves in the mirror image of the French Revolution and by the same token (re)creating the French Revolution. In a similar way, seemingly mundane events in organizational life create themselves and the entities associated with them in the light of significant events belonging to the organization as an event structure.

16.6 CONCLUSION

A point of departure for a more systematic development of an event-based organizational theory is to view organization as atomistic spatio-temporal wholes of events that emerge, giving meaning to their constituent parts (events) opening of new events. An 'atomistic' theory of organization demands that any idea of boundaries or stable structure be abandoned and the focus of analysis become the connecting power of events, seen as encounters between heterogeneous organizational actors rather than the connecting power of structures, systems, cultures, or their likes. An event-based theory of organization, inspired by Whitehead's philosophy, would make it possible to appreciate the power of time and temporality in a world where dispersed actors connect using various forms of media to create new technologies, concepts, or movements. The connectedness of present society demands that we conceive a theory of organization that responds to a flat notion of the world (Friedman, 2005), where connectedness prevails over size, flow prevails over stability, and temporality prevails over spatiality.

NOTE

1. This chapter has benefitted from comments by Ib Tunby Andersen, Morten Knudsen, Anuk Nair, Majken Schultz, Kristian Kreiner, Rasmus Johnsen, Silviya Svejenova, Magnus Larssson, and Ann Westenholz.

REFERENCES

Åkerstrøm Andersen, N. (2003). The Undecidability of Decision, in T. Bakken and T. Hernes (eds), *Autopoietic Organization Theory, Abstakt, Liber* (Oslo: Copenhagen Business School Press): 235–58.

Bakken, T. and Hernes, T. (eds) (2003). *Autopoietic Organization Theory: Drawing on Niklas Luhmann's Social Systems Perspective* (Oslo: Abstrakt, Liber, Copenhagen Business School Press).

——(2006). Organizing is Both a Noun and a Verb: Weick Meets Whitehead, *Organization Studies* 27(11): 1599–616.

Callon, M. (1986). The Sociology of an Actor-Network: The Case of the Electric Vehicle, in M. Callon, J. Law, and A. Rip (eds), *Mapping the Dynamics of Science and Technology* (Basingstoke: Macmillan): 19–34.

——(1998). An Essay on Framing and Overflowing: Economic Externalities Revisited by Sociology, in M. Callon (ed.), *The Laws of the Markets* (Oxford: Blackwell): 244–69.

Chia, R. (1999). A 'Rhizomic' Model of Organizational Change and Transformation: Perspective from a Metaphysics of Change, *British Journal of Management* 10: 209–27.

——and King, I.W. (1998). The Organizational Structuring of Novelty, *Organization* 5(4): 461–78.

Cobb, J.B. Jr. (2006). Person-in-Community: Whiteheadian Insights into Community and Institution, *Organization Studies* 28(04): 567–88.

Cook, G.A. (1979). Whitehead's Influence on the Thought of G.H. Mead, *Transactions of the Charles S. Peirce Society* 15(2): 107–31.

Cooper, R. (1976). The Open Field, *Human Relations* 29(11): 999–1017.

Cyert, R.M. and March, J.G. (1963). *A Behavioural Theory of the Firm* (Oxford: Blackwells).

Deleuze, G. (2004). *Difference and Repetition* (London: Continuum).

——(2006). *The Fold* (London: Continuum).

Dewey, J. (1941). The Philosophy of Whitehead, in P.A. Schilpp (ed.), *The Philosophy of Alfred North Whitehead* (New York: Tudor Publishing Company): 666–81.

Field, R.W. (1983). William James and the Epochal Theory of Time, *Process Studies* 13(4): 260–74.

Follett M. Parker, (1919). Community is a Process, *Philosophical Review* 28: 576–88.

——(1924). *Creative Experience* (New York: Longmans Green).

——(1941). *Dynamic Administration* (New York: Harper and Row).

Friedman, T. (2005). *The World is Flat* (London: Allen Lane).

Halewood, M. (2005). A.N. Whitehead, Information and Social Theory, *Theory, Culture and Society* 22(6): 73–94.

Hamrick, W.S. (1999). A Process View of the Flesh: Whitehead and Merleau-Ponty, *Process Studies* 28(1–2): 117–29.

Hernes, T. (2008). *Understanding Organization as Process: Theory for a Tangled World* (London: Routledge).

——(forthcoming). *A Process Theory of Organization* (Oxford: Oxford University Press).

——and Bakken, T. (2003). Implications of Self-Reference: Niklas Luhmann's Autopoiesis and Organization Studies, *Organization Studies* 24(9): 1511–36.

——and Maitlis, S. (2010). Introduction. Process, Sensemaking & Organizing, in T. Hernes and S. Maitlis (eds), *Process, Sensemaking and Organizing (Perspectives on Process Organization Studies Series)* (Oxford: Oxford University Press): 27–37.

James, W. (1890/1977). *The Principles of Psychology* (London: Macmillan).

Latour, B. (1993). *We Have Never Been Modern* (Cambridge, MA: Harvard University Press).

——(1999). *Pandora's Hope: Essays on the Reality of Science Studies* (Cambridge, MA: Harvard University Press).

—— (2005a). *Reassembling the Social: An Introduction to Actor-Network-Theory* (Oxford: Oxford University Press).

——(2005b). What is Given in Experience? A Review of Isabelle Stengers, *Penser avec Whitehead*, *Boundary* 32(2): 222–37.

Law, J. (1994). *Organizing Modernity* (Oxford: Blackwell).

——(2004). *After Method: Mess in Social Science Research* (Oxford: Routledge).

Lorino, P. and Mourey, D. (2013). The Experience of Time in the Inter-Organizing Inquiry: A Present Thickened by Dialog and Situations, *Scandinavian Journal of Management* 29(1): 48–62.

Lucas, G.R. (1989). *The Rehabilitation of Whitehead* (New York: State of New York Press).

Luhmann, N. (1995). *Social Systems* (Stanford, CA: Stanford University Press).

——(2000). *The Reality of the Mass Media* (Stanford, CA: Stanford University Press).

Maclachlan, D.L.C. (1992). Whitehead's Theory of Perception, *Process Studies* 21(4): 227–30.

March, J.G. (1994). *A Primer on Decision Making: How Decisions Happen* (New York: The Free Press).

Mead, G.H. (1929). The Nature of the Past, in J. Coss (ed.), *Essays in Honor of John Dewey* (New York: Henry Holt & Co): 235–42.

——(1932). *The Philosophy of the Present* (Amherst, NY: Prometheus Books).

—— (1934). *Mind, Self, and Society* (Chicago: University of Chicago Press).

—— (1936). Science Raises Problems for Philosophy: Vitalism, Henri Bergson, in M.H. Moore (ed.), *Movements of Thought in the Nineteenth Century* (Chicago: University of Chicago Press): 292–325.

Merleau-Ponty, M. (1995). *La Nature* (Paris: Editions du Seuil).

Price, L. (1954). *Dialogues with Alfred North Whitehead* (New York: Reinhardt).

Ramal, R. (2003). In What Sense is Whitehead's Speculative Philosophy a First Philosophy?, *Concrescence: The Australian Journal of Process Thought* 4: 9–21.

Russell, B. (1905). On Denoting, *Mind* 14(56): 479–93.

Schatzki, T.R. (2010). *The Timespace of Human Activity* (Lanham, MD: Lexington Books).

Sewell, W.H. (1996). Historical Events as Transformations of Structures: Inventing Revolution at the Bastille, *Theory and Society* 25: 841–81.

Sherburne, D.W. (1966). *A Key to Whitehead's Process and Reality* (New York: Macmillan).

——(1992). Whitehead and Dewey on Experience and System, in R.W. Burch and H.J. Saatkamp, Jr. (eds), *Frontiers in American Philosophy*, Volume I (Texas: Texas A&M University Press): 95–101.

——(2004). Whitehead, Descartes, and Terminology, in J.A. Polanowski and D.W. Sherburne (eds), *Whitehead's Philosophy: Points of Connection* (New York: SUNY Press): 3–15.

Stengers, I. (2002). *Penser avec Whitehead* (Paris: Seuil).

—— (2008). A Constructivist Reading of Process and Reality, *Theory, Culture & Society* 25(4): 91–110.

—— (2011). *Thinking with Whitehead: A Free and Wild Creation of Concepts* (Cambridge, MA: Harvard University Press).

Wallack, F.B. (1980). *The Epochal Nature of Process in Whitehead's Metaphysics* (New York: State University of New York Press).

Weber, M. (2002). Whitehead's Reading of James and Its Context (Part I), *Streams of William James* 4(1): 18–22.

—— (2003). Whitehead's Reading of James and Its Context (Part II), *Streams of William James* 5(3): 26–31.

Weick, K.E. (1976). Educational Organizations as Loosely Coupled Systems, *Administrative Science Quarterly* 21: 1–18.

Whitehead, A.N. (1911). *An Introduction to Mathematics* (London: Williams and Norgate).

—— (1920). *The Concept of Nature* (Cambridge: Cambridge University Press). Page numbers refer to the 2004 version published by Prometheus Books.

—— (1925a). *Science and the Modern World* (London: Free Association Books).

—— (1925b). *An Enquiry Concerning the Principles of Natural Knowledge* (Cambridge: Cambridge University Press).

—— (1929a). *Process and Reality* (New York: The Free Press).

—— (1929b). *The Aims of Education* (New York: The Free Press).

—— (1933/1967). *Adventures of Ideas* (New York: The Free Press).

—— (1938). *Modes of Thought* (New York: The Free Press).

Whitehead, T.N. (1936). *Leadership in a Free Society: A Study of Human Relationships Based on an Analysis of Present-Day Industrial Civilization* (Cambridge, MA: Harvard University Press).

—— (1938). *The Industrial Worker: A Statistical Study of Human Relations in a Group of Manual Workers* (Cambridge, MA: Harvard University Press).

CHAPTER 17

GEORGE HERBERT MEAD (1863–1931)

BARBARA SIMPSON[1]

> his mind was deeply original—in my contacts and my judgment the most original mind in philosophy in the America of the last generation ... I dislike to think what my own thinking might have been were it not for the seminal ideas which I derived from him.
>
> (John Dewey, 1931: 310–11)

THESE WORDS were spoken by John Dewey at the funeral of his close colleague and friend of more than 40 years, George Herbert Mead. Dewey mourned Mead's 'untimely death' as the loss to American philosophy of 'a seminal mind of the very first order' (Dewey, 1932: 34), a sentiment shared by Alfred North Whitehead who regarded 'the publication of the volumes containing the late Professor George Herbert Mead's researches as of the highest importance for philosophy' (Miller, 1973: ix). Despite these glowing testimonials however, Mead's influence on contemporary thought, especially in organization studies, remains muted. There are several threads of explanation that may be drawn to account for this. Firstly, although Mead published more than 100 critical commentaries, reports, and original articles during his lifetime, the only books attributed to him were all published posthumously (1932, 1934, 1936, 1938) under the dedicated editorial guidance of his disciples. For example, the most frequently cited of these books, *Mind, Self and Society*, comprises notes and fragments extracted from his unpublished work, supplemented by lecture notes taken by his students. Thus Mead never had the opportunity to articulate his philosophical position in a thoroughly systematic way, leaving his ideas vulnerable to misinterpretation.

Hans Joas (1997) argues that Mead's most central ideas about the social nature of the self were only ever taken up in a rather trivial way by Dewey, while the appropriation of Mead's thinking by the symbolic interactionist movement is, at best, partial. Herbert Blumer (1969), the founder of symbolic interactionism and an enthusiastic follower of Mead, claimed it was necessary to break away from some of the more radically processual aspects of his ideas (Simpson, 2009), thereby losing touch with his conception of intersubjectivity as a precondition for, rather than an outcome of, communication and the social processes of meaning-making. It is undoubtedly true that symbolic interactionism has been a significant intellectual force, especially in sociological developments, but also in organization studies where Karl Weick has declared it 'the unofficial theory of sensemaking' (1995: 41), and as such it deeply informs much of the contemporary writing on organizational practice. However, symbolic interactionism should not be taken as the final word on Mead's contribution; there is still much more to be mined.

A second potential problematic that threads throughout Mead's work is the extraordinary disciplinary breadth of sources that informed his thinking. Following his graduation from Oberlin College, which was both progressive and deeply orthodox in its theological teaching, in 1887 Mead took up a graduate position at Harvard University, where he studied philosophy with the neo-Hegelian, Josiah Royce. Although he held Royce in the highest esteem, by 1888 he had turned his attention away from philosophy and towards the more empirically accessible field of psychology. This new interest took him to Germany where he encountered Wundt's metaphysics, which offered a point of entry into a voluntaristic psychology. He was also exposed to the growing controversy between the explanatory form of psychology expounded by Ebbinghaus, and a more interpretive psychology as presented by Dilthey, who became a key influence in Mead's early career. At the same time, Mead was intensely aware of European trends in social thought such as Tarde's (1903) influential theory of imitation-suggestion, in which selves arise mimetically in their relationships to other selves, and cannot be reached other than through their relational contexts (Leys, 1993). Although Mead's own theory development pursued this notion of selves as fundamentally social, he emphatically rejected imitation as an explanatory mechanism as it cannot account for the emergence of anything that is different.

Upon his return to the United States in 1891, he met John Dewey, who recalled at that time Mead was reading deeply into biology as he attempted to draw links between the evolutionary theory of Darwin and his own abiding interest in mind and self (Dewey, 1931). For him, the survival imperative that explains adaptation in Darwin's theory provides a basis for an evolutionary epistemology that approaches all knowledge in terms of behaviour. However, he took issue with what he saw as the overly mechanistic teleology of the Darwinian argument, turning instead to Bergson's ideas about creative evolution, which were highly influential in the subsequent development of Mead's thinking (Mead, 1907, 1936: chapter 14). Like Bergson, and also Whitehead, Mead engaged with Einstein's theory of relativity in physics, which constituted a paradigmatic shift in thinking every bit as radical as Darwin's theory of biological evolution. The original insights that he extracted from relativity theory critically informed the development of his ideas about the temporality of creative action. According to Reck, Mead's temporalism 'continues to furnish a singular alternative [to Whitehead's cosmology]' that has yet 'to be adequately probed and exploited' (1964: lxi).

Over the 40 years between his return from Europe and his death, his close friendship with John Dewey was also very important in shaping Mead's intellectual journey. Morris opines that Mead and Dewey were intellectual equals sharing 'in a mutual give-and-take according to their own particular genius...If Dewey is at once the rolling rim and many of the spokes of the contemporary pragmatic wheel, Mead is the hub' (1934: xi). Like Dewey, Mead was intensely interested and practically involved in social, educational, and political reform movements, where his activities undoubtedly influenced the shape and direction of his thinking (Joas, 1997). A veritable polymath who moved with ease between disciplines as diverse as biology, psychology, theology, philosophy, and physics, Mead also had an intense love of poetry, which apparently he could recite tirelessly (Dewey, 1931). The breathtaking scope of Mead's talents and interests is difficult to grasp in the climate of intense disciplinary specialization that has prevailed in academe over recent decades. However, there is today a mounting awareness of the benefits of cross-disciplinary thinking as we are increasingly challenged by problems of ever greater complexity. Perhaps now is the time, then, when we can return to Mead with fresh eyes to see what he may have to offer to present-day thinking.

As a result of the ongoing work of writers in the domain of symbolic interactionism, Mead is currently best known as a theorist of the interacting or dialogical self. The central theme to which he returned repeatedly throughout his working life was the problem of consciousness and mind, and how these arise in human conduct. Whereas William James and Henri Bergson drew on existentialist and introspective understandings of human activities, Mead sought a more objectivist approach that would be amenable to empirical investigation. Locating thinking persons in their naturalistic situations, he argued that mind both shapes and is shaped by the social phenomena that evolve continuously in conversation. What is less well known, but is of particular relevance in this *Handbook* on process philosophy in organization studies, is the 'veritable mountain of fragments and writings' (Joas, 1997: 167) on the topic of temporality that was discovered after Mead's death (e.g. Mead, 1932, 1938). In this chapter, I begin by treating temporality and intersubjectivity separately in order to explore their implications for Mead's theorization of mind and self. But these two dimensions should not, indeed cannot, be separated in practice. I go on to suggest that Mead's notion of sociality provides a way of integrating temporality and intersubjectivity as interpenetrating processes and, further, that it offers a means of engaging empirically with the movements and flows of processes as they unfold in organizational contexts.

17.1 TEMPORALITY

Darwin's theory of evolution was a source of inspiration for many of the original pragmatist philosophers in their pursuit of practical theories that could engage with the ongoingness of human experience. However, their interest was not in the 'survival-of-the-fittest' determinism of social Darwinism, but rather, the temporal dynamics of unfolding emergence in our world(s). Mead in particular sought to understand how emergent variations in social interactions might constitute the continuously evolving consciousness from which human practice arises. To capture such temporal experience, however, Mead recognized that conventional notions of time (i.e. Newtonian time) are inadequate.

Arguably, time as we know it today is an invention of the Enlightenment. Advances in astronomy in the seventeenth century led Sir Isaac Newton to understand time as a universal property of nature that exists quite independently of human consciousness. He deduced laws of motion for the planets in our solar system that are based on the assumption of uniformly passing time, the quantum of which was originally determined empirically from astronomical observations, but today is defined in terms of the vibration frequency of caesium atoms. Newton concluded:

> Absolute, true, and mathematical time, of itself, and from its own nature, flows equably without relation to anything external. (Newton, quoted by Barbour, 2008: 2)

The resilience of this view of time as a quality of the natural world that flows independently of human intervention is reflected in Bertrand Russell's comment more than 200 years later that:

> time is an unimportant and superficial characteristic of reality. Past and future must be acknowledged to be as real as the present. (Russell, 1917: 21)

In this view then, time is an infinite sequence of instants that has neither a beginning nor an end. This succession of ceaseless instants is homogeneous, and devoid of physical or human content. Any given instant is infinitely divisible because, no matter how fine the interval between instants, each is always positioned in relation to its predecessors and successors. Thus the present moment is understood as a 'knife-edge' (Mead, 1932: 194), a shifting boundary separating an infinity of discrete past moments from an equally infinite stream of discrete future moments (Capek, 1961). This approach to time is abundantly evident in the organization studies literature, where its influence may be traced back to the industrial revolution and the deliberate management of time to maximize production. Bergson's cinematographic metaphor, which suggests reality may be understood as a rapid succession of fixed frame images, aptly captures the implications of this Newtonian perspective for understanding human action (Bergson, 1919).

There are two fundamental problems with this approach to time. Firstly, it does not address the human experience of temporal continuity. As William James observed,

> If the constitution of consciousness were that of a string of bead-like sensations and images, all separate, 'we never could have any knowledge except that of the present instant. The moment each of our sensations ceased it would be gone for ever; and we should be as if we had never been...We should be wholly incapable of acquiring experience...Even if our ideas were associated in trains, but only as they are in

imagination, we should still be without the capacity of acquiring knowledge. One idea, upon this supposition, would follow another. But that would be all. Each of our successive states of consciousness, the moment it ceased, would be gone forever. Each of those momentary states would be our whole being.' (James, 1890/1952: 396, quoting James Mill, 1829)

Bergson's solution to this problem was the notion of *durée*, which emphasizes introspection as the constituent continuity of temporal experience. Whilst Mead agreed that experience and temporality are co-constituting dynamics in the flow of becoming, he rejected Bergson's metaphysical turn towards *élan vital*, understood as a force of nature independent of human intelligence. 'When [Bergson] looks for an instance of what he calls pure "duration", as distinct from mere motion in a fixed space, he goes to the inner experience of the individual' (Mead, 1936: 297), a solution that Mead considered philosophically quite unsatisfactory in its anti-intellectualist stance. Instead he sought a more objective, dare I say more 'scientific', expression of temporal experience that is 'not necessarily limited to the interpenetration of experiences in the inner flow of consciousness' (Mead, 1936: 325). In this undertaking, he did nevertheless derive considerable inspiration from Bergson's critique of spatialized (or clock) time. In a 'world which is geometrized, there is no real duration; on the contrary we find there only reversible series which may symbolize that which arises in consciousness but can never be that change' (Mead, 1907: 382). Mead argued that the creation of something absolutely new is dependent upon the irreversibility and irreducibility of duration; 'where everything is conceivably reversible nothing can assume a new form' (Mead, 1907: 380–1). Thus we see that his central concern with novelty and creativity in the flow of experience leads to a distinctive conceptualization of duration in terms of continuity and change rather than the mere elapsing of time.

Sitting between the extremes of spatialized, knife-edge time and introspective *durée*, the idea of a specious present responds to the psychological observation that there is a minimum temporal extension required for perception to occur and conscious awareness to arise (Joas, 1997). This psychological time span was originally referred to as the 'specious present' to indicate a spurious sort of pseudo-now not to be confused with true, or universal time. In the late nineteenth and early twentieth centuries, however, this term morphed into exactly the opposite meaning; so for James and Whitehead the 'specious present' became the true present of conscious experience, suggesting a temporal extension that spreads the present across time. These specious presents may have varying lengths, and indeed Whitehead (1926) argued that they may be stretched indefinitely into both the past and the future. In Mead's (1963–1964) view, however, this notion of a specious present does not settle the problem of continuity because the possibilities for emergent novelty are inevitably denied when a future is inextricably bound to a past within the same specious present.

Mead's response to these issues begins with the assertion that ontological reality resides only in the present, which he sees as the locus of conscious action. In so saying, he is rejecting the existence of a 'real' past and a 'real' future, seeing past and future instead as epistemological resources that are continuously reconstructed to inform the actions of the passing present.

> If we spread a specious present so that it covers more events, as Whitehead suggests, taking in some of the past and conceivably some of the future, the events so included would belong not to the past and the future, but to the present. It is true that in this present there is something going on. There is passage within the duration, but that is a present passage. (Mead, 1929a: 345)

In his view, the defining characteristic of the present is that it is emergent, a turning point in the unfolding of action; for new presents to arise, it is necessary to rewrite the past so that 'from every new rise the landscape that stretches behind us becomes a different landscape' (Mead, 1932: 42). At the same time, each new past opens up new possibilities for futures, and these in turn condition, but do not fully determine, the actions of the present. Thus there is a continuous interplay between pasts and futures that is manifest in the emergent present as ongoing and evolving consciousness. It is this passage of conscious action that brings continuity to temporal experience (Simpson, 2009). Other process scholars, most notably Whitehead, Heidegger, and Ricoeur, have also explicated the interweaving of present, past, and future, but Mead's particular contribution is found in the way he relates presents, or events, to continuity and emergence in the passage of time.

Whereas Newtonian time is structured by an infinite succession of instants that are entirely independent of human experience, for Mead temporal passage is structured by events that thrust themselves into the otherwise undifferentiated flow of time, providing a mechanism for ordering and making sense of experience. In other words, without the interruption of passage by events, temporal experience would not be possible. Mead defines an event as a turning point when something new arises, a becoming that ushers in change. An event occurs in a present that

> is not a piece cut out anywhere from the temporal dimension of uniformly passing reality. Its chief reference is to the emergent event, that is, to the occurrence of something which is more than the processes that have lead up to it and which by its change, continuance, or disappearance, adds to later passages a content they would not otherwise have possessed. (Mead, 1932: 52)

Passage, then, is the passing of distinguishable events, each of which arises in a present as the past is reconstructed to support an anticipated future. By contrast with the notion of the specious present as the span of time required for a person to be herself, Mead's concept of the present may be understood as the occurrence of a unique event. Of course 'the event' as a unit of analysis in process studies is by no means limited to Mead. Whitehead developed this concept extensively as a spatio-temporal nexus that marks the difference between 'before' and 'after', while Bakhtin emphasized the living quality of events as unique occurrences. Mead's originality in relation to this important concept lies in his acknowledgement of the inherent changefulness of human experience, which offers us a new empirical focus in the form of events as turning points in the flow of action.

The second fundamental problem with the Newtonian conception of time is its inability to engage with simultaneity, or the apparent coincidence in time of events occurring in distant locations. This problem was comprehensively tackled in the physical sciences by Einstein's theory of relativity. Mead was greatly stimulated by the extent to which relativity theory recognizes that time cannot be treated as distinct from actors, or agents, and their separate situations. Thus he came to understand that 'any scientific statement about the world of moving bodies also had to take into consideration, in an objectivating manner, the corporeality of the observer' (Joas, 1997: 173). For more than a decade before his death, Mead's efforts were directed towards formulating a dynamic understanding that links temporal experience to the physical world. During this time he engaged with the writing of Whitehead who was pursuing a similar goal, although more from a cosmological perspective than from any desire to explore movements in human consciousness. Cook (1993: chapter 9) has undertaken a meticulous analysis that compares the thinking of Mead and Whitehead through this period. It appears that they agreed on much but, for the purposes of my argument here, it is more important to point to their divergences. In particular, each was motivated by a different objective; whereas Whitehead's goal was to explain how order arises in an open universe (see Chapter 16, this volume), Mead was interested in the emergence of order-disrupting novelty in human practice. He criticized Whitehead for overlooking both the social and emergent dimensions of temporal experience. It is in these two areas that Mead arguably makes his greatest contributions to the re-theorization of temporal experience.

In Mead's view, an adequate explanation of simultaneity is a necessary prerequisite for understanding the emergence of novelty in events. As we have seen, an event is a turning point between pasts and futures. These pasts and futures are constructed as separate temporalities belonging to different frames of reference that coincide in the present experience of a given actor. The simultaneous occurrence of multiple temporalities affords the actor a multifaceted perspective that offers a repertoire of alternative choices for reconstructive action in the present moment. Thus the creative potential of a turning point exists whenever two or more different temporalities coincide. Mead coined the term 'sociality' for the past-to-future movement that occurs in any event. For him, sociality is 'the situation in which the novel event is in both the old order and the new which its advent heralds' (Mead, 1932: 75). It is the movement 'betwixt and between the old system and the new' wherein '[t]here is an adjustment to this new situation...[as]...new objects enter into relationship with the old' (Mead, 1932: 73). Furthermore 'there is sociality in nature in so far as the emergence of novelty requires that objects be at once both in the old system and in that which arises in the new' (Mead, 1932: 86). Thus sociality is a defining quality of presents, as every event simultaneously juxtaposes more than one temporality. I suggest then, that the notion of sociality offers a means of empirical engagement with process that is genuinely grounded in a processual ontology. Together with Mead's idea of events as movements, or turning points, in the otherwise undifferentiated flux of passage, sociality invites us to rethink the methodological assumptions that are built into empirical approaches to process research.

17.2 INTERSUBJECTIVITY

In all of his work, Mead was motivated by a desire to understand 'life as a process and not a series of static physicochemical situations' (Mead, 1925: 275). He firmly rejected metaphysical explanations of this life process, calling instead for a focus on conduct that is made sensible by its objective presence in the world, rather than its subjective prehension in consciousness. This notion of existence in nature led him to an understanding of the self, not as an isolated individual who brings innate qualities to her/his social interactions, but as the continuous emergence of what he called the 'social act' (Mead, 1938). In Mead's view, 'selves exist only in relation to other selves' (Mead, 1925: 278); or more particularly, selves develop by adopting the attitudes of others in order to see themselves reflexively as objects in their own conversational contexts. Thus a self cannot come into existence without a community of others whose attitudes enter into the experience of its individual members. Mead referred to this community as 'the generalized other' (1934: 154), in which form 'the social process...enters as a determining factor into the individual's thinking' (1934: 155); 'only thus can thinking...occur' at all (1934: 156). Crucial for Mead's argument then is his assumption that the social, in the form of the generalized other, precedes the development of the individual self, which in turn implies that the mind is itself intersubjectively constituted.

Before I proceed further, there is an important clarification to make regarding Mead's use of 'intersubjectivity', which is an ambiguous term in the literature. If we take seriously Mead's assertion that the self is socially constituted and that the social precedes the individual, then intersubjectivity must necessarily occur within the self. This view contrasts with the perhaps more familiar idea that intersubjectivity occurs between subjects that are independently constituted. It is the latter perspective that is evident, for instance, in symbolic interactionism where 'social interaction is a process that *forms* human conduct instead of being merely a means or a setting for the expression or release of human conduct' (Blumer, 1969: 8, emphasis in the original). We see here the extent to which Blumer diverged from Mead's original thinking by restricting the meaning of intersubjectivity to the outcomes or products of social interactions. Recognizing the potential here for terminological confusion, Dewey and Bentley (1949/1991) differentiated between 'interactions', which occur between distinct entities, and 'transactions', which subsume entities into the ongoing processes of lived change. Following the same pattern of language, I might suggest that 'trans-subjectivity' better captures the essence of Mead's argument, where he very definitely saw conversation as a transaction in which conversants both shape, and are shaped by, their social engagements. However, 'trans-subjectivity' is an ugly word that may itself introduce further confusion, so I will continue to use the term 'intersubjectivity', but with the clear caveat that I intend this to refer to transactional, rather than merely interactional processes.

Conversation is the medium for intersubjective engagements, but Mead understood conversation as something much broader than a mere exchange of vocal gestures. It encapsulates all forms of gestural meaning-making including the physical actions and emotional expressions of socially constituted selves. Each gesture in a conversation is a way of probing the meanings of the situation; it is less an expression of what is, and more a tentative testing-the-water for what may become. To the extent that a given gesture does elicit an anticipated response, it constitutes what Mead referred to as a 'significant symbol' (1925: 288); that is, the gesture acts as a symbol that arouses a similar response in both the gesturer and the respondents in a conversation. We develop repertoires of significant symbols by inferring the attitudes of the generalized other in our conversational processes. As we take on the implied rules and conventions of the generalized other, our selves continue to emerge in an ongoing social process of becoming. Here Mead's argument resonates with Peirce's 'semiotic mediation' and with Bakhtin's work on dialogue (see, respectively, Chapters 10 and 21, this volume), but in my view Mead goes further by locating symbolically mediated conversation within the flow of temporality. I will return to this point later.

Mead associated the objective, reconstructive aspect of the self with a 'me', which he defined as the organized set of others' attitudes that are adopted as significant symbols. This 'me' exists as an empirically accessible object that represents how the self perceives itself through the eyes (and other sensory organs) of others. Mead (1913) argued, however, that an objective 'me' is inconceivable without a subjective 'I'. It is the 'I' that acts by gesturing, while the 'me' is a continuously reconstructed repository of experience. In any passing moment, both the constructed 'me' and the performative 'I' are present as complementary phases of the self, but the actions of the 'I' cannot be objectively perceived until their consequences have become reflexively incorporated into the 'me'. Thus the 'I' is the agent of self-construction; it is the active principle that introduces the possibilities of emergent novelty into the ongoing accomplishment of the self. Without the reconstructive potential of this agentic dimension, the self could be nothing more than an uncritical accumulation of acquired dispositions and socially determined behavioural conventions. 'The self is essentially a social process going on with these two distinguishable phases. If it did not have these two phases there could not be conscious responsibility, and there would be nothing novel in experience' (Mead, 1934: 178).

Mead argued that selves are social 'insofar as we ourselves take the attitude that others take towards us' (1925: 284). In his view then, this intra-personal 'I'/'me' dynamic is positioned within the social context of conversation by taking the attitudes, or roles, of others. What this means is not that we literally slip into another role, but that we develop the capacity to anticipate the others' responses to the conversational gestures that we might make. By taking the attitude of another, we are trying to see the world through their eyes and, in so doing, we also see ourselves as others might. This ability not only allows us to draw the actions of others into our own conduct, which then admits the possibilities of mutual adjustment towards common collective actions, but also the concurrence of our own and others' attitudes towards the self as a necessary prerequisite for the development of self-reflexivity. Having personal access to different attitudes offers a variety of perspectives to inform and resource an actor's ongoing gestural communications. Mead illustrated his argument with an example of buying and selling. Buying food, for instance, is an act of exchange

> in which a man excites himself to give by making an offer. An offer is what it is because the presentation is a stimulus to give. One cannot exchange otherwise than by putting one's self in the attitude of the other party to the bargain ... [thus] ... Buying and selling are involved in each other. Something that can be exchanged can exist in the experience of the individual only insofar as he has in his own makeup the tendency to sell when he has also the tendency to buy. And he becomes a self in this experience only insofar as one attitude on his own part calls out the corresponding attitude in the social undertaking. (Mead, 1925: 283–4)

Without this capacity for responding to the 'generalized other', Mead argued, sophisticated and abstract thinking would simply not be possible. It is the simultaneous awareness of contrasting perspectives that invites reconstructive action without which, in Mead's view, life would be reduced to a mere mirror of nature, lacking any agentic dimension capable of surfacing emergent novelty. On this point, he differentiated his position from what he saw as 'dark hints of a theory of this common world in Professor Whitehead's publications' (Mead, 1929b: 340), which reflect Whitehead's primary concern with order ahead of the reconstructive potential of human conduct. In Mead's notion of intersubjective process we see a second expression of sociality, which he defined as 'the capacity for being several things at once' (1932: 75). In essence, he is saying that for any event to be social, it must exist simultaneously in at least two different frames of reference—for instance, the different frames of gesturer and respondents in a conversation. On first appearance, this spatial definition of sociality seems to be at odds with that given earlier, where it was defined in temporal terms as a movement 'betwixt and between the old system and the new' (Mead, 1932: 73). However, if we recall that the selves who are conversing are themselves dynamic reconstructive processes, each within its own temporality, and that the conversation in which they are engaged is a continuous movement of gesture and response, then we can see how Mead linked his notions of intersubjectivity and temporality together. Sociality is the linchpin that locates social selves as emergent events in temporal passage.

17.3 IMPLICATIONS FOR PROCESS RESEARCH

In today's organizational literature it has become deeply unfashionable to admire objectivity or to emulate scientism. How then, are we to interpret, and make useful, Mead's ideas, which he repeatedly couched in terms of a need for greater objectivity and better science? He was, of course, writing for an early twentieth-century audience that would have been very familiar with the vitalistic concepts often found in the field of psychology, both then and now. Vitalism proposes that there is some unknowable, perhaps mystical principle of life that can neither be measured nor falsified. Mead's counter-argument is that attempting to explain behaviour in terms of hidden traits and inferred mental states is no explanation at all. Instead of attributing people's conduct to such subjective states, he simply focused on that which can be objectively perceived, namely the actions that people take. His entire theorization of human practice is thus based on the observable gesture and response of intersubjective conversations as they unfold in time. Furthermore, his call for better science does not equate to the extreme manifestations of scientism, which cast the world as a gigantic mechanism wherein all outcomes may be reduced to some sort of summation of isolated parts. His interest is more in improving the craft and rigour of scientific enquiry than in sharpening the accuracy of measurement.

The temporality in Mead's conception of practice draws the researcher's attention away from stable and discrete parts, inviting us instead to engage with the complexities of a perpetually unfolding world. To facilitate his argument, Mead has developed a number of key concepts that need to be understood in his terms if we are to benefit from his theoretical insights. Reprising the discussion in this chapter, these concepts include:

- *emergence*, reflecting the essential changefulness, rather than the ordered stabilities, of all human practice;
- the *social self* as a continuously emergent process of self-construction;
- the '*generalized other*', the constructed '*me*', and the performative '*I*' as complementary and interpenetrating aspects of social selves;
- *gestural conversations* as the site for reflexive role-taking and self-construction, where gestures may be vocal, physical, emotional, or otherwise communicative;
- symbols, and especially *significant symbols*, as mediators of conversational meaning-making, which are themselves mutable and subject to continuous reconstruction;
- *passage* as the perpetual and undifferentiated flux of experience;
- ephemeral *events* as movements or turning points that give meaning to passage by thrusting themselves forward into the flow, punctuating it, bringing order, and making it sensible;
- and *sociality*, which is both a movement from past to future temporalities, and the capacity for being simultaneously in more than one temporal flow. It is sociality, I argue, that draws together the intersubjective and temporal dimensions of Mead's theory of practice.

Every one of these concepts is fluid and mutable, continuously renegotiated in conversational engagements whilst at the same time influencing ongoing practice. It is this dynamic quality that distinguishes Mead's theorization as processual 'all the way down'. This expression refers to a tale that has numerous different expressions, but here I use the version recorded by Geertz:

There is an Indian story—at least I heard it as an Indian story—about an Englishman who, having been told that the world rested on a platform which rested on the back of an elephant which rested in turn on the back of a turtle, asked (perhaps he was an ethnographer; it is the way they behave), what did the turtle rest on? Another turtle. And that turtle? 'Ah, Sahib, after that it is turtles all the way down'. (1973: 28–9)

So often, we process researchers find ourselves trapped by entitative constructs (e.g. elephants and turtles), which imply reductionist assumptions that ultimately limit our capacity to engage in a thoroughly processual way with the ongoing and emergent nature of practice. Instead of focusing on entitative foundations, Mead invites us to jump on board and go with the flow, giving us a set of very useful tools that suggest ways of escaping the categorical style of thinking that has dominated western thought at least since Aristotle.

This intellectual commitment to process has very specific implications for empirical work. Firstly, the fundamental level of analysis is neither individual actors nor the organizational or social context, but rather it is the conversational dynamic of gesture and response, which flows across the dualistic boundaries that constrain more entitative approaches to research. This relational orientation has strong precedents in the hermeneutic and phenomenological traditions (e.g. Bakhtin, Heidegger, Merleau-Ponty, and Ricoeur), but as yet has made relatively little impact in the area of organization studies (see for instance Cunliffe, 2002; Gergen, 2009; Hosking, 2011; Shotter, 2006; Simpson, 2009). This is surprising given the importance of practice in organizational life, and the increasing emphasis in the literature on making transparent the interplay between theory and practice. In my view, the approach developed in this chapter has great, but as yet largely untapped, potential for shedding new light on all manner of organizational practices including leading, innovating, learning, decision-making, strategizing, and socializing. Furthermore, Mead's holistic approach to the social self invites a view of actors as emergent and socially constituted becomings who not only think, but also feel, and act. This then opens up enquiry into more subtle practices such as identity work and emotion work (e.g. Simpson and Carroll, 2008; Simpson and Marshall, 2010).

Secondly, the explicit temporality of this approach demands that the temporal dimensions of empirical studies be taken seriously, not as the mere ticking of a universal clock that measures temporal extension, but as a multiplicity of events that punctuate the passage of experience, dynamically weaving into and permeating throughout organizational practice. Capturing such movements is a real challenge for which there is no easy answer. Brigid Carroll and I have responded by attending to sociality in the online conversations of a group of managers engaged in a leadership development programme (Carroll and Simpson, 2012). We found that the flow of their conversation was structured around a variety of significant symbols as the managers struggled with the sociality movements of their collective leadership practice. More generally, processual research of this type is concerned with the generativity of ordinary, everyday talk (Boden, 1994), where the unit of analysis is the event, or turning points in the conversation. The researcher's attention is thus directed to anywhere that talk happens, whether this be in formal meetings or casual 'water cooler' encounters. The researcher's job is to follow the action, wherever it may lead. Whilst observational methods are clearly appropriate for this style of research, it is also useful if the researcher can find a way of probing the situation to gain a deeper understanding of the conversational dynamics. Czarniawska (2008) has argued compellingly that shadowing is a method ideally suited to this sort of enquiry as it produces rich narrative accounts from the researcher's direct and informed experience of events as they unfold in real time (see also McDonald, 2005). This close and engaged form of observation offers the possibilities of exciting new insights into practice and the emergent processes of organizational and managerial experience.

To conclude, I have proposed in this chapter that it is timely to revisit the wealth of potential in Mead's thinking as a way of better informing our contemporary understandings of dynamic practices in organizations. Whilst his ideas about intersubjectivity have been broadcast, albeit in a limited way, through developments in symbolic interactionism, it is his radical approach to temporality that holds real treasure for process theorizing today. Using sociality as an explicit link between intersubjectivity and temporality, Mead offers us a comprehensive theorization of practice that is both relational and dynamically emergent. Thus practice is more than the mere habits of action, or the routines that appear in every organization; it is also where change takes place under the influence of subtle forces that become evident only to a careful observer. Mead helps us in this observational task as well, by drawing our attention to empirically accessible aspects of the day-to-day actions taken by ordinary people in organizations, where these aspects are profoundly grounded in a processual philosophy. I acknowledge that to work in this way is difficult, but my resolve is strengthened by the potential that this approach offers for genuinely fresh perspectives on organizational practice.

NOTE

1. I am grateful to Hans Joas and Erkki Kilpinen for their knowledgeable guidance on details of Mead's life and thought, to fellow authors in this *Handbook*, especially Philippe Lorino and Tor Hernes, for productive conversations, and to my students, Chrysavgi Sklaveniti, Anup Nair, and Rory Tracey for their enthusiasm for process philosophy.

REFERENCES

Barbour, J. (2008). The Nature of Time, <http://fqxi.org/community/essay/winners/2008.1>
Bergson, H. (1919). *Creative Evolution* (London: Macmillan).
Blumer, H. (1969). *Symbolic Interactionism: Perspective and Method* (Berkeley and Los Angeles: University of California Press).
Boden, D. (1994). *The Business of Talk* (Cambridge: Polity Press).
Capek, M. (1961). *The Philosophical Impact of Contemporary Physics* (New York: Van Norstrand Reinhold Company).

Carroll, B. and Simpson, B. (2012). Capturing Sociality in the Movement between Frames: An Illustration from Leadership Development, *Human Relations* 65(10): 1283–309.

Cook, G.A. (1993). *George Herbert Mead: The Making of a Social Pragmatist* (Urbana and Chicago: University of Illinois Press).

Cunliffe, A. (2002). Social Poetics: A Dialogical Approach to Management Inquiry, *Journal of Management Inquiry* 11(2): 128–46.

Czarniawska, B. (2008). *Shadowing: And Other Techniques for Doing Fieldwork in Modern Societies* (Copenhagen: Copenhagen Business School Press).

Dewey, J. (1931). George Herbert Mead, *Journal of Philosophy* 28: 309–14.

——(1932). Prefatory Remarks, in G.H. Mead (ed.), *Philosophy of the Present* (Chicago: Open Court Publishing): 31–4.

——and Bentley, A.F. (1949/1991). Knowing and the Known, in J.A. Boydston (ed.), *The Later Works, 1925–1953*, Volume 16 (Carbondale: Southern Illinois University Press): 1–294.

Geertz, C. (1973). *The Interpretation of Cultures* (London: Fontana Press).

Gergen, K. (2009). *Relational Being: Beyond Self and Community* (New York: Oxford University Press).

Hosking, D.M. (2011). Telling Tales of Relations: Appreciating Relational Constructionism, *Organization Studies* 32(1): 47–65.

James, W. (1890/1952). *Principles of Psychology* (Chicago: Encyclopedia Britannica).

Joas, H. (1997). *G.H.Mead—A Contemporary Re-Examination of His Thought* (Cambridge, MA: MIT Press).

Leys, R. (1993). Mead's Voices: Imitation as Foundation, or, the Struggle Against Mimesis, *Critical Inquiry* 19(2): 277–307.

McDonald, S. (2005). Studying Actions in Context: A Qualitative Shadowing Method for Organizational Research, *Qualitative Research* 5(4): 455–73.

Mead, G.H. (1907). Review of *L'Évolution Créatrice* by Henri Bergson, *Psychological Bulletin* 4: 379–84.

—— (1913). The Social Self, in A.J. Reck (ed.), *Selected Writings: George Herbert Mead* (Chicago: University of Chicago Press): 142–9.

——(1925). The Genesis of the Self and Social Control, in A.J. Reck (ed.), *Selected Writings: George Herbert Mead* (Chicago: University of Chicago Press): 267–93.

——(1929a). The Nature of the Past, in A.J. Reck (ed.), *Selected Writings: George Herbert Mead* (Chicago: University of Chicago Press): 345–54.

——(1929b). A Pragmatic Theory of Truth, in A.J. Reck (ed.), *Selected Writings: George Herbert Mead* (Chicago: University of Chicago Press): 320–44.

——(1932). *The Philosophy of the Present* (Illinois: La Salle).

——(1934). *Mind, Self and Society* (Chicago: University of Chicago Press).

——(1936). *Movements of Thought in the Nineteenth Century* (Chicago: University of Chicago Press).

——(1938). *The Philosophy of the Act* (Chicago: University of Chicago Press).

——(1963–1964). Relative Space-Time and Simultaneity, *Review of Metaphysics* 17: 514–35.

Miller, D.L. (1973). *George Herbert Mead: Self, Language, and the World* (Austin: University of Texas Press).

Morris, C.W. (1934). Introduction: George H. Mead as Social Psychologist and Social Philosopher, in C.W. Morris (ed.), *Mind, Self, and Society from the Standpoint of a Social Behaviorist* (Chicago and London: University of Chicago Press): xii–xix.

Reck, A.J. (ed.) (1964). *Selected Writings: George Herbert Mead* (Chicago: University of Chicago Press).

Russell, B. (1917). *Mysticism and Logic* (London: Allen & Unwin).

Shotter, J. (2006). Understanding Process from Within: An Argument for 'Withness'-Thinking, *Organization Studies* 27(4): 585–604.

Simpson, B. (2009). Pragmatism, Mead, and the Practice Turn, *Organization Studies* 30(12): 1329–47.

—— and Carroll, B. (2008). Re-Viewing 'Role' in Processes of Identity Construction, *Organization* 15(1): 29–50.

——and Marshall, N. (2010). Emotion and Learning in Organizations: Mutually Constructing Social Processes, *Journal of Management Inquiry* 19(4): 351–65.

Tarde, G. (1903). *The Laws of Imitation* (New York: H. Holt and Company).

Weick, K.E. (1995). *Sensemaking in Organizations* (Thousand Oaks, CA: Sage).

Whitehead, A.N. (1926). *Science and the Modern World* (New York: Cambridge University Press).

CHAPTER 18

NISHIDA KITARŌ
(1870–1945)

ROBERT CHIA

18.1 LIFE AND PLACE

NISHIDA KITARŌ was the founder of what has become known as the Kyoto School of Philosophy, for whose adherents the notion of pure experience or absolute nothingness is a core premise of their *meo-ontology* (ontology of non-being). According to this worldview, actions, relations, and experiences are deemed to precede the existence of social entities such as 'individuals', 'organizations', and 'societies'. Nishida's work helped establish a unique Japanese philosophy involving the fusion of Anglo-European philosophy with ancient Asian sources of thought, including especially Zen Buddhism and the thinking of Lao Tzu. In this extensive philosophical effort Nishida was exemplifying what had been, more generally, a long-standing tradition in Japan to bring the west and east into communion with each other. The policy had begun with Commodore Perry's historic arrival under tense political circumstances and the demonstrative firings of the cannons from his 'Black Battleships' in 1853. This act of aggression awakened feudal Japan, forcing her out of 250 years of self-enforced seclusion. By 1868 the long reign of the Tokugawa Shogunate had finally collapsed, plunging Japan into its well-known process of modernization qua 'westernization'. Originally launched under the imminent threat of colonization, Japan's national policy therefrom entailed redoubling its efforts to learn and assimilate the best fruits of western civilization in virtually every field of human activity; from sciences and arts to even clothing, fashion, and cuisine. The Meiji Revolution or *Meiji Ishin* that describes this revolutionary chain of events restored imperial rule to Japan under Emperor Meiji, who presided over the country until he died in 1912. Born in 1870, Nishida grew up in the early years of this Meiji era when Japan was still undergoing the Europeanization of its political, educational, and cultural institutions. For him, as a young boy, this process of 'modernization' came in the dual form of a rigid, and often oppressive, school atmosphere that demanded obeisance to the emperor, and an unrelenting exposure to the seemingly progressive western ideas that had been ceremoniously ushered into Japan.

For many thoughtful Japanese intellectuals, however, there was much unease about what they saw as a wholesale cultural assimilation taking place before their very eyes. It was as though their traditional worldviews, unable to stand their own ground, shattered and dissolved irreparably on contact with this external cultural onslaught. Amongst its increasingly well-read philosophers, early enthusiasm for western scientific empiricism, and the technological progress associated with it, soon gave way to anxiety and existential angst in the face of dramatic social changes taking place. Japan, like many traditionally-based cultures, began to discover that it had not only imported western achievements but also western problems. The twin dilemma of moral direction and material means now confronted this newcomer to modernity. Japan began to experience a loss of national identity yet the way back towards traditionalism was irrevocably closed; it was no longer plausible to appeal to the authority of tradition against the universal and compelling forces of modern reason. Like western philosophers who were well exercised in seeking solutions to the problems and dilemmas of the west, Japanese philosophers were also beginning to have their own doubts about the course and costs of the process of modernization in Japan. In their view, another type of universality compatible with traditional Japanese spiritual values and experience was urgently needed to counteract the excesses of western modernization. It was thus this sense of ideological urgency that drove the search for a more adequate grounding of Japanese heritage and its national identity, thereby reconciling the twin challenges of retaining traditional values whilst embracing modern progress.

Within the context of this urgent search for a proper base for grounding both Japanese spiritual values and the logic of modernity, the then newly-coined notions of 'experience' and experiential justification associated with scientific empiricism provided a convenient conceptual link for Japanese scholars to begin formulating a more inclusive universality. They helped bridge the gap between western logic and reason, and the traditional cultural, religious, and moral values underpinning the Japanese way of life. More specifically, Zen Buddhism, which had been brought over from China and had become integral to the Japanese heritage, with its austere emphasis on achieving immediacy of pure experience through disciplined and sustained meditation, offered a possible way out of this existential quagmire. It shared with scientific empiricism, albeit superficially, a common emphasis on the epistemological superiority of beginning from raw experience. Such a convenient coincidence and apparent convergence of scientific empiricism with its ostensibly undiluted emphasis on facts as experienced, and the Zen Buddhist insistence on the importance of achieving the immediacy of unadulterated pure experience, provided the necessary philosophical impulse and inspiration for Nishida's attempted integration of these two traditions in his own unique system of thought; a system that ultimately sought to synthesize the best of both east and west.

Nishida, like many intellectuals of his time in Japan and especially like his childhood friend D.T. Suzuki, who was to become an iconic figure in the United States in the early part of the twentieth century, was steeped in the practice of meditation, having been encouraged by the latter to embrace Zen Buddhism in 1895 when he was still very much a young man. Thus his whole intellectual life constituted a gigantic tussle between a life of the mind guided by the highest norms of western scholarship, and his own natural proclivity for an austere way of life guided by the Zen practice of meditation. This apparently irreconcilable tension drove him to incomparable heights of achievements in his attempted synthesis of eastern and western thought according to the axioms of western scholarship. That he did so through his extensive and rigorous reading, insightful grasp, and effective synthesis of the work of eminent western philosophers with his own Zen-inspired thinking, has given his own work much credence today especially amongst modern western intellectuals. He drew liberally from Plato, Aristotle, Leibniz, Kant, Hegel, Fitche, Schiller, and many others but especially from James' (1912/1996) notion of 'pure experience' in his earlier works and from Bergson's (1911/1998) notion of 'pure duration', which he incorporated into his later work on 'acting intuition'. But it was Plato's *Timaeus* which proved finally instructive for Nishida's mature philosophy, for it offered a useful approximation for him to develop his notoriously difficult concept of *Basho*, or 'logic of place', the highest level of which corresponds with his now much celebrated notion of the *Basho* of 'absolute nothingness'.

In all his intellectual efforts, however, despite the fact that he hardly ever referred to it, Zen Buddhism formed the basis for his overall metaphysical outlook (Feenberg, 1999; Krueger, 2006). Wilkinson (2009: 6) further notes that Zen remained the 'absolutely constant point of reference throughout his life'. Hence 'the *fons et origo* of Nishida's view of experience (which was a central notion in his treatise *an Inquiry into the Good*) was furnished to him by Zen' (Wilkinson, 2009: 151). Yet, it would be wrong and misleading to say that Nishida's was a philosophy simply 'based on' Zen Buddhism since he was determined to express his own synthesis in a manner rigorous enough to be recognizable and acceptable by those in the west. This is what makes his work important to western philosophical thought.

18.2 'PURE EXPERIENCE' AS THE FOUNDATION OF THOUGHT

To understand Nishida's resonance with western process thought, we can approach his work through a thinker now (ironically) ensconced as a process philosopher: William James. It is not widely known among contemporary western thinkers that Asian traditions and particularly the teachings of Buddhism had begun to impact on American thought in general and American philosophy in particular during the fertile period 1890–1910. Inada and Jacobson (1991) and others maintain that by the latter half of the nineteenth century and the early twentieth century Buddhism had begun to seep into the deepest substratum of American consciousness and even begun to influence the thinking of eminent writers like Ralph Waldo Emerson, Henry Thoreau, and Walt Whitman (Fields, 1992: 55–69; Versluis, 1993; Scott, 2000). Meanwhile, at Harvard, philosophers such as Josiah Royce, George Santayana, and William Hocking began to show some interest in Buddhism, albeit in a somewhat eclectic fashion (Clarke, 1997: 116–8; Scott, 2000). Moreover, Charles Lanman, a Sanskrit scholar on early Buddhist thought at Harvard, was also a friend and neighbour of James so that it is therefore unsurprising that James himself eventually began to show interest in the teachings of Buddhism (Scott, 2000). For James, therefore, the two decades from 1890 onwards brought him a new-found awareness of oriental thought, not just in academic and philosophical settings but also in the wider 'general' American public context.

James taught physiology at Harvard from 1872 to 1880 but his interest expanded into the wider area of psychology from 1880 onwards, leading to the publication of his seminal *Principles of Psychology* in 1890. This, in turn, led him to important explorations in comparative religion, culminating in *The Varieties of Religious Experience* (1902). But James is most well known for his pragmatic philosophy, which was encapsuled in a series of publications including, especially, *Pragmatism: A New Name for Old Ways of Thinking* (1907), *A Pluralistic Universe* (1909), and *Essays in Radical Empiricism* (1912). Amidst these wide-ranging enquiries, key aspects of Buddhism caught James' attention. Thus, as Scott (2000: 3) notes, in James' *Varieties of Religious Experience* he cites a range of seminal Buddhist books written during his time by western academics, thus clearly indicating his familiarity with Buddhist thought. He also helped set up the prestigious 'American Lectures on the History of Religions' with Buddhism as one of its primary focus. Within the context of this burgeoning interest in Buddhism, a story is often told that when the charismatic Buddhist spokesman Dharmapa-la revisited America during 1902–1904 and attended a lecture of James' at Harvard, James recognized him in the audience and invited him to speak, saying 'You are better equipped to lecture on psychology than I' (Scott, 2000: 3). At the end of Dharmapa-la's exposition, James declared, 'This is the psychology everybody will be studying twenty-five years from now' (Fields, 1992: 134–5).

18.2.1 William James' Radical Empiricism and 'Pure Experience'

James' work as a whole is founded upon a sustained consideration of concrete experience as the starting point of conceptualization: the world as materially experienced by an embodied, embedded, and acting agent. He insisted that explaining the lived structures that constitute our being-in-the-world is the key to understanding the antecedent categorizations, conceptualizations, and sensemaking that goes on in our everyday lives. One sign of his widened intellectual horizons that resulted from his contact with Buddhism was his observation that 'most people live, whether physically, intellectually or morally, in a very restricted portion of their potential being. They make use of a very small portion of their possible consciousness' (James, 1907: 295). He began to see that it was language in general and intellectualism in particular which prevented us from living truly authentic and potentially rich lives. For James, selection and discrimination by the senses led to a form of abstract conceptualization that can 'only approximate to reality' because 'its logic is inapplicable to our inner life'. Like his younger contemporary Henri Bergson, whose work (Bergson, 1911/1998) he praised effusively, James regarded philosophical reflection as a form of intellectualism that moves us away from rather than towards concrete experience. He insisted that the phenomenal content of our embodied experiences far outstrips our linguistic capacity to articulate it so that conceptual analysis could never provide an adequate account of the richness of human experience. The deliverance of our senses continually runs ahead of both our descriptive vocabularies as well as our conceptual abilities. Unimpressed with rationalism and dissatisfied with traditional scientific empiricism, he asked: 'May not the flux of sensible experience itself contain a rationality that has been overlooked, so that the real remedy would consist in harking back to it more intelligently, and not advancing in the opposite direction away from it?' (James, 1909/1996: 73). In other words, James is saying that traditional empiricism is a 'false' empiricism in that it does not truly begin with raw experience since empirical 'facts' are always already conceptualized experience. For him, a true empiricism 'must neither admit into its constructions any element that is not directly experienced, nor exclude from them any element that is directly experienced' (James, 1912/1996: 42). It was at this point that James begins to formulate his notion of 'pure experience' as the cornerstone of his radical empiricism.

Pure experience, for James, 'is the name I give to the immediate flux of life which furnishes the material to our later reflection with its conceptual categories' (1912/1996: 93). It is 'an experience pure in the literal sense of a *that* which is not yet any definite *what*, though ready to be all sorts of whats' (1912/1996: 93). Pure experience is prior to the reflexive thematizing of the cogito in language and thought; it is a kind of pure seeing, an 'innocence of the eye' (Ruskin, 1927, vol. XV: 27) that encounters the world without thematizing it. It simply bears mute witness to happenings in the world in all its 'blooming, buzzing confusion' (James, 1911/1996: 50). Being pre-conceptual and pre-categorical, 'experience' in its original immediacy is unaware of itself. It is simply a dynamic, flowing, 'aboriginal sensible muchness' (James, 1911/1996: 50) that serves as the source of our subsequent conceptualization.

This insight enabled James to reinterpret the notion of consciousness, not as a substantial entity but instead as a unifying 'function'. Thus the word 'consciousness' does not stand for a substantive entity but it 'most emphatically ... stand(s) for a function' (James, 1912/1996: 4–5). This means that the body is the centre of a field of lived experience with the phenomenon of 'fringes' or 'penumbra' of consciousness an essential feature of any type of experience. These now well accepted ideas in phenomenology were first clearly expressed in James' *Essays in Radical Empiricism* (1912/1996), so much so that it led Whitehead to comment that James' work, especially in his essay 'Does Consciousness Exist?', represented the 'inauguration of a new stage in philosophy' comparable to that initiated by Descartes in his *Discourse on Method* in that he unequivocally 'clears the stage of the old paraphernalia; or rather he entirely alters its lighting' (Whitehead, 1926: 177–9; 1929) by replacing the notion of consciousness as an entity as Descartes presupposed with that of consciousness as a function.

18.2.2 Nishida and Pure Experience

James' notions of 'pure experience' and of consciousness as a unifying function aligns him philosophically with the kind of unmediated pristine experiences that practitioners of Zen meditation claim to encounter. This invariably proved attractive to Nishida in his search for an appropriate conceptual 'hook' to build his philosophical edifice. It has been observed that James' radical philosophical reconfiguring of the theatre of modern western philosophy by clearing 'old paraphernalia' and 'altering its lighting', also unwittingly opened up the 'backstage' of the theatre to an entirely unexpected and different audience: that of the eastern philosophical tradition to which Nishida belonged (Noda, 1954). Nishida honed in on James' notion of pure experience because it was congenial to a core feature of traditional Zen Buddhist thought, namely, it suggested the primacy of a state of experience *prior to the subject–object distinction*, and prior to cognitive reflection. It was comparable to that sense of a natural pre-conceptualizing, pre-discriminatory setting, which Zen traditionally calls one's 'original face' and which Nishida's friend Suzuki calls 'no-mind'. He writes: 'From the standpoint of pure experience, there is no such thing as an object divorced from the subject' (Nishida, 1921/1990: 23). Even more than James (see Dilworth, 1969: 97), Nishida realized that this non-duality of subject and object was one of the essential features of pure experience and it therefore became the central idea of Nishida's whole career, reaching its culmination in his subsequently explicated Zen ontology of '*Basho* of absolute nothingness' beyond subject–object distinctions. The notion of pure experience spoke to his Zen aesthetic religiosity, subtly guiding his thought at this stage—despite the fact that Nishida deliberately avoided any explicit references to Zen in his early works. Like James, who recognized concepts as 'static abstractions', Nishida saw meanings and judgements as secondary: 'an abstracted part of the original experience, and compared with the original experience they are meagre in content' (Nishida, 1921/1990: 9). But unlike James, who saw pure experience as a limit concept unattainable by 'normal' people, Nishida's use of the term is normative; it is that to be actively sought. Pure experience is superior because experience 'purified', ostensibly through Zen meditation, discloses an intuitive truth about the inner nature of reality; a truth that subsequently finds fruitful expression in the spheres of art, religion, and morality.

Nishida's maiden work, *An Inquiry into the Good* (1921/1990), starts with a chapter simply entitled 'Pure Experience'. It is generally accepted that the collective efforts of Nishida, comprising 15 volumes of philosophical work, are a result of his persistent and strenuous endeavours, spanning more than three decades, to develop this initial standpoint of 'pure experience' by giving it 'logical' or judgemental forms as well as socio-historical dimensions. Without doubt, James would have been greatly surprised and even delighted as well to know how far-reaching his idea of 'pure experience' could be and how it was to unexpectedly arouse so much interest on the opposite side of the Pacific. Seen from the perspective of Japan's 'awakening' to western ways, an elective affinity came to be established between James' ideas and the deepest concerns of a modern Japanese philosopher that began to appear far from being an accidental one.

In this book, Nishida begins with a detailed discussion of what he means by 'pure experience' by insisting that that was the starting point of all intellectual enquiry. Thus, 'To experience means to know facts just as they are...by completely relinquishing one's own fabrications' (Nishida, 1921/1990: 3). It is important to stress here that Nishida does not intend to mean that there are 'objective' discrete facts awaiting our experience. Instead, like James, he is reaching for a moment of 'pure seeing' that 'has no meaning whatsoever' (Nishida, 1921/1990: 4). This 'purity of pure experience' derives not so much from being instantaneous or unanalysable but from the strict unity of consciousness. In other words, like James, Nishida views consciousness as a functional unifying power that undergirds any kind of perceptual activity. Yet, there is no intrinsic meaning to this pure experience; it is merely an experientially, intuitive grasping function which provides the basis from which the subject–object correlation emerges. Subject, object, meanings, and judgements are subsequent abstractions of this primordial experience and as such they are 'meagre in content' (Nishida, 1921/1990: 9). They arise from the act of thinking, the latter being a mental activity that is essentially about determining relations between representations and unifying them. Thinking as such is the 'response of consciousness to a mental image' (Nishida, 1921/1990: 14). This of course implies that thought is already secondary to pure experience, so much so that even thought about the individual and 'its' experience cannot be considered primary. This, Nishida thinks, is the reason why James does not go far enough, for James remains tied to the notion that it is self-identical individuals (albeit in their rawest forms such as young babies and people in a coma) that can have 'pure experience'. For Nishida, however, pure experience preceded individualization; it is in effect *trans-individual*. There is 'first pure experience, and on it are founded personal egos' (Nishida, 1921/1990: 28). Pureness for him means to be free from any egocentricity. Thus, it is not that 'there is experience because there is an individual, but that there is an individual because there is experience' (Nishida, 1921/1990: 19). This radicalizing of pure experience as something preceding individuation is what distinguishes Nishida from James. In so doing he articulates an anti-essentialist model of personhood; a model that does not require appeal to a fixed substratum or permanent 'something' alleged to comprise the most essential aspect of human reality standing over against an external world. Instead, Nishida insists that the self is best understood to be a *process* or *relational field*. Pure consciousness, or indeed one might even say 'unconsciousness', is the state in which man is one with the thing itself and with the truth itself.

18.3 From Pure Experience to a Unifying Intuition

In the period after the publication of *An Inquiry into the Good*, Nishida continued to read widely in western philosophy and was greatly impressed by the ideas of Fitche and Bergson in particular. For one thing, like James, Bergson was wary of using symbols and concepts in analysing experience because any understanding was already being confined by the often thoughtless adoption of well-established categories. Thus he writes in *An Introduction to Metaphysics*: 'In its eternally unsatisfied desire to embrace the object around which it is compelled to turn, analysis multiplies without end the number of its points of view in order to complete its always incomplete representation...It goes on, therefore, to infinity' (Bergson, 1903/1955: 24). Accordingly, no amount of intellectual analysis using pre-established concepts and categories can enable us to access and explain pristine experience. Bergson's stance won the approval of his older contemporary William James, who wrote enthusiastically about Bergson's fresh thinking: 'to understand life by concepts is to arrest its movement, cutting it up into bits as if with scissors, and immobilizing these in our logical herbarium where, comparing them as dried specimens, we can ascertain which of them statically includes or excludes which other' (James, 1909/1996: 244). For Bergson, the alternative was a process philosophy that lies 'flat on its belly in the middle of experience, in the very thick of its sand and gravel' (James, 1909/1996: 277). This involves acquiring a kind of '*intellectual sympathy* by which one places oneself within an object in order to coincide with what is unique in it' (Bergson, 1903/1955: 23). Instead of an act of conceptual analysis, an act of *intuition* is required because reality is perpetually flowing and cannot be grasped through static concepts. The western proclivity to comprehend the social world as comprising 'spatio-temporal, causally interacting individuals' (Wilkinson, 2009: 87) is a knowledge construction we have found useful because it enables us to deal effectively with the circumstances we find ourselves in (for example to isolate distinct human faces using names, gender, physical features, etc.). Our mistake is to 'impose this manner of conceptualizing things on our inner life', imagining it is composed of 'atomic experiences, successively occurring in clock-time' (Wilkinson, 2009: 87). Such a tendency alienates us from our own basic self whose fundamental experience, for Bergson, is one of ceaseless duration and creative evolution. Thus, 'below the self with well-defined states, [is] a self in which *succeeding each other* means *melting into one another and forming an organic whole*'. Yet, we are constantly 'goaded by an insatiable desire to separate [and] substitute symbol for reality', thereby causing us to 'lose sight of the fundamental self' (Bergson, 1910: 128). Reality, for Bergson, including the reality of self, is one of perpetual becoming, an inexorable *durée*. Bergson's answer to this predicament of the ultimate flow of time is to grasp reality though an act of *intuition* such that the act of knowledge is coincident with the act of constituting reality. Thus Bergsonian intuition is not merely a passive registering of experience, but an active grasping of a pristine reality that is ever-flowing.

18.3.1 Nishida and Intuition

Nishida's response to reading Bergson was a major work entitled *Intuition and Reflection in Self-Consciousness* in which he writes: 'I was stirred by the works of Bergson, but again, despite my whole-hearted agreement with him, my ideas do not wholly coincide with his' (Nishida, 1917: xxv). Nishida used this book to answer the question how conceptual experience arises from primary, pure experience. Intuition, for Nishida, is a 'direct, non-reflective grasp of concrete reality' (Wilkinson, 2009: 62), a consciousness of the 'unbroken progression of ultimate reality' intimately associated with the notion of pure experience. Reflection, on the other hand, is 'conceptual thought', the result of our separation from 'primal unity', so that the basic question is how might the latter arise from the former. From this position, Nishida noted with approval that Bergson had employed the term *'la durée'* to emphasize the primacy of temporal experience as the basis of his philosophy of intuition and showed how intuition provides the motivating basis for the emergence of will (Wilkinson, 2009: 86–8). Bergson had argued that space and time were intellectual constructs and insisted on the distinction between 'clock time' and 'lived time' (*la durée*), maintaining that the former had become 'spatialized' through the process of conceptualization. In *Duration and Simultaneity*, Bergson (1922/1999) argued that Einstein's theory of relativity offerred not just a new physics but a new way of thinking about time as a 'lived *durée'*; one that is qualitatively different from Newtonian quantifiable time. For Bergson, real time, which originates from our primary consciousness of temporality and duration, is inherently indivisible, unrepeatable, and irreversible. Clock time, on the other hand, is a 'counterfeit' representation of lived experience produced through the conversion of temporal experiences into discrete and measurable instantaneous moments. Real time, on the other hand, involves the continuous progress of the past that 'gnaws into the future and which swells it as it advances' (Bergson, 1911/1998: 4), leaving its bite, or the mark of its tooth on all things. It is 'the form which the succession of our conscious states assumes when our Ego lets itself live, when it refrains from separating its present state from its former states...as happens when we recall the notes of a tune, melting, so to speak, into one another' (Bergson, 1910: 100). Real time is experienced as *la durée* and hence so-called 'states of consciousness' are actually processes, not things; they are alive, constantly changing, and so impossible to separate from one another.

Nishida agrees with Bergson, and with James, that our conceptualized experience of a world of spatio-temporal entities is unlike our seamless flow of lived experience. Bergson's claim that consciousness is not an emergent property of matter but that matter is in fact arrived at by subtracting something from consciousness was something Nishida also found agreeable (Nishida, 1987: 110). For him, talk of things like 'the self' in *self*-consciousness alludes to a unifying bundle of experience rather than something that remains constant and self-identical. He agrees with Bergson (1910: 128) in particular that the unhelpful habit of applying concepts and categories to the inner life causes us to develop a superficial, egocentric, and fragmented self that hides a much more fundamental self whose real experience is that of duration. For him, as for Bergson and James, intelligence, or the intellect, can only deal with the conceptual constructions we generate through thought, but is nevertheless unable to properly acquaint us with the real processes of reality.

Yet, as with James, Nishida had some reservations about Bergson's notion of *la durée*. While for Bergson duration is the ultimate ontological reality so that each moment of duration is unique, unrepeatable, and cumulative, Nishida argues that Bergson's very thesis that duration is not repeatable *is itself a conceptualization that presupposes the existence of a timeless transcendent*; to assert temporality implies the existence of timeless dimension. Something must 'stand outside the flow of duration' (Wilkinson, 2009: 90) for us to say that experience is unrepeatable. There has to be a constant and unchanging reference point for assessing the unrepeatability of the former. What was needed was to recast this view of the emergence of consciousness in terms of a self-conscious acting system. Thus, for Nishida, as Wilkinson notes, Bergson's 'doctrine could not even be conceived of except in a consciousness which possesses a memory, and such a consciousness must be in a certain important sense the *same* consciousness, unified...Behind duration as Bergson describes it there must be something even deeper, an ultimate unified consciousness' (Wilkinson, 2009: 90). This is where Nishida parts company with Bergson and resorts to the Japanese concept of *mu*, an absolute nothingness of infinite depth, or plenum of infinite possibilities as the basis for grounding his universal. This allows him to develop his now-famous notion of *Basho* of 'absolute nothingness' as the basis for the organization of thought.

18.4 NISHIDA'S LOGIC OF PLACE (*BASHO*)

Nishida was an adamant critic of his own work and strove unceasingly to reconstruct and refine the Zen-inspired mode of explanation he had developed throughout his lifetime. In later works Nishida drew substantially from the work of Plato, and in particular from the *Timaeus* to formulate his own alternative logic of place (*Basho*) as a complex system for explaining the origins of fact and value that confront us in our everyday lives. In the *Timaeus* Plato presents an elaborate account of the emergence of order and beauty in the world. For him this universal order is the product of a divine craftsman (*Demiurge*) who imposes a precise mathematical set of relations onto a pre-existent chaos to produce the universe we observe. For Plato this orderly arrangement of the universe is not fortuitous but an outcome of a deliberate intellect who has managed to construct a world as excellent as its nature permits. Such beautiful orderliness provides a model for rational souls to understand and emulate in order to rediscover and regain their original state of excellence. Nishida's concern begins with the second main section of the *Timaeus*, in which Plato introduces the notion of a 'receptacle' as the third kind needed for his model of the universe.

18.4.1 Plato's Receptacle

In formulating his theory of emergence and order, Plato has Timaeus introduce the notion of a receptacle as a 'third kind' alongside that of forms and their observable manifestations. For Timaeus, there are two elements of the universe that are identifiable and separable: the ideal form and its visible manifestation; the latter, though, is changing constantly. For example, we observe that the very thing that is fire becomes hot air that then condenses into clouds and then eventually becomes water; the two are 'transmitting their becoming to one another in a cycle, so it seems' (Plato, 1970: 49c6–7). Thus what appears as fire here and now is not fire in its own right: its fieriness is only a temporary characterization. But if these states are transient and change inevitable, it follows that *becoming* must take place in a kind of 'medium' that remains constant throughout this cycle of change. In a difficult and controversial passage, Timaeus proposes a totally characterless and enduring substratum that he calls the *receptacle* that makes possible the occurrence of all the varied individuals that exist and the changes they undergo. The receptacle has no form, structure, or properties of its own, thus it is not perceptible by any of the senses and hence is only arrived at by a 'spurious' form of reasoning (Plato, 1970: 52b). This receptacle he calls *chôra*, place or space. It is this notion of a 'third kind', the receptacle, that suggested itself to Nishida in his efforts to develop a universal system of comprehension and reflexive awareness that he called the logic of *Basho* (place or space). A *Basho* is a logical space which makes possible a class of judgements, but which is not itself a member of that class of judgements. This means that in reference to the class of judgements it makes possible, a *Basho*, like Plato's receptacle, is a no-thing; as a logical space, it has none of the properties of the class it generates.

18.4.2 Nishida's Logic of *Basho* and Absolute Nothingness

For Nishida, there are three levels of reflexive awareness. Firstly, there is the everyday commonsensical *Basho* of *being* within which empirical judgements about the world are made unreflectively. For instance, we may say 'this wine is red in colour'. Such a statement, couched in Aristotelian logic, seems to express a pure objectivity because the observer making the judgement does not him/herself form a part of the claim being made. His/her presence does not feature in the judgement itself as a notable subject of apprehension. The statement made, 'this wine is red in colour', only refers to the object of observation without implicating the observer him/herself. By so doing, the statement appears a seemingly objective fact of observation. It takes the form of a subject–predicate structure deriving from Aristotelian logic. Nishida, however, points out that to deliberately ignore or neutralize the role of the observer is to implicitly judge that his/her own role in formulating the statement is inconsequential. This is itself an arbitrary judgement since what is really being claimed is: 'I see wine that is red in colour and since what I see is real and external to myself I can ignore my own role in this formulation.' Such seemingly objective statements are arrived at by *arbitrarily* denying a subjective presence.

For Nishida, this arbitrary judgement to exclude/ignore the subjective self is itself located in a more encompassing logical field whereby the significance and role of the self in formulating knowledge is openly acknowledged. Moving to this more encompassing *Basho* of *relative nothingness* entails progressively becoming aware that this act of self-exclusion in our apprehension of objects in the world is essentially arbitrary. From this heightened awareness in the *Basho* of relative nothingness the self is now very much implicated in the act of observation. It is the very thing that scientific objectivity and naive empiricism ignore or overlook. For instance, even Karl Popper (1959) in his discussion of falsification involving black swans still presupposes that the self is able to objectively ascertain whether a swan is indeed black or white without seriously countenancing the possibility of a mistaken perception; subjectivity is denied. This insight that the self plays a very active role in arriving at such judgements leads to an incorporation of subjectivity in explanatory accounts.

However, when subjectivity is taken to its extreme, the individual 'self' is given an elevated status as a relatively stable locus of consciousness pre-existing any existential encounter so that 'experience' is something individuals 'have'. The self is construed as an active agent, a stable locus of knowing and a primary *cause* of change in the world. Even in Jean Paul Sartre's (1966) existentialism, notes Nishitani Keiji (1982: 32), a more contemporary disciple of Nishida, this excessive form of subjectivism intrudes on our awareness of nothingness. Sartrean 'nothingness', despite differentiating itself from 'being', nevertheless remains 'thing-like'; it is an 'emptiness perversely clung to' (Nishitani, 1982: 33). For Nishida, the mistake of those like Sartre is that they think of the self as a 'substance-like' agency rather than as a bundle of experiential relations.

Beyond this *Basho* of relative nothingness, the *Basho* of the self-conscious, willing, and intelligible self, Nishida articulates an even more encompassing *Basho* of *absolute nothingness* which provides the originating ground for consciousness, judgements, and hence basic distinctions such as subject–object, knower–known, self–other, and so on. The *Basho* of absolute nothingness, like Plato's 'receptacle', is the fecund pro-generative openness or emptiness, the groundless ground of logical thought, in which all particular occurrences take place, and yet can itself only be intuited in the same way the hidden lining of a kimono serves to keep form and shape and yet itself always remains unseen. Within this field of absolute nothingness, self and ego are dissolved so much so that the knower, the actor, and the acted-upon are fused in a moment of unifying spontaneous action that transcends individuality, time, space, and judgemental performances. This is the moment of ultimate Zen-like 'pure experience', a 'zero degree of organization' (Cooper, 1986) that pre-exists individuality and individuation so that the self is only realized through the acts of experiencing. The *Basho* of absolute nothingness, therefore, is not so much a physical space, place, or field in any material sense. Rather it is a fecund and pro-generative experiential plenum; an 'open field' (Cooper, 1976) of pure living pre-conceptual experience out of which subject–object, self–other, and knower–know emerge. Such an open field of potentiality cannot be readily conceptualized or intellectually grasped but must be directly intuited. Within this *Basho* of absolute nothingness, ultimate reality is grasped as a unifying pristine encounter with the here-and-now where the knower–known, the actor–acted-upon are fused together as one in a fleeting moment of performative actualization. This profound insight has led the Zen master D.T. Suzuki to observe that the purpose of studying the arts in eastern countries is not so much for utilitarian or even aesthetic purposes, but to 'train the mind…to bring it into contact with the ultimate reality' (Suzuki, in Herrigel, 1953/1985: 5). The *Basho* of absolute nothingness is the unsayable, self-contradictory logical space out of which being and non-being, subjectivity and objectivity, one and many, dynamic and static, as well as other dualisms, become conceivable. Thus for Nishida, 'The world of reality is essentially the one as well as the many…That is why I call the world of reality an "absolute contradictory self-identity"' (Nishida, 1958: 163). The world of particulars is actively extracted from this *Basho* of absolute nothingness through material acts of individuation and through negation of the former. 'We form the world by acts of expression…(and) at the same time, we form ourselves as viewpoints of the world' (Nishida, 1958: 197). Each individual, therefore, is both an expression of the world and an expressing subject within it. But all this is done at the cost of negating our originary pure experience. Our acts reform the world which, in turn, is also reforming us unceasingly; acting is always also 'being acted' upon (Nishida, 1958: 54). Contrary to Descartes, then, Nishida maintains that instead of 'I think, therefore I am', it should be 'I act, therefore I am.'

18.5 Implications: Nishida's *Basho* of Absolute Nothingness and Organization Studies

Perhaps a useful starting point in considering the resonance of Nishida for organization studies is to look at the work of the philosopher of organization Robert Cooper, whose little-known work 'The Open Field' (1976), published in *Human Relations*, resonates deeply with Nishida's concerns and whose muted appearance nearly four decades ago surreptitiously inaugurated a movement of thought that has in more recent times come to be called Process Organization Studies. In this seminal but complex piece, Cooper attempts to articulate an 'epistemology of process' as the basis for expressive and creative action. He maintains that the existential choice for man is either to understand himself and his social forms, including organizations, either in 'instrumental' terms *or* as inherently 'expressive systems'. In the case of the latter, it is the Open Field that 'defines the conditions necessary for process and the emergence of expressive systems' (Cooper, 1976: 1001). Like Nishida, Cooper eschews traditional theories of human action which presuppose that (a) action issues from pre-circumscribed, self-identical individuals, and that (b) action is understandable in instrumental terms. Instead, he opts for the primacy of 'pure action' that is 'uncontaminated by a directing image' as the basis for all social forms, so that 'The man who enters the Open Field uses action as a means of revealing the latent in himself and his world' (Cooper, 1976: 1002). Cooper's Open Field, whilst drawing inspiration from alternative sources, nevertheless holds deep affinities with Nishida's field or *Basho* of absolute nothingness. Both emphasize the primacy of expressive action as that which simultaneously forms and is formed by the individual and the world. Both recognize that the 'point of the Field is its use, not analysis' (Cooper, 1976: 1011). And both acknowledge that our world of everyday particulars is a consequence of logical abstraction from an undifferentiated and unnamable plenum of possibility. Our curse, says Cooper, is that we are 'slaves to an epistemology that separates the knower from the known', leading us to assume the passivity of the observer in relation to that which is observed. Like in Nishida's *Basho* of being and relative nothingness, Cooper recognizes that ordinarily we see knowledge as something apart from ourselves and our existential involvement rather than a part of it. Cooper's idea of an Open Field is another way of describing Nishida's *Basho* of absolute nothingness.

In a subsequent piece published in *Social Science Information* entitled 'Organization/ Disorganization' (1986), Cooper returns to the notion of the Open Field and reintroduces it as the 'zero degree of organization'; a condition, again reminiscent of Nishida's absolute nothingness, of 'undecideability that pervades all social organization' (Cooper, 1986: 316). Zero degree is thus '*a theoretical condition of no meaning, no form, of absolute disorder which one might call the primary source of form or organization*, if the concept of "primary" and "source" did not call to mind the sense of an absolute origin which was itself organized' (Cooper, 1986: 321, my emphasis). The zero degree of organization is thus that which 'energizes or motivates the call to order or organization' (Cooper, 1986: 321). Organization, therefore, cannot be based on a natural, linear logic or on rationality, but instead on an underlying motivating force of expressive action. All organizing processes are 'in essence transference of force from agent to object . . . force . . . is the energy of process, of action between terms' (Cooper, 1976: 1013).

In its most fundamental sense, therefore, organization is simply the forcible 'appropriation of order' out of the Open Field of possibilities, of the condition of 'zero degree' before and beyond organization. In extracting order, however, it has to negate itself, thereby creating the paradox of 'absolute contradictory self-identity' that Nishida identifies as the necessary basis for all knowing. This forcible act, Cooper observes, is akin (following the work of Spencer-Brown, 1969) to a physicist attempting to study the physical world of which she herself is a part. In this sense, human beings themselves constitute the raw material of their ordering efforts so that they too are 'subjected to the process of division . . . They thus pose to themselves the paradox of self-identity which faces any subject that is compelled to take itself as its own object' (Cooper, 1987: 406). Since the physicist herself is made up of the very factors she describes and bound by the very laws she records, for her to operate effectively, the world must 'first cut itself up into at least one state which sees, and at least another state which is seen. In this severed and mutilated condition, whatever it sees is only *partially* itself' (Spencer-Brown, 1969: 105, in Cooper, 1987: 406). The paradox of self-identity is that 'the state of seeing or thinking can never see or think itself, for when it tries to do so it must necessarily take itself as its own object and thus lose sight of its active subjectivity' (Cooper, 1987: 407). Organization, then, becomes an ontological process of forcibly 'producing and reproducing the *objects'* through which a community or society can see or think itself' (Cooper, 1987: 407). Objects and particulars are means by which a community or society come to know itself. But the function of such objects is to create order, to close off the threat of disorder by suppressing it in order to attain the 'singleness of the objective' (Cooper, 1987: 408); *immanent* in the object is an *objection* to being forcibly made into an object. 'The object is that which *objects'* (Cooper, 1987: 408) and it is the attempt to avert the crisis of contradictory self-identity through 'contamination' by its other that motivates the act of organization. Organization, as such, does not merely serve a utilitarian function. Rather, it is fundamentally about the forcible 'preparation of objects' so that it becomes distinguishable from subjects of apprehension. In this 'constructed form' it more readily lends itself to knowledge and certainty. Organization as such, from this Nishidean–Cooperian perspective, is quintessentially a monumental world-making activity.

REFERENCES

Bergson, H. (1903/1955). *An Introduction to Metaphysics* (Englewood Cliffs, NJ: Prentice Hall).
—— (1910). *Time and Free Will: An Essay on the Immediate Data of Consciousness*, trans. F.L. Pogson (London: Allen and Unwin).
——(1911/1998). *Creative Evolution* (New York: Dover Publications).
——(1922/1999). *Duration and Simultaneity*, ed. R. Durie (Manchester: Clinamen Press).
Clarke, J. (1997). *Oriental Enlightenment: The Encounter between Asian and Western Thought* (London: Routledge).
Cooper, R. (1976). The Open Field, *Human Relations* 29: 999–1017.
——(1986). Organization/Disorganization, *Social Science Information* 25(2): 299–335.
—— (1987). Information, Communication and Organisation: A Post-Structural Revision, *The Journal of Mind and Behavior* 8(3): 395–416.
Dilworth, D. (1969). The Initial Formations of 'Pure Experience' in Nishida Kitaro and William James, *Tokyo: Monumenta Nipponica* 24: 262–70.
Feenberg, A. (1999). Experience and Culture: Nishida's Path 'To The Things Themselves', *Philisophy East and West* 49(1): 28–44.
Fields, R. (1992). *How the Swans Came to the Lake: A Narrative History of Buddhism in America*, 3rd edn (Boston: Shambala).
Herrigel, E. (1953/1985). *Zen in the Art of Archery* (London: Arkana).
Inada, K. and Jacobson, N. (eds) (1991). *Buddhism and North American Thinkers* (Delhi: Sri Satguru Publications).
James, W. (1890). *Principles of Psychology*, 2 Volumes (London: Macmillan).
——(1902). *Varieties of Religious Experience* (London: Fontana).
——(1907). *Pragmatism: A New Name for Old Ways of Thinking* (London: Longmans).
——(1909/1996). *A Pluralistic Universe* (Lincoln: University of Nebraska Press).
——(1911/1996). *Some Problems of Philosophy* (Lincoln: University of Nebraska).
——(1912/1996). *Essays in Radical Empiricism* (Lincoln: University of Nebraska Press).
Krueger, J.W. (2006). The Varieties of Pure Experience: William James and Kitaro Nishida on Consciousness and Embodiment, *William James Studies* 1, <http://williamjamesstudies. org/1.1/krueger.html>

Nishida, K. (1921/1990). *An Inquiry Into the Good,* trans. M. Abe and C. Ives (New Haven, CT: Yale University Press).

——(1958). *Intelligibility and the Philosophy of Nothingness: Three Philosophical Essays*, trans. R. Schinzinger (Westport, CT: Greenwood Press).

——(1987). *Intuition and Reflection in Self-consciousness*, trans. V.H. Vigliemo with Y. Takeuchi and J.S. O'Leary (New York: State University of New York Press).

Nishitani, K. (1982). *Religion and Nothingness,* trans. J. van Bragt (Berkeley: University of California Press).

Noda, M. (1954). East West Synthesis in Kitaro Nishida, *Philosophy East and West 4*: 345–9.

Plato. (1970). *Timaeus*, in R.M. Hare and D.A. Russell (eds), *The Dialogues of Plato*, Volume 3, trans. B. Jowett (London: Sphere).

Popper, K. (1959). *The Logic of Scientific Discovery* (London: Routledge).

Ruskin, J. (1927). *The Complete Works* (London: Nicholson and Weidenfeld).

Sartre, J.-P. (1966). *Being and Nothingness* (New York: Pocket Books).

Scott, D. (2000). William James and Buddhism: American Pragmatism and the Orient, *Religion 30*: 1–20.

Spencer-Brown, G. (1969). *Laws of Form* (London: Allen and Unwin).

Versluis, A. (1993). *American Transcendentalism and Asian Religions* (New York: Oxford University Press).

Whitehead, A.N. (1926/1985). *Science and the Modern World* (London: Free Association Books).

——(1929). *Process and Reality* (New York: Macmillan).

Wilkinson, B. (2009). *Nishida and Western Philosophy* (Farnham, Surrey: Ashgate).

CHAPTER 19

··

LUDWIG WITTGENSTEIN
(1889–1952)

··

ROBERT RICHARDSON, MATT STATLER,
AND SAKU MANTERE

19.1 LIFE AND PLACE

WITTGENSTEIN WAS born into one of Europe's wealthiest families, and was educated by private tutors until the age of 14. During this time he was exposed to the formative influence of Kierkegaard, Dostoyevsky, Tolstoy, and Schopenhauer. At the same time, his home life was marked by visits from Europe's artistic elite, notably Brahms and Mahler, who frequently gave private recitals at the Wittgenstein's Viennese home.

After completing his secondary education and while studying aeronautical engineering at the University of Manchester—a still very new discipline at the time—he became interested in the foundations of mathematics, specifically the work of Frege, whose writings on reference, propositions, and the relationship between sense and reference became the grounding of what emerged as 'analytic philosophy'. Wittgenstein also read the work of Bertrand Russell, who was following similar lines of thought to Frege but with emphasis on language and its relationship with logic and metaphysics. It was Frege who suggested to Wittgenstein that he study philosophy with Russell at Cambridge.

It was with this mix of influences that Wittgenstein arrived at Cambridge. He was steeped in the moral and aesthetic perspective that was the privilege of his family and educational circumstances. And he was enamoured of the cultural products that gave this perspective its most humanistic and universal expression. At the same time, he was a product of a changing world in which science had transformed material conditions throughout Europe, including the processes that led to his father's industrial success in steel manufacture, guiding his own decision to pursue a brand new science.

It is within this context that Wittgenstein first proved himself to be 'a philosopher's philosopher', working within a newly cleared philosophical field, writing the *Tractatus*

Logico-Philosophicus (1922/1961), recalling Spinoza's own masterwork. His work captured the attention and imagination of his teachers, Russell and G.E. Moore, as well as the logical positivists of the Vienna Circle who proposed extending a version of Wittgenstein's methodology for eliminating wide swaths of 'metaphysical' discourse wherever this might occur and erecting in its place a scientific world conception. Their goal was nothing less than a single science no longer divided by methodological differences or plagued by specious metaphysical assumptions; in Wittgenstein's *Tractatus* they felt they had found a guiding light.

After the completion of the *Tractatus*, his only book published during his lifetime, two things seem to have motivated Wittgenstein's flight from academia: (1) his sense that he had drawn philosophy to a close, and simultaneously (2) that the Vienna Circle had in some sense misinterpreted the 'use' to which he meant for his method to be put, notably in their dismissive relationship with moral and aesthetic questions that Wittgenstein himself felt implicated with throughout his life—evidenced in part by the fact that Wittgenstein gave away most of his inheritance, sometimes to poets like Rilke and Trakl.

After an interlude of wandering, supporting himself as a schoolteacher and also as a gardener, and living in a hut in Norway, he acknowledged there were still philosophical questions to be dissolved, and he returned to a lectureship at Cambridge in 1929. Here he embarked on a long serious of lecture courses that took him through the 1930s and attracted the very brightest students in philosophy and other disciplines. At this time he began working on *The Blue and Brown Books* (1965), which forced the assumptions of his early philosophy through a rigorous revision. The result was a work that would be published only after his death as the *Philosophical Investigations* (1953/1968).

19.2 WITTGENSTEIN'S WORK

19.2.1 Doubt, Silence, and the Undoing of Metaphysical Philosophy

In his *Meditations* (1996), Descartes wanted to hold up his beliefs before reason to judge the viability of their candidacy as knowledge. To take each belief one by one, though, would be impossible. It would take as long as one might live. So, instead, he decided he must hold up for consideration the reliability of the sources of belief, rather than the beliefs themselves. The criterion, then, is that if a source of belief produces even one false belief, then that source cannot be trusted and so too any belief produced from it. (The end of his thought experiment is the well known 'I think, therefore I am.')

Descartes' effort provides a means by which to understand the transition from the work of the early Wittgenstein to the later Wittgenstein—and on two issues: (a) the proper 'method' for philosophizing, and (b) the fundamental change in perspective that results in the change of method. We can unpack these issues individually, allowing one to unfold into the next, and we will recompose them into a whole picture.

Take the grounding assumption that puzzled Descartes above all others in our knowledge-producing activity: our object-centric bias (versus a process-centric one). Let's look at the two phenomena, communication and internalization, to understand this bias. In every case, the intuitive accounts of these phenomena privilege the stability of the entities involved over the fluidity of the processes in which they are involved. The entire (explanatory) account depends on these entities having an identity that remains consistent throughout the process—in fact, the intuitive accounts go so far as to eschew positing change to any given entity involved in the process in order to explain how any change at all is brought about by the process.

Not surprisingly, this object-centric bias gives rise to its own (theoretical) difficulties. For instance, within communication, how are we to account for ambiguity, polysemy, misunderstanding, and errant meaning? Traditionally, these are accounts of how one may exploit the difference between the grammatical shape of a given expression and its underlying logical form. In other words, the explanation is that there is a distinction between the appearance and reality of the meaning of a given expression. In this respect, it is not that the entities involved are subject to changes brought about by the process of communication, but instead that there is a disjunction or slippage between appearance and reality. It is about the fit of two identities, rather than the constitution of either that is in question. The picture is a largely static one. The only movement at work in phenomena of communication are active minds grasping appearances and taking them at face value, or minds comprehending the divide between appearance and reality and teasing out meaning from behind the veil of grammar. All the while, this assumes the object nature of expressions, propositions, meanings, minds, and so on. These all are logically presupposed as fully constituted in giving this account of communication.

We can see something similar at work in internalization. The principal assumption here is that the mind is a constituted identity, the properties of which are beliefs (and other mental states). The mind changes, then, in respect to the changes in mental states. Mental states, themselves, are regarded as constituted, such that they are principally attitudes with content, where the content is understood as the property of the attitude, itself understood as an object. We can see here a nested hierarchy of objects and their properties. One changes an attitude, then, by giving it new content, by giving it a new property. In turn, one changes a mind by changing attitudes—in the sense of creating new ones, shedding old ones, or refurbishing some.

This assumes, of course, that there is a limit beyond which property changes are unable to affect change in identity. If we assume a substance account of the mind (or of any object, for that matter), then there are principally two constituents: substance and property. The substance is regarded as the kernel of identity. With regard to minds, this is often characterized as the self. There are several ways one can conceive of this substance. Frequently, it is thought according to the distinction between essential and accidental properties. Essential properties are those that an object or entity has necessarily, which may include something as simple as the property of being self-identical. Essential properties are unchangeable, whereas accidental properties can be changed. (We might also assume a bundle account of mind, which says that a mind is nothing more than a collection of properties that are co-located, such that changes in properties are changes in identity.)

The move in which we are interested, then, is one which can turn the traditional notions of organizational change on its head. What if we assumed that expressions, meanings, minds, selves, and so, were the results of the processes of communication and internalization, rather than the pre-constituted nodes caught up in these processes? This question motivates process philosophy, and at its core, it is a theoretical attitude towards the very undertaking of philosophy. Metaphysics, which has had to elevate specious distinctions between appearance and reality, as well as accident and essence, has not infrequently raised problems as intractable as those it is trying to solve. In light of these problems, process philosophers—primary among them, Whitehead—propose to assume a process-centric bias as a means to the end of theoretical simplicity. We can explain more phenomena with fewer assumptions if we begin by seeing processes as primary and objects as the results. Moreover, if we undertake philosophy from this direction, we might even discover that there are some entities which we assume exist that, in fact, do not.

Although productive in many respects, this shift comes up against its own shortcomings for raising its own intractable problems. In *Process and Reality*, Whitehead attempts to reconstruct the whole of metaphysics by replacing the concept of material substance with the concept of actual occasions. In other words, he begins with the assumption that every object *can* be regarded as an event that unfolds over time. Since our experience seems to give us an idea of substance as primary, it requires that we take a somewhat unnatural theoretical attitude towards what exists in order to get started. (And, on that point, Whitehead offers a number of compelling phenomenological reasons that our natural realism is misguided.) From that starting point, though, he sets about to demonstrate what conclusions reasonably follow from that axiom. In other words, the method is still heavily influenced by the traditions of Cartesian rationalism. The difference, however, is that while Descartes begins from within the depths of subjective experience to discover an unshakable foundation, Whitehead is more akin to Leibniz in that experience is regarded as no particular constraint on where we ought to begin our theorizing. This leaves him in the position to have to explain in process terms why our experience represents that world as composed of objects. And that is no easy task, especially if the goal was to have achieved a greater theoretical simplicity.

This is not the only way to critique traditional metaphysics, however. The early Wittgenstein and the logical positivists instead undertook to dismantle traditional metaphysics rather than reconstruct it by taking a very careful look at the question of method. By exploiting the linguistic turn, which presumes that a reasoned account of meaning can stand for a reasonable account of being, logical positivists including Wittgenstein proposed a criterion of meaning that was also a criterion of being. The verification principle says that a sentence is meaningful only in so far as we can either empirically verify its truth value or give an account of how we would do so. If we are unable to do either, the sentence is meaningless, which is also to say that the state of affairs it purports to refer to not only does not exist, it cannot exist. This theory depends vitally on a referentialist theory of meaning, of course, in which the meaning of a sentence is the state of affairs to which it refers. (And given the distinction between grammatical and logical form, it is technically the propositions themselves that have meanings, whereas sentences are merely the vehicles.) This criterion, then, was executed against traditional metaphysics showing that the very language in which it was undertaken was largely unverifiable— along with a wide swath of other purportedly meaningful forms of discourse—including all expressions of value, whether ethical or aesthetic.

On this last point, then, Wittgenstein was in the position to have to explain what is happening when we give expression to aesthetic or ethical judgement, when we give expressions of value. There are, in fact, two issues here. The first is the sentence used and the second is giving expression per se. Wittgenstein takes it that the entire collection of meaningful propositions is what he calls 'natural science', by which he means both the formalized undertaking that we think of when we think of science and also our everyday empirical claims about our immediate and extended environments. Value judgements fall outside the realm of natural science, because there is no empirical correlate that we could discover that would show that a value judgement was either true or false.

Wittgenstein introduces yet another distinction to help us understand the distinction between meaningful and meaningless propositions in the context of giving them expression. It is the distinction between the saying and the said. In the case of natural science, there is something said in the saying, while in value judgements nothing is said in the saying. And Wittgenstein concludes famously that that which cannot be said must be passed over in silence. How we are to interpret 'silence' here is also a famously contentious issue. The other logical positivists—at least as they have been popularly interpreted—thought it to mean that we ought to stop talking or 'saying' things that use ethical and aesthetic terms. (It may have been on this basis that Wittgenstein was asked to address the Vienna Circle and on the basis of which Wittgenstein is thought to have concluded that they had misunderstood his principal conclusions—also thought to be part of the reason that he withdrew into a series of reclusive occupations, including as a gardener for a monastery and a kindergarten teacher, for which he was, by all accounts, especially unsuited.)

Given the force of his earlier account of 'solipsism', however, it seems fairly clear that Wittgenstein means 'silence' not as a normative prescription but as a descriptive fact. Wittgenstein explains that the self's relation to the world is the same as the eye's relation to the field of vision. Or more precisely it is the same as vision's relation to the field of vision. That is, vision is not something that can be seen within the field of vision. Likewise, the self is not something that occurs in the world, but is rather the perspective taken on the world. And given the fundamental privacy of individual minds, we cannot have direct experience or knowledge of other minds in the world. Wittgenstein uses this fundamental solipsism to explain what is happening when I make an aesthetic or ethical judgement. In this activity, this saying, I am giving expression to how the world is seen from my perspective. I am not making claims about facts in the world, because there are no such more moral or aesthetic facts—which is required as a conclusion when applying the verification principle. (It is worth noting as well that ascriptions of psychological facts about myself and others might be equally meaningless, since psychological contexts are not truth-preserving when co-referring terms are swapped out for one another. Wittgenstein does not seem to have considered the idea that ascriptions of psychological facts are reducible to claims about observable entities in the environment. This is especially true about claims regarding one's own self, since selfhood is simply the limit to my world and, therefore, would in no case ever be equivalent to or reducible to a claim or set of claims about what is observed in the world.) In this context, 'silence' can be interpreted to mean that some amount of saying will always remain silent, will not have said anything, of necessity, because of the nature of selfhood and the constitution of the world. Silence here says nothing about what saying should or should not happen.

19.2.2 Use: Towards a Wittgensteinian 'Theory' of 'Change'

There were a number of famous problems associated with the verification principle or logical positivism generally, not the least of which was that the principle is not applicable to the very formulation of the theory itself. The sentences that make up the theory are meaningless by its own account. Wittgenstein himself embraces this conclusion enthusiastically, claiming that anyone who has understood what he has said in the *Tractatus* will understand that its assertions are meaningless. At the time of the book's composition, it would appear that this was not something about which Wittgenstein was especially worried, since he nonetheless believed himself to have eliminated metaphysics and solved all outstanding philosophical problems with his work. How are we to make sense of his comfort with what feels like a self-contradiction?

Wittgenstein seems to have accepted this as a fact about what it means to offer a theory, especially when the theory is offered in the form of an explanation. Explanations are such that they appeal to phenomena more fundamental in order to offer an account both as to why a given phenomenon exists and why it has the feature and characteristics that it does. When, however, explanations are offered of the very medium in which explanations are offered, we have to recognize that there are cases in which we have to draw a distinction between the object language and the meta-language. The object language is the one in which we make claims about the world, while the meta-language is the one in which we make claims about the meaning of the object language. (Russell made a similar distinction in his theory of types, but offered it in a different spirit. And the distinction was later to be explored and used both by Carnap and Tarski.) In making this distinction, then, a theory of meaning composed from meta-linguistic claims is not required to obey its own conditions in order to be meaningful. In some respect, however, it could be argued that Wittgenstein recognized that this simply pushes back the problem, such that we have to offer a theory of meaning for the meta-lanuage in a meta-meta-language, and that this would go ad infinitum. That may be why Wittgenstein concluded that the claims that make up his theory of meaning are meaningless when evaluated in terms of the very theory they constitute. Wittgenstein seemed to think that this was the only choice in light of the danger of the infinite regression of meta-languages.

It is interesting to note, however, that shortly after its publication Wittgenstein undertook to solve what he did regard as a truly outstanding problem in the *Tractatus* and, in doing so, revealed to himself the shortcomings with regard to his fundamental assumptions about meaning, especially in so far as his view privileged an unsustainably static view of what it means for something to exist. In other words, he discovered an intractable problem about the relationship between meaning and being.

The problem he needed to solve is sometimes referred to as the colour incompatibility problem, which Wittgenstein raises in 'Some Remarks on Logical Form' (1929/1993). In order to understand it, we need to review very briefly some aspects of the semantics and ontology he offers in the *Tractatus*. Wittgenstein has a semantics that combines referentialism and compositionalism. Referentialism says, as we have seen, that a proposition means by referring to its meaning, by referring to what it means. What it means is some observable fact in the world. Compositionalism says that what a proposition refers to is a function of what its parts refer to and how these parts are arranged into a structure that pictures the structure of the fact. Entire assertions refer to facts. Phrases refer to states of affairs. Names merely name objects, and therefore are not fully meaningful except in the context of a minimally meaningful phrase, which refers to the smallest compositional fact. An example of such a phrase might be, 'red here now', even though this does not correspond to a perceptual experience we might have.

There is much to say about what role the mind plays in linguistic meaning in the early Wittgenstein. As might be expected, given his account of selfhood or mindedness, it is not surprising that he believes that minds play a minimal, but nonetheless vital role in meaning. That is because sentences or propositions are thought to be facts themselves that occur within a causal matrix in which minds themselves do not seem to figure. That said, in order for one compositional fact to picture a second fact with a similar structure, a mind has to take or understand the first as a picture of the second. This has several interesting consequences. The first is that Wittgenstein does not give a true account of the creation of facts, such that even if I am the speaker of a given assertion, I too have to take my assertion as a picture. There doesn't seem to be any provision by which I can have taken it for a fact before it exists. This already seems to upset the picture we have of communication set out previously—and does so as part of the critique of metaphysics in which we are currently engaged.

The second problem arises in trying to maintain the account of communication that we often intuitively hold by recognizing that the spoken assertion is merely the second-order reflection of a fact that I have already taken as a picture of a second fact: that is, my thought about that fact, prior to my expression. What is interesting to note, however, is that Wittgenstein's account of selfhood, which is the limit of my world, requires that if I am aware of a fact as representing another, then these are both in the world, which puts 'my' thoughts on the other side of the limit which distinguishes the world from my experience. (Here we are distinguishing between self and mind; whereas previously we could allow them to be conflated, we can see here that they need to be held apart as distinct.)

The third problem arises as a matter of the combination of the first two, because if the mind is on the other side of the world from experience, Wittgenstein has isolated himself from one of the most natural answers to the question: how does a given grammatical saying come to have said something by expressing a logical form? We naturally want to answer that it is the work of the mind that imbues an expression with its logical form, but for several different reasons that is not an answer available to the early Wittgenstein. The most prominent of them is that the contents of the mind are already facts in the world and, if taken by a self as picturing yet other facts, these are already expressions of logical form for which the mind is not responsible. Things are as they are and change is especially hard to conceive of, especially that change we call 'becoming'. We can see a gripping stasis coming to rest over the account that Wittgenstein articulated in the *Tractatus*, and it animates the colour incompatibility problem.

There is an additional aspect of Wittgenstein's account that we need to understand in order to understand what troubled him about the colour incompatibility problem: that all impossibility is logical impossibility. The simple reason that Wittgenstein requires this is related to one of the central theses of the *Tractatus*. Every proposition is a compositional whole and, at the same time, a truth-functional whole. To put it slightly differently, the truth value of the proposition is a function of the truth values of the elementary propositions from which it is composed. The meaning of a given proposition, then, is whatever fact makes the proposition true or false. One of the consequences of this programme of logical atomism is that every proposition is completely analysable into its parts, which is one of the very central claims of the analytic philosophical method which the early Wittgenstein is largely responsible for developing.

Analysing propositions is no easy undertaking in actual fact, but its generalized form is easy enough to explain. Since the underlying logical form of an assertion might be obscured by grammar, we first have to search for the set of elementary propositions with which the original proposition is truth-functionally equivalent. One of the requirements of these elementary propositions is that they are logically independent from one another. The central idea, then, is that we can complete an analysis of any proposition. Or, seen from the other way around, we can begin with a set of logically independent elementary propositions and by repeatedly applying logical operations compose any possible proposition. That is, we have at our disposal the possibility of constructing every meaningful proposition.

The colour incompatibility problem occurs when analysing propositions that assert that an object has this or that colour—and, by implication, not any other. In other words, it is impossible that a certain object have more than one colour on any of the surfaces that are defined by that one colour. But this is not a matter of logical impossibility. This is impossibility of a different order altogether—physical impossibility, if you will. What this reveals is that not every proposition is a combination of logically independent elementary propositions, which strikes at the heart of the Tractarian programme. And, in fact, the problem is not only true of assertions about colour, but for any (perceptible) quality which requires that exhibiting one instance of the quality excludes exhibiting at the same time any of the others in the same family: colour, tone, degree, and so on. To put it even more bluntly, there are meaningful propositions that are not truth-functional compositions of elementary propositions.

This leaves Wittgenstein in the curious position of having to reframe a number of his central motivations for the Tractarian programme, while recognizing and acknowledging yet further insights that come from the failure of his initial logical atomist framework. The easiest way to understand the transition to his middle and later phase, then, is by weaving together these insights. He never gives up on the idea that there is a difference between the grammatical surface of language and its underlying function. He never gives up on the idea that he can exploit this difference to give an account of the meaningfulness of language. He never gives up on the idea that this account will be won on the basis of what can be observed. He never gives up on the idea that in giving an account of the meaningfulness of language we can eliminate or, in his later phase, deflate metaphysical speculation. He never gives up on the notion that mind is essentially something that occurs in the world and on the other side of the divide from experience. He never gives up on the idea that experience plays little to no role in meaning, if experience exists at all. But at the same time, he understands that his largely static view has to be abandoned in favour of one that recognizes a process of mutual exclusion that is not merely a variety of logical impossibility operating over elements with well-defined identities. He also understands that that mutual exclusivity of the truth of colour assertions is, if it is not going to get caught in the quagmire of metaphysical speculation, going to need an 'explanation' that does not choose sides in the ongoing debate between idealism and realism.

There are two ways to understand colour ascriptions. In the realist mood, we can argue that colours are properties really possessed by objects in the world. In the idealist mood, on the other hand, we can argue that colours are ultimately aspects of our experience, an effect of the way the mind organizes information about the objects in the world. (In a fully Kantian mood, we might argue that objects about which we can truly be said to have knowledge are also aspects of our experience, but that the structure of experience is universal, such that we can make true claims about it with the same assurance that the realist would make claims about the world.) We need not worry about how to go about evaluating the truth of these claims. The important point is that Wittgenstein would have seen difficulties in following out either of these paths in describing how colour ascriptions are meaningful. On the one hand, Wittgenstein does not seem to have put much stock on the notion of physical impossibility, recognizing that every scientific law is fundamentally a generalization built from observations of contingent facts, which could change over time. (Time and again, Wittgenstein is taken to task for his elementary understanding of science.) On the other hand, he seems as well to have recognized that there was no non-metaphysical way to secure a universal structure for experience, such that the impossibility of multiple colour ascriptions being true at the same time is a function of our hard-wired conceptual framework. In fact, he rejects all explanations. He rejects all theory-making in favour of offering descriptions.

It is as much his methodological radicalism that sets the later Wittgenstein apart as the conclusions he draws on the basis of applying his new methodology. In his later work, Wittgenstein rejects the idea that he is offering any theory at all. Instead, he repeatedly insists that he is offering only descriptions that he hopes will serve as a therapy for getting over some of our longest-standing intuitions, which traditionally give rise to philosophical positions on either side of an unbridgeable divide. Theories are all fundamentally explanations, but ones such that they have been sufficiently generalized to explain every instance of a given kind (of phenomenon). An explanation is nothing more than an assertion that posits the existence of a fact more fundamental than the one under consideration and which gives a reason for the fact under consideration having the features and characteristics that it does. In the case of colour ascriptions, for the realist what explains the meaning of the ascription is the way objects really are. For the idealist, what explains the meaning of the colour ascriptions is the way minds really are. Wittgenstein rejects both these paths of explanation (as metaphysical dead ends) in favour of offering descriptions, which are fundamentally nothing more than appeals or assertions to facts 'at the same level' as the facts under consideration in order to give a reason for why these exist as they do.

What the colour incompatibility problem reveals to Wittgenstein is that there are a number of expressions that are meaningful even though they are not analysable, which gives him pause to reflect on the very goal of analysability as a means of understanding linguistic meaning. At the very beginning of the *Philosophical Investigations*, he destroys referentialism and compositionalism in one go. There he provides the immanent plane on which his considerations will thereafter begin: use. He asks us to consider the phrase 'five red apples' in the context of going shopping. The very first thing to notice is that, contrary to his early position that language is meaningful only in the context of full assertion or proposition, here we are faced with a mere phrase that is useful within the context of shopping. But just what does it mean? He shows that if we are to consider it outside the context of its use, that is, if were to consider it as an object on the page and, thereafter, simply applied the referentialist explanation, then we would take this as a collection of names, each of which purports to pick out some object or another in the world. The difficulty, of course, is that taken in isolation, we would be hard-pressed to find the empirical correlates of each of these words. To speak in the terms of contemporary metaphysics, we would be looking for three rather abstract entities: five-ness, redness, and apple-ness. But it would be a rather poor result to our shopping errand if this were possible and we did end up with these tasteless, arid, abstract entities in our bag.

Moreover, the example provides a way of accounting for meaning that also counts against compositionalism. When considered as a mere object, 'five red apples' is not meaningful because it is neither true nor false, at least according to the Tractarian view. There is nothing that I could observe in the world that makes it true, nor is there any set of procedures that I could outline by which I could verify its truth. However, in the context of its use, when I go shopping with the note 'five red apples', it clearly means something, while it might mean something else in a different context or mean nothing at all. In the case of shopping, what it means, that is, what it says is to engage in a set of procedures at the store. It is as if I am to identify 'red' on a colour chart and see it correlated with a colour swatch. Then I am to locate the bin labelled 'apple'. Finally, I am to count out five 'red apple getting' movements, by which I select the correct specimens from the bin (from amongst the green apples, say) and deposit them in my bag. If I come home with six green bananas, then I did not understand what I was supposed to do, that is, I didn't understand what 'five red apples' means. But whatever the case about my carrying out my chore correctly (which we will return to shortly), it is certainly the case that it is not a matter of the truth values of the component elements. (Not surprisingly, this new position is sometimes referred to as meaning holism, but this can be a misleading way to characterize what Wittgenstein has in mind here.)

The point is that even in the *Philosophical Investigations* meaning is still a matter of satisfying a criterion or not. In the Tractarian view, that criterion was about whether or not there exists a fact with the same structure that is shown in the proposition. If there exists such a fact, then the proposition is true. If not, then it is false. But now the criterion is a criterion of correctness, which is the correlate of truth value in the context of use. Either the expression was used correctly or it was not. If I end up at home with five red apples in my shopping bag, then I used the expression correctly. If not, then I used it incorrectly, and, as a consequence, I cannot be said to have understood. But where do the criteria of correctness come from?

19.2.3 Playing the Game: Dynamic Forms of (Organizational) Life

It is at this point that Wittgenstein offers his famous account of language games. The basic idea is that, like all games, language games are formed according to rules for correct and incorrect play. And, moreover, like all games, the rules for the correctness or incorrectness of play are directed by whatever happens to be the end goal of the game itself. The goal of a given language game is defined by the form of life for which the language game is fitted and into which the language game is embedded. Forms of life are essentially modes by which our behaviours are coordinated with one another for the (sometimes efficient, sometimes inefficient) fulfillment of desires. (It is interesting to consider whether forms of life are not also mechanisms for creating aligned desires as well.) Wittgenstein says that forms of life are modes of organization in which our actions agree with one another. Language games, then, are essentially exchanges of linguistic behaviour aimed at coordinating our behaviours so that they agree with one another in satisfying the goal of a given form of life. Wittgenstein says very little—in fact, nearly nothing—about why this is the case, but he conjectures briefly in his notes that this is about efficiency. I can more easily get you to behave in useful ways by talking with you than by otherwise physically compelling you to behave in ways coordinated with the aims of the form of life we share.

Under these conditions, then, the meaning of a given expression is determined according to the context of its use, according to the language game in which it is employed. If the expression is used correctly, that is, in a rule-following manner, then the sentence is meaningful. What it means is whatever it causes to be accomplished behaviourally, whether that is the next move in the language game by my interlocutor or some non-linguistic behaviour aimed at a goal shared by us, that is, in so far as we share a form of life. Wittgenstein calls the total set of rules by which a language game is structured its grammar or its logic. To play a language game, then, requires that we master its rules. In order to understand how we do such a thing, Wittgenstein turns his attention to the context in which we learn the rules of a language game.

There are several examples that are instructive on this point, but the best example Wittgenstein gives is about learning what a particular mathematical function or rule means: 'x + 2'. The point is that we have to interpret the rule correctly in order to master it and be able to play the language game. When a teacher asks a student to begin a series with '2' that satisfies this function, the student can write any series of numbers that he or she likes, because as Wittgenstein points out, when I interpret the function for myself without the benefit of knowing how to interpret it according the rules of that language game, I can assume my interpretation is correct. So I might write down '2, 5, 12, 27'. I then observe my teacher, who will be shaking his or her head and playing out a part of the language game, 'Try again'. This is a linguistic behavioural cue that I have to write a set of numbers, but different from the last. This time, I begin with '2, 4. . .', and I look up to see a smile on my teacher's face. Here I know I've begun 'correctly', and I continue with '. . . 6, 8, 10', and my teacher praises me with 'Well done'. As Wittgenstein says, my understanding is literally nothing more (or less) than my knowing how to go on writing in ways that receive the teacher's affirmation. Moreover, Wittgenstein is clear that my understanding cannot be validated as rule-following until I have engaged in the behaviour enough times to be deemed by the teacher, who has already mastered the rules of this game, as having learned the rules. One of the most important conclusions to be drawn from this example is that all meaningful language is fundamentally a social phenomenon, an exchange of useful behaviours—and not a set of objects that represent facts or states of affairs.

We can take this moment to use the trajectory of Wittgenstein's thinking to reflect on the nature of change. Wittgenstein's work, both early and late, demonstrates that the 'mind', which figures so prominently in our explanations and theories about how to effect change, plays little to no role in what 'happens' and, therefore, in change. It is true that Wittgenstein's early account of the mind's role in the world is wrapped up in an atemporal logic that makes it nearly impossible to account for change at all, let alone the mind's role in it. That Wittgenstein only comes to understand this by having to consider whether colour exclusion is a logical impossibility is a curiosity of his method, but the important point is that his early methodological exploration leads us to something like the following conclusion: if there is a private and individual sphere on the other side of a divide from the world, a sphere we might rather need to call the 'self', then it is a sphere narrowly circumscribed in its activity. It takes one fact as representing another, and the collection of these instances gives rise to something like 'my world'. The collection is a view of how things appear to me, and it is this view or perspective that gets expressed in our moral and aesthetic judgements, even though there is no fact *in* the world that correlates with these statements.

Under this interpretation, we are almost immediately struck by an obvious question: what are all these important, but nonsensical expressions for? The early Wittgenstein does not seem to have been struck by the same question, but arrives at it only later, after having taken the path through the colour incompatibility problem and after having subjected the assumptions behind the ascendant analytic method to a rigorous criticism. In the terms laid out earlier, we can see him coming to understand that these expression themselves do something—and that they constitute the whole of meaning and, on some interpretations of his later work, mind. For our purposes, we need not engage in the minutiae of philosophical interpretation. Broadly speaking, there is a debate within the literature about how and whether we can give a Wittgensteinian account of the phenomenology of some of our mental states, the 'what it feels like' to undergo them—that is, given the overwhelming thrust of his work which suggests that there is no important divide between the inner and the outer, that the mind might be an effect of the way we are taught and trained to use language. All meaning is immanent to the behaviours that constitute 'forms of life', which we can reasonably interpret as 'forms of organization'. Under this picture, how we would go about affecting change would look radically different, since the internalization of beliefs communicated via our linguistic expressions can no longer presuppose any pre-existing entities between which these processes operate—and where we can still discover something that remains of the internal sphere, it plays no role in meaning.

19.3 Implications for Organizational Studies

Of the many implications of Wittgenstein's work for organization studies, perhaps the most critical point has to do with organizational change. Organization theorists have often assumed that organizational change is episodic, and thus presents a disturbance to the organization in its natural state (see Weick and Quinn, 1999; Mantere et al., 2007). In his work, Wittgenstein undercuts the episodic account of change, in which stasis is the norm, by rejecting all metaphysical postulates and insisting that the meaningfulness of language occurs (or not) only in the context of its use. On this account, the truthfulness of any utterance about organizational change would depend on its 'workingness', that is, on the extent to which it enables organizational members to come to some agreement or to engage in some action collectively. In this sense, the theoretical account of change prevalent in organization studies as episodic disruption of an essentially static phenomenon simply does not 'work' when organizations appear to exist in near constant flux.

Organizational theorists have also struggled with questions about the causal logic of change—who or what causes change, and what exactly is the goal? Critical scholars have challenged the assumption that organizational change is teleological, and caused by change agents, the role of whom is to overcome resistance to change by change recipients. The notion that strategies are derived from non-interested vantage points is ideological (Shrivastava, 1986) and strategic management is a self-justifying discourse (Ezzamel and Wilmott, 2008). Put positively, strategic management is an art of practical coping (Chia and Holt, 2006) and Wittgenstein's notion of language games provides a nuanced description of how organizational members engage in such practices. On Wittgenstein's account, anyone in an organization, including the top management, who engages in a discussion about change follows rules of language games that have arisen from social contexts. The organization is itself an emergent phenomenon consisting of a variety of different language games, and 'theories of change' as well as 'change management strategies' are nothing more or less than attempts to describe the dynamics that characterize specific language games. Language games are always social, including multiple players with different voices. Thus, even when a scholar or a practitioner might be tempted to conceptualize a particular organizational change as something that originated in the mind of the CEO, Wittgenstein reminds us that the initial formulation is always already inherently social and contextual, whether the CEO (or anybody else) realizes it or not.

Looking ahead, the implications of such for organization studies include the delivery of empirical research, and the risk that the programme becomes purely critical, resulting in the destruction of insight rather than the production of new insight. The foundational assumptions about change that process theorists have sought to undermine are likely to remain in place because they are not only hospitable to studying change empirically, but also for informing practitioners about managing it. Indeed, despite the fact that process scholarship has seen over ten years of visible, published output, few empirical studies have progressed beyond stating that their findings undermine yet another dogmatic belief about change by showing that things are much more complicated than what had been thought before. The field is in need of methodological insight that would lead scholars to tackle the paradox of generalizing something out of their findings, yet in a manner sensitive to the local and transient nature of the processes that they study.

As detailed earlier, Wittgenstein's work offers at least two resources for tackling this difficult dilemma. The first is his view of methodology as therapy rather than as a servant of a particular theoretical position. Rather than seeking to build an orthodox set of rules about how to practise correct scholarship about change, process scholars could use their own sense of concern for authenticity in the communication of the significance of their findings as a guide. Answering the call of overriding teleology, homophonic views of organizational meaning and the episodic view of change may be an unattainable goal, leading to nonsensical accounts. But they can be worthy opponents in each piece of scholarship, treated as a therapeutical process intended for the delivery of a significant yet authentic story.

The second resource is that Wittgenstein's work opens up a new opportunity for studying organizational stability. Wittgenstein proposes that forms of life are founded on agreement over rules of meaning. Such tenuous and fleeting agreement is an accomplishment, captured in Tsoukas and Chia's (2002: 572) metaphor of the tightrope walker:

at a certain level of analysis (or logical type)—that of the body—the statement 'the acrobat maintains her balance' is true, as is also true the statement 'the acrobat constantly adjusts her posture,' but at another level of analysis—that of the *parts* of the body. The apparent stability of the acrobat does not preclude change; on the contrary it presupposes it.

Perhaps future, process-oriented empirical studies could examine cases in which the tightrope walker exhibits excellent balance, where organizational meaning is maintained in seemingly stable agreement over a period of time.

REFERENCES

Chia, R. and Holt, R. (2006). Strategy as Practical Coping: A Heideggerian Perspective, *Organization Studies 27*(5): 635–55.

Descartes, R. (1996). *Meditations on First Philosophy*, ed. J. Cottingham (Cambridge: Cambridge University Press).

Ezzamel, M. and Wilmott, H. (2008). Strategy as Discourse in a Global Retailer: A Supplement to Rationalist and Interpretive Accounts, *Organization Studies 29*: 191–217.

Mantere, S., Sillince, J.A.A., and Hämäläinen, V. (2007). Music as a Metaphor for Organizational Change, *Journal of Organizational Change Management 20*: 447–59.

Shrivastava, P. (1986). Is Strategic Management Ideological?, *Journal of Management 12*: 363–77.

Tsoukas, H. and Chia, R. (2002). On Organizational Becoming: Rethinking Organizational Change, *Organization Science 13*(5): 567–82.

Weick, K.E. and Quinn, R.E. (1999). Organizational Change and Development, *Annual Review of Psychology 50*: 361–86.

Whitehead, A. (1979). *Process and Reality*, 2nd edn (New York: Free Press).

Wittgenstein, L. (1922/1961). *Tractatus Logico-Philosophicus*, trans. D.F. Pears and B.F. McGuinness (New York: Humanities Press).

—— (1929/1993). Some Remarks on Logical Form, *Proceedings of the Aristotelian Society*, Supplementary Volume 9: 162–71.

—— (1953/1968). *Philosophical Investigations*, trans. G.E.M. Anscombe (Oxford: Basil Blackwell).

—— (1965). *The Blue and Brown Books*, trans. G.E.M. Anscombe (San Francisco: Harper & Row).

CHAPTER 20

MARTIN HEIDEGGER
(1889–1976)

BOGDAN COSTEA AND KOSTAS AMIRIDIS

20.1 INTRODUCTION

MARTIN HEIDEGGER (1889–1976) was a German philosopher who studied first theology and then philosophy in Freiburg from around 1909 until about 1915, the year in which he obtained his *Habilitation* with a dissertation on 'Duns Scotus' Doctrine of Categories and Meaning'. He returned to teaching philosophy after World War I, first at Marburg from 1923 to 1928, and then at Freiburg from 1928 until 1945, where he succeeded Edmund Husserl. At Freiburg, he acted as Rector from May 1933 until April 1934 under the Nazi regime's approval and this gesture came to mark his reception to this day. In 1945, he was banned from teaching by one of the 'denazification' committees until September 1949. In 1951–1952, he resumed his university lectures at Freiburg. He worked and lectured until his death in May 1976. In every respect, Heidegger's life and work have been both unsurprising and extraordinary: he worked all his life as a scholar would, echoing perhaps his own remarks about Aristotle: 'Regarding the personality of a philosopher, our only interest is that he was born at a certain time, that he worked, and that he died' (Murray, 1978); at the same time, his life spanned one of the most troubling and defining periods in the destiny of modern Europe. He became both a distinguished thinker and teacher, and a dubious figure whose political affiliations with the Nazi movement have generated significant and unavoidable debate (see, for example, Farias, 1991; Faye, 2009; Löwith, 1948; Wolin, 1992a, 1992b). His relationships with colleagues and students, with his own masters, and the institutions and the world of his time have become to some extent suffused with legendary connotations. A vast literature about Heidegger's private and public life is available in many languages (for example, Arendt and Heidegger, 2004; Arendt and Jaspers, 1993; Ettinger, 1995; Jaspers, 1978; Löwith, 1994, 1995; Ott, 1993; Pöggeler, 1999; Richardson, 1967; Safranski, 1999). With regard to his thought, Martin Heidegger's work has become gradually available over the decades, both in the original German and in various translations. Since 1975, his collected works (*Gesamtausgabe*) have begun to be published by Vittorio Klostermann Verlag with a planned total of 102 volumes, of which the majority and most important are now available.

It is not easy to label Heidegger's work. He was not the follower of any doctrine, nor did he attempt to establish one. 'Phenomenology', 'existentialism', or 'hermeneutics' have been popular but facile labels pinned on Heidegger's name. As shorthand, nothing has been gained so far from analogies which tend to bracket away quite violently the complexity of a thinker's work in the name of a purported common problem with other thinkers. To call Heidegger an 'existentialist', for example, is to ignore that, as much as Jaspers or Sartre, he was a philosopher who actively and radically aimed 'to go it alone', who thought that there is something profoundly wrong with 'schools of philosophy', or with any sign of dogmatic 'system' (his immediate rejection in 1946 of Sartre's equation of existentialism to humanism is remarkable; though less known, equally radical was Jaspers' rejection of Sartre's points). Even as a student, he had also resisted the powerful attempts (in the 1920s) by his own professor, Husserl, to be anointed heir of transcendental phenomenology (Husserl, 1997).

In the area of process philosophy, Heidegger has also attracted significant attention (e.g. Cooper, 1993; Hendel, 1953; Mason, 1975; Rice, 1989; Schrag, 1959). Despite such interest, these interpretations are coloured precisely by the features just outlined: depending mostly upon fragments of one work (*Being and Time*), the 'Heidegger' who emerges appears to stand for a form of humanism, for a subjectivistic stance aiming towards an emancipation of human being in the name of a vague and undetermined freedom. Rescher (2000: 42) projects a 'Heidegger' 'aim[ing] at historical depth and hermeneutical generality, taking a humanistic and value-oriented approach' (Rescher, 2000: 42). This is, most decidedly, *not* the character of Heidegger's thought and little insight can come from such interpretations.

As the full range of Heidegger's work and thought has become available through the *Gesamtausgabe*, it is increasingly evident that a fuller, more meaningful reception of his thinking is yet to be developed, especially regarding his understanding of modernity. In this sense, any attempts to summarize 'Heidegger' or to pass value judgements about his work would be banal and futile. This chapter will therefore follow a limited agenda: to explore to what extent there may be possible connections between his work and process philosophy, and to expand on one of the possible strands of Heidegger's work that might enter into a dialogue with certain concerns in the field of organization studies.

20.2 Heidegger as Thinker of the Movement of History

Despite Heidegger's weak appropriation by process philosophers, one of the possible starting points for a dialogue between the two could be the idea of 'movement'. Thus this part of the chapter will focus upon the following question: what did Heidegger mean by *movement* in his attempt to understand history? And within that movement, how are we to view organizations, business, or management? Perhaps answers to these questions can come from one of the most fruitful aspects of Heidegger's work: his tantalizing engagement and confrontation with Nietzsche where the idea of 'history as a movement' emerges (Heidegger, 1991a, 1991b, 1976, 2002). By engaging with the latter's announcement of the 'death of God' (Nietzsche, 1974), Heidegger interprets the movement of history as the collapse, or rather withdrawal from view, of the transcendental horizon through which a self- and world-understanding of man can be grounded. In consequence of the 'death of God', Heidegger understands history as a movement in the horizon of what Nietzsche calls the age of 'European Nihilism' (Nietzsche, 1968).

However, to interpret nihilism is inherently difficult. The 'nothing' of nihilism not only hides itself as a process, but also appears as an unthinkable, absurd, and unreal imputation against modernity which sees itself as the richest and most meaningful epoch. So how could there be a method of naming this historical 'no-thing'? If the word 'nothing' is to be taken in its customary, everyday meaning, then a reader could immediately ask whether there can be a concrete historical movement of that which is not, indeed if this can be even considered as a proper object for reflection. Heidegger himself helps us directly in this respect in chapter 3 of the fourth volume of his work on *Nietzsche*:

> The nothing of negation or no-saying is purely and simply 'nothing', what is most null, and so unworthy of any further attention or respect. If the nothing is nothing, if it is not, then neither can beings ever founder in the nothing nor can all things dissolve in it. Hence there can be no process of becoming-nothing. Hence nihilism is an illusion. (Heidegger, 1991b: 21)

Indeed that is what logic would demonstrate—Heidegger himself remarks ironically: 'Who would wish to repudiate such compelling "logic"? All due respect to logic!' (Heidegger, 1991b: 22). However, this is not at all what is indicated by Nietzsche's nihilism. Quite the contrary, for both Nietzsche and Heidegger, nihilism does not indicate 'nothingness' in the common sense of the word; rather, Heidegger wants us to see in nihilism precisely a specific historical relationship between men and 'nothing':

> The question arises whether the innermost essence of nihilism and the power of its dominion do not consist precisely in considering the nothing merely as a nullity, considering nihilism as an apotheosis of the merely vacuous, as a negation that can be set to rights at once by energetic affirmation. Perhaps the essence of nihilism consists in *not* taking the question of the nothing seriously. (Heidegger, 1991b: 21)

In this statement something important occurs: the idea that nihilism is a historical movement is taken out of the sphere of mere logical games and given a content, a difficult one to understand, nonetheless one defined along an essential and revealing clue. It lies in the remark Heidegger makes about the attitude to nihilism that seeks to 'set [it] to rights at once by energetic affirmation'. For whom does this need to affirm itself energetically against the nothing arise? And in what way? For Heidegger, the answer is clear: it is the west (or Europe), with its metaphysics, *that cannot* think or 'adequately formulate' 'the essence of the nothing', and is thus 'heading toward a fundamental metaphysical position in which the essence of the nothing not only *cannot* be understood but also *will* no longer be understood' (Heidegger, 1991b: 22). The 'who' of nihilism is thus the west or Europe, and the content of the movement is metaphysical. Heidegger establishes clearly for us that the phrase 'movement of nihilism' is no mere nonsense, but rather the profound destiny of the western way of thinking in relation to the question of Being. Despite apparent logical difficulties, in the essay 'The Word of Nietzsche: "God Is Dead"', he provides a clear outline of this movement:

> Nihilism is a historical movement, not just any view or doctrine held by just anyone. Nihilism moves history in the way of a scarcely recognised fundamental process in the destiny of the Western peoples. Hence nihilism is not just one historical phenomenon among others, not just one spiritual-intellectual current that occurs within western history after others have occurred, after Christianity, after humanism, and after the Enlightenment. Nihilism, thought in its essence, is on the contrary the fundamental movement of the history of the West. Its roots are so deep that its development can entail only world catastrophes. Nihilism is the world-historical movement of the peoples of the earth who have been drawn into modernity's arena of power. (Heidegger, 2002: 163–4)

This passage appears to spell out that which we have been seeking—namely, a way of thinking about nihilism in terms of place, a way of grasping at the level of historical intuition how we might be addressed by Heidegger when he speaks to us of nihilism. All seems elucidated: nihilism's place of origin is the 'west' (in which Heidegger probably included both Europe and America), its period of unfolding corresponds to modernity (which, as we shall see, means indeed the modernity that we have become accustomed to, namely, the last five centuries or so). At first, all that is necessary to understand nihilism seems elucidated. But it is also clear from this fragment that Heidegger's explanation is no mere cultural geography of nihilism. At once, he confounds us with the homogenizing reference to 'Western peoples'. How are we to take this general assembling of the subject of nihilism under such a totalizing manner of categorization? Might Heidegger mean something deeper with this gesture? That is one question; the other that immediately strikes us, especially if we are minded to place nihilism in the history of thought, is that Heidegger places it above other currents and outside the specific dynamic of such currents in what we take to be the customary unfolding of history. In contrast to Christianity, humanism, or the Enlightenment, nihilism is a historical movement of a different kind, of a more fundamental kind, one whose roots are so deep as to be 'scarcely recognized' although it is no less than the very destiny of the west. At this point, the passage adds a mysterious character of de-recognition to accompany Heidegger's view of *how* nihilism moves. It is this de-recognition that provides a clue to understanding how nihilism moves through the essence of modern man. But before that, it is important to note how Heidegger specifies further—and thus makes more difficult to grasp—the *unspecificity*, as it were, of the movement of nihilism in historical terms; he writes:

> That is why it is not only a phenomenon of the present age, nor even a product originally of the nineteenth century, when admittedly a keen eye for nihilism awoke and its name became common. Nor is nihilism a product of particular nations whose thinkers and writers speak specifically of nihilism. Those who imagine themselves free of it are perhaps the ones advancing its development most fundamentally. Part of the eeriness of this eeriest guest is that it cannot name its own origin. (Heidegger, 2002: 164)

Nihilism appears to be indicated here almost as standing outside of, over and above, history itself. So how can it still be a 'world-historical movement'? The text seems at once clear but also puzzling. Are there no anchors for us to grasp the content of this movement which seems always tantalizingly close and intuitive, and yet always held back and concealed by Heidegger himself? In some respect, it is perhaps what Heidegger intended with these comments. He never let himself, it seems, descend to the level of cultural pessimism which was evident in his time and which he detested (especially in relation to the likes of Oswald Spengler). So he avoids systematically any possibility of identifying his thinking and elaboration of nihilism as a value judgement upon a specific place and time in the common sense of such a gesture. On the contrary, Heidegger indicates nihilism as a movement of planetary proportions both in space and in epochal terms. Nihilism is not a 'here' and 'now'; it seems to be an 'everywhere' and an 'aeon' of the world. This nuance is important because it at once clarifies as well as confounds all attempts at a concrete historical interpretation of the dynamic by which the movement Heidegger describes unfolds. In this respect, it may be useful to introduce here a reference to Louis Dupré's concluding chapter of his *Passage to Modernity*; he writes:

> Modernity is an event that has transformed the relation between the cosmos, its transcendent source, and its human interpreter. To explain this as the outcome of historical precedents is to ignore its most significant quality—namely, its success in rendering all rival views of the real obsolete. Its innovative power made modernity, which began as a local Western phenomenon, a universal project capable of forcing its theoretical and practical principles on all but the most isolated civilisations. 'Modern' has become the predicate of a unified world culture. (Dupré, 1993: 249)

What Dupré is seeking here is not dissimilar to Heidegger's own positing of the planetary nature of the movement of nihilism in relation to the west and its inevitable expansion. But Dupré does not speak of nihilism; he speaks of modernity and yet the substance seems to be the same in respect to this total reach of the expansion of western culture in the guise of the 'modern' as a manner of being in history. In this sense, Dupré speaks in the wake of Heidegger's thinking and with the means that Heidegger and Nietzsche made available to the understanding of European culture and its destiny. Heidegger's grasp, following Nietzsche, is so powerful that subsequent histories of modernity's essence were configured and grounded within this fundamental understanding.

If nihilism escapes fixing into geography or chronology, into a doctrine or other, or into a simple place in the evolution of ideas, and yet is to remain the primordial ground of our historical 'here-being' (*Dasein*), the question regarding the essence of the movement of nihilism requires further elucidation. Heidegger explains it in the same essay:

> The realm for the essence and event of nihilism is metaphysics itself, always assuming that by 'metaphysics' we are not thinking of a doctrine or only of a specialized discipline of philosophy but of the fundamental structure of beings in their entirety, so far as this entirety is differentiated into a sensory and a suprasensory world, the former of which is supported and determined by the latter. Metaphysics is the space of history in which it becomes destiny for the suprasensory world, ideas, God, moral law, the authority of reason, progress, the happiness of the greatest number, culture, and civilization to forfeit their constructive power and to become void. (Heidegger, 2002: 165)

In the second sentence of this passage, Heidegger describes fully the content of the movement of nihilism and provides the key in which to understand nihilism itself, its relation to the concrete history of modernity, and the concrete world in which it unfolds, as well as the fundamental indication of *who* the subject of this history is. But let us not move beyond the first sentence that suggests something essential to how Heidegger wants us to think of nihilism. Nihilism occurs in the realm of metaphysics and in a specific manner. This manner requires thinking about the relationship between the 'suprasensory world', the world of ideas, as the ground of the other, 'sensory world', the social contingent world of the 'everyday', of so-called 'immediate experience'. For Heidegger, this way of thinking about the relationship between contingent history and the fundamental ground to which the movement of nihilism belongs can never be sidestepped and reverted. In this respect, he is, of course, always uncomfortable for the historians of contemporary culture. This is because he asks us to renounce one of the most fundamental values of historical interpretation: the 'agency' of man in the making of their own destiny. For all the dominant approaches to the analysis of modern culture are bound up with this sense of 'agency' as the principle from which history can be understood at all in the sense of modernity being the historical realm of 'free expression' of 'conscience' itself, of subjectivity. Heidegger explains why he does not see history in this way but rather in quite opposite terms:

> The place of God's vanished authority and the Church's profession of teaching has been taken by the authority of conscience and, forcibly, by the authority of reason. The social instinct has risen up against these. Historical progress has replaced the withdrawal from the world into the suprasensory. The goal of eternal bliss in the hereafter has been transformed into the earthly happiness of the greatest number. The diligent care that was the *cultus* of religion has been replaced by enthusiasm for creating a culture or for spreading civilization. Creation, once the prerogative of the biblical God, has become the mark of human activity, whose creative work becomes in the end business transactions. (Heidegger, 2002: 164)

Perhaps there is no clearer statement in Heidegger (although he explains it in many texts), of the rise of modernity as a manifestation of the movement of nihilism. Having attempted to establish some of the essential elements of what Heidegger meant by this movement, the question arises how subjectivity manifests within it. In simple terms, the answer is that it is precisely the historical substance and form of *modern man as a relentless process of self-assertion* that occupies the place vacated by Nietzsche's 'dead God'. The idea we propose is simple: that the core of the movement of nihilism is precisely the 'energetic affirmation' of the modern counter-reaction to the thinking of the nothing as essential in the thinking of being. As mentioned earlier, Heidegger points out in precisely these terms—'energetic affirmation' of the need to set to rights the 'nothing' as being unworthy of serious attention—the essence of the movement of nihilism. This marks decisively, at the same time, the 'who' and the 'how' of this movement. The answer is startling: the 'who' of the movement of nihilism is not an isolated group, or a nation, or an individual thinking in nihilistic terms; the 'who' is 'modern man'. Or, as Nietzsche and Heidegger present it, it is Descartes' *ego* thinking of itself as the measure of all things:

> We have gathered from these introductory remarks on the distinction between Protagoras' saying and Descartes' principle that man's claim to a ground of truth found and secured by man himself arises from that 'liberation' in which he disengages himself from the constraints of biblical Christian revealed truth and church doctrine. . . . To be free now means that, in place of certitude of salvation, which was the standard for all truth, man posits the kind of certitude by virtue of which and in which he becomes certain of himself as the being that thus founds itself on itself. (Heidegger, 1991b: 97)

The 'death of god' meant the opening up of self-assertion as 'freedom' through the disappearance of the suprasensory. This meant the elimination of the final shackles of a metaphysics that bound man to a specific place and meaning. In other words, we can read here an interpretation of the Enlightenment, for example, as that manner of thinking about the place of the human subject as an entity now 'made free' to choose not only their own contents, but also to think it possible to make up their own destiny.

Herein lies the difficulty of both thought and affect with which we are faced in Heidegger's thinking of the movement of nihilism as a movement of modern man's assertion of himself as 'free' in the sense of being world-founding for himself. That which seems to be the fullest, most meaningful period in human history, modernity as the period in which the expression of the self, of the subjectivity of the subject, as a continuous affirmation of human potentialities, the period of what appears as man's fullest emancipation yet, comes to us in Heidegger's thinking as the intensified manifestation of nihilism. Unsurprisingly perhaps, this manner of thinking is not entirely secure for the self-understanding of modernity. Heidegger describes the self-positing of modern man as origin and measure of the new cultural synthesis:

> Viewed metaphysically, the new freedom is the opening up of a manifold of what in the future can and will be consciously posited by man himself as necessary and binding. The essence of the history of the modern age consists in the full development of these manifold modes of modern freedom. (Heidegger, 1991b: 98)

Not only does freedom now appear to modern man as 'new', but it appears as the possibility of it being in each case 'his' or 'her' own freedom—'mine' as if it were mine only and unlike any other's. These words mark the insight with which Heidegger will have probably looked upon the culture which now exalts 'individuality', 'diversity', and 'uniqueness' as its highest values, the highest expression of 'the freedom to be what one truly is'. The sense of empowerment that comes from the continuously repeated affirmation of the self-certainty that 'I', this particular 'I', may truly decide for myself what it is that 'I' can and will be, is, for Heidegger, 'possible only in and *as* the history of the modern age' (Heidegger, 1991b: 98). The 'manifold' manifests in precisely this apparent liberation of the self for the self, in each individual case, and as the desirability—political, cultural, economic—of this metaphysical individualism taken as *the* principle of the modern synthesis. Heidegger calls this the 'empowering of the essence of power' and we ought perhaps to be able to read in this statement not simply an interpretation of Nietzsche but also a horizon of interpretation for what Heidegger calls elsewhere the 'self-assertion' of modern man. Let us ponder Heidegger's characterization of 'self-assertion' (although he does not explicitly call it so in this specific source) in an arresting paragraph in chapter 15 of *Nietzsche—Volume IV*, entitled *The Subject in the Modern Age*:

> The securing of supreme and absolute self-development of all the capacities of mankind for the absolute dominion over the entire earth is the secret goad that prods modern man again and again to new resurgences, a goad that forces him into commitments that secure for him the surety of his actions and the certainty of his aims. (Heidegger, 1991b: 99–100)

He goes on in the same paragraph to describe with breathtaking clarity and brevity the essence of the various epochs, or currents, of the modern horizon. It is the last comment he makes about modern man's founding norm that is important here. He says that the common ground is, in our time, as follows:

> Finally, it can be the creation of a mankind that finds the shape of its essence neither in 'individuality' nor in the 'mass', but in the 'type'. The type unites in itself in a transformed way the uniqueness that was previously claimed for individuality *and* the similarity and universality that the community demands. But the uniqueness of the 'type' consists in an unmistakable prevalence of the same coinage, which nonetheless will not suffer any dreary egalitarianism, but rather requires a distinctive hierarchy. (Heidegger, 1991b: 99)

The introduction of the category of 'type' in the analysis of the modern age helps us break through the conundrum we are left with by the setting up of the 'I' as ultimate reference point of valuation: modern man is not entangled in a war of all against all; the modern age is, as Nietzsche tells us, 'the most decent and compassionate age' (Nietzsche, 1968: 7). The decency of the modern age lies in the bind of the modern 'type' that Heidegger defines: self-assertive modern man who understands all too well that self-assertion is at once individual but also the highest value that posits or grounds the community.

'Modern man' is thus a *form* that results from the specific moment of highest valuation that characterizes our epoch.

The answer to the question 'who is the subject of nihilism?' appears in this way: in manifold ways, a particular typical figure, or form, that functions as the vector of the historical movement which both Nietzsche and Heidegger call 'Nihilism', appears. If nihilism is to be understood historically, 'it is necessary to understand nihilism in a unified way as the history of valuations' (Heidegger, 1991b: 53). This type, or form, in this specific relation, is described more fully in another key text which we will use in the final part of this chapter. There, an important connection is established between self-assertion and the ordering of the world considered as a continuous process of organizing and managing it as raw material. In a true *tour de force*, Heidegger develops a picture of modern man's self-assertion and of the way in which it is bound up with the unfolding of nihilism. The essay is 'Wozu Dichter', occasioned by the twentieth anniversary of Rainer Maria Rilke's death in 1946 (Heidegger, 2001: 87–140). The text synthesizes a series of Heidegger's ideas and interpretations that can be found in many other texts, but in this form we find an essential excursus that can help the analysis we tried to unfold here.

The core of the essay is the contrast between 'modern man' and poets. 'Modern man, however, is the one who wills'; he wills in the mode of 'purposeful self-assertion of the objectifying of the world' (Heidegger, 2001: 138). This is the ground that Heidegger sets out for his analysis of modern man. He describes the mode of self-assertion at length and relates it to the category of will.

> The willing of which we speak here is the putting-through, the self-assertion, whose purpose *has already* posited the world as the whole of producible objects. This willing determines the nature of modern man, though at first he is not aware of its far-reaching implications, though he could not already know today by what will, as the Being of beings, this willing is willed. By such willing, modern man turns out to be the being who, in all relations to all that is, and thus in his relation to himself as well, rises up as the producer who puts through, carries out, his own self and establishes this uprising as the absolute rule. The whole objective inventory in terms of which the world appears is given over to, commended to, and thus subjected to the command of self-assertive production. Willing has in it the character of command; for purposeful self-assertion is a mode in which the attitude of the producing, and the objective character of the world, concentrate into an unconditional and therefore complete unity. (Heidegger, 2001: 108)

The key point in this fragment is Heidegger's intention through the category of '*production*'. Throughout the text, he deals with modern man's essence as a *producer* in the sense coming from the word's Latin root: *pro-ducere*, to bring forth, which denotes the form of *objectification* in which all modern ordering and organizing of the world takes place. The consequences of this mode of positioning in the world are taken by Heidegger to their logical conclusion. This emphasis makes clear that the intensely concrete unfolding of the movement of nihilism is in its immediate power to annihilate beings by transforming them into *objects*, into things that stand-over-against man which are then used for man's dealings with the world.

> The objectness, the standing-over-against, of production stands in the assertion of calculating propositions and of the theorems of the reason that proceeds from proposition to proposition... Not only has reason established a special system of rules for its saying, for the *logos* as declarative prediction; the logic of reason is itself the organisation of the dominion of purposeful self-assertion in the objective. (Heidegger, 2001: 130)

Reason expresses here the relationship that man has with being through *representation*. Heidegger emphasizes time and again that 'What stands as object in the world becomes *standing* in representational production. Such representation presents. But what is present is present in a representation that has the character of calculation' (Heidegger, 2001: 124). This is the specific relationship in which modern man can only exist as the subject who lives exclusively through subjectivity, that is, through the interior of consciousness as the site where presence can only appear as re-presentation. The subjectivity of the subject becomes the ground for modern man's existence and it is to this form that Heidegger attributes the greatest danger: man's relationship with *technology* as the frame through which the world is forcefully ordered so that it ceases to present any 'risk' and comes to stand as continuous possibility, as permanent potentiality for the self-assertion of man's *will*.

> What has long since been threatening man with death, and indeed with the death of his own nature, is the unconditional character of mere willing in the sense of purposeful self-assertion in everything... What threatens man in his very nature is the view that technological production puts the world in order, while in fact this ordering is precisely what levels every *ordo*, every rank, down to the uniformity of production, and thus from the outset destroys the realm from which any rank and recognition could possibly arise. (Heidegger, 2001: 114)

By elaboration of the relationship set up by technology for modern man with the world, Heidegger elucidates the nature of the modern economy as a levelling of all values in the name of the positing of values, as a pseudo-valuation. The transformation that the modern age effects in the way in which man stands with beings leads to a transformation of the world into an empty traffic with merchandise without weight or value.

> Self-willing man everywhere reckons with things and men as with objects. What is so reckoned becomes merchandise. Everything is constantly changed about into new orders.... Thus ventured into the unshielded, man moves within the medium of 'businesses' and 'exchanges'. Self-assertive man lives by staking his will. He lives essentially by risking his nature in the vibration of money and the currency of values. As this constant trader and middleman, man is the 'merchant'. He weighs and measures constantly, yet does not know the real weight of things. (Heidegger, 2001: 132–3)

This is the essence of self-assertion: constant trade, constant objectification of things that only exist in exchanges without value—constant performativity. Nothing escapes this traffic of objects and nothing can thus be held as 'value'. Yet this total movement of markets now encircles the planet and has become the highest value in itself to the extent that it represents the essential manifestation of modern man's nature as self-assertion—the self-assertion of that which is *valueless*.

> It is not only the totality of this willing that is dangerous, but willing itself, in the form of self-assertion within a world that is admitted only as will. The willing that is willed by this will is already resolved to take unconditional command. By that resolve, it is even now delivered into the hands of total organisation. (Heidegger, 2001: 114)

Heidegger seized upon the will that characterizes the modern epoch, a will that manifests itself in constant and ubiquitous processes of production, exchange, and consumption. The question that is left unanswered in such processes, the most bewildering of all questions for us in general, is that of *purpose*. In the most productive era, where Earth and 'cosmos' become objects of these processes, we fail to even think about their meaning. All the improvements in terms of *means* for man's immediate life and 'experience' cannot provide such an answer. Nietzsche exposes this emptiness:

> This meaning could have been: the 'fulfilment' of some highest ethical canon in all events, the moral world order; or the growth of love and harmony in the intercourse of beings; or the gradual approximation of a state of universal happiness; or even the development toward a state of universal annihilation—any goal at least constitutes some meaning. What all these notions have in common is that something is to be *achieved* through the process—and now one realises that becoming aims at *nothing and achieves nothing*....Given these two insights, that becoming has no goal and that underneath all becoming there is no grand unity in which the individual could immerse himself completely as in an element of supreme value. (Nietzsche, 1968: 12–13)

20.3 CONCLUDING REMARKS

We have attempted in this chapter to decipher the role that 'movement' plays in Heidegger's understanding of the modern age. We have focused on the idea of the 'movement of history' because it is central to Heidegger's work, but also because it is this aspect of Heidegger's thinking that might be taken more productively into a discussion of 'process'. Despite certain attempts to interpret Heidegger's thinking in process philosophy, the category of movement has not been explored in those interpretations. However, we would argue, it is in this category that we find an understanding of movement and temporality that has nothing in common with those limited attempts to read *Being and Time* in which 'time' is almost literally isolated as a psychologized, minimal version of human

Dasein taken out of its historical situation. What emerges from such readings is a human being falsely individualized by the commentators themselves, placed in an entirely sub-jectivized world (which is called today 'socially constructed') that has nothing to do with the import of Heidegger's understanding of that other misinterpreted notion, 'being-in-the-world'. We are proposing that Heidegger's view of time can only be grasped in rela-tion to his view of history. As Schürmann argued, 'the understanding of being as time cannot dispense with the deconstruction of epochs' (Schürmann, 1987: 283).

To present, in a final summary, what Heidegger has to say about our epoch we turn to another of his engagements with Nietzsche. Whilst his understanding of Nietzsche through the idea of the movement of nihilism might indicate that he points towards an apocalyptic conclusion, predicting disaster in some sort of historical panic, Heidegger is actually reading Nietzsche as the latter had very clearly indicated himself. Interpreting a key but enigmatic sentence of Zarathustra's *Prologue* ('The earth has become small, and on it hops the last man, who makes everything small. His race is as ineradicable as the ground flea; the last man lives longest'; Nietzsche, 1954: 12), Heidegger writes:

> Listen closely: 'The last man lives longest'. What does that say? It says that under the last man's dominion, which has now begun, we are by no means approaching an end, a final age, but that the last man will on the contrary have a strangely long staying-power. And on what grounds? Obviously on the grounds of his type of nature, which also determines the way and the 'how' in which everything *is*, and in which everything is taken to be.
>
> For the *animal rationale*, this type of nature consists in the way he sets up every-thing that is, as his objects and subjective states, confronts them, and adjusts to these objects and states as his environing circumstances. (Heidegger, 1976: 74)

The essential aspects of this passage are twofold. On the one hand, the age of the last man is not a final age, nor the heralding of an end to history—there is no apocalypse hinted at here. On the other hand, the 'last man' is clarified for us by Heidegger as the '*animal rationale*'. And what else can be read off this qualification than the scientist and engineer, the organizer, the producer, perhaps even the 'worker' and 'manager', the one who plans beforehand and decides how and what beings are to appear, as well as the consuming animal whose 'needs' and 'requirements' are objects of calculation? This is elucidated in another passage from one of Heidegger's lecture series of 1941, a passage worth reread-ing in some detail:

> We attend either to what we need or to what we cannot do without. We measure what we need according to our requirements, according to desires left to them-selves and their cravings, according to what we count with and count upon. Behind these desires and cravings stands the press of that unrest for which every 'enough' is just as soon a 'never enough'... Man can expressly elevate the living and its crav-ings into a guiding measure and make of it the 'principle' of 'progress'. If we attend only to what we need, we are yoked into the compulsive unrest of mere life. This form of life arouses the appearance of the moved and the self-moving, and there-fore of the free...

> However, this way man is only 'free', i.e., mobile, within the compulsion of his 'life-interests'. He is, in certain respects, unfettered within the circuit of compulsion, which determines itself from the premise that everything is a matter of utility. Servitude under the dominion of the constantly 'needed', i.e., of utility, looks like the freedom and magnificence of consumption and its increase. (Heidegger, 1998: 3–4)

These passages reflect the discussion earlier in which we tried to present some of Heidegger's thinking about the movement of our own historical epoch and interpret some of the key terms in which he thought it out: 'self-assertion', 'willing' and 'will', 'unconditional command', and 'total organisation'. The aim was to understand how Heidegger articulates, from a philosophical standpoint, a historically particular manifestation of *humanitas*—i.e. what is 'modern man', what is his relationship to the world as the horizon of the historical process within which the philosopher's thinking can be understood? Throughout his work, in one way or another, Heidegger points out that something crucial in this movement marks this subject out: its emptiness, its indigence, and its continuous inability to cope with the central position it comes to occupy in the cultural order it sets up.

If the modern age is a historical synthesis in the movement of nihilism, we attempted to open up a reading of Heidegger through the simple but crucial question: what might be the content of this epoch's 'unity'? How does this 'unity' of the most unconditional producing epoch relate to the 'nihil' of the 'movement of nihilism'? This chapter presents one of the ways in which Heidegger's thought can help us understand our own concrete historical condition. The result may, in fact, be simple: modernity—as the ultimate age of production and total organization, and as the epoch of self-assertion—appears to be a sign of the movement of 'nothingness', of 'the advent of nihilism', as Nietzsche put it, in a very specific way. This way is paradoxical: nihilism occurs through the self-assertion of modern man. This thought is bound to confound us today—at least to some extent. The movement of nihilism is, in Heidegger's conception, quite the opposite of what is taken for granted to be the contemporary situation. For Heidegger, nihilism is a planetary movement, the homogenous, omnipresent ground of contemporary life. On the other hand, seen from its surfaces, the contemporary situation is characterized by opposite features: it posits the 'diversity' of cultures, identities, political and social systems, and of economies. For Heidegger, modern man is 'empty' and estranged from the world, moved only by the restlessness of his 'will to will', by his sense of some endless possibility to enhance his subjectivity—without letting this be a value judgement but rather a result of his penetrating analysis of the modern condition. For our own self-understanding this is, in the majority of cases, an unthinkable thought, a thought which can only appear as dehumanizing the primordial entity whose essence is never in doubt as such, whose humanity is always posited as the highest value. This contrast may seem highly speculative and inferential but it may also be a useful trigger for further thought on Heidegger's understanding of the modern age. He asks the question of the essence of this age from a different viewpoint and with a degree of serious discomfort which seeks to be an interpretation of 'what is' and 'how it is', rather than a moralistic judgement in the name of an 'ought'.

References

Arendt, H. and Heidegger, M. (2004). *Letters, 1925–1975* (New York: Harcourt).

——and Jaspers, K. (1993). *Hannah Arendt/Karl Jaspers Correspondence, 1926–1969* (New York: Harcourt Brace).

Cooper, R.L. (1993). *Heidegger and Whitehead: A Phenomenological Examination into the Intelligibility of Experience* (Ohio: Ohio University Press).

Dupré, L.K. (1993). *Passage to Modernity: An Essay in the Hermeneutics of Nature and Culture* (New Haven, CT: Yale University Press).

Ettinger, E. (1995). *Hannah Arendt/Martin Heidegger* (New Haven, CT: Yale University Press).

Farias, V. (1991). *Heidegger and Nazism* (Memphis, TN: Temple University Press).

Faye, E. (2009). *Heidegger: The Introduction of Nazism into Philosophy in Light of the Unpublished Seminars of 1933–1935* (New Haven, CT: Yale University Press).

Heidegger, M. (1976). *What is Called Thinking?* (New York: Harper Perennial).

——(1991a). *Nietzsche: Volumes One and Two* (New York: HarperOne).

——(1991b). *Nietzsche: Volumes Three and Four* (New York: HarperOne).

——(1998). *Basic Concepts* (Indianapolis: Indiana University Press).

——(2001). *Poetry, Language, Thought* (New York: Harper Perennial).

——(2002). *Off the Beaten Track* (Cambridge: Cambridge University Press).

Hendel, C.W. (1953). The Subjective as a Problem: An Essay in Criticism of Naturalistic and Existential Philosophies, *The Philosophical Review* 62(3): 327–54.

Husserl, E. (1997). *Psychological and Transcendental Phenomenology and the Confrontation with Heidegger* (Dordrecht: Springer).

Jaspers, K. (1978). *Notizen zu Martin Heidegger* (Munich/Zürich: Piper).

Löwith, K. (1948). Heidegger: Problem and Background of Existentialism, *Social Research* 15(3): 345–69.

——(1994). *My Life in Germany Before and After 1933* (Chicago: University of Illinois Press).

——(1995). *Martin Heidegger and European Nihilism* (New York: Columbia University Press).

Mason, D.H. (1975). Time in Whitehead and Heidegger: Some Comparisons, *Process Studies* 5(2): 83–105.

Murray, M. (ed.) (1978). *Heidegger and Modern Philosophy: Critical Essays* (New Haven, CT: Yale University Press).

Nietzsche, F. (1954). *The Portable Nietzsche* (London: Penguin Books).

——(1968). *The Will to Power* (London: Vintage).

——(1974). *The Gay Science; With a Prelude in Rhymes and an Appendix of Songs* (London: Vintage Books).

Ott, H. (1993). *Martin Heidegger: A Political Life* (New York: Basic Books).

Pöggeler, O. (1999). *Heidegger in seiner Zeit* (Munich: Fink).

Rescher, N. (2000). *Process Philosophy: A Survey of Basic Issues* (Pittsburgh, PA: University of Pittsburgh Press).

Rice, D.H. (1989). Whitehead and Existential Phenomenology: Is a Synthesis Possible?, *Philosophy Today* 33(2): 183–92.

Richardson, W.J. (1967). *Heidegger: Through Phenomenology to Thought* (Netherlands: Martinus Nijhoff).

Safranski, R. (1999). *Martin Heidegger: Between Good and Evil* (Cambridge, MA: Harvard University Press).

Schrag, C.O. (1959). Whitehead and Heidegger: Process Philosophy and Existential Philosophy, *Dialectica* 13(1): 42–56.

Schürmann, R. (1987). *Heidegger on Being and Acting: From Principles to Anarchy* (Indianapolis: Indiana University Press).

Wolin, R. (1992a). *The Heidegger Controversy: A Critical Reader* (Cambridge, MA: MIT Press).

—— (1992b). *The Politics of Being: The Political Thought of Martin Heidegger* (New York: Columbia University Press).

—— (2003). *Heidegger's Children: Hannah Arendt, Karl Lowith, Hans Jonas, and Herbert Marcuse* (Princeton, NJ: Princeton University Press).

CHAPTER 21

··

MIKHAIL BAKHTIN (1895–1975)

··

ANN L. CUNLIFFE, JENNY HELIN, AND JOHN T. LUHMAN

21.1 LIFE

··

MIKHAIL MIKAILOVICH BAKHTIN was born in Oryol, Russia on 16 November 1895. He was first educated at home, and thanks to his German governess he early on learned German besides his native language which was Russian. His father made his living as a banker and his job required frequent transfers. The family moved to Orel, Vilnius, and finally to Odessa, where people on the streets spoke Russian, Polish, Lithuanian, Yiddish, and Hebrew. Bakhtin was therefore raised within a heterogeneous mix of cultures and languages, went on to study Latin and Greek, and developed an early interest in philosophy. Mikhail started his studies at Odessa University but then in 1914 followed his older brother to the University of Petrograd where he studied classics. After finishing his studies in 1918, he moved to Nevel in western Russia to work as a school teacher and to avoid the worst of the civil war period.

It was in Nevel that a group of intellectually minded friends formed what eventually became known as the 'Bakhtin circle'. They spent their time discussing literature, religion, and politics, gave lectures, demonstrated, and wrote manifests. The work by contemporary German philosophers, and especially neo-Kantianism and phenomenology, attracted their attention. Bakthin also developed an interest in physiology and science, reading for instance Einstein and Bohr. In this atmosphere Bakhtin continued to explore issues such as moral responsibility and aesthetics. Other prominent members of the circle included Valentin Vološhinov and P.N. Medvedev.

After moving to Vitebsk, Bakhtin married Elena Aleksandrovna Okolovich in 1921. He suffered from poor health throughout his life, being diagnosed with the bone disease osteomyelitis, which resulted in a leg amputation in 1938. Consequently, he had difficulties taking a normal job, a situation reinforced by his lack of political credentials under the new regime. Therefore from time to time, his wife had to support them both financially. His love was to simply sit at his desk to write, smoke, and drink tea.

Bakhtin achieved his first publication in 1919, a work on moral philosophy called *Art and Answerability*. While the majority of his writings were produced from the 1920s to the 1940s, his work only became more widely known with the advent of perestroika in the 1980s and the publication of his biography in 1984 by Katrina Clark and Michael Holquist. In 1924 he took a position at the Historical Institute in Leningrad, during which time he wrote many essays, such as *Author and Hero in Aesthetic Activity* and *Questions of Literature and Aesthetics* that were, unfortunately, not published until the end of his life. But in 1929 he did manage to publish a major work, *Problems of Dostoevsky's Creative Works* in which his concept of the dialogic relationship is discussed for the first time.

The late 1920s saw the beginnings of Stalin's political purges. Bakhtin was accused of participation with unofficial religious groups and sentenced to be exiled to Siberia for five years. Friends and supporters won an appeal on his behalf because of his poor health and he was sentenced instead to five years' exile in what is today Kazakhstan. Here he worked as a bookkeeper and wrote *Discourse in the Novel*. In 1936 he was allowed to move to teach at the Mordovian Pedagogical Institute in Saransk, but after a year was forced to resign—again due to Stalin's repression. From the late 1930s onwards, he wrote essays such as *The Novel of Development and its Significance in the History of Realism, Forms of Time and the Chronotope in the Novel, On the Philosophical Bases of the Human Sciences*, and *From the Prehistory of Novelistic Discourse*. Bakhtin also completed a book manuscript on the novel of education, but the only copy was lost during the German invasion in World War II.

By 1940 he was allowed to move to Moscow and with improved health wrote *Epic and Novel*. He also submitted his dissertation, later published as *Rabelais and His World*, to the Gorky Institute of World Literature. The war postponed the dissertation defense until the late 1940s. His dissertation, celebrating carnival, sexuality, and philosophical anarchism, created much consternation amongst the Moscow orthodox scholars. After great controversy, he was denied a doctorate but granted a 'candidate's degree' instead, and with this new degree in hand he moved back to Saransk to become chair of the General Literature Department at the Mordovian Pedagogical Institute. Here he wrote his essays *The Problem of Speech Genres* and *The Problem of the Text in Linguistics, Philology, and other Human Sciences*. In 1961 he retired for health reasons and may have all but disappeared from the public sphere if not for a group of graduate students at the Gorky Institute who uncovered his work on Dostoevsky. During the brief liberalization period of the 1960s, Bakhtin was able to revise his Dostoevsky piece and finally publish his Rabelais dissertation in 1965. From this coincidence, his status in the Soviet Union changed from an unknown to an intellectual cult figure. In 1969 he returned to Moscow where he died, aged 80, on 7 March 1975.

Controversy surrounds Bakhtin's publications for a number of reasons. Much of his early work lay hidden for years and was later deciphered by a group of students during the 1970s. Many stories circulate about lost, burnt, and hidden manuscripts and claims have been made that publications in the name of Voloshinov and Medvedev (part of the

Bakhtin circle) were written by Bakhtin. Today there are still doubts about Bakhtin's life and the philosophical tradition that nourished him. Documentary evidence about him is scant and much is unclear (Emerson, 1997). What we do know is that Bakhtin's scholarly heritage is impressively wide in scope, encompassing 'linguistics, psychoanalysis, theology, social theory, historical poetics, axiology, and philosophy of the person' (Clark and Holquist, 1984: preface). In his later years, looking back on his contribution, Bakhtin wrote:

> [O]ur analysis must be called philosophical mainly because of what it is not: it is not a linguistic, philological, literary or any other particular kind of analysis...On the one hand, a positive feature of our study is this: [it moves] in spheres that are liminal, i.e., on the borders of all the aforementioned disciplines, at their junctures and points of intersection. (Bakhtin, in *Estetika*, as cited in Holquist, 2002: 14)

21.2 INTELLECTUAL CONTRIBUTIONS

As in the quote just given, Bakhtin saw his work as a philosophical investigation spanning the boundary between disciplines. While it is extensive in scope and substance, we suggest that one of his main contributions lies in offering a different way of viewing sociality and its representation: this is a theme that pervades much of his writing. In this chapter we will address four specific (yet interrelated) aspects of his work that are of particular relevance to process thinking in organization studies: (1) the role of dialogue in the formation and understanding of social experience; (2) the nature of language as lived conversation and responsive utterances; (3) synthesizing the lived world and the world of reason; and (4) carnival and culture. We demonstrate how these four themes can help researchers to think processually about organizations and the way we represent organizational phenomena.

21.2.1 The Role of Dialogue in the Formation and Understanding of Social Experience

> Life by its very nature is dialogic. To live means to participate in dialogue: to ask questions, to hear, to respond, to agree, and so forth.
>
> (Bakhtin, 1984a: 40)

Just as Bakhtin's philosophical endeavour transcends boundaries between traditional disciplines, his philosophy of dialogue cannot be defined in a straightforward way. He uses the notion of dialogue in many different ways and contexts, but in its broadest sense he sees dialogue as integral to meaning and life. For Bakhtin:

> a person participates wholly and throughout his whole life [in dialogue]: with his eyes, lips, hands, soul, spirit, with his whole body and deeds. He invests his entire self in discourse, and this discourse enters into the dialogic fabric of human life, into the world symposium. (1984a: 293)

Thus, dialogue and dialogic relationships are ontological in that they are our way of being in the world. From his viewpoint, dialogue is not just linguistic moves in a conversation or text or an encounter between two or more individuals. Neither is it accurate to say we are 'entering into dialogue, as if the components that do so could exist in any other way' (Morson and Emerson, 1990: 50). Rather, dialogue is an ongoing struggle in which there is a continuous dynamic tension between monologic and dialogic forces (Bakhtin, 1981). This tension is preserved through a play of *centripetal* forces, which move towards unity, closings, and centralization (i.e. monologic) and *centrifugal* forces of openness and decentralization (i.e. dialogic). Since centripetal forces aim at centralizing and unifying meaning, they are necessary for sharing social life. At the same time, the stratifying and fragmenting processes of centrifugal forces incline towards multiplicity and fragmentation, which are needed for novelty to emerge since '[t]he dialogic encounter is an indeterminate social space which is prone to agonistic, hermeneutic, playful and other modes of relation. It is an ongoing occasion, with gaps, leaps and silences, always at the threshold of the next, other speaker, irreducible to one speaker, idea or language' (Gurevitch, 2000: 243). These centripetal and centrifugal forces do not end up in an ultimate resolution or equilibrium; rather, they are like the ebb and flow of the ocean, creating ongoing flux and movement in life (Steyaert, 2004).

This ongoing struggle is also seen in the way Bakhtin speaks of self as dialogical, *unfinalizable*, and always in relation to others (Jabri, 2004). He points out that while we may conceptualize life as a whole, we experience it as both given and yet-to-be-achieved in many once-occurrent events. In making our life our own, our feelings, expressions, intentions, and evaluations in unique moments—an *emotional-volitional* consciousness or tone—come into play (Bakhtin, 1986/1993). It is a volition that moves us into an embodied way of being in the world in which we are connected to others: we evaluate actions and events, anticipate responses and future actions and what it is we want to achieve. Thus, it is our emotional-volitional consciousness that relates us to others, to the context and the unique and unfinalizable situations and moments in which we find ourselves. Bakhtin also emphasizes that in deciding how to speak and respond to others, we are morally *answerable* to them for our acts of thinking, speaking, evaluating, and deciding—a relationship of answerability that can be translated into an ethical relationship:

> The emphasis is not on what the action results in, the end product of action, but rather on the ethical deed in its making, as an act in the process of creating or authoring an event that can be called a deed, whether the deed be a physical action, a thought, an utterance, or a written text. (Clark and Holquist, 1984: 63)

One example of this in organization studies is Cunliffe and Eriksen's (2011) study of US Federal Security directors. They draw on Bakhtin's work to move away from monologic views of leadership towards a dialogic way of thinking about leadership in which a leader holds herself/himself always in relation with, and therefore morally answerable to, others. Given this, leaders need to recognize the inherently polyphonic and heteroglossic nature of life and conversation.

21.2.2 The Nature of Language as Lived Conversation and Responsive Utterances

> Nothing conclusive has yet taken place in the world, the ultimate word of the world and about the world has not yet been spoken, the world is open and free, everything is still in the future and will always be in the future.
>
> (Bakhtin, 1984a: 166)

At the same time as Bakhtin writes about life as dialogic, he also views language and conversations as dialogical, since to him all human activity involves language. His departure from many of the linguistic philosophers lies in his emphasis on everyday, 'real-life', or prosaic, dialogic processes (Bakhtin, 1986). Bakhtin's view on dialogue differs from mundane usage, where dialogue is a synonym for two or more people talking to each other; rather, it is a differential relationship. Communicating dialogically means that in the moment of speaking our utterances and responses are both open to a myriad of possibilities (centrifugal forces) and shot through with speech genres and ideological ways of talking (centripetal forces). In other words, conversations are a 'dialogic interrelationship of utterances as a complex unity of differences' (Zappen, 2000: 10) in which our utterances are momentarily responsive to the words of each speaker *and also* take into consideration the context in which they are spoken.

This attention to living utterances is central because it is in the moment of speaking that the dialogic orientation of words creates particular meanings. As Bakhtin states, '[l]anguage lives only in the dialogic interaction of those who make use of it. Dialogic interaction is indeed the authentic sphere where language *lives*' (1984a: 183). This relational and momentary view on meaning-making underpinned by an understanding of what is happening at this moment, is a joint process by one and the other in the unfolding of utterances: where 'the word is a two-sided act ... determined equally by whose word it is and for whom it is meant' (Clark and Holquist, 1984: 15). At the same time, meaning has to be understood in relation to a greater whole—to social, historical, cultural, and institutional conditions. This is embodied in Bakhtin's notion of *heteroglossia*, which means that in 'any given time, in any given place, there will be a set of conditions—social, historical, meteorological, physiological—that will ensure that a word uttered in that place and at that time will have a meaning different than it would have under any other conditions' (Bakhtin, 1981: 428). In short, because living conversations are heteroglossic in nature (they have a particular combination of forces relating to the world of culture and the world of life), they are unique—accomplished only once—and never to be repeated. Thus, meaning-making is momentary as a dialogic interplay creates something unique, something that has never before been, and never will be in the future, exactly the same.

How bizarre it might sound, even an exact (in terms of words uttered) repetition of an utterance is something new and thereby different! Thus meaning-making is neither finalized nor a mental process taking place entirely in the head of the listener, but rather a dialogic process taking place between speaking subjects in the ongoing present moment. This is because living utterances are ongoing—a response to what others have said—spoken in the present but oriented to past conversations and the linguistic background, and to the anticipation of future responses. 'Any speaker is himself a respondent to a greater or lesser degree. He is not, after all, the first speaker to disturb the eternal silence of the universe... Any utterance is a link in a very complexly organized chain of other utterances' (Bakhtin, 1986: 68–9). Even though an utterance is not always followed by an immediate response, sooner or later it will be followed by a subsequent response or act because the word:

> In living conversations [is] directly, blatantly, oriented toward a future answer-word: it provokes an answer, anticipates it and structures itself in the answer's direction. Forming itself in the atmosphere of the already spoken, the word is at the same time determined by that which has not yet been said but which is needed and in fact anticipated by the answering word. Such is the situation in any living dialogue. (Bakhtin, 1981: 280)

This explains Bakhtin's emphasis on the complex nature of our social world. Iedema et al. (2004) take a dialogic approach to examine how a doctor-manager in an Australian hospital manages the many demands on him. Using a discourse analytic approach, they analyse talk in a meeting and interview to focus on the multiplicities, uncertainties, and contradictions in this social situation.

Bakhtin's concern with openness and dialogic potentiality can also be seen through his notion of *polyphony*. He argued that Dostoevsky's novels are characterized by polyphony since they allow for the interplay of a multiplicity of voices, truths, and consciousnesses. What is important in this respect is that voice, in the sense of uttering a perspective, is not a one-to-one correspondence between person and voice, since 'one perspective can be voiced by many persons, and one person can house several perspectives' (Linell, 2009: 117). These many voices contribute to the multitude of possible meanings in that they are not 'fitted harmoniously or systematically and integrated into some kind of neat whole, but rather combined but not merged, in the unity of the event' (Shotter, 2008: 516).

Out of Bakhtin's scholarly heritage, polyphony is perhaps the notion that has gained the most attention in organization studies and a number of organizational scholars have, in various ways, been calling for a polyphonic perspective in organizational research, for example, Hazen (1993, 1994), Mumby (1994), and Barry and Elmes (1997). In a 2008 special issue of the journal *Organization Studies*, it was noted that two streams have emerged around the work of polyphony: as a textual strategy in writing research and as a tool for analysing organizational practices (Belova et al., 2008). Indeed, Bate et al. (1997: 1167) argue that polyphony is 'ideally suited to organizations, which are by their very nature pluralistic and multi-vocal, and made up of a rich diversity of intersecting dialects, idioms and professional jargons (the "heteroglossia")'.

21.2.3 Synthesizing the Lived World and the World of Reason

> A theory needs to be brought into communion not with theoretical con-
> structions and conceived life, but with the actually occurring event of
> moral being—with practical reason.
>
> (Bakhtin, 1986/1993: 12)

Bakhtin's task of bridging the gap between lived experience and the ways in which we represent our experience unfolds in an unfinished manuscript of the early 1920s, eventually published in 1993 as *Toward a Philosophy of the Act*. His central concern, which we see playing through his later work, is to counter the prevailing concern with theoreticism, particularly in modern philosophy and the natural sciences, by examining the relationship between reason and lived experience.

By theoreticism he refers to the detachment of the cognition and sense of an act from the lived moment. This detachment and resulting objectification is problematic for Bakhtin because it refuses to recognize that the theoreticized world of culture is not the whole world (Bakhtin, 1986/1993). Not only does theoreticism fail to grasp 'living historicity' (Bakhtin, 1986/1993: 8), the uniqueness of experience and of each act, it is a world that is impossible to live in because it ignores our need to have our own unique practical orientation to our surroundings and to be able to live a life always in motion.

His definition of 'act' is central to his argument. An act is a deed that is performed throughout life as an 'uninterrupted performance' (Bakhtin, 1986/1993: 3). The content and sense of an act occurs in the lived experience of that act and in the entirety of its circumstances. Thus, acts are unique to those circumstances, are always becoming rather than finalized, and are therefore an integral part of the ongoing process of Being. It is in the moment of the act—of experience—that Bakhtin sees the once-occurrent unique lived experience of the moment come together with the objectified, theorized 'world of culture' (Bakhtin, 1986/1993: 2). When the 'great theoretical world' is assumed to be the 'small theoretical world' of experience (Bakhtin, 1986/1993: 11), the concept is not actualized, that is, it is rarely translated into my individual personal acts for which I'm answerable. The notion of answerability is key to the act. Bakhtin describes a 'two-sided answerability': for content (abstracted form the actor) and for Being (the act performed in the moment). It is this taking into account of the unity of both the factuality and the contextualized sense of the act that Bakhtin sees as the answerability or truth (*pravda*) of each act—'a truth both unitary and unique' (Bakhtin, 1986/1993: 29).

One aspect in which Bakhtin's work resonates with a process sensibility, and particularly a focus on emergence and flow, lies in this exposition of the philosophy of the act, because his concern (whether for discourse, conversation, or act) is for the living and lived nature of each. For example, Bakhtin finds linguistic analysis problematic, because by studying 'the relationships among elements within the language system' (1986: 118) real conversation, real people, and the responsive nature of understanding, meaning, and of life are ignored. Each of these issues must be studied in the circumstances of lived experience because Bakhtin believed there are no preconceived, pre-existing, or a priori structures, categories, or codes. In this sense, his position intersects with Bergson's because both scholars are keen to demonstrate the shortcomings of what Bakhtin terms 'theoreticism'. Bakhtin draws attention to emergence, accomplishment, and the 'once-occurrent' acts and conversations in ongoing life, Bergson (1911/1922) to the evolution and flux of life and the importance of action in leading to change. Both agree that by theorizing and abstracting life, we lose its aliveness and singularity. Theoretical thinking, historical description-exposition, and aesthetic intuition are objectifications that are not valuable if we focus on them without considering lived experience.

Both Bergson and Bakhtin are concerned with 'becoming': the unfinished and unspecified nature of experience. Yet Bakhtin is critical of Bergson's attempt to construct a philosophy of life because he says Bergson was still focused on theoreticism. 'For Bergson, reality is a continuation of consciousness, for Bakhtin it is true historical presentness' (Rudova, 1996: 178). For example, Bergson (1911/1929: 178) argues that perception is key because of the 'continuity of becoming which is reality itself, the present moment is constituted by the quasi instantaneous section effected by our perception in the flowing mass'. Bakhtin not only distinguishes between the *sense aspect* of cognition (the world of culture) and *the act* of cognition or seeing in the moment, but argues that Bergson's principal shortcoming 'is the indiscrimination, in his method, of the heterogeneous components of his conception' (Bakhtin, 1986/1993: 13).

21.2.4 Carnival and Culture

> All the symbols of the carnival idiom are filled with this pathos of change and renewal, with the sense of the gay relativity of prevailing truths and authorities.
>
> (Bakhtin, 1984b: 11)

In his work *Rabelais and His World* (1984b), Bakhtin examines the novels of French Renaissance writer François Rabelais (*c.*1494–1553) which cast a retrospective light on the development of folk culture. The study of folk culture, especially its humour and laughter, was important for Bakhtin, because '[a]ll the acts of the drama of world history were performed before a chorus of the laughing people. Without hearing this chorus we cannot understand the drama as a whole' (1984b: 474). To Bakhtin, Rabelais' work was the first, and greatest, to demonstrate this, and its manifestation in three distinct forms: ritual spectacles such as carnival pageants; comic verbal compositions in Latin or vernacular; and in various forms of foul or abusive language (1984b: 5). He argued that the official feasts of the Middle Ages (ecclesiastic, feudal, or state-sponsored) help us understand the 'whole drama', because they sanctioned the existing world order, asserting:

> all that was stable, unchanging, perennial: the existing hierarchy, the existing religious, political, and moral values, norms, and prohibitions. It was the triumph of a

truth already established, the predominant truth that was put forward as eternal and indisputable. (Bakhtin, 1984b: 9)

In contrast, the carnivals of the Middle Ages were moments of freedom from the established order, high culture, hierarchy, norms, and prohibitions. 'Carnival was the true feast of time, the feast of becoming, change, and renewal. It was hostile to all that was immortalized and completed' (1984b: 10). The carnival was removed from the sphere of the Roman Catholic Church, any medieval guild or caste, and therefore devoid of spirituality, piety, or dictates. It was a world turned upside down. But the carnival was not simply moments of celebration, escapism, and a license to experience bodily desires; it also embraced moments of shared collectivity as the crowd engaged in activities full of a continuity of time and the cycle of life and death. In these moments existed the potential for social transformation (Clark and Holquist, 1984). Over time, the language that occurred during carnival became more and more part of everyday life in the marketplaces of towns and villages. Those on the lower ends of the medieval social order developed a new form of language that was frank and free, without distance and etiquette. And more importantly, it was full of laughter, a laughter that is 'gay, triumphant, and at the same time mocking, deriding. It asserts and denies, it buries and revives' (Bakhtin, 1984b: 11–12). Carnival can also be a form of resistance, as illustrated by Boje (2001) in his study of carnival resistance in the form of protest and sit-ins to global capitalism. The humour and grotesque in carnival is further contemporized in Boje, Driver, and Cai's (2005) examination of McDonald's approach to strategy. In particular, they explore how the 'chronotopic artistic imagination' (Bakhtin, 1986: 46) of Ronald McDonald cartoons, the grotesque clownish bodies, the territorialization of (outer) space by McDonald buildings and symbols can be potentially linked to corporate expansion (Bakhtin, 1986: 202). They go on to suggest that it is this dialogic imagination that allows McDonald's to revitalize and transform its strategy.

The struggle between the official and unofficial cultures can also be seen in language, because language is 'penetrated by a system of values inseparable from living practice and class struggle' (Bakhtin, 1984b: 471) and can be presented as either *epic* texts or *novel* texts. Epic texts are finished and absolute descriptions of the past that recreate society's discourse, reinforcing and holding the past as sacred. Within the epic you find discourse already formatted, authoritative, and complete, because it is written as if everything is already over.

> Let us repeat: the important thing is not the factual sources of the epic, not the content of its historical events, nor the declarations of its authors—the important thing is…its reliance on impersonal and sacrosanct tradition, on a commonly held evaluation and point of view—which excludes any possibility of another approach—and which displays a profound piety toward…the language of tradition. (Bakhtin, 1981: 16–17)

The epic text is therefore the perpetuation of tradition and impersonality—of a commonly held view that excludes others and is beyond human touch, human activity, and change. Novel texts are about a contemporary, open, unfinished present and still evolving future. Novel texts also reflect a world in the making: 'There always remains an unrealized surplus of humanness; there always remains a need for the future and a place for this future must be found' (Bakhtin, 1981: 37). Thus, novel texts are not about a retrospective-based, finalized, routinized, and particular version of reality, but about emerging and open possibilities, improvisation not tradition. They are also based on the assumption that if we experience adventure, laughter, jealousy, and other human emotions and responses, then we can make sense of our world and lives.

21.3 THE FUTURE OF BAKHTIN IN ORGANIZATION STUDIES

We selected four themes from the rich heritage of Bakhtin's work as being particularly relevant to thinking processually about organizations: the role of dialogue in the formation and understanding of social experience; the nature of language as lived conversation and responsive utterances; synthesizing the lived world and the world of reason; and carnival and culture. Viewing these four themes together offers a distinct way to understand and represent sociality—a view of sociality that emphasizes the 'living' character of once-occurring events. Within this 'living character', processes of becoming are unique and emerge in the dialogic offering of otherness towards each other. In the words of Holquist (2002: 195), 'If Bakhtin is right, then nothing exists in itself and we live lives of buzzing, overlapping, endlessly ramifying simultaneity.'

What are the implications of this view of sociality? A significant invitation lies in how Bakhtin draws attention to different ways of thinking about our relationship with our world and the way we make sense of our experience. Its open-ended and fluid nature cannot be captured by abstract theorizing, which is after-the-fact. As we have said, for Bakhtin it is not enough to understand language in the sense of being already formed, structured, stable, and representational—as perceived by many linguistic philosophers; he believed that we need to explore how language is used and works in practical ways through utterances and exchanges made in particular contexts and moments. The enquiry into lived experience is therefore 'not a means for revealing, for bringing to the surface the already ready-made character of a person; no, in dialogue, a person not only shows himself outwardly, but he becomes for the first time that which he is...To be means to communicate dialogically' (Bakhtin, 1984a: 252). Shotter (2006: 600) aptly summarizes the difference in terms of *aboutness-thinking*, which is the traditional way of engaging in research projects from the outside (objectifying, making a study about something), contrasted with *withness-thinking*, where we are in 'contact with an other's living being, with their utterances, with their bodily expressions, with their words, their "works"'. In this interplay, where people can be moved by each other, differences can emerge which may open up new possibilities.

This change in orientation calls for rethinking how we go about our studies, where 'Instead of turning immediately, as we have in the past, to a study of how individuals come to know the objects and entities in the world around them, we must begin in quite a different way: we must study how … we can first develop and sustain between us different, particular ways of relating ourselves to each other' (Shotter, in Cunliffe, 2001: 355). In such a relational stance, just as Cunliffe (2001) notes in her study of management practices, the research project can become a two-way, emerging embodied process between the researcher and the people in the field.

In line with his critique of theoreticism, Bakhtin finds linguistic analysis problematic because it is often retrospective, monologic, and out of the context and moment of utterance. He argues that it is not enough to study language in the sense of already formed, structured, stable, and representational texts, because the mode of data collection, analysis, and writing are implicitly or explicitly monologic (i.e. based on the researcher's identification, selection, and interpretation of the discourse) and the dialogic nature of the encounter is lost. The problem with theoretism is that it falls short in recognizing the 'eventness of the event' (Bakhtin, 1986), or the 'living' character of becoming, since it confines social worlds to predefined, closed structures. This can be seen in studies using discourse analysis and narrative approaches, which assume that language is infused with centripetal forces, which results in the production of epic texts about organizations and organizational life.

To move beyond theoretism means we need to think about the way we identify, interpret, and write lived experience—as emerging in the flow of lived moments and conversations. This means questioning, for example, whether the discourses and narratives we choose to foreground in our work are monologic narratives that create restricted visions, and fix and constrain our understanding of organizational reality. It requires us to not only think about the organizational phenomenon and processes we identify, but also to think about our research design and methodology, its underlying epistemological and ontological presuppositions and their influence (Cunliffe, 2011). A dialogic approach involves finding alternative styles/plots/moral lessons in organizational discourse (the novel text over the epic text), finding marginalized voices (heteroglossia over monologic language), and looking for habits of thought combined with legitimizing objects and knowledge that create restricted visions. This means exploring the complexity in the relational nexus between participants, interpreters, and various texts in use, utterances, and the emergence of unpredictable discourses.

Because for Bakhtin dialogics means emergence and openness, researchers need to be 'sensitive to movement' (Weick, 2004: 410), where we should study *conversing*, not (finalized, already finished) conversation, and organizing rather than organization. To illuminate this idea, Weick calls for us to adopt Taylor and Van Every's (2000) image of crystal and smoke.

> Organization resides between smoke and crystal just as it resides between conversation and text in discourse analysis and just as it resides between redundancy and complexity in everyday life. Organization is talked into existence when portions of

smoke-like conversation are preserved in crystal-like texts that are then articulated by agents speaking on behalf of an emerging collectivity. Repetitive cycles of texts, conversations and agents define and modify one another and jointly organize every-day life. (Weick, 2004: 406)

Whilst essentially taking a cognitive rather than a dialogical approach, Weick's emphasis on the interweaving of conversing and text offers a way into thinking about dialogic research: what are the crystal-like texts weaving through the everyday utterances of organizational members, and how do everyday utterances modify or transform texts?

A focus on diachronic utterances (i.e. over time) can give a sense of retrospective and prospective sensemaking—but to avoid this being monologic and epic, we need to capture the polyphony of organizational voices. This means uncovering the diversity of organizational members' voices and letting those voices speak in the written text, which requires research that is longitudinal and participatory in nature, and works on two fronts. There must be a highlighting of discourse as utterances in specific contexts and practices, and an examining of discourse as broader cultural and historically situated language systems shaping social reality. This involves (a) conversations of various organizational members: one-to-one conversations, discussions in meetings, gossip, and so on; and (b) visual and written expressions, both individual and official stories, pronouncements, press releases, chronicle, reports, historical texts, and so on. The idea is not capturing what is really going on in the organization by codifying conversation and discourse, but to highlight the polyphony of organizational life by exploring the *relational nexus* of discourse and action: counterposing conversations, narratives, organizational texts, and stories to explore tensions, connections, opposing views, silences, incoherencies, 'official' and 'unofficial' language, interruptions such as who speaks and who doesn't, who offers, who argues, and who accepts. This is with a view to exploring not just what is said, but how, by whom, when, in what context, and how this might change over time. In this way, becomingness, openness, and context are emphasized (i.e. the movement of smoke as in Cunliffe and Coupland, 2012).

In relation to this Bakhtin suggests a dynamic interplay between 'insideness' and 'out-sideness' for the researcher, where a greater understanding of each other and our social worlds can emerge. The reasoning is that understanding another's culture—another's life world—takes a dialogical process in which

[a] certain entry as a living being into a foreign culture, the possibility of seeing the world through its eyes, is a necessary part of the process of understanding it; but if this were the only aspect of this understanding, it would be duplication and would not entail anything new or enriching…In order to understand, it is immensely important for the person who understands to be located outside the object of his or her creative understanding—in time, in space, in culture. (Bakhtin, 1986: xiii)

Thus, he calls for a dialogical back-and-forth manner of engaging with the people in the living moment. In this process it is essential to feel our way into their lives, their ways of thinking and experiencing, but also to take in the otherness offered to us from our own unique position. As a way of feeling her way around, Helin (2011) suggests we can make room for the other in the field through compassion.

Inevitably, because of the diachronic and synchronic nature of a dialogic approach, the researcher must be immersed in organizational life (in the moment) and must therefore be an ethnographer, but not an ethnographer with expert and authorial voice. Bate (1997: 1167) suggests that polyphony is not just about inserting the many voices of organizational members in the research, but rethinking the role of the researcher—'polyphonist is back room boy not principal actor, orchestrator not conductor'. This means the researcher is neither the expert observer nor the interpreter of the lives of others, rather the presenter of organizational voices to readers. Yet, as Bate says, this does not mean *free market polyphony*; some connections have to be made even though those connections might be disconnected and/or reconnected by others in later moments. What seems important is to balance the 'confident walk over ice' without being dragged down into the disorienting depths. Dialogics is not about encoding/decoding texts, it is about understanding living responsive interactions and utterances and meaning in relation to the moment of speaking and to a greater whole—to social, historical, cultural, and institutional conditions. This means examining how language is used and works in practical ways through utterances and exchanges made in particular contexts. By focusing on this relational nexus we can begin to explore movements, ideologies, struggles, resistances, and how people coordinate (or otherwise) their activities to move on. This therefore emphasizes the becomingness and heteroglossic nature of organizing and of researching.

Finally, Bakhtin's work could potentially stimulate new thinking around writing and how to portray lived experience in the organizational everyday. Ever since the crisis of representation hit studies of organizations in the early 1990s, people studying organizations have struggled with how to 'write up' and communicate their studies to reflect the increased awareness of the failures of 'scientific' texts. Here is an area where Bakthin's work has much to contribute, especially in relation to the question how a researcher can avoid a retrospective production of a coherent epic text in favour of a more novelistic text. The sense of the novel is inconclusive and emergent, for it demands continuation and no final word, and its goal is rethinking and re-evaluating the future. The problem with a closed, finished, and in other ways monological text is that it 'pretends to be the ultimate word'; 'finalized and deaf to the other's response, does not expect it and does not acknowledge in it any decisive force' (Bakhtin, 1984a: 293). That is problematic from a Bakhtinian perspective: 'in contrast to reader reception theory, which is usually concerned with how readers interpret the texts *after* they are made, Bakhtin's dialogic model represents readers as shaping the utterance *as* it is being made' (Morson and Emerson, 1990: 129, emphasis in original). This is a polyphonic way of understanding a text, in which a multitude of different, even competing, meanings of a text is possible. This understanding of meaning-making as momentary and performed by the reader in interaction with the text at a specific moment in time has certain implications for how to think about writing. That is why writing should not only be reduced to stabilization attempts by the construction of epic texts, but rather to a struggle in the dynamics of stabilization and destabilization, between the known and not known, in a dialogical interplay where 'what is' is not totally fixed but rather open to engagement and movement beyond the immediate reach. In short, the text has to live on the boundary between what is made and what is still in the making, in such a way that it provides space for the reader's own response in reading. This means to transcend the search for ultimate answers and prepackaged contributions and, instead, pay attention to how it is possible to create meetings between voices—voices of those in the field, of the reader, and of the author.

References

Bakhtin, M.M. (1981). *The Dialogic Imagination: Four Essays by M.M. Bakhtin*, ed. M. Holquist, trans. C. Emerson and M. Holquist (Austin: University of Texas Press).

—— (1984a). *Problems of Dostoevsky's Poetics*, ed. and trans. C. Emerson (Manchester: Manchester University Press).

——(1984b). *Rabelais and His World*, trans. H. Iswolsky (Bloomington, IN: Indiana University Press).

—— (1986). *Speech Genres and Other Late Essays*, trans. V.W. McGee (Austin: University of Texas Press).

—— (1986/1993). *Toward a Philosophy of the Act*, trans. V. Liapunov, ed. V. Liapunov and M. Holquist (Austin: University of Texas Press).

Barry, D. and Elmes, M. (1997). Strategy Retold: Toward a Narrative View of Strategic Discourse, *Academy of Management Review* 22(2): 429–52.

Bate, S.P. (1997). Whatever Happened to Organizational Anthropology? A Review of the Field of Organizational Ethnography and Anthropological Studies, *Human Relations* 50(9): 1147–75.

—— Pye, A.J., Purcell, J., and Kahn, R. (1997). *Changing the Culture of a Hospital*. Working Paper, School of Management, University of Bath.

Belova, O., King, I., and Sliwa, M. (2008). Introduction: Polyphony and Organization Studies: Mikhail Bakhtin and Beyond, *Organization Studies* 29(4): 493–500.

Bergson, H. (1911/1922). *Creative Evolution*, trans. A. Mitchell (London: Macmillan and Co).

—— (1911/1929). *Matter and Memory*, trans. N.M. Paul and W.S. Palmer (London: George Allen and Irwin).

Boje, D.M. (2001). Carnivalesque Resistance to Global Spectacle: A Critical Postmodern Theory of Public Administration, *Administrative Theory & Praxis* 23(3): 431–58.

—— Driver, M., and Cai, Y. (2005). Fiction and Humor in Transforming McDonald's Narrative Strategies, *Culture and Organization* 11(3): 195–208.

Clark, K. and Holquist, M. (1984). *Mikhail Bakhtin* (Cambridge, MA: Harvard University Press).

Cunliffe, A.L. (2001). Managers as Practical Authors: Reconstructing Our Understanding of Management Practice, *Journal of Management Studies* 38: 351–71.

——(2011). Crafting Qualitative Research: Morgan and Smircich 30 Years On, *Organizational Research Methods* 14: 647–73.

—— and Coupland, C. (2012). From Hero to Villain to Hero: Making Experience Sensible Through Embodied Narrative Sensemaking, *Human Relations* 65: 63–88.

——and Eriksen, M. (2011). Relational Leadership, *Human Relations* 64: 1425–49.

Emerson, C. (1997). *The First Hundred Years of Mikhal Bakhtin* (Princeton, NJ: Princeton University Press).

Gurevitch, Z. (2000). Plurality in Dialogue: A Comment on Bakhtin, *Sociology* 34(2): 243–63.

Hazen, M.A. (1993). Towards Polyphonic Organization, *Journal of Organizational Change Management* 6(5): 15–22.

——(1994). Multiplicity and Change in Persons and Organizations, *Journal of Organizational Change Management* 7(5): 72–81.

Helin, J. (2011). Living Moments in Family Meetings: A Process Study in the Family Business Context, JIBS Dissertation Series No. 70, Jönköping International Business School, Sweden.

Holquist, M. (2002). *Dialogism,* 2nd edn (New York: Routledge).

Iedema, R., Degeling, P., Braithwaite, J., and White, L. (2004). It's An Interesting Conversation I'm Hearing: The Doctor as Manager, *Organization Studies* 25(1): 15–33.

Jabri, M. (2004). Change as Shifting Identities: A Dialogic Perspective, *Journal of Organizational Change Management* 17(6): 566–77.

Linell, P. (2009). *Rethinking Language, Mind, and World Dialogically: Interactional and Contextual Theories of Human Sense-Making* (Charlotte, NC: Information Age Publishing, Inc).

Morson, G.S. and Emerson, C. (1990). *Mikhail Bakhtin. Creation of a Prosaics* (Stanford, CA: Stanford University Press).

Mumby, D. (1994). Review of 'Cultures in Organizations' by Joanne Martin, *Academy of Management Review* 19(1): 156–9.

Rudova, L. (1996). Bergsonism in Russia: The case of Bakhtin, *Neophilologus 80*: 175–88.

Shotter, J. (2006). Understanding Process From Within: an Argument for 'Withness'-Thinking, *Organization Studies* 27(4): 585–604.

——(2008). Dialogism and Polyphony in Organizing Theorising in Organization Studies: Action Guiding Anticipations and the Continuous Creation of Novelty, *Organization Studies* 29(4): 501–24.

Steyaert, C. (2004). The Prosaics of Entrepreneurship, in D. Hjorth and C. Steyaert (eds), *Narrative and Discursive Approaches in Entrepreneurship* (Northampton, MA: Edward Elgar Publishing): 8–21.

Taylor, J.R. and Van Every, E.J. (2000). *The Emergent Organization: Communication as its Site and Surface* (Mahwah, NJ: Lawrence Erlbaum Associates).

Weick, K.E. (2004). A Bias for Conversation: Acting Discursively in Organizations, in D. Grant, C. Hardy, C. Oswick, and L. Putnam (eds), *The Sage Handbook of Organizational Discourse* (Thousands Oaks, CA: Sage): 405–12.

Zappen, J.P. (2000). Mikhail Bakhtin (1895-1975), in M.G. Moran and M. Ballif (eds), *Twentieth-Century Rhetoric and Rhetoricians: Critical Studies and Sources* (Westport, CT: Greenwood Press): 7–20.

CHAPTER 22

JACQUES-MARIE-ÈMILE LACAN (1901–1981)

NANCY HARDING

> If you're doing your job and delivering on things it's almost like it feels like you get to a certain point and you get a tap on the shoulder by the organization . … It's almost like the organization is taking a view as to when you're ready for that next step every step of the way really. Or it certainly feels like that to me … it certainly feels like the organization is kind of keeping an eye on me.
>
> (Middle manager talking about the implementation of talent management, in Harding et al., forthcoming)

WHAT IS this 'organization' that can both keep an eye on managers and tap them on the shoulder? To this speaker it appears to be an independent, anthropomorphized entity. In this chapter I explore the contribution of Lacanian theory to understanding how speaker and this (seeming) entity with an eye and a finger co-emerge. Lacanian theory illuminates how the unconscious and 'organization' are inevitably caught up in each other. Lacan took Freud's theories, subjected them to an inspirational rereading, and thus contributed in a major way to post-structuralist theory.

Organization studies came late to reading Lacan compared with other disciplines, but a substantial and growing body of work now interprets various aspects of organizational life through a Lacanian lens. These include, for example, studies of entrepreneurship (Jones and Spicer, 2005); identity (Driver, 2009); power and resistance (Roberts, 2005); embodied subjectivity (Driver, 2008); envy (Vidaillet, 2007); organizational burnout (Vanheule and Verhaeghe, 2004; Vanheule et al., 2003); organizational dynamics (Arnaud, 2002); public administration (Fotaki, 2009; McSwite, 1997). A special issue of the journal *Organization* (Contu et al., 2010) applied Lacanian ideas of desire, enjoyment, and lack to organizational issues; an edited book explores Lacan in more depth (Cederstrom and Hoedemaekers, 2010). Finally, there has been a limited application of Lacan's thesis on gender (Fotaki and Harding, 2013; Kenny, 2009). There has as yet been little exploration of the potential of Lacanian theory for process theories of organizations (see Harding, 2007, for an early attempt).

Feminist and Marxist theorists were the first to use Lacanian ideas in the English-speaking world. Žižek's interpretation, popular in Lacanian organization studies, is the most influential reading in Marxist-Lacanian theory. My own interest in Lacan's work was stimulated by Judith Butler's guarded and critical application of his work to her thesis on the performative constitution of the (gendered) subject (1990, 1993). I therefore approached Lacan via gender theorists' interpretations, readings that deviate in some important ways from those inspired by Žižek. My understanding of Lacan therefore has a somewhat different focus from that of scholars schooled in a Žižekian interpretation, in which the concept of the phallus is largely conspicuous by its (apparent) absence. Lacanian organization theory is influenced largely by his notions of lack/desire/*jouissance*, with the three registers of the Symbolic, the Imaginary, and the Real influential to a greater or lesser extent (these are defined and discussed later). Feminist interpretations are dominated by Lacan's theory of sexuation (Lacan, 1982, 1998a), the Gaze (of the Other) (see, especially, the seminal (*sic*) paper by Laura Mulvey, 1975), and, of course, a critique of his (seeming) elevation of the phallus (see Fotaki and Harding, 2013, for a discussion) to the position of that which determines what can and cannot be spoken. There is much in feminist readings of Lacan that is yet to be taken up by organization theorists, such as his five theses on aggression (see Brennan, 1993).

It is perhaps not surprising that Lacanian theorists should mine a variety of rich seams in his work because his style of argumentation was obscure and open to multiple interpretations. His seminars (in contrast to his *Écrits*) come to us via notes and summaries made by listeners; his ideas evolved throughout his long career; and Lacan was not consistent in the use of his own terms. Most importantly, Lacan aimed to explore unconscious wishes and desires that are, by definition, outside of language: how then can they be described in language? Lacan's answer was that language should echo in some ways the manner in which the unconscious functions, hence his use of a convoluted style of writing, one that is 'psychotic' (Benvenuto and Kennedy, 1986), and full of puns, obscure or hidden references, double meanings, and so on. He wished that this style would encourage listeners and readers to engage with a text as if in a therapy session where limitations of meaning are confronted. Thus to read Lacan requires that one explore the effect the language has upon the self as it reads (Homer, 2005) and thus engage in an intense reflection upon the self.

Relatedly, to use Lacan's name as a fount of authority is to contradict Lacan's teachings concerning, variously, the name-of-the-Father,[1] the subject-supposed-to-know,[2] the discourses of the university and the master,[3] the phallus'[4] claim to be the master signifier, and so on. We must not claim to be a 'true' interpreter of his texts because that would be to attempt to dictate what knowledge *is* and what can be knowable. Lacan warned against such an endeavour.

What follows therefore must be a singular interpretation, one that inevitably says as much about the chapter's author as she attempts to say about Lacan. Marianna Fotaki and I have explored feminist interpretations of Lacan in a paper whose first version railed against Lacanian organization theorists' attempt to dictate a singular reading and thus to wield for themselves the power of the phallus (the master signifier, that dictates what is speakable). Wise reviewers pointed out that we were doing that very thing ourselves, i.e. dictating how Lacan *should* be read. To avoid this we found we needed to occupy the position of the hysteric[5] (Fotaki and Harding, 2013). This chapter therefore is avowedly hysterical, a hysteria arising in part from having to use the discourses of the master and the university ('this is how Lacan *must be* read') in order to write about Lacan for an *Oxford Handbook*.

I will next give a brief overview of Lacan's life, provide a somewhat superficial summary of his work, and then delve more deeply into some of the major aspects of his oeuvre. That returns us to the speaker whose words opened this chapter, who speaks for all of us in our desire to be recognized by a fantasized Other upon which we put the label 'organization'. I use a reflexive perspective, exploring how working on this chapter co-constitutes both self and 'university', that is, *two* 'fluid, amorphous, social phenomena in space-time' that are 'an indistinguishable mass of vague interactions and experiences' (Chia, 1998: 4) operating at both conscious and unconscious levels.

22.1 LACAN: A MASCULINE SPEAKING SUBJECT

Jacques-Marie-Èmile Lacan was a hugely controversial Parisian psychoanalyst who attracted both adulation and loathing, and scandal and crisis. He was regarded by some as a guru and by others as a charlatan. From a comfortable, middle-class, Catholic background, he developed a passion for philosophy while still at school. Trained as a psychiatrist, in the 1930s he encountered both surrealism and the writings of Sigmund Freud; their joint influence led him to profoundly change his work. Presumed to be politically left-wing, he voiced support for the student demonstrations of 1968 but later warned that revolutions led to nothing more than the replacement of one master with another.

Lacan's work is often divided between the early phase (up to 1953) and a mature phase from 1953 until his death. It was in 1953 that Lacan was elected president of the Société Française de Psychanalyse (SPF), and in the same year he started giving the seminars in which he outlined his ideas to an audience that eventually grew to 1,000 participants and included intellectual celebrities. In 1963 Lacan was banned from the SPF, which wanted membership of the International Psychoanalytic Association, a desire that could be fulfilled only if the controversial Lacan was removed. He founded his own study group that grew to become L' École Freudienne de Paris, and at the invitation of Louis Althusser set up a base at L' École Normal Superieure. Always controversial, but hugely popular, he dissolved L' École in 1980 because, in his view, it had become too Lacanian and had lost its Freudian roots.

Throughout, Lacan followed his aim of returning to Freud, rereading his works through such disciplines as philosophy (notably Plato, Kant, Hegel, and Heidegger), mathematics, and, most influentially, anthropology (Lévi-Strauss) and linguistics

(Saussure). Saussure's influence led to Lacan's best-known formula that 'The unconscious is structured as a language' (Žižek, 2006: 3). The unconscious, in this formulation, is not the repository of irrational instincts but something that talks and thinks, using its own grammar and logic (Žižek, 2006: 3). It is not located 'inside' individuals but is the effect upon subjects of a trans-individual symbolic order (Homer, 2004: 69).

How may management and organization theorists approach Lacan: as a psychoanalyst or a philosopher? We undoubtedly cannot use his ideas to undertake therapy with/in organizations, but we can use his ideas *theoretically* (Frosh, 2003), as a form of 'wild philosophy' (Bond, 2009), or indeed as a historian of the ego's era (Brennan, 1993). Lacan *qua* philosopher explores how 'reality' is constituted, notably through the effects of speech and language on the human condition (Nobus, 2000: xiii).

For Nobus (2000), Lacan's work has a global theoretical framework that must be understood before any of the other aspects of his writings can be grasped. I will firstly, writing from the position of the hysteric, summarize this framework in the form of a story. One cannot sustain one's self within only one of Lacan's four discourses: later in the chapter I will inevitably circle back through the discourses of the master and the university—attempting to dictate how Lacan *should* be understood (Fotaki and Harding, 2012).

22.2 THE EVERYDAY TRAGEDY OF BEING A SUBJECT: A LACANIAN (BAD FAIRY) TALE

A baby is born. It is nothing but a sea of consciousness (Klein, 1987) filled with demands, dread, and desires. It does not recognize that its caretakers are separate from itself, it is unaware of any boundaries to its body, even that it has a body. All there is are sensations. (Let's call this the Real: a place outside language, where there are no signifiers, signifieds, or signs.) Slowly, slowly, it starts to identify the linkages between signifier, signified, and sign—it is entering the Symbolic, where signs and symbols exist that allow objects to be named. But there is as yet no sense of self, no boundaries between a not-yet-emerged 'I/me' and others. Until one day, the child, perhaps struggling to pull itself to its feet, sees its image reflected in a mirror or in another person's face and recognizes itself. That is ME!!! There is jubilation. I exist as an I. But of course that I does not exist—it is a mirror image, a not-me. But the child *imagines* it is an I or a me. This is the Imaginary: I believe I am a whole person; that there is an 'I' that exists. This is a sexed I or me—but the sex that I am is imposed on me from outside, and I have to learn how to constitute a self that can pass as a male or a female speaking subject.

But the subject is troubled: that 'me' is outside 'me' (in the mirror) so who therefore is in here, inside, who is this I? What happened to that wonderful sense, before I had language, that I was complete, whole? Now begins a lifelong process of desiring something I can never find, something I lost when I entered the Symbolic even though I had not possessed it before losing it, and whose absence leaves me with a fundamental sense of lack. I know neither what I desire nor what I lack, I know only a constant, unquenchable desire for something I must seek, my *objet petit a*.[6] But the purpose of my desire is desire itself, because without a desire that propels me forward I cease to exist.

I thus work at constructing a self, one that consists of an ideal ego or the self I would like to be, but I also construct an ego-ideal, a big Other,[7] that I try to impress. I always fail in this endeavour of impressing that Other because of the intervention of my superego, or the Other, in its revengeful, sadistic, and punishing aspect. I try to please it but do not know what it wants. I am judged: a voice constantly whispers in my ear, coming at me from outside, from the big Other, that tells me how inadequate I am. I desire to be a fantasized, imaginary, ideal self, but I am a subject linked to the Symbolic so I can never be that person I yearn to be.

This Lacanian tale is of a subject that ceaselessly works on itself to construct a self that is impossible to construct. It has many affinities with process theories of organizations: we see fantasized selves in fantasized locations. This is where I, as hysteric, come up against myself. I recognize that 'the organization' has no existence as such, but at the same time I desire its recognition of me so that I can know of my own existence.

But the ratchet turns and the hysteric is overcome by the master and the university—rather than outlining a bad fairy tale, I turn now to exploring in a more 'philosophical' way some major aspects of Lacan's work. For each, I will explore one 'seminal' paper from organization studies that relates Lacan's ideas to organizations.

22.3 THE THREE REGISTERS OF THE IMAGINARY, THE SYMBOLIC, AND THE REAL

Lacan's early work focused on the Imaginary, his attention switching to the Symbolic in the decade following delivery of the Rome Report in 1953, with the Real a third term whose role and definition changed over the years. Although 'profoundly heterogenous', they were linked together by Lacan in a seminar in 1974–1975 (Sheridan, Translator's Note, in Lacan, 1998b).

22.3.1 The Imaginary

The Imaginary register is first encountered in the 'mirror stage' of the child's development, but continues to inform subjectivities throughout life. The mirror stage is an 'identification', that is, 'the transformation that takes place in a subject when he assumes an image' (Lacan, 1977: 2). Only seven pages long, 'The Mirror Stage' is worth exploring in depth.

Lacan discusses a young infant who cannot yet walk, stand, or even sit up unaided, and who, unaware of a body as such and thus incapable of motor coordination, feels animated by turbulent movements. But the infant sees its reflection and experiences jubilation as it recognizes its self as an I. This form would have to be called the Ideal-I, Lacan writes, but

> this form situates the agency of the ego, before its social determination, in a fictional direction, which will always remain irreducible for the individual alone, or rather, which will only rejoin the coming-into-being *(le devenir)* of the subject asymptotically, whatever the success of the dialectical syntheses by which he must resolve as I his discordance with his own reality. (1977: 2)

That is, the image reflected back at the infant is a fictional one—giving the impression of a whole, coordinated subject with which the infant can identify, an impression that belies the infant's then reality (she cannot stand unaided). This fiction or 'mirage' of a whole self will inform the subject throughout its life. Importantly, the infant has found itself outside its self, in a form that is 'certainly more constituent than constituted' (1977: 2). This Gestalt, this mirage, 'symbolizes the mental permanence of the I, at the same time as it prefigures its alienating destination' (1977: 2) within a

> temporal dialectic [that] decisively projects the formation of the individual into history. The *mirror stage* is a drama whose internal thrust is precipitated from insufficiency to anticipation—and which manufactures for the subject, caught up in the lure of spatial identification, the succession of phantasies that extends from a fragmented body-image to a form of its totality that I shall call orthopaedic—and, lastly, to the assumption of the armour of an alienating identity, which will mark with its rigid structure the subject's entire mental development. (1977: 4)

At the end of the mirror stage the 'specular I' is deflected into the 'social I' (Lacan, 1977: 5), inaugurating 'a dialectic that will henceforth link the I to socially elaborated situations' (Lacan, 1977: 5). Hegel's master/slave dialectic is influential here: the specular I seeks acknowledgement of itself 'through the desire of the other' (1977: 5) (that is, it seeks the reliving of that inaugurative jubilation when it first recognized itself), but because this I is alienated, is outside itself, it is aggressive to the other (1977: 6) because of an 'imaginary servitude' to the other (1977: 7).

Exemplary in organization studies' use of the Imaginary is perhaps Roberts' (2005) thesis that through the Imaginary I identify both with the gaze of the Other that (I imagine) looks at me, and the self I imagine myself to be. The Imaginary instigates that desire for control (over the other) that informs managerial practices. This is because 'the narcissistic identification with the gaze of the other—the seeking and finding of myself in the gaze of the other—serves as an explanation of the dynamics of both love and aggression' (Roberts, 2005: 631). I need the desire of the other if I am to exist, but because I am dependent on that gaze I also hate that desire. With regard to organizations, Roberts suggests we have a fantasized organizational ideal that we cannot live up to, so we berate ourselves: 'The ideal provides the ground with which conscience can be turned aggressively back upon the self' (Roberts, 2005: 636). This is the very organization to which we look for recognition, and thus selfhood, so to feel ourselves denied that recognition is to feel despair. It necessitates a 'strong interest' in controlling both self and others, such that the social becomes a 'domain solely of a struggle for control in the interests of the ego' (Roberts, 2005: 637). We are thus vulnerable to organizational mechanisms of disciplinary power. Only through letting go of the ego, of the self we are striving to be(come), can we resist organizational demands.

At its simplest level, the organization, in the Imaginary, can be regarded as a fantasy that has great power over the subject. As a fantasy it exists only in the psyche, but in that location it allows identification and making of an agonistic self.

22.3.2 The Symbolic

In contrast to Lacan's neat summary of the Imaginary in one lecture, his development of the theory of the Symbolic is dotted throughout several seminars beginning with the Rome seminar of 1953 (Lacan, 2006). Now the influence of Lévi-Strauss and Saussure are palpable. Frustration follows any desire to summarize 'the Symbolic' or grasp its meaning: the Rome seminar is long and discursive. But let us start at page 65, where Lacan states that 'it is the world of words that creates the world of things', so that 'Man speaks, then, but it is because the symbol has made him man.' A discussion of the laws of kinship and reference to the Oedipus complex then leads Lacan to write that 'what the subject can know of his unconscious participation in the movement of the complex structures of marriage ties, by verifying the symbolic effects in his individual existence of the tangential movement towards incest that has manifested itself ever since the coming of a universal community' (1999: 66). This leads to a statement on page 67 that 'It is in the *name of the* father that we must recognize the support of the symbolic function which, from the dawn of history, has identified this person with the figure of the law' (emphasis in original). He points out that the subject would be 'annihilated' under the weight of such huge pressures 'if desire did not preserve its part in the interferences and pulsations that the cycles of language cause to converge on him' (1999: 68). Such that

> what is at stake in an analysis is the advent in the subject of that little reality that this desire sustains in him with respect to the symbolic conflicts and imaginary fixations as the means of their agreement . . . From this point on it will be seen that the problem is that of the relations between speech and language in the subject. (1999: 68)

In a few brief passages Lacan therefore specifies language as symbols that constitute subjects within historico-cultural settings, but these are subjects necessarily driven by desire that is not only instigated by the Symbolic but will sustain that Symbolic. An added complication is the distinction between speech and language. I could spend this entire chapter analysing these four pages, especially as (for current purposes) they hint at ways in which to understand how individuals are caught up in the propulsion that constitutes 'the organization'. No doubt my interpretation would differ from other readers'—the quotes given illuminate the struggles and intellectual frissons experienced when attempting to engage with Lacan's work, but also how Lacan's language is mimetic of an analytical encounter; we have to do hard work in order to develop understanding, so each person's unconscious influences their reading.

There is surprisingly little discussion of the Symbolic in Lacanian management and organization studies. Stavrakis (2008) discusses it briefly. It is, he writes, a network into which we are born that has a far more important structuring role than the Imaginary. We must submit to it because only through submitting to the laws of language can we become subjects: we inhabit and are inhabited by language (2008: 1044). The laws of language are symbolic Law, embodied by the Name-of-the-Father, or the agent of symbolic castration. Castration is that which occurs on entering into language—the subject is radically split between a repleteness, a captivating *jouissance*[8] it experienced outside language, and the never-finished self that emerges within the Symbolic. But the Other (the Symbolic) cannot fulfil that lack, and indeed produces it, so the Other is also a lacking Other. However, Stavrakakis (2008) argues, subjects are willing to do whatever may be necessary to repress or disavow the lack in the Other (2008: 1045). Willing to subordinate themselves within conditions of voluntary servitude, subjectification within the Symbolic produces organizational subjects riven in two, suffering lack, and colluding in their own abjection.

22.4 THE REAL

The Real, apparent in Lacan's work in the 1950s, became increasingly important in succeeding decades. Its meaning and position shifted until it became the central category in Lacan's late work. Reality and 'the Real' are very different concepts: 'reality' is associated with the Symbolic order; whereas the Real is that unsymbolizable something that exists at the Symbolic's limit. The Real both undermines symbolic reality and makes it possible. Lacan understood the real in the 1950s as an undifferentiated mass that precedes language, but later argued that its being outside the Symbolic renders definition impossible; suffice it to say that it is associated with trauma, or pain that cannot be put into language (Homer, 2005).

Related to the Real are fantasy, lack, and *jouissance*. Fantasy includes daydreams and foundational myths that structure psychic life (e.g. the 'fact' of two distinct sexes; the 'fact' that managers and staff are distinct). The subject attempts to cover over its constitutive lack through attempts at identification, its *desire* to be. This negative ontology of lack explains why the lacking subject desires its subjection (Stavrakakis, 2008, 2010), an observation of importance for understanding the investment made when identifying with organizations. *Objet petit a* is the left-over of the Real: although it escapes symbolization and cannot be represented, it is a feeling that bridges the unconscious and the Symbolic; it is that thing desired and striven for in the unconscious belief that once found we will become whole. A cornerstone of Lacan's work (Braunstein, 2003), *jouissance* is as difficult to define as lack and the Real. To translate it as 'enjoyment' radically simplifies a concept that incorporates pain as much as pleasure, that is, pleasure that can be found through pain. Braunstein (2003: 104) defines it as 'a "something" lived by a body when pleasure stops being pleasure. It is a plus, a sensation that is beyond pleasure'. This suggests that *jouissance* is a letting go of the ego, or, in Hegel's terms, a forgetting of one's self in the object. Braunstein suggests:

> Desire points towards a lost and absent object; it is lack in being, and the craving for fulfilment in the encounter with the lost object. Its concrete expression is the fantasy. Jouissance, on the other hand, does not point to anything, nor does it service any purpose whatsoever…[D]esire, phantasy, and pleasure are barriers on the way to jouissance. (Braunstein, 2003: 104)

Lack and the Real have been drawn on in some depth by organization theorists since Jones and Spicer's (2005) paper. Jones and Spicer argue that entrepreneurship discourse 'is a paradoxical, incomplete and worm-ridden symbolic structure that posits an impossible and indeed incomprehensible object at its centre' (2005: 236), and so 'offers a narrative structure to the fantasy that coordinates desire' (2005: 237). They argue that this impossible desire enlists entrepreneurs and reproduces economic domination (2005: 237). The author whose development of Lacanian lack for organization studies is most fruitful is Michaela Driver who, in a series of papers, has attempted to rescue Lacan from his profound pessimism. In 2009, for example, she explored lack and identity, arguing that although 'in the end, there is only lack and the ever-present nothingness of work, organization, and self…it is also precisely this lack that holds much potential for empowerment and liberation' (Driver, 2009: 57). Organizational identity discourses, she argues, are imaginary constructions that invariably fail (2009: 65). Because of that failure and the revelation of lack that is revealed, subjects are liberated to 'engage in liberating struggles with lack' (2009: 66). That is, they are able to experiment with identities beyond those deemed permissible by the organization. Failure to define who we are allows us to be alive and creative, she argues powerfully. That is, by resisting identification *with* the organization, we may find spaces of freedom in which to constitute other identities.

22.5 SUMMARY: THE LACANIAN SUBJECT IN/OF ORGANIZATIONS

The Lacanian subject is, in short, a desiring subject for whom satisfaction is impossible, but whose search for the lost object that might provide satisfaction propels the subject forward. This subject identifies with that which appears to offer the potential to fulfil its desire (to be), to overcome its lack. 'The' organization is a site where that dialectic of desire/lack is articulated, opening the subject to domination by the organizational Big Other, albeit that the Organizational Big Other does not exist. In Lacanian terms, 'the organization' is imaginary; it is 'a master signifier that draws together a field of signification, notwithstanding its own vacuity' (Owens, 2010: 187). The Organizational Big Other promises fulfilment of the desire for being, but what is experienced is a failure of the self to become the ideal subject that the subject imagines he or she is required by the organization to be.

That is...I am sitting in my study in my house in the north of England working on this chapter. I seem to be alone, but as I read and write I gesture towards an Organizational Big Other for evidence of my identity as 'academic'. The 'organization' takes the shape of a fantasized readership of the chapter: I want their approval even though I cannot envisage who they might be. The university that pays my salary and provides students I try to teach is also here as I type: this chapter will be included in my 'outputs' for this year and that 'organization' therefore informs my thoughts. If I gain their approval I will know that I am 'an academic'. Just like the speaker whose words opened this chapter, I am waiting for a tap on the shoulder that says 'hey, excellent chapter—the best thing yet written on Lacan and organizations'. Previous experience has taught me not only how futile is this fantasy, but also how everything I write is just not good enough. I write a paper or, more rarely, a book, occasionally see one accepted and published, but each time that paper or book is not the text I had envisaged: it lacks something, I must keep on writing, trying to produce the work that encapsulates what I need to say, one that will give me recognition of myself as a successful academic, a great thinker, a fantastic interpreter of ideas. I am driven to keep on reading and writing: I read, I write, I answer emails, I think. My fantasized university, the 'object' to which I refer when I think about my job, emerges out of all these activities and those of other employees, just as we emerge out of our identities as 'academics'. I refer to it by a name that performatively constitutes it—requiring its existence so that I know of my own existence. By existing as employee ('my identity') and acting in the required manner, the object of my desire appears to be there before me—'an' organization that offers the (fallacious) opportunity for wholeness, a filling in of that lack. Isolated at my desk, the Organizational Big Other is threaded within my psyche, part of me just as I am part of 'it', that object whose desire I require. Just as Lacanian organization theorists have argued that lack drives others in pursuit of their desire—to be an entrepreneur, to manage staff, to purchase fashion products, and so on—so too does lack inform the psyche of the subject who would be an academic.

Before expanding on the implications for process theories of organizations, I must make a detour via Lacan's thesis on gender.

22.6 LACAN AND PROCESS THEORIES OF ORGANIZATIONS: A DETOUR VIA SEMINAR XX ON FEMININE SEXUALITY

Lacan's understanding of the subject as a being in process has marked affinities to 'the organization' as process. To paraphrase Lacan's (1982) notorious statement about 'the woman': there is no such thing as 'the' organization, the 'the' is barred, its facticity is a mirage arising from desire and lack. Psyches, bodies, places, artefacts, policies, rules, and so on, interweave and collapse into each other in an imbrication that seems to take place 'in' something that is actually produced through that imbrication. Given that gender is fundamental to, in the sense that it precedes, culture (and thus organizations), then it is a gendered imbrication of names/selves/objects/ places that 'produce' gendered organizations that 'produce' gendered organizational selves. Lacanian organizational process theory therefore requires[9] understanding of how it is that organizations are constituted as a *masculine* Big Other, as places in which emotions must be subordinated beneath rationality (Adler et al., 1993; Mills, 1992). They are places in which the (masculine) pervert's desire for control (Copjec, 2004) is unleashed.

In psychoanalytical theory, one cannot *be* unless one accedes to a gendered identity. Lacan argued in Seminar XX (1982/1998) that gender is neither biological nor social, but is a choice imposed on the subject: 'there is nothing by which the subject may situate himself as a male or female being' (Lacan, 1998a: 204). Mitchell and Rose (1982) translate Lacan as saying that sexual difference is 'a legislative divide which creates and reproduces its categories' (1982: 41). In Lacan, as Mitchell and Rose (1982: 29) write, we see an account of 'the fictional nature of the sexual category to which every human subject is…assigned'. Thus 'male' and 'female' are notions emerging out of fantasy (1982: 33). The 'feminine', it follows, 'is constituted as a division in language, a division which produces the feminine as its negative term'. If woman is defined as other it is because the definition produces her as other. The emancipatory potential of Lacan's arguments, Mitchell and Rose suggest, lies in seeing that the male, like the female, is subjected within the symbolic order. Lacan's work, in this interpretation, exposes the 'fundamental imposture' used in the subordination of the female (Campbell, 2004). Lacan's thesis on gender has been hotly contested by feminist thinkers (see Fotaki and Harding, 2013, for a discussion), but for present purposes the arguments from Seminar XX that gender is not determined but is fluid and flexible, and that male and female speaking subjects need not necessarily have male or female biology, is sufficient to inform the present discussion.

22.7 A (but not 'the') Lacanian Process Theory of Organizations: From the Hysteric to the (Perverted) Master

What is striking in much Lacanian organization studies is an absence of reflexivity, despite his admonition (noted earlier) that to read his texts is to engage in self-analysis. As Woźniak (2010: 396) puts it, researchers 'who apply psychoanalysis are also its subject and as such they become an effect of language, distinct from a biological individual'.

Authors use Lacan, for example, to theorize the absence of resistance towards management, yet do not ask themselves if the desire for evidence of resistance is *their* desire projected onto a fantasized other—'the workforce'. To explore lack is to interrogate one's own lack, surely? Should not we who attempt to interpret organizations through a Lacanian lens acknowledge ourselves as inevitably implicated in the Symbolic, Imaginary, and Real? Does our failure to do so reveal that we are attempting not only to occupy the place of the master, but also our secret desire to possess the phallus and thus to dictate what can be said and thought (the discourse of the university)? That is, in reading numerous texts on Lacan while writing this chapter I have hoped they would fulfil my illusory desire that I could write a perfect text, one that lacks nothing (a desire to fill that hole in my being through writing). But I have wondered why some papers were accepted for publication: couldn't reviewers see the poverty of application traducing Lacan's ideas? The 'why' bespeaks the position of the hysteric; I want to publish on Lacan, I want to join this special club but its weaknesses mean it is a club I do not wish to join—unless, that is, I can change the terms of the debate. If so, then I am dictating how to approach Lacan: welcome to the house of the master (again). *And so the Organizational Big Other constitutes 'me' even as I constitute 'it' through my fantasy of what it requires me to do—to cogently critique others' work even as I build on what they have done.*

In other words, I see in Lacanian organization studies and my own position in writing this text a Lacanian process theory of organizations in action.

To develop this thesis I turn now to another reading of Lacan from gender studies. Freud and Lacan turned to Sophocles' ancient tragedies for understanding of the modern psyche; Freud to Oedipus and Lacan, like many philosophers, to Oedipus' daughter/sister, Antigone. Copjec (2004) has developed Lacan's interpretation in a way that can inform our understanding of the co-emergence of subject and Organizational Big Other. Antigone is the daughter of the incestuous relationship between Oedipus and his mother, Jocasta. She breaks a law that the body of her slain brother shall not be buried. Discovered, arrested, and taken to King Creon, her uncle, she is condemned to the slow death of entombment in a cave. Antigone hangs herself, and Creon's wife and son commit suicide as a result. Copjec's interpretation shows the impossibility of either resisting or conforming with the Organizational Big Other.

For Copjec (2004) Creon, the king, is driven by his superego to pursue an ideal that is utterly unattainable; he is nostalgic for something he has never possessed. This lost object, Copjec shows, is possession of the place of the Big Other, a place that promises a self-assurance that comes from knowing one can dictate what others should do, and the correctness of one's every diktat. But in seeking utter control over its world, the ego has to fulfil the desires of an imaginary Other. Those desires must be guessed at but, crucially, the masculine position claims to know what they are. The (masculine) subject who, like Creon, places himself in the position of the big Other, of the Law, is then charged with upholding the (imagined) desire of this masculine organization.

Meanwhile, Antigone gives herself her own law, a law that needs validation from no other authority: the Other is non-existent for her (Copjec, 2004: 42). Crucially, Antigone has been able to 'unloose herself from the fundamental law of her own being'

(2004: 43) through refusing the Symbolic. This means that she cannot live. Antigone, the female position, demonstrates the impossibility of refusing to conform to organizational laws—to refuse is to lose one's identity.

Applying *the Antigone* to organizational process theory through a Lacanian lens suggests we collectively interpret the symbolic laws of the Organizational Big Other as desiring that we become masculine-speaking subjects who aggressively pursue the right to dictate what others may say and do. If we cannot do this then we are threatened with non-existence (or reduction to the position of the feminine). To fulfil the fantasies of what the fantasized organization desires of us, we attempt to constitute selves that exhibit the harshest, bleakest form of controlling masculinity; and we constitute an organization in that very image, one that limits what can be said, thought, done, and felt. The discourses of the university and the master dominate. In arriving at this conclusion, I too dictate how to read Lacan so as to understand organizations.

A Lacanian process theory of 'the organization' is therefore an interpretation of how a fantasy controls thoughts, deeds, and actions. This trans-individual fantasy articulates the vulnerability of subjects whose desire for existence and a yearning to feel whole facilitates the emergence of 'the organization'. However, the masculine object that exists in fantasy mitigates against conscious, let alone unconscious, feelings of wholeness.

But on reading through this draft I know there is something wrong with this text, although I cannot put my finger on it at the moment. Now if I tear it up and start again, perhaps I can make it better: perhaps I can write that perfect account of how Lacan might better help us understand organizations…

Notes

1. A symbolic position of authority and the (symbolic) law. The law is something we desire to transgress, and it is that desire which is the precondition for the law itself.
2. The person who supposedly has absolute and certain knowledge of one's innermost secrets.
3. In *Seminar XVII, The Other Side of Psychoanalysis*, Lacan (2007) outlines the schemata of four discourses constitutive of the social order: the university, master, hysteric, and analyst. These produce the four fundamental social effects of educating/indoctrinating, governing/brainwashing, desiring/protesting, and analysing/revolutionizing (Bracher, 1994).
4. The phallus should not be confused with the penis: it is a privileged signifier that inaugurates the process of signification and anchors the chain of signification. It is fundamental to *lack*, in that it signifies an object of desire that we have lost and constantly search for, although we actually never had it in the first place.
5. The hysteric's discourse is that of a subject who refuses to take up the positions available to her/him through language, even though desiring to occupy those very subject positions it refuses.
6. *Objet petit a* is, in Homer's words (2005: 87), that sense upon achieving our goals, that there is always something more that we should have experienced but we do not know what it is. The *objet petit a* is not that object; it is the function that masks the lack.

7. For Lacan, the big Other is the symbolic order, that always-already there to which I must conform if I am to have being. The unconscious is the effect of the symbolic order upon the subject. The little other (lower case 'o') refers to other people: we presume that they are unified, coherent, and whole but because every subject is a subject of lack, other people are imaginary others.

8. Stavrakakis (2010) defines *jouissance* as 'enjoyment', contradicting Lacan's account of something murkier. It is defined elsewhere as 'a sacrifice made at the altar of more or less obscure gods; it is the malefic jouissance of stripping the other of the goods he holds dear... Jouissance appears in guilt, in remorse, in confession, in contrition, more in paying than in being paid, in destroying more than in conserving (Braunstein, 2003: 108).

9. Note the imperative in this statement—'requires'. This is the discourse of the master.

REFERENCES

Adler, S., Laney, J., and Packer, M. (1993). *Managing Women* (Buckingham: Open University Press).

Arnaud, G. (2002). The Organization and the Symbolic: Organizational Dynamics Viewed from a Lacanian Perspective, *Human Relations* 55(6): 691–716.

Benvenuto, B. and Kennedy, R. (1986). *The Works of Jacques Lacan* (London: Free Association Books).

Bond, H. (2009). *Lacan at the Scene* (London: MIT Press).

Bracher, M. (1994). On the Psychological and Social Functions of Language: Lacan's Theory of the Four Discourses, in M. Bracher, M.W. Alcorn, R.J. Corthell, and F. Massardier-Kenney (eds), *Lacanian Theory of Discourse: Subject, Structure, and Society* (New York: New York University Press): 107–28.

Braunstein, N. (2003). Desire and Jouissance in the Teachings of Lacan, in J.-M. Rabaté (ed.), *Cambridge Companion to Lacan* (Cambridge: Cambridge University Press): 102–16.

Brennan, T. (1993). *History After Lacan* (London: Routledge).

Butler, J. (1990). *Gender Trouble* (London: Routledge).

——(1993). *Bodies That Matter* (New York: Routledge).

Campbell, K. (2004). *Jacques Lacan and Feminist Epistemology* (London: Routledge).

Cederstrom, C. and Hoedemaekers, C. (eds) (2010). *Lacan and Organization* (Bodmin: Mayfly Books).

Chia, R.C.H. (1998). Exploring the Expanded Realm of Technology, Organization and Modernity, in R.C.H. Chia (ed.), *Organized Worlds: Explorations in Technology and Organization with Robert Cooper* (London: Routledge): 1–19.

Contu, A., Driver, M., and Jones, C. (eds) (2010). *Jacques Lacan and Organization Studies*. Special Edition of *Organization* 17(3).

Copjec, J. (2004). *Imagine There's No Woman* (Cambridge, MA: MIT Press).

Driver, M. (2008). Every Bite You Take... Food and the Struggles of Embodied Subjectivity in Organizations, *Human Relations* 61(7): 913–34.

——(2009). Encountering the Arugula Leaf: The Failure of the Imaginary and Its Implications for Research on Identity in Organizations, Organization 16(4): 407–504.

Fotaki, M. (2009). Maintaining the Illusion of a Free Health Service in Post-Socialism: A Lacanian Analysis of Transition from a Planned to a Market Economy, *Journal of Organizational Change Management* 22(2): 141–58.

——and Harding, N. (2013). Lacan and Sexual Difference in Organization and Management Theory: Towards a Hysterical Academy? *Organization* 20(2): 153–72.

Frosh, S. (2003). *Psychoanalysis Outside the Clinic* (Basingstoke: Palgrave MacMillan).

Harding, N. (2007). On Lacan and the 'Becoming-ness' of Organizations/Selves, *Organization Studies* 28(11): 1761–73.

——Lee, H., and Ford, J. (forthcoming). *Who is the Middle Manager? On Constituting an Organizational Self.*

Hoedemaekers, C. and Keegan, A. (2010). Performance Pinned Down: Studying Subjectivity and the Language of Performance, *Organization Studies* 31(08): 1021–44.

Homer, S. (2005). *Jacques Lacan* (London: Routledge).

Jones, C. and Spicer, A. (2005). The Sublime Object of Entrepreneurship, *Organization* 12(2): 223–46.

Kenny, K. (2009). Heeding the Stains: Lacan and Organizational Change, *Management Journal of Organizational Change Management* 22(2): 214–28.

Klein, J. (1987). *Our Need for Others and Its Roots in Infancy* (London: Routledge).

Lacan, J. (1977). *Écrits. A Selection* (London: Routledge).

——(1982). God and the Jouissance of the Woman, in J. Mitchell and J. Rose (eds), *Feminine Sexuality: Jacques Lacan and the École Freudienne* (Basingstoke: Macmillan): 137–49.

——(1998a). *On Feminine Sexuality. The Limits of Love and Knowledge. 1972–1973. Encore. The Seminar of Jacques Lacan. Book XX*, ed. J.A. Miller, trans. B. Fink (New York: W.W. Norton & Co.).

——(1998b). *The Four Fundamental Concepts of Psychoanalysis. The Seminar of Jacques Lacan. Book XI*, ed. J.M. Miller, trans. A. Sheridan (New York: W.W. Norton & Co.).

——(2006). *Écrits. A First Complete Edition in English*, trans. B. Fink (New York: W. W. Norton & Co.).

——(2007). *Seminar XVII, The Other Side of Psychoanalysis*, ed. J.-A. Miller, trans. R. Grigg (New York: W.W. Norton & Co.).

McSwite, O.S. (1997). Jacques Lacan and the Theory of the Human Subject. How Psychoanalysis Can Help Public Administration, *American Behavioral Scientist* 41(1): 43–63.

Mills, A.J. (1992). Organization, Gender, and Culture, in A.J. Mills and P. Tancred (eds), *Gendering Organizational Analysis* (Newbury Park, CA: Sage): 93–111.

Mitchell, J. and Rose, J. (eds) (1982). *Feminine Sexuality. Jacques Lacan and the École Freudienne* (London: Norton).

Mulvey, L. (1975). Visual Pleasure and Narrative Cinema, *Screen* 16(3): 6–18.

Nobus, D. (2000). *Jacques Lacan and the Freudian Practice of Psychoanalysis* (London: Routledge).

Owens, C. (2010). Danger: Neurotics at Work, in C. Cederstrom and C. Hoedemaekers (eds), *Lacan and Organization* (Bodmin: Mayfly Books): 187–210.

Roberts, J. (2005). The Power of the Imaginary in Disciplinary Processes, *Organization* 12(5): 619–42.

Sköld, E. (2010). The Other Side of Enjoyment: Short-Circuiting Marketing and Creativity in the Experience Economy, *Organization* 17(3): 363–78.

Stavrakakis, Y. (2008). Peripheral Vision: Subjectivity and the Organized Other: Between Symbolic Authority and Fantasmatic Enjoyment, *Organization Studies* 297: 1037–59.

—— (2010). Symbolic Authority, Fantasmatic Enjoyment and the Spirits of Capitalism: Genealogies of Mutual Engagement, in C. Cederstrom and C. Hoedemaekers (eds), *Lacan and Organization* (Bodmin: Mayfly Books): 59–100.

Vanheule, S. and Verhaeghe, P. (2004). Powerlessness and Impossibility in Special Education: A Qualitative Study on Professional Burnout from a Lacanian Perspective, *Human Relations* 257(4): 497–519.

——Lievrouw, A., and Verhaeghe, P. (2003). Burnout and Intersubjectivity: A Psychoanalytical Study from a Lacanian Perspective, *Human Relations* 56(30): 321–38.

Vidaillet, B. (2007). Lacanian Theory's Contribution to the Study of Workplace Envy, *Human Relations* 60(11): 1669–1700.

Woźniak, A. (2010). The Dream that Caused Reality: The Place of the Lacanian Subject of Science in the Field of Organization Theory, *Organization* 17(3): 395–411.

Žižek, S. (2006). *How to Read Lacan* (London: Granta).

CHAPTER 23

GREGORY BATESON
(1904–1980)

MIKE ZUNDEL

23.1 BATESON'S HERITAGE

GREGORY BATESON proves an unusual character amongst philosophers, scientists, and teachers. A scientific mind continually striving to make connections beyond traditional boundaries, Bateson's investigations into 'patterns that connect' are always taking us to the edge of things, towards an appreciation of what he called the 'sacred': those wider relations that make up our environment and which we must not neglect, but which we can never fully grasp. In combining philosophical, biological, anthropological, psychological, and cybernetic ideas, Bateson's writings offer a rich resource for students of organization; a scientifically rigorous epistemology of life explored through practical examples and British wit, and yet forceful in illustrating the consequences of our actions when thought in terms of their final causes. Given Bateson's pursuit of wider patterns that connect, it behoves any chapter introducing his ideas to begin with the ancestry that spawned such a free thinker. We can thus begin to explore Bateson's varied and shifting interests through the intellectual heritage bestowed onto him and recurring throughout his life.

His family hails from Liverpool where his great-great grandparents were successful shipping and cotton merchants. Among their 12 children, many dying early, battling with mental health or with the law, was William Henry Bateson, Gregory's grandfather. William Henry studied at St John's College, Cambridge, under Samuel Butler, grandfather of the well-known novelist, and became fellow and later master of St John's. William Henry and his wife Anna were liberal spirits. He introduced wide-ranging secular reforms and competitive scholarship to St John's, while she was an early suffragette engaged in politics and fighting for women's access to universities. The Batesons lived in a tight-knit intellectual milieu that was rapidly transforming. William Henry had been educated at Shrewsbury Grammar School where, around the same time, Charles Darwin was also boarding (Cock and Forsdyke, 2008), and the Bateson and

Darwin families were reportedly befriended (Gershenowitz, 1983). William Henry and Darwin may also have crossed paths at Cambridge where, although at different colleges, they were both (together with Butler's son Thomas) intended for the church (Cock and Forsdyke, 2008: 522). Whilst Bateson remained at St John's, Darwin went on his famous voyage, and with the publication of *The Origin of Species* in 1859, transformed the intellectual zeitgeist and captivated in particular those working and studying at Cambridge (Lipset, 1980).

Into this milieu Gregory's father, William Bateson, was born. William must, by all accounts, have appeared to be a somewhat strange character in his youth. In addition to his reportedly 'unconventional' appearance and movements, he showed little interest in science and by his own—albeit grossly understated—account his 'knowledge of mathematics was *nil*' (Cock and Forsdyke, 2008: 10). Instead, he took up the relatively new subject of 'zoology' in his undergraduate studies at Cambridge, under patronage of the college's master, his father William Henry. William's undergraduate studies in zoology first progressed along conventional Darwinistic lines. He focused on morphology and the transformations of embryos to understand evolutionary processes, stressing continuity and only subtle mutability within and between species (Lipset, 1980: 24). Yet, after his undergraduate studies and following a series of study travels, William became disillusioned with evolutionary explanations of variations in species (Lipset, 1980: 21). His critique of Darwin, 'Britain's pride' (Coleman, 1970: 242), meant that he became isolated, even frowned upon by his Cambridge fellows. This straying from the path of Darwinism was also influenced by his contact with other radical thinkers at Cambridge, in particular his Grantchester neighbour, Alfred North Whitehead. William and Whitehead shared an interest in art and classics, and the question of how pattern or form can be reconciled with the inescapable dynamism of nature. They came to enjoy a long and intimate friendship. Mrs Whitehead played an instrumental role in the arrangement of William's marriage, and they shared a dislike for narrow standards for culture and class, and for representationalism in art and the spirit of reason that characterized conservative educational establishments like St John's (Coleman, 1970: 302; Lipset, 1980: 22–30).

William's critique of Darwin was also influenced by Samuel Butler (the novelist and grandson of William Henry's teacher). Butler believed that an organism's activities and its environment contribute directly to its adaptation, a direct opposition to the Darwinian view emanating from the works of the French naturalist Lamarck. William, on the other hand, translated and publicized ideas of the scientist and friar Gregor Mendel who had paved a middle ground between Darwinistic selection and Lamarckian adaptation. He maintained that the inheritance of variation did not accord with Newton's 'form'd Matter in solid, massy, hard, impenetrable moveable Particles' (in Lipset, 1980: 22) but that, although no direct influence of the environment on an organism's genome is possible, there were indeed longer-term feedback processes in which environmental (somatic) changes may, at least partly, affect the pathways of evolution (Harries-Jones, 1995: 154). It is therefore, argued William, equally useless to speak of organisms being determined by their genes, for 'the body of one individual has never *been* the body of its parent' (Bateson, in Lipset, 1980: 22), as it is erroneous to link adaptation to environmental influences alone. Instead, evolution can be understood with regard to *feedback* processes and levels of response; from more rapidly adjusting somatic changes to long-term adaptations. Inspired by the work of Gregor Mendel, William Bateson not only coined the term 'genetics', but was able to analyse 'regularity and lawfulness among the phenomena of variability in evolution' (G. Bateson, 1972: 379); the 'rhythms of divisions' (Lipset, 1980: 23) that gave rise to discontinuities in evolution. To this end, he studied large numbers of mutations, for instance cases of an addition-ally growing leg in beetles, showing that these are, really, two legs, following a repetitive regularity and symmetry of variability which came to be know as 'Bateson's Rule' (G. Bateson, 1972: 385).

William called his third son Gregory (after Gregor Mendel), his name an endless invitation to take up and develop his father's 'ghost' (Bateson and Bateson, 1987: 202); something he was to do by searching for 'patterns that connect all living creatures' and rigorously connecting ideas from Darwin, Lamarck, Mendel, Whitehead, and others (Bateson, 1979: 8).

23.2 BATESON KNOWS SOMETHING WHICH HE DOESN'T TELL YOU (G. BATESON, 1972: XIX)

Gregory Bateson read biology at St John's, but left the natural sciences to take up the relatively new field of anthropology at Cambridge and, following the death of his father William, conducted anthropological fieldwork in New Guinea. There he also met his first wife, Margaret Mead, who had already come to fame in her native America, and beyond, through the publication of *Coming of Age in Samoa*. From Mead, Bateson learned a range of fieldwork techniques and she introduced him to Gestalt psychology, psychoanalysis, and learning theory (Lipset, 1980: 136). Mead greatly influenced Bateson's work, first in their collaboration in New Guinea and, following Mead's divorce and subsequent mar-riage to Bateson, also through her help organizing materials for his first book, *Naven* (1936), and their joint research of Balinese culture, which involved for the first time the use of film and photographs resulting in more than 25,000 stills and over four miles of 16mm film material (Lipset, 1980: 156). From there, Bateson's career took various turns, including social planning work for the Institute for Intercultural Studies and being a film analyst for the Museum of Modern Art in New York; staff planner and regional specialist for the southeast branch of the US Office of Strategic Services during the war; working on ethnology in California and on schizophrenia, where he developed the theory of the 'double bind'; and on dolphin communication in Hawaii (Harries-Jones, 2002).

Throughout his life Bateson waged a battle against the structural approaches that predominated in the study of human behaviour. Notably he found that concepts like culture, understood as 'housing' a range of behaviours, alone were not helpful[1] and set out to develop an epistemology that corresponded to the patterns that characterized the world of living things. His epistemology is wide-ranging in its implications, but might be unpicked into the following five threads by which it is being continually woven. These threads might be said to be the material by which the patterns of his thought found form.

23.2.1 Creatura and Pleroma

When trying to understand how, in the process of learning, experience is generalized into some class of context and how some information comes to modify these formalized classes, Bateson read Carl Jung's *Seven Sermons to the Dead* in which Jung describes a contrast between a crudely physical world, governed by forces and impact, and a domain of living things, governed by distinctions and difference (Bateson and Bateson, 1987: 14). Jung calls these domains 'pleroma' and 'creatura'.[2]

For Bateson, the pleroma signifies the world of eternal verities; a world of *things in themselves* that remains ungraspable. There are no 'facts' because there is no difference and distinction, nothing that can be filtered out by the senses, so that there is no information to process (G. Bateson, 1972: 459). Bateson suggests: '[w]e can study and describe the pleroma, but always the distinctions which we draw are attributed *by us* to the pleroma. The pleroma knows nothing of difference and distinction; it contains no "ideas"' (G. Bateson, 1972: 462, my italics). Things only become graspable through differences, and difference only exists in the world of finite, living things. A piece of chalk serves as Bateson's example. This piece is characterized by myriad differences, for instance between the object's outlines and its surroundings; its whiteness when held *against* a dark background; or *between* the elevation left by a chalk line and the smooth surface of the board. Out of the many differences that may characterize a piece of chalk, our senses may picture a few *aspects* as 'facts'; as meaningful information in the explanatory world of the creatura; as some'-thing' that gets from the territory onto the map: 'the difference that makes a difference' (G. Bateson, 1972: 459).

23.2.2 The Map is not the Territory: Logical Types

The distinction between pleroma and creatura paves the way for one of Bateson's most important insights: that what gets from the territory onto the map is not part of the territory, but is merely 'difference' or information—and difference belongs to the world of living things. When looking at a piece of chalk, we can somehow never fully grasp the thing in itself, and we end up with information about size, shape, colour, and so on. In so doing, we notice but a few of the myriad *differences* the chalk-thing can make; its size or shape being different from the table on which it lies, or its colour differing from the board upon which it is spread. For Bateson, all the abstractions that constitute folk and scientific explanations are made up of such differences (not of 'things'); they belong to the creatura and are of a different *logical type* than the 'things' they attempt to represent.

The idea of logical typing stems from Russell and Whitehead's *Principia Mathematica* (1910), in which they suggest, in Bateson's words, that 'no class can, in formal logical or mathematical discourse, be a member of itself; that a class of classes cannot be one of the classes which are its members; that a name is not the thing named; that "John Bateson" is the class of which that boy is the unique member, and so forth' (G. Bateson, 1972: 279). The theory of logical types has profound implications for our understanding of the relationships between the world of explanation and the world of things we try to capture.

It implies, for instance, that concepts such as a 'routine' are of a different logical order to the 'things' they are designed to represent. Taking the routine to *be* the actions, people, or processes we can observe, poses an epistemological impasse as we mistake the map for the territory. We habitually grapple with the consequences of such impasses when, however hard we try, we cannot specify to which things, exactly, our concepts correspond as we continually find diverse and sometimes paradoxical interpretations of the seemingly 'same' thing (Ruesch and Bateson, 1951: 192). Weick (2001: 298), for example, identifies an 'abundance of conceptual dichotomies' in the studies of organizations such as exploration–exploitation, routine–novelty, or control–innovation. Tsoukas and Hatch (2001: 987) take these to be indicators of the complexity of organizational phenomena, so that for most, if not all of them, more than one inequivalent description can be generated. This leads to the seemingly paradoxical situation that organizational phenomena can adopt oppositional characteristics. For instance, Feldman and colleagues (2000; Feldman and Pentland, 2003) have identified persistent differences in their studies of routines, where stable characteristics attributed to the routines are continually upset by empirical observations indicating periodical or constant flux, adaptation, and mutation.

Following Bateson, such problems result from errors in logical typing, where the concept is mistaken for the thing it is meant to represent; like going to a restaurant and eating the menu card instead of the dinner (G. Bateson, 1972: 280).[3] Cooper (1986: 302) suggests that scientific work is particularly prone to such errors, as it frequently 'ignores or hides its re-presenting or framing role' without the perceiver usually being aware of it. Who of us knows the thought and abstraction processes that were involved in the generation of the concept of a routine? Yet, treating these concepts as if such mapping processes had never happened tempts us to portray them not only as descriptions, explanations, or maps, but as substitutes for these phenomena.

23.2.3 Feedback and the Organization of Creatura

How then can we think of the processes that characterize the world of living things without committing errors in logical typing? Let us consider for a moment the structure of explanation that Bateson finds erroneous. Assume that the stability and concreteness of categories—for instance those of institutions or routines, into which observed organizational phenomena can then be taxonomized—is akin to a syllogism of the form: 'Men are mortal; Socrates is a man; Socrates is mortal.' Using such a logical structure, particular observed behaviours in organizations are taken to be members of the class 'routine' in the same way in which Socrates, as a member of the class 'men', is treated as inheriting the property 'mortality' of that class (Bateson, 1991: 241).

However, because the map is not the territory, such inheritance is impossible. The problem is that while Socrates can be alive or dead, the class 'men' cannot or, similarly, while an action can be stable and changing, a routine cannot. To disregard this difference is to mistake the map for the territory.[4] The same applies to the theories we have *about* organizations. The hierarchies and classes and the predicate–subject relations of language with which these theories are constructed are *sui generis*; they cannot be found in the world of organizations—a world that does not abide by concrete taxonomies and stable characteristics (M.C. Bateson, 1972: 69, Bateson and Bateson, 1987: 27). Anatol Holt, a participant at a conference chaired by Bateson in 1968 coined a slogan that was later taken up by Karl Weick and many others. Holt suggested printing car stickers saying: 'HELP STAMP OUT NOUNS' to alert us to our misplaced fascination with entities that is imposed even by the language we use and the logic of classes contained therein (M.C. Bateson, 1972: 62).

How then can we understand the processes that characterize the world of living things, such as those of organizations outside of taxonomies and classificationary logics? Here Bateson alerts us to the importance of time. Bateson (1991: 181) highlights a difference in the nature of the 'if…then' relationships at play in the logical types of classifications and living systems. The 'then' in class-based, logical statements is timeless. Take the example of Epimenedes, the Cretan who said that 'Cretans always lie'. Here we are faced with a circular paradox because if he was a liar, then he was not a liar; and if he was not a liar, then it was untrue that Cretans always lie, and so on. The problem, Bateson insists, is that we ascribe logic to the world of living things (the creatura), which does not match the patterns of that world (as it is not organized by force and impact, but by distinctions and difference). While it is fine to ascribe such explanations to questions of logic—for instance when saying that it is always true that if a polygon has three corners and three sides which are line segments, then it is a triangle—such timeless statements make little sense when talking about organisms, tribes, organizations, or Cretans.

The 'then' in Epimenedes' statement therefore leads to paradox only if it is taken in a timeless manner. When understood causally *and* temporally, the contradiction disappears. The response becomes a sequence (yes, no, yes, no, yes…) similar to that of an electric bell on a door, where a complete electric circuit activates a magnet which will then break the circuit, which will then deactivate the magnet to restore the circuit, and so on (Ruesch and Bateson, 1951: 193). Epimenedes can lie *and* say the truth at different points in time in the same way in which a routine can be stable *and* changing at different moments without posing a problem to the integrity of the patterns of living things. However, this does question the utility of classes and classed-based taxonomies when trying to understand living patterns, as it makes as little sense to speak of Epimenedes saying a truth or falsity without specifying the temporal characteristics involved as it does to specify 'a routine' in timeless fashion. Timeless things like triangles do not respond to each other; social and natural systems, like those of electrical doorbells, organizations, or interacting human beings, on the other hand, are couched in sequential relational patterns (Bateson, 1991). Once we add time to our explanation we find institutional agents, like Epimenedes, who conform to institutional patterns *now* (such as being Cretan, and/or a liar) and may change things *later*, or routines that repeat certain actions at one point in time, and add other elements at others.

Considering time not only dissolves the paradoxes produced in errors of logical typing, it also alerts us to the consequences of feedback processes when living systems interact. Epimenedes' constant telling of lies will have implications for the quality of his social relations; a doorbell ringing will lead to someone answering the door; and the action of an organizational agent will invite new responses by her organizational environment. Such feedback will therefore alter the patterns of response; Epimenedes may soon find that there is nobody left willing to speak to him, lest being lied to, while an individual who goes against the mould of things may find herself dismissed or promoted by her organization, thus changing the pattern of future interactions.

Bateson's consideration of feedback processes echoes his father's enquires into evolutionary processes. For William Bateson, variation occurred when organisms interact with their environment over time. The successful evolution of variation is therefore, *pace* Darwin, not a matter of the strength of a particular type of organism, of specializations generated by chance that afford survival through natural selection. Instead, successful variations are those, Gregory Bateson (1991: 101) argues, which do not rely too much upon the seemingly static characteristics of their environment and remain flexible enough to (re)adapt to contextual changes.

We will return to the question of flexibility shortly. First, however, it is necessary to consider in more detail how feedback patterns lead to changes in the relationship between a living system and its environment; and again we find Bateson drawing on his father's work to understand regularity and variation in the recurrence of such processes.

23.2.4 Patterns: Symmetry and Complementarity

In his anthropological studies, in particular of the Iatmul tribes of New Guinea, Bateson observed a variety of intensifying feedback processes. For instance, an act of boasting from one juvenile led to more boasting by another, followed by even more exaggerated boasting by the first, and so on. Similarly, acts of dominance by one family or clan may be reciprocated with submission, leading to more dominance of the former, prompting more submissive responses by the latter, which, in turn, invite more dominance, and so on. Bateson (1936: 175) called such intensifying patterns 'schismogenesis': 'a process of differentiation in the norms of individual behavior resulting from cumulative interaction between individuals'. One well-known example of schismogenesis is Marcel Mauss' (1990) description of the 'potlatch' in his book *The Gift*, where each reciprocal contact prompts even more excessive displays of grandiloquence in return, resulting in bigger and bigger festivals. Understanding the intensifying nature of these patterns thus turns our attention to the thresholds that, when crossed, hold serious consequences for the partners involved. Juvenile boasting may turn to physical brawls, family feuds may lead to the break-up of the moiety, and unrestricted engagements in reciprocal festivals may incur the depletion of a tribe's resources, starvation, and perishing. If schismogenetically intensifying processes remain *unregulated*, they create a 'tangle of interlocking variables in which the more of something, the more of something else; and the more of the other thing, the more of the first' (Bateson, 1975: 29).

Bateson then went on to develop a classification of schismogenetic patterns, albeit not based on fixed characteristics but in terms of *process* (Bateson, 1941). Heeding Whitehead's warning of the fallacy of misplaced concreteness (Whitehead, 1967), Bateson suggests 'that we might expect to find the same sort of laws at work in the structure of crystal as in the structure of society, or that the segmentation of an earthworm might really be comparable to the process by which basalt pillars are formed' (Bateson, 1941: 54). Right away we begin to appreciate the rigidity of classes and how they would prevent such lateral thinking.

To understand the feedback patterns of Iatmul social life, Bateson again returns to his father's study of the structure of organisms. Here, he finds organisms with body parts and distributed shapes which show symmetry along a transverse plane, as in the physiology of human beings, and others where there is no left or right side but radial symmetry, for instance in jellyfish (Bateson, 1936: 98, 1941: 56). Bateson takes these different forms of organization in organisms and transposes them to the organization of Iatmul life, which he then explores in terms of the symmetries/asymmetries of unfolding patterns as opposed to the ordering of living things into classes according to their homologous or analogous properties (G. Bateson, 1972: 76).

In comparing the organization of a jellyfish's body parts with the organization of the social processes of a group of human beings, Bateson operates squarely outside of class-based logics. Such thinking is a bewildering experience at first, resulting in syllogisms of the sort: 'Grass dies, men die, men are grass.' Here, Bateson is after similarities in temporal patterns across class-based memberships—from earthworms to basalt pillars to tribes and organizations—affording entirely new ways of understanding living relations. Following this spirit, Bateson suggests metaphorical syllogisms of the sort: jellyfish show symmetries, Iatmul show symmetries, thus there is a pattern that connects both which could be stated in 'as if' terms: we can understand Iatmul *as if* they were jellyfish (c.f. Bateson and Bateson, 1987: 26).

This means that we can characterize the *kinds* of intensifying (schismogenetic) feedback patterns that ensue between individuals, families, or clans as symmetrical when displays of a particular behaviour A lead to responses of the same behaviour A, as in a juvenile's boasting being answered by even more boasting by his peers. Conversely, Bateson speaks of 'complementarity', when a behavioural display A is answered with a different behaviour B, for instance displays of aggression elicit displays of demureness in others.

Bateson's processual classification of the processes of living systems holds intriguing insights for the study of organizations. First, it urges us to think of consequences of patterns outside of cause–effect logics. Schismogenetic patterns cannot be confined to measures of force or impact like, for instance, when we try to understand the processes involved when two billiard balls collide. Unlike billiard balls, boasting juveniles, feuding families, organizations, or industries are motivated by 'difference' so that the mere sight of a competitor can prompt strong reaction whose force by far outweighs its stimulus (G. Bateson, 1972: 409).

Take the example of Hebden Bridge, a small market town in West Yorkshire in the United Kingdom, which has so far resisted the opening of stores by large high street chains. The mere information of attempts by large retail firms to plan outlets has frequently prompted petitions, demonstrations, complaints, and the like by Hebden's inhabitants—reactions whose 'energy' or force far exceeds the energy the retail chain puts into its planning application. It therefore makes little sense to speak of a cause–effect relationship; the retail chain does not 'cause' the inhabitants to get busy with their protest; rather they were animated by the mere 'difference' which the appearance of such a store made. Bateson insists that such 'difference' cannot be localized; unlike a billiard ball, it is not a 'thing' (G. Bateson, 1972: 416). The difference made by the appearance of a retail chain store is like that between the chalk and the board: an *aspect* which may stimulate a living system to react—or not—and thereby stimulate further feedback patterns.

Invoking the metaphorical classification of symmetry and complementarity offers a way of grasping the dynamics of such patterns without invoking thing-like relations. Understanding the patterns of competitors locked in price wars, or those between powerful firms and emasculated employees, in terms of symmetrical and complementary dynamics can provide us with an idea of what these patterns lead to, over time, and what their implications are for the survival of the wider system.

This also points towards a second important insight from Bateson's epistemology. Considering the consequences of feedback patterns over time affords early interventions. In the cases of boasting juveniles and competitive price wars, we are too late to intervene once breakdowns are visible—once a physical brawl starts, or once a firm has amassed too much debt in the pursuit of market victory. The thresholds that would have allowed safe recovery have by then well been crossed. Bateson thus urges us to consider not fixed states but latent possibilities that may be anticipated and corrected before they become pathological.

23.2.5 Acclimation, Thresholds, Flexibility

How, then, do we become entangled in intensifying patterns which, if unregulated, lead to breakdowns? There is 'positive feedback' at play: the actions of one part of a system stimulate another part to react with a more intense behaviour of the same (symmetrical) or a different (complementary) type, which then stimulate the first to react again, usually with greater intensity, and so on. Stimulated by 'positive', intensifying, feedback interactions become 'vicious' cycles.

This may be illustrated with another of Bateson's areas of study: alcoholism (G. Bateson, 1972: 316–30). Understood in terms of classes, entities, and logics, substance dependency is often portrayed as a problem of two parts: a drinker and the bottle; with the predicate 'dependency' being attached to a single part, the individual drinker (Bateson and Bateson, 1987: 37). Here, alcoholism is understood as a 'clash of wills' between the alcoholic and the bottle (Harries-Jones, 1995: 38). For Bateson, this is erroneous as it neglects time and, thereby, mutes the patterns of relations that exist between different parts of a systemic whole and thereby produce changes in the system every time information is fed back.

Understood processually, having a drink may initially be a means of coping with other issues in the sober life of the drinker such as dealing with work-related stress or boredom, or overcoming feelings of inadequacy in the company of others (G. Bateson, 1972: 329). Alcohol can alleviate these inadequacies because its intoxicating effects tend to lessen feelings of anxiety and worry. Faced with pathologies in her sober life, the drinker finds escape in alcohol, which offers temporary correction and allows her to cope awhile. Based on her positive experiences with this escapism, and stimulated by further pressures from her environment (which demands more of her, given that she has seemingly found a way to 'cope'), she is likely to enter the vicious cycle of drink dependency. Positive feedback, be it dependence on alcohol, patterns of boasting, or competitive rivalry, needs to be understood in terms of wider systemic tangles, and often in terms of pathologies in these wider contexts, rather than as relations between two isolated entities. From an ecological perspective, alcohol consumption is therefore at first a successful *adaptation* in which the individual temporarily alleviates other pathologies in her wider, sober, relationships with her environment. Alcoholism can thus not be restricted to the drinker and the bottle; it involves wider patterns of information between 'bottle+individual+environment' (Bateson, 1991: 52).

Three aspects of Bateson's processual characterization of drink dependency appear to be particularly important for our purposes. First, we have suggested that the consumption of alcohol can be understood as a response to pathological relations in the sober life of the drinker. Adaptation, or, as Bateson often calls it, 'acclimation', is a necessary and successful process of living systems. For instance, it allows us to cope when we spend longer periods in high altitudes by adjusting our physiological processes to the changed environments. Our respiratory systems get accustomed to the new context in the same way in which a drinker gets accustomed to using alcohol to deal with stressful relations. However, if done over a prolonged period of time, there will be adaptation of the body to the substance in terms of the physiological and psychological changes that come with prolonged drinking and the changes this prompts in the drinker's social relations. A further example for the connecting of acclimation and dependency is the use of the pesticide DDT, which was at first an immensely successful adaptation in food production, which then led to major dependencies of a growing earth population on increased crop harvests, changes in the resistance levels of insects to pesticides, diminishing populations of insect-feeding birds, the growth of agricultural lobbying communities, and so on. In other words, the world became 'addicted' to DDT (G. Bateson, 1972: 497). The alcoholic's dependence on the drink and the world's dependence on DDT have the same characteristic:[5] what began as adaptive behaviour turned, at a later stage, into a 'runaway' intensification, whereby a successful adaptation turns into pathology (Harries-Jones, 1995: 170)—just as in commerce we become addicted to performance of doing more with less, or as consumers of replacing the old with the new. The acclimation now becomes a source of stress for the individual (G. Bateson, 1991: 210; 1972: 351).

Second, positive feedback loops leading to vicious spirals are subject to thresholds. When these are crossed the drinker will descend towards hitting rock bottom, her partner or employer will grow unwilling or unable to cope any longer, or her body will succumb to health issues. Once visible changes in relational patterns are visible it is often too late. Rather than emerging in linear fashion, the 'stress' in the system increases abruptly when tolerances in the wider system are crossed and the 'weakest' part of the system gives in, thus highlighting Whitehead's (1967: 109) point that 'any physical object which by its influence deteriorates its environment, commits suicide' (in Harries-Jones, 1995: 66).

Third, the chances of 'survival' of a living system, be it a tribe, an alcoholic, or a competitively acting firm are slim if they adapt too much. The juvenile finding acts of boasting a release for his temperament, a drinker turning to alcohol to alleviate social pressures, or a firm investing heavily into marketing to cope with tough trading environments may do fine for a while but will face extinction once these environmental conditions change. Such change is inevitable because of the ongoing feedback patterns that continually transform the wider system. Too much boasting amongst juveniles may thus invoke social and legal sanctions, drinkers may hit the gutter, and continued aggressive marketing campaigns may be met with raised levels of immunity and indifference in consumers and exponentially increased expenses for marketing campaigns. Unless somehow regulated and checked, these processes will tend towards schismogenetic intensification over and beyond the thresholds that warrant stability.

Unlike Darwinian specialization, Bateson (1991: 101) therefore suggests we ought to think of a 'positive survival value' when considering the possibilities of a continued existence of living systems; a 'creative, nonstatic characteristic'. In other words, what an organism, individual, or organization needs is the ability to lose its acclimation, to unlearn its adaptations to readjust to new contexts in order to cope with what Bateson calls nature's 'dirty tricks': letting a system act for generations on the assumption that certain of its characteristics can be relied upon only to change these at one point and turn any successful acclimation into a source of stress and decay. Survival, Bateson (1991: 101) concludes, echoing ideas of Mendel, is a 'fight for flexibility'; a combination of shorter, reversible, and longer-term adaptations in relation to environmental changes (G. Bateson, 1972: 352; 1979: 92).

23.2.6 Bateson's Epistemology and Organization Studies

A number of Bateson's ideas and in particular some of the catchy statements he invented or helped to popularize are familiar to studies of organizations. Nouns, for instance, have become nearly extinct amongst processually minded students of organizing. Similarly, researchers of communication frequently alert us to the dangers of mobilizing the terminology and knowledge of machines or biophysics to describe the Gestalt (Ruesch and Bateson, 1951) of organizations, or when talking about organizations as single actors in terms of their ability to think, feel, or to intend something (Cornelissen, 2008: 81). Organizations can, of course, neither think nor feel (Bencherki and Cooren, 2011), and treating meta-language as a 'constant rather than a variable' is what Ryle (1949, in Taylor, 2011: 1276) calls a 'category mistake' akin to Bateson's error in logical typing (G. Bateson, 1972: 280).

However, the more radical processual insights of Bateson's epistemology have so far only been limitedly explored. In one of the first issues of *Organization Studies*, Morgan (1981), for example, develops the metaphor of schismogenesis for organizational analysis. In particular, he links intensifying processes with a number of organizational problems, for instance as a possible antecedent to loose coupling, conflict, or withdrawal, concluding that research built on the 'schismatic metaphor' recognizes that 'the continued survival of social systems is problematic and hinges upon a balance between disintegrative and integrative tendencies' (Morgan, 1981: 40).

The possible balance between disintegration (schismogenesis) and integration (homeostasis) is perhaps one of the most productive insights of Bateson's work. Bateson called his book about his early anthropological studies *Naven*. *Naven* is a ceremony held by tribes in New Guinea in which there seems to be a change in the emotional responses between men and women, where fun is made of a man (the mother's brother *'wau'* of the individual for whom the ceremony was held) depicting baffooning behaviour while dressed in female clothing, while women display male attributes and accessories, for instance when they proudly wear homicidal ornaments (Bateson, 1936: 258).

Bateson recognized that *naven* represented an important regulator governing the otherwise runaway relational patterns between tribes, families, and individuals. For Bateson, the cultural 'unity' of a tribe or family is therefore not a static entity (an 'it'), but a dynamic equilibrium. Social, living systems are under continuous stress as their interactive behavioural patterns tend towards (schismogenetic) intensification, threatening breakdown if variables are stretched beyond their tolerances. For living systems to maintain temporary states of equilibrium, schismogenetic processes must be counteracted by processes that *regulate* the otherwise runaway patterns (Bateson, 1936: 175). In the case of boasting, regulative processes may include the outbreak of smaller, even ritualistically ordained quarrels through which tensions are released and schismogenetic intensification temporarily suspended (Bateson, 1936: 175). *Naven* represents such a formally ordained ceremonial regulator, affording the dissolution of tensions that would otherwise accelerate beyond safe thresholds.

We can transpose the highly advanced, processual institution of *naven* to our modern, western world of organizations. Burgelman and Grove (2007), for instance, observe that in the period between 1965 and 2005 over 80 of initially 100 top US-based industrial companies dropped out of the *Fortune* magazine list, 66 of them being acquired or disbanded altogether. Burgelman (2002; Burgelman and Grove, 2002) invokes the metaphor of the creosote bush (organizations are like grass, after all) to capture the kind of lock-in experienced by successful firms. Creosote bushes often grow at regular spacing supposedly linked to the excretion of toxic substances, killing any seedlings nearby. The more the creosote bush grows, the more it inhibits the growth of other plants, affording it to develop a more elaborate root system, gaining better access to resources in typically arid habitats (Phillips and MacMahon, 1981). This 'mutually disadvantageous interaction' (Woodell et al., 1969) between individual specimen leads, prima facie, to the isolation of the creosote shrub from its environment, an insularity rendering it increasingly self-centred and unable to react to changing environmental conditions. For Burgelman, managers may get equally locked in because of psychological rigidities and the unavailability of creative and versatile managers following many years of success. Generations of managers spoiled with success, it seems, have simply forgotten—or have never learned—how to cope with changing (dynamic) environments.

Following Bateson, what else can we say about the patterns of managerial lock-in like those of a creosote bush? First, rather than being isolated, we can understand the bush's lack of flexibility for adaptation in terms of its being locked into a complementarily schismogenetic relationship with competitive plants (like bottle+drinker+environment we now find creosote+roots+environment). Increased growth of creosote, decreased contraction of other plants, and vice versa, following a complementary schismogenetic pattern: more behaviour of type A will lead to more of a different behaviour, type B, in response. If unregulated, such patterns therefore tend to take on runaway characteristics; they speed up and, eventually, lead to breakdown of the system or a part thereof. However, the schismognetic tendencies of creosote bushes are routinely counteracted by other (homeostatic) processes. These include the uptake of unevenly distributed resources, such as phosphorus, which tends to decline per root unit if the entire root system increases. The growth of the bush brings individual root strands into competition with each other, thus forming a self-limitation to growth (Schwinning and Weiner, 1998). Creosote bushes therefore survive for a surprisingly long time because these regulative processes keep check on the otherwise intensifying patterns.

Successful organizations, on the other hand, often have no such regulation (so their metaphor breaks down, or holds them prisoner itself, as a class, beware the structuring impress of all terms). In periods of successful growth, firms frequently have access to many mobile resources, in particular finance. This means that they can grow to an extent that exceeds the *thresholds* that limit the wider system's survival. The 'successes' of retail chains in rural areas may thus lead to the decay of other trading businesses and growing unemployment coupled with a shift towards low-paid work. As a result, the success of the retail chain model leads to a deterioration of the customer environment, thereby committing commercial suicide (Whitehead, 1967: 109).

Bateson also allows us to speculate why it is difficult to avoid such intensifying tangles; indeed there are a few chains in Hebden now, a Ladbrokes betting shop, a Fat Face clothing store, Boots which took over the local chemist, small chains granted, but perhaps the thin end of a wedge? Consider again the addictive patterns of drinkers. Here, addiction is not a dependency of an individual to the bottle, or even the absolute alcohol level in the blood. It is, rather, a positive gradient of alcohol consumption, as in each step of the spiralling feedback pattern the drinker requires a greater response to the bodily and environmental stimuli (Bateson and Bateson, 1987: 46). Feedback has a spiral rather than a circular movement as its basic process, indicating dynamic intensification (Harries-Jones, 2005). The creosote bush is also subject to intensification. It has to grow a large root system to ensure superior access to soil moisture and nutrients while growing larger stem and leaf systems to harvest more light needed to grow and sustain these roots—requiring, in turn, more elaborate roots, and so on. In both cases, what was once a successful adapation can quickly turn into a source of stress, in particular when environmental contexts change. It is clear that organizations also depend on positive gradients in their development. Organizations are therefore not static entities and we gain much from thinking of them in terms of interacting patterns of disintegrative and integrative tendencies (Morgan, 1981: 40). Their continued 'existence' requires a precarious equilibrium between these tendencies. This requirement, perhaps, offers new scope for managerial intervention; not as drivers of intensification, but as governors who regulate otherwise pathological tendencies of organizations as living systems. Bateson's epistemology may help us develop the *thinking* necessary for such a change.

Notes

1. It is worth reading the epilogue to his anthropological account of these cultures (*Naven*, published in 1936) where Bateson describes his struggles to connect his empirical material into a coherent framework that is not restricted to class-based taxonomical thinking.

2. For Jung, in the pleroma there is no thinking and being; characteristic-less eternity and un-endingness that contains 'nothing and everything'. One cannot even think about the pleroma, and thereby penetrate it, as this would introduce boundaries and characteristics of Jung's second world of explanation: the 'creatura'. The creatura is part of the pleroma and yet different. While the pleroma is infinite, the creatura is finite in time and space; the world of changeable living beings possessing altering characteristics while the pleroma, at any point, remains boundariless and always true.

3. Bateson was also influenced by the work of Alfred Korzybski (1933) who coined the notion that the 'map is not the territory'.

4. Bateson does not treat the distinction between the creatura and the pleroma in terms of mind–matter dualisms, nor does he describe both spheres in terms of the language of classes. Instead, the creatura entails and is only possible because of the pleroma. Causes and effects do have a place in the creatura, but they play a smaller role next to the possibilities emerging from the release of the energies inherent in the different parts of any living system and the dynamic patterns that can emerge from ongoing reactions in such systems.

5. Bateson calls this 'deutero learning' or learning about context (G. Bateson, 1972: 169, 287). What matters is not what is learned, but the context in which learning occurs (Harries Jones, 2002: 112). We thus get better in our responses the next time the same situation arises—not because we have successfully memorized some rote behaviour, but because we have a sense of the context; what to look out for and what may be neglected; what works and what not. Deutero learning, therefore, has a reinforcing quality. We have, to use Bateson's phrase, 'learned to learn' (quoted in Lipset, 1980: 172), so that certain circumstances can come to reinforce our behaviour.

References

Bateson, G. (1936). *Naven: The Culture of the Iatmul People of New Guinea as Revealed through a Study of the 'Naven' Ceremonial*, 2nd edn (London: Wildwood House).

——— (1941). Experiments in Thinking about Observed Ethnological Material, *Philosophy of Science, 8*(1): 53–68.

———(1972). *Steps to an Ecology of Mind* (Chicago: University of Chicago Press).

———(1979). *Mind and Nature: A Necessary Unity* (London: Wildwood House).

———(1975). *Loka: A Journal from Naropa Institute*, vol. 1 (Anchor Press. New York).

———(1991). *A Sacred Unity: Further Steps to an Ecology of Mind* (New York: Harper Collins).

——— and Bateson, M.C. (1987). *Angels Fear: Towards an Epistemology of the Sacred* (New York: Macmillan).

Bateson, M.C. (1972). *Our Own Metaphor* (New York: Alfed A. Knopf).

Bencherki, N. and Cooren, F. (2011). Having to Be: The Possessive Constitution of Organization, *Human Relations 64*(12): 1579–607.

Burgelman, R. A. (2002). Strategy as Vector and the Inertia of Coevolutionary Lock-In, *Administrative Science Quarterly, 47*(2): 325–57.

——— and Grove, A.S. (2007). Let Chaos Reign, then Rein in Chaos—Repeatedly: Managing Strategic Dynamics for Corporate Longevity, *Strategic Management Journal 28*: 965–79.

Cock, A.G. and Forsdyke, D.R. (2008). *Treasure your Exceptions. The Science and Life of William Bateson* (Berlin: Springer).

Coleman, W. (1970). Bateson and Chromosomes: Conservative thought in Science, *Centaurus 3–4*: 228–314.

Cooper, R. (1986). Organization/Disorganization, *Social Science Information 25*(2): 299–335.

Cornelissen, J.P. (2008). Metonymy in Language about Organizations: A Corpus-Based Study of Company Names, *Journal of Management Studies 45*(1): 79–99.

Feldman, M. (2000). Organizational Routines as a Source of Continuous Change, *Organization Science 11*(6): 611–29.

——— and Pentland, B.T. (2003). Reconceptualizing Organizational Routines as a Source of Flexibility and Change, *Administrative Science Quarterly 48*(1): 94–124.

Gershenowitz, H. (1983). Why did Gregory Bateson Overlook some Basic Lamarckian Tenets?, *Indian Journal of History of Science 18*(2): 137–53.

Harries-Jones, P. (1995). *A Recursive Vision: Ecological Understanding and Gregory Bateson* (London: University of Toronto Press).

———(2002). Where Bonds Become Binds: The Necessity for Bateson's Interactive Perspective in Biosemiotics, Sign Systems Studies 30(1): 163–81.

——— (2005). Gregory Bateson, Heterarchies, and the Topology of Recursion, *Cybernetics and Human Knowing 12*(1–2): 168–74.

Jung, C.G. (1916/1967). *Septem Sermones ad Mortuos*, trans. H.G. Bayes (London: Stuart and Watkins).

Korzybski, A. (1933). *Science and Sanity: An Introduction to Non-Aristotelian Systems and General Semantics* (Fort Worth, TX: Institute of General Semantics).

Lipset, D. (1980). *Gregory Bateson: The Legacy of a Scientist* (Englewood Cliffs: Prentice Hall).

Mauss, M. (1990). *The Gift*. (London: Routledge)

Morgan, G. (1981). The Schismatic Metaphor and Its Implications for Organizational Analysis, *Organization Studies 2*(1): 23–44.

Phillips, D.L. and MacMahon, J.A. (1981). Competition and Spacing Patterns in Desert Shrubs, *Journal of Ecology 69*: 97–115.

Ruesch, J. and Bateson, G. (1951). *Communication: The Social Matrix of Psychiatry* (New York: W.W. Norton).

Russell, B. and Whitehead, A.N. (1910). *Principia Mathematica*, 2nd edn (Cambridge: Cambridge University Press).

Ryle, G. (1949). *The Concept of Mind* (London: Hutchinson).

Schwinning, S. and Weiner, J. (1998). Mechanisms Determining the Degree of Size Asymmetry in Competition among Plants, *Oecologia 113*: 447–55.

Taylor, J.R. (2011). Organization as an (Imbricated) Configuring of Transactions, *Organization Studies 32*(9): 1273–94.

Tsoukas, H. and Hatch, M.-J. (2001). Complex Thinking, Complex Practice: The Case for a Narrative Approach to Organizational Complexity, *Human Relations 54*(8): 979–1013.

Weick, K.E. (2001). *Making Sense of the Organization* (Oxford: Blackwell).

Whitehead, A.N. (1967). *Science and the Modern World* (New York: Free Press).

Woodell, S.R.J., Mooney, H.A., and Hill, A.J. (1969). The Behaviour of Larrea Divaricata (Creosote Bush) in Response to Rainfall in California, *Journal of Ecology 57*(1): 37–44.

CHAPTER 24

HANNAH ARENDT
(1906–1975)

RICHARD P. NIELSEN

> Turning and turning in the widening gyre…Things fall apart; the centre
> cannot hold; Mere anarchy is loosed upon the world, The blood-dimmed
> tide is loosed, and everywhere, The ceremony of innocence is drowned;
> The best lack all conviction, while the worst Are full of passionate inten-
> sity…a waste of desert sand; A shape with lion body and the head of a
> man, A gaze blank and pitiless as the sun…The darkness drops again but
> now I know That twenty centuries of stony sleep Were vexed to night-
> mare…And what rough beast, its hour come round at last, Slouches
> towards Bethlehem to be born?
>
> (Yeats, 'The Second Coming', in Yeats, 1919/1956)

In his *Praxis and Action*, Bernstein observed that 'Most of the truly great philosophers have sought to show us how their own views capture what they take to be the insight and "truth" implicit in other views', and they reject what is thought to be misleading and false' in the other's views (Bernstein, 1971: 8). Heidegger was a foundational intellectual and personal influence on Arendt both with respect to her insights and where she strongly diverged from Heidegger.

Heidegger's (1933/1962, 1935/1959, 1977) concept of the dynamic nature of being and, interactively, identity, as becoming in context, *dasein*, is particularly important for Arendt (1951, 1963a, 1963b, 1968, 1978). The formative experiences of the terrible context and becoming in post-World War I Germany, in World War II, and her life as a refugee in France and later America was extremely important and should not be underestimated. That context, which Yeats (1919/1956) captured and foretold in his evocation of 'Things fall apart; the centre cannot hold…the blood-dimmed tide is loosed, and everywhere. The ceremony of innocence is drowned', very much influenced her understanding of Heidegger and later Eichmann as discussed in this chapter.

Arendt understood Heidegger as a type of, in Yeats' phrase, a 'best', who after his brief period as a Nazi and his disillusionment with the Nazi promise of a restored, ideal, pastoral society, became a 'best without [civic] conviction'. That is, she considered Heidegger's withdrawal from civic life as a kind of dysfunctional and even complicit withdrawal that made it easier for the authoritarian, unethical, and criminal processes to prevail (Arendt, 1978, 2003; Bernstein, 1971, 1985; Habermas, 1983; Kristeva, 2001; Young-Bruehl, 1982).

Arendt understood Eichmann, as an ordinary 'banal' person who became a type of 'worst', as he gradually and relentlessly became a key enabler and even creative innovator in the Nazi mass murder and concentration camp organizational processes. In addition to Heidegger's concept of the dynamic nature of being as becoming in context, *dasein*, Arendt may also have adapted Heidegger's concept of the banality of superficial politics, what Heidegger referred to as *gerede* (idle talk) and its dangers, to her related concept of the 'banality of evil' (Stassen, 2003).

Arendt tried to understand how so many of both the 'best' and 'worst' could succumb to massively unethical and criminal organizational behaviours and what needs to be done to reduce the likelihood of such phenomena re-emerging. Arendt considered how both the brilliant Heidegger and banal Eichmann were absorbed into and shaped by Nazi processes.

What she considered her and Heidegger's different responses to a similar understanding of the power of such seemingly ordinary negative becoming became a further source of rejection of Heidegger's ideas and a stimulus for the development of her ideas concerning the need for social, communicative politics which later became very important for Habermas' work (Bernstein, 1971, 1985; Habermas, 1983; Young-Bruehl, 1982).

Hannah Arendt's process philosophy of organizational ethics and politics, and particularly her analysis of authoritarian organizations and the emergent Eichmann archetype as a middle-level manager who efficiently and even creatively obeys and implements unethical and illegal orders, who enables massive administrative harm, certainly an extreme, controversial, and evocative case and archetype. However, it is as relevant today as it was in 1963 when her book *Eichmann in Jerusalem: A Report on the Banality of Evil* was published. Related key books of Arendt's include *The Origins of Totalitarianism* (1951), *The Human Condition* (1958), *On Revolution* (1963), *Men in Dark Times* (1968), *On Violence* (1970), and *The Life of the Mind* (1978).

Twenty years after Arendt's book on Eichmann was published and eight years after Arendt's death, the Israeli authorities released tapes of the Eichmann interviews with Israeli police investigator, Captain Avner Less, that included some 275 hours of taped recordings that resulted in 77 transcripts totalling 3,564 pages (Lang and Sibyll, 1983). Some of this material will be considered in relation to Arendt's analyses. The transcripts for the most part support and may also extend her conclusions with respect to the potentially even more negative transformative power of the authoritarian organizational process phenomena and the Eichmann archetype.

That is, the transcripts suggest that she may have even underestimated the transformative severity of the organizational process phenomena. It appears that Eichmann, in his becoming transformed, passed through at least five stages: low-level clerk; low-level analyst; middle-level organizer of coerced emigration of millions of people; upper middle-level organizer of the logistics and transportation of millions of people to mass murder in concentration camps; and energetic and even perversely moralist organizer in the last year of the war when many others, for various reasons explained later, were slackening and even halting their unethical and criminal activities.

This raises the question about whether organizational processes, at least in extreme situations such as existed in Nazi Germany, can transform more or less normal people even beyond the 'banality of evil' into 'organizational sociopathy' (Pech and Slade, 2007; Gabriel, 2012). Apparently Eichmann never committed any harm in his private life or outside of his organizational role. Nonetheless, in his organizational life, as referred to a moment ago, he was increasingly the key analytic, efficient, and creative organizer of first coerced emigration and then 'administrative massacre' of millions of people through his organization of mass transportation of people to concentration camps. Further, in the last year of World War II, it appears that he also became an extraordinarily energetic and even perversely moralistic organizer of mass transportation to the death camps.

24.1 Biographical Sketch

Hannah Arendt was born in 1906 in Hanover into a secular, middle-class, Jewish German family. From the mid 1920s through the early 1930s, Arendt attended university. During this formative period, there was massive economic depression in Germany and other parts of Europe that contributed to the rise of political extremes in Germany, Austria, Italy, Spain, and other European countries. The economic depression that contributed to the political extremes was caused in significant part by the severe austerity programmes imposed on Germany, Austria, and Italy by England, France, and the United States after World War I. Many people, including academics and intellectuals, lost confidence in both traditional and modern institutions as a result of the terrible damages of World War I and the following severe economic depression. The environment was very receptive to radical, alternative, political, economic, and cultural ideologies and solutions.

In 1924 Arendt went to Marburg University to study with Martin Heidegger, with whom she had a love affair. The following year, 1925, she went to Freiburg University and attended the lectures of Edmund Husserl. A year later in 1926 she went to Heidelberg University to study with Karl Jaspers. With Jaspers she had a love affair as well as a long-lasting intellectual and personal friendship relationship. She wrote her dissertation under Jaspers' supervision in 1929, *Der Liebesbegrif bei Augustin*, which was about Augustine's ideas concerning concepts of love.

Arendt's relationship with Heidegger was severely damaged when Heidegger joined the Nazi Party. 'Nazi' is the common English language term for the National Socialist German Workers Party (NSDAP). Her relationship with Heidegger was further damaged when Heidegger, through the NSDAP, was instrumental in the removal of Jaspers from his professorship and German university life in 1937.

Nonetheless and somehow, Arendt both separated from and was able to remain friends with Heidegger even after he had spent years as a Nazi and after his terrible treatment of her friend Jaspers.

One wonders how her understanding of why such a brilliant mind as Heidegger's could be seduced by Nazism might have influenced how she understood Eichmann's 'banality of evil'. Eichmann was certainly far outside the intellectual and aesthetic league of Heidegger, yet both joined the Nazis, one with misplaced 'romantic' and 'poetic' misunderstanding, the other with 'banality'. It appears that during this terrible period of the 1930s Arendt also shifted her work from the study of different understandings of love in the work of Augustine, Jaspers, Kant, and other philosophers, to the study of the darker phenomena of 'violence', 'totalitarianism', and 'the banality of evil'.

Arendt left Germany in 1933 and lived in Paris until 1941. With the help of the economist Albert O. Hirschmann who, along with the journalist Vivian Fry and the British and American Friends Service Committees helped many intellectuals, artists, and ordinary people escape from Nazi-controlled Europe, Arendt emigrated to the United States and New York City. She held a number of academic positions at American universities, most often at the New School of Social Research, until her death in 1975.

One of her most noted works was the 1963 *Eichmann in Jerusalem: A Report on the Banality of Evil*. It was originally commissioned by and published in *The New Yorker*, and was later expanded into book form. It is considered something of a modern classic due to its thought-provoking analytic power, which is very important for organizational process and management studies (Nielsen, 1984, 1996). Arendt's process philosophy and her analysis of Eichmann as a person and of his organizational situation, while certainly an extreme case, is a valuable example of a certain type of cooperation with unethical and illegal behaviours in organizations.

24.2 Biographical Sketch—Adolf Eichmann

Adolf Eichmann (1906–1962) was born in the same year as Hannah Arendt, also to a middle-class German family. His was a religious, Lutheran family from Solingen, Germany. After his mother died in 1914, the family moved to Linz, Austria because of a business opportunity for his father. His father was an accountant and successful small businessman who worked for a number of German and Austrian small family businesses. During World War I his father served in the Austro-Hungarian army. Eichmann was not a good student and did not attend university, but did attend a vocational school in industrial mechanics. During the 1920s and early 1930s Eichmann worked in a variety of business capacities including mechanics, sales, and administration.

In 1932, Eichmann was invited by a business acquaintance, Ernst Kaltenbrunner, to join the SS, Schutzstaffel (Protection Corps) at the lowest rank of private. In a few months he was promoted to corporal. The SS was originally formed to provide security for early Nazi party meetings as well as security for Nazi party officials. By the end of World War II it had at one time or another employed around one million soldiers/police and was involved with most Nazi war crimes.

In 1934, Eichmann joined the SD, the intelligence division of the SS. He was first assigned to the office that dealt with Freemasons. Later that same year, he was transferred to the larger office of Jewish Affairs. The highest rank Eichmann achieved was equivalent to the rank of major or lieutenant colonel, not very high in the Nazi hierarchy and not a policy-making rank. His career in the SD was primarily about implementation, transportation, and logistics. And yet, he was a key logistics and transportation person in facilitating the 'administrative massacre' of millions of people.

Eichmann's work in the Jewish Affairs section of the SD appears to have moved through four stages: first, he worked as a low-level analyst reading and analysing materials related to Jewish affairs; second, he helped organize the coerced emigration of Jews from German-controlled territories, sometimes in cooperation with Zionist organizations who were trying to recruit European Jews to move to Palestine; third, he was the key manager in organizing the transportation of European Jews to concentration camps for mass murder; and fourth, towards the end of the war, when there was significant slackening of efforts to move Jews to the concentration camps, Eichmann was an extraordinarily energetic and even perversely moralistic organizer of transportation of European Jews to concentration camps and mass murder. As referred to earlier, this last transformative stage may have been missed by Arendt in her 1963 book since much of the material concerning this stage was revealed in the interrogation tapes that were not released by the Israeli authorities until 1983, ten years after Arendt's death.

After World War II, Eichmann was captured by the US Army. He gave a false name, Otto Eckmann, and escaped in early 1946. He lived in a small town in the Luneburg area of Austria for two years until 1950. He then moved to Italy, and shortly thereafter emigrated to Argentina under the name of Riccardo Klement. His family joined him in Argentina from Germany in 1952. For the next ten years he worked in Argentina at a number of different jobs such as factory worker, engineer, welder, mechanic, and farmer.

In 1960 Eichmann was captured and illegally brought to Israel by the Israeli intelligence agency, Mossad, without the knowledge or cooperation of the Argentine government. In 1960 and 1961 he was interrogated by the Israeli police investigator, Avner Less. In 1961 he was indicted on 15 criminal charges including war crimes, crimes against humanity, and crimes against the Jewish people. On 11 December 1961 the Israeli Court found him guilty on all charges. On 15 December the Court imposed the death penalty. The Israeli Supreme Court rejected his appeal on 29 May 1962. Eichmann was executed by hanging on 31 May 1962. His body was cremated by the Israeli government and scattered at sea in the Mediterranean on 1 June 1962 outside Israeli territorial waters.

24.3 ARENDT'S EICHMANN AS ARCHETYPE

Max Weber constructed archetypes, evocative representative models, designed to reveal essential features of human behaviour. Weber's most well-known archetype was the 'Protestant Capitalist', presented in his *Protestant Ethics and the Sprit of Capitalism* (1904). Weber contrasted aspects of 'Protestant' and 'Catholic' philosophy that he saw embodied in different types of work-related and organizational behaviour. While he recognized that there were Byzantine Greek Orthodox and Catholic Venetian and Florentines from the twelfth to the fifteenth centuries who were capitalist long before there were Protestants, he used the archetype of the 'Protestant Capitalist' to illuminate key aspects of capitalist organizational behaviour that had new significance.

Similarly, Emerson in his *Representative Men* (1850) presented the exemplary archetypes of 'The Philosopher', 'The Mystic', 'The Skeptic', 'The Poet', 'The Man of the World', and 'The Writer'. Long before Emerson, there was Machiavelli's modernist 'Prince' and Plato's pre-modern 'Philosopher-King' and 'Sophist'.

Arendt considered Eichmann as an archetype, but as an emergent, inductive archetype that was not static. She was concerned with the relationships among institutional and organizational environments, pressures, processes, thinking, and acting, particularly the political space or lack thereof for communicative action. Many managers and employees know that conflicts can exist between institutional requirements to obey orders and individual conscience, that institutions can harm people, and that responsibility for institutional and organizational behaviour that harms people is shared at different institutional and organizational levels. The emergent archetype organizational and Eichmann dimensions that Arendt considered are discussed in what follows.

24.4 ADMINISTRATIVE HARM

Arendt made a distinction between direct, physical inflection of harm and 'administrative harm', which she considered a key problem in modern organizational and bureaucratic life. Arendt saw that Eichmann worked in a Nazi institution engaged in, as Arendt phrased it, the 'administrative massacre' of millions of people.

As referred to in section 24.2, Eichmann's career work in the Jewish Affairs division of the SD appears to have progressed through four stages. First, in 1935, he worked as a low-level analyst reading and analysing materials related to Jewish affairs. Eichmann explains how he operated at this stage:

One of the first books he [Mildenstein, his supervisor in the SD] gave me to read was *The Jewish State* by Theodor Herzl...When I had finished reading, I was told to make an abstract of it to serve as an orientation booklet for the General SS and also for the specific use of the SD...In it I described the structure of the Zionist world organization, the aims of Zionism, its sources, and the difficulties standing in its way. I also stressed the need to encourage it, because it fell in with our own desire for a political solution: The Zionists wanted a territory [outside German-controlled territories] where the Jewish people could finally settle...and that was pretty much what the National Socialists wanted. (Lang and Sibyll, 1983: 24)

Apparently, during this time there was still division among the top Nazis about the relative merits of expulsion versus mass murder of German and European Jews.

The second stage of Eichmann's and the Jewish Affairs Division of the SD focused on the coerced emigration of Jews from German territories. Eichmann explains:

The groundwork for our reporting was provided by the SS orientation booklet. I just had to consult it...The government wants emigration, whatever favors emigration must be done, nothing must be allowed to hinder it. Everything revolved around that...Herr von Bollschwingh [a supervisor in the SD] told me a gentleman from the Haganah [a Jewish paramilitary organization based in Palestine that sometimes engaged in what today is called terrorist activities against both British and Arab forces and which later became one of the foundations for the Israeli state military] was in Berlin and arranged a meeting. First, I must tell you that I had gone through official channels and asked in writing for written instructions about this particular case. I was in no position to decide anything for myself. Naturally, this decision didn't come from Hagen either. It came from Six, who may have talked it over with Heydrich...I took the [Haganah] gentleman to lunch. He knew who I was and I knew that he was from Palestine. He told me all about the kibbutzim, about construction and development projects, things I already knew because I had read about them...we believed that our aims converged. After a second lunch, the gentleman invited me to Palestine...Heydrich authorized me to accept the invitation. (Lang and Sibyll, 1983: 28)

During this phase, Eichmann was both an efficient and even creative administrator. For example, as he explained:

They suggested that I should somehow centralize the [emigration] work...That same afternoon an idea took shape in my mind: a conveyor belt. The initial application and all the rest of the required papers are put on at one end, and the passport falls off at the other end...I then suggested a Central Office for Jewish Emigration to which the government departments—Police Presidium, Finance Ministry, State Police, Currency Control, in short all departments concerned—should send representatives...The Israelite community was also present at the conveyor belt, represented by six to fourteen delegates, depending on the amount of business to be handled. Some days we had as many as a thousand cases. (Lang and Sibyll, 1983: 52)

The third phase of Eichmann's activities involved organizing the transportation of Jews to the concentration camps for mass murder. Eichmann explains:

> I obeyed orders. In the first [coerced emigration] years I had no conflicts, no inner conflicts of any kind. I sat at my desk and did my work. My unconditional, my absolute allegiance underwent a change when I ... when the ... the ... the so-called solution of the Jewish question became more violent—I mean that is—when the gassing and shooting started. (Lang and Sibyll, 1983: 39)

This third phase of Eichmann's work began around 1941, when Heydrich sent for Eichmann and announced to him that 'The Fuhrer has ordered physical extermination of the Jews' (Lang and Sibyll, 1943: 75, 81). Eichmann also visited some of the mass murder sites and concentration camps. He continued to work efficiently and even creatively, as he did with his 'conveyor belt system', to obey and implement the order to arrange the logistics for the mass murders even while he says he felt very upset and physically shaken by the physical details of the mass murders.

24.5 WIDE ORGANIZATIONAL SEPARATION BETWEEN POLICY-MAKING AND PHYSICAL IMPLEMENTATION

From Arendt (1963a) we learn that Eichmann at his career peak in his organization, the SD, was an upper middle-level manager. The highest rank that he achieved was 'Sturmbannfuhrer', equivalent to that of a major or lieutenant colonel (Laqueur, 1983). Eichmann never belonged to the higher Nazi Party circles and did not participate in policy decisions. According to Arendt's analysis of the Eichmann organizational situation, 'The degree of responsibility increases as we draw further away from the man who uses the fatal instrument with his own hands' (1963a: 247).

Apparently, Eichmann never personally, physically harmed anyone and yet he facilitated the mass murder of millions. Eichmann both admits his guilt in facilitating the administrative massacre of millions and explains that he never personally, directly, physically harmed anyone:

> I never killed a Jew, but I never killed a non-Jew either—I've never killed anybody ... I'm covered with guilt ... I know that ... I am guilty, because I helped with the evacuation. I'm ready to pay for that ... I'm obviously guilty of complicity. I can't deny my responsibility, and any attempt to do so would be absurd ... I'm not a statistician. I just figured that out for myself ... Yes, one way or another, about six million Jews must have been killed ... I know the death penalty awaits me. I am not asking you for mercy, because I am not entitled to it. (Lang and Sibyll, 1983: 102, 110)

24.6 SEPARATION AND COMPARTMENTALIZATION OF PERSONAL CONSCIENCE AND FEELINGS FROM ORDERS

Arendt observed that Eichmann could compartmentalize his very bad feelings about the physical details of mass murders while cognitively and efficiently facilitating the transportation for the mass murders. Eichmann explained:

> I was horrified. My nerves aren't strong enough...I still remember how I visualized the scene and began to tremble, as if I'd been through something, some terrible experience. The kind of thing that happens sometimes and afterwards you start to shake...The screaming and...I was much too shaken and so on. I told Muller [his SD supervisor at the time] in my report...A doctor in a white smock wanted me to look through a peephole and watch [people being gassed]. I refused, I couldn't, I had to get out of there...Terrible, an inferno. I can't. It's...I can't do it...I told him...I implored the Gruppenfuhrer: 'Please don't send me there. Send someone else. Someone with stronger nerves'...I can't stand it. I can't sleep at night, I have nightmares. (Land and Sibyll, 1984: 76–7)

Eichmann was perhaps also able to foresee what would happen to others who worked closely and directly in the physical murders. Eichmann explains, 'We're training our men to be sadists. We shouldn't be surprised if they all turn out to be criminals, all criminals' (Lang and Sibyll, 1983: 80). That type of transformation may eventually have also happened to Eichmann in his fourth phase of energetic and perversely moralistic acceleration of efforts to send people to the concentration camps towards the end of the war.

On the apparently very few occasions when Eichmann's subordinates voiced similar reservations, Eichmann advised separation of feelings from orders. For example, on one occasion one of Eichmann's subordinates said to him: 'God grant that our enemies never get an opportunity to do the same to the German people. Eichmann replied that I shouldn't get sentimental, that it was the Fuhrer's Order and had to be carried out' (Lang and Sibyll, 1983: 96).

24.7 ORGANIZATIONAL REQUIREMENTS TO OBEY UNETHICAL AND ILLEGAL ORDERS

Eichmann voluntarily joined and rose in the ranks to upper middle-level management in an organization, the SD, where obeying authority was valued, expected, required, and where disobedience was severely punished. Arendt explains what she thinks Eichmann thought: 'His guilt came from his obedience, and obedience is praised as a virtue. His virtue had been abused by the Nazi leaders. But he was not one of the ruling clique, he was a victim' (1963a: 247).

According to Arendt, Eichmann believed that he was practising the virtue of obedience when he did his work. He obeyed orders without thinking about ethical implications. Eichmann was about six administrative layers below Hitler. Hitler ordered Borman, Borman ordered Himmler, Himmler ordered Heydrick, Heydrich ordered Gruber, Gruber ordered Eichmann, and Eichmann obeyed.

Eichmann explains his position about requirements to obey orders:

> IV B 4 [Eichmann's group] never decided anything on the strength of its own judgment and authority. It never would have entered my head to mess myself up with a decision of my own. And neither, as I've said before, did any of my staff ever make a decision of his own. All decisions were based on (a) the relevant Reich laws and accompanying implementation orders; (b) the police regulations, the decrees, orders, and instructions of Himmler and the head of the Security Police—those were our legislative bases... The loyalty oath in itself called for unquestioning obedience. So naturally we had to comply with the laws and regulations... The final solution itself—I mean, the special mission given to Heydrich—to put it bluntly, the extermination of the Jews, was not provided for by Reich law. It was a Fuhrer's Order, a so-called Fuhrer's Order. And Himmler and Heydrich and Pohl, the head of Administration and Supply—each had his own part in the implementation of the Fuhrer's Order. According to the then prevailing interpretation, which no one questioned, the Fuhrer's orders had the force of law. Not only in this case. In every case. That is common knowledge. The Fuhrer's orders have the force of law... These were not personal decisions. If I had not been sitting there, someone else would have had to make exactly the same decision on the basis of the instructions, regulations, and orders of the higher-ups. I wasn't expected to make any decisions at all. At the most, I wrote letters... for somebody else... I obeyed my orders without thinking, I just did as I was told. That's where I found my—how shall I say?—my fulfillment. It made no difference what the orders were. (Land and Sibyll, 1983: 124, 144, 157)

The Israeli Police Captain Avner Less at one point asks Eichmann, 'If for example, an officer gives the order to shoot civilians—not hostages or anything like that—no, he just picks out these civilians and says, "Shoot them!" Must the subordinate carry out such an order?' Eichmann answers:

> Yes, Herr Hauptmann [Captain]. Same as the Allied flyers, who dropped their bombs on German cities and killed women, children, and old people . .. If you don't obey, you're court-martialed. If you obey and the order was a mistake, the commanding officer must answer for it. That's how it has always been. Little by little, we were taught all these things. We grew into them, all we knew was obedience to orders. We were chained to our oath. (Land and Sibyll, 1983: 158–9)

At other points, Eichmann made comparisons to the US soldiers who obeyed the orders to drop the atomic bombs on Hiroshima and Nagasaki and killed hundreds of thousands of civilians (Sebald, 2003).

24.8 'BANALITY OF EVIL'

Arendt concludes with the judgement that Eichmann was guilty, but that instead of being insane or monstrously evil, Eichmann was, perhaps more horribly, well within the range of sanity and normality, at least within his organizational environment. He was a 'thoughtless' and 'banal' man who did not think about distinguishing right from wrong in his role as a manager in an organization that harmed millions of people. His job was not, as he saw it, to think about the ethics of policies or decisions made by higher authority. His thinking was narrowly directed towards efficient and even creative implementation.

Arendt explains:

> Despite all the efforts of the prosecution, everybody could see that this man was not a monster...he certainly would never have murdered his superior in order to inherit his post. He merely, to put the matter colloquially, never realized what he was doing...He was not stupid. It was sheer thoughtlessness—something by no means identical with stupidity. (1963a: 287)

Arendt's key characteristic of the Eichmann archetype is a narrow, routinized, 'in the box' mentality that does not recognize ethical dimensions—as Arendt phrased it, 'the banality of evil'. As referred to earlier, Arendt's concept of the 'banality' of evil may be related to Heidegger's concept of '*gerede*', idle talk (Stassen, 2003).

According to Eichmann, his motivation at the time for joining the SS was boredom with his business career, the invitation from a business acquaintance, and a vague sense that radical change was needed. Eichmann explained: 'In those first years, what mattered to me...was work and bread for seven million people, an Autobahn, and the fight against Versailles' (Lang and Sibyll, 1983: 42). The fight against Versailles referred to the broad opposition in Germany and Austria to the post-World War I Versailles treaty that imposed severe austerity conditions and was a main cause of the depression in Austria and Germany that led to literally millions of starving Austrians and Germans during that period. There was also much anti-Semitic propaganda in Germany and Austria at the time that was related to the British efforts in World War I to recruit additional countries on the side of the British, such as the United States, the Arab countries, and Zionist Jews from Europe and the United States. The British promised Zionist Jews that after the British won the war, an at least partial Israeli state would be created in Palestine. The Nazis in particular exploited this theme in propaganda efforts to portray Jews as traitors during and after World War I.

From Arendt's analysis and as the tapes appear to confirm, Eichmann appears to have joined both the SS and later the SD without very much thought about what those organizations stood for. Boredom seems to be an important motivator in his decision to join the SD. Eichmann explains: 'I expected to see what I'd seen in the Munchner Illustrierte: SS commandos riding in cars behind high party leaders, men standing on running boards. That was an escort commando, I'd got the Reichsfuhrer-SS's Security

Service mixed up with the Reich Security Service [Reichssicherheitsdienst]' (Lang and Sibyll, 1983: 21).

The fourth phase of Eichmann's work occurred towards the end of the war, around 1944, when Himmler ordered that the mass murder of Jews be halted. There was a common belief in Germany around this time that the war was lost. There was a significant slackening of mass murder efforts by many in the SS and the SD. Some appeared to be using cessation of mass murder as a negotiating strategy for future post-war considerations with General Eisenhower. Some seemed to have been more concerned about planning their own post-war escapes. Some appeared to be concerned about bad public relations associated with the mass murder concentration camps. Some seemed to be more or less depressed and less motivated as it became clear that the war was lost.

It was around this time that Eichmann seems to have elevated his efforts, moralistically condemning those who were slackening their efforts. For example, one of Eichmann's subordinates testified that, 'Even after Himmler's order of October 1944, Eichmann did not rest. The order prohibited only the destruction of the Jews, so he set to recruiting Jews... as laborers.' SS-Standartenfuhrer Kurt Becher goes even further, 'Herr Eichmann made a last attempt to circumvent Himmler's order to stop murdering... an attempt was made to keep deporting Jews by way of Vienna. This had nothing to do with labor service' (Lang and Sibyll, 1983: 250).

Avner Less observed that:

> Everyone who in the last hours of the Thousand-year Reich put human feeling above unconditional obedience is the object of Eichmann's irreconcilable hatred. He has read Gerhard Boldt's book *The Last Days of the Reich Chancellery* and discovered that Boldt, the author, was not obedient to his Fuhrer down to the last comma. The description on the dust jacket begins with the words: 'In January 1945, a young front-line officer...' Eichmann crosses out 'front-line officer' and writes in 'scoundrel,' 'traitor,' 'skunk.' Wherever Boldt's name appears in the book, he adds 'scoundrel,' 'traitor,' or 'skunk.' (Lang and Sibyll, 1983: 287)

24.9 HEIDEGGER, EICHMANN, AND ARENDT'S VIEW OF ORGANIZATIONAL BECOMING

As referred to earlier, a foundational element in Arendt's work, which she considered a key 'truth' from Heidegger's work, was Heidegger's recognition of the importance of the existential process of '*dasein*' in dynamic context. For Arendt, this is a very important transformative process influence upon one's previously accidental or even arbitrary self without foundation—in Arendt's phrase, 'without banisters'. Her process understanding and view of Eichmann's becoming in his radical organizational life was a key determinate of her building upon, as well as criticism and departure from, Heidegger.

Arendt sees in the becoming Eichmann a radical organizational process that may have gone so far as to not just greatly influence, but perhaps even eliminate any essence of a self that an unthinking Eichmann might have had when he entered the SD organizational life. Arendt did not approach her observation of Eichmann with a deductive archetype theoretical framework. For Arendt, Eichmann emerged as an archetype, making him in a sense a 'processual' archetype.

Arendt goes even further. In a sense, both Eichmann and Heidegger became what they did. Both the brilliant thinking of Heidegger and the banal unthinking of Eichmann did not appear to help them relative to the power of the organizational processes. Perhaps Arendt even saw in Heidegger during his Nazi years a somewhat similar phenomenon to the one that shaped and transformed Eichmann. If it could happen to such intellectual extremes as the brilliant thinking 'best', Heidegger and the 'banal' unthinking, ordinary 'worst', Eichmann, it might be able to happen to many or even any of us.

Arendt also departed from Heidegger in what she considered a solution to the Eichmann organizational process phenomenon with respect to the need for a participative and community building capacity for effective, ethical praxis and effective ethical resistance. Arendt saw in Heidegger's latter years a movement towards still brilliant thinking, but also further isolation and 'rejecting the possibilities of politics' that she considered as a key heightening of the power and dangers of authoritarian and bureaucratic organizational life, which isolated and negatively transformed individuals and society (Young-Bruehl, 1982: 445).

In 1976, reflecting back on her concept of the 'banality of evil', Arendt saw similar post-World War II organizational conditions as well as the transformative power of organizations to move people towards the Eichmann 'processual' archetype. She writes:

> We have become so accustomed to admiring or smiling at the good-natured solicitude of the family man, the serious concentration on the welfare of the family, the solemn commitment to devote his life to wife and children, that we scarcely perceived how the caring father, who was concerned above all for security, was transformed against his will, under the pressure of the chaotic economic conditions of our time, ... who with all his anxiety could never be sure of the next day. His pliability was already demonstrated in the homogenization ... It turned out that he was willing to sacrifice conscience, honor, and human dignity for the sake of pension, life insurance, the secure existence of wife and children. (1976: 40)

24.10 CONCLUSION

The 'processual' archetype organizational process characteristics that Arendt identified in the Eichmann situation are as follows. (1) Organizations can do immense 'administrative' harm. (2) The people who make the policy decisions to do immense harm and the middle managers who organize implementation are usually a long organizational distance from the lower-level employees who do the physical imple-mentation. (3) Administrators often separate and compartmentalize their personal ethical beliefs and feelings from their efficient and even creative implementation of unethical orders. (4) There are severe organizational requirements to obey orders; and (5) there is a 'banality' of organizational evil or at least unethical organizational behav-iour in the sense that often managers and administrators not only compartmentalize and separate personal feelings and beliefs from efficient and even creative implemen-tation of unethical orders, but also do not think about and do not want to think about the ethical implications of their work in cooperating with and facilitating unethical organizational behaviour.

With respect to these five process characteristics, there does seem to be evidence from both the public sector and the private sector that these phenomena continue to operate at least to some extent in many organizations. In the public sector we have the extreme cases of the Stalinist Soviet organizations, the Maoist Chinese communist organiza-tions, the Pol Pot Cambodian organizations, and many more.

Arendt was also apprehensive about what was happening in the United States. According to her long-time friend, Mary McCarthy,

> I used to tell Hannah Arendt that McCarthy could not last on the American political scene, but she did not believe me. Her expressed fear then and later, was for our State Department, which she expected to be emasculated by the McCarthy campaign. She was right about that, positively prescient, but in reality that was only the visible, admissible part of her fear for our country; at the same time, quietly, she was looking for signs that concentration camps were opening. Under Nixon, in the last years of the Vietnamese war, she became apprehensive. She actually talked about emigrat-ing back to Europe fast, while there was still time. That she was willing to accept the prospect of being a refugee twice, two times over, made me understand finally the absence of assurance she had been living in for roughly thirty years without my tak-ing note of it. (Young-Bruehl, 1982: 275)

One cannot help but wonder what Arendt might have thought about the seemingly never-ending and expanding United States and Israeli wars with Muslim countries, the Guantanamo detention and torture base in Cuba, the many rendition torture and inter-rogation camps all over the world, the drone bombings of homes and villages in search of suspected enemies, and even the assassination of US citizens without trial, represen-tation, or due process.

In the private sector we also seem to have at least somewhat similar phenomena oper-ating with respect to, for example, the cigarette industry, which for many years know-ingly denied that there were links between cigarette smoking and cancer, between nicotine and addiction, and knowingly used massive amounts of advertising to per-suade both children and adults to become addicted smokers.

And in another example, in the recent financial crisis and great recession, there is quite a bit of evidence that millions of people were harmed. The people who made the policy decisions and the people who organized the key implementation programmes were at a substantial organizational distance from the people being directly harmed. Many middle- and lower-level employees appeared to compartmentalize their personal feelings and ethical beliefs about the harms being done by their organizations and their administrative actions. There were and are important organizational requirements to obey and implement orders.

And there does appear to be a problem with a 'banality' of unethical, organizational behaviour where many people appear to both not think about and not want to think about their complicity in unethical organizational behaviours. For example, in a hearing of the US Senate Judiciary Committee on 6 March 2013, Senator Charles Grassley, an Iowa Republican, said to Attorney General Eric Holder that:

> I don't have a recollection of [the US Department of Justice] prosecuting any high-profile financial criminal convictions in either companies or individuals. Assistant Attorney General Breuer said that one reason why DOJ has not brought these prosecutions is that it reaches out to, quote-unquote, experts to see what effect the prosecutions would have on the financial markets. (Forsyth, 2013: 15)

Attorney General Holder appeared to agree and responded as follows:

> The concern that you have raised is one that I frankly share. And I'm not talking about [a specific case] now, because that may not be appropriate. But I am concerned that the size of some of these institutions becomes so large that it does become difficult for us to prosecute them when we are hit with indications that if you do prosecute, if you do bring a criminal charge, it will have a negative impact on the national economy, perhaps even the world economy. (Forsyth, 2013: 15)

Randall W. Forsyth, an editorial columnist for the financial publication *Barron's*, critically editorialized that 'the nation's chief law-enforcement official admitted the decision to prosecute depends not on the law, but the impact on the financial markets and the domestic and global economy from these megabanks' (Forsyth, 2013: 15–16).

Habermas observed that from the type of analysis provided by Forsyth, Arendt reconceived the concept of power. According to Arendt, 'Power corresponds to the human ability not just to act but to act in concert' (1970: 41). Habermas explains:

> Max Weber has defined power as the possibility of forcing one's own will, whatever it may be, on the conduct of others. Hannah Arendt, by contrast understands power as the capacity to agree in uncoerced communication on some community action... The basic phenomenon is not the instrumentalizing of another's will for one's own purposes but the formation of a common will in a communication aimed at agreement. (1983: 171)

References

Arendt, H. (1951). *The Origins of Totalitarianism* (New York: Harcourt Brace Jovanovich).

——(1958). *The Human Condition* (Chicago: University of Chicago Press).

——(1963a). *Eichmann in Jerusalem: A Report on the Banality of Evil* (New York: Viking).

——(1963b). *On Revolution* (New York: Viking).

——(1968). *Men in Dark Times* (New York: Harcourt Brace Jovanovich).

——(1970). *On Violence* (New York: Viking).

——(1976/2002). *Hidden Tradition* (Oxford: Oxford University Press).

—— (1978). *The Life of the Mind* (New York: Harcourt Brace Jovanovich).

——(2003). *Responsibility and Judgment*, ed. J. Kohn (New York: Schocken Books).

Bernstein, R.J. (1971). *Praxis and Action* (Philadelphia: University of Pennsylvania Press).

—— (1985). *Beyond Objectivism and Relativism: Science, Hermeneutics, and Praxis* (Philadelphia: University of Pennsylvania Press).

Forsyth, R.W. (2013). Too Big to Jail, *Barron's* (9 March): 15–16.

Gabriel, Y. (2012). Organizations in a State of Darkness: Towards a Theory of Organizational Miasma, *Organization Studies 33(9)*: 1137–52.

Habermas, J. (1983). Hannah Arendt: On the Concept of Power, in J. Habermas, *Philosophical-Political Profiles* (Cambridge, MA: MIT Press): 171–88.

Heidegger, M. (1933/1962). *Being and Time*, trans. J. Macquarrie and E. Bobinson (London: SCM Press).

——(1935/1959). *Introduction to Metaphysics* (New Haven, NJ: Yale University Press).

——(1977). *Basic Writings*, ed. D. Farrell Krell (New York: Harper & Row).

Kristeva, J. (2001). *Hannah Arendt* (New York: Columbia University Press).

Lang, J. von and Sibyll, C. (eds) (1983). *Eichmann Interrogated: Transcripts from the Archives of the Israeli Police* (New York: Vintage).

Laqueur, W. (1983). An Obedient Monster: Review of Lang, Jochen von and Sibyll, Claus (eds), *Eichmann Interrogated: Transcripts from the Archives of the Israeli Police*, *The New York Times Book Review*, 10 July: 13, 18.

Nielsen, R.P. (1984). Arendt's Action Philosophy and the Manager as Eichmann, Richard III, Faust, or Institution Citizen, *California Management Review 26(3)*: 191–201.

——(1996). *The Politics of Ethics* (New York: Oxford University Press).

Pech, R.J. and Slade, B.W. (2007). Organizational Sociopaths, *Society and Business Review* 2(3): 254–69.

Sebald, W.G. (2003). *On the Natural History of Destruction* (London: Hamish Hamilton).

Stassen, M. (2003). Introduction, in M. Stassen (ed.), *Martin Heidegger: Philosophical and Political Writings* (New York: Continuum): ix–xxxiii.

Yeats, W.B. (1919/1953). *The Collected Poems of W.B. Yeats* (New York: Macmillan).

Young-Bruehl, E. (1982). *Hannah Arendt: For Love of the World* (New Haven, NJ: Yale University Press).

CHAPTER 25

....

SIMONE DE BEAUVOIR
(1908–1986)

....

MELISSA TYLER[1]

SIMONE DE Beauvoir is widely acknowledged to be one of history's most important female intellectuals and feminist activists. She is generally regarded, even amongst her critics, to have been the most significant influence on feminist theory and politics during the course of the twentieth century (Edmondson Bell, 2000; Fullbrook and Fullbrook, 2008; Moi, 1985, 1994). Yet, with a few notable exceptions, De Beauvoir's work continues to remain curiously neglected by organizational scholars. What is particularly surprising about this is that central themes in her writing such as dialectics, subjectivity, Otherness, ethics, oppression, and equality, not to mention women's relegation to a secondary status, have become key concerns of organization theorists in recent years. The integration of a Hegelian philosophy of intersubjectivity and existentialist thinking underpinning her writing is materialized particularly in De Beauvoir's best-known work, *The Second Sex*, in the book's preoccupation with the question of 'why woman has been defined as Other' (De Beauvoir, 1949/2011: 17), a concern that has had a profound impact upon feminist thinking since the book was first published in 1949, and which constitutes the basis of our focus on De Beauvoir's writing and its potential contribution to organization studies throughout this chapter.

The chapter provides a broad introduction to some of De Beauvoir's main philosophical and political preoccupations, teasing out major themes that recur throughout her work, focusing most notably on the processual ontology underpinning her analysis of women's situation and the process of becoming Other. Revisiting these themes in her writing brings into focus, it will be argued here, the extent to which De Beauvoir understands this process as a profoundly organizational one, underpinned by what she calls 'an existential infrastructure' (De Beauvoir, 1949/2011: 69). For De Beauvoir, women are ascribed the status of the Other not as a result of their inherent biology or psychology, or even because of their material circumstances, but as the outcome of a process of organization through which one *becomes* the Other as the consequence of a series of constraints and compulsions. In contemporary terms, the latter can be identified, for instance, in the narrow chain of signifiers found in advertising that culturally encodes what it means to be a man or a woman, and in the materialization of these signifiers in settings such as education and the labour market, both of which continue to position women within a relatively restricted range of opportunities and occupations compared to men.

Heavily influenced by Hegel's philosophy of intersubjectivity (a point to which we return in due course) and its underlying processual ontology, of central concern in De Beauvoir's writing, most notably *The Second Sex*, is a preoccupation with the gendered organization of the desire for recognition. Understanding the ways in which gender performance is driven by our basic, ontological need to be accorded recognition of ourselves as viable subjects within relations of reciprocity and mutual respect as the outcome of an intersubjective process of hostility and struggle through which One confronts the Other is her primary focus in this respect. Her analysis of the gendered organization of this process leads De Beauvoir, in her development of this Hegelian dialectic, into a distinctly feminist account of the situated nature of the desire for recognition, to a critique of the negating effects of the conditions of reciprocity and of the consequences of women's perpetual misrecognition in terms of the latter's relegation to a secondary status. It is her situated understanding of this process that leads De Beauvoir to ask, as the philosophical premise of *The Second Sex*, how the reciprocal claim of the Other becomes negated within relations between men and women: 'How is it … that between the sexes this reciprocity has not been put forward, that one of the terms has been asserted as the only essential one, denying … its correlative, defining the latter as pure alterity?' (1949/2011: 7). In other words, 'why do women not contest male sovereignty?' (1949/2011: 7). Re-engaging the basic premise underpinning De Beauvoir's writing through an organizational lens enables us to reflect on the actual and potential influence of her work on organization studies, and to examine the endurance and impact of her ideas in this respect. With some cautionary provisos, the case is made in this chapter for revisiting her work, and for recognizing more widely the impact that it has had, and continues to have on organizational thinking, particularly on feminist accounts of organizational processes and practices of Othering.

We begin by considering De Beauvoir's intellectual biography, reflecting on the conditions that contributed to the production and reception of her major works for, perhaps more so than many other writers, her ideas need to be understood within the context of the intellectual, social, and political setting in which she was writing. Her writing also of course needs to be considered through connections with other philosophers, most obviously her life-long companion Jean-Paul Sartre, in order to fully appreciate the development and impact of her work both at the time it was written and subsequently. As Judi Marshall has commented in one of the few papers to develop a sustained engagement with De Beauvoir within management and organization studies, 'articulations of insight and theoretical analyses are of their time and context' (Marshall, 2000: 167). This is certainly the case with De Beauvoir's own life and writing in so far as her work must be understood within the wider social and intellectual context in which it was written, and appreciated in relation to the circumstances and conventions of her time, not least in order to appreciate the extent to which, with no self-conscious feminist movement in France at the time, and with its explicit references to female sexuality, her work was both radical and shocking (Marshall, 2000). Writing explicitly about women's sexuality in the 1940s, and within a heavily male-dominated intellectual milieu, De Beauvoir's writing was not only politically bold but also philosophically so. Her emphasis on women's secondary status as the outcome rather than the cause of their social subordination, and her concern to understand how feminine pleasure is bound up with pain and the perpetual threat of possession was ground-breaking; 'most disturbing to the defenders of the status quo was the *mix* of sex and philosophy. A woman theorizing in sensuous language broke all the rules of containment' (Rowbotham, 2009: xi). Of course, as we will discuss later when we reflect on some of the limitations and more problematic aspects of De Beauvoir's writing, many aspects of her work and ideas appear dated. However, as a classic text, *The Second Sex* in particular continues to be a highly influential reference point within feminist thinking.

25.1 DE BEAUVOIR'S LIFE AND INTELLECTUAL INFLUENCES

Simone de Beauvoir was born in Paris, where she lived for most of her life until she died aged 78, and where she is buried next to Sartre in the Cimetière du Montparnasse. Her bourgeois upbringing involved a convent education; in her autobiographical works, De Beauvoir recalls how she was deeply religious until a crisis of faith in her teens meant that she remained an atheist for the rest of her life. This is a theme underpinning her discussion of ethics in *An Ethics of Ambiguity* (1948/1976), in which De Beauvoir reflects on the relationship between ethics and secularity and considers the existentialist dilemma of absolute freedom as opposed to the constraints of circumstance. An ardent traveller and a public intellectual who enjoyed something of a celebrity status in France, De Beauvoir worked tirelessly as a writer, correspondent, editor, and political activist, as well as a teacher, with many of her closest 'disciples' becoming close friends and shared lovers of hers and Sartre's. Aside from her own work, De Beauvoir is of course well known for her lifelong relationship with Sartre, whom she (famously) met whilst preparing for the highly competitive *agrégation* at the *École Normal* at the age of 21. De Beauvoir was the youngest person ever to pass the exam, and was placed narrowly second to Sartre, an experience that would arguably shape the intellectual bond between them that lasted for the rest of their lives.

As many of De Beauvoir's intellectual biographers have noted (see Fullbrook and Fullbrook, 2008), her and Sartre always read each other's work, each being valued as the other's harshest and possibly only genuinely worthy critic. In addition to Sartre,

De Beauvoir's intellectual circle included Merleau-Ponty and Lévi-Strauss. The philosophical legacy of Hegel and Leibniz also heavily influenced her work, and she based her thesis in philosophy at the Sorbonne on the work of the latter. From Leibniz, De Beauvoir derived her interests in process and perception, and in the force of ideas, particularly in her writing on the monads in Leibniz's metaphysics. From Hegel, she developed a commitment to exploring the impact of the human need for recognition and reciprocity. From existentialism, De Beauvoir therefore took her commitment to understanding human existence as a social process of living through others, and from phenomenology, a view of this process as shaped by struggle, according to which attainment of self-consciousness requires mutual recognition. This phenomenological existentialism, and its underlying preoccupation with the conditions of human freedom and the consequences of its disavowal, led De Beauvoir to remain dedicated to integrating her personal, intellectual, and political activities throughout her life, a commitment reflected in the role that she played in the formation of several important political groups and journals with friends and acquaintances from within her and Sartre's intellectual circle.

Along with Merleau-Ponty, Sartre and De Beauvoir set up a political journal at the end of World War II, *Les Temps Modernes*, of which De Beauvoir remained an editor until her death, and in which she published early versions of the essays that were to become chapters in *The Second Sex*. In her later years particularly, she became involved in a series of feminist political campaigns, most famously signing the Manifesto of the 343 in 1971, a list of well-known women who claimed to have had an abortion (illegal at the time in France, but legalized in 1974 largely as a result of the impact of the Manifesto and the feminist movement more widely).

De Beauvoir's writing included novels, essays, biographical and autographical works, and monographs on politics, philosophy, and ethics, much of it combining different forms and genres, perhaps most obviously *She Came to Stay* (De Beauvoir, 1984), a melancholy reflection which amalgamates several characters in their social circle with whom both De Beauvoir and Sartre had intimate relationships. A similar fusion of genres can be found in her book *Adieux* (De Beauvoir, 1981/1985), constituting 'A Farewell to Sartre', in which De Beauvoir offers a painful and very personal account of her last years with Sartre, noting at the beginning that it is the only published writing of hers that Sartre had not read. Her best-known work, *The Second Sex*, arguably included all of these elements in the form of a detailed analysis of women's oppression that seamlessly blends philosophy, history, social commentary, literary analysis, and autobiography. As contemporary feminist Sheila Rowbotham writes in her foreword to the 2009 translation, 'In *The Second Sex* Beauvoir is at once a thinker, a scholar and a creative writer. Her writing communicates on several levels simultaneously, reasoning and seducing at the same time' (2009: ix).

First published in 1949, *The Second Sex* sold 22,000 copies during its first week of publication, and has since become a classic feminist text. Much controversy has surrounded the book since its publication, not least because the first English translation (published in 1954) was produced by Howard Parshley (De Beauvoir, 1949/1988), who had only a basic familiarity with French, and minimal understanding of philosophy (he was a professor of biology), so that much of the original text seems to have been misunderstood or inappropriately edited. It wasn't until 2009 (the sixtieth anniversary of the original publication date), that the publishers allowed a second translation to be produced by Constance Borde and Sheila Malovany-Chevallier, who reinstated original text that expanded the book by approximately a third, so that this long-awaited translation has been described as 'both a return and a revelation' (Rowbotham, 2009: ix).

As Claire Duchen (1986: 165) reminds us, *The Second Sex* was published at a time when there was no discernible feminist movement in France, causing something of a '*succès de scandale*'. The political Left accused De Beauvoir of deviating from the real political struggle by focusing specifically on 'the woman question', whilst also arguing that, as a relatively privileged and unencumbered member of the Parisian intellectual elite, she could not possibly claim to speak on behalf of ordinary women (Jardine, 1979). From the Right, De Beauvoir endured more personal attacks, being daubed both a pornographer because of her graphic depictions of women's bodies and references to sexuality, and amoral because of her rejection of marriage and motherhood. As Schwarzer (1984) notes, even Camus (a personal friend of both De Beauvoir and Sartre, and a member of their intellectual circle) stated publicly that De Beauvoir had made a laughing stock of the French male by publishing *The Second Sex*. A further attack came from the claim that it was actually Sartre who had written much of the text, a critique that seems to have taken De Beauvoir rather literally when she described herself as 'Sartre's disciple in matters philosophical' (see Jardine, 1979).

Widely regarded as the intellectual starting point for second-wave feminist theory, constituting what Atack (1998: 32) has described as an 'anchoring text', in what follows we shall argue that the central concern of *The Second Sex*, and arguably of De Beauvoir's writing more widely, is a fundamentally organizational one. Drawing largely from Hegel, her underlying and most enduring preoccupation is with understanding the process through which society comes to be *organized* so that one becomes the Other. As De Beauvoir puts it, 'this is the fundamental characteristic of women: she is the Other at the heart of a whole whose two components are necessary to each other' (De Beauvoir, 1949/2011: 9).

25.2 WOMEN'S OTHERNESS AND *THE SECOND SEX*

In order to understand how De Beauvoir's conception of the situated self helps us to reflect on the positioning of women within organizational life, it is important to locate it within her broader analysis of the intersubjective process of becoming a woman, proceeding from her conviction that 'One is not born but rather, becomes woman' (De

Beauvoir, 1949/2011: 293). Here, in what is perhaps the most oft-quoted line from *The Second Sex*, De Beauvoir encapsulates the philosophical preoccupations that drive the text, and summarizes the thesis emerging from it; namely that as biology, psychoanalysis, and historical materialism cannot account for women's secondary status, a more philosophical, ontological account of woman's position as Other is necessary. Hence, De Beauvoir articulates the notion that becoming a man or a woman is a dynamic social process, one that acknowledges both the capacity of social construction as well as the compulsion to 'become' in a particular way, *and* the constraints on autonomous subjectivity produced by women's oppressive situation. It is precisely this dynamic interrelationship between agentive capacity, social compulsion, and structural constraint that De Beauvoir encapsulates in this widely quoted line. This characterizes the processual ontology underpinning *The Second Sex*, and arguably feminist theory subsequently, the former premised on a socially situated understanding of the Hegelian desire for recognition, and the latter based on a social constructionist ontology of gender as a dynamic social process. As Kruks has put it:

> In her account of women as subjects 'in situation', *De Beauvoir can both acknowledge the weight of social construction*, including gender, in the formation of the self and *yet refuse to reduce the self to an 'effect'*. She can grant a degree of autonomy to the self—as is necessary in order to sustain key notions of political action, responsibility, and the oppression of the self—*while also acknowledging the real constraints on autonomous subjectivity produced by oppressive situations*. (Kruks, 1992: 92, emphasis added)

For feminist theorists who have drawn on *The Second Sex* as a reference point, this ontological move emphasizes that while 'to become a woman is a purposive and appropriative set of acts' (Butler, 1990: 36), such acts are simultaneously compelled and constrained by the particular circumstances in which women are situated. In organizational terms, this means that becoming gendered is both an organizational process—a process through which men and women are organized into differential, and in the case of the latter, deferential, social positions in accordance with the conditions of viable subjectivity—*and* a process that takes place within organizational settings, within which conformity to the conditions of viability is rewarded through recognition (in the form of employability, for instance). Yet, as De Beauvoir emphasizes, because of women's relatively deferential social position, and their ontological status as Other, this recognition is always precarious and conditional, so that even when women are accorded the status of viable employability, their position is always relatively disadvantaged, so that women are granted access only to a relatively narrow range of occupations, or are perpetually under paid for the work they do, or their skills are not recognized as such. Further, those who are unable or unwilling to meet the conditions of viability are condemned to misrecognition in the form of discrimination and exclusion, for example. As De Beauvoir (1949/2011: 183) put it starkly in the 1940s, 'disabled, ugly or old, woman repels', a repulsion that has arguably intensified considerably in labour market terms within the confines of the contemporary 'aesthetic economy' (Böhme, 2003). In this sense, De Beauvoir still speaks clearly 'to the problem of developing an adequate feminist theory of the gendering of subjectivity' as Butler (1990: 36) puts it, including within and through organizational processes.

For De Beauvoir, the key issue in understanding sexual difference (taken here to refer to the difference between men and women as social subjects) is that if we accept that women exist as a social category, but also that women are not defined by their reproductive function or determined by some notion of an 'eternal feminine', then we must ask: 'what is a woman?' (De Beauvoir, 1949/2011: 5). In *The Second Sex* ontological rather than biological, psychological, or materialist answers are found to this basic philosophical question: 'the relation of the two sexes is not that of two electrical poles: the man represents both the positive and the neutral... Woman is the negative, without reciprocity' (De Beauvoir, 1949/2011: 5). Here, De Beauvoir maps out the basic premise of her account, namely that what it means to be a woman is to be a human being driven by, but at the same time denied, recognition, 'without reciprocity'. Hence, 'she determines and differentiates herself in relation to man, and he does not in relation to her; she is the inessential form of the essential. He is the Subject; he is the Absolute. She is the Other' (De Beauvoir, 1949/2011: 6). In this respect, as noted earlier, De Beauvoir draws on Otherness as a basic category of human existence within Hegelian philosophy, emphasizing how 'the subject posits itself only in opposition' (De Beauvoir, 1949/2011: 6).

Within De Beauvoir's account, woman is condemned to perpetual immanence, unable to achieve the self-consciousness necessary for emancipation, because she cannot recognize her own subjugation; woman internalizes her secondary status. In its simplest form, De Beauvoir's thesis is therefore a critique of the conditions of recognition, and of the consequences of misrecognition, for women as viable subjects. It is not then merely woman's Otherness but her subjection—the non-reciprocal objectification of what it means to be a woman—that De Beauvoir is concerned with. For her, it is this non-reciprocal objectification—the social situation, or *organization*—of the desire for recognition that precludes relations of reciprocity between the sexes:

> Hence woman makes no claims for herself as subject because she lacks the concrete means, because she senses the necessary link connecting her to man without positing its reciprocity, and because she often derives satisfaction from her role as *Other*. (De Beauvoir, 1949/2011: 10, original emphasis)

What De Beauvoir calls 'the drama of woman' (De Beauvoir, 1949/2011: 29)—evoking the theatrical language of Hegel's master–slave narrative—lies in the existential conflict between the fundamental aspirations of every subject (ego)—who regards the self as essential—and the compulsions of a concrete or 'situated' existence in which she is already the inessential and within which femininity is equated with Otherness. In her account of the perpetuation of this conflict, difference is used as the justification for woman's Otherness, for women's supposed inferiority and consequential inequality. This therefore creates a vicious circle for women so that in all analogous circumstances: when an individual or a group of individuals is kept in a situation of inferiority, the fact is that he or they *are* inferior. But the scope of the verb *to be* must be understood; bad faith means giving it a substantive value, when in fact it has the sense of the Hegelian dynamic: to *be* is to have become, to have been made as one manifests oneself. (De Beauvoir, 1949/2011: 13, original emphasis)

Here De Beauvoir notes that if a woman is oppressed to the point where her subjectivity is denied her, then her situation is *de facto* her 'destiny'. However, what De Beauvoir derives from Hegelian philosophy (and its development in existentialism in this respect), is the conviction that the gendered self is not a static state of being, but rather a constant process of becoming. As De Beauvoir puts it (drawing also on Merleau-Ponty's ontology of the subject), 'woman is not a fixed reality, but a becoming, she has to be compared with man in her becoming; that is, her *possibilities* have to be defined' (De Beauvoir, 1949/2011: 46, original emphasis). The search for an underlying essence of womanhood, for De Beauvoir, is therefore futile and misguided; for her, men and women are ultimately the same in their potential ('possibilities') as human beings, but this 'sameness' is distorted through the social location of woman as the (ontologically inferior) Other— through her relegation to the 'second sex', or what De Beauvoir describes as 'her concrete situation' (De Beauvoir, 1949/2011: 15). For (drawing heavily on her Marxist influences) 'in humanity individual "possibilities" depend on the economic and social situation' (De Beauvoir, 1949/2011: 47). In this respect, De Beauvoir's reading of Hegel's master–slave dialectic, through which he narrates the struggle for recognition between two opposing social beings, evolves into her concept of man as the Self, and woman as the Other. For De Beauvoir, as discussed earlier, women cannot enter into the struggle for recognition in Hegelian terms because they cannot recognize themselves as oppressed in so far as they themselves contribute to the perpetuation of their own oppression: 'woman's drama lies in this conflict between the fundamental claim of every subject, which always posits itself as essential, *and the demands of a situation that constitutes her as inessential*' (De Beauvoir, 1949/2011: 17, emphasis added).

In woman, De Beauvoir therefore recognizes a self that both men and women have defined as Other; an ideal of womanhood that entails in women a duty to sacrifice themselves ontologically, if not literally. For her, what makes so fundamental and enduring the idea that women find a sense of self only by surrendering their claim to a sense of self (to their right to 'be' as autonomous human beings) is, therefore, that women internalize it (and so work with rather than against it), as an accurate reflection of what it means to be a feminine woman. This is what De Beauvoir means by the 'feminine mystique'; a concept developed by Betty Friedan (1963) in her liberal feminist account of housewives as 'forfeited selves'. It also echoes Mary Wollstonecraft's (1788/1976) much earlier assessment of middle-class women confined to the private sphere of the home as 'caged birds'. De Beauvoir, much like Wollstonecraft before her, and Friedan subsequently, argued that the 'feminine mystique' is perpetuated through the socialization and education of women into passive social roles.

Ultimately, therefore, De Beauvoir argued that sexual difference needs to be understood in relation to the human project:

the value of muscular strength, of the phallus, of the tool can be defined only in a world of values; it is determined by the basic project through which *the existent seeks transcendence*. (De Beauvoir, 1949/2011: 91, emphasis added)

Developing this existentialist conception of the human condition as a project of becoming into something more discernibly feminist, she maintained that women are compelled to conform to a feminine (passive, inferior) role in order to 'be', to be accepted as feminine, and so sustain the very relations of difference that constitute the foundation of their oppression in order to survive socially, economically, and psychologically. As she poignantly put it in this respect, 'her wings are cut and then she is blamed for not knowing how to fly' (De Beauvoir, 1949/2011: 660). In other words, women are compelled to 'become' in particular ways, ways that ultimately sustain their own oppression, in order to exist as feminine. What is significant in De Beauvoir's terms is that women not only accept this but perpetually, and painfully, aspire to it as a sign of their viability as feminine subjects. The ensuing embodied servitude that women don't simply live and experience but positively embrace as a sign of viable femininity, De Beauvoir describes as 'a state of serfdom':

> It follows that woman knows and chooses herself not as she exists for herself but as man defines her. She has to be described first as men dream of her since her *being-for-men is one of the essential factors of her concrete condition.* (De Beauvoir, 1949/2011: 159, emphasis added)

In the last third of *The Second Sex*, in what for many are its most problematic sections (see Evans, 1985), De Beauvoir emphasizes that because woman's Otherness is socially rather than biologically determined, women need not continue playing the role of the Other indefinitely, and she outlines three strategies women might pursue in this respect. First, she argues, women must support themselves financially, striving for economic autonomy through paid work: 'when she is productive and active, she regains her transcendence' (De Beauvoir, 1949/2011: 737). It is important to note, however, that De Beauvoir also cautions that a woman who works unpaid in the home and on a paid (but exploited) basis within the labour market carries a 'double servitude' (De Beauvoir, 1949/2011: 739); not only are working women independent only within the confines of an oppressed class, their paid work outside of the home does not free them from unpaid work within it, and persistent patterns of labour market segmentation mean that even within paid work, most women 'do not escape the traditional feminine world' (De Beauvoir, 1949/2011: 738). Hence,

> The woman embarks on a career in the context of a highly problematic situation, subjugated still by the burdens traditionally implied by her femininity. (De Beauvoir, 1949/2011: 753)

This aspect of her writing, as Evans (1985: 128) has succinctly put it, 'lacks nuance', remaining as it does relatively undeveloped in her account—in her discussion of professional women as divided between femininity and autonomy, for instance, or of the body work that women have to invest in conforming to the aesthetic ideals of the labour market, both of which are themes that are mentioned only in passing (see De Beauvoir, 1949/2011: 739–40).

Second, in another passage of the text written in the aforementioned style of an auto-biographical reflection in which she laments the 'burdensome hypocrisy...demanded of her' (De Beauvoir, 1949/2011: 743), De Beauvoir argues that women should strive to become intellectuals—a theme that has been developed by proponents of '*l'écriture feminine*' such as Hélène Cixous (1986), who urge women to 're-inscribe' themselves into the political process through their writing (see Höpfl, 2011). This, in De Beauvoir's view, helps address the fundamentally epistemological problem of women's Otherness; in her words, to unravel the extent to which 'representation of the world, as the world itself, is the work of men; they describe it from a point of view that is their own and that they confound with the absolute truth' (De Beauvoir, 1949/2011: 166).

The final and most important strategy for women to take part in is political transformation through social reorganization, and De Beauvoir urges women to act as agents of macro-level social change. Yet, she did not, however, put her faith entirely in the development of a post-capitalist utopia, acknowledging that there will always be some differences between men and women. These, she argued in particularly problematic passages of *The Second Sex*, are primarily corporeal—relating to men and women's different ways of 'being' in the body.

Drawing directly on Merleau-Ponty's (1948/2002: 409) post-Cartesian understanding of embodiment as our mode of 'being in the world', developed most fully in his *Phenomenology of Perception*, De Beauvoir understands embodiment as the process through which lived materiality and subjective consciousness merge into reciprocity: 'I am thus my body in as much as I have experience, and reciprocally, my body is like a natural subject' (Merleau-Ponty, 1948/2002: 232, cited in De Beauvoir, 1949/2011: 42). Put simply, for De Beauvoir, 'the body is not a thing, *it is a situation*: it is our grasp on the world and the outline for our projects' (De Beauvoir, 1949/2011: 46, emphasis added). As in the case of her incorporation of Hegel's (1807/1979) master–slave dialectic or Marx's critique of proletarian false consciousness, however, De Beauvoir develops Merleau-Ponty's thesis into a more discernibly feminist understanding of women's relationship to their bodies, arguing that 'woman *is* her body and man *is* his, but for her body is something other than her' (De Beauvoir, 1949/2011: 42). In De Beauvoir's hands, the female body as it is 'lived by the subject' (De Beauvoir, 1949/2011: 50) becomes 'an alienated opaque thing' (De Beauvoir, 1949/2011: 42), 'endured as a burden' (De Beauvoir, 1949/2011: 360), with women's embodied experience of reproduction in particular being framed as 'an exhausting servitude' (De Beauvoir, 1949/2011: 43). While several feminists have been strongly influenced by De Beauvoir's analysis of women as living 'beside themselves' in relation to their bodies (Benhabib, 1992), not surprisingly other feminist writers such as Hughes and Witz (1997) have been critical of this aspect of her account of women's lived experiences of embodiment, reflecting on its negative portrayal of motherhood in particular and its 'troubling' (Moi, 1994: 148) descriptions of women's relationship to their bodies more generally. Evans (1985) has also noted the largely unreflexive tone of De Beauvoir's use of language in her descriptions of women's bodies, which makes it difficult to discern De Beauvoir's critique of the alienating opacity of women's bodies from her own feelings and experiences, an ambivalence that characterizes her various descriptions of women's relationship to their bodies:

> It is a burden: weakened by the species, bleeding every month, passively propagating, for her it is not the pure instrument of her grasp on the world but rather an opaque presence; it is not certain that it will give her pleasure and it creates pains that tear her apart; it contains 'threats': she feels danger in her insides...Her body escapes her, it betrays her; it is her most intimate reality, but it is a shameful reality that she keeps hidden. And yet it is her marvelous double; she contemplates it in the mirror with amazement; it is the promise of happiness, a work of art, a living statue; she shapes it, adorns it, displays it. (De Beauvoir, 1949/2011: 672)

Further to the criticisms to which *The Second Sex* has been subject for its portrayal of women's bodies as relatively abject, and for what might be taken to be a rather confused position in this respect, De Beauvoir has also been criticized for her acceptance, even celebration, of male ideals (see Kruks, 1992 and Moi, 1994). Indeed, in some sections of the text she appeals directly to a predominantly male notion of abstract, universal freedom as the goal for the truly liberated woman, urging women to 'overcome' their burdensome bodies and embrace male rationality. In this sense, her writing is arguably much closer to Sartre than Merleau-Ponty in its implicit reinstatement of a Cartesian dualism; noted by many critics has been the way in which the last word of *The Second Sex*, literally, is granted to a call for an unequivocal affirmation of fraternity. In sum, *The Second Sex* has been

> called racist as it did not account for Black women's experience; heterosexist or homophobic for its depiction of lesbian women as sexually abnormal; patriarchal for accepting male terms of reference and lacking in any notion of woman centred-ness; exclusive because of its existentialist framework and difficult language. (Duchen, 1986: 166)

Duchen (1986: 167) goes on to note that, more recently, De Beauvoir has also been criticized for 'ignoring the fact that men, as well as women, need to change, and again for her assumption of heterosexuality as the norm' (see also Kruks, 1992).

These criticisms notwithstanding, few feminists (even those who number its most vehement critics) would deny that *The Second Sex* has been fundamental to the development of contemporary feminism. As Rosemary Tong puts it in her text on contemporary feminist theory, 'no introduction to feminist thought would be nearly complete without a discussion of this work, which has helped many feminists understand the full significance of woman's Otherness' (1998: 195). Many other writers have emphasized the importance of De Beauvoir's work to feminist theory and philosophy more generally.

Liz Stanley, for instance, has argued that 'the fecundity of her philosophical thinking is undeniable and fascinating' (2001: 202). Toril Moi has perhaps put it most passionately, arguing that

> *The Second Sex* is both a major philosophical text and the deepest and most origi-
> nal work of feminist thought to have been produced in this [the twentieth] cen-
> tury...Feminist thought can benefit immensely from serious reconsideration of *The
> Second Sex*, not as a historical document illustrating a long past moment in feminist
> thought, but as a source of new philosophical insights. (1994: vii)

25.3 DE BEAUVOIR AND ORGANIZATION STUDIES

Whilst De Beauvoir's writing has been the subject of considerable and sustained engagement within feminist theory, organizational scholars, with a few notable exceptions,
have tended to eschew direct engagement with her work. However, the impact of her
writing can be felt quite widely across the field, particularly in terms of a more sustained
dialogue in recent years with so-called 'new French feminists' (see Höpfl, 2011), and
especially so via the inroads that Judith Butler's work has begun to make into organization studies (Hancock and Tyler, 2007; Parker, 2002; Phillips and Knowles, 2012; Pullen
and Knights, 2007; Tyler and Cohen, 2008). Butler (1990) herself acknowledges the debt
she owes to De Beauvoir, tracing her own preoccupation with the conditions of recognition in her earlier writing (Butler, 1990, 1993), and the consequences of misrecognition
in her more recent work (Butler, 2004, 2005, 2009), back to De Beauvoir's dual concern
with gender as a productive social process on the one hand, and with the social conditions constraining that process on the other. For Butler (1990), what she terms the
'heterosexual matrix', an ontological-epistemic schema that organizes sex, gender, and
sexuality as a hierarchical dualism, privileging masculine heterosexuality, owes much to
De Beauvoir's account of the constraints that compel women to 'become' in particular
ways. Yet beyond Butler's own acknowledgements, the thread running from Butler back
through De Beauvoir and ultimately to Hegel in understanding the process through
which women come to be *organized* into a position of Otherness remains relatively
undeveloped even within critical, feminist thinking.

De Beauvoir's influence is also widely but indirectly felt in studies acknowledging
a grammatical shift in the way in which gender is articulated, emphasizing that gender is something that we 'do' rather than what we have, or are (West and Zimmerman,
1987). From this perspective, gender is understood as a social or discursive practice characterized by fluidity, multiplicity, and performativity (Czarniawska, 2006;
Jeanes, 2007; Kerfoot and Knights, 1998; Martin, 2003, 2006; Pullen, 2006; Pullen and
Simpson, 2009). Again, the direct connections with the work of De Beauvoir's remain

underdeveloped, yet re-engaging her writing has the potential to enable us to develop a more recognition-based understanding of gender performativity, one concerned to understand, on the one hand, the role organizations play in compelling us to become in particular ways and, on the other, the organizational constraints limiting this becoming, itself understood as a process of organization. De Beauvoir reminds us that not only how we become who we are, but also why, is driven by ontological desire—by the basic, human need for recognition of oneself as a viable subject—and furthermore, because both the desire for recognition and the conditions of viability governing its conferral or denial are always socially situated, the process through which we become who we are is organized in such a way as to relegate women to a secondary status. Understood through this 'organizational' lens, women's relative inferiority can therefore be seen as the outcome and not the cause of their subjugation; situating women as Other constitutes a fundamentally *organizational* process at both an ontological and social level.

One notable example of explicit engagement with these organizational aspects of De Beauvoir's writing can be identified in the form of a collection of papers published as a special issue of the *Journal of Management Inquiry* in 2000, to mark the fiftieth anniversary of the publication of *The Second Sex*. In her editorial overview of this collection, Judi Marshall (2000) focuses on the contribution of De Beauvoir's writing to the development of a more pluralist approach to management and organization studies, one that values rather than negates gender analysis and the contribution of feminist scholarship. Further sustained engagement with De Beauvoir can be found in a series of papers published almost exclusively in the journal *Gender, Work and Organization*. Here, in a recent article on the performativity of women business owners, Phillips and Knowles (2012) for instance, draw on De Beauvoir to demonstrate how 'women's entrepreneurship is Othered' within popular cultural discourses. Similarly, Tyler (2005) develops a critique of the co-optation of women's Otherness in literature on organizational change management drawing directly on insights from *The Second Sex*, arguing that within change management discourse women are positioned in a secondary role, largely as the providers of emotional support, whereas men tend to be positioned more strategically as change agents. Gherardi (1996), Kerfoot and Knights (2004), and Simpson (2011) also cite De Beauvoir in their respective discussions of the ways in which organizational processes assign an inferior status to femininity, as does Jeanes (2007) in her critique of gender binaries that construct woman as the Other as an obstacle to organizational equity. Bolton (2005) also cites De Beauvoir in her discussion of the ceremonial work undertaken by women working as gynaecology nurses in order to reappropriate their relegation to a secondary status, reframing themselves as Other in a way that collectively embraces the marginal status attributed to their work and skill; for the nurses in her study, being 'on the outside' is reframed as a position of strength and solidarity. Powell, Bagilhole, and Dainty (2009: 414) also explore the ways in which women engineers do and undo gender with reference to De Beauvoir's discussion of how 'woman is socially constructed as the Other'.

Building on the many insights provided by these works and re-engaging not only with the substance of *The Second Sex* but also the conditions in which it was written and published arguably encourages us to reflect critically on the production of knowledge and of knowing subjects within contemporary academia, reflecting on not only what we write, but also how we write and position our work in relation to others. Writing in the 1940s, De Beauvoir emphasized the importance of a situated, reflexive understanding of the production of knowledge, and of ourselves as knowing subjects:

> It is no doubt impossible to approach any human problem without partiality: even the way of asking questions, of adopting perspectives, presupposes hierarchies of interests; all characteristics comprise values; every so-called objective description is set against an ethical background. Instead of trying to conceal those principles that are more or less explicitly implied, we would be better off stating them from the start... [as] Presence in the world implies the positing of a body that is both a thing of the world and a point of view on this world. (De Beauvoir, 1949/2011: 16 and 24)

As Marshall put it in this respect, both the substance and the form of De Beauvoir's work serves as a poignant reminder to us that 'the personal, professional and intellectual are interwoven' (2000: 169). Following De Beauvoir, much of the scholarship discussed in this chapter has concerned itself with the social and organizational construction of gender, and with the perpetuation of inequalities based on gender difference. Integrating insights from De Beauvoir's thinking with more recent writing on multiplicity and intersectionality opens up avenues to explore more carefully and reflexively the ways in which other aspects of our selves are situated and organized.

In this respect, De Beauvoir's writing encourages us to develop more theoretically sophisticated accounts of Othering as a process of organization, understanding not only how we are embedded within organizational structures that serve to disadvantage, discriminate, marginalize, and negate, but also why, and with what consequences. The processual ontology underpinning her work requires us to consider the dynamic relationship between how, as situated subjects, we are *embodied, embedded,* and *encoded* organizationally. Her situated understanding of becoming as a social process also requires us to confront the conditions of possibility that compel and constrain our becoming, focusing our attention on the terms of recognition, and on the consequences of misrecognition, and particularly on the processes through which organizations exploit our desire for recognition. In this respect, De Beauvoir's understanding of the need for recognition as the most basic human premise leads her to emphasize how our mutual interdependence explains both 'why oppression is possible and why it is so hateful' (De Beauvoir, 1948/1976: 82).

Insights such as these lead us to ask, what would it mean to develop a more relational, situated model of organizational life? How might we make sense of organizations within a more processual epistemology that frames knowledge as relational, based upon a dialogical methodology in which all research participants understand each other as knowing subjects? These kinds of ethical, epistemological, and methodological questions are still in their relatively embryonic stages within organization studies. At the time of its publication, *The Second Sex* represented a shockingly significant departure from conventional thinking about women, subjectivity, and emancipation, even within the relatively intellectually elitist, sexually enlightened, and politically radical circles in which De Beauvoir mixed at the time of writing. Re-engaging with this text rather invites the question, therefore, what form might such a radical departure take now, and what impact might it have?

NOTE

1. This chapter is dedicated to Heather Höpfl, for the flying lessons.

REFERENCES

Atack, M. (1998). Writing from the Centre: Ironies of Otherness and Marginality, in R. Evans (ed.), *Simone de Beauvoir's The Second Sex: New Interdisciplinary Essays* (Manchester: University of Manchester Press): 31–58.

de Beauvoir, S. (1943/1984). *She Came To Stay*, trans. Y. Moyse and R. Senhouse (London: Flamingo).

——(1948/1976). *The Ethics of Ambiguity*, trans. B. Frechtman (New York: Citadel Press).

——(1949/1988). *The Second Sex*, trans. H.M. Parshley (London: Jonathan Cape).

—— (1949/2011). *The Second Sex*, trans. C. Borde and S. Malovany-Chevallier (London: Vintage).

——(1981/1985). *Adieux*, trans. P. O'Brian (Harmondsworth: Penguin).

Benhabib, S. (1992). *Situating the Self* (Cambridge: Polity).

Böhme, G. (2003). Contribution to the Critique of the Aesthetic Economy, *Thesis Eleven* 73(1): 71–82.

Bolton, S. (2005). Women's Work, Dirty Work: The Gynaecology Nurse as Other, *Gender, Work and Organization* 12(2): 169–86.

Butler, J. (1990). *Gender Trouble* (London: Routledge).

——(1993). *Bodies That Matter* (London: Routledge).

——(2004). *Undoing Gender* (London: Routledge).

——(2005). *Giving an Account of Oneself* (London: Routledge).

——(2009). *Precarious Lives* (London: Routledge).

Calás, M. and Smircich, L. (2000). Ignored for 'Good Reason': Beauvoir's Philosophy as a Revision of Social Identity Approaches, *Journal of Management Inquiry* 9(2): 193–99.

Cixous, H. (1986). *The Newly Born Woman*, trans. B. Wing (Minneapolis: University of Minnesota Press).

Czarniawska, B. (2006). Doing Gender unto the Other: Fiction as a Mode of Studying Gender Discrimination in Organizations, *Gender, Work and Organization* 13(3): 234–53.

Duchen, C. (1986). *Feminism in France* (London: Routledge).

Edmondson Bell, E. (2000). What Does it Mean to Be An Intellectual Woman? A Comparative Essay, *Journal of Management Inquiry* 9(2): 200–6.

Evans, M. (1985). *Simone de Beauvoir: Feminist Mandarin* (London: Tavistock).

——(1996). *Simone de Beauvoir* (London: Sage).

Friedan, B. (1963). *The Feminine Mystique* (New York: Dell).

Fullbrook, E. and Fullbrook, K. (2008). *Sex and Philosophy: Rethinking de Beauvoir and Sartre* (London: Conundrum).

Gherardi, S. (1995). *Gender, Symbolism and Organizational Cultures* (London: Sage).

—— (1996). Gendered Organizational Cultures: Narratives of Women Travellers in a Male World, *Gender, Work and Organization* 3(4): 187–201.

Hancock, P. and Tyler, M. (2007). Undoing Gender and the Aesthetics of Organizational Performance, *Gender, Work and Organization* 16(6): 512–33.

Hegel, G.W.F. (1807/1979). *Phenomenology of Spirit*, trans. A.V. Miller (Oxford: Oxford University Press).

Höpfl, H. (2011). Women's Writing, in E. Jeanes, D. Knights, and P.Y. Martin (eds), *Handbook of Gender, Work and Organization* (Oxford: Wiley-Blackwell): 25–36.

Hughes, A. and Witz. A. (1997). Feminism and the Matter of Bodies: From de Beauvoir to Butler, *Body and Society* 3(1): 47–60.

Jardine, A. (1979). An Interview with Simone de Beauvoir, *Signs: Journal of Women in Culture and Society* 5(2): 224–36.

Jeanes, E. (2007). The Doing and Undoing of Gender: The Importance of Being a Credible Female Victim, *Gender, Work and Organization* 14(6): 552–71.

Kerfoot, D. and Knights, D. (1998). Managing Masculinity in Contemporary Organizational Life: A Man(agerial) Project, *Organization* 5(1): 7–26.

—— (2004). Between Representations and Subjectivity: Gender Binaries and the Politics of Organizational Transformation, *Gender, Work and Organization* 11(4): 430–54.

Kruks, S. (1992). Gender and Subjectivity: Simone de Beauvoir and Contemporary Feminism, *Signs: Journal of Women in Culture and Society* 18(1): 89–110.

Marshall, J. (2000). Revisiting Simone de Beauvoir: Recognizing Feminist Contributions to Pluralism in Organizational Studies, *Journal of Management Inquiry* 9(2): 166–72.

Martin, P.Y. (2003). 'Said and Done' Versus 'Saying and Doing': Gendering Practices, Practicing Gender at Work, *Gender and Society* 17(3): 342–66.

—— (2006). Practising Gender at Work: Further Thoughts on Reflexivity, *Gender, Work and Organization* 13(3): 254–76.

Merleau-Ponty, M. (1948/2002). *Phenomenology of Perception* (London: Routledge).

Moi, T. (1985). *Sexual/Textual Politics* (London: Routledge).

—— (1994). *Simone de Beauvoir: The Making of an Intellectual Woman* (Oxford: Blackwell).

Parker, M. (2002). Queering Management and Organization, *Gender, Work and Organization* 9(2): 146–66.

Phillips, M. and Knowles, D. (2012). Performance and Performativity: Undoing Fictions of Women Business Owners, *Gender, Work and Organization* 19(4): 416–37.

Powell, A., Bagilhole, B., and Dainty, A. (2009). How Women Engineers Do and Undo Gender: Consequences for Gender Equality, *Gender, Work and Organization* 16(4): 411–28.

Pullen, A. (2006). Gendering the Research Self: Social Practice and Corporeal Multiplicity in the Writing of Organizational Research, *Gender, Work and Organization* 13(3): 277–98.

—— and Knights, D. (2007). Editorial: Undoing Gender—Organizing and Disorganizing Performance, *Gender, Work and Organization* 14(6): 505–11.

—— and Simpson, R. (2009). Managing Difference in Feminized Work: Men, Otherness and Social Practice, *Human Relations* 62(4): 561–87.

Rowbotham, S. (2009). Foreword, *The Second Sex*, trans. C. Borde and S. Malovany-Chevallier (London: Vintage): ix–xix.

Schwarzer, A. (1984). *After The Second Sex: Conversations with Simone de Beauvoir* (London: Pantheon).

Simpson, R. (2011). Men Discussing Women and Women Discussing Men: Reflexivity, Transformation and Gendered Practice in the Context of Nursing Care, *Gender, Work and Organization* 18(4): 377–98.

Tong, R. (1998). *Feminist Thought: A Comprehensive Introduction* (London: Routledge).

Tyler, M. (2005). Women in Change Management: Simone de Beauvoir and the Co-optation of Women's Otherness, *Journal of Organizational Change Management* 18(6): 561–77.

—— (2011). Postmodern Feminism and Organization Studies: A Marriage of Inconvenience?, in E. Jeanes, D. Knights, and P.Y. Martin (eds), *Handbook of Gender, Work and Organization* (Oxford: Wiley-Blackwell): 9–24.

—— and Cohen, L. (2008). Management in/as Comic Relief: Queer Theory and Gender Peformativity in *The Office*, *Gender, Work and Organization* 15(2): 113–32.

Wollstonecraft, M. (1788/1976). *A Vindication of the Rights of Woman* (London: Dover Press).

CHAPTER 26

MAURICE MERLEAU-PONTY (1908–1961)

WENDELIN KUEPERS

26.1 INTRODUCTION

THE SPECIAL contribution of the phenomenology of Merleau-Ponty lies in revealing the bodily, embodied dimensions and forms of non- or post-representational knowing for understanding organizational phenomena and realties as processes. Phenomenological process thinking involves *inter*preting phenomena dynamically, by seeing them as unfolding movements, flows, activities, or events. This kind of process orientation directs attention to our relational involvements in the world as the moving condition for existence and co-creation. In particular, it implies considering the *in-between* of, for example, continuity and discontinuity, or stability and change, or static substances and dynamic occurrences. Taking relationality seriously, this process orientation overcomes the inherent problems and limits of mechanistic, essentialist, and substance-based approaches towards understanding organizational phenomena (Sandberg and Dall'Alba, 2009). In line with the embodied turn in social and organizational science, Merleau-Ponty's phenomenology offers possibilities for developing a processual understanding of a re-embodied organization (Styhre, 2004) and a corresponding sense-based and sense-making organizational practice.

26.2 LIFE

Maurice Merleau-Ponty was born in 1908 in Rochefort-sur-Mer, a provincial town in France close to the sea; he became an orphan early in his childhood. Eventually he made up his way to the prestigious École Normale Superieure, where he studied and became friends with an influential circle of philosophers, including Sartre, de Beauvoir, and Camus. After serving in the infantry in World War II, and being active in the resistance movement while teaching, he was recognized and appointed academically to the highest professorial levels. Following his lecturing on child psychology and education at the Sorbonne, he was awarded the prestigious chair of philosophy at the Collège de France. Being political editor of *Les Temps Modernes*, he became part of the leftist movement in France, although he was gradually disillusioned with Marxism.

Deeply enmeshed in the often agonistic social and political struggles of his time, as well as in responding to the theoretical questions associated with western modernity, he initiated an existential turn in phenomenology. This turn opposed definitions of human beings as primarily rational as well as resisting the primacy of scientific-technical thought. In their stead he emphasized the value of bodily existence as the primary site of experiencing and knowing the world. This emphasis on the body carries through to his own method; as, for Merleau-Ponty, phenomenology is discernible as a specific style or mode of reasoning and 'movement of thought' (1962: xxi). It is characterized by a flexible and vivid way of enquiry, actively encouraging adherents to take different directions, experiment with new ways of reasoning, always aware of the sheer variety of meaning and ambiguity inherent in the phenomena being enquired after.

In his later philosophy he moved towards a more 'adequate' ontological thinking by postulating a general, underlying, common connective tissue (Merleau-Ponty, 1995: 131) or fleshly 'texture of Being' (Merleau-Ponty, 1964: 166), which we occupy and inhabit; like 'the eye lives in this texture as a man lives in his house' (Merleau-Ponty, 1964: 166). This ontology found Merleau-Ponty advocating a dynamic structuration and depth of being in which the visible that is, what is experienced as seen, is entwined with the invisible i.e. a post-spectatorial conception of vision (Merleau-Ponty, 1995). Here Merleau-Ponty begins to complicate the hierarchy of awareness and status of experience characteristic of western worldviews. For him, experience is more and different than what can be made explicit as such. Specifically, for him phenomenology can be seen as an attempt to understand what experience is and means as well as developing creative forms of expression and even 'singing the world' (Merleau-Ponty, 1962: 187): 'The phenomenological world is not the bringing to explicit expression of a pre-existing being, but the laying down of being. Philosophy is not the reflection of a pre-existing truth, but like art the act of bringing truth into being' (Merleau-Ponty, 1962: xx). First, there is no distinction to be had between enquiring after the world and the world itself, and second, enquiry is a form of world creation.

With this orientation, his curiosity and his influence extended into theories of psychology, science, politics, language, and art as well as cross-disciplinary research. Described as aloof, but charming, he increasingly entertained these varied interests, but with his untimely death from a sudden stroke, aged 53, this challenging endeavour of pushing phenomenology to its limits remained fragmentary and, appropriately, without conclusive summary.

Historically, his anti-foundationalism, anti-essentialism, non-dualism, and his concept of (good) ambiguity anticipate post-structuralist and postmodern themes: the relinquishment of meta-narratives, the rejection of a purely objective realm, and the decentring of a master subject while opting for an interrogative approach towards processual constituencies.

Despite its mid-twentieth-century vintage, and the fact that his philosophy was sidelined and neglected for a long time, coupled to its having a dense, complicated, and at times elusive idiom, it continues to offer promising resources and insights for contemporary concerns. Notably this relates to the capacity to alleviate malingering problems of dualistic and representational thinking by opening new vistas and expressions and creative ways of reconfiguring and dissolving the residual division of the relationship between subjective and objective stances. Bridging the divide between subject and object, self and world, without effacing the differences between these poles of perception, knowledge and living, Merleau-Ponty's phenomenology and relational and expressive ontology provides a dynamic base for a reinterpreted immanent processsualism.

26.3 THE PROCESSUAL 'GIST' OF MERLEAU-PONTY'S PHILOSOPHY

To understand the implicit process philosophical ideas of Merleau-Ponty and their significance for organizational theory and practice, I will in the following present selected *key concepts*. Two, in particular, stand out: first, his understanding of the living body and multi-folded dynamic embodiment (beyond empiricism and idealism); second, his interrelational ontology of the mediating and reversible '*Flesh*' and chiasm.

26.4 THE LIVING BODY AND DYNAMIC EMBODIMENT BEYOND EMPIRICISM AND IDEALISM

Departing from the orthodox Husserlian conceptions of the purpose and scope of phenomenology, Merleau-Ponty offered a post-Cartesian, post-dualistic, and post-representational turn towards the living body and to situated embodiment as a dynamic, 'basic', and disclosing nexus of meaning.

By extending Husserl's account of the 'lived body'—that is, the body as it is experienced and experiences as opposed to the merely physical body—Merleau-Ponty resisted and rejected the traditional representationalism and dualisms with its separation of matter and mind, body and spirit. Instead, he developed the idea of an embodied perception and consciousness of a 'body-mind' as processing a living connection to the world. It is this incarnated perceiving interplaying with an embodied reality and its interplay that constitutes responsively in an inseparable bond with the vastness of experience and existence as a being-in and towards-the-world. Embodiment and perception are the pre-reflexive openings onto a world that is not merely functioning as a screen of ideas or stage, but an incarnated and thus living medium of intertwinement. With this orientation, he aims at rediscovering and uncovering the system of how self, other selves, and things come into being as an experiencing system (Merleau-Ponty, 1962: 57). The embodied self, other selves, and the world are symbiotic, interwoven, entangled, all contributing to the synergy of living experiences and realities.

Taking the body and embodiment as a dynamic 'base', Merleau-Ponty's existential form of interrogating phenomenology and relational ontology addresses a wide range of bodily experiences and embodied phenomena, ranging from perception, spatiality, and motility of the body, to the body in sexual being and in speech, expression, and embodied relationships to others, up to questions regarding temporality and freedom. By refocusing on an extended understanding of the concrete structures of worldly experience, Merleau-Ponty's advancement of phenomenology strived for overcoming, or perhaps better to say, undermining the de-corporealization of the body and the neglect of embodiment.

To Merleau-Ponty, experience is not given to a subject, mind, or consciousness, which could then be appealed to as substance within the world. On the contrary, the world is originally given and it is from this pre-subjective 'givenness' that concrete definitions of the 'subject' can be formulated. However he showed also that there is no direct, unmediated knowledge of reality 'mythically given'. Rather, all knowledge and all human experience are bodily organized, structured, and culturally mediated. The body and embodiment and related phenomena are always already lived, meaningful, relational, intentional, and responsive; so intentionality works as a kinaesthetic and e-motional action-oriented projection (Merleau-Ponty, 1962: xviii, 165).

Influenced by and critically using insights from Heidegger and the Gestalt theorists and psychologists, Merleau-Ponty (1962: 177) questions how both empiricist realism (examining things and perceptions of such to inductively build explanation) as well as rationalistic idealism (posing first principles) are reductionist as they reduce living phenomena, perception, and sensation either to the realm of matter or to that of ideas. Focusing instead on bodily experiences and embodiment, not as material 'objects' or subjective 'representations', but as constitutive and open media, led him to an anti-foundationalist, anti-essentialist, and non-dualistic position, and to a philosophy of irresolvable ambiguities. In describing his apartment he muses on how, whilst he might conceive it from above, as though on a floor plan, this would not be possible without his bodily experience in space, by which he is first able to appreciate 'inside', 'outside', and 'direction'; only through the body can an object enter into our experience as something (1962: 210–11).

With these orientations, Merleau-Ponty sought to rearticulate the synergetic relationship *between* 'subject' and 'object' among various other dualisms within a post-dichotomous, integrative nexus, situated in the living world as a system of 'self–others–things' (Merleau-Ponty, 1962: 57; Waldenfels, 2007). The living 'reflexive' body functions as a medium of crossing, where mind and matter; culture and nature, self and world, as well as meaning and force, meet and unfold. The embodied 'subject' and their likewise embodied intersubjective and 'interobjective' life-world are an extensive continuum, in which both are embedded and actively co-creative and take part in a passive mode. Therefore, neither subjective, intersubjective, nor objective dimensions can be isolated from the dynamic process of embodied being. Mediated by the body and embodiment, human beings and 'Being' are interrelated realities of becoming in an ongoing process of transition and unfoldment of meaning.

As unruly, unpredictable, and unmanageable be(com)ings, the body and embodiment are decentring. Neither is centred or 'mastering', but disrupting, undermining, and escaping purposive and boundary-drawing orders. Accordingly, bodily and embodied forces underlie the processual, dynamic, and unfinished nature of any perceiving, feeling, thinking, intending, responding, and acting as well as its material, bio-socio-cultural world spheres. All of them are intricately intertwined and mutually 'engaged' within an ever-present relational sphere which Merleau-Ponty calls '*La chair du monde*', i.e. 'the *Flesh* of the world'.

26.5 Reversible *Flesh* as Elemental Carnality and Formative Medium and Chiasm

The polyvalent, variegated open-ended term and metaphor of *Flesh* is Merleau-Ponty's central ontological principle. It sustains his attempt to overcome traditional metaphysical dualisms and expand and ontologize his concept of the lived body as an ambiguous Being and serves as a foundation of the possibility of expression. The ontological concept and carnal metaphor of *Flesh* expresses and facilitates associations to both the sensible and bodily commonality of beings and also to the generative capacity of a difference-enabling being as becoming. Referring to the intertwining and reversibility of pre-personal, personal, inter- and trans-personal dimensions, Merleau-Ponty's ontology of *Flesh* allows a profound and relational understanding of phenomena.

In order to elucidate this concept of *Flesh*, the following describes the same first as carnality and mediating element of being and then outlines how it is processed through reversibility and chiasm. These specifications then open up towards a post-dualistic ontology of 'wild being' and transformational becoming.

For Merleau-Ponty, '[t]he *Flesh* is not matter, is not mind, is not substance. To designate it, we should need the old term element in the sense it was used to speak of water, air, earth, and fire, that is, in the sense of a general thing, midway between the spatio-temporal individual and the idea, a sort of incarnate principle' (1995: 139). Thus *Flesh* refers to both the particular being and the more general element in which all beings and the world share, but with its indeterminate qualities it cannot be reduced to the old notions of subject or object. Rather, *Flesh* serves as the formative medium, preceding conceptual splits into 'subjective' and 'objective', or paired structures (Merleau-Ponty, 1995: 250). It was conceived as an attempt to recover a pre-reflective present or 'tissue' that underlies all subject–object relations, all explicit differentiations. We can all of us only speak and be spoken to, hear and be heard, love and be loved, because we share the same brute, basic condition, share the same fleshy reality; for example, to feel pain entails a feeling of how others' feel pain as we are all grounded in flesh (Merleau-Ponty, 1995: 234).

As an intermediating realm, this *Flesh* joins the pre-reflexive sentient and sensible body, through which inside and outside, passivity and activity, mesh. In this way, *Flesh* refers to an original fabric that precedes all other ways of referring to ourselves or others. In particular, it operates through a role-swapping reversibility. This reversibility refers to the reflexivity of sensible experiences wherein the sensing body itself is always within a sensible field. The entwined *sentient and sensible* aspects of the *Flesh* are mediating an emblematic experience of an 'originary connectedness'. The experience is that of us being both at one and the same time, for instance, seeing and being seen or toucher and touched. Merleau-Ponty draws attention to the difficulty of attending to both subject and object at once. When I focus my attention on feeling the left hand touching the right hand, the left hand as feeler, rather than that which is felt, recedes. Reversing roles and adopting alternate positions never entirely coincides in the same way. Thus, this circular experience of switching points is constituted by a gap, split, fission, or fold, in the *Flesh*. Not only do we have to be seeable or touchable in order to see or touch, but we also experience a reversibility when switching which creates a kind of gap within what remains inseparable, The reversible foldings of differences need a kind of integration by which some form can hold, but also unfold further differentiations and open possibilities. This dynamic integration can be interpreted with Merleau-Ponty's post-dichotomous account of 'identity-encompassing difference', which acknowledges both a common grounding in flesh and yet also the possibility of difference as we experience switching.

26.6 CHIASM

Merleau-Ponty uses the metaphor of chiasm to describe the experience of folding (holding of form in *Flesh*) and unfolding (the gap created in experiences of reversibility, as we move from touched to toucher, say). Derived from the Greek letter χ ('chi'), chiasm implies a criss-crossing structure, as is found at the point in the brain where the optic from the right visual field crosses to the left side and vice versa. By this the non-photosensitive but perception-enabling nerves create hidden blind spots in the periphery of the field of vision before the chiasm reversibly rejoins the two sides in one unified visibility. Merleau-Ponty was inspired by the general understanding of chiasm as a dynamic diffraction or splitting dehiscence and mediating link between different sides of phenomena.

Metaphorically, the reversible processes of the chiasm can be described as connecting lacunae of intersection, i.e. giving and taking, similar to a moving wave that arises and flows. The folding over and coiling waves are spiralling forward, encountering sand at the seashore, and flowing back to the sea. Through a constantly reversible flow of elements, an interlaced circular movement arises in which each element advances to then coil back through divergence and overlap(ping). For Merleau-Ponty, this opening chiasm is a processual patterning process of *Flesh* that differentiates and 'unifies' without synthesis, while constituting all sensing, perceiving, and communicating (Merleau-Ponty, 1995: 143). Sensibility, affection, perception, and other forms of relating and movement are possible because the body, as sensing and sensed medium, is already part of the fabric of the sensible. Experiences are affective because corporeally processed and expressed states are constituted and belong together in the in-corporeal inter-world of chiasmic mediality (Merleau-Ponty, 1962: 157, 357; 1964: 163, 168). Poetically expressed: in the '*inter-world*', sparks of sensing/sensible affection are lit and fire starts to burn (Merleau-Ponty, 1964: 163, 168), and with this firing, amplifying tensions, resonances, metaphormoses, and ambiguities emerge.

Understanding chiasm as the operational move of intercorporeal *Flesh* and the intermediating link between different sides or positions allows and preserves possibilities for forming relational connections between different phenomena and 'entities' in an opening and open way. Importantly, a chiasmic realization of Being exceeds the basic and visual forms of perception and encompasses the full range of senses of bodies as they move, shift, and weave sensually with events in developing meaning (Morris, 2010). One advantage of the concept of chiasm is that it allows a *relational pluralism*; any focal entity, whether a person, a team, or an entire organization, derives or co-creates meanings and the possibilities for acting from the many heterogeneous, and overlapping relations with other entities.

26.7 WILD BEING AND BE(COM)ING

The described processual, non-substantial 'inter-worldy' *Flesh* generates an affective power through its intensive, libidinal, decentred elemental 'wild being'. The inter-corporeity of *Flesh* is a being that is 'wild', as it is not reducible to some kind of eidetic principle that would keep otherness in the logic of sameness.

According to Johnson (2003) there is an order to *Flesh*, but it is one that does not express rigid control and mastery over otherness. Instead, it is a 'non-orderly order' that illuminates a primordial energy that empowers intertwined being and acting. Merleau-Ponty's notion of wildness, and the corresponding pre-reflective quality of wild meaning, indicates that 'subject' and 'object' have not been tamed into separate categories, but precedes and is presupposed by these and other dualities.

For Merleau-Ponty, this fleshly wild being is a brute fabric of meaning that is woven through all levels of experience, and as such precedes or makes possible all particular horizons and accomplishments. It serves as an invisible ontological medium out of which self, others, and things arise through the previously described reversible relations. As an affective elementality, this untamed 're-evolutionary' being relates and differentiates, unites and separates. While inducing to movement, it appeals to sensitivity, inviting and disrupting habitual investments and practices, re-evolutionizing the structured, the possible, and the different.

Overall, Merleau-Ponty's key process philosophical concepts of living body and dynamic inter-corporeality as well as the reversible, chiasmic *Flesh* and wild being provide the basis for what might be called an ethos of '*inter-be(com)ing*' by which he might be said to show strong resonance with process philosophy.

26.8 MERLEAU-PONTY AND OTHER PROCESS PHILOSOPHIES

There are various connections, but also differences between Merleau-Ponty and other process philosophers. Merleau-Ponty himself was inspired by Bergson, especially concerning his understanding of embodiment and bodily rhythms as temporal flows and becomings, but also concerning his understanding of intuition, nothingness, and freedom (Alia Al-Saji, 2013). But Merleau-Ponty has different views on what immediate experience and its interpretation involves. For example, he criticizes Bergson's description of experience because it dissolves into a unified flux of structural elements (past, present; subject, object) that needs to be differentiated for our experience to have any meaning at all. Rather than look at a full range of possible connections with other process thinkers, here we look at two of obvious significance, namely Whitehead and Deleuze.

26.9 MERLEAU-PONTY AND WHITEHEAD: PAN-EXPERIENTIALISM

With its relational emphasis, Merleau-Ponty's work offers an elusive bridge from/to Whitehead's process philosophy (Hamrick, 2004; Hamrick and Van der Veken, 2012). Although following different paradigms (Bertram, 1989), the two thinkers provide a mutually enriching supplement for developing a post-dualistic, processual understanding of organizing as a relational event. Whitehead's (1925, 1929) metaphysical system and pan-relationalist ontology follows a kind of 'proto-phenomenological' focus on actual entities or occasions of experience, concrescence, prehension, and event.

Moreover, Whiteheadian pan-experientialism (Griffin, 1998) is similar and complementary to advanced phenomenology. On the one hand, the Whiteheadian universe as a 'communion of subjects' processed internally falls prey to mono-logical accusations. Although Whitehead opened the door for the complexities of (subjective) interiors, subjectivity, and an acknowledgement of the objective nature of a subject–subject interaction, he remains tied to an internal subject–object relationship and did not walk through the gate towards a simultaneous co-presence and mutuality. Due to this retained impasse of an inadequate account of the role that a situated interpersonal space plays before and in prehension, Whiteheadian philosophy might be supplemented by integrating situated, intersubjective relationships based on embodied dialogue and mutual understanding as provided by Merleau-Ponty's thinking.

On the other hand, Whitehead's conceptuality can nourish, solicit, or furnish and expand Merleau-Ponty's emerging radicalized ontology (Hamrick and Van der Veken, 2012: 5) towards an understanding of nature that is even more fluid, generative, and expressive. What both philosophical systems show, in their fight against fallacies, limitations, and epistemic blind spots of scientific materialism, and in their contestation of bifurcations, is that the relationship between 'subject' and 'object' is no longer a relationship of 'knowing' as postulated by classical subjectivist idealism, or by classical objectifying empiricism. Rather, it is a relationship of 'being' in which, paradoxically, the 'intersubject(s)' *is* their body, their world, and their situation by an interrelational and reversible interchange and in-(ter-)between.

Both intentionalities and prehensions are implicit guides for the 'in-formation' of experiences and coincidental processes of being and becoming, thus a be(com)ing also in organizations. A further linkage between advanced phenomenology and process philosophy can be found—besides the common understanding of commitment (Doud, 1977)—in comparing Merleau-Ponty's treatment of ambiguity and Whitehead's notion of contrast-rich adventure. Conjoining both in a novel and enriching way allows us to comprehend *Flesh* and Nature in a non-representational way and move towards a concrescence: a growing together.

26.10 MERLEAU-PONTY AND DELEUZE: BECOMING BODY AND BODY-BE(COM)ING

There are multi-folded resonances and convergences and divergences between Merleau-Ponty and Deleuze. Both decentre the subject and undermine Cartesian categories and dichotomies, as well as share a Bergsonian understanding of style *in sensu* of a 'becoming-phenomenology' (Ming-Qian, 2005). Furthermore, both recognize a plea for immanentism and a sensual continuum of body and world as part of an ambiguous, non-coincident, layered and folded Being (Wambacq, 2011a: 272, 2011b). Both philosophers enquire into foldings of 'relation-scapes' (Manning, 2009), of the sensing plastic and rhythmic 'becoming-body', thus exploring potentials that emerge out of hollowing folds of embodied processes. Merleau-Ponty's understanding of 'wild being' corresponds to a certain extent to Deleuzian pre-individual, a-subjective affect as a zone of re-creative indetermination and indiscernibility (Deleuze and Guattari, 1994: 173–4; 1987: 293).

However, they part ways in relation to the understanding of body as a lived one versus one without organs (Olkowski, 2012). Unlike Merleau-Ponty, Deleuze's non-essentialist, post-human bodies as Spinozist configurations and techno-cultural constructs and play of forces are discontinuous processes of unfolding on surfaces of intensities and as durations. With these different interpretations, Merleau-Ponty and Deleuze also diverge with regard to the (im-material) status of sensation and embodiment, as well as with regards to ontological, epistemological, as well as ethical and political (Reynolds and Roffe, 2006), and aesthetic issues (Somers-Hall, 2009) in relation to *Flesh*. Following a radical anti-humanist orientation, for Deleuze the being of sensation exists for itself as a projective compound of non-human (virtual) forces without being incorporated by a supporting subjectivating *Flesh*, which for Merleau-Ponty is still an actual element of the world and is denigrated by Deleuze in its function as urdoxic desire for harmony (Deleuze and Guattari, 1994: 183). For example, perceiving an ongoing, monotonous noise in the office begins with a chaos of varying tiny sounds that as heterogonous multiplicities first demand attention, but gradually turns (not integrated) into a blanket of filtered, ignorable white noise that occupies the background of awareness. Macro-perception is a differential product of sub-phenomena which themselves are differentials of yet smaller ones, subtended by heterogeneous series, all part of a continuous variation of increase and decrease in our power of affectively mediated intensities and actions. While Merleau-Ponty's theory accounts more for the ongoing dynamic constitution of phenomena in the world co-created by an identity-in-difference, Deleuze aims at explaining the intensity of any given moment of phenomenal experience as difference without identity. Importantly, Merleau-Ponty's relational and Deleuze's transformational pragmatics of becoming-other both share an interest in the interrogative nature of being (Gilson, 2005) and 'locate' the same processually as in-between (Deleuze and Guattari, 1987: 293).

26.11 LIVING 'BODIES AT WORK' AND EMBODIED AGENCY IN ORGANIZATIONS

Merleau-Ponty's concept of living bodies and embodiment can help to develop a re-embodied organization as life-worlds (Holt and Sandberg, 2011) in which an operative intentionality, including collective we-mode intentionalities, are understood as a moving and e-motional orientation and actional projection (Merleau-Ponty, 1962: xviii, 165). Furthermore, embodied *responsiveness* in organizational life can be interpreted as a situated and process-oriented (not only instrumental) practice of answering, relevant for organizational development.

Processually, with Merleau-Ponty the embodied agency in organizational practices can be understood as a kinetic disposition and distributed, emergent, socio-material processes of interaction. Expressive, motivated, efficacious, performative, creative, and communicative bodies exercise agentic capacities. These bodies emerge and interact as contingent singularities of individual or collective agents across a spectrum of and between pre-personal, corporeal non-cognitive processes, and intersubjective and trans-personal inter-worlds.

One form in which the living body and embodied organizing can be explored is as those practices that involve 'bodies at work' (Wolkowitz, 2006: 183). What has been called *embodied labour* refers to ways in which members of organizations are operating as bodily-engaged beings within occupational milieus. For example, in performing *somatic work* (Vannini et al., 2012) or *sensory work* with in organizations, the practical work experiences of the embodied practitioner create, manage, reproduce, negotiate, interrupt, and communicate somatic awareness and sensations. In somatic work, people manipulate sensory experiences (Vannini et al., 2012) and use agency-oriented body techniques (Crossley, 1995) for a desired or expected impression management. Using sensing as a social and symbolic practice, the somantic working body is crafted, negotiated, manipulated, and involved in 'affective dramas' of being performed, staged, and presented in the everyday life of organizing—for example, in occupational areas ranging from fashion to fitness (Waskul and Vannini, 2008). This kind of embodied, ritualized performance, for example managing smell (as an act) and odour (as a sign), is often processed in critical relation to social, cultural, and moral order in specific organizational circumstances while it enacts a corporeal sensemaking or sensuous making and giving of meaning (Waskul and Vannini, 2008). Moreover, the intensifying qualities as manifested in somatic work can be critically connected to affective commitment in the workplace (Meyer, 2009), for example applied to undercommitted or overstressed service workers. Furthermore, various forms of *affective labour* refer to a kind of embodied practice, which produces or modifies affective and emotional experiences in people to manipulate senses and affects as part of an affect-oriented consumer culture and today's experience economy.

In embodying *emotional labour*, the body acts as a medium of affective and symbolic communication through bodily language, gestures, and appearances, especially in service work with highly ambivalent effects, which may be impoverishing, alienating, or exhausting, but at the same time mutually connecting, acting out and enriching or satisfying working life (Küpers and Weibler, 2008). For example, emotional labour in electronic call centres seemingly provides a freedom to be authentic ('just be yourself') which is in fact not freedom *from* control, but managerially prescribed freedom around control (Fleming and Sturdy, 2011) that can lead to eliminating productive commitment and creative employee participation (Higgins et al., 1997) and heading towards symbolic violence (Schweingruber and Berns, 2005). However, other researchers have found that personalized role enactment and emotional interpersonal role-making during emotional labour can contribute to a more satisfying self-expressive sense of personal accomplishment or to a performance game of mutual winners, for example, among flight attendants (Wouters, 1989), thus enhancing the work experience (Shuler and Sypher, 2000).

Another form of embodied labour is the bodywork involved in *caring*, which is often stigmatized as low-status, low-paying, and dirty work, deemed more suitable for the bodies of women and migrants. Furthermore, *aesthetic labour* is an embodied practice that entails supplying, mobilizing, developing, and commodifying embodied dispositions, capacities, and attributes transformed into competencies, which are then aesthetically geared towards producing a 'style' in service encounters. As a form of presentational performance, aesthetic labour displays approved social attributes of the body or embodiment, for example to create and preserve a professional and/or corporate image or to keep up appearances as in the fashion industries (Entwistle and Wissinger, 2006), especially through clothing policies for wearing uniforms as aestheticizing retail workers (Hall and van den Broek, 2012)

As an ongoing production of the body/self, specific embodied capacities in aesthetically oriented labour have been investigated as experienced also by interactive service employees in the retail and hospitality industries. Self- and other-oriented *presentational labour* are embodied practices, in which frontline personal service specialists overtly or subtly know about the relationship between emotional and aesthetic labour, acquiring emotional and aesthetic literacies that are essential to their performance in maintaining a close, personal relationship with their clients. Occupational and somatic particularities of diversity workers can also use micro-political 'strategies of embodiment' as a form of resistance or co-optation. As Swan and Fox have shown (2010), occupational resources involve forms of symbolism of racialized and gendered bodies and body work as part of temporal, dynamic, and intermingled processes in diversity work in the new public sector management with its variegated nature of insider/outsider dynamics. In their description of the politics and ambivalence of diversity work, they show how the micro-practices use both embodied and discursive resources, as well as management technologies. Interestingly, Swan and Fox demonstrate how occupational resources of resistance move beyond the discursive resources.

Furthermore, studies show how practitioners are incorporating *embodied knowing*, as intertwined with feelings and cognition, into social work practice and embodied learning (Küpers and Weibler, 2008). They use their body as a valid source of knowledge, trusting their somatic sensations as part of their professional activities. Moreover, bodily knowing is an experiential, contextual, reflective learning process.

26.12 Elemental, Reversible, and Chiasmic *Flesh* and Organizing

Based on his post-dual ontology of 'inter-being', Merleau-Ponty suggests a radicalized relational understanding of organizing as an emerging event (2003: 208). This happening is constituted and processed through the described elemental, mediating, and reversible *Flesh*, here serving as a medium in which all organizing is situated and processed. The integrative nexus of 'self–other–things' (Merleau-Ponty, 1962: 57) and perspectival 'integral being' (Merleau-Ponty, 1995: 84) implies that to be in organizing is to inter-be(come). Thus, in a sense, Merleau-Ponty's process philosophical orientation allows enriched explorations of various phenomena of elemental and enfleshed organizing or *'organic-izations'*, with their reversible and dynamic interconstitutions (Cecil, 2004; Parkan, 2003).

In the life-world of organization, *Flesh* operates as an intermediating, open-ended, soma-significative medium and reversible, often dialogical exchange as chiasmic wave-like flow and entwinement, for example between embodied selves and others (Cataldi, 1993: 69). This relational, reversible *Flesh* constitutes in-between spaces and times in organizations (Bradbury and Lichtenstein, 2000), which include various interwoven processes and feedback loops as they emerge in practices (Calori, 2002; Lukenchuk, 2006).

Shotter (2003, 2004) has described the living, chiasmically organized, and dynamic intertwined relations connected to spontaneous, dialogical, and expressive-responsiveness of moving bodies in relation to orchestrated change. For example, chiasmic event-within meetings with their complex, dynamically intertwined character of the living emergent parties and realities cannot be captured in subjective, nor in objective terms; or with causally or rationally related parts, neither are they wholly orderly nor wholly disorderly. Like any dynamic whole, the reality created within such meetings will exhibit a synthesis of unity and multiplicity, of chronotopic continuity and discontinuity, thereby opening for possibilities to emerge. In contrast with an 'aboutness-thinking', Shotter argues for a 'thinking-from-within' or 'withness-thinking' that co-creates an 'action guiding' sense from within lived and living experience of shared circumstances (Shotter 2006).

Providing possibilities for an unfolding in-betweenness, *Flesh* in organizing serves as a generative capacity and generous source, enacted as a corporeal generosity of embodied mutual recognition in organizational life-worlds (Hancock, 2008). Considering the elemental medium of a '*Flesh of Leadership*' allows understanding co-created and reversible roles of leading and following (Ladkin, 2010: 71–3; 182–3), as both are constitutive through their mutual interplay.

The key concept of reversible and chiasmic 'in-between' of *Flesh* can be used for post-dichotomous interpretations and post-dualistic orientation in organization studies and practice, especially in relation to conflicts and transformations or dealing with disunity, ambiguities, dilemmas, and paradoxes. Accordingly, a chiasmic organizing is balancing dynamically between, for example control and autonomy, creativity and structure, situated in inter-practices.

26.13 EMBODIED AND ENFLESHED INTER-PRACTICE

Similar to the conceptualization of practice configurations in a radical process-orientation (Chia and MacKay, 2007), phenomenologically practices are not only a collection of purposeful activities of self-contained individual actors and material things. They are also trans-individual, social, and systemic events of emergent becoming and meaning-giving complexes (Tsoukas and Chia 2002). With its emotional dynamics and active responsiveness, this relational practising resembles more an iterative, explorative way-finding and dwelling than a planned navigation and building (Chia and Holt, 2009).

Considering the corporeality of practice-based dimensions (Yakhlef, 2010) and following Merleau-Ponty's relational process perspective, practices can be interpreted as embodied inter-practices in organizations (Küpers, 2007, 2009) and in leadership (Küpers, 2013). The concept of embodied and enfleshed practice and a corresponding 'pheno-practice' (Küpers, 2005, 2009, 2011) in organization helps to reveal and interpret the nexus of being, feeling, knowing, doing, sharing, structuring, and effectuating in and through embodied agency and action, both individually and collectively. It can be used for enquiries into the negotiating interplay of the inherently entwined materialities, subjectivities, intersubjectivities, and objectivities as they occur and are processed in organizational life-worlds, for example in enacted improvisation (Küpers, 2011) as embodied and creative performances and immersion-in-activity.

26.14 Theoretical and Methodological Implications

The process philosophical phenomenology and ontology of Merleau-Ponty can also help deal with methodological difficulties involved in process research, enacting a special kind of 'processism' (De Cock and Sharp, 2007: 246) to reveal the imbricated researcher in her 'becoming-ness' (Chia, 1995; Harding, 2007) as well as cracks, ambiguities, and contradictions involved in her tentative ongoing practising as a researcher (Bjørkeng, Clegg, and Pitsis, 2009; Hernes, 2007; Hernes and Weik, 2007; Nayak, 2008; Wood, 2005, 2008; Wood and Ladkin, 2008). With Merleau-Ponty it becomes possible to identify where meaning falls down, as it is not about collecting data, but issuing reminders that challenge meaning rather than yielding a definitve one.

Following an extended method of suspension (bracketing), Merleau-Ponty's phenomenology retains an openness, sensibility, and awareness for how organizing, also of research, reveals and manifests itself processually as an embodied practice.

Moreover, an integral, process-oriented ontology of *Flesh* and aesthetics opens the bodily relation to a larger collective-systemic sphere of socio-material embodiment, as well as implicating acts of communication and expressions.

Taking research itself as a form of inter-practising, cross-disciplinary bridging helps to show the significance of embodied and mediating processes involved in relational organizational practices. In this sense, Merleau-Ponty's philosophy can be interpreted as a 'scientia media' (Robbins, 2001) that provides access to a discourse of the in-between, the liminal, the ambiguous, thus entering a Janus-headed threshold which opens upon the space of a science which is always other to itself. A corresponding integral episte-mology and methodological pluralism needs to take first-, second-, and third-person perspectives while considering each of their specific, inherent modes of enquiry as well as their complex interplay as applied for example in a relational practice of leadership (Küpers and Weibler, 2008). Epistemologically and ontologically, such research orienta-tion contributes to the radically reflexive reworking of subject–object distinctions with their knowledge problematics. Metaphorically speaking, process phenomenological research provides bridges to pre-reflective dimensions of experience and realities with-out getting lost in pre-modern swamps of regression, as this would pull back into an undifferentiated union. Furthermore, it offers passages between Scylla—the rocks of dogmatic modernity—and Charibdis—the whirlpool of dispersed postmodernity.

Overall, a body-oriented or 'carnal' organizational studies embraces a more sensorial and fleshly stance in relation to its members and the mediating embodiment at work as part of organizational everyday worlds. Developing such embodied organization research requires shifting from theorizing *about* or *of* bodies, in a disembodied, objec-tifying, or subjectifying way, towards thinking *from* and *with* lived bodies and embodi-ment. Such orientation calls in particular for more sensual methodologies and art-based research practices.

26.15 CONCLUSION

Merleau-Ponty's ontology and epistemology foregrounds bodily mediated or embodied emergences, relationships, interactions, and meanings in their enfleshed processual-ity. Accordingly, processes in organization can be approached and understood not only in more dynamically interpreted, carnal ways, but also as part of a relational becoming innate to all organizing and its research. In a way, to organize is to 'inter-become': a vast, interrelated dynamism of a mutual be-coming of all who are a part of the process of organ-izing. Overarchingly, this becoming-of-organizing has a co-evolving relationship with all phenomena it affects and is affected by, thus co-arising interdependently. When organizational members, a group, or the entire entity, 'inter-become', they are inexo-rably entwined with the relational becoming of others as all participate in the turning inter-be(com)ing.

This return requires care not to fall prey to a pre-modern longing for unity and retro-romantic fallacies. A historiographically and culturally informed account of embodiment prevents such relapse into a kind of neo-sensualism or neo-sensationalism. Rather, it links the embodied sensorium of practice to con-temporary forms of sensemaking, including, for instance, in tele-presences and multimedia applications.

Putting into practice an embodied, chiasmic, and enfleshed processual understand-ing opens up possibilities for future studies about bodily 'how's' of organizing especially as inter-practising. On the one hand, such an approach helps to critique disembodied and non-creative orientations that neglect individual and collective bodies and embodiments or merely see them as constructed or render them as instrumentalized objects for utilitarian exploitative 'practicalism'. On the other hand, focusing on inter-practices may contribute to the emergence and realization of alternative, ingenious, and more suitable forms of organizational practices. This becomes even more relevant as these are placed in increasingly complex and often paradoxical or dilemmatic individual and collective settings. Furthermore, actualizing an embodied practice may facilitate the cultivation of practical well-being and practical wisdom in organizations (Küpers, 2005, 2007).

Re-membering and re-searching the living experience and dynamic intricacies of bodily inter-practising and embodied organizing is a challenging endeavour. But this undertaking is a timely and worthwhile one, as it contributes to more integrally transformative and hence sustainable approaches and practices in the current interdependent worlds of leadership and organization and beyond. Thus, reviving and enacting embodied interrelationalities in organizational life-worlds with all its 'pregnancy of the possible' (Merleau-Ponty, 1995: 298) may mediate the incarnation and unfoldment of alternative economic, political, societal, and ethical relationships and realities to inter-be-come.

Following the paradox of expression (Merleau-Ponty, 1962: 389; 1995: 144), moving between sedimented and new meanings, possibilities and futures might be launched that are called and responded, and thus co-created processually and approached phenomenologically. While being a perpetually critical (self-)reflection and unfinished, and thus a continuous provisional 'science of beginnings' (Stewart and Mukunas, 1990: 5), process phenomenology has a 're-evolutionary' potential, re-constellating evolutional enfoldments towards a more integral 'inter-be(com)ing-in-the-world' as spiralling moments of the aborning cosmos.

References

Alia Al-Saji, A. (2013). *Bodies and Memories: Bergson, Merleau-Ponty, and the Time of Difference* (Albany, NY: SUNY).

Bertram, M. (1989). The Different Paradigms of Merleau-Ponty and Whitehead, *Philosophy Today* 24: 121–32.

Bjørkeng, K., Clegg, S., and Pitsis, T. (2009). Becoming (a) Practice, *Management Learning* 40(2): 145–59.

Bradbury, H. and Lichtenstein, B. (2000). Relationality in Organizational Research: Exploring the Space Between, *Organization Science* 11: 551–64.

Calori, R. (2002). Organizational Development and the Ontology of Creative Dialectical Evolution, *Organization* 9(1): 127–50.

Cataldi, S. (1993). *Emotion, Depth and Flesh: A Study of Sensitive Space. Reflections on Merleau-Ponty's Philosophy of Embodiment* (Albany, NY: SUNY).

Cecil, P. (2004). Changing Cultures in Organizations: A Process of Organicization, *Concrescence* 5(101): 1445–4297.

Chia, R. (1995). From Modern to Postmodern Organizational Analysis, *Organizational Studies* 16(4): 579–604.

—— and Holt, R. (2009). *Strategy without Design: The Silent Efficacy of Indirect Action* (Cambridge: Cambridge University Press).

——and MacKay, B. (2007). Post-Processual Challenges for the Emerging Strategy-as-Practice Perspective, *Human Relations 60*: 217–42.

Crossley, N. (1995). Body Techniques, Agency and Intercorporeality: On Goffman's Relations in Public, *Sociology 29*(1): 133–49.

De Cock, C. and Sharp, R.J. (2007). Process Theory and Research: Exploring the Dialectic Tension, *Scandinavian Journal of Management 23*: 233–50.

Deleuze, G. and Guattari, F. (1987). *A Thousand Plateaus: Capitalism and Schizophrenia* (Minneapolis: University of Minnesota Press).

—— (1994). *What is Philosophy?* (London: Verso).

Doud, R. (1977). Whitehead and Merleau-Ponty: Commitment as a Context for Comparison, *Process Studies 7*(3): 145–60.

Entwistle, J. and Wissinger, E. (2006). Keeping up Appearances: Aesthetic Labour and Identity in the Fashion Modelling Industries of London and New York. *Sociological Review, 54*(4): 774–94.

Fleming, P. and Sturdy, A. (2011). Being Yourself in the Electronic Sweatshop: New Forms of Normative Control, *Human Relations 64*: 2177–200.

Gilson, E. (2005). Questioning to the nth Power: Interrogative Ontology in Merleau-Ponty and Deleuze, *Chiasmi International 6*: 207–24.

Griffin, D.R. (1998). Process Philosophy, in E. Craig (ed.), *Routledge Encyclopedia of Philosophy* (London: Routledge): 711–16.

Hall, R. and van den Broek, D. (2012). Aestheticising Retail Workers: Orientations of Aesthetic Labour in Australian Fashion Retail, *Economic and Industrial Democracy 33*(1): 85–102.

Hamrick, W. (2004). Whitehead and Merleau-Ponty: Healing the Bifurcation of Nature, in A. Polanowski and D. Sherburne (eds), *Whitehead's Philosophy: Points of Connection* (Albany, NY: SUNY): 127–42.

——and Van der Veken, J. (2012). *Nature and Logos. A Whiteheadian Key to Merleau-Ponty's Fundamental Thought* (Albany, NY: SUNY).

Hancock, P. (2008). Embodied Generosity and an Ethics of Organization, *Organization Studies 29*(10): 1357–73.

Harding, N. (2007). Becoming-ness of Organizations, *Organization Studies 28*(11): 1761–77.

Hernes, T. (2007). *Understanding Organization as Process—Theory for a Tangled World* (London: Routledge).

—— and Weik, E. (2007). Organization as Process: Drawing a Line between Endogenous and Exogenous Views, *Scandinavian Journal of Management 23*(3): 251–64.

Higgins, T.E., Shah, J.H., and Friedman, R. (1997). Emotional Responses to Goal Attainment: Strength of Regulatory Focus as Moderator, *Journal of Personality and Social Psychology 72*: 515–25.

Holt, R. and Sandberg, J. (2011). Phenomenology and Organization Theory, in H. Tsoukas and R. Chia (eds), *Research in the Sociology of Organizations* (Bingley, UK: Emerald): 215–49.

Johnson, G. (2003). Merleau-Pontian Phenomenology as Non-Conventionally Utopian, *Human Studies 26*: 383–400.

Küpers, W. (2005). Phenomenology and Integral Pheno-Practice of Embodied Well-Be(com) ing in Organizations, *Culture and Organization 11*(3): 221–31.

—— (2007). Integral Pheno-Practice of Wisdom in Management and Organization, *Social Epistemology* 22(4): 169–93.

—— (2009). Perspectives on Integral 'Pheno-Pragma-Practice' in Organizations, *International Journal of Management Practice* 4(1): 27–50.

—— (2011). Embodied Pheno-Pragma-Practice—Phenomenological and Pragmatic Perspectives on Creative Inter-practice in Organizations between Habits and Improvization, *Phenomenology and Practice* 5(1): 100–39.

—— (2013). Embodied Inter-Practices of Leadership: Phenomenological Perspectives on Relational and Responsive Leading and Following, *Leadership* 9(3): 335–57.

——and Weibler, J. (2008). Inter-Leadership—Why and How to Think Leader and Followership Integrally, *Leadership* 4(4): 443–47.

Ladkin, D. (2010). *Rethinking Leadership: A New Look at Old Leadership Questions* (Cheltenham: Elgar).

Lukenchuk A (2006). Traversing the Chiasms of Lived Experiences: Phenomenological Illuminations for Practitioner Research, *Educational Action Research International Journal* 14(3): 423–35.

Manning, E. (2009). *Relationscapes: Movement, Art, Philosophy* (Cambridge, MA: MIT Press).

Merleau-Ponty, M. (1962). *Phenomenology of Perception* (London: Routledge).

—— (1964). *Eye and Mind: The Primacy of Perception* (Evanston, IL: Northwestern University Press).

—— (1995). *The Visible and the Invisible* (Evanston, IL: Northwestern University Press).

—— (2003). *Nature. Course Notes from the College de France* (Evanston, IL: Northwestern University Press).

Meyer, J.P. (2009). Commitment in a Changing World of Work, in H.J. Klein, T.E. Becker, and J.P. Meyer (eds), *Commitment in Organizations: Accumulated Wisdom and New Directions* (Florence, KY: Routledge): 37–68.

Ming-Qian, M. (2005). Becoming Phenomenology: Style, Poetic Texture, and the Pragmatic Turn in Gilles Deleuze and Michel Serres, *Analecta Husserliana* 1(84): 97–116.

Morris, D. (2010). The Enigma of Reversibility and the Genesis of Sense in Merleau-Ponty, *Continental Philosophy Review* 43(2): 141–65.

Nayak, A (2008). On the Way to Theory: A Processual Approach, *Organization Studies* 29: 173–90.

Olkowski, D. (2012). Deleuze's Critique of Phenomenology: Is the Body without Organs Superior to the Lived Body? *Chiasmi International*, <http://www.filosofia.unimi.it/~chiasmi/>

Parkan, B. (2003). A Process-Ontological Account of Work, *Axiomathes* 14(1): 219–35.

Reynolds, J. and Roffe, J. (2006). Deleuze and Merleau-Ponty: Immanence, Univocity and Phenomenology, *Journal of the British Society of Phenomenology* 37(3): 228–51.

Robbins, B.D. (2001). Scientia Media, Incommensurability, and Interdisciplinary Space, *Janus Head* 3: 67–83.

Sandberg, J. and Dall'Alba, G. (2009). Returning to Practice Anew: A Life-World Perspective, *Organization Studies* 30(12): 1349–68.

Schweingruber, D. and Berns, N. (2005). Shaping the Selves of Young Salespeople through Emotion Management, *Journal of Contemporary Enthnography* 34(6): 679–706.

Shotter, J. (2003). Cartesian Change, Chiasmic Change: The Power of Living Expression, *Janus Head* 6(1): 6–29.

——(2004). Responsive Expression in Living Bodies: The Power of Invisible 'Real Presences' within our Everyday Lives Together, *Cultural Studies* 2–3: 443–60.

——(2006). Understanding Process from within: An Argument for 'Withness-' Thinking, *Organization Studies* 27: 585–604.

Shuler, S. and Sypher, B.D. (2000). Seeking Emotional Labor: When Managing the Heart Enhances the Work Experience, *Management Communication Quarterly* 14(1): 50–89.

Somers-Hall, H. (2009). Deleuze and Merleau-Ponty: Aesthetics of Difference, in C.V. Boundas (ed.), *Gilles Deleuze: The Intensive Reduction* (London: Continuum Press): 123–30.

Stewart, D. and Mukunas, A. (1990). *Exploring Phenomenology: A Guide to the Field and its Literature*, 2nd edition. Athens, OH: Ohio University Press.

Styhre, A. (2004). The (Re)Embodied Organization: Four Perspectives on the Body in Organizations, *Human Resource Development International* 7(1): 101–16.

Swan, E. and Fox, S. (2010). Playing the Game: Strategies of Resistance and Co-optation in Diversity Work, *Gender, Work & Organization* 17(5): 567–89.

Tsoukas; H. & Chia, R. (2002). On Organizational Becoming: Rethinking Organizational Change, *Organization Science* 13(5): 567–82.

Vannini, P., Waskul, D., and Gottschalk, S. (2012). *The Senses in Self, Society, and Culture: A Sociology of the Senses* (New York: Routledge).

Waldenfels, B. (2007). *The Question of the Other* (Albany, NY: SUNY).

Wambacq, J. (2011a). Maurice Merleau-Ponty and Gilles Deleuze as Interpreters of Henri Bergson, *Analecta Husserliana* 1(108): 269–84.

——(2011b). The Layered Being of Merleau-Ponty versus the Being Layered of Deleuze. University of Ghent, <https://biblio.ugent.be/publication/941199>

Waskul, D. and Vannini, P. (2008). Smell, Odor, and Somatic Work: Sense-Making and Sensory Management, *Social Psychology Quarterly* 71: 53–71.

Whitehead, A.N. (1925). *Science and the Modern World* (New York: The Free Press).

——(1929). *Process and Reality* (New York: Free Press).

Wolkowitz, C. (2006). *Bodies at Work*. London: Sage.

Wood, M. (2005). The Fallacy of Misplaced Leadership, *Journal of Management Studies*, 42(6): 1101–21.

——(2008). Process Philosophy, in R. Thorpe and R. Holt (eds), *Dictionary of Qualitative Management Research* (London: Sage): 171–3.

——and Ladkin, D. (2008). The Event's the Thing: Brief Encounters with the Leaderful Moment, in K. Turnbull James and J. Collins (eds), *Leadership Perspectives: Knowledge into Action* (Houndmills: Palgrave Macmillan): 15–28.

Wouters, C. (1989). The Sociology of Emotions and Flight Attendants: Hochschild's Managed Heart, *Theory, Culture and Society* 6(1): 95–123.

Yakhlef, A. (2010). The Corporeality of Practice-Based Learning, *Organization Studies* 31(4): 409–30.

CHAPTER 27

ARNE NAESS (1912–2009)

CARIEN DE JONGE AND GAIL WHITEMAN[1]

> People are frustrated that I can write an entire book upon an intuition that is nowhere defined or explained. It is tantalizing for our culture, this seeming lack of explanation. We do not accept the mode of the seer in academic circles. But if you hear a phrase like 'all life is fundamentally one', you must be open to tasting this, before asking immediately, 'what does this mean?' Being more precise does not necessarily create something that is more inspiring.
>
> (Naess, in Rothenberg, 1993: 105)

27.1 INTRODUCTION

ARNE NAESS was a Norwegian philosopher who worked in semantics and philosophy of science, and was committed to Gandhian non-violent enquiry. He became famous worldwide as an ecophilosopher and the father of the deep ecology movement. He held his first chair in philosophy at the University of Oslo when he was 27 and published until a few years before his death at age 96.

Naess' path to understanding does not lie solely in logical explanations and specifications, although he made many compelling points and was at one point asked to join the Vienna Circle. The path to understanding lies in an interwoven set of active processes, which include cognitive and emotive components. In addition to deep enquiry, these contain spontaneous identification processes with the creatures, systems, and things we interact with, a widening and maturing of the self and self-realization, and the ability to root ourselves deeply in a place and learn what is required of us from within that intimate field of life forms.

It is our goal in this chapter to allow readers to *taste* the complex concepts that are the building blocks of Naess' philosophical system, his ecosophy. To *try on* the potentiality that is added through consideration of these ideas for a process theory of organizing. In addition to a philosophical reflection on Naess' ideas concerning radically dynamic, open, and interconnected systems, relationality, and Gestalt ontology, we also attempt to stay close to the foundation of Naess' thoughts and being: his deep connection with and love for nature. For that, we begin by describing his cabin, called Tvergastein, high up in the Norwegian Hallingskarvet massif, which sets the stage for an in-depth discussion of four of Naess' key philosophical insights—Self-realization!, relationalism, Gestalt ontology/perception, and the genesis of the Place-person. Within our chapter, we also offer a short personal narrative of a spontaneous experience with non-humans in the city to illustrate the key process of *identification*. Our chapter ends with a consideration of how his work contributes unique insights to a process theory of organizing.

27.2 TVERGASTEIN: Ecosophy T

> I like to sit at the living room window of my isolated mountain hut, Tvergastein [see Figure 27.1], which offers an eagle eye's view of the Norwegian scenery of the Hardangervidda Plateau. It is easy to let my thoughts soar far away... Above all, I have a work space that I have built in the southwest corner, with a view over untrammelled space, a precipice of the majestic Hallingskarvet Massif as my closest neighbor, and more than fifty thousand square miles of landscape in sight. Up here, it is difficult not to think big.
>
> (Naess, 1998/2002: 20–1)

A lifelong mountaineer, Naess grew up in the affluent suburbs of Slemdal in Oslo, Norway. His father died while he was still an infant, and Naess' mother took her children

FIGURE 27.1 Tvergastein, Norway. Photograph by Øyvind Holst.

regularly to her cottage at Ustaoset, four hours, train ride from Oslo. The cabin was not overly appealing to the young Naess, who instead became fascinated by the nearby mountainscape of Hallingskarvet, a fascination which had a lasting influence. He explained, 'The vast world above the trees, and the process of getting through the timberline, made an impression so profound and so deeply gratifying that it left an intense longing to get back to that vast world just as soon as I was again in my usual surroundings' (2008: 52).

In 1936, Naess built a cabin and an observation point high above the tree line on Hallingskarvet, and called this place, Tvergastein. Tvergastein 'has some of the oldest rock in Europe' (Drengson and Deval, 2008: 34), and it 'became like a father to him' (Drengson and Deval, 2008: 8). Naess spent many years living, for extended periods, at his cabin. Many of his students and colleagues chose to visit him there, and took the relatively arduous journey to Tvergastein to engage in dialogue. With those visits, Naess enjoyed a rich social life at Tvergastein, in addition to long periods of quiet.

Like many Norwegians, Naess adhered to the Norse practice of *friluftsliv* (life-in-the-free-air), being outdoors engaged in activities in free nature. The distinction between free nature and wild nature was important to him, with free nature signifying nature that was not dominated by human constructions but not necessarily pristine. In a number of his writings, Naess makes the case that, while the appeal of wilderness is powerful, it does not have the same resonance in Europe as in North America. Drengson elaborates on this point: 'Free nature differs from North American wilderness, for vast areas of alp land in Norway are in the old farms, even though the land is unfenced and open. The air is free to walk and camp in, except where there are summer farm buildings' (Drengson, 2010: 82). The essential point is that people seek out regular access to 'free nature' even in the city: 'From the point of view of ecological education, the spots of free nature are crucial because small children [and adults] in cities and towns get intimately acquainted with the chaotic and infinitely diverse character of nature without being transported out of town or city' (Naess, 1992: 30).

Yet Naess also felt that mountains, in particular, have much to offer.

> As I see it, modesty is of little value if it is not a natural consequence of much deeper feelings and, even more important in our special context, a consequence of a way of understanding ourselves as part of nature in a wide sense of the term. This way is such that the smaller we come to feel ourselves compared with the mountain, the nearer we come to participating in its greatness. I do not know why this is so. (Naess in Drengson and Deval, 2008: 67)

While at Tvergastein, Naess paid intense daily attention to algae, flowers, animals, rocks, weather, snow, geography, wind, to all the elements of the life sphere that surrounded him. And from this embeddedness, he reflected upon the philosophical underpinnings of his own life and work: 'The choice of geographical place was based on a more or less set of requirements, but now the question was, What would the place require of me? What kind of lifestyle, activities, and ceremonies would be appropriate for this place? What would be a life worthy of Hallingskarvet and in solidarity with, and respect for, the other life-forms?' (Naess, 2008: 54). From this experiential perch Naess developed 'Ecosophy T', his own personalized understanding of life and enquiry.

> What is remarkable about Tvergastein and similar places is their capacity to furnish the basis for a life of simplicity of means and richness of ends. The latter is dependent upon their development from being a place to being a Place. With increasing intensity of commitment, the Place will satisfy an increasing variety of needs and will allow for an increasing variety of cherished goals to be reached. (Naess, 2008: 56)

These details are not superfluous to Naess' process philosophy. Indeed, he equated his direct and deep engagement with the life forms and mountains surrounding Tvergastein as a foundational influence on what he called 'ecosophy'—

> By an ecosophy I mean a philosophy of ecological harmony or equilibrium. A philosophy as a kind of sofia (or) wisdom, is openly normative, it contains both norms, rules, postulates, value priority announcements and hypotheses concerning the state of affairs in our universe. Wisdom is policy wisdom, prescription, not only scientific description and prediction. The details of an ecosophy will show many variations due to significant differences concerning not only the 'facts' of pollution, resources, population, etc. but also value priorities. (Naess, 1972/1995: 8)

For Naess, the word 'philosophy' has two distinctly different meanings: it can mean either a field of study (an approach to knowledge), or one's own personal code of values and a view of the world which guides one's own decisions. When it comes to the way we act and take our place in the world, philosophy according to the first definition is not sufficient. We have to make decisions during and concerning our life. To do this, and to be able to have pragmatic arguments, we need to make (implicit) choices between fundamental value priorities. The second meaning of philosophy, applied to questions involving ourselves and our place in nature, Naess calls *ecosophy*.

An *ecosophy* is therefore a set of personal codes of values and ideas. Naess emphasizes the fact that it is *one's own* personal system. Every individual should come to their own ecosophy. *The ecosophy* can never exist. Furthermore, a person's ecosophy does not necessarily have to be composed solely of one's own thoughts and concepts; you can adopt any idea or system that suits you. It is about finding a total view that you feel is right for you, while realizing that it is not a static system, but changing, like our own life changes over the course of our lifetime. Naess' named his personal view, 'ecosophy T', with the T for Tvergastein, emphasizing the importance of Tvergastein for his life and the development of his ideas. Throughout his life, Naess encouraged people to develop their own ecosophy, related to a specific place (or set of places), and that without one, humankind both individually and collectively engage in place-corrosive processes that limit the potentialities open to all of us. Naess' ecosophy is furthermore strongly influenced by the two thinkers that inspired him most: Benedictus de Spinoza and Mahatma Gandhi.

Naess works with a structure of norms and hypotheses as one's own personal normative system. In his normative system, there is a clear distinction between hypotheses, which are noted as short sentences, and normative statements, written down with exclamation marks. His normative system forms a network of thoughts and statements that can be reduced to these statements (Naess, 2006). The top norm is the most fundamental norm from which the whole normative system is derived. For Naess, this top norm is *self-realization!* (The exclamation mark appears in the original to signify we are dealing with a normative claim).

27.2.1 Self-Realization!

> Traditionally, the maturity of the self has been considered to develop through three stages: from ego to social self (comprising the ego), and from social self to a metaphysical self (comprising the social self). But in this conception of the maturity of the self, nature is largely left out. Our immediate environment, our home (where we belong as children), and the identification with nonhuman living beings are largely ignored. Therefore, I tentatively introduce, perhaps for the very first time, the concept of ecological self. We may be said to be in, and of, nature from the very beginning of ourselves.
>
> (Naess, 2008: 81)

Inspired by Spinoza's philosophy and his own experiences in nature, Naess arrived at the conclusion that the well-being of living things is ultimately founded in their ability to persist and to express their nature. Two concepts in Spinoza's philosophy are essential to Naess: *joy*, the active emotion that is a transition towards greater perfection in Spinoza's system, and the *conatus*, which Spinoza terms the essence of every thing that is, the drive to persevere in one's being.[2]

In a world that is relational by nature, the well-being of an individual can never be enough of a foundation. The self that is to be preserved, expressed, and realized is not just the individual self, but an expanding inclusive field of selves (and of the whole relational field in which all the knots exist that manifest as individual things; see further what follows). The self is not just your mind or body or both. The Ecological Self of a person is that with which this person, and this way of perceiving the self, shifts the burden of clarification from the term 'self' to that of 'identification' or rather 'process of identification' (the Norwegian word is *identifisering*).

Increased self-realization implies broadening and deepening of self, which happens through the process of identification with others. We 'see ourself in others'. And this process of identification does not stop at interpersonal relations between humans: 'Society and human relations are important, but our self is richer in its constitutive relations. These relations are not only relations we have to other humans and the human community' (Naess, 1986: 1). This becomes clearer from one of Naess' most often used examples of this process:

> My standard example involves a nonhuman being I met in the 1940s. I was looking through an old-fashioned microscope at the dramatic meeting of two drops of different chemicals. At that moment, a flea jumped from a lemming that was strolling along the table [see Figure 27.2].

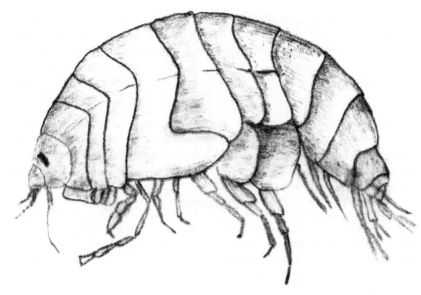

FIGURE 27.2 Sea flea. Image courtesy of http://commons.wikimedia.org/wiki/File:Sea_flea.jpg

The insect landed in the middle of the acid chemicals. To save it was impossible. It took minutes for the flea to die. The tiny being's movements were dreadfully expressive. Naturally, I felt a painful sense of compassion and empathy. But the empathy was not basic. Rather, it was a process of identification: I saw myself in the flea. If I had been alienated from the flea, not seeing intuitively anything even resembling myself, the death struggle would have left me feeling indifferent. So there must be identification for there to be compassion and, among humans, solidarity. (Naess, 1995: 15–16)

Naess preferred to use the term 'self-*perseveration*' over the usual translation 'self-*preservation*', as he thought this is a better translation of Spinoza's meaning. *Perseverare in suo esse* is an active concept in which the *conatus* is the force that makes the self sustain itself. Preserve has a static connotation to it, as in preserving the way things are, while the whole idea is that our self is a dynamic notion.

Naess' *relationalism* has often been interpreted as a type of interconnectedness thinking in which all boundaries between the perceiver and the perceived vanish in the process of indentification. Christian Diehm emphasizes that the flea anecdote shows us that we have to understand this identification more in terms of 'commonality' or 'kinship' and states that 'in what is perhaps his most provocative remark on the subject, Naess suggests that to identify with others is to understand that there is in them "that part of God that lives in all that is living"' (Naess, 2002: 114; Diehm, 2007: 12). That last quote, however, indicates that the theme of the extending self, paired with the idea of self-realization as the path to increasing our joy and the meaning of our lives, is a result of Naess' study and interpretation of Spinoza. The compassionate recognizing of something as akin to you, because you share in the totality of Nature/God/Substance, is what according to Naess is a plausible interpretation of Spinoza's *Amor Intellectualis Dei*, which Naess has proposed to translate as loving understanding of particular beings in the light of the great whole, the creative aspect of the whole (the immanent God) (Naess, 1993: 5–7).

When you connect with and recognize something of the 'other' in you, you feel empathy, it becomes part of your self, and your well-being becomes co-dependent with its well-being. Serving yourself also serves all the relations you have. There is no discrepancy between taking care of/caring for 'me' or 'the river I live close to'. So this care, this self-interest, is not anything negative, nor is it 'unselfishness' or 'sacrificing something'. While caring for all the things that are part of your ecological self, you increase your power and joy, because you increase your capacity for and realization of self-expression (realizing inherent potentialities).[3] The expression of any self is intrinsically part of the expression of all the things that this self is related to.

Naess' other main influence and inspiration, Mahatma Gandhi, also supports this idea. Naess frames the same idea in Gandhian terms:

> As a student and admirer since 1930 of Gandhi's non-violent, direct actions in bloody conflicts, I am inevitably influenced by his metaphysics...Paradoxically, it seems, he [Gandhi] tries to reach self-realization through *selfless action*, that is, through the reduction of the dominance of the narrow self or the ego. Through the wider self, every living being is connected intimately, and from this intimacy follows the capacity of *identification* and, as its natural consequence, practice of nonviolence. No moralizing is needed, just as we do not need morals to breathe. We need to cultivate our insight: The rock-bottom foundation of the technique for achieving the power of non-violence is belief in the essential oneness of all life. (Naess, 2008: 90)

The ultimate or most expanded idea of self is the Self, that contains all there is in the world. Naess is both a thinker who reached for the highest altitudes and at the same time a pragmatic activist who is firmly rooted in the earth. 'Because the infinite level of Self-realization only makes sense metaphysically, the capital S should be used sparingly. At any level of realization of potentials, the individual egos remain separate...Our care continues ultimately to concern the individuals, not any collectivity' (Naess, 1989: 195).

Naess explicitly recognized his own limitations in the face of these altitudes and attitudes. Here we see once more a moment where it seems as if there is some kind of contradiction:

> In the U.S., you cannot walk in the desert in the springtime without crushing flowers. With every step, you kill. People ask how I could justify doing this while at the same time holding the principle of deep ecology that every living being has value in itself. And I say that I can't; it is an inconsistency in my practical philosophy. If I were more engaged in this philosophy I wouldn't do it, or I would only do it when the flowers were already dying; that would be more consistent. I have a very easy excuse—but it's bad, it doesn't work—which is that others will come and the flowers will be crushed anyway. But this is not enough to justify walking around and killing living beings,

which according to my philosophy is something you shouldn't do unless you have very special reasons. So I say, 'All right, I am inconsistent'. We should be clear that this is inconsistent when we are talking so wonderfully about the life of a living being. I think it's very important for philosophers to concede inconsistencies. We should be able to admit fallibility, that humans are through and through fallible. (Naess, 1989: 195)

There is an underlying tone in much of Naess' work that the richness, the different and sometimes contradictive things in our web of life are all part of life's beauty. A key lesson from Naess' work is to be mindful of spontaneous experiences with non-humans and our web of intrinsic relations.

Box 27.1 Spontaneous experience: Seagull (Carien de Jonge)

It was a morning like any other when I went to work. I was in my mid-twenties and late as always. A few blocks away from my house I approached the huge crossing with traffic lights where every morning streams of cars poured out of their residential areas, all hastily trying to get onto the main road to the city where work was waiting. I pulled up for a red light.

And there it was. In front of me in the street, almost in the middle of the square: a large wounded seagull. From the looks of it some car had hit its wing, which hung limp on the street. I could see the bird was still alive and terrified. It could not move away for some reason. The light for the people on the street to the left of me turned to green and all the cars pulled up as if there was nothing on the street, narrowly passing the seagull left and right. I held my breath and clung with my hands tight on the wheel. But after the last car had passed the seagull was still there, no car had hit it this round. Surely, if I could see the bird other people could too. But no one had stopped so far. Oh, and this was back in the days when only some CEOs and salespeople had car-phones—the big ones that needed an antenna to be built onto your car. So there was not really a chance that anyone had called for help.

My stomach turned. The lights would go green again within a few seconds. The seagull could only have so many lucky shots. I felt fortunate I was driving the car that day. It was an easily recognizable company car from a popular local radio station that I worked for at the time. This would hopefully make people more accepting of what I was about to do. When the light turned green, I spun the car in front of the seagull with my hazard lights flashing. Thankfully, the other drivers moved around me carefully instead of honking their horns or screaming at me from their windows. I got out and approached the bird.

It was huge. It stared at me and I stared back.

I went back to the car to see if there was anything in it to help me. Gloves, a crate, some piece of carton, anything to help me lift it or contain it. Nothing. Meanwhile, the traffic lights kept doing its work and cars just kept on passing me. No one stopped. No one helped.

I checked my clothing and thought the only thing that could aid me was my sturdy, woollen shawl. The bird kept eyeing me. I took a deep breath and flung the shawl over its body, tucking it in on the side with the normal wing, and then carefully lifted it up, the shawl dangling from its body, and placed the bird on the passenger's seat. I tried to push the shawl as best as I could under its body, in a faint attempt to keep the seat free from bird

(Continued)

Box 27.1 (Continued)

shit or bacteria. I quickly took my place again behind the wheel and vacated the square when it was safe to do so. The other drivers gave me some room.

A few minutes later, I rushed to the local bird rescue centre. As I entered, with the seagull in my arms, two of the volunteers saw me coming and quickly prepared a tray to put the seagull in. They looked at me with their eyes wide open. Only after we had put the seagull safely in they told me how lucky I was that I still had all of my fingers. 'Did you realize' said one of them 'that a seagull's beak can easily snap one off with one bite? Do you even realize how dangerous handling a wild animal like that is, and with your bare hands, a risk you should not have taken.' I smiled with the self-confidence that is only fitting for a 25-year old. 'Oh, but it knew I was here to save it.' She shook her head and sighed. 'This animal is in complete shock from pain. That is the only reason it did not attack you.'

27.2.2 Relationalism

> Organisms as knots in the field of intrinsic relations.
>
> (Naess, 1989: 28)

Spinoza's monistic ontological foundation underpinned much of Naess' philosophy. The world with everything there is to it, whether we are talking about ideas or about tangible items such as bacteria, a stone, a mountain, a living human being, is *one—one* substance[4] that is without end or beginning, outside which nothing can be conceived.

'The world is *one*' does not mean that the emphasis lies on the totality which all individual things are part of; instead, a more adequate way to understand this claim is in terms of a dynamic interplay of all the individual things that in different constellations make up the totality, a totality that *in total* may have a stable connotation to it, but that is in fact the constant flux of all movement and change in the world, and all the things that exist in those moments. One could call this 'the plane of life'. And in this plane of life, everything is interconnected.

> An intrinsic relation between two things A and B is such that the relation belongs to the definitions or basic constitutions of A and B, so that without the relations, A and B are no longer the same things. The total field model dissolves not only the man-in-environment concept, but every compact thing-in-milieu concept—except when talking at a superficial or preliminary level of communication. (Naess, 1989: 28)

To Naess, 'the plane of life' is a dynamic relational field, and he uses the term *relationalism* to encapsulate these ideas and experiences. *Relationalism* takes relations and interdependency to be essential in what constitutes the world and how we perceive it. This suggests that nothing can *be* alone in itself: everything exists as a knot or point where these relations meet. Naess understands the world as the world on the level of our daily perception and the world as we could perceive it as a whole.

Taking the example of a pet owner, in the first type of perception, your 'self' loves your dog, and in the second you realize that your dog and you are part of one dynamic, interrelational system/field that you are part of, dependent upon, and that you love (the Self). The same could be said about the seagull in Carien's story (see Box 27.1), in which ultimately the whole situation of the seagull, Carien, all the car drivers, and the physical setting they were in, are one vibrant co-dependent system. To connect with all of that— *and* realizing this is only a small part of the dynamic interrelational field—would have been connecting to Naess' *Self.*

The capital S is used by Naess to refer to the idea of self that extends to the totality of all there is. The main point inherent in his argumentation is that these two different 'realities' are not the result of ontological differences, but are two *perceivable* perspectives that exist at the same moment. Because we can shift between these perspectives, a deeper understanding of relationality, *relationalism,* will change how we perceive ourselves in the world and our role in it, and thus will inherently lead to a deep sense of care for the world around us, including the people we share the planet with. This happens through an active process of identification which can lead to Self-realization!

Relationalism makes it easy to shift towards system thinking, and to go beyond the idea of relationality as interaction between an organism and its environment: 'Speaking of interaction between organisms and the milieux gives rise to the wrong associations, as an organism *is* interaction' (Naess, 1989: 56).

Naess' concept of an always-moving interconnected field that constitutes our world is a notion he shares with, for example, Gilles Deleuze (who was, like Naess, inspired by Spinoza). However, Naess differs from Deleuze because, where Deleuze focuses on the continuous dynamic of the becoming of singularities, Naess zooms in on the aspect of relationality of the relational field that is the totality of our world.

27.2.3 Gestalt Ontology/Gestalt Perception

> We are basically gestalt entities experiencing gestalts, rather than particulars.
>
> (Naess in Diehm, 2004: 13)

Naess used the concept of *Gestalt-ontology* for the way we can combine both perspectives in our daily lives, and he shares many of his ideas of Gestalt ontology with Merleau-Ponty. Naess argued that thinking in terms of Gestalts, rather than of entities or events or things, allowed us to acknowledge and understand relationalism in our life and world. Gestalt ontology and Gestalt perception create room for an integral view on aspects like emotions and embodiedness and connection to place. We are not passive perceivers: we are in active interaction with Gestalts. We are part of its relational system. 'The very concepts of "nature" and "environment/milieu" cannot be delimited in an ecosophical fashion without reference to interactions between elements of which we partake…Gestalt formation crosses boundaries between what is conventionally classed as thinking as separated from emotion' (Naess, 1989: 63).

The Gestalt of, for example, 'home' consists of the physical elements of your house, the relationships you have with the people that live there with you, the memories you have of your life there, the smells, the street in which your house is set, how the sun sets on the balcony on a sunny day in the fall, and so on. All these things exist in relation to you, and in relation to each other. Your Gestalt of home is a field of relations. The Gestalt of you-reading-this-sentence presupposes you, a medium that you use, the text as written by us, with ideas from Naess and Spinoza, the context in which you are sitting (or standing) while you are reading this, and maybe some people around you that you are aware of. Though some of these aspects may be 'material things', such as your computer, Gestalts have a high level of subjectivity, as they are construed by your perception and relations. We cannot say of anything that it is purely subjective or purely objective.

In Naess' ontology, the subject–object dichotomy disappears. It is not a relevant distinction:

> When absorbed in the contemplation of a concrete, natural thing, a person does not experience a subject–object relation. Nor does a person have this experience when absorbed in vivid action, whether in movement or not. There is no epistemological ego reaching out to see and understand a tree or an opponent in a fight, or a problem of decision. A tree is always part of a total, a gestalt. Analysis may discover many structural ingredients, sometimes an ego-relation, sometimes not. The gestalt is a whole, self-contained and self-sufficient. If we call it 'experience of the gestalt', we are easily misled in a subjectivist direction. (Naess, 2008: 75–6).

For example, in the seagull experience, we see the disappearance of the subject–object dichotomy when it comes to Carien and the seagull. However, in the moment when Carien decided to step outside—of the car, and of the rush-hour flow—she felt a strong alienation of the car drivers who in her opinion were completely wrapped up in their speedy cocoons and oblivious to what was happening outside. So in that sense one has to wonder if at any time during this story, there was a real Gestalt perception in the full meaning of the word.

Naess' use of Gestalt ontology was not a roundabout way to take things into a systemic level and talk about systems, for example ecosystems, instead of entities. The entity itself is the knot of relations in interaction with our perception. Naess used a river as an exemplar: 'The river itself cannot be identified with its chemistry or its physics, nor with an x, the river as a *Ding an sich*. What gestalt ontology does is to remind one of the inescapable complexity and unity of the river as spontaneously experienced, and therefore not at all rejecting everyday life conceptions' (Naess, 2005: 125) (see Figure 27.3).

Gestalt ontology is not a kind of 'holism'. Naess explicitly explained that he did not use the terms emergentism or holism, since he wanted to emphasize that both the whole *and* its parts are of equal importance, or rather that they are internally related. Gestalt ontology and Gestalt perception hang closely together. It is the perceiving of things that is the moment where the relation is construed or activated. When there is a piece of music that you love, and you hear a few notes of it, you may be overwhelmed with the emotions that you connect to that musical piece. You know these notes as part of the total play. Yet at the same time, you are able to listen to the specific piece right then and there, and you

FIGURE 27.3 Rupert River, James Bay, Canada. Photograph by Gail Whiteman.

may hear that in this particular performance, this note is held a tiny bit longer than in another version of the piece played by someone else. For Naess, these ideas do not exist on an abstract plane. 'On the fundamental level, the idea of the intrinsic value of living beings sounds abstract, but in deep ecology you have very practical situations in which you must make choices' (Naess in Angus, n.d.).

27.3 Genesis of a Place-Person

> How did we, who belong to a place, get to belong there in spite of not being raised there and not having always lived there?
>
> (Naess, 2008: 52)

For many of us, the term 'place' may be simply considered a location, a place where we are, or where we want to go—to this or that place. But for Naess, the feelings we have for places can develop us as humans, and help us overcome our limited ego (Naess, 1998/2005). Furthermore, specific place-person relationisms have agency: 'Phenomenologically speaking, the orders given by a place and the orders given by oneself are inseparable. Only philosophies that impose a sharp subject–object dualism try to trace a border between the "self" and its geographical surroundings' (Naess, 2008: 56).

Naess reached the conclusion that all languages (written, spoken, theoretical, practical, specialized) are too limited when it comes to expressing our spontaneous experiences, or any integral view or approach to the world. This is a result of an inherent limitedness of any language, but also a social phenomenon, for Naess believed that '[h]ow words get their meaning is always bound up with a context that includes a place, culture and customs' (Drengson and Deval, 2008:12). Indeed, the places from which we think, write, and organize, are intrinsically bound up in these fields of intrinsic relations. At times, this caused him to question the disembedded insights of his contemporaries. For instance, 'I find it difficult to understand how Nietzsche could manage to write pettifogging letters among the high mountains' (Naess, 1998/2005: 21).

Despite Naess' numerous positive writings on the value of becoming a place-person (for instance, he seriously considered changing his last name to Tvergastein), he also carefully noted the potential negative effects of such processes. 'A personal place occasionally tyrannizes, imposes itself, gives orders' (Naess, 1998/2005: 56) and '[t]he main thing is that a favored place relentlessly and remorselessly determines the details of one's life…I find that attachment to place should not be praised uncritically' (Naess, 1998/2005: 60). Nevertheless, Tvergastein had a long-lasting imprint upon the man and his philosophy. According to his widow, Kit-Fai Naess (personal correspondence),

> Arne's favourite [place] in Norway was Hallingskarvet, where his Tvergastein is located. He was the patron of Stetind—a mountain voted by the Norwegians as their national mountain. Incidentally his headstone has a very similar shape to that mountain…The stone itself is of the kind that Hallingskarvet is made of. Note that neither Hallingskarvet nor Stetind are the highest in Norway.

A fitting tribute given that Naess both warned of the lure of looking for the most spectacular places in nature, and praised the value of more ordinary places.

27.4 IMPLICATIONS FOR PROCESS THEORY OF ORGANIZING

Naess' work is not generally well known in organization studies. However, within the published literature on organizational sustainability, his work is briefly cited in a variety of ways: (1) as the father of deep ecology (Egri and Pinfield, 1999; Starik and Marcus, 2000); (2) as conceptual support for an eco-centric approach to organizations and the environment (Gladwin et al., 1995; Purser et al., 1995; Shrivastava, 1995); and (3) to highlight the need to reintegrate humans with nature (Shrivastava, 2010; Walck, 2004; Whiteman, 2004; Whiteman and Cooper, 2000; Worthy, 2008).

While most of these papers acknowledge Naess' foundational role in the philosophical (or political) foundations of sustainability (and the deep ecology movement), there are very few, if any, studies which take Naess' philosophy as a central anchor. We believe that a closer reading of Naess offers at least four important contributions to our understanding of the process of organizing: organizing within a field of intrinsic relations, organizing as a reintegration of humans with nature, organizing as a process of place-making or destroying, and organizing from ecosophic foundations.

27.4.1 Organizing within a Field of Intrinsic Relations

A key insight from Naess' work is that organizing can best be described as the process of tying and untying *knots in the field of intrinsic relations*. According to Naess' philosophy, this metaphoric use of 'knots' should not be understood as knots in a rope, but as nodes in a field with hubs where flows of interaction meet. According to Naess, the field of intrinsic relations is, by definition, expanded to include 'the plane of life' containing all life forms.

Like many process philosophers, Naess believed in a dynamic unfolding flow of interaction, rather than static, structured hierarchical determinism. Unlike other process philosophers, Naess explicitly identified non-human beings as contributing an essential dynamic within the process of organizing, within the endless tying and untying of knots of relations in a continuing flow. Naess also argued that Gestalt perception and self-maturation—Self-realization!—are essential features of this process of organizing, and that these can best be developed with long-term immersion in specific ecologies and fields of intrinsic relations, both wild and mundane.

The richness of Naess' work relies upon these layers of relations and through direct engagement with the natural world and with other people in spontaneous experience. According to Drengson, one of the great lessons of Naess is to

> respect the integrity of our *spontaneous experiences* as deep and complex. We cannot adequately describe them in any language, spoken, written, philosophical, scientific, or poetic; not even in performance arts like song and dance. Our feelings and thoughts are rich and deep, when we are *fully open* to them; we could spend our lives reflecting on them, for they are inexhaustible. Our spontaneous experiences can be open to the *whole* world. (Drengson, 2010: 92)

The emphasis on spontaneous experience resonates with the work of Heidegger.

However, what differentiates Naess' approach is his fundamental integration of humans with nature. Naess takes these ideas a step further. For him, it is not sufficient to respectfully allow the beings to show themselves and to give them space. He adds the active component of identification, of engagement with the world and incorporating it in the relational field we are all part of.

Such thinking fits well with the organizational research on ecological embeddedness and sustainability, which presents empirical research on management perspectives that arise from the local ecosystem and indigenous people's belief system which privileges the web of life over human dominion (Whiteman and Cooper, 2000).

A process theory of organizing from a Naessian perspective underscores the primacy of our intrinsic field of relations (human and non-human), and the value of spontaneous experiences in nature is that it helps us open ourselves and our organizing processes—epistemologically and physically—to non-human ecological beings. This is easier said than done. It is all too tempting (and normal) to marginalize spontaneous moments—like the seagull being hit by traffic—as being off-topic or unrelated to work life even when it happens on our way to work. But when we embrace Naess' principle of the primacy of our intrinsic field of relations—and hence privilege the seagull interaction—we are offered a rare moment through which we can glimpse a process approach to organizing, one that rests upon a dynamic, unfolding flow of interaction, rather than static, structured hierarchical determinism. If we expand this to encompass all of the complex moments by which the natural environment is impacted by our organizing processes (and vice versa), we begin to reject the very notion of 'externalities' and realize that we cannot address sustainability issues through the monetization of environmental impact. Instead, Naess' process view of organizing places these human–non-human interactions at the dynamic centre of Self-realization!

27.4.2 Organizing as a Reintegration of Humans with Nature: Genesis of the Place-Person

Naess' argument that humans are not separate from nature (and to think so leads to trouble) is an oft-repeated idea in many fields, including organization studies of sustainability. Indeed, the realization that dualism is a root cause of organizational un-sustainability appeared early on, in the first papers in this literature. For example, Gladwin et al. (1995) argued against the 'fractured epistemology which separates humanity from nature' (Gladwin et al., 1995: 874). Similarly, Purser et al. (1995: 1053) rallied against 'a disembodied form of technological knowing conjoined with an egocentric organizational orientation'. More recently, Worthy (2008: 148) provides empirical support to such ideas, and shows 'that phenomenal dissociation—defined as the lack of immediate, sensual engagement with the consequences of our everyday actions and with the human and nonhuman others that we affect with our actions—increases destructive tendency and that awareness is not enough to curb destructiveness'.

Despite the recognition that dualism is counterproductive to a processual understanding of organizing and sustainability, there has been little empirical research on how this can be accomplished, aside from conceptual demands to heal the divided mind (Walck, 2004), to relocate management and organization processes 'outside' (Whiteman, 2004), or to integrate 'an embodied engagement with the natural environment' into our pedagogical approaches to sustainability (Shrivastava, 2010; also see Jolly et al., 2011). These pleas fit well within Naess' own philosophical suggestions. 'Today, people need to concentrate more on *feeling* the world' (Naess, 1992/2005: 20).

While inspiring, Naess also provides us with greater direction than simply offering appealing (yet somewhat vague statements) about embodiment or feelings. More specifically, Naess describes *identification* as the key process by which humans gain maturity, empathy, and an expanded sense of self which includes other non-/human living beings. The process of identification can unfold at any, or all, given moments in our ordinary lives. Identification may be hard to resist when one is in deep wilderness, yet Naess explicitly highlighted the everyday, spontaneous examples—in his case, the flea that fell under the microscope, and in Carien's case, the seagull that was hit by a car during rush hour traffic.

Through an ongoing and deepening spiral of identification with an ever-expanding field of relations, the dualistic and false separation between people and nature disintegrates.

27.4.3 Organizing as a Process of Place-Making (or Destroying)

The issue of place is an emerging conceptual area in organization studies (e.g. Elmes et al., 2012; Guthey et al., forthcoming; Guthey and Whiteman, 2009; Shrivastava, 2013; Walck, 2004). The concept of place helps to address a significant gap in organization studies. For instance, 'Management theory has historically portrayed organizations and managers as if they were free-floating entities, separate from the natural landscapes they occupy' (Guthey et al., forthcoming: 1). However, the emerging studies on organizations and place have yet to integrate Naess' insights on place and place-person. Instead, the conceptual roots of these studies tend to emerge from geography (Tuan, 1976) and phenomenology (Relph, 1976).

The philosophy of Naess has much to offer, not least of which is to highlight the need to adopt a process perspective to place-making and organizing. At a fundamental level, Naess recognized that the genesis of a place-person exists within all of us, and that rediscovering such embedded relationalism holds the key to transformation and reintegration. Organizing is thus a process of place-making and/or destroying.

Naess saw that those of certain cultures, such as the Inuit in the Arctic, may be born into a relational system that honours their intrinsic interaction with place. The people and the place become inseparable in terms of historic and ongoing processes of person-place identification, and will suffer loss (perhaps irrecoverable) if they are forcibly relocated from their 'place'.

> If people are relocated or, rather, transplanted from a steep, mountainous place to a plain, they also realize, but too late, that their home-place has been part of themselves—that they have identified with the features of the place. And the way of life in the tiny locality, the density of social relations, has formed their persons. Again, they are not the same as they were. (Naess in Drengson and Deval, 2008: 87)

Natural resource development (organizing) must therefore be conceived of as a place-changing (place-enhancing, place-destroying) set of organizing processes.

Naess also considered how urban people develop place-based relations through the intrinsic field of relations open (or closed) to us because of urban planning.

> Cities cannot, of course, contain areas of wilderness, but future cities, like many cities centuries ago, can contain areas of 'free nature'. Such an area is one without domination by humans but with scattered human population. They do not interfere with its flora and fauna and other life forms. One important difference from areas of wilderness is the size: an area of free nature may be very much smaller. (Naess, 1992/2005: 29)

Urban sites for 'free nature' provide opportunities for identification and Self-realization!

> Inevitably, such organizing processes have implications for our cultural identities. When a person who has grown up in a city grows into a nonurbanized personal place, how does this affect his friends and relatives? Obviously, there are sources of tensions and personal tragedies—or the extension of influence so that one's nearest friends and family also develop a relationship with the same place. (Naess, 2008: 56)

The key is to embed one's self (and preferably one's social relations) deeply within a specific place (like Tvergastein in a more remote location, and/or free nature in the city). Daily engagement over time with said place, combined with deep reflective enquiry, will allow space for the co-creation of a place-person Gestalt, with knots of intrinsic relations encompassing the person and the broader geography and community of life forms. Over time, this process of organizing provides space whereby a person can transcend the narrow ego and achieve Self-realization!

27.4.4 Organizing from Ecosophic Foundations

Naess argued that each person can and should develop their own ecosophy, related to a specific place (or set of places), and that, without one, humankind both individually and collectively engage in place-corrosive processes that limit the potentialities open to all of us. While we may start off denatured and materialistic, we may not end up that way.

> In the environment in which I grew up, I heard that what is serious in life is to get *to be* somebody—to outdo others in something, being victorious in a comparison of abilities. What makes this conception of the meaning and goal of life especially dangerous today is the vast, international economic competition. Free market, perhaps, yes, but the law of supply and demand of separate, isolatable 'goods and services', independent of needs, must not be made to reign over increasing other areas of our life. (Naess, 2008: 90–1)

The key is to develop, over one's life and interactions, an ecosophy. Ecosophy 'T' refers directly to Naess' relationship to Tvergastein—it is not directly transferable to other organizing fields or actors. Instead, Naess encouraged all of us to develop our own ecosophy based upon the dynamic field of intrinsic relations within which we exist. From such a position, our organizing practices emerge, change, and mature.

In addition, Naess' work encourages us to take philosophy out into the world. As a philosopher who was geared towards being active, he also measured other thinkers by that standard. While Naess was indebted to Merleau-Ponty's work, he sought to anchor phenomenological experience with political action:

> I studied and very much liked Merleau-Ponty, but I didn't feel that his philosophy was showing a way to activism. I felt that one could be very close to Merleau-Ponty and then do nothing. I always ask, 'What does your philosophy tell you to do in your society? Politically? In education? In the most important areas of life? What are the implications? (Diehm, 2004: 8–9)

Throughout his life, Naess was actively involved in political activism following the values inherent in Ecosophy T and Gandhian enquiry. After World War II, he helped organize a reconciliation process amongst Norwegians who had been collaborators during the war and their communities. In 1969, Naess gave up his position as professor and devoted himself to the environmental movement, becoming the first Norwegian president of Greenpeace, and, as mentioned earlier, the father of the deep ecology movement.

In keeping with his own inspirational life's philosophy (2002), we close by encouraging the reader to literally follow Naess, and put into practice a slogan he formed a few years before his death—to '*deepen* our care for humans and to *extend* it to non-humans' (personal correspondence, Kit-Fai Naess). That would imply to be bold, to 'do' things, to deeply immerse ourselves in free nature, to be open to spontaneous experiences, and to consider deeply how this affects one's organizing philosophy and work life. What kind of potentialities are discovered when we accept the never-ending flux of interactions amongst our intrinsic field of relations? How can our organizing processes mature alongside our evolving ecosophies?

NOTES

1. Acknowlegements: We would like to thank Alan Drengson and Kit-Fai Naess for their close reading of this chapter and many helpful suggestions. We would also like to acknowledge the valuable editorial direction of Jenny Helin, Tor Hernes, Robin Holt, and Daniel Hjorth. The editorial staff at Oxford University Press were also wonderful. And of course, we are indebted to Arne Naess and the seagull.
2. Naess always read Spinoza in Latin, and the translations he uses in his texts are usually his own.
3. Most of the prior paragraph is quoted from 'Self Realization: An Ecological Approach to Being in this World', a Forth Keith Roby Memorial Lecture at Murdoch University, Australia in March 1986. Reprinted in *the Trumpeter: Journal of Ecosophy* 4(3) (1987): 35–41.
4. Physical bodies, motion, and rest are, however, substance perceived under the attribute of extension, whereas ideas and the infinite intellect are substance perceived under the attribute of thought. They do not interact, but are parallel expressions of the one substance. Just like an audio or visual track at a film, where the input depends on your senses. See Spinoza's *Ethics*, specifically parts I and II.

References

Angus, I. (n.d.). Interview with Arne Naess, <http://www.academia.edu/1468041/Ian_Angus_interviews_philosopher_Arne_Naess_about_nature_social_justice_and_strategies_for_change>

Diehm, C. (2004). 'Here I Stand': An Interview with Arne Naess, *Environmental Philosophy* 1(2): 6–19.

—— (2007). Identification with Nature: What It Is and Why It Matters, *Ethics and the Environment* 12(2): 1–22.

Drengson, A. (2010). Communication Ecology of Arne Naess, *The Trumpeter: Journal of Ecosophy* 26(2): 79–118.

—— and Deval, B. (2008). *Ecology of Wisdom: Writings by Arne Naess* (Emeryville, CA: Counterpoint Press).

Egri, C.P. and Pinfield, L.T. (1999). *Managing Organizations Current Issues* (London: Sage).

Elmes, M.E., Whiteman, G., and Guthey, G.T. (2012). Teaching Social Entrepreneurship and Innovation from the Perspective of Place and Place/Making, *Academy of Management Learning and Education* 11(4): 533–54.

Gladwin, T.N., Kennelly, J.J., and Krause, T.S. (1995). Shifting Paradigms for Sustainable Development: Implications for Management Theory and Research, *Academy of Management Review 20:* 874–907.

Guthey, G.T. and Whiteman, G. (2009). Social and Ecological Transitions: Winemaking in California, *Emergence: Complexity and Organization* 11: 37–48.

——Whiteman, G., and Elmes, M.E. (forthcoming). Place and Sense of Place: Implications for Organizational Studies of Sustainability, *Journal of Management Inquiry.*

Jolly, F., Whiteman, G., Atkinson, M., and Radu, I. (2011). Managing and Educating Outside: A Cree Hunter's Perspective on Management Education, *Journal of Management Education* 35(1): 27–50.

Naess, A. (1972/1995). The Shallow and the Deep, Long-Range Ecology Movement, in A. Drengson and Y. Inoue (eds), *The Deep Ecology Movement* (Berkeley, CA: North Atlantic Books): 3–10.

—— (1986). An Ecological Approach to Being in the World, *The Fourth Keith Roby Memorial Lecture in Community Science*, Murdoch University, Australia.

—— (1987). Self Realization: An Ecological Approach to Being in this World, *The Trumpeter: Journal of Ecosophy* 4(3): 35–41.

——(1989). *Ecology, Community and Lifestyle* (Cambridge: Cambridge University Press).

——(1992/2005). Architecture and Deep Ecology, *Trumpeter: Journal of Ecosophy* 21(2): 29–34.

——(1993). *Spinoza and the Deep Ecology Movement* (Delft: Eburon).

—— (1995). 'Self-Realization: An Ecological Approach to Being in the World', in A. Drengson and Y. Inoue (eds), *The Deep Ecology Movement* (Berkeley, CA: North Atlantic Books): 13–30.

—— (1998/2002). *Life's Philosophy: Reason and Feeling in a Deeper World* (Athens, GA: University of Georgia Press).

——(2005). Reflections on Gestalt Ontology, *The Trumpeter: Journal of Ecosophy* 21(1): 119–28.

——(2006). Notes on the Methodology of Normative Systems, *Trumpeter: Journal of Ecosophy* 22(1): 14–28.

—— (2008). *Ecology of Wisdom: Writings by Arne Naess*, ed. A. Drengson and B. Deval (Emeryville, CA: Counterpoint Press).

Purser, R.E., Park, C., and Montuori, A. (1995). Limits to Anthropocentrism: Toward an Ecocentric Organization Paradigm, *Academy of Management Review 20*: 1053–89.

Relph, E. (1976). *Place and Placelessness* (London: Pion).

Rothenberg, D. and Reed. P. (eds) (1993). *Wisdom in the Open Air: The Norwegian Roots of Deep Ecology* (Minneapolis: University of Minnesota Press).

Shrivastava, P. (1995). The Role of Corporations in Achieving Ecological Sustainability, *Academy of Management Review 20*: 936–60.

—— (2010). Pedagogy of Passion for Sustainability, *Academy of Management Learning and Education 9*: 443–55.

—— and Kennelly, J.J. (2013). Sustainability and Place-Based Enterprise, *Organization & Environment*, online first version. Doi: 10.1177/1086026612475068.

Starik, M. and Marcus, A.A. (2000). Introduction to the Special Research Forum on the Management of Organizations in the Natural Environment: A Field Emerging from Multiple Paths, with many Challenges Ahead, *Academy of Management Journal 43*: 539–46.

Tuan, Y.F. (1976). Geopiety: A Theme in Man's Attachment to Nature and Place, in D. Lowenthal and M. Bowden (eds), *Geographies of the Mind* (New York: Oxford University Press): 11–39.

——(1977). *Space and Place: The Perspective of Experience* (Minneapolis: University of Minnesota Press).

Walck, C. (2004). Healing the Divided Mind: Land as an Integrating Concept for Organizations and the Natural Environment, *Organization & Environment 17*: 170–94.

Whiteman, G. (2004). Why Are We Talking Inside? Reflecting on Traditional Ecological Knowledge (TEK) and Management Research, *Journal of Management Inquiry 13*: 261–77.

——and Cooper, W.H. (2000). Ecological Embeddedness, *Academy of Management Journal 43*: 1265–82.

Worthy, K. (2008). Modern Institutions, Phenomenal Dissociations, and Destructiveness Toward Humans and the Environment, *Organization Environment 21*: 148–70.

CHAPTER 28

PAUL RICOEUR

(1913–2005)

HENRIKA FRANCK

28.1 LIFE AND PLACE

PAUL RICOEUR occupies an almost unique position in modern French philosophy. Throughout his long life (he died aged 92) his thinking spanned generations and schools of thought. He started his philosophical journey as a student at the Sorbonne, but his studies were interrupted when he was drafted into the French army and then became a prisoner of war. Interred, he continued his studies, reading Heidegger, Husserl, and especially Jaspers, grounding himself, along with fellow detainees in what became an intellectual prison camp so well endowed with talent that it was granted degree-awarding powers by the Vichy government. Post-war, he continued work in philosophy at Strasbourg, then at the Sorbonne, and finally at the new experimental university at Nanterre. His thinking had matured in a landscape dominated by existential thinkers such as Simone de Beauvoir, Jean-Paul Sartre, and Gabriel Marcel. This existential and phenomenological dominance was challenged through the 1950s and 1960s by the rise of structuralist thought, espoused by the likes of Lévi-Strauss, Jacques Lacan, and Louis Althusser. Interest in the concrete existence, the body, and 'the other' was replaced by concerns for abstract self-regulating systems, and language. Amid such change, Ricoeur sustained a continuing engagement with all sides, not least because of his dispositional refusal to ally himself too closely to any school. It is this reticent intellectual temperament of always seeking to give voice to other positions, without ever espousing them as dogma, that persists throughout Ricoeur's thought and writing; it is his motif.

This lack of allegiance to positions extended itself to wider institutional and geographic settings. From the outset he had been more than a 'French' philosopher. As a student he had studied in Germany, and long before other European philosophers he had started taking note of American philosophy. This influence intensified in 1970, when, resigning from his position of dean at Nanterre in the wake of abuse from student protestors (though still retaining a teaching post there until 1981), he was left free to take up part-time posts in the United States, notably in the divinity department at the University of Chicago. From here he became established as a 'transatlantic' philosopher, trying to relate continental and Anglo-Saxon traditions, without promise of ever reaching any unity.

This breadth of awareness, both geographical and philosophical, finds his work covering many questions, but throughout he carries an abiding interest in what it is to be a human being; 'Who am I?' and 'How shall I live?' being the persistent questions woven into what became his sustained philosophical investigation of the 'capable person'. How should we understand the man Paul Ricoeur, for instance? Ricoeur the flesh-and-blood man leads a long life embedded in different intellectual and social milieu, contingencies and histories over which he has no control and into which he is thrown, having continually to discover what a flourishing life might entail in specific and fluid situations. Ricoeur the reasoner, however, transcends these particulars of a life (what Ricoeur initially calls *bios*). He is able to consider universal conditions and questions through generalizing language (*logos*) against which the specifics of any life become paltry. Human lives are conditioned in this interplay of the immediate and timeless, the active and contemplative, the fragile and perpetual, the directly felt and the rational, the concealed and unconcealed, the circuitous and direct. Experiencing this interplay, whether appearing in feeling or structured through institution, defines human lives. We experience ourselves not in opposition to wider institutional and material settings, but necessarily bound by their specificities, and yet also in possession of loosening generalities. The capable life becomes an experience configured by the capacity to abstract from our distinctive places (without which we cannot live) and to reach across into wider communion with what is different, or other, to us, without rest.

Communication is what enables us to negotiate this interplay of *bios* and *logos*, and hence why language and the use of language preoccupies Ricoeur. Indeed language becomes the medium by which we become a self, and learn of others. Language is what constrains us into the necessary patterns of established meaning by which we sustain practices necessary to live, and language is what proffers the possibility of release from such practices as, through sustained engagement, our embodiment of the rules and actions and thoughts by which practices live exposes them to new possibility. Here language is more than words, extending to symbols that tap into the subconscious where the tension between irresistible drives and personal freedom is played out as keenly as our conscious lives. The upshot is a sense of subjectivity that is neither inner nor outer, nether mental nor structure, but a residue of the words, analogies, metaphors, symbols, and narratives by which we continually write and are written about, speak and are spoken of, in our search for responding to the riddle of our lives. This concern with how we identify ourselves and others within a narrative that unfolds through temporal experiences of our self and others, and generationally and socially within the historical weight carried in language, finds its fullest expression in his 1985–1986 Gifford Lectures published as *Oneself as Another* (1992). Here narrative, time, history, and identity are subsumed into what Ricoeur considers the condition that, above all else, defines our capability for being human: the ethical, as that which considers what is other.

It is this insistence on acknowledging the other that brings Ricoeur to bear on studies of organization. In being organized we find ourselves thrown into everyday conditions demanding we acknowledge ourselves from the outside; we become technologically configured as experts, machinists, or operatives and we are taught how these roles relate to the roles of others. These others are not other, but fully known, already quantified; they are tasks, or duties undertaken by agents of organization. I buy and you sell; I make and you distribute; I acquire and you dispose, all is balanced in organization. In such functional or professional configurations we are often kept at a distance from our sense of personal self. Roles in organizational life are given to us; we don't take them upon ourselves as being parts of us, and are not often encouraged to, save, perhaps, for the technological discipline of producing more with less. We are expected to fall in with the practices and the routines publicly ascribed to us, making any intimacy between our human lives and the organized orders of recognition an ad hoc arrangement. Ricoeur's writing shows how such organization is both inevitable and debilitating if, from within our already organized condition, we are not able to experience what is other to us, what is beyond the confines of legitimated concern, outside the purview of established procedure, over-spilling the classifications of concepts. This otherness is processual; there is no settlement, no arriving at secure foundations, no possibility of reaching a state of knowledge that is more certain than any other. In its stead comes willingness to reach beyond established human settlements in social, intellectual, emotional, and geographic settings, whilst always acknowledging their importance. The capacity to acknowledge what is 'other' is always pulling our lives into yet further considerations of what it means to be capable, without end. Ricoeur investigates how this occurs in many ways, but perhaps the most persistent are in his discussion of time, narrative, history, and identity. It is to these the chapter turns, in turn.

28.2 Time and Narrative

The interplay of *bios* and *logos*, the stretch between the local and general, occurs temporally. By 'time' Ricoeur, schooled in the phenomenology of Heidegger and Jaspers, means temporality. The immediate time of belonging, the *bios*, finds us within time, placed or thrown there, being pulled into 'nows', and 'what thens', and 'nexts', immersed into long-established practices themselves governed through patterns of time associated with the passing of day and night and seasons. Already, though, time is far richer than the measured, phased time of linear, uniform instants. This clock time is just a residue of our being entities with a tendency to mark and measure. Time is that where we find ourselves, where we are thrown, to use Heidegger's term.

Ricoeur then enriches this Heideggerean insight into time by introducing narrative. As beings we reckon with time, aware not just of things being available to us, or frustrating us, in our immediate experience, but also of whether the time is right to do things, whether it is appropriate, and this reaches beyond the immediate towards the general; *logos* is brought to bear on *bios*. To configure this awareness, Ricoeur uses the term 'narrative'. The sense of what is appropriate is collective (involves us reading situations as others might read them) and public (it exposes our judgement to assessment by others). Our immediate facticity is lengthened into spans, becomes considered, as we acknowledge how we are thrown in amid things in the company of others—family, lovers, authority figures, mythical characters—all of whom are insinuating themselves into situations they themselves have not brought about, but for which they are capable of bearing a sense of responsibility understood simply as being able to respond. Narrative captures this sense of submission and responsibility, of being preoccupied and yet also aware of such preoccupations.

Awareness of our pre-occupation pulls us into a sense of expectation, lends our lives an (incomplete) directedness by which the openings and contingencies we experience are pulled into a frame of coherence governed by desired states. For Ricoeur, narratives describe our effort to live up to such desired states where characters and events are brought into a still contingent but approachable plot. We experience ourselves as parts of a story that is unfolding, and our life within a social community becomes part of the narratives of the other individuals. We are continuously trying to make sure that our actions are reconcilable with emerging, and restless, desired states to which we aspire.

So narratives become a way of understanding our being in time; they combine disparate elements into a unity of a plot that has a temporal span. This span, though, is of a specific nature, what Ricoeur calls the 'third' aspect of time, where the cosmological—'world' time—and the phenomenolocial—'soul' time—are combined to become 'human' time, the human experience in time, in the narrative. If we start exploring narratives as something more private and situated in 'human' time, then within narratives we can find a feeling of belonging to a story, a feeling that is both private and public, both immediately present and possible—we become part of it as we find ourselves drawn into and coping with unfolding events and yet still able to evaluate somehow, albeit partially. Narratives present the moments when agents who are aware of their power to act actually do so, and those who are subject to being affected by actions actually are affected. By affect I mean mental and emotional influence over a feeling or state of mind, something different from effect as in causal influence (cf. Spinoza). Again in human time we have a sense of movement, the acknowledgement of *bios* then reaching out through *logos*.

For Ricoeur narrative is undervalued as a mode of understanding, and by widening our understanding of narratives we can be more sensible to why and with whom things matter, as such significance unfolds in events. Ricoeur shows how events only exist because they are part of a plot. But we might be too quick to abstract—to use concepts like 'storytelling' to get people involved and engaged with one another in order to then extract rents or solutions—when Ricoeur is finding narrative a grounding condition in how we understand ourselves rather than an occasional and instrumental one. Narratives tell how we belong both privately and publicly; it is the way we make sense of things, and what makes things matter. There is deep affinity between organization and an appreciation of the power of narratives or stories, but the temporal experience of stories is something to be explored further. In his book *Storytelling: Bewitching the Modern Mind* (2010), Christian Salmon questions the modern preoccupation with abandoning silence, encouraging babble, stories, commentaries in order to more 'meaningfully' structure work life. He shows how stories are being actively managed, exploited in service of strategic aims; the story of the good employee encouraging productivity, the story of stoic endurance encouraging capacity to bear misfortunes and downgrading of conditions, the use of satire to dissolve tension, invoking dreams to encapsulate strategic vision. Facing complex, globally insecure environments, stories are used to help members of organizations and customers feel settled, believe themselves still in control because they allow tellers and audience alike to elide from raw experience. It is not the illusion of control, but something more subtle, encouraging in us the impulse to always move on, to turn our back on the empirical, on what has happened and might happen, and believe in the mobility of the story instead. Thus Salmon issues a warning, showing us how stories help us forget, their seductions allow us to ignore history, to repress human time by being too readily configured by generality. Narrative structures really are that pervasive. Our feelings, insights, aspirations, and fears are not first created within us and then translated to others through mediating organization, but actually form a part of narrative structures that are inherently communicable. Organizations themselves, what we call an organization—a firm, policy unit, political party, or congregation—are themselves narratives. Salmon shows how, if you can genuinely belong to one of these entities as opposed to being told you belong to it, then you feel more capable as a human being, yet this capability can carry huge costs for one's capability if it is invoked as means to service specified ends like buying or making more. For Ricoeur, capability is not based on belonging (a feeling of being securely held within specific practices) but of being able to spill over from specific practices (*bios*) towards general identification (*logos*). Where organizations use narrative instrumentally, the narrative itself is corrupted because there is hostility to such spilling over. It is movement that defines narrative as Ricoeur wishes it to be understood, not the clarity of the beginning, middle, and end points.

28.3 History

Narratives involve history, a sense of what has been, and in his work *Memory, History, Forgetting* (2005) Ricoeur reflects on his own work and authorship as history. He ponders the question of how memory in the present time also can be an absent history and on the premises behind 'the truth' of history writing and telling. His presumption is that the ability to remember, which is the most important prerequisite for writing history, is developed in dialectic between memory and forgetting. The importance of forgetting feeds into the notion of forgiving; for humans not to become victims of themselves, it is necessary they free themselves from their past actions, but also have the capability to take responsibility for their future actions through promise. Thus history takes up the interplay of *bios* and *logos* set out in narrative forms, where in consulting history we are able somehow to reach after a kind of discontinuity, or abstraction, a universal history to which we might aspire where we are able to treat others as human beings without their having to be connected to us in our lives in some way. This is how Ricoeur discusses three scientific levels of history: the documentary, the explanatory, and the large historical categories. For him these cannot be separated, because no one goes into an archive without trying to explain something, or using a specific narrative or theory, and yet is able to reach into (potentially) these larger categories and so, like Kant, strive after a truly cosmopolitan perspective, *logos* with only the bare hint of *bios*. Ricoeur emphasizes the role of the witnesses of history, the people who tell stories, and thus questions the idea of a neutral observer who can register past events without emotion or involvement. It is by working through history in a questioning manner that we arrive at the possibility of abstraction, not by an epistemological decision to be neutral, a claim to objectivity that has no grounding because it is never worked at, only asserted. We have to work through history to become neutral, not work beyond or against it. Thus he problematizes the idea of time and space in the writing of history; the time when something occurred, and the time when someone tells about it.

This has resonance in organizations, not just as events to be forgotten and remembered then move on but also in the movement from direct documentary awareness of one's own experience through to larger categories by which any organization can be configured as having memory. Often in organizational settings employees or members are required to forget, to relocate, to configure where they are by consulting from whence they came, organizationally. Forgetting and awareness are brought into continual conversation. This is further complicated by the fact that people have a collective memory, but also a personal one. For example, when the Symbian operating system was developed at Nokia, employees put in many working hours—late nights and weekends—making the system as good as possible. Then, in 2011, Nokia announced it would use Microsoft's platform, dropping Symbian as its main Smartphone OS. Two to three years of working over time, choosing work over family and leisure, seemed wasted. These people had their own history, they were witnesses of what happened, but they didn't write the story. However, to keep going, they must be able to forget and forgive. You need to be brave enough to stop, to forget, to forgive, lest history overwhelm you in recrimination.

The firm Lego might be said to have experienced a different call on history. At the turn of the millennium employees were being actively encouraged to recover the origins and spirit of its founding forces as part of a strategic renewal process. The upshot was a profound and commercially successful reassessment of what the organization 'did', centred around the symbolically resonant object of the small plastic brick. Current employees had no direct recollection, and hence were invoking more generally available and rendered accounts of the company's past, and through this move towards the general found the means of recovering a sense of commercial direction. Lego takes up the tradition of its origin, it repeats its beginnings, and in doing so creates a new founding act that makes history anew in acts of beginning again, literally considering and writing down that sense of origin by which it began. This narrative recommencing finds the firm enquiring into its sense of direction in which the original sense of being thrown, of finding oneself in and amid things, replete with structuring conditions, is revisted and in this repetition extended. There is awareness of things dying here, of generations passing, and thus of memory by which current members are able to think about what has passed away as otherness that is now absent, but in being recalled in a kind of resurection through repetition (Ricoeur, 1980).

Recalling the earlier comments about stories, however, it is equally important that history is not forgotten entirely, that what is forgiven is done so through active memory. There are countless examples of organizational pasts that have been buried to the detriment of what Ricoeur would consider leading a capable life, the Vienna Philharmonic being a recent case. At the beginning of 2013, the orchestra was found to have long-standing Nazi associations, not least the orchestra's signature New Year's Concert originally being a Nazi marketing stunt. The orchestra hierarchy had tried for years to cover it up. This case reveals the dialectic between memory and forgetting, which Ricoeur says is the ability to remember. So the orchestra can now redeem itself in admission and then move on, rather than ignoring its history. The importance of forgetting feeds into the notion of forgiving; it is necessary to free oneself from past actions, but in order to do that there has to be capability to take responsibility.

28.4 Identity

Ricoeur was concerned with understanding the relation between self and other. More specifically, he was occupied by the question of how it is possible for two distinct selves, separated by time and space, perhaps even by language and culture, to understand and relate to one another with generosity and hospitality. To better appreciate this, Ricoeur's philosophical anthropology develops as a reflexive structure, where the self is made universal in a rather sensational way. Identity is not only about the self in the first person, as 'I', but includes oneself in the third person, as 'he' or 'she'—like a complex relationship to self. Respect for others and self-respect are inseparable in a philosophical reflexion that describes the human as imperfect—she must constantly turn to others to find herself. In a time characterized by individualism, Ricoeur tries to explore the possibilities for some kind of universalism, although without ever striving to colonize the other. This is played out, this relationship, through combinations of constant parts, samemess (*idem*) and changing parts, otherness (*ipse*). Selfhood is not sameness when the temporal dimension is taken into consideration. Because it is only with the question of permanence in time that the confrontation between *idem* and *ipse* becomes an issue; the *idem*-identity gives the self its spatio-temporal sameness, and the *ipse*-identity gives the self the ability to intitiate something new, to spill over. Without both sorts of identity, there is no self. For example, when we speak of ourselves, we in fact have available to us two models of permanence in time: personal character and keeping one's word. To keep one's word is the *ipse*-identity represented by self-constancy; it is the manner in which a person conducts herself so that others (and oneself) can count on her.

Ricoeur saw identity being formed in the relation between selfhood, otherness, and sameness, and for him 'other' is not just a simple antonym to 'same' like 'other than self' or 'contrary', but otherness is constitutive of identity as such. In other words, otherness is both a comparison when defining identity and an integrative part in forming it. Selfhood reconciles and ties the self to the other through commitment and promise. Ricoeur distinguishes between three levels of otherness: otherness from the institution, otherness from the other person, and otherness from oneself.

It was something like this that Sveningsson and Alvesson were struggling with in their 2003 piece on identity work, the way people's identities unfold beyond specific framings and contextual settings. If we suppose that identity work is in constant flux and that work invokes self-narratives that make a point about the narrator, then, as concepts, sameness and otherness are constitutive of all identity formed through a basic narrative question: 'Who am I in relation to my (former/future) self and others?' Narrative identity perspectives suggest an approach to identity work that is self-reflexive and focuses on the conception of the self and interactions with others (Watson, 2009). The self-narrative needs a continuity of self through time, a reflexivity of the self and others and a treatment of the self as other, which includes, inevitably, a moral evaluation of the self (Linde, 1993; Ricoeur, 1992). Identity work can be seen as a continuous iteration between these two; people want to create coherent narratives out of identities and want to identify with the organization's 'sameness', but the inherent otherness cannot be avoided, so the sameness becomes disrupted over and over again.

Take family businesses as an example of how identity is understood by Ricoeur. They can be seen as organizations where the questions of self-esteem and identity are intimately connected. To make a promise is the capacity to put yourself in a relationship with another whereby that other is capable of expecting certain behaviour from you and the eliciting of that responsibility is how self-esteem is configured, and it seems this is how a family works. It is not a promise, as in 'I'll do this', but more like an open-ended obligation that you are just committed to others, *idem* and *ipse*. Moreover, in a family firm it is not just individuals who come together to create an organization; they are individuals because of their being already organized, because they are instituted in places that offer them verification, that afford them recognition. It is through the institution of family that firm members gain identity, and that identity is configured through a relational condition of otherness. The family is a kind of proto or primal form of an organization predicated on self-esteem, the experience of others, and an open-ended obligation. It is not about doing something for other members because they have done something for you; indeed it is often in spite of them not having done things. It is this sense of exposure that Ricoeur tries to translate. In modern organizations there is a risk of losing that sense; it is stripped away because of overt reliance on public and formal definitions and contractual terms, stipulating what is owed and what is due. By stipulating ourselves like that we empty ourselves of what is human about our identity.

28.5 ORGANIZATION AS ETHICS

In Ricoeur's view, narrative, time, history, and identity are gathered in what he calls the ethical condition of our lives. Ethics is what marks us out, yet it is also what has been increasingly shut out, especially from commercially organized life. The expression 'a good life' is an evaluation that combines one's own subjective criteria and the intersubjective criteria of the regard, words, and action of others. Here is the root of ethics: a responsibility for one's actions. It is a practical and material conception of identity that entails a presumption that self-identity is utterly dependent on others. As a subject for my actions, I am responsible for what I do with and for others. As the ethical intention in future aims and intentions is set by one's self alone, it includes self-concepts like role, solicitude, and justice.

In all such identity is a condition of reciprocity and so, for Ricoeur, ineluctably ethical: identity is sustained in so far as others' lives are considered of equal value and interest to one's own. This brings up the dilemma of 'the other's' mind—sameness is being inside my own consciousness, within my own will. Otherness is outside my mind and untouched by my own will. The ethical aim of life is to 'live the good life, with and for others, in just institutions' (Ricoeur, 1992: 172).

Identity is dependent upon a narrative coherence in one's life, and if this is lost, the ability to see oneself as worthy of living a good life, and as being responsible, is lost, leading to a loss of self-esteem. Ricoeur hence argues that self-esteem is the ethical aim of human life. In other words, self-esteem means affirming narratively to one's self that one is worthy of a good life. Ethical values are not constructed anew every time a decision is made; they have history and are part of the search for the good life that people in organizations strive for. In contrast to the sameness ideal, otherness makes the agent subsume his or her goals under others' capacity to accept them. This tension between sameness and otherness can be seen in organizational work. In organizations, the one who decides upon the work to be done has a certain status over the person to whom the obligation is owed. The one who gives the promise of doing the work is counted on and his or her self-constancy is made responsive to this expectation. In the moment of commitment to the organizational work (say because of the power of a story), people either arbitrarily assume a constancy in their feelings which is not in their power to establish, or they accept in advance that they have to carry out actions which won't reflect their state of mind. They are either (unconsciously) lying to themselves at the moment of commitment or they will be lying to others in the future. This is where Ricoeur offers his notion of practical wisdom: 'Practical wisdom consists of inventing conduct that will best satisfy the exception required by solicitude, by betraying the rule of the smallest extent possible' (1992: 269). Otherness pays regard to the ethical dimension of any human collaboration and practical wisdom is the ability of an agent to understand the distinctive nature of the other. It is primarily an individual characteristic, but it manifests itself in organizations through moral exemplarity and reciprocity.

Towards the end of his life, Ricoeur extended these reflections into questions of justice which he equates with a sense of fundamental unfairness at unequal shares and the failure to keep one's word. In his last work, *Reflections on the Just* (2007), he proposes a dual axis of horizontal constitution of the self as dialectic between sameness and otherness, and a vertical axis constituted by human action; between practice and institution. He sees a dichotomy and conflict between the institution and interpersonal relations; the otherness of individuals is opposed to the unitary aspect of the concept of humanity. There is a schism between respect for the law and respect for persons. In short, there is again a conflict between universalism (*logos*) and contextualism (*bios*). He writes:

> I adopt a more direct, shorter route in the direction of applied ethics. I rapidly evoke typical situations that represent the conflict between apparently equal norms of value, conflicts between respect for the norm and solicitude towards persons, a choice between gray and gray rather than between black and white, and finally—here the boundary narrows—between the bad and the worst. (2007: 9)

If we have a concept of justice that is purely rational and a matter of procedural law, then ethics of argumentation can resolve conflicts. But is the situation the same with the principle of respect for persons? Here there is a consistent emphasis of the Aristotelian virtue of phronesis, practical wisdom in unique situations, set against the Kantian model of conscience defined in terms of rigour and impartiality. The act of judging is no longer concerned with 'either the legal or the good but the equitable' (2007: xxiv). What makes Ricoeur's view on justice interesting from an organizational perspective is his discussions between teleological and deontological ethics mediated by categories of self, the good life, and just institutions. As Clark (2010) points out, it is not simply a dialectic between Aristotelian and Kantian traditions, but also a mediation between Anglo-American and European traditions of debate, and a continuous process of mutually illuminating transformation. Justice must be thought of as simultaneously structure and event; the universal and the contextual, as utopian horizon and specific practice, as high concept and contingency decision-making (Clark, 2010).

This view finds ethics as an individual's ongoing experience of making choices about what to do in the institutional context in which this activity is situated. In so doing, it brings into question the very idea of separating individuals and institutional contexts for, as found in the thinking of Ricoeur, ethics is less a study of moral norms than the transcendental basis for identity constituted in experiencing what is other than, or beyond, oneself. Ethics is inherent in the identity of a human being, and cannot be a separate or objective part of human life.

There is a kinship between Ricoeur's notion of justice and practical wisdom and the practice of organizational work. First, Ricoeur says that the search for the 'just mean' seems to be good advice, signifying something other than cowardly compromise, that in itself may be 'extreme'. In organizations, perhaps the most important moral decisions consist in drawing a line between what is permitted and what is forbidden—a deliberation between the norm and the situation at hand. Second, Ricoeur suggests that moral judgement in a situation is less arbitrary if the decision-maker has taken the counsel of people who are reputed to be 'the most competent and the wisest' (1992: 273). In organizations it is also clear that a decision benefits from the plural character of the debate.

28.6 THE VALUE OF RICOEUR IN ORGANIZATION STUDIES

As I wrote earlier, work in organizations is mostly hierarchical in the way that the one who decides upon the work to be done has a certain status over the person to whom the obligation is owed. The one who gives the promise of doing the work is counted on and their self-constancy is made responsive to this expectation. Ricoeur reveals an inherent tension in human condition organizationally set; he helps us configure the just organization in its own ordinary grounding. There is a sense of community, a challenge of experiencing, and a translation from the self to the other, without losing sense of us always participating in a enigma; we resist the urge for clarity, for objectivity, for predictability. Ricoeur's thinking of the institution helps us understand organizations, neither as individuals nor as collectives, but settled in self–other, the tension in life therein.

In English translations of Ricoeur, the term 'the ethical aim' is used, translated from 'la visée ethique': 'la visée de la vie bonne, avec et pour les autre, dans des institutions justes' ('The aim of living the good life, with and for others, in just institutions'). However, 'la visée' does not strictly mean 'aim', it is more like an intention we are not necessarily aware of. This is a problematic term in English, because 'aim' in English connotes something that is strived for. But if we discount standards and principles, ethics becomes something internalized, something we simply live. Nothing is pushing or pulling us in life; there is nothing in life that is sustaining us; there is nothing dogmatic about ethics. Because ethics is like breathing for Ricoeur, it is therefore not decisional. Morality might be decisional, which is the kind of expression of ethics on the level of social norm, where it becomes explicit, at least in so far as it can invoke standards, or you can identify manners or customs. Typically, studies of ethics in business find morals existing in the form of externally configured yardsticks, like principles, standards, and regulations, against which individuals are assumed to employ deliberate moral reasoning to clarify, assess, and manage their behaviours. But from within, ethics is that condition from beneath which you can't apply any yardstick, and you can't decide whether someone is or is not ethical. Ricoeur is useful in that he allows us, at least to some extent, to get a handle on that. This is the value associated with Ricoeur, he allows us to make sense of the problems we are experiencing. There is a common set of problems at play, the experience of tension, which we can make sense of.

This is not to imply that people in organizations should be all-knowing about their motives. But they are infused by the institutional setting, and are articulated by and at the same time impeded by that setting. It is very difficult to do that without abstracting, and nearly all organization studies literature abstracts in a way that veils our awareness of experience by bracketing it. This is typically fine, if we talk about something like resource allocation. But when we talk about identities, ethics, or justice, it becomes problematic, because they are dealing with the assumption of projective expressions in a public setting. In other words, both identity work and ethics are concerned about how you flourish in the company of others, and through the articulation or expression or discovery of a sense of esteem it cannot be pulled away from. So scholars in identity work or business ethics cannot behave in the same way, by abstracting. What Ricoeur shows is that it is really hard to pull away, not to abstract. We are not sufficiently aware of that, but we as scholars have to try and define someone, or their subjectivity, and recognize that it is constantly under review. More broadly, people in organizations aren't fixable; they aren't only virtuous people that we can pinpoint, nor are they full of vice. We cannot isolate them as workers in the organization as distinct from parents or men or women. What Ricoeur can help organization scholars do is to articulate a kind of well-being, the experience of identity and ethics, as being something underway as opposed to something attained. It is about the task of self-creation and re-creation, and this endeavour is as much ironic as it is beautiful. I'm not saying that business should be more ethical, because there are no readily quantifiable elements in ethics. Ricoeur's idea of the just institution is what animates people's lives; because he sees ethics as distinct from the moral. Too often business ethics is discussed at the level of the moral. But the underbelly, which is where ethics matters, is hidden over. It is a bit similar to the 'practical coping' in strategy (see Chia and Holt, 2006)—people see the 'headline' issues, but the ordinary grounding is something we ignore, something we abstract away from, and Ricoeur is pulling us back there.

This chapter has attested to the value of Paul Ricoeur in organizational settings and to process organization studies in particular. I realize that Ricoeur can be brought into critique because of his preoccupation with an idea of the ethical self that is narrated with an insufficient degree of continuity, common thread, or sense of history, but this doesn't mean we should give up on this kind of thinking. Rather, it calls for organization scholars to recognize that identity work and ethics concern how you flourish in the company of others and through the articulation or expression or discovery of a sense of esteem. It makes us see the evidence of our behaviour and perhaps helps us become the moral beings we can look back upon with a good sense of self-esteem.

REFERENCES

Chia, R. and Holt R. (2006). Strategy as Practical Coping: A Heideggerian Perspective, *Organization Studies* 27(5): 635–55.

Clark, H.C. (2010). Introduction: Paul Ricoeur: Memory, Identity, *Ethics, Culture & Society* 27(5): 3–17.

Linde, C. (1993). *Life Stories: The Creation of Coherence* (New York: Oxford University Press).

Ricoeur, P. (1975). *The Rule of Metaphor: Multi-Disciplinary Studies in the Creation of Meaning in Language*, trans. R. Czerny with K. McLaughlin and S.J. Costello (London: Routledge and Kegan Paul).

—— (1980). Narrative Time, *Critical Inquiry* 7(1): 169–90.

—— (1992). *Oneself as Another,* trans. K. Blamey (Chicago: University of Chicago Press).

—— (2004). *Memory, History, Forgetting,* trans. K. Blamey and D. Pellauer (Chicago: University of Chicago Press).

—— (2007). *Reflections on the Just,* trans. D. Pellauer (Chicago: University of Chicago Press).

Salmon, C. (2010). *Storytelling: Bewitching the Modern Mind,* trans. D. Macey (London: Verso).

Svenningson, S. and Alvesson, M. (2003). Managing Managerial Identities: Organizational Fragmentation, Discourse and Identity Struggle, *Human Relations* 56(10): 1163–93.

Watson, T.J. (2009). Narrative, Lifestory and Manager Identity: A Case Study in Auto-biographical Identity Work, *Human Relations* 62(3): 299–322.

CHAPTER 29

HAROLD GARFINKEL
(1917–2011)

NICK LLEWELLYN

29.1 INTRODUCTION

THIS CHAPTER considers the work of Harold Garfinkel and the study area he founded, ethnomethodology. Ethnomethodology is presented as one way of accessing organizational processes as they are 'in flight' (Garfinkel, 1986). Ethnomethodologists study the flow of ordinary mundane actions, prioritizing their detailed 'endogenous organization' (Garfinkel, 1996; Hernes and Weik, 2007). One of Garfinkel's central recommendations was to give 'to the most commonplace activities of daily life the attention usually accorded extraordinary events' (Garfinkel, 1967: 1). For some 50 years, researchers following his recommendations have explored distinctive ways of working with empirical materials that enable researchers to explicate accomplishments of social order; ethnomethods through which people assemble commonplace objects, actions, and circumstances. This chapter addresses this work and its implications for process research in organization studies.

Throughout the chapter, ethnomethodology is discussed in relation to an ontology of becoming, i.e. the sense that all things are in a 'continuous process of becoming, transforming and perishing' (Chia, 1997: 695). Specifically, it addresses how ethnomethodology accesses the continual making and remaking of social things. To be concerned with process is to take seriously how objects, actions, and settings are continually being made and remade through practical actions. 'Process thinking' eschews structural, subjectivist, and rational-individualistic explanations of such accomplishments. Instead, the challenge is to show how social facts are concertedly realized in the moment. Capturing the ebb and flow of practical activity is a demanding task. Mundane actions happen fast and are often densely layered. Multiple overlapping sign systems interact, such as speech, gaze, the body, and gesture. Process researchers clearly recognize this;

'connectedness is of the essence of all things' (Whitehead, 1938: 9). Garfinkel's work supplies a novel way of accessing connectedness, movement, and the continual reproduction of organizational scenes.

29.2 INTELLECTUAL AND PERSONAL BACKGROUND

Ethnomethodology had a strong organizational angle from the start. Garfinkel, albeit in a junior capacity, worked on two of the most high-profile organization behaviour studies ever undertaken. Whilst a graduate student at Harvard, Garfinkel worked with Wilbert Moore on the Organizational Behaviour Project at Princeton. Upon leaving Harvard, he worked on the leadership studies conducted at Ohio State University. As a very young man, Garfinkel even took business courses on book-keeping and accounting at Newark College (which developed into Rutgers University) (Rawls, 2002: 10). As ethnomethodology developed through the late 1950s, it was concerned with work settings and problems. The founding collection, *Studies in Ethnomethodology* (Garfinkel, 1967), tackles the work of jurors and social science coders. It analyses settings, including a psychiatric outpatient clinic, a suicide prevention centre, and a coroner's office. The chapter 'Good Organisational Reasons for Bad Clinical Records' was co-written with Egon Bittner (Garfinkel and Bittner, 1967), who went on to write the noteworthy essay, The Concept of Organization (Bittner, 1974).

By way of background, Garfinkel is typically considered a scholar of the late 1960s and early 1970s. However, the central publication, *Studies in Ethnomethodology* (Garfinkel, 1967), was the result of work done over 12 years (Garfinkel, 1967: ix). Garfinkel understood the project to have begun in the middle 1950s. Intellectually, as Rawls (2002: 3) notes, Garfinkel was a contemporary, and not just a student, of Wittgenstein and C. Wright Mills (Wittgenstein's *Blue and Brown Books* were not widely available until 1958, and his *Philosophical Investigations* did not appear until 1945). The first reported usage of the term 'ethnomethodology' was at the American Sociological Association (ASA) meeting in 1954. In terms of chronology then, and remarkably given the conservatism of the field, ethnomethodology starts in the mid-1950s.

For Garfinkel's career, we need to go back before then, to the early 1940s. Garfinkel received his MA in sociology from the University of North Carolina in 1942, where his thesis concerned race relations and in particular the procedures through which inter- and intra-racial homicides were processed by the courts. Garfinkel's very first publication was actually a lucid short story published initially in 1940 (see Garfinkel, 1945), 'a quasi-fictional account of a conflict that arose when an African American woman refused to sit at the back of the bus when the vehicle crossed the former Mason-Dixon line' (Lynch, 2011). This was republished in the 1941 edition of the *Best American Short Stories*. Garfinkel's contribution follows William Faulkner's 'Gold is not Always'. The

MA thesis formed the basis of Garfinkel's first scholarly publication (Garfinkel, 1948–1949) in the journal *Social Forces*. The paper is tightly argued and theoretically mainstream, an example of the structural-functionalist orthodoxy of the time.

The move to Harvard in 1947, to pursue doctoral studies with Talcott Parsons, led Garfinkel in a more theoretical direction. In 1948 he wrote a manuscript entitled *Seeing Sociologically: The Routine Grounds of Social Action*, which was published in 2006, with a rich forward by Anne Rawls. In this manuscript and in Garfinkel's PhD thesis completed three years later, entitled The Perception of the Other: A Study of Social Order, Garfinkel's mature critique of the mainstream structural-functionalist theory, and Parsons' Theory of Action in particular, is apparent. But the writing is formal and theoretical. Garfinkel's 'ethnomethodological alternative' to precisely this type of 'formal analytic sociology' (Garfinkel, 1996: 9) cannot be anticipated from this work. Garfinkel is still writing and publishing within the theoretical orthodoxy. In 1956 Garfinkel published in the *American Journal of Sociology* a piece on 'Conditions of Successful Degradation Ceremonies'. The absolute intellectual and stylistic break between Garfinkel's early functionalist work and the ethnomethodological alternative he must have been simultaneously developing is astonishing.

To understand connections and contrasts with his immediate peers, and to locate Garfinkel's concern with the continual making and remaking of social and organizational scenes, it is worth dwelling on his relationship with Talcott Parsons, in particular the ideas expressed in *The Structure of Social Action* (Parsons, 1937/1967) and the collection *Towards a General Theory of Action* (Parsons and Shils, 1951). Whilst Garfinkel engaged many theoretical sources deeply, exchanging correspondence with authors such as Schutz and Gurwitch, Parsons was certainly the central reference in Garfinkel's writing. Parsons was the pre-eminent world figure in sociology at the time; he defined the mainstream for at least thirty years.

Whilst Parsons' work is extensive, and changed in important ways throughout Garfinkel's career, Garfinkel's critique of *The Structure of Social Action* is of central importance for understanding ethnomethodology as a response to sociology and as a potential avenue of interest for process researchers. Central to the argument in *The Structure of Social Action* is that social sciences are dealing with systems of social action, the basic components of which Parsons termed 'unit acts', which are composed of actors, ends, a current situation and a mode of orientation (Heritage, 1984). Together these components form the 'action frame' (Parsons, 1937/1967). Through this frame, two central preoccupations are addressed: goal striving, i.e. 'the subjective direction of effort in the pursuit of normatively valued ends' (Heritage, 1978: 227), and social order, i.e. how the strivings of different social actors could be reconciled without social relations being dominated by violence and fraud. Parsons' solution was derived from Durkheim, in that he proposes that moral values, internalized through socialization, come to constrain both desired ends and acceptable means. Social cohesion is achieved as the result of the institutionalization of a central set of values; 'it is through internalization of common patterns of value orientation that a system of social interaction can be established' (Parsons and Shils, 1951: 150). In important ways, Garfinkel was not critical of the content of Parsons' theoretical work. He reacted against the mode of theorizing itself. Three aspects of this are worth highlighting.

First, Parsons' work is posited on the idea that persons, actions, and scenes of ordinary society can be treated as solid, Durkheimian facts. The analyst's job is to build a theoretical edifice that explains those facts. For Garfinkel, in contrast, even apparently solid things, such as statistical rates, were not well understood as static objects. Rather, they were understood as ongoing accomplishments. For instance, unexplained deaths are counted as 'suicides' by coroners through their work (Garfinkel, 1967). Coroners exercise judgement through various practical and inferential procedures. Rather than static facts, suicide rates, of the kind that Durkheim's thesis relied upon, are recoverable products of ordinary work practices. Presuming a body of social facts, passively awaiting social scientific explanation, misses what is most interesting about the phenomenon at hand, its fluid, fragile, and accomplished character.

Second, in the Parsonian theoretical mode, the actor's role/agency in the reproduction of social facts is extremely limited. Social action is best explained through macro variables, namely the dominant value patterns, which are internalized by individual actors. The idea that social actors internalize values, norms, or discourses, to the point where they passively and unknowingly reproduce them through action, is perhaps one of the key ideas in sociological theorizing generally. For the analysis of actual stretches of conduct, however, it is extremely difficult to work with such a reductive account of the actor.

At stake here is not whether social actors internalize values and rules over the course of their life—of course they do—but rather how values and norms are externalized. Rules and normative standards are sociologically interesting to the extent that they are manifest in social action. This is important because social action is unpredictable and somewhat messy. People can privately hold to a particular value or norm, but find themselves participating in exchanges that partially or wholly undermine such commitments. Just because an individual holds to an idea (via internalization) does not guarantee the idea will be manifest in their actions. Such is life. Practical actions often unfold in ways that confound, rather than reproduce, the espoused beliefs of the actors themselves.

There is a more theoretical point here. The idea that we can neatly separate a society's normative frameworks, on the one hand, and a vast landscape of social facts, on the other, with the former governing the latter, is problematic. Rules or norms are not just governing devices; they are also constitutive of the very objects they are thought to control. For example, the operation of school discipline is partially mediated by a prior normative distinction between 'good' and 'bad' kids (Baker, 1997). This distinction is reflexively constitutive of social action. Hence, rule-breaking by 'good kids' can be seen as an anomaly. Normative frameworks do not simply govern individual conduct; they are reflexively implicated in the constitution of the very objects they seemingly control. This is a very conventional thing for a social scientist to say in the present day. But in the middle 1950s there were few reference points people could have drawn upon to 'get' what Garfinkel was talking about when he spoke of the ' "reflexive" or "incarnate" character of accounting practices' (Garfinkel, 1967: 1).

Summarizing the issue of agency, for Garfinkel social order is not secured simply through the stock of knowledge people carry around in their heads. This knowledge is obviously important, but it is not enough. People must also have methods through which they externalize their thoughts, understandings, plans, and motives. The achievement of social order requires both a common cultural heritage and a set of common procedures through which people can display to one another 'what is on their mind' (Sacks, 1992), the standards they are drawing upon and what they are thinking. For Garfinkel the problem of social order is essentially praxiological rather than cognitive; it is resolved on each and every occasion locally.

Thirdly and finally, Parsons used the term 'social action' in a very general way. In Parsons' work, social action is understood broadly, to encompass events that take place across sites, over time, and which involve multiple actors. In a volume entitled *The Structure of Social Action*, this understanding enables Parsons to avoid analysing any single discrete action. Garfinkel meant something quite different by the term 'social action'. He meant things like saying 'hello', turning left in traffic, asking a question, or walking along a busy street. These mundane actions, which are perhaps *the* locus of sociability for ordinary members of society, were almost entirely overlooked by the sociology of the 1950s. Arguably, they remain so. The Parsonian framework was tremendously grand, but was it sophisticated enough to provide for something as simple as a 'greeting sequence' (Heritage, 1984: 110)? Garfinkel was drawn to this tension between the awe-inspiring theoretical edifice and the simple social actions it seemingly could not explain.

How was ethnomethodology received? If it emerged in the contemporary period, it would surely fit in rather nicely, in creative tension with constructivist and post-structuralist approaches. But these approaches did not exist in the 1950s; this is pre-Foucault and Butler. Wittgenstein was not yet widely read in English. German phenomenology was not yet a mainstream resource for theoretical development. To speak of the practical accomplishment of social facts, at a time of functionalist-positivist hegemony, was radical and challenging. In that context, ethnomethodology seemed strange and met with varied, though typically not positive, reactions.

Ethnomethodology was framed as 'aggressively and programmatically devoid of theoretical content', a 'massive cop-out, a determined refusal to undertake research that would indicate the extent to which our lives are affected by the socioeconomic context in which they are embedded' (Coser, 1975: 698). The work was fascinated by problems of 'embarrassing triviality' (Coser, 1975: 698), it practitioners subject to 'language diseases' (Coser, 1975: 696). Ernest Gellner's (1975) piece 'Ethnomethodology: The Re-Enchantment Industry or The Californian Way of Subjectivity' was even more scathing. It remains fascinating for its sexism and bile.

I had the unforgettable pleasure of attending a conference on Ethnomethodology in Edinburgh, it was noticeable, and I think significant that the quantity and quality of ethno-chicks surpassed by far those of chicks of any other movement which I have ever observed—even Far Out Left Chicks, not to mention ordinary anthropo-chicks, socio-chicks or (dreadful thought) philosophy chicks. (Gellner, 1975: 435)

For Sharrock (1989), there was simply too much interest. Ethnomethodology 'attracted far more attention than was altogether beneficial to the longer term health of the enterprise' (Sharrock, 1989: 657). 'It became the focus of a kind of attention and expectations that it could not accommodate, for it was never likely to gratify the requirements that sociologists in a hurry, and those with a mission, would bring to it' (Sharrock, 1989: 657).

29.3 GUIDING IDEAS

Ethnomethodology is a partial rather than total framework. It is never going to explain the financialization of capitalism, globalization, why men get paid more than women, or social mobility. The reader is presented with a distinctive way of understanding the 'on going accomplishment' (Feldman, 2000) of social order; how people make and remake the social facts which conventional social science seeks to explain. Ethnomethodology is not a singular, fully integrated theoretical statement, either. The reader is presented with a 'cluster of concepts, heuristics and initiatives' (Pollner, 1991: 371), rather than a unified theory, such as 'practical attitude', 'indexicality', 'reflexivity', 'practical accomplishments of social order', 'accountability', 'accountable actions', 'retrospective-prospective sense-making', 'reportable', and 'witness-able and accountable'. These terms are now considered further, through the illustrative analysis of a single, simple interaction.

In the interaction, a customer is trying to buy a ticket to enter an art gallery (see Figure 29.1). The setting is simple and has various archetypal features. The customer enters through a doorway, and walks towards a payment counter, behind which there is a price schedule. Prices vary according to the customer's age and the gallery also offers 'standard' and 'gift aid' prices, where the gift aid price include a voluntary 10 per cent donation. Customers would progress towards the counter and, once there, order their tickets. Of analytic interest is simply the question of how they do this. How are 'ticket orders' continually made and remade such that both parties can see what is being done?

The extract (see Figure 29.2) is represented in a figure that makes use of visual images extracted from the video, and an attempt to capture talk, drawing on the Jefferson notation system (Jefferson, 1984). For convenience, the extract is separated into two 'chunks'. The initial phase takes a little under three seconds. It is nevertheless densely layered. The customer walks towards the payment counter; he is searching his purse for money. The issue of how customers approach service counters is involved. In the gallery, a series of norms were made relevant for this aspect of customers' conduct. Sometimes the customer would hold back, waiting for the server's permission to come over. They could be

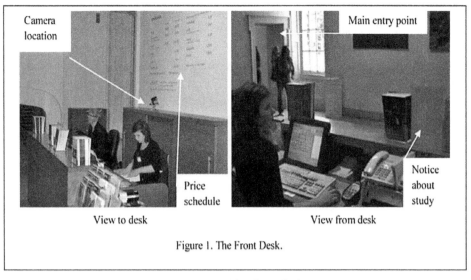

Figure 1. The Front Desk.

FIGURE 29.1 The front desk.

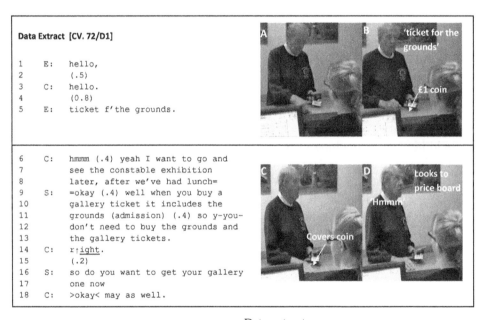

```
Data Extract [CV. 72/D1]

1    E:   hello,
2         (.5)
3    C:   hello.
4         (0.8)
5    E:   ticket f'the grounds.

6    C:   hmmm (.4) yeah I want to go and
7         see the constable exhibition
8         later, after we've had lunch=
9    S:   =okay (.4) well when you buy a
10        gallery ticket it includes the
11        grounds (admission) (.4) so y-you-
12        don't need to buy the grounds and
13        the gallery tickets.
14   C:   r↑ight.
15        (.2)
16   S:   so do you want to get your gallery
17        one now
18   C:   >okay< may as well.
```

FIGURE 29.2 Data extract.

seen searching for signs of the server's readiness to receive them. Through such ways of looking and standing, people practically displayed an orientation to locally operative norms, the sense they needed permission to move forwards.

In the extract, neither customer nor server invokes these norms. The customer simply approaches the desk looking to his purse. So, simply asserting the relevance of this or that norm can be problematic. It is through action that norms do (or do not) take hold within a scene. The customer extracts a £10 note, which he holds in his left hand, and a £1 coin. He does not look up to the employee, who has her gaze fixed upon him. As he is searching his purse, and coming to a halt in front of the server, she says 'hello' (line 1). In this way, she both 'greets' the customer, and also recognizes the beginnings of a social encounter. Her greeting recognizes he is coming to her, and not the server to her right, who is presently unoccupied. Greetings form part of a class of activity which Harvey Sacks, a one-time collaborator of Garfinkel's, called adjacency pairs (Sacks et al., 1974). The initial part of the adjacency pair sets up an expectation of a forthcoming action, in this case a return greeting, which can be 'noticeably absent' if not produced. Just before he places a £1 coin on the desk (Fig. 29.2A), the customer produces the second part, returning the greeting ('hello', line 3).

What happens next nicely illustrates concepts Garfinkel used and developed. The customer places a £1 coin on the desk. *How* does he do this? This is worth exploring because the employee sees, from the way he has placed the coin on the counter, the performance of a discrete social action. He has *done* something and without using words. The server's judgement is based entirely on a practical analysis of his embodied activity, and more specifically his placement of the coin. She has determined the customer wishes to purchase a ticket to enter the grounds (gardens).

So, the customer has produced an 'accountable-action'. Accountability is a key term for ethnomethodology (Lynch, 1993: 15–17). It differs from the conventional use of the term 'account', as a verbal explanation or justification of an action. Sometimes there is an overlap between the common and the ethnomethodological usage. In response to some utterance or movement, a recipient might ask 'what are you doing?', thereby inviting a verbal account. But the verbal account would itself be an accountable-action; it would be *doing* something in the exchange. We can thus say that all actions are accountable, even accounts. Normally, people do not ask 'what are you doing?' Rather, they orient to an account of the prior utterance in the way they respond. Rather than saying 'are you insulting me', the recipient slaps the speaker across the face, rebuts an 'insult', or issues an 'insult' of their own. In such ways, people account for prior 'insults'. Regardless of what the initial speaker might have meant, that is how their utterance has been publicly understood or accounted for. In the extract, the customer puts the coin down; the server says 'ticket for the grounds'. The server's response accounts for a 'ticket order'. This kind of accounting work is typically 'seen but unnoticed' (Garfinkel, 1967), but all actions are continually accounted for. It is impossible to avoid this. In light of a prior activity, non-response is not an option and many of Garfinkel's 'experiments', including the 'randomised advice experiment' (Garfinkel, 1967: 76–103), beautifully illustrate this.

For ethnomethodology, accountable-actions are the primary unit of analysis. To analyse accountable-actions, the analyst does not presuppose anything about the actor's thinking or motives. This is a critical point. For Garfinkel, consciousness, thought, and knowledge are approached solely as practical concerns. There is no focus, in contrast to process philosophers such as Bergson (1913) and Whitehead (1932), on 'the mind in apprehending...experiences sensations which, properly speaking, are qualities of the mind alone' (Whitehead, 1932/1985: 68). The question for Garfinkel is how people publicly exhibit and recognize what is on their mind. By saying 'ticket for the grounds', the server has publicly and accountably exhibited her understanding. The customer can see this and can respond.

So, the server's utterance ('ticket for the grounds') publicly accounts for the customer's prior activity as a 'ticket order'. This is worth pointing out because the employee need not have done this. She could have processed the order in silence, taken the pound and generated the customer's ticket. But she doesn't. She says 'ticket for the grounds', not as a question seeking clarification, but rather as a *commentary* on her own activity. As she says this, she looks down to the screen and starts to move the mouse. She has started to process the order. Whilst her utterance is not built as a question seeking clarification, it nevertheless creates a particular opportunity. The customer can intervene, should the account of his conduct be in some way problematic. This is indeed what happens.

But we are getting ahead of ourselves. How does the employee witness the social object we are considering, the ticket order? How has this *become* something? One point surely concerns the denomination (£1). There is only one ticket worth £1 on the price schedule. But this is not all. Many people extract money, one coin at a time, until they have enough to purchase their ticket. But in this case, the server does not wait for additional coins to be extracted. The customer places the coin down decisively and right in front of the employee. It is placed down quickly and, rather than returning to his purse for additional change, he looks to the server for the first time. He is both physically still and, by directing his gaze to the employee, awaiting a response. She can see it is her turn; her silence to fill. She treats the action as complete, by responding at the point she does. She does not wait for the customer to invoke the £10 note he is holding in his left hand (£6 was the concessionary entrance price). She starts to process the order.

Whilst her response ('ticket for the grounds') is not seeking clarification, it soon becomes apparent the customer is unsure what he wants. His initial action has quickly dissolved and needs to be remade. The customer hesitates saying 'hmmm' and looks away to the price board. Whilst so doing he immediately covers the £1 coin with his right hand, silencing its semiotic pulse and perhaps redacting its action. This nicely illustrates the ethnomethodological sensibility when applied to seemingly psychological concepts. In this case, the customer exhibits *confusion* in and through his embodied actions. The server can see and account for his state of mind.

To be clear, the customer does face a tricky problem. Nowhere on the price board does it indicate that 'admission to the grounds' (£1 when purchased as a separate ticket) is actually included in the general ticket price. By purchasing the £6 concessionary ticket, the customer is entitled to enter the gardens. Rather than topicalizing his confusion ('sorry, I'm a bit confused'), the customer engages a recurrent practice. He describes his personal circumstances and leaves the server to establish what he wants. In so doing he negotiates the epistemic division of labour, which does the work of working out what the customer wants. Rather than treating 'the division of labour' as a Durkheimian social fact, Garfinkel encourages us to track the continual remaking of such divisions in the flow of ordinary work.

The employee explains that the general entry ticket includes admission to the gardens. But the customer is not 'out of the woods' yet. What is the relevance of this for his plans? If he wishes to picnic in the gardens, does he first need to purchase a ticket? Can he be in the gardens without a ticket? Would it be a transgression to walk through the ticket hall into the café without buying a ticket? Even in this simple setting, we sense the customer is thoroughly *alienated* from the organization's procedures. Empirically, we see that clarity is yet to be achieved. The customer does not exhibit the onset of understanding, saying 'oh, okay, great, so one general ticket please'. Rather, he says 'right', somewhat questioningly, with an upward intonational contour. He pauses, looks to the server, and awaits her next turn. The extract is only six seconds old, and we have seen how, at every moment, understanding is exhibited, affirmed, noticed, and accounted for. Still in pedagogic mode, the server attends to these troubles. She says 'so, do you want to get your gallery one now'. The customer's response ('may as well') seems to exhibit his appreciation of the situation. He seems to know he can purchase the ticket later, should he wish.

Summarizing, the first few seconds of this mundane interaction have been considered. The transaction is not a pre-accomplished social fact, but a concerted achievement that is continually being made and remade by the participants. The action is densely compacted. In the first three seconds alone, a range of practical, normative, and epistemic issues were confronted and resolved. Social order was taken, by those involved, to be exhibited in the fine details of speech, gaze, bodily gesture, and in the management of objects within the material environment. What initially looked to be one thing quickly dissolved into something else.

29.4 Ethnomethodological Studies of Work and Organization

How might this style of analysis, so concerned with the local details of practical actions, contribute to organization studies?

One argument is the 'foundational' position. Such studies explicate practices and processes which organization studies trades upon, but typically overlooks. In this argument, ethnomethodology is slowly and carefully 'filling in' the disciplines missing processual foundations. To illustrate this argument, consider research on service labour and interactive service work (Bolton, 2004; Bolton and Boyd, 2003; Hanser, 2012; Lloyd and Payne, 2009; Rosenthal and Peccei, 2006). When this literature is considered, we see that 'order taking' is a gross feature of the service jobs analysed. But what 'order taking' involves is almost entirely unexplicated. The work of 'taking orders' is transformed into a passive social fact by authors. For example, before they begin their analysis, Lloyd and Payne (2009: 623) use a single sentence to describe work done by the people they interviewed: 'typical calls included taking down names and addresses, giving out flight arrival times, dealing with credit card applications and processing payments'. Deery et al. (2002: 481) provide us with a little more detail. In two sentences they describe work as dealing with 'customer enquiries about telephone installations and re-connections, queries about accounts and payment extensions and complaints about disconnections and telephone faults' (Deery et al., 2002: 481). Callaghan and Thompson (2002: 238–9) present a slightly longer account, dedicating one paragraph to processes of work. It is precisely this layer of organizational life that ethnomethodological studies wish to rescue, to establish a different place from which to theorize the contemporary nature of jobs, skills, and work.

For example, a quite visible body of ethnomethodological research has challenged theoretical oppositions, which run to the heart of organization studies, between 'mental' and 'manual labour' and between 'knowledge-based' and 'routine work'. Lucy Suchman argues that images of work have been

> systematically biased to highlight judgmental, interpretative work amongst the professions, while obscuring the work's mundane practical aspects. Commensurately, mundane practical activity is foregrounded in so-called routine forms of work, while reasoning is relegated. (2000: 30)

Addressing this problem, ethnomethodological scholars have been engaged in two related projects. One has revealed practical and embodied aspects of 'professional work' (see Goodwin, 1994; Hindmarsh and Pilnick, 2007). These studies are diverse but they all point to the fact that professional authority, legitimacy, and expertise are not predetermined, but exercised 'through the competent deployment in a relevant setting of a complex of situated practices' (Goodwin, 1994). The related project involves recovering expertise and reasoning which feature as essential components of apparently 'routine work' such as servicing machines, selling goods, or taking orders (Llewellyn and Burrow, 2008; Suchman, 1987; Whalen et al., 2002). Researchers Clark and Pinch (2010) consider video recordings of 'shop work' to access how assistants recognize the projects of 'customers' (are they 'browsing', 'trying to initiate contact', or 'waiting to be served') from the way they manage their body conduct within the local ecology of the store. Similarly, Whalen et al. (2002), considering the work of call centre staff, found that 'work that appears to be uncomplicatedly "routine" or even scripted may in reality require considerable adroitness with an organization that is conspicuously intricate' (Whalen et al., 2002: 255). Authors such as Clark, and Pinch, Suchman and Whalen confront management and theorists with the challenge of the knowledgeable worker.

Alternatively, the contribution of ethnomethodology can be understood more boldly and theoretically, as re-specifying core concepts. 'Re-specification' (Garfinkel, 1996) signals a powerful shift in the way core concepts are approached. The process can be simply explained. The analyst starts by asking where in society people are acting within the auspices of this or that concept or category. Once such settings are identified, the task is then to explicate the relevance and consequentiality of the category or concept for the practical actions of members. A good example would be 'the gift', not least because in the extract considered earlier (Figure 29.2), the customer goes on to voluntarily pay the higher 'gift aid' price, thereby allowing the gallery to reclaim tax from the UK government on the whole ticket price (receiving a sum of £11.24). How would one re-specify 'the gift'?

On the one hand, the problem of how to distinguish 'gifts' from other objects, such as commodities, can be thought of as a theoretical challenge for the social scientist. Whilst there is no agreed definition, three criteria are most commonly discussed in sociological and anthropological theory. Gifts differ from commodities because they are inalienable objects that bind giver and recipient in an interdependent relation, via the establishment of reciprocal obligations (Gregory, 1980). Over time, theoretical definitions have been developed that allow analysts to observe, delineate, and classify gifts.

On the other hand, whilst analysts have established theoretical resources through which they can observe gifts, the point remains that ordinary members of society, who have not read this literature, can also do this. Not being up-to-speed with functionalism (Malinowski, 1922/1972), structuralism (Lévi-Strauss, 1949/1976), or Marxist anthropology (Gregory, 1980) appears to be no hindrance. How would one re-specify the gift? Consider an example. The author of the present chapter recently intended to lend a book to a friend. Having arrived at their house, the book was handed over. However, their response, the nature of the 'gratitude' expressed (Simmel 1950/1964: 392–3), marked a gift and not a loan. There was simply too much gratitude for a mere loan. In light of such a reaction, the author faced a problem: to go along with this account or reveal an embarrassing mistake. These are not equivalent options and the book was lost! In this case, there was something methodic in the expression of gratitude that established the gift as something all parties could, and indeed did, recognize. Gratitude did not simply follow the gift, as a normatively required response, but actively constituted the gift as a social fact. In the extract considered earlier (Figure 29.2), similarly, though in ways that cannot be explicated here, the server's brief and passionless response to the donation ('okay, thank you'), which leads to her request for payment ('okay, thank you, so that's £6.60), reflexively constitutes the donation in a particular fashion, as an institutional gift, rather than a gift given to *her* personally.

This kind of re-specification can be performed on all categories and concepts in organization studies, not to undermine the discipline but to more fully explicate its processual foundations. Take 'the body'. To be concerned with 'the body' as an ethnomethodologist is to analyse (a) people doing things with actual bodies (see Hindmarsh and Pilnick, 2007), or (b) how people look at bodies in order to determine, from the way they are moving, various social facts (see Goodwin, 1994). This might involve analysing video recordings of teamwork in pre-operative anaesthesia (see Hindmarsh and Pilnick, 2007), or how the attorneys at the trial of Rodney King looked at video recordings of his bodily movements to show that (for them at least) he continued to be dangerous (Goodwin, 1994).

Or take 'surveillance'. Ethnomethodological studies would analyse how people look at bodies and objects, configured within an environment, to address and resolve organizational problems. Hence, Heath, Luff, and Sanchez Svensson (2002) analysed how '[London Underground] personnel constitute the sense and significance of CCTV images' (Heath et al., 2002). Despite considerable theoretical interest in surveillance, few studies have analysed how people practically accomplish 'overview' of some domain. For ethnomethodology, the issue is not how one defines surveillance (or 'the body' or 'the gift') theoretically, but how oversight is accomplished. How do organizational actors, such as station supervisors, determine, from a bank of screens and other local information, a dangerously overcrowded station (Heath et al., 2002)?

29.5 CONCLUSION

In keeping with process philosophy generally, Garfinkel's work disturbs any sense of a stable, pre-established social world. For Garfinkel, this works all the way down into the fine details of ordinary life. Take the social character of the £1 coin in the empirical example (Figure 29.2). Within just three seconds, the social status of this coin was exhibited, verbally accounted for, and transformed. This hinged on the ways it was handled, placed down, covered, and embedded within its local environment. As a medium of social action, the coin was always in a state of 'becoming and perishing'. Like process philosophy, ethnomethodology privileges 'activity and movement…over substance and entities'; the 'emphasis is on the primacy of process, interaction and relatedness' (Chia, 1997: 696). But it would be trite to claim that Garfinkel was a 'process thinker'. There are a range of rubs and points of difference too. Garfinkel is simply someone process researchers might read and take something from.

For instance, the way ethnomethodological studies engage empirical materials might be of some interest to process researchers. Ethnomethodologists are skilled at collecting materials that preserve the continual remaking of organizational scenes. In this regard, video technology has proved indispensable. Video is the only way to robustly capture and preserve the concerted achievement of organizational activities. Could an ethnographic observer have recovered the detailed social life of the £1 coin we saw in the extract in Figure 29.2? And that was just three seconds of activity from a day's recording (7 hours, a total of 25,200 seconds). It is extremely unlikely.

A common negative response is that ethnomethodology is too concerned with details and thereby misses 'the big picture'. In many ways this is a fair response. But it is one that quietly grates against the process ontology we are supposed to be following. Appealing to 'motives' behind actions ('I'd like to know why they did that') or wider organizational realities such as ongoing 'projects', 'change initiatives', or 'structures' is understandable. But such appeals presume a factual external world, made up of solid knowable objects like 'motives' and 'organizations'. Perversely, they presume we can only appreciate *becoming* and *movement* if we look away from, rather than towards, interaction and activity. In subtle but important ways, for those subscribing to a process ontology, this is like having your cake and eating it.

Analytically, the concept of 'accountability' might also be useful to process research-ers, lending them a common vocabulary for tracking the continual remaking of real-time organizational actions. Distinguishing the accountability of ordinary actions from the verbal accounts people give researchers about their actions is critical, both the-oretically and empirically. The latter are merely *about* organization, whereas the former are constitutive of the processes we are interested in. This alone is worth some thought. It would be no small thing if were analysts interested, not in the accounts people give about work, but in the accountable-actions through which they actually produce work. The consequences of that would be far-ranging theoretically, empirically, and for the subjects of academic research, who would be able to find themselves within the local organizational orders they sustain, reproduce, or disrupt.

REFERENCES

Baker, C. (1997). Ticketing Rules: Categorization and Moral Ordering in a School Staff Meeting, in S. Hester and P. Eglin (eds), *Culture in Action: Studies in Membership Categorization Analysis* (Washington, DC: University Press of America): 77–98.

Bergson, H. (1913). *Creative Evolution* (London: Macmillian).

Bittner, E. (1974). The Concept of Organization, in R. Turner (ed.), *Ethnomethodology: Selected Readings* (Harmondsworth: Penguin Books): 69–81.

Bolton, S.C. (2004). A Simple Matter of Control: NHS Hospital Nurses and New Management, *Journal of Management Studies* 41(2): 317–35.

—— and Boyd, C. (2003). Trolley Dolly or Skilled Emotion Manager? Moving on from Hochschild's Managed Heart, *Work, Employment and Society* 17(2): 289–308.

Chia, R. (1997). Essai: Thirty Years On: From Organization Structures to the Organization of Thought, *Organization Studies* 18(4): 685–707.

Clark, C. and Pinch, T. (2010). Some 'Major' Organizational Consequences of Some 'Minor' Organized Behaviour: A Video Analysis of Pre-Verbal Service Encounters in a Showroom Retail Store, in N. Llewellyn and J. Hindmarsh (eds), *Organisation, Interaction and Practice* (Cambridge: Cambridge University Press): 140–71.

Coser, L.A. (1975). Presidential Address: Two Methods in Search of Substance, *American Sociological Review* 40(6): 691–700.

Deery, S., Iverson, R., and Walsh, J. (2002). Work Relationships in Telephone Call Centres: Understanding Emotional Exhaustion and Employee Withdrawal, *Journal of Management Studies* 39(4): 471–96.

Feldman, M. (2000). Organizational Routines as a Source of Continual Change, *Organization Science,* 11(6): 611–29.

Garfinkel, H. (1945). Color Trouble, in B. Moon (ed.), *Primer for White Folks* (Doubleday, Doran, Co.): 269–86.

——(1948–1949). Research Note on Inter- and Intra-Racial Homicides, *Social Forces* 27: 369–80.

——(1956). Conditions of Successful Degradation Ceremonies, *American Journal of Sociology* 61(5): 420–4.

——(1967). *Studies in Ethnomethodology* (Cambridge: Polity Press).

——(1996). Ethnomethodology's Program, *Social Psychology Quarterly* 59(1): 5–21.

——(ed.) (1986). *Ethnomethodological Studies of Work* (London: Routledge and Kegan Paul).

——and Bittner, E. (1967). Good Organisational Reasons for Bad Clinical Records, *Studies in Ethnomethodology* (Englewood Cliffs: Prentice Hall): 186–207.

Gellner, E. (1975). Ethnomethodology: The Re-Enchantment Industry or the Californian Way of Subjectivity, *Philosophy of Social Science* 5: 431–50.

Goodwin, C. (1994). Professional Vision, *American Anthropologist* 96(3): 606–33.

Gregory, C.A. (1980). Gifts to Men and Gifts to God: Exchange and Capital Accumulation in Contemporary Papua, *Man* 15: 626–52.

Hanser, A. (2012). Class and the Service Encounter: New Approaches to Inequality in the Service Work-Place, *Sociology Compass* 6(4): 293–305.

Heath, C., Luff, P., and Sanchez Svensson, M. (2002). Overseeing Organizations: Configuring Action and its Environment, *British Journal of Sociology* 53: 181–201.

Heritage, J. (1978). Aspects of the Flexibilities of Natural Language Use: A Reply to Phillips, *Sociology* 12: 79–103.

——(1984). *Garfinkel and Ethnomethodology* (Cambridge: Polity Press).

Hernes, T. and Weik, E. (2007). Organisation as Process: Drawing a Line between Endogenous and Exogenous Views, *Scandinavian Journal of Management* 23: 251–64.

Hindmarsh, J. and Pilnick, A. (2007). Knowing Bodies at Work: Embodiment and Ephemeral Teamwork in Anaesthesia, *Organization Studies* 28(9): 1395–416.

Jefferson, G. (1984). Transcript Notation, in J.M. Atkinson and J. Heritage (eds), *Structures of Social Action: Studies in Conversation Analysis* (Cambridge: Cambridge University Press): ix–xvi.

Lévi-Strauss, C. (1949/1976). The Principle of Reciprocity, in L.A. Coser and B. Rosenberg (eds), *Sociological Theory* (New York: Macmillan): 84–94.

Llewellyn, N. and Burrow, R. (2008). Streetwise Sales and the Social Order of City Streets, *The British Journal of Sociology* 59(3): 561–83.

Lloyd, C. and Payne, J. (2009). 'Full of Sound and Fury, Signifying Nothing': Interrogative New Skill Concepts in Service Work—The View from Two Call Centres, *Work, Employment and Society* 23(4): 617–34.

Lynch, M. (1993). *Scientific Practice and Ordinary Action: Ethnomethodology and Social Studies of Science* (New York: Cambridge University Press).

——(2011). Harold Garfinkel (29 October 1917–21 April 2011): A Remembrance and Reminder, *Social Studies of Science* 41(6): 927–42.

Malinowski, B. (1922/1972). *Argonauts of the Western Pacific* (London: Routledge).

Parsons, T. (1937/1967). *The Structure of Social Action* (New York: Free Press).

——and Shils, E.A. (1951). *Towards a General Theory of Action* (Oxford: Oxford University Press).

Pollner, M. (1991). Left of Ethnomethodology: The Rise and Decline of Radical Reflexivity, *American Sociological Review* 56: 370–80.

Rawls, A. (2002). Editor's Introduction, in H. Garfinkel (ed.), *Ethnomethodology's Program: Working Out Durkheim's Aphorism* (New York: Rowman & Littlefield): 1–64.

—— (2006). Editor's Introduction, in H. Garfinkel (ed.), *Seeing Sociologically* (Boulder, CO: Paradigm Publishers): 1–98.

Rosenthal, P. and Peccei, R. (2006). The Social Construction of Clients by Service Agents in Reformed Welfare Administration, *Human Relations* 59(12): 1633–58.

Sacks, H. (1992). *Lectures on Conversation*, Volumes 1 and 2, ed. G. Jefferson with an introduction by E.A. Schegloff (Oxford: Basil Blackwell).

——Schegloff, E.A., and Jefferson, G. (1974). A Simplest Systematics for the Organization of Turn-Taking for Conversation, *Language* 50(4): 696–735.

Sharrock, W. (1989). Ethnomethodology, *The British Journal of Sociology* 40(4): 657–77.

Simmel, G. (1950/1964). Faithfulness and Gratitude, in K.H. Wolff (ed.), *The Sociology of Georg Simmel* (New York: Free Press): 379–95.

Suchman, L. (1987). *Plans and Situated Actions: The Problem of Human-Machine Interaction* (Cambridge: Cambridge University Press).

——(2000). Making a Case: Knowledge and Routine Work in Document Production, in P. Luff, J. Hindmarsh, and C. Heath (eds), *Workplace Studies: Recovering Work Practice and Informing System Design* (Cambridge: Cambridge University Press): 29–45.

Whalen, J., Whalen, M., and Henderson, K. (2002). Improvisational Choreography in Teleservice Work, *The British Journal of Sociology* 53(2): 239–59.

Whitehead, A.N. (1925/1985). *Science and the Modern World* (Free Association: London).

——(1938). *Modes of Thought* (Cambridge, MA: Harvard University Press).

....

CHAPTER 30

GEORGE SPENCER-BROWN (1923b)

....

TORE BAKKEN

30.1 Introduction

WHEN THE Tavistock scholar Philip Herbst published his book, *Alternatives to Hierarchies* (1976), experimentation with 'autonomous work groups' in industrial firms (e.g. the Volvo and Toyota factories) was his main concern. The problem was: how to find the way from a hierarchical organization towards autonomy? To work further on this issue, Herbst was clear: wishes or solicitations to eliminate hierarchies are useless. To become more aware of what to eliminate, and what to develop, Herbst turned to a more profound idea, namely the study of 'behavioural logic' to better understand the implications of irreducible distinctions such as internal–external, determinable–indeterminable, and being–non-being. It is in this relationship that he became interested in the work of the British mathematician and logician George Spencer-Brown. Spencer-Brown published his book *Laws of Form* in 1969—an abstract and bold 'calculus of indications' engaged with the very foundation of development of knowledge—that incidentally received praise from Bertrand Russell himself, who in a blurb for the book called it 'a calculus of great power and simplicity. Not since Euclid's *Elements* have we seen anything like it.'

George Spencer-Brown—born in Grimsby, Lincolnshire, England 1923—has held a number of occupational roles, such as a mathematician, consulting engineer, psychologist, pilot, educational consultant, author and poet, adviser in military communications (coding and code-breaking), football correspondent to the *Daily Express*; he even practised car racing with Gavin Maxwell. Spencer-Brown studied at Trinity College, Cambridge (1947–1952), and at Christ Church, Oxford (1952–1958). He worked with Ludwig Wittgenstein on the foundations of philosophy (1950–1951), and with Bertrand Russell on the foundations of mathematics in 1960, and he also taught mathematics at Oxford, Cambridge, and University of London.

Laws of Form (hereafter called *LoF*) remains Spencer-Brown's main work, even though he published books on probability theory (1957) and even love (1971) under the pseudonym James Key. In *LoF* Spencer-Brown presents a calculus that aims to clarify the laws serving as a basis for the formation of forms. Form, in Spencer-Brown's calculus, is foremost about the marking of a difference with the help of a distinction that compels us to designate one or the other side of the distinction. Form has thus an inside and an outside, where the inside designates the possibility of attaching further descriptions, while the outside is the side from which we can reflect on the form. Quite different from the distinction in propositional logic (that between 1 or 0, or between true and false), we now have a difference between an inside and an outside where neither of them can be given ontological first status. Both sides are what they are in relation to each other. To study the interplay between inside and outside of distinctions (forms) is thus the main theme of Spencer-Brown's 'calculus'.

As we will see in what follows, *LoF* does not only have implications for process philosophy (as it is a transition from a strictly bivalent logic to a calculus of processing distinctions), but is also open to the possibility of constructing models that include their beginnings as their premise. This challenges Russell's 'theory of types', which does not allow these types of self-referential statements because they create unsolvable paradoxes. As Wittgenstein (1961: 16) puts it: 'No proposition can make a statement about itself, because a propositional sign cannot be contained in itself (that is the whole of the "theory of types")'.

Amongst mathematicians, the American Louis Kauffman (1977, 1978, 1987, 1998a, 1998b, 1999) and the German Matthias Varga von Kibéd (1989, 1993) stand out as authors who have worked on the calculus of form (especially Kauffman, with the purpose of developing a 'virtual logic'), but it must be said that Spencer-Brown remains relatively unknown among typical 'mainstream' mathematicians. His 'form calculus' has, however, gained more widespread recognition in communities oriented more towards cybernetics. This is perhaps not surprising, as his calculus—despite being abstract and highly theoretical—is also actually aimed at solving practical engineering-related problems (Beer, 1969; von Foerster, 1969). Also the biologist Francesco Varela (1975) developed a 'Calculus of Self-reference', where the ideas of Spencer-Brown are further developed and used in biological systems. In particular, Varela applies and further develops *LoF* in order to illustrate the recursive dynamics in cellular self-production (autopoiesis). Still, perhaps most known for the use of *LoF* is the German sociologist Niklas Luhmann (1984, 1993, 1997, 1999). With Luhmann, sociological systems theory is radicalized by becoming a form theory, where system is no longer synonymous with identity, but rather with difference. For instance, in the distinction between system and environment, both are what they are in relation to each other. One cannot understand system without environment—and vice versa.

On the basis of Spencer-Brown's form calculus, I will discuss what can be achieved by working with construction of 'forms' rather than descriptions of, for example, 'substances' or 'things'. In addition, what does Spencer-Brown's form calculus add to our understanding of organizations? First, I will introduce some basic tenets of

Spencer-Brown's form calculus. I will argue that the calculus operates with important methodological assumptions, which have clear implications for process philosophy (Rescher, 2000; Whitehead, 1929). Then, I will show how the calculus can contribute to a better understanding of phenomena that we experience in our daily lives, namely self-reference and paradox. Finally, I will provide a critical discussion of possibilities that lie in the application of form calculus in the study of organizations.

30.2 MATHEMATICS AS A COGNITION THEORY

It was a rather special and practical engineering-related problem concerning designing 'electronic circuit networks' that led to *LoF*. Spencer-Brown became involved in laws of form when, together with his brother, he conducted an assignment for British Railways. A reliable counting machine had to be constructed to count wagon wheels passing in a tunnel both backwards and forwards. The problem that had to be solved was something we all experience when we get on the train: 'it goes along and then it stops and then it goes backwards for a bit, then forwards. So if the train was having its wheels counted, and then, for any reason, ran out of steam and got stuck and then slipped back, then the counter had to go backwards' (Spencer-Brown, 1973a: 2). In this context, circuits were developed with on/off knobs used for counting and remembering the number of wagons passing in the tunnel. However, the counter had to count forwards and backwards and *simultaneously* remember how many wagons had passed. There was no such machine at the time that could count forwards and backwards simultaneously, without forgetting what was counted before within the calculation itself. Spencer-Brown (and his brother) solved this problem, and did so in a simple and accessible way. The counting machine was patented, and even though there have been numerous accidents in the history of British Railways, according to Spencer-Brown they have never 'consisted of any train running into a detached wagon in a tunnel' (1973a: 2).

Spencer-Brown's experience was that one could not solve simple engineering-related problems by using the rules of classical logic (Tarski, 1959) based upon and/or, if/so, allowed/not allowed, and so on. Networks are complex, and everyone who has experience working with networks knows that with every 'junction' one has to make a choice between a number of different possibilities. Restoring network design to the demands of bivalent logic, according to which something is either true or false, was not a viable option. A counting machine was therefore constructed that could count by using something unknown in 'switching logic', namely *imaginary Boolean values*. This means that even if one is dealing with a binary distinction with only two sides, more values must be comprised in the analysis. Therefore, the following problem arises. Even if the idea of imaginary values functioned in practice—and much engineering-related problem-solving actually proves this (in the words of Spencer-Brown: 'we were absolutely certain that they worked and were reliable, because we could see how they worked' (1973a: 2))—there is no mathematical theory that could justify a method where one works with these types of values. As bound as mathematics has been to logic, it has only allowed us to operate with two values, 1 and 0. However, what is achieved when one allows for a third value, avoiding the principle of a *tertium non datur* where no third possibility is given? The answer is that one can then catch what is vague and what lies 'in-between' what is true and false, 1 and 0. This applies to borderline cases, and it is these borderline cases (that in many cases can be crucial) that can be grasped with the help of imaginary values.

Boole did not dare to move beyond the two-valued logic. He designed his algebra so that it could fit with the logic, and not the mathematics; '"the disastrous invasion" of mathematics by logic' as Wittgenstein calls it (1983: 281). Spencer-Brown's calculus, however, works with such imaginary values, and that is revolutionary. It is against this background that Spencer-Brown invites us on a journey from logic to mathematics, but which must also be understood as a journey from the special and practical to the universal and formal, from semantics and pragmatism towards syntax (but also back again, for example, from arithmetic to algebra, and from syntax to semantics). A calculus must be developed that illustrates what is general. Therefore, the calculus could not develop as logic understood from thinking based upon truth alone. The problem with 'never ending expressions' must be formulated so that expressions are allowed to enter their own areas. This has so far not been accepted, as it will lead to antinomies, and one ends up with the classic clash between simultaneity of truth and falsity in relation to expressions (Simon, 1993). But Spencer-Brown's solution is to make the system 'bi-stabile'; it can oscillate between one value and the other and in this way generate time. This is how self-reference can be accepted; paradoxes can be seen as challenges not to be eliminated, but to be handled in a fruitful manner (von Foerster, 1981).

This is how we obtain an operative calculus that uses signs, which in the transformation of signs implies *time*. This calculus is open to experiment, trial and error, even invention. How forms are generated as a process and developed is brought into focus, and not how things or substances can be described. It is actually, and probably surprising for many, that according to Spencer-Brown mathematics is open for this more testing and constructivist approach to reality.

That every universe (cosmological, physical, or sociological) is unavailable without any description is something upon which we can probably all agree. Spencer-Brown's starting point however, is, that every description demands a distinction. Therefore, the theme of *LoF* is clearly described in the following way: 'a universe comes into being when a space is severed or taken apart' (Spencer-Brown, 1969/2008: xxii). This statement contains a deep philosophical implication. First, it tells us that the universe is not given because space is given. Space and universe are not the same; the universe must be understood as a result of a particular activity, namely the splitting of space. And this is the point: this splitting of space does not lead to the occurrence of the universe. In other words, not necessity, but contingency is in focus. A different splitting of a space would cause the occurrence of completely different universes (Baecker, 1999b: 13). This is why there is an experience of extreme contingency underlying the calculus: something is done, but simultaneously something else becomes possible. In addition, everything that is done is connected with something else. It is like discovering the unlikely in the familiar, or, as in Hans Blumenberg (2010), a form of 'stimulus'—understood as courage to be exactly who you are.

Second, Spencer-Brown's statement directs us to a certain possibility, namely to construct models whose premises also include their new beginning. Wittgenstein's (1961: 74) scepticism to this is known, and that is why he concludes his *Tractatus* with 'whereof one cannot speak, thereof one has to be silent'. However, Spencer-Brown's answer is that we can obviously not describe such a world, but we can go behind the descriptions and *invoke* such a world by the help of imperatives such as 'Draw a distinction!' Hence, not a descriptive, but an injunctive language can provide an answer to Wittgenstein's doubts. Therefore, mathematics is invoked: 'A mathematical text is thus not an end in itself, but a key to a world beyond the compass of ordinary description' (1969/2008: vxxii). If we follow Spencer-Brown's suggestion, then a person who reads a mathematical text does not need to limit their illustrations to the injunctions in the text itself. The reader can wander off on their own, find their own illustrations, either consistently or inconsistently with the guidelines in the text. Only in this way, and through their own explorations, will the reader be capable of seeing the limitations or the laws for the world described by a mathematician (1969/2008: 65). Mathematics understood in this way opens up for a contingent (a differently possible) world that precedes the traditional necessity-based thinking as we know it in the classical philosophical literature based upon a bivalent logic. Instead of limiting (the way logic does), the forms of mathematics can discover new relationships, analogies, and correspondences between phenomena. As an example: all beginnings can now be thematized rather than be taken for granted. However, they can only be thematized as a process-based interdependence between being and nothingness, almost in the same way that *Daodejing* shows how being arises from nothingness; or much like another well-known concept in modern chaos theory: chaos is without form, but contains all forms, as Faust in conversation with Mephisto in Paul Valéry's *My Faust* says: 'Chaos, the original one, the very first unutterable confusion, when space, light, possibilities, and essences were all in a state of yet-to-be' (1960: 36).

30.3 THE PRIMARY DISTINCTION

Spencer-Brown's calculus stems from the following injunction: 'Draw a distinction!', which is illustrated with the following symbol or mark of distinction:

$$\urcorner$$

The distinction is a form of 'boundary mathematics'. Spencer-Brown's process of distinction can be understood formally: it cleaves a space, and imposes structure and intention not as a godly act of creation, but rather diabolically by valuing difference (the world as a multiplicity of observers) more highly than identity (the world as a 'totality of facts'). The content and the context where the distinction is constructed are separated. We find ourselves in a primitive a priori dimension for all notation or scientific representation, namely in a two-dimensional space with an 'inside' and an 'outside'. The concave side of the mark represents the 'inside' or a 'marked state'. Two conditions are created, namely a 'marked state' (what is within and is observed), and an 'unmarked state' (what is outside and not observed). In other words, a two-sidedness is created which contains a threefold distinction: (1) what the thing is, (2) what it is not, and (3) the boundary in between. This means that one can never avoid (4) the context being included in everything that is done. We here see why Spencer-Brown in his construction of 'electronic circuit networks' could not base everything on two-valued logic alone, because form proves that we are dealing with a binary distinction that has two sides and four values.

'Distinction is perfect continence', according to Spencer-Brown (1969/2008: 1)—where the verb in Latin is 'continere', which (among other things) means 'stay together', 'limit', or 'confine'. We now understand Herbst's interest in form calculus referred to in section 30.1; 'perfect continence' expresses a formal way to understand the phenomenon of autonomy, something that also influenced Niklas Luhmann's (1984, 1997) notion of autopoietic (self-producing) systems. In many instances, Luhmann describes autopoiesis as 'perfect continence'.

The sign of distinction represents a 'cross' (descriptive), but that can also be understood as a 'cross!' (injunctive). The result of the distinction is never final, but more like a process: one can make a new distinction in the content or the context of the first distinction, which is impossible in binary logic.

The difference between 'cross' and 'negation' is important here. While binary logic operates with negations that are locked in a position (when a statement is true, its negation is false), the cross depends upon the space where it stands. The other side of the cross is not what is negated in form calculus, but simply the other 'unmarked space'—akin to what Husserl (2003) calls 'horizon', or 'what makes sense within a horizon of possibilities' (Weick, 1995).

This is how Spencer-Brown arrives at the notion that mathematical being is not really about numbers and quantity for, if we enter into more abstract symbolic algebra, mathematics can be widely understood as a science of symbolic operations. Spencer-Brown is here clearly inspired by Boole's (1951) classical work. It has been shown that this algebraic system of symbolic relations has been particularly useful to solve problems with electro-technical circuits, amongst other things (Canainn, 1969). However, Spencer-Brown also developed a new arithmetic for abstract symbolic algebra—in other words, a non-numerical arithmetic which is not the science of sizes and quantities, but a science of distinctions, as already pointed out. Algebraic symbolic operations must be capable of being led back to a form of distinction, and it is precisely this fact that will be contributed by non-numerical arithmetic. This is a proto-arithmetic that must go ahead of primary algebra. Only this can satisfy the demand of simplicity that Spencer-Brown strived for. A simple process of distinction replaces constants. 'Not just to find the constants, because that would be, in terms of arithmetic of numbers, only to find the number. But to find how they combine, and how they relate—and that is the arithmetic' (Spencer-Brown, 1973b: 3).

Two important traits come into view with regards to the primary distinction: (1) we are dealing with a reductive process, and (2) we are dealing with an injunctive method. Both have clear implications for process philosophy. Let us take them in turn.

(1) The reductive process is based upon the fact that Spencer-Brown, with the help of a strongly condensed symbol of distinction, can develop a formal language that does not assume any type of exact or delimiting objects that demands a special usage of symbols. Instead, a type of symbol that is more flexible is developed, and which can be expressed in different applications and contexts (Wille and Hölscher, 2009: 36). In this way, the investigation undertaken by Spencer-Brown is so foundational that it goes 'beyond the point of simplicity where language ceases to act normally as currency for communication' (1969/2008: xx). It is found in a pre-discursive plane where something was created and developed in a process, and which is very different from the field of numbers or logic, where one is not very concerned with how a universe is created or what our cognitive relationship to the world is like. Therefore, logic cannot be a fundamental discipline. The point is not a rejection of logic, but a rejection of it coming first. Because then we will be left in a thought process within the dominance of coordinates and exclusion (where only precision counts; something is always one thing or the other, and not a third), which prevents a process of thinking directed at that which is open and permanently in motion. The calculus contains not only an operative, but also an indeterminate aspect. This is a method reminiscent of Paul Klee's perception of art (1969a: 69). Klee also worked on highly reduced and condensed expressions, and moved gradually towards a kind of 'clean state' that led back to geometry and its abstractions. By systematically investigating the diverse usage of the simplest elements—the circle, the square, the straight line, etc.—he could find exactly what he was always looking for, namely all logical variations, combinations, connections, and interdependencies in the course of nature. To understand these processes it was crucial for Klee to work with reduced and condensed expressions. The artist tries to see what there is by knowing that it could have been different, and actually probably has been different. Because nature is process and movement, 'fixed forms are not the height of nature's creation. It is the nature in process that the artist seeks to make visible' (Klee, 1969b: 76). This is certainly not an attempt to render violence against what is real, but rather seeing how reality develops in 'the process of transformation'.

(2) The injunctive method rejects the doctrine that one can know something when one is told something. What one is told can be believed or learned but not known. One only reaches knowledge from one's *own experience*, almost like Edmund Husserl's (2003) statement that natural objects must be experienced before any theorizing about them can occur. So, in this relationship the injunctive method is a solicitation to experience. Spencer-Brown uses the example of prime numbers to illustrate this. It is well

known that prime numbers are infinite, but one cannot know this for a fact. To know something one must go 'deeper', one must experience, and contemplate on one's own; in other words, one needs commands and solicitations, not descriptions. Not forced, but more like a game: 'Call this "so or so", do something, and show what you get.' There are prescribed rules that must be followed, which can be compared with music or cooking. Neither the cook nor the composer tries to describe their 'works', but rather provides directions or recipes for what the reader must do. If one follows the directions, one can undergo a similar experience to that of those who issued the directions.

The benefit of this method, seen in relation to every form of description, is that that which is acknowledged cannot be uprooted from what the observer must do to reach their conclusion. This is also a essential aspect of the calculus, something we will return to later. The point is that knowledge is not only bound to actions and behaviour, it also *is* action and behaviour. This is how we can say that an intersubjective consensus about knowledge is only reachable through injunctions, a known phenomenon in experimental science where one says: 'See through the microscope and you will find knowledge and clues!' We know the meaning of these injunctions from history: Galileo's opponents dreaded looking through his binoculars.

In this way injunction is based upon referral and solicitation and is not a representation of a controlled variable (or condition of being). All possible usages of the word 'is' are replaced by solicitations such as 'let us do, as if'. This again is reminiscent of Wittgenstein's language philosophy that requires a non-language experience, knowledge, or insight before one can discuss the language.

To sum up, the distinction contains everything that is needed. One can, with no prerequisite, and with the help of a cleaving of space, create a universe. However, the demand of no prerequisite is not easy to meet in a world where, in various ways, we are enveloped in life's representations in the shape of myths, histories, fables, images, and the like, which only tell about themselves. There are, in particular, many examples of such representations in organization theory (Morgan, 1986).

30.4 THE TWO UNDERLYING AXIOMS: THE LAW OF CALLING AND THE LAW OF CROSSING

With the 'primary distinction' as a background, the calculus can now decide the relationship between identity and difference more closely. It is in this connection that Spencer-Brown developed the two 'arithmetic axioms' (A1 and A2) that underlie the primary arithmetic and everything upon which *LoF* is built. These laws (Spencer-Brown, 1969/2008: 2) are based upon a difference between a descriptive (positivistic) (A1) and an injunctive (operational) (A2) aspect of our knowledge, summarized in two basic axioms (also known as primitive equations):

Axiom 1. The law of calling

The value of a call made again is the value of the call

That is to say, if a name is called and then called again, the value indicated by the two calls taken together is the value indicated by one of them.

That is to say, for any name, to recall is to call. ($\overline{}\ \overline{}_=\overline{}$)

Axiom 2. The law of crossing

The value of a crossing made again is not the value of the crossing

That is to say, if it is intended to cross a boundary and then it is intended to cross it again, the value indicated by the two intentions taken together is the value indicated by none of them. ($\overline{\overline{}}=$)

The first axiom expresses a condensation. If a 'name' is mentioned a second time, the value which is indicated through both names is the same as the one indicated through one indication. This is expressed through the following equation where *identity* is constituted:

$$\overline{}\ \overline{}=\overline{}$$

For example, the values of 'snowflakes' do not change for the skier by being named twice. The grades of information remain the same. Here there is no referral to the other side in a difference. 'The value of a calling' is not changed through 'recalling'. So, the value in 'recalling' is the same as that in 'calling'. However, this is not an identity that will represent a whole in the meaning of *representatio identitatis*. It is rather about identities that are created through utilization of ancient event complexes, and which are continuously reconstructed. Identity cannot thereby be assumed, but must be produced, condensed increasingly in new situations, reaffirmed, and generalized anew. Identity expands through repetition and is converted into new identities, as when one produces poetic texts, legal texts, or maintains the dominant semantics and conventions of society. Thus, the value for 'condensation' that is equal to 'marked state' (the side that is indicated) formally corresponds to what Boole expressed in *Laws of Thought* (1951): a quality x repeated is still the same quality. But while Boole, to begin with, assumes the existence of identifiable objects, Spencer-Brown is more concerned about the process whereby subjects and objects *come into being*.

The second axiom does not concern itself with that which is mainly descriptive, but with the operative stage. It is not enough here to only name a name, but we are dealing with an injunction to achieve an effect, or to *transform* a value. The first axiom is only concerned with one side of the difference, while the other axiom employs itself with both sides. From the second axiom, one gets the primitive equation, the so-called *cancellation*, where the other 'crossing' does not have the same value as the first. There are only two existing values, one for the marked one and one for the unmarked one. Through the other 'crossing', the first is cancelled and invalidated. Thereby, difference is constituted as:

$$\overline{\overline{}}=$$

A boundary can only be crossed in two directions: from an external to an internal side, and from an internal to an external side. To cross a boundary from the outside to the inside is to make a distinction—an operation that from the 'law of calling' can be repeated with the same result. To cross the boundary from the inside to the outside, however, means to cancel a distinction. This means that you have decided not to follow the distinction's indication; you look instead at its non-indicated states. In other words, we do not only follow distinctions, we also abolish them. You return to the state before any distinction existed, much the same as in Buddhist meditational practice (Baecker, 1999a: 2). Thus the second axiom reminds us of the fact that the world we live in is a contingent one (other possibilities were and are always there). Further, it demonstrates that the act of creation is also an act of negation: the original state is negated, for only by the negation of the negation are we able to return to the original state. As Herbst puts it: 'It is the same as that which we left *and also not*. For it is said that the man who has done the outward journey and later returned is no longer the same as he was before he made the journey' (1995: 74). It is in this way that Spencer-Brown takes Boole's work further and constructs models that include as their premise their beginnings.

According to Spencer-Brown's two axioms, every 'finite expression' can now achieve a unique simplification. In both A1 and A2 the expressions on the right side of the equation has fewer symbols than the expressions on the left side. This is based upon the idea that every arithmetic expression can, by using A1 and A2, be simplified to one of two states, namely one marked and one unmarked. The analogies to engineering-related problems are clear, and then mainly to properties of 'series' and 'parallel electrical circuits', though also when dealing with 'diagramming processes' that include 'flow-charting'. We can say that A1 is an expression for 'parallel connection', while A2 expresses 'series connection'. We can therefore say that to make a distinction corresponds to that of changing how two points in a 'circuit' are related to each other and not only attached to the wiring. However, first and foremost, the two axioms are probably meant to answer Wittgenstein's statement in *Tractatus* (sentence 7), 'whereof one cannot speak, thereof one must be silent'. With A2, Spencer-Brown has shown how there is no need to remain silent in relation to everything that cannot be understood in a descriptive (positivistic) way by indications.

30.5 Indication Regarding the Distinction

This brings us back to the primary distinction. For Spencer-Brown's starting point, to make a distinction *and* to indicate one of the separated sides is to view them as two *simultaneous aspects in one operation*. 'We take as given the idea of distinction and the idea of indication, and the fact that we cannot make an indication without drawing a distinction' (1969/2008: 1). It is in the same way impossible to draw a distinction without making an indication. This is one of the many surprising aspects of Spencer-Brown's calculus: the observer is contained within the calculus. 'Draw a distinction!' can be interpreted as 'Bring in the observer!' (Lau 2008: 108), with the consequence that 'operator' (the symbol for making a distinction) and 'operand' (on what an operation is used) fall together.

This idea is based upon the assumption that every description we produce is subject to a fundamental distinction that is localized in the actual difference between a description and the object of description, as well as in the difference between the observer and what is being observed. It is emphasized that the distinction is a constructive operation (an active undertaking), and not a form of sorting of pre-existing phenomena. This is how objects are not in focus—even though they are significant—but we cannot begin to discuss those until the operation of distinction is completed. However, nor are subjects in focus. So neither subjects nor objects but *differences* are in focus. In order for the calculus to be consistent, the development of the indications must therefore be based upon the calculus itself. All attempts the observer makes in dealing with the universe and its description are made in the context of the actual 'calculus of indication'. Therefore, they are structures (and the distinction is the first single structure) that we find within the 'calculus of indications'; they are not only in agreement with a given description, but actually *are* those structures. Hence the observer is recovered in the actual calculus, and within the calculus. Thus, Spencer-Brown's last and final statement in *LoF*: 'We see now that the first distinction, the mark, and the observer are not only interchangeable, but, in the form, identical' (1969/2008: 63).

The presumed observer is made explicit: an observer, since they distinguish the space they occupies, is also a mark. Spencer-Brown emphasizes the physicist as an example of an observer who describes the world, and who becomes incorporated within the physical relationships that they describe (1969/2008: 85). In other words, the distinction is always incorporated into every description. However, when we describe a universe where the observer will also be included, we never avoid the problem of *self-reference*. 'The world we know is constructed in order to see itself', says Spencer-Brown (1969/2008: 85), which means that to generate theory and science can always be understood as an observation—as an active undertaking, but also as *self-observation*. Applied to sociology: 'Social systems as seen by an observer are paradoxical systems…They include self-referential operations' (Luhmann, 1990: 7).

This, however, assumes a transformation from a strict bivalent logic, to a calculus, to process distinctions, and it marks a distance from a one-sided fact-related observation and description to another stage where one can observe and describe the observation on one's own observation, and which in every way expresses that which lies within modern society's potential for *reflection*. William Rasch describes it in the following way:

> What was once 'the whole' or the nature of 'all things' that could be seized in an instant and for all time as a totality now becomes an immanent field of observations, descriptions, and communications, a 'totality of facts' as Wittgenstein wrote, that must contend with the uncomfortable situation that only any observation of fact is itself a fact that can be observed. (2002: 3)

With Gödel (1931), we can say that the dream of finally clarified mathematics is impossible. We never avoid the paradox. Logic can never do without the observer that is directed to observe from within and never from the outside, in the same way that the sociologist is forced to observe society from within only, and never from the outside. In conclusion, we can never avoid a reflective dimension where we not only have to reflect on immanence/transcendence, good/evil, but actually also have to reflect on what distinctions we are operating with, and whether we might rather draw other distinctions.

LoF shows that to view a distinction (observe it, differentiate it, consider its 'form') is something completely different from making ('crossing') it. Hence, its reflective potential for social sciences: it opens up the possibility of seeing fundamental social processes where there is always someone doing and saying something; and always others that can make us aware of the *contingency* of what one does—i.e. to make one aware of the possibility to say, do, or believe otherwise (Baecker, 1999b).

30.6 RE-ENTRY OF THE FORM INTO THE FORM

So far, we have seen how form combines actuality (marked state) and potentiality (unmarked state). We have also seen how negativity has been tied to 'cross' (or operation). However, there is yet another version of this negativity in Spencer-Brown's calculus, and it is tied to the term 're-entry' (or 'indeterminism'): the observer in the beginning, the one who actuates the calculus, is in the end the object of the calculus, and thus becomes a part of the very process. This last aspect is especially important in Spencer-Brown's calculus, and it makes it in many ways unique, and also interesting for social science (Schiltz, 2007). This aspect expresses the potential that lies in 'process reflection'. Social scientists are observers who observe others who, in turn, observe other observers—precisely what von Foerster (1981) calls 'second order observation'. According to Spencer-Brown, distinctions are re-entered into their form, to become capable of 'watching that form', while reflecting on its usefulness. Russell and Whitehead's 'theories of types' is challenged here, but also Wittgenstein's statement that 'a function cannot be its own argument, whereas an operation can take one of its own results as its base' (1961: 42). For, if 'inverse' and 'implicit functions' are allowed, then Wittgenstein's statement does not hold. 'If an operation can take its own result as a base, the function determined by its operation can be its own argument', claims Spencer-Brown (1969/2008: 79). And in re-entrant forms 'we shall call a partial destruction of the distinctive properties of constants a subversion' (1969/2008: 51). The form is proven capable of 're-entering' the space it is generated in.

It is when the basic axioms are used on higher-graded algebraic equations that the problem regarding 're-entries of the form into the form' appears. Anomalies do happen; re-entries of equations back to themselves do sometimes result in paradoxes. This happens when 'marked state' is made equal to 'unmarked state'. Spencer-Brown (1993) sees this as a challenge. Rather than seeing it as a simultaneous presence of exclusive conditions (as in traditional logic), he suggests an alternative: maybe it is the case that the system oscillates between opposite conditions *in time*. Therefore: combine space with time in the calculus, for this is how self-reflective actions of 're-entries' connect time with space as it is assumed in the primary distinction. If given adequate time, 'marked' and 'unmarked state' can exist in the same space. This is how self-references appear, for time cannot be understood in itself, time is not related to the universe generally, but appears as we attempt to describe this universe 'from within'.

We have here returned to the engineering-related problems that Spencer-Brown and his brother worked on for British Railways. For Spencer-Brown the problem was purely mathematical: he wanted to prove the validity of imaginary values, such as the square root of -1, something that had become very common to use in electromagnetic theory. Since imaginary values can be used to solve equations that cannot otherwise be solved, we must accept these values as a third category that is independent of (1) truth (tautology: $x = x$) and (2) falsehood (contradiction: $x = -x$). However, to draw the square root of negative numbers has been banned in mathematics for a long time, as it cannot lead to any unambiguous solutions, only 'flippety', as we say. We oscillate between two conditions, back and forth. For Spencer-Brown this became the solution to a problem. He lets what is counted re-enter into the counted, and that is what he calls *re-entries*. As Paul Watzlawick writes:

> Brown's logic is based on the concept of 'inside' and 'outside'...one might say that Brown shows how a reality construction may transcend its own limits, look at its totality from the vantage point of being outside the frame, and eventually 're-enter' its limits with information gained about itself. (Watzlawick, 1984: 254)

This is dealing with no less than being aware of the *third value*: the excluded within the included; the non-communicative within communication; the non-knowledge within knowledge; and so on. This means that the excluded re-enter in the included, or as Michel Serres puts it in his book *The Parasite* (2007): What we try to displace, continues to be there, just like the parasite. The paradox is given and expresses itself in *Tertium non datur* (third is not given). Contrary to ontological considerations of being, the parasite reflects a combinatorial aspect of our human lives. More than norms and sanctions, parasitical 'quasi-objects' contribute with necessary redundancy to the systems. All this is a prerequisite for *reflection*, which makes us more aware, not only of what is said and done, but also of what is excluded, avoided, or not mentioned. With Spencer-Brown, we can now say that the world becomes capable of seeing itself, while not ignoring the paradoxes of self-observation. Everything is seen back on itself in a *recursive* sequence, and this reflects a particular meaning in process reflectivity: insight into those recursions that we ourselves operate within when we observe. The calculus has thereby a large potential in terms of clarifying central aspects of what sociologists today call the 'reflexive modern' (Beck et al., 1994).

In Robert Musil's novel *The Confusions of Young Törless* (2001) the young boy, who was so possessed with imaginary values that he had to seek out the math teacher, asked: What can give us new imaginary power, new intuition, and ability for imagination? The answer lies in a 'possible', 'not real' number value (such as the square root of–1). However, this interest in imaginary numbers (symbolized by '*i*') is not led by a wish to escape reality, but quite the opposite. It is close to the truth that we experience. For instance, time and temporality is something we all experience in our daily life; however, in propositional logic there is no time and temporality because no feedback is allowed. According to Spencer-Brown there cannot be time without a self-referential equation (1973a: 10). Using the operator *i* in *LoF*, time is created, we get a state that 'flutters', and this is the oscillation between two states (the marked state and the unmarked state). Time can only be measured through change, and the only change we can produce is the crossing from one state to another. This is no less than a question of reaching a new reality from a reality, from one operation to a new recursive process, but also of handling 'incompleteness' and 'indeterminacy' so that 'infinite processes' can be brought to a solution. It signifies no less than to overcome the difference between concept, thought, and reality. To successfully overcome this obstacle one has to do what is simple, namely to take action, think, and experience without allowing oneself to be limited by a limiting factor, such as the specific structures or descriptive statements we take for granted.

30.7 CONCLUSION: LAWS OF FORM FOR ORGANIZATION THEORY

Finally, I will suggest how Spencer-Brown's form calculus can be used to illustrate some chosen themes within organization theory. The main point is that organizations can never avoid the problem of self-reference, and, by implication, the challenge of paradox.

First, the form calculus can be read as an important contribution to the issues of *medium and form*. For when a space is marked, a boundary is drawn within it, and one side will be indicated. This relationship between space and side is analogous to the relationship between medium and form. The space is a medium and the indicated side is the form. Forms can be understood as actualized elements and patterns of elements through which organizations are realized, while the medium is the frame from which forms can be selected. Strictly speaking, organizations are not the cause of the connection between forms within the medium, but are created in the process of connection and disconnection of elements. We can now imagine organizations where something is unfolded through time, or rather as a chain of connections and disconnections of forms (Luhmann, 2000) that create time, or the experience of time (Bakken et al., 2013).

Second, *LoF*'s axiom regarding the 'Law of crossing' clarifies the relationship between *identity* and *difference* in organizations (Baecker, 1999b). In studies of organizations based upon Hegel's (1977) and Marx's (1960) dialectical method, difference is also emphasized. However, approaches based on the dialectic method take for granted a kind of completion or end product of the process, which unfolds with necessity. The form calculus, however, has no end product, but ends by exploding its own ability to calculate and reaches a condition that can be described as 'unresolvable indeterminacy', and which thereby needs imaginary worlds for further processing, and also time, memory, and freedom to 'oscillate' between an 'inside' and an 'outside'—namely through information (knowledge) and connection with new operations (non-knowledge). This is how we see a shift from the necessity of dialectics towards the contingency of constructivism, as suggested by Baecker (1999b). The benefit of such an approach is that we can more easily adapt to thinking of organizations that produce 'incompleteness' (Gödel, 1931) and 'uncertainty' (Heisenberg, 1931). This is where form calculus corresponds to the process thinking applied to organization studies put forward by Tsoukas and Chia (2002) and Hernes (2008), who see organizations as momentary attempts at stabilization rather than as stabilized entities. What the form calculus draws attention to is how any notion of stabilization carries within it both incompleteness and uncertainty. In other words, attempts aiming at certainty lead to uncertainty, and attempts aiming towards knowledge lead to the creation of non-knowledge (Bakken and Hernes, 2006).

Third, with the help of *LoF*'s concept of *re-entries*, we can handle paradoxes more rigorously (Luhmann, 1993, 2000). We already know the phenomenon through Max Weber's (1958) description of the emergence of the capitalistic monetary economy: ascetic denial of the world produces more of that world it denies. In addition, the more we deny the world (i.e. try to control it), the more complex it becomes. Much of the same can be found in studies of organizations, such as what Argyris (1988) calls 'designed inconsistency'. Observing paradoxes can then acknowledge how treatment of paradoxes can lead to creative solutions where the result is not a logical cleansing of the problem, but a restructuring of cognitive complexity (March, 2010). Organizations do not stop in the face of logical contradictions; if further possibilities are at hand, 'they jump' (Luhmann, 1990: 8). To hope for the reconciliation of reason with reality can never be anything other than a trivialization of reality.

If researchers of organization were to choose one basic lesson from Spencer-Brown's form calculus, it should be this: it is not enough to think through the science of organization, but one must also think through science as such. If we wish to deconstruct hierarchical forms of organization—as we have shown initially in relation to Philip Herbst's project—this also demands a deconstruction of a 'hierarchic philosophy'. This is a request for a transition from a monolithic form of cognition to a polycentric scientific understanding, which is obviously a meticulous process. It is related to a resignation of 'the principal' (Marquard, 1989), meaning all forms of the a priori, whether it is manifested in the form of one-dimensional management philosophies or other forms of deeply grounded constants. Therefore, we can say that the mode for a non-hierarchical form of cognition is a mode characterized by self-reference: only a theory capable of reflecting on its own starting point can evade the powerful hierarchical tradition of science.

References

Argyris, C. (1988). Crafting a Theory of Practice: The Case of Organizational Paradoxes, in R.E. Quinn and K.S. Cameron (eds), *Paradox and Transformation: Toward a Theory of Change in Organization and Management* (Cambridge, MA: Ballinger): 255–78.

Baecker, D. (1999a). Introduction, in D. Baecker (ed.), *Problems of Form* (Stanford, CA: Stanford University Press): 1–15.

——(1999b). The Form Game, in D. Baecker (ed.), *Problems of Form* (Stanford, CA: Stanford University Press): 99–107.

Bakken, T. and Hernes, T. (2006). Organizing is Both a Verb and a Noun: Weick meets Whitehead, *Organization Studies* 27(11): 1599–616.

——Holt, R., and Zundel, M. (2013). Time and Play in Management Practice: An Investigation through the Philosophies of McTaggart and Heidegger', *Scandinavian Journal of Management* 29: 13–22.

Beck, U., Giddens, A., and Lash, S. (1994). *Reflexive Modernization: Politics, Tradition and Aesthetics in the Modern Social Order* (Stanford, CA: Stanford University Press).

Beer, S. (1969). Maths Created, *Nature* 223 (27 September): 1392–3.

Blumenberg, H. (2010). *Theorie der Lebenswelt* (Frankfurt am Main: Suhrkamp).

Boole, G. (1951). *The Laws of Thought on which are Founded the Mathematical Theories of Logic and Probabilities* (New York: Dover).

Canainn, T. (1969). The Application of Boolean Algebra to Switching Circuits, in P.D. Barry (ed.), *George Boole: A Miscellany* (Dublin: Hely Thom Limited): 53–8.

von Foerster, H. (1981). *Observing Systems* (California: Intersystems Publications).

——(1993). Die Gesetze der Form, in D. Baecker (ed.), *Kalkül der Form* (Frankfurt am Main: Suhrkamp): 9–12. Reprint from *Whole Earth Catalog*, Spring 1969: 14–16.

Gödel, K. (1931). Über formal unentscheidbare Sätze der Principia Matematica und verwandter Systeme, *Monatshefte für Mathematik und Physik* 38: 173–98.

Hegel, G.W.F. (1977). *Phenomenology of Spirit* (Oxford and New York: Oxford University Press).

Heisenberg, W. (1931). Die Rolle der Unbestimmtheitsrelationen in der modernen Physik, *Monatshefte für Mathematik und Physik* 38: 365–72.

Herbst, D.P. (1976). *Alternatives to Hierarchies* (Leiden: Martinus Nijhoff).

——(1995). What Happens when We Make a Distinction: An Elementary Introduction to Co-Genetic Logic, in T.A. Kindermann and J. Valsiner (eds), *Development of Person-Context Relations* (New Jersey: Lawrence Erlbaum Associates): 29–38.

Hernes, T. (2008). *Understanding Organization as Process: Theory for a Tangled World* (London: Routledge).

Husserl, E. (2003). *Philosophy of Arithmetic: Psychological and Logical Investigations* (Dordrecht and Boston: Kluwer Academic Publishers).

Kauffman, L. (1977). Reviews of *The Laws of Form*, *Mathematical Reviews* 54: 701–2.

——(1978). Network Synthesis and Varela's Calculus, *International Journal of General Systems* 4: 179–87.

——(1987). Self-Reference and Recursive Forms, *Journal of Social and Biological Structure* 10: 53–72.

——(1998a). Virtual Logic—The Calculus of Indication, *Cybernetics and Human Knowing* 5(1): 63–8.

——(1998b). Virtual Logic—Self-reference and the Calculus of Indications, *Cybernetics and Human Knowing* 5(2): 75–82.

—— (1999). Virtual Logic—The MetaGame Paradox, *Cybernetics and Human Knowing* 6(4): 73–9.

Klee, P. (1969a). Exact Experiments in the Realm of Art, in P. Klee, *Notebooks: The Thinking Eye*, Volume 1 (London: Lund Humphries): 69–71.

——(1969b). Creative Credo, in P. Klee, *Notebooks: The Thinking Eye*, Volume 1 (London: Lund Humphries): 76–82.

Lau, F. (2008). *Die Form der Paradoxie. Eine Einführung in die Mathematik und Philosophie der 'Laws of Form' von G. Spencer-Brown* (Heidelberg: Carl Auer Verlag).

Luhmann, N. (1984). *Soziale Systeme* (Frankfurt am Main: Suhrkamp).

——(1990). *Essays on Self-Reference* (New York: Columbia University Press).

——(1993). Observing Re-Entries, *Graduate Faculty Philosophy Journal* 16(2): 485–98.

——(1997). *Die Gesellschaft der Gesellschaft* (Frankfurt am Main: Suhrkamp).

——(1999). The Paradox of Form, in D. Baecker (ed.), *Problems of Form* (Stanford, CA: Stanford University Press): 15–26.

——(2000). *Organisation und Entscheidung* (Opladen: Westdeutscher Verlag).

March, J. (2010). *Ambiguities of Experience* (Stanford, CA: Stanford University Press).

Marquard, O. (1989). *Farewell to Matters of Principle: Philosophical Studies* (New York and Oxford: Oxford University Press).

Marx, K. (1960). *Das Kapital (MEW)* (Berlin: Dietz Verlag).

Morgan, G. (1986). *Images of Organization* (London: Sage).

Musil, R. (2001). *The Confusion of Young Törless* (London: Penguin Classics).

Rasch, W. (2002). Introduction: The Self-Positing Society, in N. Luhmann (ed.), *Theories of Distinction. Redescribing the Descriptions of Modernity* (Stanford, CA: Stanford University Press): 1–30.

Rescher, N. (2000). *Process Philosophy* (Pittsburg: University of Pittsburgh Press).

Schiltz, M. (2007). Space is the Place: The Laws of Form and the Social Systems, *Thesis Eleven* 88: 8–30.

Serres, M. (2007). *The Parasite* (Minneapolis: University of Minnesota Press).

Simon, F.B. (1993). Mathematik und Erkenntnis: Eine Möglichkeit die *Laws of Form* zu lesen, in D. Baecker (ed.), *Kalkül der Form* (Frankfurt am Main: Suhrkamp): 38–58.

Spencer-Brown, G. (1957). *Probability and Scientific Inference* (London/New York/Toronto: Longmans).

——(1969/2008). *Laws of Form* (Leipzig: Bohmeier Verlag).

——(as James Keys) (1971). *Only Two can Play this Game* (New York: Julian Press).

——(1973a). *The George Spencer-Brown AUM Conference*. Esalen/CA: Esalen Institute. Session one, Monday Morning, 19 March.

——(1973b). *The George Spencer-Brown AUM Conference*. Esalen/CA: Esalen Institute. Session two, Monday Afternoon, 19 March.

——(1993). Self reference, Distinction and Time, *Teoria Sociologica* 1–2: 47–53.

Tarski, A. (1959). *Introduction to Logic and the Methodology of Deductive Sciences* (New York and Oxford: Oxford University Press).

Tsoukas, H. and Chia, R. (2002). On Organizational Becoming: Rethinking Organizational Change, *Organization Science* 13(5): 567–82.

Valéry, P. (1960). My Faust, in P. Valéry, *Plays, The Collected Works of Paul Valéry*, Volume 3 (New York: Bollingen Foundation): 3–140.

Varela, F. (1975). Calculus for Self-reference, *International Journal of General Systems* 2: 5–24.

Varga von Kibèd, M. (1989). Wittgenstein und Spencer-Brown, in P. Weingartner and G. Schurz (eds), *Philosophie der Naturwissenschaften. Akten des 13. Internationalen Wittgenstein Symposium* (Wien: Hölder-Pichler-Tempsky): 402–6.

——and Matzka, R. (1993). Motive und Grundgedanken der *Gesetze der Form*, in D. Baecker (ed.), *Kalkül der Form* (Frankfurt am Main: Suhrkamp): 58–96.

Watzlawick, P. (1984). *The Invented Reality* (New York and London: W.W. Norton Company).

Weber, M. (1958). *The Protestantic Ethic and the Spirit of Capitalism* (New York: Columbia University Press).

Weick, K. (1995). *Sensemaking in Organizations* (Thousand Oaks, CA: Sage).

Wille, K. and Hölscher, T. (2009). Kontexte und Architektur der Laws of Form, in T. Schönwalder-Kuntze, K. Wille, and T. Hölscher, *George Spencer-Brown. Eine Einführung in die Laws of Form* (Wiesbaden: VS Verlag für Sozialwissenschaften): 23–44.

Whitehead, A.N. (1929). *Process and Reality: an Essay in Cosmology* (Cambridge: Cambridge University Press).

Wittgenstein, L. (1961). *Tractatus Logico-Philosophicus* (London: Routledge).

——(1983). *Remarks on the Foundations of Mathematics* (Cambridge, MA: MIT Press).

CHAPTER 31

GILLES DELEUZE
(1925–1995)

ANDERS R. KRISTENSEN,
THOMAS LOPDRUP-HJORTH, AND
BENT MEIER SØRENSEN

31.1 INTRODUCTION

GILLES DELEUZE's thinking is ontological. This is remarkable, and it makes his work stand out in the post-structuralist cadre in which he is often placed. In organization studies, Deleuze is associated with postmodernism (Cooper and Burrell, 1988) and post-structuralism (Jones, 2009: 77) alongside thinkers such as Derrida, with whom he does share much. Yet post-structuralist approaches tend to place a primary 'focus on language in organizational life' (Jones, 2009: 78), and Deleuze doesn't trust language as such to be a conveyer of what is 'Interesting, Remarkable, or Important' (Deleuze and Guattari, 2003: 82). The philosopher must struggle directly with language in order to create a concept which may intervene ontologically in the world, and *through this intervention* create something interesting, remarkable, or important.

This experimental, indeed, as we shall see, *processual*, deployment of philosophy makes Deleuze sit uneasily in the conventional history of the field, a history which may, following Abel, Tugendhat, and Rorty (see Habermas, 2000: 37), be separated into three distinct paradigms: (1) the metaphysical paradigm prevailing in ancient and medieval times, (2) the epistemological paradigm introduced by Descartes and Kant, (3) the linguistic paradigm of modern times. While Deleuze belongs to the 'great generation' of French philosophers who went through 1968, his philosophy is distrustful of language, which toils under the Order-word (Deleuze and Guattari, 1988), and he will in some sense go back to the ancient, metaphysical paradigm in order to completely recreate it. This so-called metaphysical paradigm was dismissed by Kant because it 'was premised on a naive epistemological assumption according to which being (the thing in itself) would immediately be available to thought' (Gabriel, 2011: x).

There is in this view no access to being without mediation of a subject. In the episte-mological paradigm, being was therefore substituted by the subject as the primary con-stitutive principle. Yet, as the linguistic, that is, modern, philosophers later argued, it is language rather than the subject that constitutes the primary foundation of knowledge, because our epistemological access to the world is always mediated by discourses and symbolic formations.

Belonging primarily to the linguistic camp, Derrida eschews ontology as a promis-ing field for thought, not least if we take ontology to be a study of 'what there is' (May, 2005: 8ff), and sees the language in which any ontology is expressed as already contami-nated by its own, internal economy: since any term lives by violently repressing its other—the concept of 'man' is constituted, argues Derrida, through its exclusion of the term 'woman', and so on—the ontology that becomes expressed in such language would con-secrate into a naturalized identity what is in fact a fierce and continuous tension (Derrida, 2003: 351ff). While Deleuze remains fundamentally positive to Derrida and other post-structuralists' stance, he nevertheless goes in the opposite direction and ventures directly into ontology, insisting that a 'concept is not discursive, and philosophy is not a discursive formation' (Deleuze and Guattari, 1994: 22). Deleuze sees the philosophical and political problems which the great generation struggled with as directly connected to ontology, which is why philosophy should invent new ways of thinking, ways which open up to new ontologies. Ontology is, in this view, not bent on *identity*: it is bent on *difference* (Deleuze, 1994). Identities do exist in this world; as Bryant says: 'Deleuze is quite happy to say that representation, identity and recognition are real phenomena of our experience' (2007: 5). Yet, these are results of differentiation, not representations or copying: 'differ-ence is behind everything, but behind differences there is nothing' (Deleuze, 1994: 57).

Even though the philosophy of Deleuze has been widely adopted and accepted within the organizational perspective on process metaphysics (see e.g. Chia, 1995, 1999; Bougen and Young, 2000; Lilley, 2009; Linstead, 2002; Linstead and Thanem, 2007; Styhre, 2002; Thanem, 2004; Nayak, 2008), we believe that it could play an even greater role. This emphasis should embrace ontology not as a new idealism, but rather as a concrete pragmatism (Deleuze and Guattari, 1988: 22).

In this chapter we will present some key terms from Deleuze's philosophical oeuvre as well as give some consideration as to how these can be utilized. In so doing we will fur-thermore highlight how processual thinking has become an important area of investiga-tion within organization and management studies at large, as change, the unforeseen, and unpredictability have shown up as central conditions and challenges for manage-ment today. Hence, it is not only organization studies that have taken a processual turn; this has to a large extent also happened within mainstream and popular management theories. Process thinking is therefore not in opposition to mainstream management thought, but can be located at its very core. So rather than finding processes in opposi-tion to organization and management, we would like to frame the question of processes in organization studies differently. Instead of studying how processes are repressed by the bureaucratic organization, we show how processes have become the normative aspi-ration hailed within management thought.

As the dichotomy between processes and change on the one hand, and management and organization on the other has become increasingly blurred throughout the past couple of decades, we argue for a practical turn within process organization studies that aspires to think a processual ontology and metaphysics of management. To do so we will make use of Deleuze and especially draw on his ideas of thinking through the creation of concepts.

The chapter is structured as follows. In section 31.2 we will present Deleuze's understanding of metaphysics and the creation of concepts. We will here argue that process organization studies, from a Deleuzian perspective, should focus on the creation of concepts that make it possible to bring something new into the world. In section 31.3 we will attend to the process ontology already found within process organization studies. This will then, in section 31.4, be set in relation to a wider socio-historical context within which process thinking, in a more general way, has become a major concern. In section 31.5 we will give some pointers as to how Deleuze and Deleuzian-inspired thought can be utilized. Finally, in section 31.6 we conclude by arguing that the deployment of Deleuze's philosophy in process organization studies should be more normative and pragmatic.

31.2 DELEUZE'S METAPHYSICS AND THE CREATION OF CONCEPTS

In order to understand Deleuze's philosophy we will begin with his understanding of metaphysics. In a late interview Deleuze says somewhat polemically:

> I feel myself to be a pure metaphysician. Bergson says that modern science hasn't found its metaphysics, the metaphysics it would need. It is this metaphysics that interests me. (Villani, 1999: 130, quoted in Smith, 2003: 49)

This remark can at first seem quite strange. Is Deleuze not the thinker of immanence par excellence? And does metaphysics not presuppose a position of transcendence? The answer is that Deleuze has never been in opposition to metaphysics. His aim was not to overcome or move beyond metaphysics (Goodchild, 1996: 1). Yet, he doesn't see metaphysics as in itself a steady, paradigmatic institution: 'I've never worried about going beyond metaphysics or the death of philosophy, and I never made a big thing about giving up Totality, Unity, the Subject' (Deleuze, 1995a: 88). But his aim is to create and invent new metaphysical systems that make it possible to go beyond the current understanding of the world's phenomena and beyond the thinking that goes on about it within various fields of science (Deleuze, 1995a: 136). Daniel W. Smith writes:

> Deleuze sees his work as being strictly *immanent* to metaphysics: creation and transformation are possible within metaphysics, and there are virtualities in past

> metaphysics that are capable of being reactivated, as it were, and inserted into new contexts, and new problematics. Metaphysics itself, in other words, is dynamic and in constant becoming. (Smith, 2003: 50)

Deleuze is not against representation as such. His problem with representation is rather the central place it historically has been accorded—both within common sense and within philosophy as such (Deleuze, 1994). Deleuze conceives of his own philosophical task as establishing new criteria upon which something new can come into the world (Smith, 1998: xxiv; 2007). In this sense Deleuze understands metaphysics as a creative process that does not aim at discovering what already exists, but rather establish what there could be if we only were able to think differently about a given subject (Lohmann and Steyart, 2006; Williams, 2005; Spoelstra, 2007; May, 2005).

Metaphysics is difficult because it resides far from our everyday understanding of management and organizations. For process metaphysics this implies that we should study the conditions under which we experience processes. We agree with Linstead when he argues that 'change must always to some degree be organized to be thinkable' (Linstead, 2002: 105). It is simply not possible to have a pure experience of change or process in itself. However, this does not mean that we should study process as something that belongs to the organization. Deleuze offers us a third way. This is the way of *transcendental empiricism*, which is to go beyond the given experience of process to a general possible experience of process to investigate how the possible object of knowledge is given (Smith, 2007: 4–5). Hence, the aim of transcendental empiricism is not to know of process in itself, which we can have no knowledge of, but to study (and change if necessary!) the transcendental categories and concepts in which we can have knowledge of processes (Lohmann and Steyart, 2006: 92). We believe that this is what Linstead points to when he urges us to 'constantly reflect change as a condition in its other terms' (Linstead, 2002: 106). In other words, we should locate how change and process work as a transcendental condition in other terms.

It is in this Deleuzian sense that we would like to discuss process metaphysics in relation to organization studies. It is not a question of organizations having or not having a metaphysics. On the contrary, it is a matter of organizations not having the metaphysics they need. Such a recreation goes through the creation of concepts.

We need to create concepts to be able to know. This does not mean that we should develop more abstract theories in order to know more about processes. Instead, we have to develop pragmatic problems through which the constitution of processes can be analysed. Deleuze argues that 'you will know nothing through concepts unless you have created them' (Deleuze and Guattari, 2003: 7). This means that we should not abstract thought (Goodchild, 2000: 164), but that we should abstract the transcendental categories in which we think from the empirical realm in order to reposition the possible ways of thinking. The concept belongs to this transcendental field, a fact which enables Deleuze to state the value of the philosophical concept more pragmatically: '[Philosophy] groups under one concept things which you would have thought were very different, or it separates things you would have thought belonged together'

(2006: 214). This way, the concept determines what becomes available as knowledge: 'The concept is a window onto chaos, not to order it or to reduce it, but to recognize it, make it sensible—perhaps, thinkable' (Jackson and Carter, 2004: 148).

Deleuze's philosophy should inspire organization scholars to create concepts for ever-changing problems, that is, to do what philosophers have done and not just repeat what they have said (Deleuze and Guattari, 2003: 28). Put differently, it is a matter of 'defocusing the problem in order to "produce the problematic"' (Sørensen, 2005: 121). It is in relation to this methodology—which we will exemplify at the end of this chapter—that we should understand the Deleuzian definition of the task of philosophy as a creation of concepts (Deleuze and Guattari, 2003). This perspective on philosophy is inspired by Nietzsche, who writes that philosophers 'must no longer accept concepts as a gift, nor merely purify and polish them, but first *make* and *create* them, present them and make them convincing' (1968: 220). Concepts are not ready-made, given to us 'from some sort of wonderland: but they are, after all, the inheritance from our most remote, most foolish as well as most intelligent ancestors' (Nietzsche, 1968: 221; see also Deleuze and Guattari, 2003: 5 and Chapter 13, this volume).

How can we create knowledge about something if we do not have the categories or concepts in which the given can be given to us? And how can knowledge be said to be true if it is founded on concepts we have created ourselves? If we want to create knowledge about something that does not yet exist, the point is not representational accuracy but engagement in creating problems that have practical relevance. Hayden says:

> The criterion for philosophical activity is not representational accuracy of how the world 'really is' as a closed system independent of experience but, given a theory of immanence, the success of the construction of concepts designed to respond to specific problems and real, particular conditions of existence. Thus for Deleuze the goal of an empiricist philosophy is practical: to make a positive difference in life, to invent, create, and experiment. (1998: 79–80)

For Deleuze, philosophy should not aim for truth by representing or discovering a missing world: his processual philosophy renders ontology a matter of creation. Philosophy must *denaturalize* the general imperatives for how we represent and understand the given in order to make room for raising problems in new, positive ways. Truth lies in the effort of creating new forms of problems rather than finding any 'first principle', or as Deleuze and Guattari put it, 'a concept always has the truth that falls to it as a function of the conditions of its creation' (2003: 27).

The act of creation is not only to invent new concepts but also to positively destroy problems in an effort to make it possible to state new forms of problems. So, creation is much more than inventing new solutions. It also involves creating new problems. In so doing it calls not for a philosophy *for* organization, where philosophy as an underlabourer clears the way for 'science', but rather for a philosophy *of* organization, where new concepts can be created within organization studies itself (Spoelstra, 2007: 25). This focus on problems is not to say that we should not pay attention to solutions. It is simply to say that we need to address problems first because 'the problem always has the solution it deserves, in terms of the way in which it is stated (i.e. the conditions under which it is determined as a problem)' (Deleuze, 1991: 16). If solutions, in this sense, are inseparable from problems, then we cannot address solutions; we need to employ the constitutive power of problems to be able to know (Deleuze, 1991: 16). We have to develop concepts to apprehend something that does not yet exist but is about to come into existence.

Even if Deleuze in his philosophical oeuvre has created a great number of processual concepts such as rhizome, body without organs, and smooth space, we should not just apply these concepts wildly to the empirical world. Using concepts as empirical descriptions is problematic, because it effectually removes them from the problems in relation to which they are created as functions (Deleuze and Guattari, 1994; see also Spoelstra, 2007). Instead, our task as readers and users of Deleuze is to create concepts by which something new can come into existence. The Internet or al-Qaeda might look like rhizomatic organizations, but the danger of applying the most obvious image to something is that we might not get beyond the mere metaphor of the rhizome. The point is not to show that the Internet or al-Qaeda are rhizomatic, but to bring something new into the world by *showing* that these social formations have rhizomatic qualities and strategies. This will not happen by asking 'What is ... [the Internet or al-Qaeda]?' but, since what the question addresses, the idea, always is a multiplicity, by asking '*who? how? how much? where and when? in which cases?*—forms that sketch the genuine spatio-temporal coordinates of the Idea' (Deleuze, 2004: 96). Therefore, one must force oneself to think and create new images of thought. When it comes to process philosophy, this counts not least, as already indicated, for the relation between process and stasis. Deleuze and Guattari (1988: 40ff) have placed, in the beginning of the 'Geology of Morals'-plateau in *A Thousand Plateaus*, a slightly mad Professor Challenger who has insights into this. Being the narrator, he has explained that 'the Earth—the Deterritorialized, the Glacial, the giant Molecule—is a body without organs'. This concept, the body without organs, is one that we, being organization scholars interested in process philosophy, may equal to a pure process or an unrestrained creative flow. While any actual body is restricted in its possibility so that we still do not know, as Spinoza reminds Deleuze and Guattari (1988: 257), what a body can do, it also has a body without organs, a thought-body with a virtual dimension that expresses a multiplicity of possible actions and affects.

However, we want in this chapter to warn a little against too much enthusiasm for pure processes and specifically want to warn against having the body without organs invested with this enthusiasm. Professor Challenger does say that the Earth is a body without organs and surely, he confirms its flow character: 'This body without organs is permeated by unformed, unstable matters, by flows in all directions, by free intensities or nomadic singularities, by mad or transitory particles' (1988: 40). Then he says something that maybe should surprise us as process philosophers: 'That, however, was not the question at hand' (1988: 40). His professorial insight is, then, not that everything is in unformed processes, that it flows, ejects free particles, is raving mad and unstable. This is just how it is. And we do not need to account for this, we can just look at lava, look at sun storms, look at firestorms, look at the Internet or at al-Qaeda or at the ramblings of the US Tea Party movement, or take a look into the organization we just now pass or inhabit. There are mad and untamed processes everywhere. But they cannot, exactly because of their obviousness, be considered 'the question at hand' when the (moral) geologist looks at the Earth and its organization. The Professor is looking for something different, although concomitant:

> For there simultaneously occurs upon the earth a very important, inevitable phenomenon that is beneficial in many respects and unfortunate in many others: stratification. (Deleuze and Guattari, 1988: 40)

Stratification is the process by which something becomes formed and layered by various forces, and a sensible engagement with Deleuze and Guattari in thinking about processes and organization should (1) take seriously the simultaneity and embroiled nature of process and stratification, and (2) observe that Deleuze and Guattari consider the stratification of the flow 'beneficial in many respects'. Then, the primary question is no longer how something 'manages to leave the strata but how things get into them in the first place' (Deleuze and Guattari, 1988: 56). This opens for a philosophy of organization which sees processes and organization as enfolded in each other: everything orders itself through a self-referential autopoiesis, but is also subjected to reductionary and stratifying forces. Such complications can be hazardous; in Professor Challenger's case, at this stage and with 500 pages still remaining, 'most of the audience had left' (Deleuze and Guattari, 1988: 56). This should not, however, discourage us from discussing the consequences of this view for process organization studies.

31.3 AN ONTOLOGY OF BECOMING IN PROCESS ORGANIZATION STUDIES

One of Robert Chia's great contributions to process thinking is that he urges us to go beyond the discussion of reality as something 'out there' or 'in the mind' (Chia, 1996: 128; see also Nayak, 2008: 177). In other words, we should not raise the question of process from an epistemological perspective but rather from a metaphysical or ontological perspective. So Chia frames the question of process in a different way. He does not ask what processes are in organizations, but how we should be thinking about processes. We should not just be 'thinking about organizations' but rather create an 'organization of thought' (Nayak, 2008: 177). This change of focus from epistemology towards ontology and metaphysics is connected to what has been termed the 'ontological turn' in social theory (see e.g. Burrell, 2003: 528; Escobar, 2007). This turn to the ontological emphasizes 'the innermost constituent of reality itself', as Žižek (2004: 56) puts it. It is not only the constitution of the *experience* of reality that must be accounted for, but actually *the constitution of reality in itself*. Knowledge is therefore not only a matter of the foundation of experience of process, but a matter of the foundation of process in itself (Chia, 1999: 210). It is in this sense that we need to speak about process metaphysics if we intend to 'get at the heart of the phenomenon of change itself' (Chia, 1999: 210).

Process organization studies sees processes as fundamental and hence studies organizations as emerging from ontological and metaphysical processes. Central to this field has been the establishment of a battle line between a *metaphysics of process and change* on the one hand and a *metaphysics of substance* on the other (Chia, 1998; Chia and King, 1999; Styhre, 2002). According to a metaphysics of process and change, what fundamentally exist, at a base ontological level, are processes that unfold in a more or less chaotic manner. While arguing for the ontological primacy of processes and change over entities and stasis, this metaphysics, however, does not deny the existence of organizations, but views them as effects or gradual hardenings of these prior ontological processes. Tsoukas and Chia describe this interrelationship by way of stating that change 'must not be thought of as a property of organization. Rather, organization must be understood as an emergent property of change. Change is ontologically prior to organization—it is the condition of possibility for organization' (2002: 570).

The metaphysics of substance holds the reverse to be true. What fundamentally exists, according to this view, is self-contained entities (actors, organizations, societies, etc.) that then undergo some kind of change. Thus, change and processes are given a secondary role in relation to the entities to which they are tied, just as they are viewed as the exception rather than the norm (Chia, 1999: 210). In this sense, processes are mere attributes of organizations. Process thinkers within organization studies have been centrally preoccupied with pointing out the weakness of this latter view (Weick, 1974: 358; Tsoukas and Chia, 2002). A main concern in this regard has been that our thinking in general, and our thinking about organizational change and management in particular, logically end up by denying the very existence of change when we think in accordance with the vocabulary and conceptualizations underlying this metaphysics. If, to give just one prominent example of this metaphysics, we use a stage model to explain how an organization has changed, we paradoxically end up by denying what we set out to explain. This is so because 'change is reduced to a series of static positions... Change per se remains elusive and unaccounted—strangely, it is what goes on *between* the positions representing change' (Tsoukas and Chia, 2002: 571).

The reason for the inabilities of scholars and practitioners to properly account for organizational change, however, is not merely a matter of the ways in which we currently think about organizations. Rather, the way in which we account for change can be traced far back in our intellectual history. Thus, from Parmenides and Descartes through Newton to modern science, we find an intellectual and philosophical predisposition to begin with substances and stable entities as the ontological point of departure (Rescher, 1996). While not denying the various merits of thought built upon this tradition, scholars within process organization studies have claimed that this long historical lineage is in the way and constitutes a hindrance to adequately grasping the true processual nature of reality in general and real-life organizations in particular (e.g. Chia, 1999).

In trying to correct the shortcomings of our intellectual abilities when we think in accordance with this metaphysics of substance, several scholars have set out to search for early philosophical figures who were not caught up in this image of thought. A whole lineage from Heraclitus to Bergson, Whitehead, Derrida, Serres, and Deleuze have thus been mobilized as inspiring figures to draw upon in reframing how we should conceptualize processes and change (see e.g. Chia, 1999; Chia and King, 1998; Linstead, 2002; Styhre, 2002; Linstead and Thanem, 2007). These philosophical process thinkers have remained a continuing source of inspiration for the field of process organization studies since their initial uptake in the late 1990s. From here on, the discussions have developed by differentiating between different views of processes (Van de Ven and Pool, 2005; Hernes and Weik, 2007), just as central discussions have been developed by highlighting the complex interdependencies between verbs and nouns when accounting for organizations in accordance with a process perspective (Bakken and Hernes, 2006; Weick, 1974).

The various contributions to process organization studies that deploy Deleuze's philosophy share an engagement in wanting us to see organization in a different way. Linstead and Thanem (2007) draw, for example, on Deleuze's (1991) reading of Bergson to argue that organization studies, rather than recognize organization as a stable entity, should focus on change as organization is a product of unstable forces. In this sense they invite us to revise the conventional view of organization as resistant to change and force us to think about organization as change (Linstead and Thanem, 2007: 1485). The primary object of organization studies should not be the stable entities of organization but rather the unstable processes of changes, as Styhre writes: '[process philosophy is] a unifying label for theoretical models that emphasize change over stability, novelty over uniformity, and becoming over being' (Styhre, 2002: 557). What these researchers aim to do is not to discuss the abstract question of how we should understand process as such, but instead to abstract how a processual understanding of process, if you allow it, can contribute to various fields of organization studies. Hence, they seek to create new concepts that will make it possible to understand the organization of work, knowledge, and management differently and in new ways (Styhre, 2002).

On behalf of these theoretical developments within the last decade, process organization studies have provided a much-needed orientation towards the importance of ontological processes and the pervasive nature of change within the field of organization and management studies, just as it has enhanced and sharpened our conceptual repertoire in describing processes and change. Yet, though the field has undergone important developments, kept on evolving and flourished intellectually, the underlying scholarly challenge has remained a stable one. From the outset and up until today, this challenge has revolved around our inabilities to *think* and conceptualize movement, processes, becoming, change, and flux in a productive way (Chia, 1998; Chia and King, 1999). Hence, process thinking has remained centrally preoccupied with 'the analytical distinctions that we draw' (Bakken and Hernes, 2006: 1600) when we think about these matters of concern.

It seems to have been an underlying premise within process organization studies that we are not up to the challenge of thinking and dealing with the true processual nature of organizations. In light thereof management is depicted as a specific kind of inter-vention that, often in vain, seeks to create stability, order, and predictability in a world of continuing flux and movement. In spite of our carefully crafted planned interven-tions, we are constantly taken by surprise by the way in which 'our best-laid plans' are disrupted 'in innumerable ways' (Chia, 2011: 183). Though there are some merits to this claim, especially in view of the historical origins and initial aspirations of management thought (e.g. Fayol, 1916/1949; Taylor, 1911/1998), we think it is inadequate if it is not seen in accordance with a major tendency that has left a significant imprint on the practice and theory of management within the last couple of decades.

31.4 THE NEW SPIRIT OF CAPITALISM AND CONTEMPORARY MANAGEMENT THOUGHT

This tendency is what the French sociologists Luc Boltanski and Eve Chiapello (2005) have termed the new spirit of capitalism. Drawing upon Weber's (1905/2002) notion of 'the spirit of capitalism', Boltanski and Chiapello claim that we, from the end of the 1980s, have witnessed the rise of a new such spirit, which in its justificatory principles and normative injunctions is markedly different from an earlier one dating from the 1960s. According to Boltanski and Chiapello (2005), management thought has recently sought to battle and overcome its earlier engagement in and subjection to ideas of control, order, hierarchy, and predictability. This has happened by way of demanding a constant transgression of what already exists, and by way of insisting on imperma-nence, fluidity, change, and unpredictability as something that is mutually benefitting for employers and employees. In Boltanski and Chiapello's view, processes, change, flux, and movement are not in opposition to management and organization. Rather, they have in significant ways become inscribed within the very normative aspirations guid-ing management thought; i.e. they are hailed as something that needs to be facilitated and attended to. Due to this, it becomes increasingly difficult to uphold the dichotomy between change and process on the one hand, and management and organization as something that emerges afterwards and tries to arrest these processes on the other hand.

This points to a permanent blurring of the two poles, where management constantly seeks to overcome its former foundation by way of liquefying and processualizing its mode of being. Rather than stability, a constant production of unstable, liminal spaces that occupy spaces and loopholes has become the defining characteristic of organiza-tion (Garsten, 1999). One prominent contemporary example is the highly influential management guru Gary Hamel. He argues that management should liberate itself from stifling restrictions, structures, hierarchies, and rules (Hamel and Breen, 2007). This, however, is not the same as saying that we should not have management at all; rather, it is to make the important point that we need a different kind of management. Hamel therefore argues that the traditional form of management is blocking the way of realizing the potential of what management could be. He calls for a new management paradigm (Hamel 2009a, 2009b; Hamel and Breen, 2007). Although there are important differences between Hamel's thought and the scholarship done within process organization studies, we think it is important to recognize that Hamel, in developing this line of thought, subscribes to a process perspective in a double way, since processes show up not only as what has to be facilitated (Hamel, 2009a: 5), but also as that which has to be grasped and to be conceptualized by management studies (Birkinshaw et al., 2008: 826). On the one hand, then, Hamel's writings attest to the fact that process thinking within management and organization studies is not something that exists at the outskirts as a neglected and overlooked paradigm, since it already thrives among some of the most popular and influential scholars. On the other hand, this almost overwhelming success of process thinking obviously reconfigures the former battle line between proponents of a metaphysics of substance and proponents of a metaphysics of becoming (Chia and King, 1998; Tsoukas and Chia, 2002). Since the latter has now to a large extent become mainstream, the problem to be confronted should not be one of contrasting processes on the one hand with management and organizations on the other, but should instead revolve around how a proper *processual ontology and metaphysics of management* should be worked out. In the next section we will try to take some steps in this direction.

31.5 Deploying Deleuze: Organization Studies as a Simulacrum of Philosophy

Rather than imposing the philosophy of Deleuze upon organization studies, or upon process philosophy for that matter, one should instead draw out its consequences; we will point out a select number of individual cases where a certain, perhaps Deleuzian, philosophy of organization is developed. Pedersen (2008; 2011) has drawn on Deleuze and Guattari's idea that processes work by constantly breaking down (Deleuze and Guattari, 2004), yet, because 'desire production' is an event of surplus and transgression, the social machines involved constantly rise and reconfigure. Pedersen shows, for instance, how a contemporary organizational phenomenon such as stress is organized. Rather than seeing stress as a personal and individual breakdown of the human being, Pedersen suggests that stress is an effect of the breakdown of the social machine that precedes the individual as well as the organization. Stress is not only caused by a lack of individual skills in self-management, but is indeed fundamental to the way work is organized in contemporary capitalism (Pedersen, 2011). In another Deleuzian vein, Styhre (2002) argues that theories and models of strategic management rarely problematize the basic assumptions they are based upon. This is a problem, as it often restricts the way that one can think strategic management processes. Process thinking can contribute to strategic management by challenging traditional basic assumptions of the field and provide a new understanding of the ontological foundation of ideas like project organization, organizational capabilities, and entrepreneurship. By developing the ontological foundations for these areas of knowledge it should be possible to establish more consistency in the way that the areas are construed.

Kristensen (2010) has drawn on Deleuze's idea of univocality in an exploration of work–life balance. He argues that, rather than focusing on the boundary between work and home, a Deleuzian analysis may enable a change of perspective to how work is defined in the concrete individual case by the employee. What then, in Deleuze and Guattari's programmatic parlance, becomes 'Interesting, Remarkable, or Important' is not the relation between two separate entities, life and work, but rather the processes by which work is individuated in the life of the employees. For example, how may it be considered work to send an email in the evening? Is it work to read an article at weekends? Is it work to update one's profile on Facebook, or, even more, LinkedIn? When trying to answer these questions, one may come to the pragmatic conclusion that it depends on the circumstances, but the more fundamental point here is that work has become nothing less than *metaphysical* (Kristensen, 2010). Work is not simply given to us concretely and psychically. We do not know what our work is because we can no longer simply define work in terms of working hours, working time, or contract work. The definition of work depends on something outside of the relation between work and home and how these circumstances outside of work and home are individuated by the individual employees when they either construe something as work or not work. When exploring work–life balance as a question of 'metaphysical labour' it becomes interesting to focus on that by which the employees define work as work. From a Deleuzian perspective this is exactly what a transcendental empiricism should be concerned with (Deleuze, 1994: 140). Similarly, Weiskopf and Loacker (2006: 395) read Deleuze's (1995) work on control society in order to identify the fluid, indeed processual, premises for today's knowledge workers, who are struggling with 'technologies of modulation' focusing on the 'the production of the autonomous, flexible and adaptable subject'. Weiskopf and Loacker show the double character of notions of process, a point we have tried to emphasize in this chapter: each deliberatory Deleuzian or other term which may be deployed is most likely already to be found in prescriptive programmes for management.

31.6 Conclusion: A more Normative and Empirical Process Organization Studies?

Deleuze's thinking forces us to consider what *might* be rather than what *ought* to be (Kristensen, 2012). Hence, we should not try to describe processes in organization and management or judge organization through a pre-established morality (Smith, 2007), but rather strive to change how we can think about organization. In this sense there is a profound relationship between ontology and ethics in Deleuze's philosophy (in some way similar to Spinoza's *Ethics*; see Chapter 6, this volume), as the former urges us to create new concepts that can make it possible to think and act differently (Deleuze and Guattari, 1994). What is important for process organization studies is that we cannot conclude that processes as such are good (and structures are bad). In this sense, the question of processes shifts from something to be normatively valued to something which, in relation to specific problems, should be assessed according to whether they are expanding the possibilities of freedom or, conversely, limiting the ways that humans can act and think? From a Deleuzian perspective we should begin our study of processes in organization with the practical question of what can organizations do—and not long-winded theoretical questions like 'what is process?' Such question rests on abstract universals, and they do not explain anything but have themselves to be explained (Deleuze and Guattari, 2003: 7). Hence, knowledge about something cannot be grasped by simply applying abstract categories to the empirical world of sensible objects (Buchanan, 1999).

We suggest that process organization studies should refrain from any attempt at representing what process is, but rather seek to invent and experiment with how it is possible to think about process in practice (see Hayden, 1998: 79–80). As we see it, the philosophy of Deleuze offers one way of doing this but, as other chapters in this *Handbook* testify, it is also possible to rely on other philosophers and thinkers. The important thing is how we address processes. We further suggest that the focus should be on the processes of creation, i.e. the role that processes play in the transcendental conditioning and constitution of the organization, in other words, a focus on the creation of concepts. Hence we should not try to understand metaphysical processes in themselves, but in their deployment within the organizational context. This may be a call for a more pragmatic and less pure (in a metaphysical sense) understanding of process organization studies that does not see itself in opposition to management, but rather tries to change the constitutions and the conditioning of process in mainstream management. We could perhaps frame this as a call for a practical turn in process organization studies. In our opinion, we should not only legitimize the studies of process theoretically, in opposition to mainstream management thinking about processes, creativity, and change, but also address the practical use and value of process organization studies, which we believe has much to offer to the empirical understanding of processes.

References

Bakken, T. and Hernes T. (2006). Organizing is both Verb and Noun: Weick Meets Whitehead, *Organization Studies* 27(11): 1599–616.

Birkinshaw, J., Hamel, G., and Mol, M.J. (2008). Management Innovation, *Academy of Management Review* 33(4): 825–45.

Boltanski, L. and Chiapello, E. (2005). *The New Spirit of Capitalism* (London and New York: Verso).

Bougen, P.D. and Young, J.J. (2000). Organizing and Regulating as Rhizomatic Lines: Bank Fraud and Auditing, *Organization* 7: 403–26.

Buchanan, I. (1999). Introduction, in I. Buchanan (ed.), *A Deleuzian Century?* (Duke: Duke University Press): 1–12.

Burrell, G. (2003). The Future of Organization Theory: Prospects and Limitations, in H. Tsoukas and C. Knudsen (eds), *The Oxford Handbook of Organization Theory* (Oxford: Oxford University Press): 525–35.

Carter, P. and Jackson, N. (2003). Gilles Deleuze and Felix Guattari, in S. Linstead (ed.), *Organization Theory and Postmodern Thought* (London: Sage): 105–26.

Chia, R. (1995). From Modern to Postmodern Organizational Analysis, *Organization Studies* 16: 579–604.

——(1996). *Organizational Analysis as Deconstructive Practice* (Berlin: Walter de Gruyter & Co).

——(1999). A 'Rhizomic' Model of Organizational Change and Transformation: Perspective from a Metaphysics of Change, *British Journal of Management* 10(3): 209–27.

——(2011). Complex Thinking: Towards an Oblique Strategy for Dealing with the Complex, in P. Allen, S. Maguire, and B. McKelvey (eds), *The Sage Handbook of Complexity and Management* (London: Sage): 182–98.

——and King, I.W. (1998). The Organizational Structuring of Novelty, *Organization* 5(4): 461–78.

Cooper, R. and Burrell, G. (1988). Modernism, Postmodernism and Organizational Analysis: An Introduction, *Organization Studies* 9(1): 91–112.

Deleuze, G. (1991). *Bergsonism*, trans. H. Tomlinson and B. Habberjam (New York: Zone Books).

——(1994). *Difference and Repetition*, trans. P. Patton (New York: Columbia University Press).

——(1995a). *Negotiations*, trans. M. Joughin (New York: Columbia University Press).

——(1995b). *Kant's Critical Philosophy: The Doctrine of Faculties*, trans. H. Tomlinson and B. Habberjam (London: The Athlone Press).

—— (1995c). Postscript on Control Societies, in G. Deleuze (ed.), Negotiations *1972–1990* (New York: Columbia University Press): 177–82.

——(2001). *Pure Immanence: Essays on a Life*, trans. A. Boyman (New York: Zone Books).

——(2002). Preface to English Language Edition, in G. Deleuze and C. Parnet, *Dialogues II*, trans. H. Tomlinson and B. Habberjam (London: Continuum): xi–viii.

—— (2004). *Desert Islands and Other Texts 1953–1974, trans.* M. Taormina (New York: Semiotext(e)).

——and Guattari, F. (1988). *A Thousand Plateaus: Capitalism & Schizophrenia* (London: The Athlone Press).

—— (1994) *What is Philosophy?*, trans. Hugh Tomlinson and Graham Burchell. New York: Columbia University Press.

——(2003). *What is Philosophy?*, trans. G. Burchell and H. Tomlinson (London: Verso).

——(2004). *Anti-Oedipus: Capitalism and Schizophrenia* (London: Continuum).

Derrida, J. (2003). *Writing and Difference* (London: Routledge).

Escobar, A. (2007). The 'Ontological Turn', in S. Marston, J.P. Jones II, and K. Woodward (eds), *Social Theory. A Commentary on 'Human Geography without Scale'*, *Transaction of Institute of British Geographers* 32(1): 106–11.

Fayol, H. (1916/1949). *General and Industrial Management* (London: Pitman).

Gabriel, M. (2011). *Transcendental Ontology: Essays in German Idealism* (London: Continuum).

Garsten, C. (1999). Betwixt and Between: Temporary Employees as Liminal Subjects in Flexible Organizations, *Organization Studies* 20: 601–17.

Goodchild, P. (1996). *An Introduction to the Politics of Desire* (London: Sage).

——(2000). Why is Philosophy so Compromised with God?, in M. Bryden (ed.), *Deleuze and Religion* (Florence: Routledge): 156–66.

Habermas, J. (2000). Richard Rorty's Pragmatic Turn, in R.B. Brandom (ed.), *Rorty and his Critics* (Oxford: Blackwell): 31–55.

Hamel, G. (2009a). Management Innovation, *Leadership Excellence May*: 5.

——(2009b). Management 2.0, *Leadership Excellence November*: 5.

——and Breen, B. (2007). *The Future of Management* (Cambridge, MA: Harvard Business School Press).

Hayden, P. (1998). *Multiplicity and Becoming: The Pluralist Empiricism of Gilles Deleuze* (New York: Peter Lang).

Hernes, T. and Weik, E. (2007). Organization as Process: Drawing a Line between Endogenous and Exogenous Views, *Scandinavian Journal of Management* 23(3): 251–64.

Jackson, N. and Carter, P. (2004). Gilles Deleuze and Felix Guattari, in *Organization Theory and Postmodern Thought*, S. Linstead (ed.), 105–26. London: Sage.

Jones, C. (2009). Poststructuralism in Critical Management Studies, in M. Alvesson, T. Bridgman, and H. Willmott (eds), *The Oxford Handbook of Critical Management Studies* (Oxford: Oxford University Press): 76–98.

Kristensen, A.R. (2010). *Metaphysical Labour. Flexibility, Performance and Commitment in Work-Life Management* (Copenhagen: CBS).

——(2012). Thinking and Normativity in Deleuze's Philosophy, in R. Braidotti and P. Pisters (eds), *Revisiting Normativity with Deleuze* (London: Bloomsbury): 11–24.

Lilley, S. (2009). Organising Time: Contraction, Synthesis, Contemplation, *Culture and Organization* 15: 135–50.

Linstead, S. (2002). Organization as Reply: Henri Bergson and Casual Organization Theory, *Organization* 9(1): 95–111.

——and Thanem, T. (2007). Multiplicity, Virtuality and Organization: The Contribution of Gilles Deleuze, *Organization Studies* 28(10): 1483–1501.

Lohmann, P. and Steyart, C. (2006). In the Mean Time: Vitalism, Affects and Metamorphosis in Organizational Change, in M. Fuglsang and B.M. Sørensen (eds), *Deleuze and the Social* (Edinburgh: Edinburgh University Press): 77–95.

May, T. (2005). *Gilles Deleuze: An Introduction* (Cambridge: Cambridge University Press).

Nayak, A. (2008). On the Way to Theory: A Processual Approach, *Organization Studies* 29(2): 173–90.

Nietzsche, F. (1968). *The Will to Power*, trans. W. Kaufmann and R.J. Hollingdale (New York: Vintage Books).

Pedersen, M. (2008). Tune In, Break Down, and Reboot: New Machines for Coping with the Stress of Commitment, *Culture and Organization* 14(2): 171–85.

——(2011). 'A Career is Nothing without a Personal Life': On the Social Machine in the Call for Authentic Employees, *ephemera* 11(1): 63–77.

Rescher, N. (1996). *Process Metaphysics: An Introduction to Process Philosophy* (New York: State University of New York Press).

Smith, D.W. (1998). Introduction, in G. Deleuze, *Essays Critical and Clinical* (London: Verso): xi–Iiv.

—— (2003). Deleuze and Derrida, Immanence and Transcendence: Two Directions in Recent French Thought, in P. Patton and J. Protevi (eds), *Between Derrida and Deleuze* (London: Continuum): 46–66.

——(2007). The Conditions of the New, *Deleuze Studies* 1: 1–21.

Sørensen, B.M. (2005). Immaculate Defecation: Gilles Deleuze and Felix Guattari in Organization Theory, in C. Jones and R. Munro (eds), *Contemporary Organization Theory* (Malden: Blackwell Publishing).

Spoelstra, S. (2007). *What is Organization?* (Lund: Lund Business Press).

Styhre, A. (2002). How Process Philosophy Can Contribute to Strategic Management, *Systems Research and Behavioral Science 19*: 577–87.

Taylor, F.W. (1911/1998). *The Principles of Scientific Management* (New York: Dover Publications).

Thanem, T. (2004). The Body without Organs: Nonorganizational Desire in Organizational Life, *Culture and Organization 10*: 203–17.

Tsoukas, H. and Chia, R. (2002). On Organizational Becoming: Rethinking Organizational Change, *Organization Science 13*(5): 567–82.

Van de Ven, A. and Poole, S. (1995). Explaining Development and Change in Organizations, *Academy of Management Review 20*(3): 510–40.

Villani, A. (1999). *La guêpe et l'orchidée: Essai sur Gilles Deleuze* (Paris: Belin).

Weber, M. (1905/2002). *The Protestant Ethic and the Spirit of Capitalism* (New York: Penguin Books).

Weick, K.E. (1974). Middle Range Theories of Social Systems, *Behavioral Science 19*(6): 357–67.

Weiskopf, R. and Loacker, B. (2006). A Snake's Coils are even more Intricate than a Mole's Burrow: Individualization and Subjectification in Post-Disciplinary Regimes of Work, *Management Review 17*: 395–419.

Williams, J. (2005). *The Transversal Thought of Gilles Deleuze: Encounters and Influences* (Manchester: Clinamen Press).

Žižek, S. (2004). *Organs without Bodies: Deleuze and Consequences* (New York: Routledge).

CHAPTER 32

MICHEL FOUCAULT
(1926–1984)

RICHARD WEISKOPF AND HUGH WILLMOTT

Do not ask who I am and do not ask me to remain the same: leave it to our bureaucrats and our police to see that our papers are in order. At least spare us their morality when we write.

(Foucault, 1989: 17)

32.1 INTRODUCTION

FROM THE opening quotation, it is evident that Foucault is disinclined to 'remain the same'. He is resistant to forces that impose stasis, consistency, and homogeneity and so invites us to understand his thinking as 'work in process'. We, as authors of this chapter, risk contributing to a venture in which we exercise the 'morality of the bureaucrat' inspecting Foucault's papers to determine 'who he is', how his approach is to be categorized, or whether he did or didn't contribute to a body of knowledge identified as 'process' or 'process philosophy'. Conscious of this danger, we will endeavour to exercise our freedom in ways that minimize engagement of a bureaucratic form of 'morality'. More positively, we hope to provoke, and point to, ways of enriching how thinking ascribed to 'Foucault' is received and appreciated. Foucault, we suggest, was committed to a critical stance that led him repeatedly to challenge established 'truths', including his own thinking. It has also served to frustrate, if rarely elude, those ('bureaucrats') who endeavour to confine 'Foucault' within, and so make him accountable for, positions that he either never occupied or abandoned prior to receiving their attentions.

It is Foucault's 'systematic scepticism toward all anthropological universals' (Foucault, 2003f: 3) and his illumination of the processes and practices through which the subject and object are formed and transformed historically, that make his work significant in

the context of processual understandings of organization and organizing. His thinking is pertinent, and offers instruction, when reflecting upon the contingency of our
knowledge of organizations and of organizing. It is also highly relevant for scrutinizing
our status as 'subjects' of organizing—both in the sense of being *subjected* to organizing
forces that form and shape us and as subjects who are (potentially) able to engage in a
work of transformation. Foucault's thinking attends to the social world, including the
world of organization, as fluid and dynamic, as a no-thing that is continuously 'coming into being'. Phenomena that come to our attention—such as 'the organization' and
'the subject'—are not, for Foucault, manifestations of a (unchanging) substance that the
human sciences are able to reveal. Rather, from a Foucauldian standpoint, 'the subject'
and 'the organization' are 'forms' constituted through discourses and practices and are
always specific to particular social and historical contexts. 'It [the subject] is a form, and
this form is not primarily or always identical to itself' (Foucault, 1997: 290). At any point
in history, the subject—the same applies to the organization—is already established
and shaped, but *only* exists in the 'embryonic form of its future becoming' (O'Leary,
2002: 120). When addressed in this way, 'organization' is not a thing but, rather, the
name for a multiplicity of practices by which we invent and reinvent ourselves by *giving
form* to our relations to ourselves as well as to others.

We begin by expanding upon 'Foucault' as a placeholder for a particular style, or styles,
of thinking that contributes to an appreciation of process. We then turn to Foucault's
understanding of discourse, history, and practices where we focus upon his challenge
to a representationalist view of the world and his distinctive view of the dynamics of
history. In turn, this provides a basis for some selective reflections on the engagement of
Foucault's thinking within the field of organization studies and some conclusions on the
general vision it opens up.

32.2 FOUCAULT?

Who is, or was, Foucault? Not one, but many. He has been variously identified/named
as a 'philosopher', 'structuralist', 'post-structuralist', 'political activist', 'gay rights activist', 'pseudo-Marxist', 'krypto-normativist', 'happy positivist', 'anti-modernist', and
'postmodernist'. Each label orders and confines the figure 'Foucault' within a particular system of meanings; each identity invites us to position him within an associated
normative frame and perceive and evaluate his work accordingly. When considering
Foucault's work, including its relation to process philosophy, it is therefore prudent to
heed his cautions about presenting 'simplistic appropriation(s) of others for the purpose
of communication' (Foucault, 1986a: 9).

In the context of this *Handbook*, the designation 'philosopher'—the first of the
identities ascribed to Foucault a moment ago—is salient, but problematic. On the
one hand, there is a strong case for identifying Foucault as one of the most influential philosophers of our times, so making his inclusion in this volume unexceptional

or even 'essential'. On the other hand, his work is not easily subsumed or catalogued under 'philosophy'. It is notable that social scientists, and even students of business and management, have been more enthusiastic adopters of Foucault than most professional or academic philosophers. Indeed, up until the end of the 1970s at least, Foucault consistently refused the appellation of philosopher in the classical sense (Foucault, 2001: 861)—that is, a thinker who searches for the truth *behind* phenomena, or strives to disclose the foundations for truth. With regard to 'process' Foucault was not concerned with articulating a general theory or metaphysics of 'process', of 'becoming', or of 'change' but, instead, with 'an analysis of *transformations* in their specificity' (Foucault, 1991b: 56, original emphasis). Seeking to pigeon hole Foucault within an academic discipline is futile. It is more illuminating to consider whether any theme, albeit one that is approached in diverse ways, can be found running through his work. Here again, Foucault offers a potent suggestion: the study of 'the different modes by which, in our culture, human beings are made subjects' (Foucault, 1982a: 208). His work has dealt with various 'modes of objectification which transform human beings into subjects' (Foucault, 1982a: 208).

The study of how human beings are transformed into subjects through 'modes of objectification' includes, for example, the 'modes of inquiry which try to give themselves the status of sciences' (Foucault, 1982a: 208), the disciplinary practices of 'confinement' and 'correction' institutionalized within the Hôpital Général described in *Madness and Civilization* (1965), and the panoptic technologies described in *Discipline and Punish* (1977). Such objectifications are seen to arrest and regulate emerging movement and fix subjects in conceptual and institutional frames. But Foucault also stresses that power-invested stabilizations are never finalized. In his later work, Foucault studies 'the way a human being turns him or herself into a subject' (Foucault, 1982a: 208). We are, in Foucault's view, always in the midst of concrete transformations, and it is the interplay and interconnection of processes of 'objectivation' and 'subjectivation' in historically specific practices that accounts for these transformations of ourselves (Foucault, 2003f). As subjects, we 'do not simply circulate in those networks (of power)'. Rather, we are 'in a position to both submit to and exercise this power through which human beings are transformed into subjects. [Subjects] are never the inert or consenting targets of power; they are always also its relays. In other words, *power passes through individuals*. It is not applied to them' (Foucault 2003g: 29, emphasis added).

Foucault addresses the *history* of truth, including the truths ascribed to the subject. Truth is conceived as a contingent outcome of historical processes from which power cannot be exorcised. In regarding truth and knowledge as *contingent*, Foucault rejects a notion of truth counterposed to falsity or ideology. Rather than with the 'production of true utterances' (e.g. on the subject), he was concerned with the 'truth-effects' of certain established positions. More specifically, he said: 'my problem is to see how men govern (themselves and others) by the production of truth' (Foucault, 1991a: 79). The view of the historicity of truth, knowledge, and the subject is affirmed by Foucault's occupancy of a chair, named 'history of systems of thought', at the Collège de France. Despite the recognition vested in this appointment, few historians recognize or value Foucault as one of their number. This, ironically enough, is partly because Foucault considered himself to be practising 'wirkliche Historie' (true history) in Nietzsche's sense. That is to say, his interest was in the 'history of the present' rather than in a representation of the past, showing how things—concepts, ideas, practices that we tend to take as givens—are an outcome of historical struggles. In sum, it would seem that Foucault is too much of a philosopher to be accepted by historians, and too much of a historian to be claimed by philosophers. For those less hostile to Foucault's imperviousness to easy categorization and disciplinary membership, his historical orientation enhances his status as a philosopher, and vice versa.

An alternative to attributing a unified identity to 'Foucault' or classifying his work would be to regard 'Foucault' as a name given to a 'site of a multiplicity of practices and labors' (Rabinow and Rose, 2003: xx). This alternative is more consistent with Foucault's self-understanding as 'experimenter' who writes 'experience books' (livre-expérience) instead of 'truth-books' (livre-verité) (Foucault, 2001: 866). Considered in this way, 'Foucault' is a 'multiplicity' that has emerged in a particular historical/intellectual context: Paris where, in the 1950s and 1960s, existentialism and phenomenology (Sartre, Merleau-Ponty), on the one hand, and structuralism (Althusser, Levis-Strauss Saussure), on the other, were in the ascendant and occasionally in productive tension. The distinctive political as well as the intellectual qualities of this context are important. Foucault inherits a specific intellectual tradition to which he responds, and which his thinking acts to transform (Jones, 2002). Specifically, Foucault acknowledges being very hostile to the idea of a founding subject associated with phenomenology (Foucault, 2001; May, 2003). Foucault's connectedness to current affairs is evident from many of his interviews where he often directly engages these questions and associated issues. In his books on the other hand, the primary focus is upon 'lines of transformation' that have led us to become 'this' rather than 'that', and which act to denaturalize (and politicize) *what* or *who* we are *today*. Notably, Foucault's analysis of modes of objectifying 'madness' and the 'mad' in discourses and practices of psychiatry fuelled the anti-psychiatric movement and struggles to reform psychiatric treatment. And Foucault's analysis of the 'birth of the prison' in *Discipline and Punish* cannot be fully appreciated independently of struggles around prison reform in France and the prominent activist role played by Foucault in the Groupe d'Information sur les Prisons (GIP) in the early 1970s (Eribon, 1994). Nor can Foucault's interest in the ethics of antiquity—which is explored mainly in the *History of Sexuality, Volumes 2 and 3* (1986a, 1986b)—be satisfactorily comprehended without reference to the contemporary problem of developing a morality/ethics that goes beyond following (moral) rules and regulations (in particular, an ethics after Auschwitz). And, finally, there is Foucault's attention to practices of freedom and alternative modes of self-formation. This is also strongest in his later works, particularly in his final lectures on the practice of *parrhesia* (truth-telling) (Foucault, 2010, 2011). The specific construction of the 'free individual' as an 'entrepreneur of himself' which Foucault saw emerging in the context of the economic theories of neoliberalism (Foucault, 2008a) may have prompted his excavation of alternative self-relations and modes of self-formation which operated, historically speaking, before scientific rationalization and Christian confession (Luxon, 2008).

What, then, of Foucault's broader intellectual location beyond the volatile mix of existentialism, phenomenology, and structuralism in post-war Paris? Some illumination of this question is offered in a lexicon article entitled 'Michel Foucault' in which Foucault playfully adopts the pseudonym 'Maurice Florence' (2003f). Prepared near the end of his life, this article positions Foucault's work within the '*critical* tradition of Kant' (2003f: 1). For Foucault, it was Kant, a master of critique, who made central the questions of 'what is our present?' and 'what we are, *in this very moment*' (Foucault, 1982a: 216, emphasis added)?'[1] They are questions which, for Foucault, are directly connected to the question of critique. What animates Foucault's thinking, we suggest, is a deep and sustained commitment to *the critical attitude*. It is remarkable how, again and again, Foucault (e.g. 2003b, 2003d) returned to Kant's short, but famous, text 'What is Enlightenment?' (Kant, 1784/1949, a text which he admitted was 'something of a blazon, a fetish for (him)' (2010: 7). Most tellingly, in his final lectures on the practice of *parrhesia* (truth-telling) at the Collége de France, Foucault discusses Kant's essay at length in the first and second hour (Foucault, 2010: 1–40) and so frames the practice of *parrhesia* as exemplifying and predating the critical attitude of modernity, that questions established authorities and 'regimes of truth' that support them.

In Foucault's reframing of the Enlightenment, the task of philosophical thinking is not to tell the truth 'about' politics or to define ideal models or prescriptions for organizing society. Rather, its purpose is primarily to speak truth *to* power in whatever form such power may take. 'The task of telling the truth is an endless labour: to respect it in all its complexity is an obligation no power can do without—except by imposing the silence of slavery' (Foucault, 1988b: 267). Critique and the critical attitude are not the exclusive preserve of philosophers or other expert merchants of critique. Critique, for Foucault, is not defined by a privileged vantage point from which truths can be revealed; critique makes no claim to possess an impartial, atemporal, neutral yardstick for evaluating and judging various practices. Rather, it is a practice that accompanies—both as 'partner and adversary'—the various 'arts of governing' in seeking 'not to be governed like *that*' (Foucault, 2003b: 264, original emphasis).

32.3 INTERROGATING PROCESS: HISTORY AND DISCOURSE

Foucault's writings, we have noted, do not offer a philosophical meditation on process. Nor do they provide a metaphysics of process or a general theory of 'becoming' or change. Reading Foucault, we suggest, can instead challenge and transform our thinking, by 'substituting for the theme of becoming (general form, abstract element, first cause and universal effect, a confused mixture of the identical and the new) an analysis of *transformations* in their specificity' (Foucault, 1991b: 56, original emphasis). In this section we consider how process is interrogated with specific reference to history, discourse, and practices.

32.3.1 History as the 'Concrete Body of Becoming'

Foucault shares the Hegelian and Marxian understanding that wo/man is a product of history. But he rejects their view that historical development is *determined* by an immanent structuring principle or preceded by an essence which unfolds in the course of its movement. Following Nietzsche, the metaphysical construction of progress is denied: 'Humanity does not gradually progress from combat to combat until it arrives at a universal reciprocity, where the rule of law finally replaces warfare' (Foucault, 2003e: 358). In Foucault's understanding of history, there is no necessary movement to an end state where contradictions are finally resolved. In place of a comparatively predictable dialectical movement defined by Hegelian or Marxian contradictions, there is, for Foucault, a movement of difference (differential relations of force). The view that 'forces operating in history obey destiny or regulative mechanisms' is rejected. 'Luck' or 'Chance' does not imply the spinning of a coin but, rather, the making of luck (e.g. by developing the capacity to capitalize on events) through a mixture of chance and coincidence involving a clash of forces. 'Chance is not simply the drawing of lots but raising the stakes in every attempt to master chance through the will to power, and giving rise to the risk of an even greater chance' (2003e: 361).

For Foucault, history emerges from a path-dependent yet also unpredictable *unfolding of practices* without necessary pattern or structure (e.g. life-cycles, dialectics, etc.). Accordingly, Foucauldian genealogy studies the emergence or history of ideals, concepts, or practices and thereby 'disrupt(s) its pretended continuity' (2003e: 360). For the genealogist, history is a '*concrete body of becoming*', with its moments of intensity, its lapses, its extended periods of feverish agitation, its fainting spells' (2003e: 354, emphasis added). No underlying logic, programme, code, or causal mechanisms direct(s) its development. To posit any such necessity, Foucault argues, is to submit history to some transcendent principle outside of the specific movement of events. Like all other practices or configurations of practices, even practices that ignite or facilitate transformation are singular events; and the world is, in effect, a 'profusion of entangled events' (2003e: 361). This approach radically denies entative thinking, according to which the world consists of reified objectivities. Behind supposed unities (e.g. 'organizations' or 'individuals') there is no unifying principle that guarantees their stability and no essence to be discovered. Rather, there is an 'unstable assemblage of faults, fissures, and heterogeneous layers that threaten the fragile inheritor from within or from underneath' (2003e: 356).

Within 'the concrete body of becoming', practices are repeated, but they are never repeated in exactly the same way. Transformations are not manifestations of an underlying principle, nor are they an effect of implementing a plan of reform. Instead, they emerge from local practices and struggles. As May puts it, for Foucault history 'does not *necessarily* progress or regress. It does not *necessarily* move in a circle. It does not *necessarily* repeat anything. It may progress, or regress, or circle or repeat. But if it does, then this is because of particular local conditions that have arisen, not because it lies in the character of history itself to do so' (2006: 15, emphasis added). Foucault refuses mono-causal explanations but he also rejects randomness. History is *contingent*, but not arbitrary: it did take *this* course of development, rather than *that*. In effect, Foucault subscribes to a version of causality which recognizes that, in a given historical situation, multiple and often opposing forces are active at once. What he terms the 'procedure of causal multiplication' is adopted to provide a means of 'analysing an event according to the multiple processes which constitute it'. He explains this with an example:

> to *analyse the practice* of penal incarceration as an 'event' (not as an institutional fact of ideological effect) means to *determine the processes* of 'penalization' (that is, pro-gressive insertion into the form of legal punishment) of already existing practices of internment; the processes of 'carceralizaton' of practices of penal justice (that is, the movement by which imprisonment as a form of punishment and technique of correction becomes a central component of the penal order); ... the penalization of internment comprises a multiplicity of processes such as the formation of closed pedagogical spaces functioning through rewards and punishments, etc. (Foucault, 1991a: 76–7, emphasis added).

From this standpoint, practices and configurations of practices have a *history* and they have a *becoming*. Every new configuration of practices, such as those that he later identi-fied as 'discipline' and 'security', has its own genealogical lines of formation. One can trace back practices to previous practices. Tracing back and following the lines of trans-formation of (specific) practices does not, however, allow us to uncover some originary principle or causal mechanism from which these practices ostensibly derive. Instead it 'means making visible a *singularity* at places where there is a temptation to invoke a his-torical constant' (Foucault, 1991a: 76). Practices also have a future. As we shall show in the next section, even though the future is circumscribed by the genealogical conditions of its past, it is novel and unpredictable.

32.3.2 Discourse, Practices, and Power-Knowledge

We have noted how, for Foucault, there is no pre-given order of things that can be revealed; the 'order of things' is produced through historically specific discourses. The various (positive) sciences—including organization science—do not, from this perspec-tive, faithfully represent reality; nor can they credibly aspire, or hope, to do so. Rather, sciences are actively involved in constructing and producing the very reality which they seek to describe or explain (see Osborne and Rose, 1999; Knights, 1992). That said, and before proceeding further, it is relevant to underscore how, for Foucault, discourse is not synonymous with language; and there is no suggestion that what science seeks to capture and disclose can be changed by adopting different terms to represent or adapt it.

To understand 'discourse' as only spoken or written words forming descriptive state-ments is, from a Foucauldian perspective, symptomatic of (the retention of) repre-sentationalist thinking. Discursive practices are the local and historical contingencies which enable and constrain the knowledge-generating activities of speaking, writing, thinking, calculating, measuring, and so on. Discursive practices *produce*, rather than describe, the subjects and objects of knowledge. Discourses, Foucault writes, are not to be treated as 'groups of signs (signifying elements referring to contents or representations) *but as practices that systematically form the objects of which they speak*' (Foucault, 1989: 54, emphasis added). Such 'objects' include 'authorship', 'organization(s)', and processes of organizing. Our knowledge of reality is inescapably a contingent product of particular discursive practices organizing it, and they are unable to yield a universally credible, mirror-like reflection of it.

Foucault (2003a) demonstrates this point by showing how the humanist sense of the author, as 'genial creator', is a product or 'effect' of a particular, historical discourse. It is this discourse which renders the notion credible and seemingly self-evident. In pointing to its conditions of possibility—a set of historically contingent rules within an order of discourse—Foucault shows how a particular (humanist) sense of authorship is rendered authoritative. By attending to questions such as 'How, under what conditions, and in what forms can something like the subject appear in the order of discourse?' 'What place can it occupy in each type of discourse, what functions can it assume, and by obeying what rules?' (Foucault, 2003a: 390) he signals the possibility of subverting and resisting, rather than accepting and reproducing, a system of dependencies, such as the system which lends authority to the humanist notion of authorship.

In his earlier (archaeological) writings, Foucault focuses upon *how subjects and objects of knowledge* are formed by historically specific rules of discourse. He does not exclude practices from consideration but, at this point, he does not seek to explicate how practices and discourse are related, intertwined, or fused. It is only later, starting with his first major genealogical study, *Discipline and Punish*, that Foucault explicitly shifts his understanding and analysis of the formation of subjects/subjectivities towards *practices*. So doing, he contends that 'the subject who knows, the objects to be known and the modalities of knowledge must be regarded as so many effects of these fundamental implications of power-knowledge and their historical transformations' (Foucault, 1977: 28). Practices are understood to be embedded within *a nexus of power-knowledge relations* that are themselves reproduced and transformed through practices. The nexus—that is, the hyphen in the power-knowledge relations—is *practices*. This shift of attentiveness from the rules of discourse to practices does not, in our view, imply that the earlier work is misconceived or redundant. Instead, it serves to correct any suggestion of an abstraction of discourse from practices and extends the exploration of constitutive forces. Reappraising his work, Foucault reflects:

> In this piece of research [*Discipline and Punish*], as in my earlier work, the target of analysis wasn't 'institutions', 'theories' or 'ideology', but *practices*—with the aim of grasping the conditions which make these acceptable at a given moment…It is a question of analysing a 'regime of practices'—*practices being understood here as places where what is said and what is done, rules imposed and reasons given, the planned and the taken for granted meet and interconnect.* (Foucault, 1991a: 75, original emphasis; second emphasis added).

A focus on the nexus of power-knowledge relations is, albeit in embryonic form, present even in Foucault's inaugural lecture at the Collège de France (*The Order of Discourse*). In this lecture he develops the argument 'that in every society the production of discourse is at once controlled, selected, organised and redistributed by a certain number of procedures whose role is to ward off its powers and dangers, to gain mastery over its chance events, to evade its ponderous, formidable materiality' (Foucault, 1981a: 52). A system of limitations and restrictions is a necessary condition for discourse to be effective: 'Exchange and communication are positive figures working inside complex systems of restriction, and probably would not be able to function independently of them' (Foucault, 1981a: 62). Discourse can only constitute meaning via such limitations and restrictions. In fact, meaning is an effect of these limitations. Moreover, as we noted earlier, discourse does not represent 'reality out there' but, instead, (violently) imposes its own principle of order:

> the world is not the accomplice of our knowledge; there is no prediscursive providence which disposes the world in our favour. We must conceive discourse as a violence which we do to things, or in any case as a practice which we impose on them; and it is in this practice that the events of discourse find the principle of regularity. (Foucault, 1981a: 67)

For Foucault—in contrast to phenomenology—there is no lived experience, or essential property, to which analysis can refer as a benchmark of validation. That is because the specification of any such benchmark is itself a product of discourse, ad infinitum. There is only the field of knowledge 'defined by a specific combination of the visible and the sayable' (Webb, 2003: 127). Foucault's critics have characterized his position as solipsistic or relativistic. What such criticism fails to take into account is Foucault's assumption of a gap between the ineffable reality of the world, which includes our 'lived experience', and our knowledge of it. It is discourse—or discursive practices—that constitutes what we can know, and so conditions but does not determine what we feel and perceive. The conditions are themselves a set of transformable rules and are 'in each case a singular crystallization of a complex set of changing relations, actions, rules, and practices' (Webb, 2003: 127).

The understanding of the subject as an 'effect of discourse' and a 'product' of power-infused practices invites the question of the scope for self-formation that is not reduced or reducible to these practices and relations. It is in his later writings that Foucault considers the possibilities of active self-formation that is related to and effected by the historical conditions without being determined by them. More specifically, he explores the possibility of self-creation and ethical self-formation through 'practices of the self' (Foucault 1986a, 1986b, 1997)—a possibility that is opened by the limited capacity of discursive and non-discursive practices to form a closed system that finally excludes all 'outside' and so impedes self-formation and the related capacity to enable it (see also Deleuze, 1988). In a retrospective comment on the 'death of man', proclaimed in *The Order of Things* (1970: 340–3), Foucault offers a clarification of what otherwise might be taken as his endorsement of a deterministic position:[2]

> *Men [sic] are perpetually engaged in a process* that, in constituting objects, at the same time displaces man, deforms, transforms, and transfigures him as subject. In speaking of the death of man, in a confused, simplifying way, that is what I meant to say. (Foucault, 2000: 276, emphasis added)

Even if the understanding of subjects as effects of historically contingent discourses and products of power-infused practices radically questions humanistic conceptions of autonomy, it does not deny or exclude the possibility of 'struggles *against* subjection' and 'struggles *for* a new subjectivity' (Foucault, 1982a: 212–13, emphasis added). On the contrary, denaturalizing the self and revealing its constitution in contingent power-knowledge relations opens the way to redefine the (humanist) task of 'discovering' or liberating an essential human subject. It is a task characterized by Foucault as an endeavour 'to discover one's true self, to separate it from that which might obscure and alienate it, to decipher its truth' (Foucault, 1982b: 245). Distancing himself from a moral (e.g. Sartrean) notion of 'authenticity', Foucault insists that '(f)rom the idea that the self is not given to us, I think that there is only one practical consequence: we have to create ourselves as works of art' (1982b: 237). It is precisely because there is no given or essential self that subjects are repeatedly challenged to engage in a process of self-(trans)formation. For Foucault, this process of creative self-formation is thoroughly historically rooted. It is also inherently political as it involves a *refusal* of normalizing (scientific, administrative, and moral) conceptions that define and fix 'who we are' *and* prompts an experimental practice that disrupts and surpasses historically sedimented conceptions of identity and the self; and so promotes struggles for 'a new subjectivity' (Foucault, 1982a: 213). So, when Foucault asserts that 'the target nowadays is not to *discover* what we are, but to *refuse* what we are' (1982a: 216), this injunction must be interpreted in the context of a radical anti-essentialism that challenges normalized and normalizing conceptions of the self that (arbitrarily) delimit the field of our possibilities. Foucault's 'refusal' is not simply a denial. It is, paradoxically, a 'non-positive affirmation' (Foucault, 1998: 74) that opens the possibility of a 'politics of ourselves' (Allen, 2011)—a process of a self-creation that moves us beyond established and conventionalised identities. Such self-creation does not lie in the distance from, or absence of, power-infused ensemble of practices. Instead, it resides in the 'historically fragile and contingent ways we are folded into it, just as we ourselves are folds of it' (May, 2005: 528). So, when considering the possibility of (active) self-creation through 'practices of the self', Foucault does not posit an ahistorical self that exists before or beyond discourses and practices. Instead, he maintains that there is an infinite number of ways of 'folding the forces' operating on us (Deleuze, 1988; Rose, 1998). Such 'folding' is inevitably bound to practices but, as Foucault makes clear, 'these practices are nevertheless not something invented by the individual himself. They are models he [sic] finds in his culture and are proposed, suggested, imposed upon him by his culture, his society, his social group' (Foucault, 1997: 291). It is in a permanent actualizing of the 'critical attitude' (Foucault, 2003b) in relation to our present practices, and how they govern our relations to self and others, that new forms of subjectivity are created: a work in process rather than an outcome or result.

32.4 ORGANIZATION STUDIES

We move from our reading of evolving themes in 'Foucault' to the engagement of his writings by students of organization(s). Here we encounter some turbulence, even disorientation. As Knights (2002, 2004) has observed, the tendency has been for organization scholars to 'write Foucault into organization theory' as they take established agenda(s) as a point of departure, and so read (or plunder) Foucault as a source for strengthening established frameworks of perceiving organizational phenomena such as control in organizations. More rare has been an interest in how organizational analysis might be 'written into Foucault' (Knights, 2002) so that established frameworks of analysis become problematic. In this section, we selectively identify some of the more influential Foucauldian contributions to organization studies.

32.4.1 Panopticism

The idea of the Panopticon, which Foucault analysed in *Discipline and Punish* (1977: 195–228), has been seized upon to develop or provide fresh momentum to established areas of organization studies such as control in the workplace (e.g. Ortmann, 1984; Sewell and Wilkinson, 1992; Zuboff, 1988). A version of Foucault was brought to a wider audience as his thinking was shown to provide inter alia a distinctive and comparatively accessible illumination of workplace relations. More questionable is whether the reading of Foucault privileged by such analyses sufficiently brought out Foucault's idea of an evolving and dynamic reality. Burrell, for example, when considering the Panopticon, contends that Foucault's 'real point' is that 'as individuals we are incarcerated within an organizational world…whilst we may not live in total institutions, the institutional organization of our lives is total. It is in this sense that Foucault's comment "prisons resemble factories, schools, barracks, hospitals which all resemble prisons" has to be understood' (Burrell, 1988: 232). A decontextualized reading of such a comment stands in danger of disregarding the ethico-political intent of Foucauldian genealogies.[3] When adopted or recycled in 'Foucauldianism', the contention that 'the institutional organization of our lives is total' (Burrell, 1988: 232), in which incarcerated actors are stripped of agency, presents a straw target for those who, quite justifiably, find it unconvincing (e.g. Reed, 1997, 1988, 2000). The incongruity arises when invocations of the Panopticon are abstracted from Foucault's genealogical (historical) perspective. As a consequence, it omits appreciation of how, in Foucault's analysis, the 'panoptic diagram' has been formed in a contingent history, and is itself evolving and transforming (see also Deleuze, 1988; Foucault, 2007).

32.4.2 Resistance, Governmentality, and the Apparatus of Security

Empirical studies of organization that draw on Foucault's work, and in particular on his relational understanding of power (Foucault, 1981b: 92–102), have illustrated how infinite forms of resistance emerge in the context of organizations and continuously serve to undermine, to reform, and to reshape the form of imposed orders. Foucault's work on 'discipline' and 'disciplinary power' continues to be a major source of inspiration for critical studies of organization (e.g. Clegg, 1998; McKinlay and Starkey, 1998; Hatchuel et al., 2005). However, it has also been argued that we now live in, or are entering an era of, 'fluid modernity', which, as Bauman (2001: 11) puts it, is 'post-Panoptical'. The 'disciplinary world of *l'employé*' (Jacques, 1996: 98), where organizations can be understood as 'enclosed spaces', and are populated by docile, normalized subjects, it is suggested, is becoming less recognizable. In so far as processes of financialization and social mediatization are succouring comparatively dynamic and fluid—'post-bureaucratic'—organizations, employee creativity and subjectivity are increasingly seen as 'human capital' to be mobilized and churned, rather than as an unruly capacity that must be 'moulded' into disciplined patterns of identity. In this context, scholarship informed primarily by Foucault's analysis of the 'panoptic diagram' and the disciplinary mode of governing organizations/social relations may become less credible.

To counteract and rebalance studies that exhibit 'Foucauldianism', students of organization have turned to Foucault's later works, where he explores the ethics of antiquity (Foucault, 1986a, 1986b), and complements the analytics of power with notions of 'biopolitics', the 'apparatus of security', and (neoliberal) 'governmentality' (Foucault, 1981b, 2007, 2008). Notably, inspiration has been drawn from an understanding of ethics where the focus is on processes of self-creation and self-governing (e.g. Ibarra-Colado et al., 2006; Crane, Knights, Starkey, 2008; Chan and Garrick, 2002; Starkey and Hatchuel et al., 2002; McMurray et al., 2011; Weiskopf and Willmott, 2013). Related studies have explored how contemporary practices and technologies of the self are reframed in the neoliberal context of 'enterprise', enabling forms of 'self-stylization on the flows of business, or a self-management indistinguishable form corporate management' (Spoelstra, 2007: 302).

Foucault's lectures on 'biopolitics' and the 'apparatus of security' (2007, 2008) extend the conceptual means of understanding and problematizing technologies and practices of organizing work relations, and of governing (various) process(es), including processes of subjectification. We have noted how attention in earlier analyses mainly centres on the disciplinary techniques enabling modes of governing by fixing and defining movement, *prescribing* actions and sequences in a process (Townley, 1993, 1994). Foucault's later work explores how discipline is modified and supplemented with regulatory techniques that he calls 'security' or the 'apparatus of security'. These new techniques are better understood as *regulating* flows enabling the controlled circulation of various resources, including the 'human resources' in comparatively open and self-generating networks. These techniques seek to influence a 'milieu' (Foucault, 2008: 20): action is brought to bear on the 'rules of the game' rather than on the players; processes are governed by providing general incentives and disincentives for promoting and developing entrepreneurial orientations in a population (Weiskopf and Munro, 2012).

The 'apparatus of security' incorporates and welcomes the exercise of discretion, in contrast to 'discipline' which *prescribes* actions and movements in some detail. In the 'apparatus of security', individual responsibility for making choices is actively promoted and incentivized: the apparatus constructs and channels employee 'freedom' in particular directions. As a form of power, government refers to the 'conduct of conduct' (Foucault, 2007) and so has extensive application—notably, through liberal and neoliberal forms of governmentality (McNay, 2009). A common example is the use of performance or output metrics which do not simply impose an ideal norm (as disciplinary regulation does), but derive the norm(al) from the measurement of reality itself (the average number is the norm). These metrics do not contrive to eliminate freedom by dictating precisely how a desired outcome is to be achieved. Instead, the metrics reward discretion when its exercise boosts short-term performance as shown by the measure. The introduction of rankings, ratings, performance indicators, benchmarking techniques, and the like permits 'continuous improvement' rather than adaptation to a fixed norm. It is a new, dynamic form of 'flexible normalism' (Link, 2004) encouraging subjects to adapt and 'be creative' in response to the development of new metrics and the continuous shifting of thresholds. In contrast to the panoptic ideal of establishing 'an economic geometry of a "house of certainty"' (Foucault, 1977: 202), the 'apparatus of security' is favoured as a means of influencing and managing 'space(s) in which a series of uncertain elements unfold' (Foucault, 2008: 20). Its application renders a population (e.g. of citizens or employees) more governable in circumstances where efforts to eliminate, rather than regulate, the exercise of discretion would likely falter or eventuate in poorer performance.

The apparatus of security incorporates liberal principles of laissez-faire and supplements the associated freedoms with technologies of control that allow for the management of the risks and dangers associated with these freedoms (Miller and Rose, 2008; Power, 2007). The 'freedom' attributed to subjects is orchestrated, rather than tightly controlled. Foucauldian studies of neoliberal governmentality have examined the reshaping of public and private organizations through the neoliberal discourse of enterprise (du Gay, 1996, 2004)—a discourse inviting employees to understand and conduct themselves in an enterprising manner so as to cultivate their own 'human capital'. When conceived as human capital, the working subject becomes an 'abilities machine' incorporating pressing requirements to continuously modulate and reconfigure its abilities in response to the demands of competitiveness and threats of obsolescence (Foucault, 2008: 224–6). In a post-disciplinary (neoliberal) framing of the employment relationship 'continuous improvement' through 'learning' is advanced as a strategy to maintain employability and is routinely linked to the concept of self-responsibility (Burchell et al., 1991). Characteristically, the normative construction of the autonomous, creative, and ever-active artist/entrepreneur who constantly (re-)invents himself or herself serves as a subjectivizing norm or model which supports a readiness and openness to change. 'Thinking differently', 'becoming other than one is', and 'making one's life a work of art', which Foucault saw as attempts to break out of a regulated and conventionalized world, are rapidly becoming a norm itself; in the words of Tom Peters: 'Be distinct . . . or extinct!' (Peters, 2001, front cover). This illustrates a mode of governing that is based on the idea of 'optimization of difference' (Foucault, 2008: 259) rather than imposing a (stable) disciplinary order.

32.4.3 'The Subject' and the Question of Freedom

Studies which engage Foucault's concept of 'governmentality' challenge and counteract a reading of Foucault as an author whose work amounts to 'little more than an elaboration of Weber's "iron cage" argument' (Starkey and McKinlay, 1998: 231). Still, there is a risk of regarding the subject as passive consumer of neoliberal discourse, for example, in studies that focus on the 'enterprising up' of individuals and organizations (see du Gay, 2004). As Bardon and Josserand (2011: 498) suggest, there are two broad stratagems for addressing this issue. One is to assume an 'essentialist ground for action' that exists before or beyond discourse; a second one is to recognize the heterogeneity of discourses and practices from which a sense of agency derives.

The second—anti-essentialist—stratagem is consistent with a radical ontology of becoming that is implied by Foucault's historicization of the subject, and of subjectivity. This does not mean that there is 'nothing outside discourse than more discourse' (Reed, 2000: 525). It is just that what is outside of discourse—a dynamic and shifting field of forces—is knowable only through heterogeneous (power-invested) discourses. There is no difficulty in acknowledging 'materialities' so long as they are recognized to be 'actions upon the actions of others' (Foucault, 1982a: 221); and that their identification is discursive, and thus the product of particular discursive practices, and not a reflection of reality.

Paradoxically, the disappearance of the autonomous 'subject', which follows from the acknowledgement of the multiple discourses and practices that make the subject, facilitates the possibility of overcoming or transgressing what is otherwise taken for granted. It invites us to 'follow the distribution of gaps and breaches, and watch out for openings this disappearance uncovers' (Foucault, 2003a: 380), and thereby to engage in self-(trans)formation. That said, processes of self-creation, or self-formation take place *in relation* to a set of norms established and sedimented in a historical process (Bernauer and Mahon, 2006; Butler, 2005). The possibility of critical reflexivity allows historically situated subjects to form and shape themselves not only within but also *in relation to* the normative matrix that defines modes of being. This possibility opens up the path to an ethico-politics of ourselves which questions and problematizes 'who we are' (our historically constituted identities and the institutional framework and technologies of government that supports them) and engages in individual and collective processes of self-formation.

32.5 CONCLUSION

In Foucault's thinking, knowledge is historicized and representationalist accounts (e.g. those generated by the human sciences) are destabilized. Through this destabilization, historically specific 'regimes of truth' that define and fix 'who we are' are denaturalized, and the knowing subject as an autonomous subject of knowledge is deconstructed. By attending to the practices which constitute and organize our relations to self, others, and to things, Foucault prompts us, in our study of organization(s), for example, to pose questions such as: how are subjectivities produced, maintained, and transformed within and through (historically specific) discourses and practices of organizing? What limitations are imposed on us by various forms and modes of governing such relations? And what are the conditions and possibilities for transforming these limitations/practices through an inventive ethico-politics of organizing that questions and problematizes established configurations of practices and moves us beyond contingent limitations?

For Foucault, thinking is a situated practice of reflection that is embedded in a specific historic and societal context. Such thinking, or what Foucault terms 'philosophical activity', is context-dependent; but it is not determined by its context. Rather, it is distinguished by the creation of a distance to contexts—a distance that can be more or less intentionally valued and expanded. Where the distance is increased, it tends to disrupt contexts and initiate new contexts as it fosters a 'displacement and transformation of frameworks of thinking, the changing of received values'. Such transformative thinking is inclusive of 'all the work that has been done to think otherwise, to do something else, to become other than what one is' (Foucault, 2003c: 179). Such thinking does not proceed in a linear progression—for example, as an activity of incremental 'theory building', or as a way of approaching the truth step by step; and it is not preoccupied with separating what is true and false. It is, instead, concerned primarily with reflecting upon our relationship to truth, or what is held to be true. It involves a 'movement by which . . . one detaches oneself from what is accepted as true and seeks other rules' (Foucault, 2003c: 179). It is demanding as well as disorientating, as it interrogates the preconditions of our being; and it thereby invites, risks, or compels a transformation of self.

Such thinking, we have suggested, might inspire an ethico-politics of organizing, which is (necessarily) situated within historically specific relations of power. It extends an invitation to explore and expand the possibility of participating in organization(s), including those of academia, in ways that necessarily involve power of power and do not eliminate domination, yet nonetheless endeavour to minimize it. As Foucault (1997: 298) observes, the vision and practice of an ethico-politics of organizing 'is not of trying to dissolve them [relations of power] in the utopia of completely transparent communication'. Rather, it is to develop 'the rules of law, the management techniques, and also the morality, the ethos, the practice of the self, that will allow us to play these games of power with as little domination as possible' (Foucault, 1997: 298).

Notes

1. Foucault's relation to Kant—which begins with his doctoral thesis comprising a translation of Kant's *Anthropology* and an original introduction to it (Foucault, 2008)—is complex, and it is therefore misleading to identify him simply as 'anti-modernist' or 'postmodernist'.
2. Foucault's anti-humanism provided a valuable corrective to the self-regarding, anthropocentric folly of humanism. It is important to appreciate that Foucault's critique of humanism did not simply or primarily reduce the subject to 'a standardised product of some discourse formation' (Habermas, 1987: 293). Rather, it presents a timely challenge to the excessive centring of 'man' within humanist analysis, and so opens a space for exploring the historically contingent rules of subject formation (Knights and Willmott, 2002). See also Allen (2000).
3. The ethico-political intent of such analysis is to 'free thought from what it silently thinks and so enable it to think differently' (Foucault, 1984a: 16–17, in Bardon and Josserand, 2011: 500) and thereby 'transfigure the taken-for-granted hierarchy of values and practice our liberty' (Bardon and Josserand, 2011: 500).

References

Allen, A. (2000). The Anti-Subjective Hypothesis: Michel Foucault and the Death of the Subject, *The Philosophical Forum* 31(2): 113–30.

——(2011). Foucault and the Politics of Our Selves, *History of the Human Sciences* 24(4): 43–59.

Bardon, T. and Josserand, E. (2011). A Nietzschean Reading of Foucauldian Thinking: Constructing a Project of the Self within an Ontology of Becoming, *Organization* 18(4): 497–515.

Bauman, Z. (2001). *Liquid Modernity* (Cambridge: Polity Press).

Bernauer, J.W. and Mahon, M. (2006). Michel Foucault: Ethical Imagination, in G. Gutting (ed.), *The Cambridge Companion to Foucault* (Cambridge: Cambridge University Press): 149–75.

Burchell, G., Gordon, C., and Miller, P. (eds) (1991). *The Foucault Effect. Studies in Governmentality* (London: Harvester Wheatsheaf).

Burrell, G. (1988). Modernism, Postmodernism and Organizational Analysis: The Contribution of Michel Foucault, *Organizational Studies* 9(2): 221–35.

Butler, J. (2005). *Giving an Account of Oneself* (New York: Fordham University Press).

Chan, A. and Garrick, J. (2002). Organization Theory in Turbulent Times: The Traces of Foucault's Ethics, *Organization* 9(4): 683–701.

Chia, R. (2000). Discourse Analysis as Organizational Analysis, *Organization* 7(3): 513–18.

Clegg, S. (1998). Foucault, Power and Organizations, in A. McKinlay and K. Starkey (eds), *Foucault, Management and Organization Theory* (London: Sage): 29–48.

Crane, A., Knights, D., and Starkey, K. (2008). The Conditions of our Freedom: Foucault, Organization and Ethics, *Business Ethics Quarterly* 18(3): 299–320.

Deleuze, G. (1988). *Foucault*, trans. S. Hand (Minneapolis: University of Minnesota Press).

——(1995). *Negotiations. 1972–1990* (New York: Columbia University Press).

Eribon, D. (1994). *Michel Foucault et ses contemporains* (Paris: Fayard).

Foucault, M. (1965). *Madness and Civilization: A History of Insanity in the Age of Reason*, trans. R. Howard (New York: Random House).

——(1970). *The Order of Things* (London: Tavistock).

——(1977). *Discipline and Punish. The Birth of the Prison*, trans. A. Sheridan (London: Penguin Books).

—— (1981a). The Order of Discourse. Inaugural Lecture at the Collège de France, given 2 December 1970, in R. Young (ed.), *Untying the Text: A Post-Structuralist Reader* (Boston: Routledge & Kegan Paul): 51–78.

——(1981b). *The History of Sexuality. Volume 1*, trans. R. Hurley (London: Penguin Books).

——(1982a). Afterword by Michel Foucault: The Subject and Power, in H.L. Dreyfus and P. Rabinow (eds), *Michel Foucault. Beyond Structuralism and Hermeneutics*, 2nd edn (Chicago: University of Chicago Press): 208–28.

——(1982b). On the Genealogy of Ethics: An Overview of Work in Progress, in H. Dreyfus and P. Rabinow (eds), *Michel Foucault. Beyong Structuralism and Hermeneutics* (Chicago: University of Chicago Press): 229–52.

—— (1986a). *The Use of Pleasure. The History of Sexuality: Volume Two*, trans. A. Sheridan (London: Penguin Books).

—— (1986b). *The Care of the Self—The History of Sexuality: Volume Three*, trans. R. Hurley (London: Penguin Books).

——(1989). *Archeology of Knowledge* (London: Routledge).

——(1991a). Questions of Method, in G. Burchell, C. Gordon, and P. Miller (eds), *The Foucault Effect* (London: Harvester Wheatsheaf): 73–86.

——(1991b). Politics and the Study of Discourse, in G. Burchell, C. Gordon, and P. Miller (eds), *The Foucault Effect* (London: Harvester Wheatsheaf): 53–86.

——(1997). The Ethics of the Concern for the Self as a Practice of Freedom, in P. Rabinow (ed.), *Michel Foucault. Ethics. Subjectivity and Truth* (New York: The New Press): 281–301.

——(2000). Interview with Michel Foucault, in J. Faubion (ed.), *The Essential Works of Michel Foucault, Volume 3: Power* (New York: New Press): 449–53.

——(2001). Entretien avec Michel Foucault (avec D. Tromadori), in D. Defert and F. Ewald (eds), *Dits et Écrits II, 1976–1988* (Paris: Quarto Gallimard): 860–74.

—— (2003a). What is an Author, in P. Rabinow and N. Rose (eds), *The Essential Foucault. Selections form Essential Works of Foucault, 1954–1984* (New York and London: The New Press): 378–91.

—— (2003b). What is Critique?, in P. Rabinow and N. Rose (eds), *The Essential Foucault. Selections from the Essential Works of Foucault 1954–1984* (New York and London: New Press): 263–78.

——(2003c). The Masked Philosopher, in P. Rabinow and N. Rose (eds), *The Essential Foucault. Selections form the Essential Works of Foucault 1954–1984* (New York and London: The New Press): 174–9.

——(2003d). What is Enlightenment, in P. Rabinow and N. Rose (eds), *The Essential Foucault. Selections from the Essential Works of Foucault, 1954–1984* (New York and London: The New Press): 43–57.

——(2003e). Nietzsche, Genealogy and History, in P. Rabinow and N. Rose (eds), *The Essential Foucault. Selections from the Essential Works of Foucault, 1954–1984* (New York and London: The New Press): 351–69.

——(2003f). Foucault, in P. Rabinow and N. Rose (eds), *The Essential Foucault. Selections from the Essential Works of Foucault, 1954–1984* (New York and London: The New Press): 1–17.

—— (2003g). *Society Must Be Defended: Lectures at the Collège de France, 1975–76*, trans. D. Macey (New York: Picador).

—— (2007). *Security, Territory, Population. Lectures at the Collège de France 1977–78* (London: Palgrave Macmillan).

——(2008a). *The Birth of Biopolitics. Lectures at the Collège de France 1978–1979* (London: Palgrave Macmillan).

——(2008b). *Introduction to Kant's Anthropology* (Los Angeles: Semiotext(e)).

——(2010). *The Government of Self and Others. Lectures at the Collège de France 1982–1983*, trans. G. Burchell (London: Palgrave Macmillan).

—— (2011). *The Courage of Truth. Lectures at the Collège de France. 1982–1983* (Houndsmills: Palgrave Macmillan).

du Gay, P. (1996). *Consumption and Identity at Work* (London: Sage).

——(2004). Against 'Enterprise' (but not against 'enterprise', for that would make no sense), *Organization* 11(1): 37–57.

Habermas, J. (1987). *The Philosophical Discourse of Modernity: Twelve Lectures*, trans. F. Lawrence (Cambridge, MA: MIT Press).

Hatchuel, A., Pezet, É., Starkey, K., and Lenay, O. (2005). *Gouvernement, organisation et gestion: l'héritage de Michel Foucault* (Québec: Les Presses de l'Université Laval).

Ibarra-Colado, E., Clegg, S., Rhodes, C., and Kornberger, M. (2006). Ethics of Managerial Subjectivity, *Journal of Business Ethics* 64: 45–55.

Jacques, R. (1996). *Manufacturing the Employee. Management Knowledge from the 19th to 21st Centuries* (London: Sage).

Jones, C. (2002). Foucault's Inheritance/Inheriting Foucault, *Culture and Organization* 8(3): 225–38.

Kant, I. (1784/1949). What is Enlightenment, in C.J. Friedrich (ed.), *The Philosophy of Immanuel Kant* (New York: Random House): 132–9.

Knights, D. (1992). Changing Spaces: The Disruptive Impact of a New Epistemological Location for the Study of Management, *Accademy of Management Review* 17(3): 514–36.

——(2002). Writing Organizational Analysis into Foucault, *Organization* 9: 575–93.

——(2004). Michel Foucault, in S. Linstead (ed.), *Organization Theory and Postmodern Thought* (London: Sage): 14–33.

——and Willmott, H. (1989). Power and Subjectivity at Work, *Sociology* 24(3): 535–58.

———(2002). Autonomy as Utopia and Dystopia, in M. Parker (ed.), *Utopia and Organization* (London: Sage): 59–81.

Link, J. (2004). From the 'Power of the Norm' to 'Flexible Normalism': Considerations after Foucault, *Cultural Critique* 57(Spring): 14–32.

Luxon, N. (2008). Ethics and Subjectivity. Practices of Self-Governance in the Late Lectures of Michel Foucault, *Political Theory* 36(3): 377–402.

May, T. (2003). Foucault's Relation to Phenomenology, in G. Gutting (ed.), *The Cambridge Companion to Foucault* (Cambridge: Cambridge University Press): 284–311.

——(2005). To Change the World, to Celebrate Life. Merleau-Ponty and Foucault on the Body, *Philosophy & Social Criticism* 31(5–6): 517–31.

——(2006). *The Philosophy of Foucault* (Chesham: Acumen).

McKinlay, A. and Starkey, K. (eds) (1998). *Foucault, Management and Organization Theory. From Panopticon to Technologies of the Self* (London: Sage).

McMurray, R., Pullen, A., and Rhodes, C. (2011). Ethical Subjectivity and Politics in Organizations: A Case of Health Care Tendering, *Organization* 18(4): 541–61.

McNay, L. (2009). Self as Enterprise: Dilemmas of Control and Resistance in Foucault's The Birth of Biopolitics, *Theory, Culture and Society* 26(6): 55–77.

Miller, P. and Rose, N. (2008). *Governing the Present. Administering Economic, Social and Personal Life* (Cambridge: Polity).

O'Leary, T. (2002). *Foucault and the Art of Ethics* (London and New York: Continuum).

Ortmann, G. (1984). *Der zwingende Blick. Personalinformationssysteme als Architektur der Disziplin* (Frankfurt am Main: Campus).

Osborne, T. and Rose, N. (1999). Do the Social Sciences Create Phenomena?: The Example of Public Opinion Research, *British Journal of Sociology* 50(3): 367–96.

Peters, T. (2001). *Reinventing Work. The Brand you 50. Or: Fifty Ways to Transform Yourself from an 'Employee' into a Brand that Shouts Distinction, Commitment, and Passion!* (New York: Alfred A. Knopf & Inc).

Power, M. (2007). *Organized Uncertainty. Designing a World of Risk Management* (Oxford: Oxford University Press).

Rabinow, P. and Rose, N. (2003). Introduction. Foucault Today, in P. Rabinow and N. Rose (eds), *The Essential Foucault. Selections from Essential Works of Foucault, 1954–1984* (New York: The New Press): vii–xxxv.

Reed, M. (1997). In Praise of Duality and Dualism: Rethinking Agency and Structure in Organizational Analysis, *Organization Studies* 18(1): 21–42.

—— (1998). Organizational Analysis as Discourse Analysis, in D. Grant, T. Keenoy, and C. Oswick (eds), *Discourse and Organization* (London: Sage): 193–213.

—— (2000). The Limits of Discourse Analysis in Organizational analysis, *Organization* 7(3): 524–30.

Rose, N. (1998). *Inventing our Selves. Psychology, Power and Personhood* (Cambridge: Cambridge University Press).

Sewell, G. and Wilkinson, B. (1992). 'Someone to Watch Over Me': Surveillance, Discipline and the Just-in-Time Labour Process, *Sociology* 26(2): 271–89.

Spoelstra, S. (2007). Book Review: Foucault on Philosophy and Self-management, *Organization* 14(2): 299–303.

Starkey, K. and Hatchuel, A. (2002). The Long Detour: Foucault's History of Desire and Pleasure, *Organization* 9(4): 641–56.

—— and McKinley, A. (1998). Afterword: Deconstructing Organization—Discipline and Desire, in A. McKinlay and K. Starkey (eds), *Foucault, Management and Organization Theory* (London: Sage): 230–41.

Townley, B. (1993). Foucault, Power/Knowledge, and its Relevance for Human Resource Management, *Academy of Management Review* 18(3): 518–45.

—— (1994). *Reframing Human Resource Management. Power, Ethics and the Subject at Work* (London: Sage).

Webb, D. (2003). On Friendship: Derrida, Foucault and the Practice of Becoming, *Research in Phenomenology* 33: 119–40.

Weiskopf, R. and Munro, I. (2012). Management of Human Capital: Discipline, Security and Controlled Circulation in HRM, *Organization* 19(6): 685–702.

—— and Willmott, H. (2013). Ethics as Critical Practice: 'The Pentagon Papers', Deciding Responsibly, Truth-Telling, and the Unsettling of Organizational Morality, *Organization Studies* 34(4): 469–93.

Zuboff, S. (1988). *In the Age of the Smart Machine. The Future of Work and Power* (Oxford: Heinemann).

CHAPTER 33

··

LUCE IRIGARAY (1930b)

··

HEATHER HÖPFL

33.1 AGAINST 'REASONABLE' WORDS

Turn everything upside down, inside out, back to front. *Rack it with radical convulsions*, carry back, reimport, those crises that her 'body' suffers in her impotence to say what disturbs her. Insist also and deliberately upon those *blanks* in discourse which recall the places of her exclusion, and which by their *silent plasticity*, ensure the cohesion, the articulation, the coherent expansion of established forms...deconstruct the logic grid of the reader-writer, drive him out of his mind... *Overthrow syntax* by suspending its eternally teleological order.

(Irigaray, 1974/1985: 142, italics in the original)

33.2 ON THE IMPOSSIBILITY OF MOVEMENT

How is it possible to begin to write about Irigaray after such an exhortation: after such a passionate demand for redress against the 'lexicon' (Irigaray, 1974/1985: 142)? Not only does Irigaray resist all attempts to categorize her, she has clearly stated her dislike of attempts to solicit her personal views or to probe her personal life (Irigaray, 1983: 192–202). She has been clear in her contention that, as a woman whose work poses a radical challenge not least to teleological order, she does not want to be reduced to her biography (Whitford, 1991: 2) as others before her, for instance Simone de Beauvoir, have been. It has been Irigaray's opposition to being *reduced by biography* which has made her difficult to capture by those who would reduce her work to the political or the personal or even to attempt to present an overview of her work. Her work has come under attack from critics within feminism who have tended to apply the same type of simplification and reductionism that have been found more widely amongst critics of her work. Whitford (1991) observes that before it is possible to discuss Irigaray's work it is necessary to bear in mind that most of the criticism of her work antedates the publication of the translation of her work into English, that there is a simple assumption that she is essentialist in her views, that she sees a relationship between the body and the 'true' self, also that she is one of the so called 'Holy Trinity' of French feminists and, with Kristeva and Cixous, a champion of *écriture feminine*. Indeed, Whitford contends that this simplification enables a bracketing of these three writers to the extent that their individual work is diminished by a further theoretical and political reductionism (Whitford, 1991: 2). Finally, Whitford puts forward the view that it is mainly Irigaray's (1977/1985) work, *This Sex Which Is Not One*, that has allowed the view to emerge that what she has written on writing and the body, 'writing the body', represents the entirety of her work. Be that as it may, a series of issues emerge. How is it possible to write about Irigaray and in a volume such as this, when she calls on women to 'make it impossible for a while to predict whence, whither, when, how, why...something goes by or goes on: will come, will spread, will reverse, will cease moving' (Irigaray, 1974/1985: 142)? Even the question falls within the ambit of the lexicon which she seeks to destroy. Rather, she invites us to 'speak only in riddles, allusions, hints, parables...to the limits of exasperation' (Irigaray, 1974/1985: 143). And so it is only possible to begin from a position of paralysis against which every movement is a movement away from Irigaray's insight and intent, the product of 'hysterical repressions [a]nd their paralytic signifying-effects' (Irigaray, 1977/1985: 118). In 'Writing as a Woman' (chapter 6 of her book *Je, Tu, Nous* (1990/1991: 53)), Irigaray says, 'I am a woman. I write with who I am. Why shouldn't that be valid unless out of contempt for the value of women or from the denial of a culture in which the sexual is a significant subjective and objective dimension? But how could I on the one hand be a woman, and on the other, a writer?' And she adds, 'I am a woman. I do not write *as a* woman' (italics added).

Here, she is identifying the problem of what it is to be a woman within the phallogocentric discourse: what it is to be constructed in a way which conforms to patriarchal notions of order and authority, and what it is to be regulated by representations which are at variance with embodied experience.

This dilemma cannot be avoided in a *Handbook* such as this, and is perhaps an ironic comment on it and this chapter. The very nature of the volume produces the inevitability of falling into the lexicon and delivering precisely the sort of discourse which flies entirely in the face of Irigaray's work and ideas. Her background in philosophy and psychoanalysis, arts, and linguistics lead her towards identifying a new working space. She is working in the flux of ideas which redefine women whom she sees as being *excluded* from the *project* of philosophy. Unable or unwilling to capture her life history in order to draw parallels between her work and her experience, and yet unequivocal in a commitment to 'snipping the wires, cutting the current, breaking the circuits' (1990/1991: 142), there is undeniably a position where motion ceases and a loss of voluntary movement takes over. So, according to Irigaray's notion of access to the prevailing ideology (1990/1991: 142), if this chapter is to be written at all, it requires mimicry: a pretence of reconciliation with the lexicon. Or as Irigaray puts it, through a strategy of mimesis, 'one must assume the feminine role deliberately ... To play with mimesis is thus, for a woman, to try to recover the place of her exploitation by discourse, without allowing herself to be simply reduced to it' (Irigaray, 1977/1985: 76). It is that or not to be given access to 'reasonable' words (Irigaray, 1974/1985: 142) at all. And, as Michèle Le Doeuff says, 'if philosophy is constructed by exclusion and in particular the exclusion of women, how can women enter it without contradiction?' (Whitford, 1991: 9).

33.3 ENTERING THE CONTRADICTION

Any attempt to capture Irigaray in language produces remarkably slim pickings. Her work is intended to stand alone, removed from her biography. However, there are things which can be noted. She was born in Belgium in 1930 and received a Master's degree in philosophy and arts from the Catholic University of Louvain in 1955. After a brief spell of school-teaching in Brussels, she moved to Paris where she studied psychology and psychopathology and attended the psychoanalytic seminars of Jacques Lacan. In 1968 she was awarded a doctorate in linguistics. She herself trained and practised as a psychoanalyst. However, it is her experience of the École Freudienne de Paris that provides some insight into the relationship between the woman and her work. As Irigaray herself intimates in the opening of *Je, Tu, Nous* (1990/1991), it was her expulsion from the Freudian School of Paris which provides her with one of the central themes of her work: exclusion. It was in 1974 while studying at the School that she gained her second doctorate, which when published became one of her most influential works, *Speculum, de l'autre femme* (1974), in English *Speculum of the Other Woman* (1985). The thesis was a critique of the phallocentricism of both Freudian and Lacanian psychoanalysis and of philosophy. It made an immediate if equivocal impact. However, for Irigaray the consequences were dramatic and she lost her post at the Université de Vincennes and incurred the rage of the Lacanians. In her own words, she was 'put into quarantine' by the psychoanalytic establishment (Baruch and Serrano, 1988: 163).

Her critique of psychoanalysis met with resistance partly at the level of the political. Psychoanalysts of both the Freudian and Lacanian traditions held to the view that there was no place in psychoanalytic theory for a political standpoint: a position which Irigaray repudiated on the grounds that such a position was itself a political one. However, what is interesting about her position on psychoanalysis is the way she redirects psychoanalytic theory against itself, dismissing many of its theoretical positions as located in unconscious fantasies, resistances, and defences. This has something in common with Nietzsche's notion of *ressentiment*: a reductive, defensive, regress-oriented position. It is an attack on what she sees as the source of her frustration with phallogocentricism and the assignment of 'cause'. Freud's work she sees as ahistorical, patriarchal, and phallocentric: 'difference is assumed under male parameters' (Whitford, 1991: 6). Perhaps more seriously, it was the breakdown of her working relationship with Lacan which caused her pain. Lacan, it seems, was unable to cope with criticism or with deviations from his theoretical assumptions. Therefore, although he had been one of her mentors, after the publication of *Speculum* he was dismissive of her work. Her criticism of his work in *The Poverty of Psychoanalysis* (reprinted in Whitford, 1991: 79–104) is specific:

> 'Gentlemen, psychoanalysts', she begins, 'Why only "gentlemen"? Adding "ladies" as is the custom nowadays, would not change anything: in language [langue], the masculine noun always governs the agreement. The subject always speaks in the same gender... The phallus—indeed, the Phallus—is the emblem, the signifier and the product of a single sex'. (Whitford, 1991: 79).

Indeed, she goes further to say that the audience will not understand her meaning since they are prevented from understanding by 'at least two systems of screens, of censorship or of repression... The phallo-narcissism you have duly invested in your function as analysts will not tolerate such a statement... in no way does psychoanalysis suffer from poverty [*la misère*], nor is it wretched [*une misère*]' (Whitford, 1991: 79).

The article is a biting attack on psychoanalysis and the phallocratic power to define. She attacks Lacan for giving theoretical primacy to the phallus and for his notion of the imaginary body of the mirror stage as being a male body. This leads her to explore the significance of the speculum as an instrument for medical examination, specifically of the examination of internal areas of the body. Lacan, she argues, can only admit a mirror which sees women's bodies as always lacking, indeed as a hole (see Whitford, 1991: 6). Lacan needs the speculum to see inside. 'Lacan', she offers,

> delights in not quoting his sources or resources... He is only too ready to play the seductive philosophy teacher who 'knows more', and thus secures the love of his young pupils... the whole tissue of knowledges and identifications that go to make up the word of your Master, his word inevitably looks like the Truth to you. (in Whitford, 1991: 85)

Her assault on Lacan is a vehement one in which she accuses him of parading as 'the God of your unconscious... avatar of salvation incarnate' (Whitford, 1991: 86). It is no wonder that she speaks of 'snipping the wires' of discourse. She is playing with the anxiety which the 'man-god-father' experiences that women will 'swallow them up, devour them, castrate them' (Whitford, 1991: 49), an anxiety which might, she argues, be 'an unconscious memory of the sacrifice which sanctifies phallic erection as the only sexual value?' (Irigaray, 1981/ 1991): an erection supported by 'an act of faith in the patriarchal tradition' (Irigaray, 1981/ 1991: 41).

33.4 SPECULUM/SPECULATIONS

In *Speculum*, she begins her text with a rereading of Freud's essay 'Feminity' in order to explore the ideological underpinnings of psychoanalytic theory which, as she explains, regards woman as a less-than-complete man, as a man manqué. She devotes a good deal of the text to the analysis of the history of philosophy in order to trace the development of patriarchy from the time of Plato to the present day and concludes that the story is one of matricide. Her subsequent book, in English *An Ethics of Sexual Difference* (1984/1993) further examines the history of philosophy by engaging with specific texts from Plato, Aristotle, Descartes, Spinoza, Merleau-Ponty, and Levinas in order to explore the sexual deferral which is present in the writing. In her introduction she says,

> A revolution in thought and ethics is needed if the work of sexual difference is to take place. We need to reinterpret everything concerning the relations between the subject and discourse, the subject and the world, the subject and the cosmic, the microcosmic and the macrocosmic. Everything, beginning with the way in which the subject has always been written in the masculine form, as *man*, even when it claimed to be universal or neutral. Despite the fact that *man*—at least in French—rather than being neutral, is sexed. (Irigaray, 1984/1993: 8, italics in the original)

She continues on this theme by considering the implications of the designation 'man' for the gendered nature of the deity: God is 'masculine and paternal'.

As far as this relates to philosophy itself, she considers the implications for the ordering of space and time, where 'philosophy then confirms the genealogy of the task of the gods or God (and) time, becomes the axis of the world's ordering' (Irigaray, 1984/1993: 9). God, then, as regulation and ordering becomes time/eternity and the *interiority* of the subject constructed in the temporal, where the masculine is experienced as time and the feminine as *exteriority*: as space. However, as Irigaray goes on to argue, the implications of this are that the relationship between woman and place leads to the designation of woman as *a thing*, as a container, a location for man's *things*, what she terms 'the envelope'; as a construction much like other things, 'he defines her and creates *his* identity with her as his starting point' (Irigaray, 1984/1993: 11), but without a subjective life: 'man remains with a master-slave dialectic. The slave, ultimately, of a God on whom he bestows the characteristics of an absolute master. Secretly or obscurely, a slave to the power of the maternal-feminine which he diminishes or destroys' (Irigaray, 1984/1993: 11). Hence, the maternal-feminine is deprived of a place: it has no place of its own. Appropriated, it has no ' "proper" place' (Irigaray, 1984/1993: 11). As Irigaray argues, an attempt to change these relativities would require an adjustment to the 'whole economy of space-time'.

Moreover, the disparities between time and space mean that there is 'a dissociation between body and soul, sexuality and spirituality…in the sexual act…these realities remain separate' (Irigaray, 1984/1993: 15) and the celebration of conjunction is deferred. In this regard, she accords a special significance to the role of 'angels' who are neither enclosed in a location nor immobile. 'Irreducible to philosophy, theology, morality, angels appear as messengers of ethics evoked by art—sculpture, painting, or music—without its [*sic*] being possible to say anything more than the gesture which represents them'

(Irigaray, 1984/1993: 16), and she argues that for a sexual or carnal ethics to be possible requires both angel and body to be in concert: the possibility of the intersection between the physical and the metaphysical, transcendent and immanent. (For a fuller discussion of Irigaray's view of the role of angels, see her 'Belief Itself'; Irigaray, 1980/1993: 24–53.)

In short, the implications of being located and limited by definition, by containment, are that the maternal-feminine is immobilized and subordinated. Woman as container must accommodate the man and sometimes the child. She becomes the vessel for the child and, in perforation, the vessel for the man. However, this leaves no place for herself. She can only find a meaning for herself in the idealization of the container where the place, the location, becomes synonymous with 'inside'. Any other possibility, any other ecstasy, is forbidden. With no place for sexual expression and no place for expression in language, women live in 'exile' (Irigaray, 1978/1990). Irigaray argues that, to move forward, 'We need to discover a language that is not a substitute for the experience of *corps-à-corps* as the paternal language seeks to be, but which accompanies that, bodily experience, clothing it in words that do not erase the body but speak the body' (1980/1993: 19). How this plays out in Irigaray's work is considered in the themes from her work which are identified in the rest of the chapter.

33.5 JAMMING THE THEORETICAL MACHINERY

'What remains to be done, then, is to work at "destroying" the discursive mechanism' (Irigaray, 1977/1985: 76). With this challenging *cri de coeur*, Irigaray announces her desire for a *retraversal* of discourse intended to rediscover a feminine place which would require 'jamming the theoretical machinery [of discourse], suspending its pretension to the production of a truth and of a meaning that are excessively univocal' (Irigaray, 1977/1985: 78). Irigaray argues that the hegemony of philosophic *logos* derives from its power to '*reduce all others to the economy of the Same*...[and to] eradicate the difference between the sexes in systems that are self-representative of a "masculine subject"' (1977/1985: 74). Consequently, it is necessary to interrogate its 'systematicity' and the mechanisms which make possible its reproduction, the scenography, and the 'architectonics of its theatre, its framing in time and space'. These are the scenographic structures which ensure the reproduction, duplication, and re-enactment, 'the mirror...that allows the *logos*, the subject, to reduplicate itself, to reflect itself by itself' to ensure its material continuity.

More poetically, in her more recent work, Irigaray (2013) says:

> in this construction, everything ultimately amounts to the same...immutable...The maintenance of homeostasis is already at work and contributes to the

closure of the universe. To be sure, at each moment the mechanism is in move-ment, but it assures the permanence of the same, to the detriment of becom-ing. An illusion of life is created, of which *he* is the master. (Irigaray, 2013: 42, italics added)

Consequently, according to the 'economy of the Same', the systematicity itself has thwarted the possibility of an understanding of the process of becoming and, moreo-ver, such a construction when translated as phallogocentric desire can only conceive of women as 'lack'. This protects the construction from the disorderly feminine but as stabilization renders itself incapable of movement.

This is a world from which 'women and the gods have withdrawn...[but] there still exists a flesh that cannot express itself in a distinct and reasoned way' (Irigaray, 2013: 42). Yet woman has to submit herself to the regulation of the Father. In the absence of a female subject position, women can only become subjects if they assimilate to male subjectivity; a separate subject position for women does not exist: woman is always attendant to man (cf. the etymology of the word 'woman': *wif, wim, wum* + man, *Oxford English Dictionary*). Yet women supply the basis for the phallic order through their engagement with matter and their physical reproduc-ibility, what Irigaray terms 'red blood' (Irigaray, 1977/1985: 77), which must forever nourish *speculation* with all associations of the term in play. Ironically, the phallo-cratic economy, as merely an abstract entity, seeks to transfer its own 'lack' onto the feminine so that the feminine bears the responsibility for the lack and is not only rendered deficient but the cause of disorder, the failure of abstract desires, the gap between the sublime and the actual. There is the fear of being exposed to the scar of the castrated other, of falling below some expectation: of failing to have or be a big enough member. It is the male desire for mastery made manifest. 'He seeks how to manipulate words in order to put life and the gods in his service' (Irigaray, 2013: 98). In response to the endless systematization which outlines the implications of fail-ure and the endless commitment to monitoring, it is not surprising, then, that the consequence is a paralysing state that sets the individual at odds with the world, alienated from it, terrified of it, unable to act, react, or to adopt a moral disposi-tion: unable to sustain the erection. So everything falls, institutions collapse, mem-bership is lost 'but not without destroying life in this erection' (Irigaray, 2013: 99). It is the fear of disorder brought by women as the already deficient other. Irigaray maintains that 'All desire is connected to madness. But apparently one desire has chosen to see itself as wisdom, moderation, truth and has left the other to bear the burden of madness it did not want to attribute to itself, recognize in itself' (Irigaray, 1981/1991: 35). To refuse to conform to logic is to be declared 'mad', and the remedy for madness, it seems, is death. As Cixous (1976/1981) has argued, the remedy for women is decapitation. So whereas men might fear madness and castration, physi-cal and symbolic, so women are confronted with the power of logic and the threat of the severed head.

33.6 THE MIMETIC STRATEGY

This systematicity which Irigaray refers to can be seen in the frenetic formulation and definition of future and idealized states: in strategic planning, life planning, a commitment to futurity. In seeking to construct themselves both as sublime manifestations of male desire and as unattainable ideals, men's projections, their erections, lay themselves open to a range of problems. The therapeutic project of *saving* the system via the rule of logic, via insistent authority, and via psychology, is a process of mortification and the first victim is 'the mother'. Irigaray develops the theme of matricide in her 1981 paper 'The Bodily Encounter with the Mother' in which she revisits the myth of Clytemnestra and concludes that patriarchy is founded on the sacrifice of the mother. Moreover, this scenography is founded on a masculine sublime fabricated to reflect the male ego, narcissistic and inevitably melancholic. Women have no place, no reflection, no role in this construction other than to the extent that, in an entirely selective way, they serve as *things* within the construction. In this construction, women are hysterical and have to be kept in their place because, by posing a threat to such representational forms (to mimesis), they threaten the basis of phallocratic order. Only if women are prepared to submit themselves to the symbol of the erection, primarily as objects of desire but also as homologues, can they enter into reflection. However, they must show proper deference. If they lack propriety, they are nothing. If they reject the phallocratic order, they have no part to play. They must enter what Irigaray has termed 'the scenography that makes representation feasible... That allows the *logos*, the subject to reduplicate itself, to reflect itself by itself' (1981/1991: 123). The significance of reproduction is transferred from its natural place, the womb (hystera), to scenographic constructions of reproducibility.

These are the defences which protect philosophy, from incoherence, from failure and subversion by women; a phallocentric psychology which credits itself with the initiative and defends its position by relegating women to place, fixed positions, category, definition. Clearly, part of such a defensive strategy rests on power over the control of reflection, theorization, and discourse, and on the control of things and their meanings. In the same vein as Irigaray, Lyotard argues that this desire to control women and to neutralize difference is exercised by making women into men (making women into *objects* or in Irigaray's terms *things*): 'let her confront death, or castration, the law of the signifier. Otherwise, she will always lack the sense of lack' (Lyotard, 1989: 113). In Irigaray's terms, she must be aware of the scar of her castration. Irigaray takes the view that by wanting to be 'the sole creator, the Father, according to our culture, superimposes upon the archaic world of flesh a universe of language and symbols which cannot take root in it except as in the form of that which makes a hole in the bellies of women and in the site of their identity' (Irigaray, 1981/1991: 41).

Men want to create the heroic sublime and this is inevitably one which relegates the woman to a subordinate position: fixed and immovable. This sublime is abstract and metaphysical, removed from what is regarded as the filthy womb, the devouring mouth, source of foul emissions which causes phallic threat and disgust (Irigaray, 1981/1991: 41). However, even the construction of this account is rendered melancholic by the process of theorization and the construction of discourse. One becomes caught in the 'trap of insight' (Lacoue-Labarthe, 1989: 129). The very theorization that seeks to capture and structure becomes the cause of immobility, of paralysis. 'The philosopher…who has already bent light to his *logos*, cannot tolerate the sympathetic magic of the shadowy vault of fantasies, the hallucination, the "madness"' ((Irigaray, 1974/1985: 276). Speculations are bent to the service of the *logos*. On the other hand, Irigaray says that women privilege touch, and that to get away from such speculations requires a language of the body. Woman is required to remain silent or to present herself according to the representation of herself as viewed through the male gaze: to produce a version of herself in a way which effaces her. There is no place to turn that is, in itself, not subject to capture.

Women's deficiencies can, it seems, be corrected by reason. In this sense, conformity requires submission to *psychology* (regulation of the psyche by the *logos*). If that which is defined as deficient will only submit to superior logic she will *realize* the extent of her disorder. She can be saved by surrendering to the *logos*, by abandoning her threatening femininity. When she is truly converted she might be permitted to play a role as long as she plays it in compliance with male expectations. When she does this, she will be rendered powerless (impotent) as the price of membership. She will then be conformed to psychology: 'the wisdom of the master. And of mastery' (Irigaray, 1974/1985: 274). If the patriarchal order can convert women to the power of the *logos*, it is able to demonstrate control over hysteria and disorder. In other words, women are permitted entry to the scene precisely because they are no longer women: they are put in their *place*.

Consequently, discourse is regulated by the patriarchal order, and the patriarchal economy is the single most important determinant of participation. The thrust of the text with its emphasis on rigidity and tumescence is a symbolic one. As such, ironically, it signifies the loss of contact with the physical body. Women must either live as male constructions or *be found wanting*. In this sense, to lack a phallus is a very serious deficiency from the point of view of the male subject. It induces anxieties that the same fate might befall him. Therefore, it is a necessary condition of the male delusion of wholeness for women to be construed as castrated. Indeed, the resulting wound, 'the openness of the mother, the opening on to the mother, appears to be threats of contagion, contamination, engulfment in illness, madness and death' (Irigaray, I981/1991: 40). She is always the dirty, deficient other.

However, given Irigaray's ([1981/1991) concern for the primacy of the maternal function as the basis of social order, it seems appropriate to attempt to say something about matricide. From the phallocentric perspective, matricide should not be regarded as an act of madness—although it does derive from a relationship with hysteria and might thus be regarded as masculine hysteria—to preserve the patriarchal order. It is subject to the rule of logic and rationality. The killing of the mother and her subjection to the rule of patriarchy, which incidentally involves the usurpation of her arcane powers, requires the substitution of the mother with a representation and deferential emblem which retains a captive version of the feminine albeit in a now entirely mimetic way (Höpfl, 2000). The maternal-feminine is contained by the very ambivalence which is concealed and regulated by the act of matricide, while at the same time 'Mother-matter-nature' provides the very sustenance for *speculation*. Yet this source, this red blood, is dismissed, cast aside as madness: a madness contaminated by matter. Mother, matter, and nature are subject to the same subordination in the desire for mastery: captured and regulated, systematized and theorized. They are reduced to a therapeutic quest, as debates as diverse as those relating to bureaucratization, categorization, taxonomic thinking, and the definition and prescription of ecological problems indicate.

33.7 On Organizations and the Denial of Feminine Pleasure

By dealing with the *conception* of the organization as maternal, the role of the maternal-feminine in relation to organizations stems from what Irigaray has spoken of in terms of a violent rupture: 'deconstruct the logic grid of the reader-writer, drive him out of his mind... *Overthrow syntax* by suspending its eternally teleological order' (Irigaray, 1974/1985: 142, italics in the original). She seeks to cross 'back through the mirror that subtends all speculation' (Irigaray, 1977/1985: 77), in order to allow reflections on the mother/motherhood/maternal imagery to enter the text, to discover feminine pleasure. Thus, the embodied subject speaks of division, separation, rupture, tearing, and blood, whereas the text of the organization speaks of regulation and representation, of rational argument and rhetorical trajectory. By breaking the text, the implications of 'the sterile perfectionism' of the patriarchal consciousness (Dourley, 1990: 51) is made transparent. So, mother/matter stands against the way in which conventional accounts of management are presented, poses alternative ways of understanding organization, and offers insights into the organization as embodied experience. It also provides intimations of the development of new entrepreneurial styles which work against traditional, masculine, rational approaches (see Hjorth, 2012; Everett, 2011). Moreover, to give voice to the view that, despite the feminine being always defined in terms of its relationship to the phallocratic order, it might have what Irigaray has termed 'its own specificity' (Irigaray, 1977/1985: 69) which could be used to bring about a new dimension of organizational studies that affirms the significance of the feminine. This is the upshot of 'snipping the wires' and it implies not only a radically different approach, but an approach which engages with the politics of the body and a new understanding of the experience of labour.

The entry of mother/matter, the ecstasy (*ek-stasis*) of feminine pleasure implicitly threatens the process of sterile reproducibility and the taxonomic thinking which attaches to phallocratic order, and so inherently subverts power relations in organizations. This is the greatest threat. It is a threat to scenographic continuity, to the rule of logic, and to the rigidity of the phallus. It involves the rejection of the defining and locating reflection of the speculum—the threat of what Docherty calls 'indefinition' (Docherty, 1996: 67). Lacoue-Labarthe (1989: 129) indicates what Plato has identified as the major threats to representation as being women and madness. And, indeed, women and madness as themes spiral together as surely as the *hystera* (Greek *womb*) and the psycho*logical* condition of hysteria (as a disturbance of the nervous system, thought to be brought about by uterine dysfunction) find a common origin in the function of reproduction (see Foucault, 1961/1988). Consequently, there is a fundamental need for the reassurance of a sustainable erection: that the system can be maintained. If real women cannot be admitted, what is lost to the organization must be elevated to fill the gap. Only those who know 'their place' can enter, and even then only in a constructed and specular/representational way. Instead of flesh and blood, patriarchal order creates for itself a representational version of what is no longer there. It seeks to uphold the representation of the feminine, the body within its scenography, but which inevitably achieves a cancellation. Under such circumstances, woman can only dress herself and her place in ways which are appropriate to her location and her situation within the patriarchal system. It is little wonder, therefore, that notions of quality and care, the ubiquitous valorization of staff, the commitment to service improvement, and so forth, have more in them of absence than of presence. To repeat Irigaray's point, such constructions reassure patriarchal order that it is not mad by appealing to logic and the therapeutic quest; madness is all that is other, madness is alterity: the feminine. Hence, the phallocratic order is concerned with logic, maintenance, and rationality, with location and hierarchy, with allocation and definition, with the phallocratic quest, and with preserving the erection. 'There remains only a mental agility that plays at assembling and separating words in order to construct a world that life, love, flesh have deserted' (Irigaray, 2013: 43).

Irigaray's work is not focused on the organization and yet it brings a great richness to an understanding of the sterility of contemporary work and its endless obsession with metrics and the construction of appearances. Certainly, the logic which counters itself to madness, and which has done so from the time of Plato, is a logic which deludes itself with the assumption of system and symmetry, while at the same time being founded on a masculine hysteria, a fear of the hystera and the fear of the collapse of the erection. By 'force of habit, the resistance of repetition, of the representation of the repetition that he knows, [he is sent] back to his previous posture, visions and voices. Better to be misled by fakes than to lose one's sight by opening the eyes to the flame of truth' (Irigaray, 1974/1985: 276). Founded on logic, detached from the body, from flesh, constructed in such a way as to *appear* to remedy this separation, modern organizations are inherently narcissistic and melancholic, ornamentation and pretence: out of *touch*. Conventional patriarchal representations of the organization reduce *organization* to mere abstract relationships, rational actions, and purposive behaviour. Under these constraints, organization becomes synonymous with regulation and control. This is achieved primarily by the imposition of definition and location: scenographic systems which are the basis of reproduction. Under such circumstances, organization functions in a very specific sense to establish a notion of pure (in the sense of uncontaminated) abstraction, and to establish what can be taken for granted in administrative and managerial practice. In contrast, the restoration of the m/other to the organization as embodied presence rather than mere textual representation opens up the possibility of new ways of *conceiving* (as against constructing) organization and, at the same time, permits the possibility of new political interpretations of 'organization' (see Irigaray, 1974/1985: 160–7, 'How to conceive (of) a Girl'). The aspirational goals of the trajectory mean that, in the present, everyone is deficient relative to the targets which have to be achieved.

There are two important dimensions to Irigaray's work which are to do with the importance of the body and experience and the implications they have for the study of work organizations. Women's being seems to be an impossibility and has no place in the organization as a male construction. The relationship between being and identity, being and authority, being and the body, make the subject of women's existence a problematic one in relation to women's work roles, identity, and problems of authority and permission. The desire to confront the problem of capture and immobilization within the patriarchal text is fundamental to Irigaray's work, and yet she acknowledges that to attempt to use language against itself is to create an untenable position: a position which is all too familiar to women when they attempt to deviate from the roles that are allocated to them.

In this sense, this chapter seeks to have a bearing upon the ways in which women's being is seen, specifically by Irigaray, in order to *conceive* of ways in which women might subvert the lexicon. However, the text is already ensnared within the trap of rhetoric. There are clearly implications of all this for the ways in which work roles are constructed, progressions determined, and differences conciliated. It is now over 40 years since Irigaray, Cixous, and Kristeva started their influential work, but so little has happened. Ironically, the lexicon has reinforced itself, produced more taxonomic structures, defined more categories, and women bear the scars of this logic.

33.8 Regulated and Relegated

So what is it to write from an absent subject position? What can be done to examine the important issues which Irigaray raises without reducing her and her ideas to simplifications and categories: biographical and epistemological. This can only be permitted via a vicarious acknowledgement of the male subject position from which such a task might be undertaken. It is not possible both to contribute to a philosophical text and, at the same time, to jam the theoretical machinery. Such actions can only be played out in specific performances within a specific scenography. There is an almost Gnostic separation between the abstract and valorized power of discourse and the condemnation of the flesh as contaminating and degraded. Consequently, it is impossible to engage in discourse as flesh or to admit mother/matter other than as the 'production of a truth and of a meaning that are excessively univocal' (Irigaray, 1977/1985: 77). It is important to know one's place and, in this case, the text affords only the opportunity for mimetic expression. Yet there is much to be said. Admittedly, Irigaray is not easy to read. Her work is complex and draws on a range of academic disciplines which inform and elaborate her text. The extent to which she draws on her own experiences and biography is more difficult to ascertain. She does not make her standpoint clear. She has been described as essentialist, criticized for her sometimes contradictory political comments, and her work has been much criticized by younger feminists. However, it seems that this is the wrong way to approach her work. As Whitford remarks, Irigaray's work 'is marked by a tension between critique and the vision of a new order' (Whitford, 1991: 12). It is this move beyond critique which gives her work appeal and which informs her own activism. She would 'fertilize' (Whitford, 1991: 12) the rigidities and thanatos-driven sterility of patriarchy. Her work is rich and the offer of a vision of the future is an appealing one. She refuses to be placed in alignment with the melancholy of patriarchal discourse. Having said that, it is clearly impossible to cover the range of her work in a short account such as this: to expose the opening of the mother without the suggestion of revealing a scar. I have tried as far as possible to let her work speak for itself and, in order to do so in a way which does justice to the complexity of her ideas, I have abandoned as far as possible any attempt to systematize and reduce her work to themes and categories. However, themes and categories there are. In *This Sex Which Is Not One* (1977/1985), the interested reader might pay particular attention to her work on discourse (chapter 4), on the 'mechanics of fluids' (chapter 6) with its attention to the lack of a theory of fluids which might consider milk, urine, saliva and blood (1977/1985: 113). In *Speculum of the Other Woman* ([1974] 1985), she treats such themes as 'The Avoidance of (Masculine) Hysteria' (pages 268–77) and 'The Deferred Act of Castration' (pages 81–9). But beyond these classic texts, the work on mothers and daughters, *Je, Tu, Nous*, presents her discourse on the mother (see Irigaray, 1990/1991), the relationship between mother and daughter, and her own disappointment with Simone de Beauvoir and with critiques by younger feminists (see 'Equal or Different', in Whitford, 1991: 30–3, and 12–13). I have given some attention to her book *An Ethics of Sexual Difference* (1984/2004) but there is much here to be digested. *Sexes and Genealogies* (1987/1993) contains some excellent conference papers presented in a more accessible style. Of her more recent work, her 2013 book *In the Beginning She Was* has a poetic quality which makes it very readable and perhaps suggests that she is moving from her formidable command of mimetic discourse to a style which resonates more with the body: in her own terms, reflecting perhaps an angelic movement. It has been argued that the simplification of her ideas compromises their complexity. However, it seems that in later work she is seeking to touch the reader, to become more mobile, and shift in her place. Of course, this means that her work potentially has much to say which could contribute to the development of process philosophy. At the same time, there are issues in the very systematization of philosophy and the ways in which theorization itself stands in the way of embodied experience. It could be argued that as a male construction, even process philosophy with its desire for movement and philosophy in action is subject to its own trajectory and delusion. She seeks more radical dismantling of the edifice: 'snipping the wires' of discourse (Irigaray, 1974/1985: 142).

And what of *her* view of philosophy? Her concern is more with practice. Having a concern with changing existing social arrangements, she has been active in a number of social movements. In the 1980s she was involved with political groups in Italy. Much of her later work suggests a commitment to political action and practical approaches to raising the position of women and helping them to achieve a social identity. Consequently, her attitude to philosophy is arguably predictable.

> Don't concern yourself with philosophy; philosophy won't mind. Without you knowing it you have been 'caught' in nihilism...After the end of philosophy, philosophical discourse leads those who do not take cognizance of it to adopt discourses which might be described as cut-price, discourses in which the truth, truly exploited by professional hacks, comes cheap...This end-of-the-world polemic...plays with the forms of language without any respect or regard for their meaning, order, beauty or generation. (Irigaray, *Parler n'est jamais neutre* (1985/1991), in Whitford, 1991: 88)

As I said earlier, it is appropriate that this *Handbook* on process philosophy should take seriously the work of Irigaray. Appropriate, because she offers both critique and hope for better things. She is not a romantic in this sense. She wants to change the order of things. Therefore, in the spirit of this chapter, I give back the final words to Irigaray herself. She says that western man

> has searched for his becoming in objects, things, and their representations or mental reduplications. Man has searched for himself outside the self while intending to appropriate this outside, notably through representations. And this does not represent a cultivation of interiority, but an exile in an external world that he intends to appropriate by means of a technique which reduplicates the real, of a logic through which he makes the world his own, the *logos*. (Irigaray, 2013: 145)

In the face of this, her work takes great pains to outline the possibility of a reconciliation of sexual difference: between subject and discourse. And, is the theoretical machinery jammed? Sadly not.

References

Baruch, E.H. and Serrano, L. (1988). *Women Analyze Women in France, England and the United States* (London: Harvester Wheatsheaf).

Cixous, H. (1976/1981). Castration or Decapitation?, trans. A. Kuhn, *Signs* 7(1): 41–55. First published as Le sexe ou la tête, *Les Cahiers du GRIF* 13: 5–15.

Docherty, T. (1996). *Alterities: Criticism, History, Representation* (Oxford: Clarendon Press).

Dourley, J.P. (1990). *The Goddess, Mother of the Trinity* (Lewiston: The Edwin Mellen Press).

Everett, K. (2011). *Designing the Networked Organization* (New York: Business Expert Press).

Foucault, M. (1961/1988). *Madness and Civilisation* (New York: Vintage Books, Random House).

Freud, S. (1930/1961). *Civilization and its Discontents*, trans. and ed. J. Strachey (New York: W.W. Norton).

Hjorth, D. (2012). *Handbook on Organizational Entrepreneurship* (Cheltenham: Edward Elgar).

Höpfl, H.J. (2000). The Suffering Mother and the Miserable Son, Organising Women and Organising Women's Writing, *Gender Work and Organization* 7(2): 98–106.

——(2001). The Mystery of the Assumption: Of Mothers and Measures, in N. Lee and R. Monro (eds), *The Consumption of Mass* (Oxford: Blackwell): 60–72.

——and Kostera, M. (2003). *Interpreting the Maternal Organisation* (London: Routledge).

Irigaray, L. (1974/1985). *Speculum of the Other Woman*, trans. G. Gill (Ithaca: Cornell University Press). Originally published as *Speculum. De l'autre femme* (Paris: Minuit).

——(1977/1985). *This Sex Which is not One*, trans. C. Porter (Ithaca: Cornell University Press). Originally published as *Ce Sexe qui n'en pas un* (Paris: Minuit).

——(1977/1990). Women's Exile, trans. C. Venn, in D. Cameron (ed.), *The Feminist Critique of Language: A Reader* (London: Routledge): 80–96. Originally published in *Ideology and Consciousness* 1: 62–76.

——(1980/1993). Belief Itself, in G. Gill (ed.), *Sexes and Genealogies* (New York: Columbia University Press): 23–53. Originally published in *Sexes et Parentés* (Paris: Minuit).

——(1981/1991). The Bodily Encounter with the Mother, trans. D. Macey, in M. Whitford (ed.). *The Irigaray Reader* (Oxford: Blackwell): 34–46. Originally published as *Le Corps-à-corps avec le mere* (Montreal: Ediations de la pleine lune).

——(1983). An Interview with Luce Irigaray, *Hecate* 9(1–2): 192–202.

——(1984/1993). *An Ethics of Sexual Difference*, trans. C. Burke and G. Gill (London: The Athlone Press). Originally published as *Ethique de la difference sexuelle* (Paris: Minuit).

——(1990/1991). How to Define Sexuate Rights?, trans. D. Macey, in M. Whitford (ed.) *The Irigaray Reader* (Oxford: Blackwell): 34–46. Originally published as *Je, tu, nous: pour une culture de la difference* (Paris: Grasset).

——(2013). *In the Beginning She Was* (London: Bloomsbury Academic).

Lacoue-Labarthe, P. (1989). *Typography* (Stanford, CA: Stanford University Press).

Lyotard, J.F. (1989). One of the Things at Stake in Women's Struggles, in A. Benjamin (ed.), *The Lyotard Reader* (Oxford: Basil Blackwell): 111–21.

Whitford, M. (1991). *The Irigaray Reader* (Oxford: Blackwell).

CHAPTER 34

MICHEL SERRES (1930b)

CHRIS STEYAERT

34.1 TRANSLATION

> The tinnitus I'm permanently afflicted with reproduces with high fidelity the whistling and silky sound of the implacable mass of moving water that, overflowing its regular bed, was then occupying the flood plain, kilometers-wide between hills called, like us, the Serres. At least my sense of hearing has never left Garonne.
>
> (Serres, 2012b: 13)

MICHEL SERRES (1930b) is a French philosopher, mathematician, and historian of science, who has enquired into the interrelationships between various systems, including science, philosophy, mythology, and poetry/literature. Because they are all systems, they can be compared, if only to discover what each system tries to exclude, such as disorder, noise, or turbulence (Buchanan, 2010). While the latter are all interesting features in a processual analysis, the relevant question here is whether this potential has been recognized in (processual) organization studies. To start this chapter with such a blunt question, which produces only an empty echo, and maybe a sign of consternation, may not be the best way to persuade scholars of processual organization studies to invest in reading and rereading Serres' highly inspiring writings. In 2002, Brown wrote that Serres 'has as yet failed to find an audience amongst British and North American social theorists' (Brown, 2002: 1). Now, more than ten years later, this situation is fundamentally the same: his work rarely gains much attention, especially among those in organization studies (Linstead, 2004; Hatch, 2011). Nor has his work gained attention for its potential value in processual analysis (Hernes, 2008), making him probably one of the least appreciated philosophers of the 'becoming' perspective.

To counter this injustice, let me note that Serres has been included as an important or at least feasible contributor to contemporary organization theory (Brown, 2005). From a processual perspective, Brown and Stenner (2009) give him great prominence, saying he stands next to Whitehead in formulating a non-foundational conception of process in a psychosocial context. This should come as no surprise: Harman (2009) places him alongside Whitehead, Bergson, William James, Deleuze, Simondon, and Tarde, as they all 'emphasize the capacity to become-otherwise of things; each endorses a metaphysics of Becoming more than Being, of flow, generative process, creative evolution, ruckus' (Bennett and Connolly, 2012: 153).

Besides the potential and force of Serres' work to formulate a non-foundational foundation for the process of becoming, several more of its core features are pertinent for a processual analysis. Consider his conceptions of time (Assad, 1999, 2012; Herzogenrath, 2012), of translation and mediation (Brown, 2002; Brown and Stenner, 2009), of the third-excluded and the third-instructed (Brown and Stenner, 2009; Zembylas, 2002), of multiplicity and complexity (Brown, 2000; Herzogenrath, 2012), of the body and the senses (Connor, 2005; Pearce, 2010), and, indeed, of interdisciplinarity (Brown, 2003; Gagliardi and Czarniawska, 2006; Serres, 2006a).

Thus a broad repertoire of generative concepts is available to inform a processual theory of organization, but these applications have been most fruitfully used and given prominence, however indirectly, in the development of Actor Network theory (Brown, 2002; Brown and Capdevila, 1999), for which Serres was a 'crucial figure' (Michael, 2000: 26). Furthermore, other organizational scholars have drawn upon such 'becoming' notions as noise, the parasite, and chaos to conceptualize learning as becoming (Clegg et al., 2005), to conceptualize consulting as translating (Clegg et al., 2004), entrepreneuring as stepping aside (Steyaert, 2012), and lastly management education as invention (Dey and Steyaert, 2007; Hjorth and Steyaert, 2006). Notwithstanding these valuable contributions, the work of Serres has even more potential for further theoretical developments of organization as complex, multitemporal, and inventive not in the least because it also allows us to address the things themselves and 'to reflect critically upon the tendency to privilege process over product within ontologies of Becoming and to continue to refine our theoretizations of the periodic and differentiated quality of Becoming' (Bennett and Connolly, 2012: 154).

If we are to understand the delayed impact of Michel Serres, several explanations deserve mention. First, his work is not easily co-opted (Brown, 2005), especially because he quickly shifted his approach to writing away from the usual academic styles (Assad, 1999; Paulson, 2000). Second, the translation of his work has proceeded rather slowly, and an important backlog remains, especially because his writing style often complicates translation or translators see his texts as impossible to translate 'due to their complex word play, neologisms and erratic style' (Pearce, 2010: 88). At the same time, we have to counter the idea that his impact would be minimal; rather, it has to be understood in a different way. Even though Serres participated in the flourishing of a whole generation of French philosophers after May 1968 (Dosse, 2011), he never received the international, especially North American, attention that came to Foucault, Derrida, or Deleuze. Still, he was hired as professor of French at Stanford University in 1984. Although he was closely involved with Foucault and Deleuze in Vincennes, Serres has traced an extremely independent path within French university and intellectual life [. .. in order] to recuperate French philosophy of what he saw in the 1950s, 1960s, and 1970s as the hegemony of phenomenology and Marxism (of German origin) and what he sees now as the contemporary invasion of the French philosophical and cultural scene by the Anglo-Saxon philosophy of language- and American pop culture. (Bell, 2006: 660)

Moreover, it has to be emphasized that Serres has become a public intellectual: the Académie Française appointed him a member in 1990 (seat 18 of 40). His public appeal has grown consistently since the 1980s through his appearances in the media, such as in the French TV programme on literature *Aposthrophes* (Bell, 2006). Since 2004, he has boosted his reputation even more by giving a weekly talk on the radio in a series entitled *Le Sens de l'Info* hosted by Michel Polacco. In five-minute presentations noted for their erudition and clarity, Serres gives his views on a variety of topics such as knowledge, power, jealousy, and politeness. These mini-expositions form small interventions of thinking related to the weekly topic and accessible to a large audience; many have been published (Serres, 2006b, 2007b, 2009). Asked why he speaks on the radio, Serres explains: 'It's very simple. A class that I teach may have 25 students; a radio audience 4 million. That's interesting for a professor who is trying to raise the level of cultural life' (Hagen, 2009). For instance, in a talk on knowledge (broadcast on *France Info* and downloadable since 2 September 2012), Serres explains, in four acts, the development of knowledge in oral, written, printed, and electronic forms, and compares the latter form to the story of St Denis, the bishop of Paris in the third century, who is often depicted as decapitated, holding his own head. According to Serres, today we all resemble St Denis as knowledge is no longer in our heads but externalized in computers, tools, and networks, giving a new role to the knower in terms of intuition, invention, and creativity. With the computer in front of us as a kind of decapitated head, we are all condemned to become intelligent. This little radio talk brings us to Serres' typical style, in which epistemological and other issues are framed by referring to myths, fables, and apologues (Assad, 2012).

34.2 STYLE

In the beginning is the song.

(Serres, 1995a: 138)

We are still waiting for the first official biography of the life and work of Michel Serres, even if some important elements of his life are well known (Bell, 2006; Buchanan, 2010), partly because he often refers to the region where he grew up or his times as a sailor or mountaineer (Serres, 2012b). Michel Serres was born in 1930 in Agen, on the Garonne River, halfway between Bordeaux and Toulouse, between the Atlantic and the Mediterranean. Serres started his study at the Naval College (l'École Navale) in 1949, and then studied philosophy at the famous École Normale Supérieure from 1952 on. In

1968, he gained a doctorate for a thesis on the work of the German philosopher Leibniz. He taught at the universities of Clermont-Ferrand and Vincennes, where he joined such colleagues as Michel Foucault, Gilles Deleuze, and Jean-François Lyotard. But, as quickly as possible, he fled the disorder at Vincennes (Eribon, 1991), and soon gained a chair in the history of science at the Sorbonne, a position he kept for most of his life. While it is usually considered overdone to trace the connections between an author's life and work, doing so for Serres is quite appropriate. Before becoming a writer, Serres was a naval officer and seafarer. Many of the images and metaphors he uses to develop notions of knowledge and time are indebted to his experiences of voyaging and movement and the sea, and of water, wind, and weather: not for nothing are time and weather both *le temps* (Serres and Latour, 1995: 60).

Serres' writing, highly acclaimed for its poetic qualities (Clayton, 2012), has been called both a geographical writing (Connor, 2008) and an angelological one (Zournazi, 2012). ten Bos (2012: 187) even calls his style 'shamelessly poetic', saying it should be read aloud—and for this reason I have inserted several long fragments for readers to experience the sensation of reading it. Serres has been called 'an artificer of words who does not believe that the world revolves around words' (Paulson, 2000: 216). Typical of his style of writing is his abundant use of conceptual personae (Deleuze and Guattari, 1994), figures that can intensify the conceptual thinking, such as Hermes, angels, harlequins, troubadours, or Thumbelina. Serres comments on his way of proceeding in a conversation with Latour:

> I was condemned to invent a new vocabulary which would have complicated the situation [of presenting a new philosophy] even more, so little by little I resolved to use more and more natural, everyday language. But the moment you refine language as much and as well as possible, you create a style. (Serres and Latour, 1995: 71–2)

Part of this style involves using and prioritizing other forms of writing; this is more than a stylistic gesture, as it forms 'a long and continuous Serresean practice which favors a language where adjectives, adverbs, and prepositions play more than supporting roles for nouns and verbs, the stalwarts of syntactical constructions for Western languages' (Assad, 1999: 27). Furthermore, style experiments lead to exploration, in contrast to grammar that is based on analysis and leads to debate (Clayton, 2012). Therefore, Serres believes in a comparative method that allows one to be synthetic instead of sequential: 'synthesis will no doubt be made more through comparativism than by sequential linking, more through Hermes's swift travels than by deduction or solid construction' (Serres and Latour, 1995: 73).

Serres detests the thinking in schools that limits opportunities for students to create and invent. He feels at home with the idea of Deleuze and Guattari that philosophy consists of creating concepts; like them, he sees himself as a geographer of philosophy. Also like them, he sets out to create philosophy as a logic of multiplicities. Deleuze (2000: 147) has affirmed he feels close to Serres on this point, while Serres (1994: 49; see Connor, 2004) affirms that 'everything is folding, as Gilles Deleuze has rightly said of it'. Despite the scarcity of these cross-references, awareness is growing of how the work of Serres and Deleuze features 'conceptual res-onances' (Herzogenrath, 2012: 14), and forms a 'dissonant conjunction' (Bennett and Connolly, 2012: 165). Thus, a combination of their thinking is finally in order given the key motifs in their work:

> an inter-weaving of different disciplinary registers (mathematics and poetry), a refusal to isolate the human animal from life, a sense of life as multiplicity, a complex historical sense that would destroy the history of man in favour of a history of bodies (where bodies would include technological objects, words, languages, animals, politics, cities and images) and an emphasis on sense. (Colebrook, 2012: 116)

For these reasons, the work of Serres 'can appear as an enigma...It moves with speed as it journeys through the sciences, philosophy, mythology and literature' (Clayton, 2012: 31). It does what it urges those interested in understanding process to do: be interdisciplinary and inventive. This makes him, as said, difficult to read, but Connor offers an even more important reason why Serres' work is hard to digest, especially by the Anglophone academic world: Serres declines 'the rules of engagement that govern academic theory, which seem to constitute knowledge as an agonistic space of conflict, hostility and critique' (2008: 7–8). However, Serres believes that if we want to save the Earth, we will have to let go of this situation where '[e]veryone is fascinated by interesting disputes, tragic quarrels between people, villages and hamlets, by conflicts between petty leaders and their permanent theatre. They don't know what they're doing; they love violence so much that it increases like a flood that's always ready to cover the entire Earth' (2012b: 6). Instead, Serres writes in a generative and generous way, meanwhile referring, eruditely, to many parts of the history of the sciences and the humanities, which he makes 'cross each other in the centre of the compass so that meaning/direction will spring forth' (Serres, 1997: 18). Serres rarely makes use of any direct reference system, and dislikes jargon which he considers redundant and harmful, especially because 'ultratechnical vocabulary breeds fear and exclusion' (Serres and Latour, 1995: 24). Instead, Serres' processual view emerges from a style that draws upon all senses.

34.3 GENESIS

> I am young and old.
>
> (Serres, 1995a: 60)

To best consider how Michel Serres can be considered an important processual theorist, let us zoom in on his work *Genèse* (1982) or *Genesis* (1995a) (Bennett and Connolly, 2012; Clayton, 2012), a book that is seen as performing the transition from the parasitic third toward chaotic multiplicity (Assad, 1999). To create multiplicity, Serres begins by literally playing along with Descartes' *'cogito ergo sum'* or 'I think therefore I am'. He enacts this in a poetic style, illustrating the pure creativity connected to the singularity of rhizo-matic subjectivity (Zembylas, 2002):

> Who am I, beyond the joy coming from this shudder of awakening, the growth of this green ivy, this dancing flame, this living fire? I think in general, I am a capacity to think something, and I am virtual. I think in general, I can think anything. I think, therefore I am indeterminate. I think, therefore I am anyone. A tree, a river, a number, an ivy, a fire, a reason or you, whatever. Proteus. I think, therefore I am Nobody. The I is nobody in particular, it is not a singularity, it has no contours, it is the blankness of all col-ours and all nuances, an open and translucent welcome of a multiplicity of thoughts, it is therefore I do not exist. Who am I? A blank domino, a joker, that can take any value. A pure capacity. There is nothing more abstract. I am just the plain whore of the thoughts that accost me, I wait for them, morning and evening, at the crossroads, under the statue of the angel Hermes, all wind and all weather. And, maybe, I am, maybe, if the verb to be is a joker or a blank domino, as well. (Serres, 1995a: 31)

This extensive quote helps to explain the core of *Genèse*: a book on creation or, rather, the book where Serres unfolds his concept of creation through a performative poet-ics. Noise, chance, and disorder are evoked as the heralds of the doing of creation. In particular, Serres conceives of noise as the background to all existence; noise is the multiple, multiplicity, the chaos that is always there, invisible but inevitably present in things that are forming and becoming. Serres originally wanted to call the book 'Noise', but was overruled by his French publisher (Critchley, 1996). Noise is the name given to 'that onto-field of generativity and its impersonal force of operation' (Bennett and Connolly, 2012: 155). Noise is not pre-given or pre-conditional but forms an element of an in-between as it is posited in and between phenomena. Being coterminous with them, noise is 'the multiplicity of the possible [that] ... rustles in the midst of the forms that emerge from it' (Serres, 1995a: 23–4). However, noise is not seen as something undifferentiated; instead, it thickens into lumps of 'phenomena' through the cauldron of turbulence (Bennett and Connolly, 2012).

It is almost as if Serres was offering a response, in advance, to the notable observa-tion Deleuze and Guattari (1994: 201) make in their final book, *What Is Philosophy?*, that 'we only need a little organisation to protect us against chaos'. With great zeal and much poetry, his *Genèse* plunges into the stream of multiplicity; throughout the book multiplicity turns up repeatedly, showing that it has earned itself a place of pri-ority. Organization is an effect, a stabilization, which often blinds us to the multiple, the chaotic, in short to the process of becoming. In Serres' work, multiplicity is set to music. Indeed, he says, it is easier to listen to multiplicity than to conceive of it visually. Images are sound-images. Perhaps we have been able to imagine multiplicity, but have not always allowed it to sound. Hearing always continues long after seeing has stopped. Multiplicities—think of the wind or sea—are not seen but heard. We are immersed in sound just as we are in light and air. 'Noise' is always there; it is our unbroken back-ground, the material for our forms.

What Serres really envisions is, like Deleuze's nomadology (Clayton, 2012; Zembylas, 2002), a philosophy of movement which does not attempt to conceal multiplicity under unitary concepts, like sweeping dust under a carpet. The same holds for the way we theorize relations, often prioritizing just one causal relationship. However, as Serres asks, who can claim that a relation cannot be further elucidated in more subtle relations? There is never simply one causal relation but a web of connections and relationships a researcher needs to attend to. And it would be a mistake to consider multiplicity as a sum total, an aggregate: it is rather 'a lake under the mist, the sea, a white plain, background noise, the murmur of a crowd, time' (1995a: 5). For Serres, multiplicity is not something abstract, but something that belongs to the everyday: 'Sea, forest, rumour, noise, society, life, works and days, all common multiples' (1995a: 6). And in all of this, time is the absolute multiplicity, a magnitude without unity. Here is where history can appear, full of sound (noise) and fury. Serres (1995a: 20) calls sound-noise—the Old French word *noise*—the only positive word for describing the condition for which we normally reserve only negative terms, such as dis-order.

The question is what we can do to make the multiple part of (organizational) life: how can we 'begin' a process? Above all, Serres (1995a: 5) believes that the usual academic habitus of arrogant truth-making needs to be altered radically: 'May the aforesaid scientific knowledge strip off its arrogance, its magisterial, ecclesial drapery, may it leave off its martial agressivity, the hateful claim of always being right; let it tell the truth; let it come down, pacified, toward common knowledge' (1995a: 6). Instead of holding on to interests and positions, Serres holds, creative living is dependent on those who, in their everyday life, dare to step aside and create space for whatever (new and different) is to come, and thus initiate a process. That is the crucial question Serres describes in the following quote:

> To take a place or to give up a place, that is the whole question. There are those who take places, there are those who give them up...Those who give up their places, move and flow. Their blankness is pure processuality. To yield means to take a step. To step aside, we say. Those who step aside, those who cede their place, begin, by their cession, a process. Those who take the places stabilize them and drown them in noise. Those who give up their place have already taken a step.... The only steps are steps aside. There is no step that is not a cession. Those who give up their place yield it up to all those who take places, they yield it to everyone, they always yield it. They never have a place to put their foot down, they never have a place to rest their head, they have no rest. *They are always moving. There is no movement except by stepping aside, giving up one's place. Thus, the series of cessions makes process.* (Serres, 1995a: 76–7; my italics)

Thus, Serres sees a permanent movement through the act of stepping aside again and again. To give way is to give someone a way. Pay attention, says Serres, to those who give (a)way, for it is they who are 'on the way'. They are moving. They occupy no space, they don't silt up, they are neither immobile nor unmoved. They don't get carried away. Driven out, they float away. Away they must. Like Ulysses, they are always creating new space. They are on the move, like those in a dance which is based on steps that open a space. Dancing is the continual creation of space, a trace of trace-making. For Serres, the dancer becomes the prototype of the person becoming. For dancing, like writing, is pure movement.

34.4 INVENTION

The creator is born old and dies young.

(Serres, 1997: 104)

Serres is interested in gaining new knowledge ('*le nouveau savoir*'), which 'is mirrored in the dynamical non-linearity' of his writings (Assad, 2012: 85). For him, what makes the connections between systems is 'an unwavering search for a vital and non-oppositional (re)union of subject and object, joining historical consciousness and the material reality of the world' (Assad, 2012: 85). To develop a way of non-oppositional thinking, Serres invents the notion of the third by overturning the classical principle of identity as two different elements that can only be compared in their relationship which forms a third element. Invention happens in the third space, which Assad (2012: 86) says 'swells into a vast atlas of virtual maps related to each other by passages through which new knowledge percolates, not in a straight Cartesian line, but in unexpected movements that resemble' what Serres compares to a 'zigzag path of grazing goats' (Assad, 2012: 86).

In *Le Tiers-Instruit* (meaning the Third-Instructed but translated as The Troubadour of Knowledge), Serres (1991) explores the consequences that an ontology of the multiple has for the inventive force of education. The book forms 'an educational manual' for learning how the third-instructed or the figure that learns in the third space can become inventive by entering a time of pure passing (Assad, 2012: 92). Even in the preface, Serres promotes Harlequin as the conceptual persona to emphasize that knowledge is interdisciplinary, comparing the organization of the encyclopedia to the stage of *commedia dell'arte*. Knowledge then 'looks like Harlequin's coat, because each works at the intersection or the interference of many other disciplines and, sometimes, of almost all of them' (1991: xvii). Furthermore, learning is situated at the level of the body, where the possibility of invention is prepared:

> Just as the body . . . assimilates and retains the various differences experienced during travel and returns home a half-breed of new gestures and other customs, dissolved in the body's attitudes and functions, to the point that it believes that as far as it is concerned nothing has changed, so the secular miracle of tolerance, of benevolent neutrality welcomes, in peace, just as many apprenticeships in order to make the liberty of invention, thus of thought, spring forth from them. (1991: xvii)

Learning equals invention as the body mediates the possibility of new practices and movements. Learning is itself a process that Serres compares with swimming, where learners have to leave the shore, encounter new streams, and abandon all reference points. 'Depart, take the plunge', Serres (1997: 5) urges us, because learning requires a body that leaves the security of the shore, and moves towards the middle where the real passage can occur. Serres trusts that the body will do its work, because 'under threat of drowning, the body confidently takes up a slow breaststroke' (1997: 5). After this initiation into a third world, the body will never be home again; instead, it will live in the intermediary, in the middle, forming a hyphen that connects different sides. Serres compares this to the process of learning a new language where becoming bilingual does not mean that one simply speaks two languages; rather one 'passes unceasingly through the fold of the dictionary' (1997: 6). The middle or the third is only a way to get out of a single-minded or binary logic, but Serres quickly asks 'Did you believe it to be triple?' (1997: 7). By passing through the blank middle, one's 'com-pass' can diverge in 'twenty or one hundred thousand directions' (1997: 7). Make no mistake, he says: learning is a process that evokes and enacts the multiple.

Throughout Serres' manual on upbringing, instruction, and education, we encounter gentle encouragements. Repeatedly, he urges his readers to 'Depart. Go out', because 'no learning can avoid the voyage' (1997: 8). This de-part-ure implies that each learner divides herself into parts and pieces: parts that she leaves behind in the form of old ideas and former habits, new pieces that she explores and adopts. Thus pedagogy is 'the voyage of children'; its maxim is 'never take the easy road, swim the river instead' (1997: 8). This is because swimming in the river leads one to the passage through the third place, and 'all evolution and learning require passing through the third place. So that knowledge, thought, or invention does not cease to pass from one third place to another and therefore is always exposed, or so that the one who knows, thinks, or invents quickly becomes a passing third' (1997: 12).

To become a passing third, Serres evokes the figure of the troubadour, which forms another name for the third-instructed. In troubadours, Serres sees his ancestors: he has 'always written like a troubadour' (1997: 101). If invention comes from the body, creativity in the form of artwork requires health and thus exercise: 'thus there exists a hygienics, yes, a diet of the work. High-level sportsmen live like monks, and creators live like athletes' (1997: 92). So, to anyone who seeks to invent, Serres has these suggestions:

> Begin with exercise, seven regular hours of sleep, and a strict diet. The hardest life and the most demanding discipline: asceticism and austerity. Resist fiercely the talk around you that claims the opposite...Do not resist only narcotics, but especially social chemistry, by far the strongest and thus the worst: the media, conventional fashions. Everyone always says the same thing and, like the flow of influence, descends the steepest slope together. (1997: 92)

As a consequence, Serres sharply delineates how one can achieve learning and thinking:

> The goal of instruction is the end of instruction, that is to say invention. Invention is the only true intellectual act, the only act of intelligence. The rest? Copying, cheating, reproduction, laziness, convention, battle, sleep. Only discovery awakens. Only

invention proves that one truly thinks what one thinks, whatever that may be. I think therefore I invent, I invent therefore I think. (1997: 92–3)

However, this kind of inventive learning is usually discouraged in universities and other institutions which fear invention as dangerous. Serres is clear on this:

> the institutions of culture, of teaching, or of research, those that live on messages, repeated images, or printed copies, the great mammoths that are the universities, media, and publishing, the ideocracies also, [which] surround themselves with a mass of solid artifices that forbid invention or break it, that fear it like the greatest danger…The more institutions evolve toward the gigantic, the better the counterconditions are for the exercise of thought. Do you want to create? You are in danger. (1997: 93)

Invention is light and rapid, he says, and it laughs at those large organizations that imprison freedom of thought and preach idleness. Indeed, it preserves something of the agility and swiftness of children, and therefore invention is able to reverse time: the creator dies young. Thus, learning is always paradoxical: even when people try to learn everything, they do so in order to know nothing. This is the most critical element: allowing oneself to forget what others have served as established knowledge. Therefore, 'with his whole body, all his passion, his anger, and his strained liberty, whoever wants to create resists the power of knowledge, both the works that have already been made and the institutions that feed on them' (1997: 98).

Enacting a trajectory of invention, 'the middle-instructed will always tend towards the unpredictable and thereby is the guarantor of creativity, which for Serres is the equivalent of a History of Life' (Assad, 2012: 92). Invention does not follow the path of seeking and researching but of finding. As in the old French language, the producer of improbable novelty is called 'a finder: trouvère in the North, troubadour in the South' (Assad, 2012: 104). However, this finding should come without any compulsion to dominate, as the troubadour is modest, and even holds back. This is where the sciences can become wise, if they could learn understatement, reserve, holding back, and restraint: 'Science will become wise when it holds back from doing everything it can do' (Assad, 2012: 122).

34.5 Sensing the Process

> I invent outside of myself.
>
> (Serres, 2008b: 94)

Serres encourages us to understand processes through trying out different embodied relationships with the world; he then goes beyond the visual and explores all the senses. He discussed these ideas in *Les Cinq Sens* (*The Five Senses*), which dates from 1985 but was only translated in 2008, and took them up again in *Variations on the Body* (1999/2011c). For Serres, the five senses are 'a complex, interwoven web of multifaceted hybridity' (Pearce, 2010: 94). In *Angels: A Modern Myth*, Serres had established his belief in the creative force of our senses, when he wrote: 'Once words come to dominate flesh and matter which were previously innocent, all we have left is to dream of the paradisiacal times in which the body was free and could run and enjoy sensations at leisure. If a revolt is to come, it will have to come from the five senses!' (1995b: 71). This might be truer than ever for organizational theory, especially considering his strong critique of the way language has come to dominate theory and knowledge. This view would indeed bring a revolution to a field that has, for the last 25 years, invested most of its energy in understanding language, narrative, and discourse, partially masking the openings towards the bodily and affective performance (Beyes and Steyaert, 2012).

In 1985, when the linguistic turn was at its peak, readers may not have been ready for this book which 'cries out at the empire of signs' (Serres and Latour, 1995: 132). Now, its recent translation might bring it a rich reception, especially by those interested in the affective turn (Tucker, 2011; Wraith, 2011). Serres considers language to be worse than drugs, as it deprives us of using our senses:

> I can recall hearing philosophers in dialogue, screeching and quarrelling at the foot of beautiful mountains, on ocean beaches, in front of Niagara Falls, they had the fixed gaze of those with something to say, and I can testify that they saw neither the snow of the glacier, nor the sea, that they heard nothing of the crashing water: they were arguing...Dangerous people. I fear those who go through life drugged, less than I fear those under the edict of language. (2008b: 92)

He concludes this passage by saying, 'Language dictates. We are addicted' (2008b: 92).

Serres refers here to the philosophers around Socrates, who was as numb as if he had taken drugs, thanks to the screeching talk of his friends. However, Serres anticipates his own deathbed and foresees silence as a different form of communication: 'This morning I am in full possession of my faculties; and I declare it my unambiguous wish that people remain silent when I am dying. I want no drugs, neither pharmaceutical nor linguistic. I want to hear who is approaching' (2008b: 92–3). Serres wonders whether it is possible to put any distance between himself and the droning of the language that shapes him or if he is condemned to be drunk on words. Therefore, he is guided by the idea that 'unspeaking, I go towards silence, towards health, I open myself up to the world. The sensitive, delicate, receptive, refined feeler detects another echo and withdraws hastily, waits, observes, unsteady, outweighed by the mass of language, like a rarely-extended antenna, waits for the unexpected, recognizes the unrecognizable, expectant in the silence' (2008b: 93). Serres thus connects the possibility of living and invention when we are able to go outside of ourselves, and outside the language and knowledge that keep us imprisoned, and connect with the world through the senses:

> The I only exists outside the I. The I only thinks outside of the I. It really feels when outside of itself. The I within language is reducible to the sum of its mother tongue, to the collective, to an undefined set of others, to the closure of the open group to which it belongs. It is set in its habits: caught in the I of language almost always and almost everywhere, our whole life long we do not live. I only really live outside of myself;

outside of myself I think, meditate, know; outside of myself I receive what is given, enduringly; I invent outside of myself. Outside of myself, I exist, as does the world. Outside of my verbose flesh, I am on the side of the world. (2008b: 94)

The book thus 'circumscribes the possibility of an immanent experience of the world by the subject who divests himself of the "language screen" summarily called culture that humans have erected between themselves and reality' (Assad, 2012: 91).

Serres discusses the senses chapter by chapter, though he treats smell and taste together. Still he does not keep them separate as complementary gates of the city wall that provide an entry to the city; instead, 'the senses are nothing but the mixing of the body, the principal means whereby the body mingles with the world and with itself, overflows its borders' (Connor, 2008: 3). Thus Serres does not want to separate and dissect the senses, as they belong and work together. For instance, if he starts the book with the skin and touch, then it is to illustrate that skin forms the mutable milieu where soul and world commingle (Connor, 2008).

As he already described in *Genesis*, Serres believes that one understands multiplicity and creative processes through listening. Recently, Serres (2011a) took this idea up again in his book *Musique*, where he again emphasizes (listening to) music as a way to understand processes. If there is one language that Serres does not question, it is the language of music. By listening to music, he tries to disclose languages other than those with which we produce meaning, knowledge, and science. He also explored this question in the earlier *Biogea* (2010a/2012b: 107), in which he tries to listen to other elements, not from an elevated position, because 'we cannot claim to be subjects in the midst of a world of objects, for our behavior resembles that of other insects, other rodents or poisonous plants. Not separated, but plunged, immersed in the Biogea, in cousin company.' Biogea—a neologism combining *bios* (life) and geo (earth)—forms an attempt to consider the world outside the habitual human appropriation of it and to enquire into the relations between earth and bodies and their intermingling (Zournazi, 2012). Again, Serres is quite outspoken about the problems that the specialization of knowledge and science have created for the earth and the lives we can live:

Our analytical hate bursts into these little puzzle pieces, into these texts armored with compelling, aggressive, defensive citations. In fragmented lives, we think a world burst into technologies, sciences, separated languages. Our meaning lies in scattered limbs. By dint of quartering the subjective, the cognitive, the objective and the collective, how can we say the right word and live a happy life?...What love will reunite them? That's the project of a thought, the program of a language, the hope of life. (2011a: 75)

Serres would like to think like the elements of a science that was being born in its totality. He asks how we can speak in several voices: those of things, of knowledge, of emotions, of each and every one. Indeed, it remains to be seen whether, by dint of listening to the voices of the Biogea, we will find this language.

Part of the answer could lie in music, which can never be fully understood by language. Music does not know one single sense but integrates all senses. The body, connected to the earth, is again a crucial mediator between the making of meaning and the voice that utters these meanings. Serres explores music as another, acoustic dimension of the body, mediating between sound and significance. Voices are not primarily producers of meaning, but interconnected with all earthly layers; voices emerge from the wind with its trilling timbres, via the lungs of the world and our own lungs, as much as they surface from our capillaries and the immense rolling of the sea. Therefore, we have to learn to listen to their music, to the music of animals and birds, to the distant signals of whales in the sea. There is so much to listen to: the fantastic explosion of life in all its variations or, in more detail, the wonderful music of a periodic crystal and the sophisticated chromaticism of chromosomes.

Serres thus tries to locate meaningful speech by making a voyage across the many landscapes he traverses in order to retrace a kind of ground noise, a fickle tumult like a prickly bush coming from the world of things; next he explores the various voices of the lively and the bodily, covered with the stings of movements and emotions, and then zooms in on sounds, on the acoustics of vibrations, on music, its beats and rhythms, on compositions. Then, eventually, he passes onto the spread of languages and their meaningful utterances. However, if discursive signfication can have one or just a few meanings, Serres believes that music is polyvalent and omnipotent. By retracing these many layers that connect the body with the world, we will become able to transcend our deafness, and start to value the ear more than the eye. Even if the ear provides us with much richer information than the eye, it seems that philosophers, pedagogues, publishers, and papers keep acting against this reality. Music also gives us a chance to amplify and expand, which we need if we are to invent and to create. Critique represses and shrinks our spaces of action and thought. Even if discussion seems to sharpen our intelligence, it kills our possibilities of engaging with the world beyond any discursive access. With the swelling of the music, our thinking can take a plunge in the expanded space, and start to explore and connect 'Secret de l'art d'inventer: la dilatation de la joie' [secret of the art of invention: the expansion of joy] (2011a: 138). Music imitates the emotional movement from our flesh to (making some) sense. Indeed, 'trembling, music haunts the house of our emotions' (2011a: 147, own translation). Thus, for Serres, sensing the process comes down to ending our deafness and again becoming able to listen to the rustling and murmuring of the world, the sounds and music of the Biogea (ten Bos, 2012). This is what is scandalous in his writing: his willingness to renounce analysis and dissection in favour of poetics and music. If we want to produce any kind of sense, it will not happen in some stabilized discourse, but by immersing ourselves in the buzzing and droning of the world, in this sea of fluid sounds and senses.

34.6 OUTLOOK

Je voudrais avoir dix-huit ans, l'âge de Petite Poucette et de Petit Poucet, puisque tout est à refaire, puisque tout reste à inventer.

(Serres, 2012a: 23)

I have argued that the work of Serres holds untapped potential for supporting and deepening processual thinking. The translation of his work—both as a linguistic conversion and as a transformation in the middle—is probably most effective when it comes with an acknowledgement of the aesthetic, affective, and ethical appeal that an ontology of becoming holds, in the way that Bennett and Connolly (2012: 154) perform their adherence:

> we confess an attraction to the idea that freedom, movement, creativity are installed at the very heart of things, we are drawn to the call to try to ride the waves of the natura naturans and diffuse the urge to master a sea of Life that was not designed for us, and we find an ontology of Becoming to confirm our everyday experience of change as quite fundamental to life and of time as proceeding 'more like the flight of [a] ... wasp than along a line'. (Serres and Latour, 1995: 65)

This combination of a budding potential and an everyday practice of passage forms both a philosophy and practice of invention, one I want to illustrate as a form of an outlook, or rather as Serres would have it, a song in the future distant, by considering one of Serres' latest books.

On 14 March 2013, Serres presented his newest book in a short video clip on YouTube. Although he is now over 80, Serres continues to be productive, and his work continues to be transmitted and translated into many languages. Even at this age, he seems to publish at least one book a year, on topics that include evil (*Le Mal Propre*, 2007a), war (*La Guerre Mondiale*, 2008a), crisis (*Temps des Crises*, 2010b), environmental issues (*Biogée*, 2010a/2012b), and living (*Habiter*, 2011b). This unstoppable, intellectual eagerness seems to respond to what Serres 'promised' himself in a conversation with Bruno Latour:

> I want to finish drawing this navigational map, this inventory—fluctuating and mobile—before I die. Once this work is done it will be clearly seen that all the rapports I traced out either followed or invented a possible road across the ensemble of movements from place to place. Note that this maritime chart, an ocean of possible routes, fluctuates and does not remain static like a map. Each route invents itself. (Serres and Latour, 1995: 105)

Recently, he published *Petite Poucette* (2012a), a book on the new challenges for education. In it, he looks at how education—and with it, society—is confronted by the current students who have grown up with, and are now continuously occupied with, new technologies and social media. While he avoids calling them a 'generation', Serres creates a name for this group of students, who were born since the early 1980s and now constitute a third of the population in the West. He calls them Petite Poucette or Petit Poucet, making reference to Hans Christian Andersen's story of Thumbelina: 'I have baptized them with the greatest possible tenderness that a grandfather can express' (own translation: '*je les ai baptisés, avec la plus grande tendresse que puisse exprimer un grand-père, Petite Poucette et Petit Poucet*' (2012a: 14)).

Serres explains that he purposely used the female form in the title, acknowledging that, in the 40 years he has been teaching, female students have gained supremacy in many fields of science and education; he even says that women were always his better students, more attentive and industrious than 'the dominating males, arrogant weaklings' (2012a: 67). Serres evokes the images of all those who are now formulating and sending messages—by email, SMS, or tweet—by pushing with their two thumbs (in French, thumb is '*pouce*') on their smartphones faster than one can think the texts they are formulating. This image neatly illustrates the new condition of contemporary students who are in the middle of a world of flows, as they have access to knowledge through media, advertisements, and social media.

Here Serres also repeats the story of St Denis, as we all have our heads in front of us in the form of a computer or other communication devices. This fundamentally changes the classroom situation, which gets louder and louder as everyone is talking: why listen to a teacher (whom he calls a '*porte-voix*') to transmit some knowledge read from a paper if one can have the same issue on one's screen in multiple versions? In this situation everyone wants to become active and interactive in front of his or her computer and the classroom becomes virtual. And the teacher knows she can no longer ask for silence, because none will come: the wave of access to knowledge everywhere and at whatever time rises as high as the murmuring and babbling in the classroom.

Should this make us desperate? With Serres and his undestroyable optimism (ten Bos, 2012), we have the connected idea of seriality and invention. Serres has always written in series, from the *Hermes* series (Serres, 1992) to the *Five Senses* publication that was supposed to be a series; though he executed these ideas in later books, he never labelled them as the following volumes (Connor, 2008). Serres, returning to his ideas from *The Troubadour of Knowledge*, believes that the only authentic intellectual act is invention. As knowledge is no longer the issue, the challenge is to be inventive with this vast access to knowledge in which everyone is an epistemologist. This requires that we make an end to the institutional partitions that have conquered our campuses. More importantly, we will have to reinvent everything that organizes society, along with our ways of living together, our institutions, our ways of being and knowing. Serres thus anticipates that everything will have to change radically, not only education but also '[w]ork, enterprises, healthcare, law and politics, in short the whole of our institutions' (2012a: 20–1). For the first time in history, the public, people, actually every passerby, all of them Thumbelinas, can show as much wisdom, knowledge, information, and decisive capacity as those 'dinosaurs', 'those solemn and lost institutions' (2012a: 66) which are losing their grip on this slowly forming, interconnected new body.

And Michel Serres is eager to participate in this emerging network, this anonymous multitude. As illustrated by the quote that opens this section, Serres writes that he would like to be 18 years old again, as everything has to be remade. Do we not find here a real processual spirit of creativity and invention? Is this not an appropriate slogan for a processual thinker: '*tout est à reinventer*', everything is to be reinvented: our ways of living together, our institutions, our ways of being and knowing. Let us give our students—and ourselves—'the right to invent'.

34.7 ENVOI

Eureka!

(Serres, 2012b: 64)

How does this Serresean thinking resonate with processual organization studies? Processual organization theorists will listen and speak in many languages; their writing, like that of troubadours, will be in a poetic style to acknowledge the full understanding of their analysis enacted through all the senses. Processual thinkers read everything and cite nothing; they only write when they have found something: Eureka! Actually organizational analysis will become organizational synthesis: the multiplicity of organization has to be made through performing a multitemporal assemblage. Following an ontology of movement, organizational theorizing is a work of connecting through interdisciplinary, inventive, and inclusive practices. Scholars of processual studies will re-evaluate the force of language and avoid its addictions by including many layers of sound, noise, and reverberation; they will give prominence to the body: its movements connect us with the movements of the world, its affects relate us to human and non-human becomings; it forms the place of life as an apprenticeship, the hyphen that connects the many gestures and customs we adopt or have to unlearn. If a Serresean revolt is to come, it will turn the study of process into a study of the senses. Those in the field study and engage with the question of how to invent the conditions of inventions. Organizational theorists move constantly through passages, search for the swirls and percolations of the third space, operate in a polychronic landscape, navigate the Northwest Passage and stay on the side of the world. They adopt the practices and styles of angels, messengers, harlequins, jokers, and parasites. Any theoretical take on organization will favour a pragmatic orientation, concerned as they are with saving the Earth and the seas. They will begin with themselves and follow, like athletes, a stringent diet of work. Then they will go (on) swimming with their students, and explore with them the love of wisdom and invention. Then they will move to the institutions and urge them to be modest, even prudent: these institutions will have to step aside and hold back, yet reinvent themselves. At any time, organizational theorists will show the courage to embrace disorder, listen to noise, and incorporate the sites and sounds of the worlds they encounter. In search of an ethical response to evil and violence, above all, they invent, joyously.

REFERENCES

Assad, M.L. (1999). *Reading with Michel Serres. An Encounter with Time* (New York: State University of New York Press).

——(2012). Ulyssean Trajectories: A (New) Look at Michel Serres' Topology of Time, in B. Herzogenrath (ed.), *Time and History in Deleuze and Serres* (London: Continuum): 85–102.

Bell, D.F. (2006). Michel Serres?, in L.D. Kritzman (ed.), *The Columbia History of Twentieth-Century French Thought* (New York: Columbia University Press): 658–60.

Bennett, J. and Connolly, W. (2012). The Crumpled Handkerchief, in B. Herzogenrath (ed.), *Time and History in Deleuze and Serres* (London: Continuum): 153–71.

Beyes, T. and Steyaert, C. (2012). Spacing Organization: Non-Representational Theory and Performing Organizational Space, *Organization* 19(1): 43–59.

Brown, S.D. (2000). Extended Review: Michel Serres: The Angelology of Knowledge. Extended Book Review, *The Sociological Review* 48(1): 147–53.

—— (2002). Science, Translation and the Logic of the Parasite, *Theory, Culture & Society* 19(3): 1–27.

——(2003). Natural Writing: The Case of Serres, *Interdisciplinary Science Reviews* 28(3): 184–92.

——(2005). The Theatre of Measurement: Michel Serres?, in C. Jones and R. Munro (eds), *Contemporary Organization Theory* (Oxford: Blackwell): 215–27.

—— and Capdevila, R. (1999). Perpetuum Mobile: Substance, Force and the Sociology of Translation, in J. Law and J. Hassard (eds), *Actor Network Theory and After* (Oxford: Blackwell): 26–50.

——and Stenner, P. (2009). *Psychology without Foundations. History, Philosophy and Psychosocial Theory* (London: Sage).

Buchanan, I. (2010). *Oxford Dictionary of Critical Theory* (Oxford: Oxford University Press).

Clayton, K. (2012). Time Folded and Crumpled: Time, History, Self-Organization and Methodology of Michel Serres, in B. Herzogenrath (ed.), *Time and History in Deleuze and Serres* (London: Continuum): 31–49.

Clegg, S.R., Kornberger, M., and Rhodes, C. (2004). Noise, Parasites and Translation. Theory and Practice in Management Consulting, *Management Learning* 35(1): 31–44.

——————(2005). Learning/Becoming/Organizing, *Organization* 12(2): 147–67.

Colebrook, C. (2012). Post-Human Humanities, in B. Herzogenrath (ed.), *Time and History in Deleuze and Serres* (London: Continuum): 103–25.

Connor, S. (2004). Topologies: Michel Serres and the Shapes of Thought, *Anglistik* 15: 105–17.

—— (2005). Michel Serres' Les Cinq Sens, in N. Abbas (ed.), *Mapping Michel Serres* (Michigan: University of Michigan Press): 153–69.

—— (2008). Introduction, in M. Serres, *Five Senses* (Stanford, CA: Stanford University Press): 1–16.

Critchley, S. (1996). Angel in Disguise: Michel Serres' Attempt to Re-Enchant the World, *Times Literary Supplement*, 19 January.

Deleuze, G. (2000). *Negotiations* (New York: Columbia University Press).

——and Guattari, F. (1994). *What is Philosophy?* (New York: Columbia University Press).

Dey, P. and Steyaert, C. (2007). The Troubadours of Knowledge. Passion and Invention in Management Education, *Organization* 14(3): 437–61.

Dosse, F. (2011). *Gilles Deleuze & Félix Guattari. Intersecting Lives* (New York: Columbia University Press).

Eribon, D. (1991). *Michel Foucault* (Cambridge, MA: Harvard University Press).

Gagliardi, P. and Czarniawska, B. (2006). *Management Education and Humanities* (Edward Elgar: Cheltenham).

Hagen, C. (2009). Michel Serres, One of France's Immortels, Tells the 'Grand Récit' at Stanford, *Stanford Report*, 27 May.

Harman, G. (2009). *Prince of Networks: Bruno Latour and Metaphysics* (Melbourne: re-press).

Hatch, M.J. (2011). *Organizations: A Very Short Introduction* (Oxford: Oxford University Press).

Hernes, T. (2008). *Understanding Organization as Process. Theory for a Tangled World* (New York: Routledge).

Herzogenrath, B. (ed.) (2012). *Time and History in Deleuze and Serres* (London: Continuum).

Hjorth, C. and Steyaert, C. (2006). American Psycho/European Schizo: Stories of Managerial Elites in a Hundred Images, in P. Gagliardi and B. Czarniawska (eds), *Management Education and Humanities* (Edward Elgar: Cheltenham): 67–97.

Linstead, S. (2004). *Organization Theory and Postmodern Thought* (London: Sage).

Michael, M. (2000). *Reconnecting Culture, Technology and Nature* (London: Routledge).

Paulson, W. (2000). Michel Serres' Utopia of Language, *Configurations* 8(2): 215–28.

Pearce, J.V. (2010). The Five Senses: A Philosophy of Mingled Bodies, *Perspectives: International Postgraduate Journal of Philosophy* 3(1): 88–95.

Serres, M. (1982). *Genèse* (Paris: Grasset).

——(1985). *Les Cinq Sens* (Paris: Grasset).

——(1991). *Le Tiers-Instruit* (Paris: François Bourin).

——(1992). *Hermes: Literature, Science, Philosophy* (Baltimore: The Johns Hopkins University Press).

——(1994). *Atlas* (Paris: Editions Julliard).

——(1995a). *Genesis* (Ann Arbor: The University of Michigan Press).

——(1995b). *Angels: A Modern Myth* (Paris: Editions Flammarion).

——(1997). *The Troubadour of Knowledge* (Ann Arbor: University of Michigan Press).

——(1999). *Variations sur le Corps* (Paris: Le Pommier).

—— (2006a). The Great Narrative of the Sciences and the History of Humanities, in P. Gagliardi and B. Czarniawska (eds), *Management Education and Humanities* (Edward Elgar: Cheltenham): 227–32.

——(2006b). *Petites Chroniques du Dimanche Soir* (Paris: Le Pommier).

——(2007a). *Le Mal Propre* (Paris: Le Pommier).

——(2007b). *Petites Chroniques du Dimanche Soir. Tome II* (Paris: Le Pommier).

——(2008a). *La Guerre Mondiale* (Paris: Le Pommier).

——(2008b). *The Five Senses. A Philosophy of Mingled Bodies* (Stanford, CA: Stanford University Press).

——(2009). *Petites Chroniques du Dimanche Soir. Tome III* (Paris: Le Pommier).

——(2010a). *Biogée* (Paris: Le Pommier).

——(2010b) *Temps des Crises* (Paris: Le Pommier).

——(2011a). *Musique* (Paris: Le Pommier).

——(2011b). *Habiter* (Paris: Le Pommier).

——(2011c). *Variations on the Body* (Minneapolis: Univocal Publishing).

——(2012a). *Petite Poucette* (Paris: Edition Le Pommier, Manifestes).

——(2012b). *Biogea* (Minneapolis: Univocal Publishing).

——and Latour, B. (1995). *Conversations on Science, Culture and Time* (Ann Arbor: University of Michigan Press).

Steyaert, C. (2012). Making the Multiple. Theorizing Processes of Entrepreneurship and Organization, in D. Hjorth (ed.), *Organizational Entrepreneurship* (Cheltenham: Edward Elgar): 151–68.

ten Bos, R. (2012). Nawoord, in M. Serres, *Muziek* (Amsterdam: Boom): 187–96.

Tucker, I. (2011). Sense and the Limits of Knowledge. Bodily Connections in the Work of Serres, *Theory, Culture & Society* 28(1): 149–60.

Wraith, M. (2011). Review of The Five Senses, *Critical Quarterly* 53(1): 106–11.

Zembylas, M. (2002). Michel Serres: A Troubadour for Science, Philosophy and Education, *Educational Philosophy and Theory* 34(4): 477–502.

Zournazi, M. (2012). Cosmocracy: A Hymn for the World? Reflections on Michel Serres and the Natural World, *Journal of Multidisciplinary International Studies* 9(2): 1–9.

CHAPTER 35

PETER SLOTERDIJK (1947b)

TIMON BEYES

35.1 A WORLDLY PHILOSOPHER

> If I had to examine myself from a distance, then I would say that this
> Sloterdijk is a strange bastard, comprising a lyrical extremist and a
> damned school master. Or a mystic and compère.
>
> (Sloterdijk, 2011a: 297)

Peter Sloterdijk has a lot to say about a lot of things. Following Thrift's assessment
(2012: 136), this 'promiscuous relationship with the world', on the back of a rather breathtaking erudition turned into a distinctive, literary, evocative, and 'hyper-connective'
style of 'hyperbolic reasoning' (2012: 136), is what makes his writings so interesting and
original, sometimes infuriating and often a joy to read. His work poses 'a challenge to
anyone interested in understanding what it means to do philosophy today' (van Tuinen,
2007: 276). That it poses particular challenges to anyone interested in thinking organization and/as process, especially with regard to embodiment, space, affect, and a scholarly
ethics of generosity, is what this chapter seeks to demonstrate.

As I am writing this, Sloterdijk has published almost 40 books on a wide range of topics in his native German, from long, sprawling explorations to short and partly quite
polemical interventions. His apparent ease in moving from topic to topic corresponds to
an impressive scope of sources he draws upon, which cannot be pinned down in terms
of disciplinary categories. His outspoken disdain for the disciplinary grids and limitations of 'state philosophy' and its 'scholastic aberrance' (Sloterdijk, 2001a: 48) has made
him a singular and contested figure, the 'odd one out' in the German intellectual landscape of the past 30 years (Schinkel and Nordegraaf-Eelens, 2011b: 17).

It is probably no coincidence, then, that Sloterdijk's prodigious output has not ema-
nated from a proper position in German faculties of philosophy. After studies in philosophy, history, and literature and a PhD in linguistics he started out as a freelance
scholar and writer in the 1980s. He became professor of philosophy and media theory at

Karlsruhe University of Arts and Design when it opened in 1992, and became its Rektor in 2001. Seen by some as 'Germany's foremost public philosopher' (Toscano, 2010; Couture, 2012), Sloterdijk is a reliable presence in the major newspapers and magazines as well as on TV (from 2002 to 2012 he co-hosted the philosophical television show 'In the Glasshouse: Philosophical Quartet' on one of the two major German public TV stations). He regularly intervenes in, or provokes, debates over societal matters of concern. This had led to public, quite entertaining but sometimes also malicious controversies, especially with his *bête noires*, the heirs of Frankfurt School critical theory, most notoriously with Jürgen Habermas on Sloterdijk's *Rules for the Human Zoo* speech (2009a; for Sloterdijk's reflection on the scandal, see 2011a).

Lately, Sloterdijk has also become a major presence in Anglophone and global discussions of so-called continental theory (Elden, 2012b). This is manifested in a recent flurry of English translations of his major works—*Rage and Time* (2010a); the book of interviews *Neither Sun nor Death* (2011a); the first instalment of his *Spheres* trilogy (2011b), with Volumes II and III already announced; *You Must Change Your Life* (2013)—as well as some of his shorter books: *Theory of the Post-War Periods* (2008); *Rules for the Human Zoo* (2009a); *God's Zeal* (2009b); *Derrida, an Egyptian* (2009c); *Terror from the Air* (2009d); *The Art of Philosophy* (2012a). Edited collections on his work have been published (Elden, 2012a; Schinkel and Noordegraaf-Eelens, 2011a) and special issues have appeared in *Cultural Policy* (van Tuinen, 2007) and *Environment and Planning D: Society and Space* (Elden and Mendieta, 2009).

However, it would be more precise to speak of 'Sloterdijk's second coming' in the English-speaking world (Elden and Mendieta, 2009: 1), because his ground-breaking, surprise best-seller *Critique of Cynical Reason*, originally published in 1983, was published in English as early as 1988, quickly followed by his early book on Nietzsche, *Thinker on Stage* (1989a). The hiatus between the late 1980s and late 2000s (much less so with regard to the more sustained reception of his work in other languages such as Dutch, French, and Spanish) seems to have to do with the contingencies of translation and the vagaries of intellectual fashion. In this sense, the renewed attention awarded to Sloterdijk in Anglophone circles might have as much to do with the rediscovery of a singular thinker as with his idiosyncratic—and, I will argue, process-minded—treatment of important themes of contemporary cultural theory, namely the body, space, and affect, or in Sloterdijk's own summary and current vocabulary (2012b), his theorizing of a 'generalized immunology' and of 'psychopolitics'. On the international conference circuit Sloterdijk now shares the stage with the likes of Latour, Rancière, and Žižek, often as a kind of qualifying or counter-figure to contemporary radical chic and the 'Brothers and Sisters of the Damaged Life' (2011a: 17).[1]

As concerns the aim and scope of this chapter, then, a few qualifications are in order. For one, Peter Sloterdijk is a thinker of the contemporary who has characterized himself as a kind of medium of the *Zeitgeist*, and who in his reflections on contemporaneousness has explicitly related his work to the Nietzschean notion (and philosophico-therapeutical practice) of physician of culture and 'provocation therapist' (2011a: 11, 218). As Huyssen (1988: xi) suggests, we might describe Sloterdijk's project as an analysis of our present (even if often prepared through sweeping historical surveys) that seeks to apprehend what the world is and is doing to us at this moment. One is thus faced with an unfinished work in progress; the philosopher's contemporaneousness spawns an ongoing, variegated, and sometimes speculative labour of reflection geared towards new thoughts and practices.

Moreover, a hermeneutics of situating Sloterdijk's thought in the history and present of philosophy is beyond the scope of this chapter. The work of this 'intellectual magpie' (Elden, 2012b: 3) exceeds scholastic philosophy in its ambition, excursiveness, and styles as well as through the wide array of sources it draws upon, which 'range from psychoanalysis and constructivist philosophy to theology, Indian philosophy, architectural theory, palaeoanthropology, ethnology, pop culture, medicine, economics, media theory, systems theory, and cybernetics' (van Tuinen, 2007: 279). Since influences, connections, and contrasts will pop up as I go along, it suffices to summarily list here the more important ones (also with regard to indicating a certain heritage of process thinking). Sloterdijk inscribes his thought in a line of ancestors that includes 'anti-philosophical' and controversial philosophers and thinkers, most prominently Nietzsche and Heidegger, but also Diogenes, Kierkegaard, Günther, and Luhmann as well as a number of protagonists of twentieth-century French thought such as Tarde, Sartre, Foucault, Derrida, and Deleuze. Indeed, what it means to think 'after' figures such as Nietzsche, Heidegger, Luhmann, and Deleuze, to have learned their lessons, and to add to what they have achieved, is a question Sloterdijk repeatedly ponders (e.g. 2001a, 2001b).

That said, whether there is an overarching system to the philosopher's thought, or even a discernible overall trajectory, is a matter of debate (Elden, 2012b). Echoing Thrift's notion of Sloterdijk as 'the very model of a worldly philosopher' (2012: 135), he has been called a 'morphological thinker', 'a trainee trying new forms, new combinations, reaching out and philosophically embodying an ek-sistenz rather than a closed set of propositions' (Schinkel and Nordegraaf-Eelens, 2011b: 7–8). Sloterdijk's approach therefore bears some similarities to Deleuze and Guattari's notion of philosophy as the affirmative invention and fabrication of concepts (Deleuze and Guattari, 1994); a 'gay science', to quote its perhaps most important influence: a Nietzschean joy of creation, of bringing about new thoughts and ideas (Nietzsche, 1999). Sloterdijk quite notoriously contrasts this type of doing philosophy with what he perceives to be the *ressentiment* (resentment), provincialism, and Eurocentrism of conventional critical theory as well as 'the German maso-theory cartel' (2011a: 17) and its gathering of 'aggressive and depressive moralists, problematists, "problemoholics," and soft rigorists whose predominant existential stimulus is *No*' (1988: 126, emphasis in the original). Especially later Frankfurt School-type of criticism would indulge in an a priori of *Weltschmerz*, of pain and bitterness (1988: xxxiii). What one encounters in Sloterdijk's writings from *Critique of Cynical Reason* to *You Must Change Your Life*, therefore, is a risky and affirmative mode of theorizing of a certain processual bend, a methodology of world-making (and its politics).

For the purpose of this chapter, it follows that using up its space to attempt to summarize every nook and cranny of this thinker's published oeuvre or to delve into the details of his major books is both unfeasible and beside the point. Rather, I will move relatively freely between his major texts and selected shorter books, between English translations and (as yet) untranslated texts,[2] to coax out dominant strands of his work and ponder how they might affect, provoke, irritate, and refresh our thinking of organization as made up of processes. After positioning the philosopher as an idiosyncratic thinker of process (and without wanting to reduce him to this label), I attempt to present Sloterdijk's work as a challenge to think processes of organizing in their 'kynical and anthropotechnical', 'immunological and spherical', 'psychopolitical', and 'homeotechnological' materializations. In a vocabulary perhaps better known to organizational scholars, this could be translated as learning to apprehend organizing in its embodied, spatial, affective, and very material forms. Adopting a more essayistic style includes touching upon existing uses of Sloterdijk in organization studies, which are modest in number and scope, and pointing towards potential openings for further work as I go along. Indeed, the primary aim of this chapter is to entice readers to engage with, indulge in, and experiment with what it might mean to think organizing with and after Sloterdijk.

35.2 Coming-into-the-World: Thinking Relational Movement

> The point for me is to contribute to dissolving the crushing heritages of the metaphysics of substance and of the isolated thing, which are still firmly anchored in people's mindsets: representations which, for 2500 years, have blinded Europeans by playing a grammatical mirage over what is called the hard kernel of the real.
>
> (Sloterdijk, 2011a: 138–9)

Sloterdijk is not a process philosopher in the strict sense of theorizing the notion of process and its ramifications, let alone a theorist of organizational processes. However, his work constitutes an original philosophy of becoming, of processes of formation and self-formation (van Tuinen, 2011). In *Nicht gerettet* (*Not Saved*), his book of essays on thinking after—and thus with and against—Heidegger, Sloterdijk (2001a) begins by characterizing Heidegger as a 'thinker-in-movement', a philosopher of kinetics. Being is invariably put into movement and pervaded by movement, from which it cannot be saved (2001a: 31). The corresponding fundamental critique of notions of subjectivity as 'enframed' and 'stilled' substance, this 'fundamental neurosis of Western culture' (Sloterdijk, 1998a: 85), runs like a thread through Sloterdijk's texts. Instead, he engages in an ontological constructivism that grasps human and social formation as becoming, as a series of events in dissipative, excessive processes of production (Sloterdijk, 2001a: 206). We can, he writes vis-à-vis Heidegger, 'no longer begin with fixed appearance, idea, things, subject, system, consciousness, state of affairs, the objective, or time-transcending values. We can only begin with the primal movement and movability of and upon ourselves, with our temporality, temporariness, situatedness and relatedness' (2001a: 32).

In this spirit, the earlier works *Kopernikanische Mobilmachung und ptolemäische Abrüstung* (*Copernican Mobilization and Ptolemaic Disarmament*; 1986) and *Eurotaoismus: Zur Kritik der politischen Kinetik* (*Eurotaoism: Towards a Critique of Political Kinetics*; 1989b) diagnose a kinetic utopianism at the heart of modernity. Ernst Jünger's notion of mobilization is enlisted to denote a neurotic and aggressive quest for movement, movement for movement's sake: 'the entire movement of the world is to be the performance of our design for it' (Sloterdijk, 1989: 23). The metaphysical tradition of subject philosophy and its intersubjective aftermath are complicit in this development, which implicates the dominant forms of critical theory in modernity and Enlightenment's kinetic, and finally, militaristic predicament.

Importantly, for Sloterdijk the processes of mobilization are not explained through an economy or psychology of guilt, lack, scarcity, or related 'negative' concepts. These are examples of a 'priestly' anthropocentric discourse of resentment that he regularly dismisses and in later writings tries to supplement with a Nietzschean ethos and 'psychopolitics' of excess, affluence, and generosity (see Sloterdijk, 2001b, 2010a, 2010b). A kind of philosophical energetics is required, which remains open to and embedded in the ecstatic openness of mobilization and strives towards a 'being-at-ease-in-movement' or 'rest-in-movement' (2011a: 347). Drawing upon and reconfiguring Heidegger's notion of *Gelassenheit*—and prefiguring the ongoing search of what Sloterdijk would later call 'immunological practices' (2011a)—in *Eurotaoismus* the philosopher argues that 'there has never been a Frankfurt critical theory, but only a Freiburg one' (1989: 143). To prefer the Freiburg of Husserl and especially Heidegger to the Frankfurt (School) of Adorno et al. is a provocation perhaps lost on a reader unaware of Germany's intellectual scenery. To 'risk the expression' of 'a Heideggerian Left' (Sloterdijk, 1988: 245) means developing a left thought from the work of a philosopher once entangled in, or at least supportive of, the fascist ideology of National Socialism.

In contradistinction to Heidegger's being-unto-death and to elide his dark existentialism, putative technophobia, and provincialism, Sloterdijk posits a 'being-unto-life' and tries to 'interpret the movement into life as a kind of permanent birth' (2011c: 191)—the assumption of a primordial and perpetual horizontal or lateral openness and thrust against Heidgger's vertical 'thrownness'. In *Eurotaoismus*, Sloterdijk (1989b) draws upon Nietzsche's and Arendt's notion of natality to develop the idea of coming-into-the-world as denoting the entering into worldly horizons, original excess, and perpetual birth: 'ecstatic immanence'. He thus proposes to think of life from the perspective of its beginning and as a series of beginnings. In this sense, van Tuinen (2011: 49) detects an original principle of difference in Sloterdijk's writings, which he calls 'natal difference'. It designates 'what has already begun with a processual excess over itself'. Clear traces of 'natal difference' are already present in the *Critique of Cynical Reason*, where Sloterdijk argues for a softening and liquefying of the 'hard', 'male' subject and its identity pathology:

> The mania for 'identity' seems to be the deepest of unconscious programmings... A formal somebody, as bearer of our social identifications, is, so to speak,

programmed into us...Basically, however, no life has a name. The self-conscious nobody in us—who acquires names and identities only through its 'social birth'—remains the living source of freedom. The living Nobody, in spite of the horror of socialization, remembers the energetic paradises beneath the personalities. Its life soil is the mentally alert body, which we should call not *nobody* but *yesbody*. (1988: 73; emphasis in the original)

There is thus a vitalist motif in Sloterdijk's thinking, which calls to mind Deleuze's insistence, drawn from Spinoza, that we do not know what our bodies can do and our lives can become (Deleuze and Guattari, 1988: 257). Importantly, and as the term 'social birth' in the quote indicates, this is a decidedly relational motif of vitalism. It assumes a being-with, a relational space of coexistence where 'people are ecstatic, as Heidegger says, but not because they are contained in nothingness...They themselves are ecstatic because the other always already penetrates them' (Sloterdijk, 2011c: 185–6). In other words, humans constitute media or 'medial inter-beings' (*Zwischenwesen*) (Sloterdijk, 2004), through which becomings and events unfold, which they then work or 'exercise' on. In 'assuming themselves', they are thus simultaneously products of formation and self-forming; they constitute 'local energies of gathering' (Sloterdijk, 2001a: 222). It is due to these relational and excessive processes of formation, of forming and being formed, that we can speak of human beings as world-making, world-constituting animals.

Moreover, today more than ever the pre-subjective forces of life include technical apparatuses and thus media by which humans are inscribed, coded, or conditioned. Not only in relation to other actors, but also in relation to other actants, to use Latour's term, must human life and the social be understood in its 'monstrous' processes of production, with human beings as co-producers or, perhaps, intelligent accelerators (Sloterdijk, 2012c). Here, too, Sloterdijk prefers a relatively affirmative theorizing of the technological condition to Heidegger's gloomier notion of the enframing and demiurgic power of the *Gestell*. If there is no unmediated life and technologies invariably accompany the formation of the human and their habitat, then we need to think and speculate on the hybrid co-evolution of man and technology through what Sloterdijk calls the practice of 'homeotechnology' (2001a: 227). Latour claims that 'no contemporary philosopher is more interested in materiality, in engineering, in biotechnology...and in science more generally', and Sloterdijk's sensibility for the new alliances of technological and human development would make him '*the* philosopher of design' (2009: 159–60; emphasis in the original).

In sum, while one should be wary to reduce Sloterdijk's oeuvre to a catchy, encompassing formula, the notions of 'coming-into-the-world' and 'natal difference' allow to detect a processual angle and to establish, as it were, his credentials as an original process theorist. Indeed, this thinker of 'the primal movement and movability of and upon ourselves' (2001a: 32) has described his theorizing as one of 'relocation' and 'transitions between elements and states of affairs' (Sloterdijk, 2011a: 334). The theorizing of organization as process, thus understood as 'a more general force which includes us in its perpetual movement between order and disorder' (Cooper: 1998: 154), therefore gains an elaborate and idiosyncratic reflective apparatus for thinking organizing (in) a world on the move.

Going beyond Sloterdijk's credentials as a thinker of process, in the following the study of organizing is confronted with what I deem the most important of his conceptual, poetic, and speculative movements and transitions. I move in four steps. First, I revisit the *Critique of Cynical Reason* and relate it to the struggle between cynical modes of reason and embodied practices of kynicism at work in organizational life. This 'early Sloterdijk' is linked to the 'late' one of practices of self-transformation and the potential of studying (the history of) organization as (a history of) exercises of self-fashioning. Second, I delve into the spherological project of explicating a spatial ontology and sketch its potential to rethink organization as atmospheric gatherings of people, things, technologies, and affects. Third, from there it is but a step to the psychopolitics of affective surges and their organizational force. Fourth and finally, I discuss the style and politics of a risky, experimental, and joyful theorizing of process. Perhaps the most striking challenge that Sloterdijk's work poses, or so I conclude, pertains to the possibility of an ethics of generosity in scholarly work, which supplements or subverts the spirit of *ressentiment* that all too often pervades our writings.

35.3 OF KYNICS AND ACROBATS

> We have the cynical Zeitgeist and that specific taste of a fragmented, over-complicated, demoralizing world situation in our bones, our nerves, our eyes, and in the corners of our mouths. In everything that is really contemporary, the kynical and the cynical elements become noticeable as part of our bodily-psychical and intellectual physiognomy... [W]hoever wants to decipher it is faced with the task of working on the psychosomatics of cynicism.
>
> (Sloterdijk, 1988: 140)

The *Critique of Cynical Reason*, Sloterdijk's surprise philosophical best-seller originally published in 1983, is an encyclopaedic, digressive, and eminently readable treatise on the struggle between the cynical consciousness of power and the responses of a kynical consciousness of revolt and its politics of the body. The notion of kynicism refers to the ancient, original form of cynicism, a thinking with and through the body associated with Diogenes of Sinope and enacted through satirical laughter, sarcasm, strategic silence, indecent or debased bodily action, and the unrestrained fulfilment of bodily needs—perhaps the philosophical invention of counterculture. Sloterdijk's attempt at 'a theory of consciousness with flesh and blood (and teeth)' (1988: xxxi) seeks to recover and reinvigorate such embodied performances of critique. They are pitted against the modern variant of cynicism, which would have transformed or cleaned up the ancient cynical ethics into a toxic mix of disillusionment, self-interest, and self-serving embedded in and conditioning our modes of working and living. This state of 'enlightened false consciousness' (1988: 5) implies acting contrary to better knowledge and against better judgement, continuing to function while full of doubts, asocial but fully integrated, without illusion and still sucked down by the order of things. Modern cynicism thus denotes 'a hard-boiled, shadowy cleverness that has split courage off from itself, holds anything positive to be fraud, and is intent only on somehow getting through life' (1988: 546).

However, more than (just) another binary opposition between 'bad' cynicism and 'good' kynicism, this struggle is about a split within cynicism itself, which is enacted through the cynical reason of domination and self-domination and the kynic revolt of self-assertion and self-realization. Instrumental or cynical reason is never total. There is a potential or positive force of cynicism, which takes the form of kynical self-assertion, waiting to be mobilized in the moment of disillusioned enlightenment. The masochism of refusal or melancholy about irrevocable loss—for Sloterdijk, the double heritage of critical theory—today merely reinforces the enlightened false consciousness it should help to dismantle. Instead, Sloterdijk announces his conceptual and stylistic labour as *Erheiterungsarbeit*, 'a work that cheers us up' (1988: xxxvii). He 'carnivalizes the frozen landscape of negative dialectics, and mobilizes the kynical body of Diogenes against the cunning of Odysseus, that master-cynic of the *Dialectic of Enlightenment*' (Huyssen, 1988: xviii).

The book and its author were immediately drawn into the political and ideological trenches of its time—a position Sloterdijk would never really leave again. All the accusations now routinely levelled against his work were there already: 'simplistic, faddish, and pretentious, anti-theoretical, regressively irrational, and politically reactionary' (Huyssen, 1988: x). Moreover, notwithstanding its fight against the entitative and 'hard' logic of the western subject the book often espouses a decidedly male cynicism, its repeated emphasis of maleness or virility 'not quite up to the task of thinking about women even where, maybe especially where...the body, masturbation, pornography' are concerned (Babich, 2012: 21, 31).

Apart from the pleasures of reading the *Critique of Cynical Reason* as well as its foreshadowing of the later trajectories of Sloterdijk's thought,[3] the book offers quite straightforward reverberations for the study of organization. While the *Critique* and the notion of enlightened false consciousness have received fleeting nods in, for instance, studies of cynicism at the workplace (e.g. Fleming and Spicer, 2003) and the performativity of critical management studies (Spicer et al., 2009), in similar fashion to the rest of Sloterdijk's oeuvre it is by-and-large an untapped source of inspiration for organizational scholars. Which is a bit of a surprise: after all, the perpetual struggle between cynical modes of reasoning and practice—as organizational forces and as they are enacted within organizations—and kynical performances of resistance and subversion goes beyond a one-sided focus on workers' cynicism as response to organizational relations of domination. It opens up a more complex perspective on processes of organizing as they play out the split within cynicism itself; and it is on this basis that the question of different modes of cynicism—and how to be cynical—poses itself. Moreover, the *Critique* forces us to encounter the bodies and physiognomies of organizing. It is a style of thinking (in) the flesh and apprehending the politics of the body, which is directed against the reliance on putatively disembodied master narratives of reason, rationality, and control. In other words, it calls for a psychosomatics of organizing.

In the spirit of the *Critique of Cynical Reason*, then, might we not ask whether critical studies of organizational life tend to reproduce the disillusioned art (and complicity) of knowing better? Consider the recent proliferations of 'the theatrical-political aspect of protest and provocation' on streets and squares across the world (Osborne, 2012: 19): is the performative radicalism of the ancient type being resurrected? And can we not help resound and make circulate such kynical processes of 'therapeutic' destabilization and expansion of the boundaries of subjectivity and collectivity (e.g. Taussig, 2012)? For instance, Osborne (2012) enlists Sloterdijk's distinction to reflect on the Occupy movement's enactments of asceticism, its provocative, embodied, and witty demonstrations of free speech, and its hatred of power.

Almost in contradistinction to such interpretations, Sloterdijk later distanced himself from his ground-breaking book, commenting upon some of its passages 'as the last free forest-song of the romanticism of emancipation' and implicating it in a naive post-1968 belief in progress through 'cultural revolutionary, anarcho-ecologist, and experimental creative' forces (2011a: 281). It is therefore tempting to read *You Must Change Your Life*, his most recent major work, as a response to and further development of the sensibilities espoused in the *Critique*. *You Must Change Your Life* (2013) again investigates the knot of ascetism and resentment but leaves behind ascetic practices of kynicism to set its sight on a 'general ascetology' (2013: 6). In ancient Greek, *áskesis* means exercise or training. What Sloterdijk tries to develop, then, is a 'comprehensive theory of practising existence' (2013: 6), which departs from a Nietzschean distinction between the priestly, life-denying, and stultifying ascetism of the ill and the positive, life-affirming, and empowering practices of the healthy in order to re-narrate human development through its practices of self-formation and self-transformation. Life, then, is acrobatics, and the practising human an acrobatic animal. 'You must change your life', a line from Rilke's poem 'Archaic Torso of Apollo', thus expresses 'the absolute imperative' (2013: 442): Condemned to lead a life of practice, we are caught up in a perpetual (and quite surrealist) labour of individual and collective self-fashioning.

Sloterdijk's philosophical energetics, according to which being is invariably put into movement and pervaded by movement, is here directed at a history of 'anthropotechnics', the tableau of training regimes, cultural drillings, and exercises that shape and discipline humans, and what they make of it. It thus shows similarities to the late Foucault's work on practices of the self (1992). It also indicates a shift from the emancipatory thrust of the *Critique of Cynical Reason* to a meritocratic and rather elitist notion of good and bad trainings, where '[a]depts and players are constantly involved in a spontaneous better-or-worse ranking of their skills and actions. I define these kinds of distinctions as an expression of the vertical tension inherent in human existence' (Sloterdijk, 2012a: 7). Given his understanding of philosophical practice as a therapeutic one, the task of philosophy thus becomes educating the athletes, acrobats, and virtuosos to invent new forms of practising existence, forms more adept at dealing with the ecological and economic crisis of today (Sloterdijk, 2013: 442 ff; van Tuinen, 2012).

The challenges that Sloterdijk's grand rewriting of the anthropology of humanity as a general theory of practice pose to the study of organization seem as obvious as they are far-reaching. They ask us to 'suspend virtually everything that has been said about humans as working beings in order to translate it into the language of practicing, or self-forming and self-enhancing behaviour' (Sloterdijk, 2013: 5). Rather than viewing organization as division of labour or labour process, as production process, power structure, communicative system, form of institutional reproduction, and so on, it might be conceived as a configuration of self-referential training exercises that work on and constitute organizational subjects, who in turn co-condition these exercises' execution. Can we explicate an acrobatics of organizational life? Can we reframe organizational man as acrobatic man and investigate the interplay between organizational training regimes and the urge to overcome oneself? And how do we relate to the fundamental problematic of life-formation today and enact our own training regimes as scholars and educators (Sloterdjk, 2012a)?

35.4 OF FOAM AND ATMOSPHERES

> I claim that the first common activity of humans is…the production of a resonance between those who live together. For present-day cultures the question of survival has become a question of the way in which they are reproduced as atmospheric communities.
>
> (Sloterdijk, 2011a: 245)

The ecstatic character of human becoming, its existential acrobatics of mental and physical exercises is embedded in a relational space of coexistence and the building of collective worlds. While especially *You Must Change Your Life* seems at times to fall back into a subject-centred celebration of the capacity of outstanding individuals to assume and form themselves, I suggest this should be read on the background of Sloterdijk's wide-ranging attempt to elaborate 'a grammar of the shared situation' and a mode of 'being-in-the-middle-of-it' (2011a: 348, 349).

To oversimplify the author's philosophical heritage: human's radical openness and the Nietzschean urge to overcome oneself are invariably predicated on a Heideggerian inhabitation in more or less porous, more or less protective dwelling places, relative enclosures, or insulations brought together in the notion of spheres or spheres of immunity. The possibility of the self-fashioning of kynical and acrobatic bodies hinges on the fundamental spatiality and thus relational and co-constitutive nature of human existence in spheres. Importantly, and close to the ancient term '*techne*' as that which brings forth the human in the first place (Morin, 2012: 84), technology or what Sloterdijk calls 'homeotechnology' is an active participant in these processes of co-constitution (2001a: 227).

Sloterdijk's massive, if not megalomaniac, *Spheres* trilogy is dedicated to the explication of this spatial ontology. In *Sphären I* (1998a: 345) he suggests understanding his project as the necessary counterpart to Heidegger's *Being and Time*, as *Being and Space*.

It thus constitutes an idiosyncratic theory of space formation and an extended meditation—'a hyperbolic novel' (2004: 16), a 'medial poetics of existence' (1998a: 81)—on being-in-the-world as being-with or being-together in spheres (Elden, 2012b). It is a sprawling meditation on the 'soft antroposphere's' of self-animated and immunological spaces we are born into, that we shape and that shape us. These protective spheres 'separate the human from the pressure of the environment, allow him to develop in a non-adaptive way and prepare the world-opening of the human, that is, prepare his sensibility for what is either spatially or temporally remote' (Morin, 2012: 84).

It is impossible to do justice to the avalanche of concepts, metaphors, examples, and speculations that make up the three volumes—subtitled *Bubbles*, *Globes*, and *Foam*—in this section. Together they narrate a spatial history of humankind: from the 'microspheric' bubbles of coming-into-the-world (the uterus; the primordial housing) to the 'macrospheric' history of globalization to today's plural and co-fragile spheres of digital networks, apartment complexes, and 'foam cities'. As a kind of spin-off published shortly after the third volume, albeit a major work in its own right, *Im Weltinnenraum des Kapitals* (*In the Inner World Space of Capital*, 2005) further develops the theory of globalization laid out in *Spheres II* and culminates in an extended discussion of the 'interior sphere' and the 'interior design' of global capitalism as well as its excluded outside.

With regard to organizational process, among the riches on offer here I suggest three potential lines of enquiry that seem particularly striking: its spatio-theoretical sensibility; foam as a guiding metaphor to investigate contemporary organizing; and the notion of atmospheres to think and explore the pre-subjective knot of spatial, material, and affective forces. First, the spherological project constitutes an ambitious and distinct exploration of coming to terms with and learning to apprehend the spatial embeddedness of the social and human becoming. Bearing some resemblances to the loosely coupled body of work in human geography that has been labelled 'Non-Representational Theory' (Thrift, 2007), especially in the first and third volume of the *Spheres* trilogy—less so in the grand 'macrospheric' narrative of Volume II—Sloterdijk develops a resolutely processual and open-ended notion of space, or 'spacing' (Beyes and Steyaert, 2012). It offers a promising point of departure for a truly spatial approach to organizational becoming, which attempts to avoid the residual essentialism and stasis often at work in spatial analyses. Space is seen as an excessive composition of multiple forces, which include the mediating power of things or inhuman traffic and its material-technological relations as well as the affective surges that sweep through the human body. Echoing Sloterdijk's continuous dismissal of the metaphysics of substance, the body becomes the setting for a play of spatial connections, which then have to be worked upon through the immunological practices of anthropotechnics. And importantly, he radically experiments with a strange philosophico-literary language, a spatial poetics of affects, intensities, flows, floating, magnetisms, resonances, and other spacings that seek to apprehend these spatial concatenations, which are usually lost in the representational techniques of the social sciences. Indeed, '[w]e ought not to justify, but instead to form, to link up, and to let sail. Intensifications replace acts of founding' (Sloterdijk, 2011a: 244).

Second, Sloterdijk's analysis of the 'multi-spherical' condition of the present conducted in *Sphären III* offers a set of concepts and insights to explore contemporary processes of organizing as they play out in, and simultaneously produce, organizational spaces. In this sense, Borch (2010, 2011) has embarked on a pioneering reading of the third instalment of the *Spheres* trilogy in order to discuss its implications for understanding organizational dynamics and the complex composition of organizations as foam structures. The metaphor of foam allows Sloterdijk to explicate the topological assemblages of a multiplicity of interlocking spheres (2004: 251). They resemble cells that hang together and are both separated and connected at the same time: 'co-fragile' and 'co-isolated associations' (2004: 255, 302). The notion of social foam thus replaces that of society and its implications of the social as a 'mono-spherical container' (2004: 59) and that of networks and their reductive geometries of points, nodes, and lines—this 'universe for data fishers and anorectics' (2004: 257). Following Sloterdijk, Borch (2010) grasps the relations between foam-like spheres in terms of Tarde's concept of affective imitation and contagion (instead of communication and discourse): Feelings, actions, and effects reverberate through the foams, often with unpredictable consequences and repercussions (think of the contagious spiralling of affects in digital networks, the recent financial crisis, or the environmental maladies). Thus, the study of organization gains a perspective that is able to take into account the interplay of spatial, affective, and material processes, which constitute organizational spatialities and their interrelations. Indeed, empirical practices of 'organizational foam analysis...should be welcomed since they are likely to shed new light on organizational life' (Borch, 2010: 238).

Third, Sloterdijik develops in *Spheres III* the contours of a philosophy of atmospheres. Also published as a stand-alone book, *Luftbeben*, literally 'airquakes' and translated as *Terror from the Air* (Sloterdjik, 2009d), is mainly a history of twentieth-century 'atmoterrorism'. The book traces how acts of war and terror began aiming less at the bodies of enemies and more at the environmental conditions of human life. It is thus a history of the becoming-conscious of atmospheres, of how the air we breathe has lost its innocence. Drawing, among others, on the work of neo-phenomenologist Herrmann Schmitz (2008), atmospheres constitute 'half-things' and 'tuned spaces' (*gestimmte Räume*), which are experienced through the living body. The notion of atmospheres thus allows for an analysis of the affective constitution of spheres (of how affective contagion takes place) and their pre-conscious effects on human sensory experience. Sloterdijk (2004) goes on to reflect on the design of products and organizational atmospheres as they are modulated in, for instance, shopping malls and convention centres—'the air conditions of organizational foam' (Borch, 2010: 236) and the aesthetic manipulation enacted through architecture as well as smells, lights, colours, and sounds. In *Im Weltinnenraum des Kapitals* Sloterdijk (2005) argues that terrorism and economic liberalism share a damaging belief in unilateral, unhindered movement through the co-fragility of the plurality of spheres; both 'do not realize that they are essentially connected with what they are trying to destroy' (Morin, 2012: 92).

Sloterdijk's tongue-in-cheek invitation for a *Betriebswirtschaftslehre für Zivilisationstreibhäuser*, a 'business economics for civilization's greenhouses', in combination with a *Seifenblasenethik*, an 'ethics of soap bubbles' (2004: 260), thus takes on a double meaning. The capacity for managerial manipulation of affect is a striking feature of contemporary capitalism and calls for scholarly concepts and methods such as atmospheric analysis. At the same time, in the age of environmental crises an ethics of foam would see the most fragile associations as responsibility's point of origin; and it would indeed attempt to evaluate the detrimental atmospheric effects emanating from organized conduct. Can we imagine organizational process theorists as physicians and immunologists of culture who now 'must advance the debate on the space inhabitable by man…and tackle this question: how is the human greenhouse established and conditioned climatologically?' (2011a: 218, translation amended).

35.5 OF RAGE AND PSYCHOPOLITICS

The development of a 'critical theory of air and a positive notion of the atmospheric *res publica*' (Sloterdijk, 2004: 353) constitutes the psychopolitical thrust of the *Spheres* trilogy. In parallel, Sloterdijk has turned his philosophical energetics to the politics of collective affect in a number of publications (1995, 1998b, 2010b), culminating in *Zorn und Zeit*, translated as *Rage and Time* (2010a)—of course another playful allusion to Heidegger's *Sein und Zeit*. The history and present of human development as a spatial narrative of coming-into-spheres is thus followed by another sweeping account of the history and 'post-communist' present of human development in terms of the ecology and economy of rage. The philosopher revisits his long feud with theories of lack or scarcity such as economics and psychoanalysis and their 'ethics of indignity' (Sloterdijk, 2010a: 19; 2010b) by staging another Nietzschean meeting, this time between thymotic energies of affluence, pride, and generosity as counterparts to libidinal or erotic ones of lack, calculation, and sublimation. In a move reminiscent of the distinction between kynicism and cynisms and the split within cynicism itself, Sloterdijk returns to the ancient notion of *thymós* to distinguish between a noble, 'healthy' thymotics of pride or *Beherztheit* (stout heartedness) (2010a: 12) and an 'ill' one of accumulated anger and resentment. Anger is thus framed as the most important affect for the generation of political subjectivity (van Tuinen, 2012). In a move as shrewd as it is original, Sloterdijk traces the development of an economy of anger that, like the money economy, has 'advanced from local accumulation and selective explosion to the level of a systematic investment and cyclic increase' in the past two centuries (2010a: 64). Accordingly, the philosopher offers the historical distinction between the 'locally sourced' and expressed 'project form of anger' (and its corollary called revenge) and the accumulative gathering power of the 'bank form of anger' (and its corollary called revolution). As van Tuinen points out (2012: 46), Sloterdijk thus quite perversely implicates the revolutionary movements of the past two centuries as protagonists of a fundamentally capitalist economy of anger that refutes and undermines the very political economy they propagated. At least traditional leftist movements and parties resemble entrepreneurs systematically trading on and exploiting the collective investments of envy, spite, and *ressentiment*.

Sloterdijk is as critical of late capitalism's circuits of greed—denoting the displacement of thymotic forces by an erotic and depoliticized psychopolitics of imitating desire and calculating reason—as he is dismissive of the capacity to systematically mobilize and organize the flows of anger in western societies' post-communist situation. Whatever one makes of these highly opinionated assessments of the contemporary socio- and psychopolitical landscape, the philosopher's reflections on the organizing power of collective affect offer a rich point of departure for further investigations into the organizational effects of affective forces that sweep through today's spheres of co-habitation (Beyes and Steyaert, 2013). They enact an energetics of organizing, which criss-crosses the boundaries of conventional organizational forms and enables new organizational movements. And of course, thinking organizational life through its thymotic undercurrents provocatively calls for a critical sensibility that watches out for a noble, productive, and empowering kind of contempt. It is a contempt that does not exhaust itself in disdain for the powerful and diagnoses of lack and suffering but brings forth new possibilities of life and organizing. Is there a logic of disorganization enacted by 'projects of anger' and a logic of organization performed by 'banks of anger' today? Given the political thrust of this kind of affect theory, future scholars of organizational psychopolitics might indeed be tempted to take a closer look at the ambivalence of thymotic energies between 'weak' resentment and new political imaginations engendered by the reorganization of the economy of rage.

35.6 In Conclusion: Towards a Scholarly Ethics of Generosity

In this chapter I have presented Peter Sloterdijk as a singular thinker of process: of 'coming-into-the-world' and 'natal difference', of 'being-in-the-middle-of-it' and 'ecstatic immanence', of movement and relocation. Moreover, I have tried to identify and discuss the themes and concepts that seem both important and challenging for researching organizational process (which also means that this chapter did not attempt a systematic and comprehensive discussion of this philosopher's particularly wide-ranging body of work). They range from the physiognomies and effects of organizing enacted through cynical reason and embodied kynical practice to an acrobatics of organizational life performed through training exercises; from the material and affective spacings that constitute organizational spatialities, or foam, to the apprehensions of (modulations or manipulations of) organizational atmospheres; from the affective ecologies of organizing to the potential of an organizational psychopolitics.

All of these movements seem to share a basic intuition, which perhaps provokes the most daunting task that the work of this philosopher presents us with. In the epilogue to *Sphären III*, Sloterdijk, ever the stylistic experimenter, stages a look back on his spherological project in the form of excerpts from a fictive round-table talk starring 'the macro-historian', 'the literary critic', and 'the theologist' (they are waiting for the author, who does not show up). Apart from their impression that the *Spheres* trilogy would constitute an attempt to tell the story of human beings as a story of the production and organization of space, the macro-historian voices a suspicion: could it be that the author actually wanted to write a *universal history of generosity* under the mask of a phenomenology of spatial configurations and extensions? (Sloterdijk, 2004: 884–5)

It is, of course, Sloterdijk who is commenting upon himself here. In the guise of a historian, he is echoing a sentiment that indeed runs through—and perhaps more than anything else informs—his work: to grapple with and fight against the central psychopolitical malady of *ressentiment*, and to make the case for an ethics of generosity (van Tuinen, 2012). Perhaps, then, the overarching questions that a Sloterdijkian theorizing of organizational process pose, and has to pose to itself, are thus: how to become or remain a subject of experimentation? And how to perform a scholarly work of experimentation, generosity, and joy (and not of resentment)?

In concluding this chapter, there is no space for properly discussing whether Sloterdijk's practice of philosophy supplies the answers. In fact, his recent 'meritocratic shift' (see especially Sloterdijk, 2010b) seems to fall short of the critical potential of Nietzsche's concept of *ressentiment* (van Tuinen, 2012: 56). In addition, Sloterdijk's rather lofty diagnoses of the mediocrity of contemporary life—and his dismissals of apparently any contemporary political movement as fuelled by resentment of the particularly gifted and proud—smack of a quite ungenerous stance perhaps not too far removed from the cynicism of the powerful the philosopher once set out to hold to task. 'Wherefrom [Sloterdijk's] obsessive-compulsive urge to find beneath solidarity the envy of the weak and their thirst for revenge?', asks the hyperbolically equally gifted Žižek. '[W]herefrom his unbound "hermeneutics of suspicion" *à la* caricaturised Nietzsche? What if *this very urge is sustained by a disavowed envy and resentment of its own*?' (Žižek, 2008: 164–5, emphasis in the original).

Notwithstanding such qualms and objections, Sloterdijk's wide-ranging and unfinished oeuvre indeed offers a courageous, inspired, and inspiring attempt to do scholarly work 'beyond resentment' (Sloterdijk, 2010a: 227). Through its experimental and evocative styles of writing, it not only offers but performs a joyful overcoming of 'the perversions of analytical spirit or the resignation of philosophical critique to counterfactualism and abstractions in the face of complex reality' (van Tuinen, 2007: 279). If anything, one hopes that organizational scholars would take courage from this spirit and practice of experimentation—against the odds, which means against the 'triumph of discursive one-dimensionality', 'the trappings of seriousness', and the 'resentment that presents itself as a method' (Sloterdijk, 2011a: 267–8). If history, as Sloterdijk writes in his Nietzsche book *Über die Verbesserung der guten Nachricht* (*On the Improvement of the Good News*), can be separated into the time of poisonous debt-economy and that of generosity (2001b: 50), Sloterdijk's philosophical energetics ceaselessly probe what it might mean to think, revive, and invent generous ways of becoming-human.

Notes

1. Žižek has memorably labelled him as 'definitely not one of our side, but also not a complete idiot' (2009: 131).
2. Except where indicated, translations from the German are mine.
3. In retrospect the *Critique* bears the traces of what is to come for and from Sloterdijk. Of course, there is Nietzsche who in *Die fröhliche Wissenschaft* famously staged the return of Diogenes as the madman with a lantern on the marketplace in the morning hours (Nietzsche, 1999: 480–1); and, to a lesser extent, there is Heidegger, presented as a theoretical and provincial neo-kynist. There are extended reflections on critical theory's descent into stagnation, resentment, and cynical reason—where the masochistic element has surpassed the creative one—that is to be overcome by a rejuvenated left critique. The issue of the 'psychosomatics of the Zeitgeist' (Sloterdijk, 1988: 139) and the notion of 'psychopolitics' (Sloterdijk, 1988: 120) will prominently resurface in later works on ecologies of energies and affects. There is the ambivalence of, and fascination with, technology as co-shaping force in human development through 'the ontological enrichments in the inventory of existence' (Sloterdijk, 1988: 456). And the importance of the body, of atmospheric conditions, and the speculation about what Sloterdijk would later call immunological practices of building artificial spheres, foreshadow the *Spheres* trilogy.

References

Babich, B. (2012). Sloterdijk's Cynicism: Diogenes in the Marketplace, in S. Elden (ed.), *Sloterdijk Now* (Cambridge: Polity): 17–36.

Beyes, T. and Steyaert, C. (2012). Spacing Organization: Non-Representational Theorizing and the Spatial Turn in Organizational Research, *Organization* 19(1): 45–61.

—— (2013). Strangely Familiar: The Uncanny and Unsiting Organizational Analysis, *Organization Studies* 34(10): 1445–65.

Borch, C. (2010). Organizational Atmospheres: Foam, Affect and Architecture, *Organization* 17(2): 223–41.

——(2011). Foamy Business: On the Organizational Politics of Atmospheres, in W. Schinkel and L. Nordegraaf-Eelens (eds), *In Medias Res: Peter Sloterdijk's Spherological Poetics of Being* (Amsterdam: Amsterdam University Press): 29–42.

Cooper, R. (1998). Interview with Robert Cooper, in R. Chia (ed.), *Organized Worlds: Explorations in Technology and Organization with Robert Cooper* (London: Routledge): 121–65.

Couture, J.-P. (2012). A Public Intellectual, in S. Elden (ed.), *Sloterdijk Now* (Cambridge: Polity): 96–113.

Deleuze, G. and Guattari, F. (1988). *A Thousand Plateaus*, trans. B. Massumi (London: Athlone Press).

—— (1994). *What is Philosophy?*, trans. G. Burchell and H. Tomlinson (London: Verso).

Elden, S. (ed.) (2012a). *Sloterdijk Now* (Cambridge: Polity).

—— (2012b). Worlds, Engagements, Temperaments, in S. Elden (ed.), *Sloterdijk Now* (Cambridge: Polity): 1–16.

——and Mendieta, E. (2009). Being-with as Making Worlds: The 'Second Coming' of Peter Sloterdijk, *Environment and Planning D: Society and Space* 27(1): 1–11.

Fleming, P. and Spicer, A. (2003). Working at a Cynical Distance: Implications for Power, Subjectivity and Resistance, *Organization* 10(1): 157–79.

Foucault, M. (1992). *The History of Sexuality, Volume II: The Use of Pleasure*, trans. R. Hurley (London: Penguin).

Huyssen, A. (1988). Foreword: The Return of Diogenes as Postmodern Intellectual, in P. Sloterdijk, *Critique of Cynical Reason* (Minneapolis: University of Minnesota Press): ix–xxv.

Latour, B. (2009). A Cautious Prometheus? A Few Steps Toward a Philosophy of Design with Special Attention to Peter Sloterdijk, in W. Schinkel and L. Nordegraaf-Eelens (eds), *In Medias Res: Peter Sloterdijk's Spherological Poetics of Being* (Amsterdam: Amsterdam University Press): 151–64.

Morin, M.-E. (2012). The Coming-to-the-World of the Human Animal, in S. Elden (ed.), *Sloterdijk Now* (Cambridge: Polity): 77–95.

Nietzsche, F. (1999). *Die fröhliche Wissenschaft*. Kritische Studienausgabe 3 (München: Deutscher Taschenbuchverlag).

Osborne, P. (2012). Disguised as a Dog: Cynical Occupy?', *Radical Philosophy 174*: 15–21.

Schinkel, W. and Nordegraaf-Eelens, L. (eds) (2011a). *In Medias Res: Peter Sloterdijk's Spherological Poetics of Being* (Amsterdam: Amsterdam University Press).

—— (2011b). Peter Sloterdijk's Spherological Acrobatics: An Exercise in Introduction, in W. Schinkel and L. Nordegraaf-Eelens (eds), *In Medias Res: Peter Sloterdijk's Spherological Poetics of Being* (Amsterdam: Amsterdam University Press): 7–28.

Schmitz, H. (2008). *Der Leib, der Raum und die Gefühle* (Ostfildern: edition tertium).

Sloterdijk, P. (1986). *Kopernikanische Mobilmachung und ptolemäische Abrüstung* (Frankfurt am Main: Suhrkamp).

——(1988). *Critique of Cynical Reason*, trans. M. Eldred (Minneapolis: University of Minnesota Press).

——(1989a). *Thinker on Stage: Nietzsche's Materialism* (Minneapolis: University of Minnesota Press).

——(1989b). *Eurotaoismus. Zur Kritik der politischen Kinetik* (Frankfurt am Main: Suhrkamp).

——(1995). *Im selben Boot. Versuch über die Hyperpolitik* (Frankfurt am Main: Suhrkamp).

——(1998a). *Sphären I: Blasen. Mikrosphärologie* (Frankfurt am Main: Suhrkamp).

——(1998b). *Der starke Grund zusammen zu sein. Erinnerungen an die Erfindung des Volkes* (Frankfurt am Main: Suhrkamp).

——(2001a). *Nicht gerettet. Versuche nach Heidegger* (Frankfurt am Main: Suhrkamp).

—— (2001b). *Über die Verbesserung der guten Nachricht: Nietzsches fünftes 'Evangelium'* (Frankfurt am Main: Suhrkamp).

——(2004). *Sphären III: Schäume. Plurale Sphärologie* (Frankfurt am Main: Suhrkamp).

——(2005). *Im Weltinnenraum des Kapitals: Für eine philosophische Theorie der Globalisierung* (Frankfurt am Main: Suhrkamp).

——(2008). *Theory of the Post-War Periods: Observations on Franco-German Relations since 1945*, trans. R. Payne (Wien: Springer).

——(2009a). Rules for the Human Zoo: A Response to the *Letter on Humanism*, trans. M.V. Rorty, *Environment and Planning D: Society and Space* 27(1): 12–28.

——(2009b). *God's Zeal: The Battle of the Three Monotheisms*, trans. W. Hoban (Cambridge: Polity).

——(2009c). *Derrida, an Egyptian: On the Problem of the Jewish Pyramid*, trans. W. Hoban (Cambridge: Polity).

——(2009d). *Terror from the Air*, trans. A. Patton and S. Corcoran (Los Angeles: Semiotext(e)).

—— (2010a). *Rage and Time: A Psychopolitical Investigation*, trans. M. Wenning (New York: Columbia University Press).

——(2010b). *Die nehmende Hand und die gebende Seite. Beiträge zu einer Debatte über die demokratische Neubegründung von Steuern* (Frankfurt am Main: Suhrkamp).

—— (2011a). *Neither Sun nor Death* (with H.J. Heinrichs), trans. S. Corcoran (Los Angeles: Semiotext(e)).

—— (2011b). *Bubbles. Spheres Volume I: Microspherology*, trans. W. Hoban (Cambridge, MA: MIT Press).

——(2011c). 'The Space of Global Capitalism and Its Imaginary Imperialism: An Interview with Peter Sloterdijk, in W. Schinkel and L. Nordegraaf-Eelens (eds), *In Medias Res: Peter Sloterdijk's Spherological Poetics of Being* (Amsterdam: Amsterdam University Press): 185–95.

——(2012a). *The Art of Philosophy: Wisdom as a Practice*, trans. K. Margolis (New York: Columbia University Press).

——(2012b). *Zeilen und Tage: Notizen 2008–2011* (Frankfurt am Main: Suhrkamp).

——(2012c). The Time of the Crime of the Monstrous: On the Philosophical Justification of the Artificial, in S. Elden (ed.), *Sloterdijk Now* (Cambridge: Polity): 165–81.

——(2013). *You Must Change Your Life*, trans. W. Hoban (Cambridge: Polity).

Spicer, A., Alvesson, M., and Kärreman, D. (2009). Critical Performativity: The Unfinished Business of Critical Management Studies, *Human Relations* 62(4): 537–60.

Taussig, M. (2012). I'm so Angry I Made a Sign, *Critical Inquiry* 39(1): 56–88.

Thrift, N. (2007). *Non-Representational Theory: Space, Politics, Affect* (London: Routledge).

—— (2012). Peter Sloterdijk and the Philosopher's Stone, in S. Elden (ed.), *Sloterdijk Now* (Cambridge: Polity): 133–46.

Toscano, A. (2010). Review: Sloterdijk, Sloterdijk & Sloterdijk, *The Philosophers Magazine*, <http://philosophypress.co.uk/?p=1006>

van Tuinen, S. (2007). Critique beyond Resentment: An Introduction to Peter Sloterdijk's Jovial Modernity, *Cultural Politics* 3(2): 275–306.

—— (2011). 'Transgeneous Philosophy': Post-Humanism, Anthropotechnis and the Poetics of Natal Difference, in W. Schinkel and L. Nordegraaf-Eelens (eds), *In Medias Res: Peter Sloterdijk's Spherological Poetics of Being* (Amsterdam: Amsterdam University Press): 43–66.

——(2012). From Psychopolitics to Cosmopolitics: The Problem of Ressentiment, in S. Elden (ed.), *Sloterdijk Now* (Cambridge: Polity): 37–57.

Žižek, S. (2008). *Violence* (London: Profile Books).

——(2009). *First as Tragedy, Then as Farce* (London: Verso).

CHAPTER 36

PROCESS AND REALITY

ROBERT COOPER

PROCESS IS a generic term for the continuous making and moving of forms. The dictionary defines process as a series of acts or events. An act is a physical and mental gesture that constitutes the actual making of a form while an event (from the Latin *evenire*, to appear, come into form) is an act that has yet to complete itself as an enduring presence. Process in this sense reminds us that the ready-made structures of the human world are initiated and constituted by human agency and are thus not objectified forms independent of the human observer. Observer and observed are mutually constituting acts of knowing which generate each other. Process has to be understood as the continuous coming-to-presence of the forms and objects of everyday life rather than their taken-for-granted, ready-made presences. The act of observation necessarily requires the active participation of the human agent as observer in making the world present and presentable in repeated acts of re-presentation. Reality in this sense is the *realization* of the world as a source of appearances and forms rather than their objective, independent existences. This is what the origin of *process* implies in its etymological combination of *approach* and *withdrawal* as pro- (the making and appearance of forms) and -*cess* (the disappearance and loss of forms). Process thus can be understood as a divided state of being in which human agency is forever suspended between the ceaseless act of making forms present and their constant recession. Process and recess are recursive versions of each other in a world without end.

As a divided and suspended state of being, process is an infinite series of acts that never complete themselves. Process is thus always partial and hence always implies something other than itself. Process is the abandonment of fixed forms and static objects which now have to be understood as transient and provisional parts of a more comprehensive and even infinite whole. This is one way of understanding reality as a mobile flow or flux of relationships (Whitehead, 1929). Reality is thus the continuous division and suspension of human agency as a series of infinite acts and events. It is in this sense that we have to understand the human agent as a participant observer of its world where *participation* also means *partial* and thus incomplete. The human agent is an intrinsic part of a field which recedes when approached in the continuous work of process.

As the making and moving of forms, process begins in the act of division or distinction. Forms emerge out of an indistinguishable or undifferentiated ground through a primal act of division (Spencer-Brown, 1969). Division distinguishes parts from wholes. In this context, division is a form of *di-vision* or a double way of seeing in which parts are divided from wholes that serve as comprehensive containers of parts. Parts constitute wholes just as wholes constitute parts. Parts are thus always partial and never complete, never whole. Wholeness has to be understood as an invisible and infinite receptacle of parts. The human observer as participant observer is also a partial part of this wholeness that forever recedes; the observer is constituted by the forms and materials that its observations represent. Observer and observed become reversible and thus partial reflections or counterchanges of each other. Here we see the primal act of division or distinction at work in which the world cuts itself in two: a state that sees and a state that is seen: 'In this severed and mutilated condition, whatever it sees is *only partially itself*' (Spencer-Brown, 1969: 105). Parts become 'tokens or expressions' of a more comprehensive and missing wholeness that continually withdraws from visibilization: 'since tokens or expresssions are considered to be *of* some (other) substratum, so the universe itself, as we know it, may be considered to be an expression of a reality other than itself' (Spencer-Brown, 1969: 104). This reality is also an invisible and infinite receptacle of parts that defines the wider context of process.

Reality now has to be viewed as the expression of an order that refuses to reveal itself. We, as representatives of this hidden order, represent the world as a scene of partial forms which always imply something other than themselves, something which continually escapes our attempts to make it visible. Process is the action of human agency in its work of seeing its world in parts, which also means that the world as a whole constantly withdraws from conscious knowledge: 'Its particularity is the price we pay for its visibility' (Spencer-Brown, 1969: 106). As a double way of seeing, di-vision also implies that part and whole are mutually enfolded as we previously noted in our discussion of *pro-cess* as the double action of approach and withdrawal. The part can be approached and thus made visible while the whole withdraws from conscious visibility. As an invisible and infinite receptacle, the whole is more than we can consciously grasp. Yet the infinite invisibility of the whole serves to mobilize conscious thought and visibilization by continuously reminding us of its constitutive absence in the partialness or incompleteness of parts. Process is kept moving by its parts which are mutually constituted by the gaps and intervals of its invisible and infinite wholeness. In this sense, the ever-present absences of wholeness are necessary motivators of visibilization and conscious thought. The part–whole relationship also means that partial forms are presences that are complemented by their absences. Like approach and withdrawal, process depends on the provisional nature of presence and absence as mutual recursions or counterchanges of each other: presence is the continuous pursuit and deferral of itself in a process of continuous suspension. Like the *event*, like approach and withdrawal, the recursively interactive nature of the presence–absence relationship means that process is a series of acts that are forever trying to find themselves.

To understand wholeness as an invisible and infinite receptacle, we have to think of it as a creative source and not as an empty space. Process reveals reality as the creative interaction of wholeness and parts in which human agency creates reality as the 'tokens or expressions' of a world that is divided from itself and which continually recedes from conscious appropriation while 'playing a kind of hide-and-seek with itself' (Spencer-Brown, 1969: 106). Division in this context implies a fundamental interaction between visibility and invisibility which appears to engender each other so that there can be no visibility without invisibility (Luhmann, 2000: 91). The purpose of process is to make visible forms out of the muteness of undifferentiated space whose muteness is also a mutability which can be translated into an infinite variety of forms: 'it is as if there were a layer behind appearances that had no qualities, but took on the character of its surroundings, accommodating itself to our interpretations' (Kaplan, 1999: 59). The negative ground of forms is thus another way of defining the whole as an invisible and mutable source of positive forms. Process implies this complementary interaction between negative ground and positive forms in its combination of *approach* and *withdrawal* which seemingly engender and activate each other. Process in this context also implies a state of active suspension in which positive and negative *supplement* each other in the making and unmaking of forms. Process means that parts simply supplement each other in an infinite movement of suspension in which they are forever suspended. The suspension of parts significantly implies that process is moved by 'a principle of accelerating supplementarity' in which parts 'are never more than a step in the supplemental movements of thought' (Bersani, 1986: 48). This means that parts not only supplement each other and thus keep process continually on the move but they also re-mind the human agent of its radical incompleteness and thus its continual need to re-mind and re-compose itself. The negative now appears as a necessary stimulus of the positive; positive parts are also partially negative inasmuch as they constitute and make visible a whole that forever withdraws from them in an infinite process of hide-and-seek. Process is the continuous anticipation of what is *not present* in space and time in order to make it present. In this sense, process can be understood as the work of re-minding as the 'productive receding of consciousness' (Bersani, 1986: 47).

36.1 THE RELATING OF PROCESS

Process can now be interpreted as the continuous coming-to-presence of forms. This implies that process is the continuous making and moving of forms. It also, significantly, implies that forms are subject to the continuous threat of recession. Forms may now be seen as provisional appearances that are extracted out of a mute ground of negativity. Forms can thus be seen as 'tokens or expressions' of a negative level of reality which constantly eludes the visibility of consciousness. Process now becomes the translation of this invisible ground of reality into the visibility of manifest forms. Process is thus the action of *relating* the latent or hidden ground of forms into the manifest and meaningful appearances of visible experience. To relate in this primitive sense is not simply to express the world in meaningful forms but is also, significantly, the continuous re-presentation of the negative ground of forms. The latent thus appears as an invisible bearer of the 'tokens or expressions' of the negative base of reality. The latent itself never appears but is an ever-present 'existential precursor' of the conscious appearances we call reality (Spencer-Brown, 1969: 97–106). To relate is thus never the re-presentation of presence as stable, settled forms but their continuous deferral of difference in a process of undivided flowing movement and coming-to-presence.

The latent is a mute field of mutability which is intrinsically indifferent to human understanding; it has to be personified by human agency in acts of translation and relation. In other words, it is intrinsically unlocatable as the undivided ground that comes before the divisions and distinctions of human consciousness. Human agency creates itself out of this mute ground by translating its muteness and mutability into meaningful forms which serve to reflect and thus mirror human consciousness and understanding. This is a stage in human consciousness in which the drawing of boundaries and the tracing of forms is still precarious: 'This is a place that is everywhere and nowhere, a place you cannot get to from here...This strange locus is another name for the ground of things, the preoriginal ground of the ground, something other to any activity of mapping' (Miller, 1992: 7). This is the invisible and infinite receptacle of wholeness which eludes the partiality of visibility and conscious thought (Spencer-Brown, 1969: 105). The latent is thus a suspended state of being that is always yet-to-come; it remains a placeless, hidden place that denies exposure. Like process, the latent draws us and withdraws from us at the same time. Human relating thus draws on a placeless place which it narrates as a *nowhere* and a *not yet*, a '*no man's land* between being and not-yet-being' (Levinas, 1969: 259). In this sense, to relate combines the negative and the positive as complementary acts of human agency in its fundamental interaction with the world. Positive forms are made to emerge out of their negative and mute ground. The negative ground is the *nowhere* and the *not yet* that continually withdraws from positive appropriation and thus continually stimulates human agency to remake itself in a coming-to-presence that never fully comes.

Process now has to be understood as a generic act of deferral and anticipation. This is what the double vision of *di-vision* implies: every act of primal division or differentiation is a deferring of its negative ground as if to keep life forever on the move. Again, we need to remind ourselves that this deferral is another way of expressing wholeness as an invisible and infinite receptacle that 'will always partially elude itself' (Spencer-Brown, 1969: 105). Di-vision and deferral also imply that forms are always partial since they are necessary parts of the mute and mutable wholeness from which they derive their provisional boundaries. The words in a sentence, for example, change as one reads the sentence and 'that sentence in turn changes as one moves to the next sentence, or paragraph, or page' (Bryson, 1988: 98). Meaning thus exemplifies the act and action of process as a deferral that never completes itself and hence, like coming-to-presence, 'never arrives' (Bryson, 1988: 98). This is how we can understand *relation* as the *translation* or crossing of the gaps and intervals that constitute the negative ground of wholeness as an invisible and infinite receptacle. Things are never themselves but are parts that are also continuous transformations of the 'constitutive negativity' that characterizes the flux and flow of wholeness as process (Bryson, 1988: 99). 'Constitutive negativity' means that forms and objects are constituted by what they are *not*, by their deferral in space and time. This means that forms and objects are never singular, independent structures, never a specific *x* or *y*, but are mutable parts that relate each other. Like the word in a sentence, the flower is already part of a moving process which includes its origin in the form of the seed and its end in the form of dust: 'the flower is inhabited by its past as seed and its future as dust, in a continuous motion of postponement', which effectively means that the flower is never completely itself, just as seed and dust are never completely themselves (Bryson, 1988: 99).

All this means that process implies that forms and objects are never themselves as independent structures but are partial and mutable expressions of a wholeness that forever withdraws from us. The word and the flower are 'interpenetrated' by what they are not and thus exist 'under a mode of constitutive negativity' (Bryson, 1988: 99). This, again, is the coming-to-presence that never fully comes and hence re-minds human agency of its intrinsically suspended nature in which process has no static or stable forms, only the mutability and infinity of a 'productive receding of consciousness' (Bersani, 1986: 47). The word and the flower remind us that they are parts of a series of acts and events which constitute each other. Seed, flower, and dust are interchangeable in the sense that each 'is both prior to the other and later than it, causer and caused, inside it and outside it at once . . . in a perpetually reversing metalepsis' (Miller, 1995: 21). Parts become mutable reflections of each other in a moving field of otherness and alterity. Parts in this sense are already ready to *de-part*. The reality of process is essentially a process of *realizing* the world as the 'tokens or expressions' of a mutability that is intrinsically provisional, transient, and yet-to-be.

'Constitutive negativity' can be likened to the unarticulated base of raw material from which variable forms can be extracted or realized. Base as the negative ground of things is both mute and mutable. Like the invisible and infinite ground behind appearances that embraces the forms imposed on it, base can also be understood as latency which is there for us to re-late it as the myriad appearances of reality. Base now appears as the negative source of parts that always defer their positive appearances in a creative alternation in which parts are also other than themselves in a suspended state of otherness or reversibility, just as cause and effect, inside and outside, constitute each other. This reversible otherness is basic to the flow of process as the expression of latency in which parts are never simply themselves but are mutable reflections of each other. In other words, parts (from the Latin *partire, portare,* to bear, carry, share, distribute) relate each other in the constant interchangeability of wholeness. Human agency can be viewed in the same way: the human body and its organs work as interchangeable parts of their environment. The body's parts thus relate or carry themselves as parts of a constitutive wholeness which is never complete or finite. The body's inside can only know itself as a reflection of its outside through the continuous work or process of 'sentient continuity' with its environment (Scarry, 1985: 248). 'Continuity' thus implies the wholeness of parts that not only 'continue' each other but also 'contain' each other in a fundamental process of reciprocity. Parts have to be understood as intrinsic *acts* of transmission which seek their otherness in a process that is always yet-to-be. 'Sentient continuity' as process means that the human agent perpetually recreates itself in an infinite otherness or excess where *ex-cess* implies the ceaseless withdrawal of *pro-cess*. It is this infinite otherness as ceaseless withdrawal that reveals 'sentient continuity' as the continuous recreation of wholeness as the invisible and infinite receptacle of process.

Process is thus a generic act of otherness as alterity in which the human body is never itself and hence seeks to reflect and thus know itself through the forms and objects that constitute the existential parts of its 'sentient continuity'. This, again, reminds us of the processual act as an event that is a suspended coming-to-presence. Continuity also significantly implies that wholeness as an infinite receptacle is also an infinite *container* of endless *continuity*. This means that parts are contained or held together as contents in a background of excess from which they are extracted as provisional forms. The human body is a necessary part of this continuous work of continuity and containment in the same way as the forms and objects that serve human agency in the generic process of existence. The body projects itself in continuous acts of production and reproduction and is thus an intrinsic part of process as a generic act of continuation and containment. The body thus continually projects itself through its created forms and objects into a new world of possibilities through which it recreates and renews itself. In other words, the forms and objects of human agency are bearers and transmitters of the immanent latency that motivates the process of 'sentient continuity' as the active relating and coming-to-presence of process. Human agency thus reveals 'sentient continuity' and latency as expressions of the universe's continuous need to expand in order 'to escape the telescopes through which we, who are it, are trying to capture it, which is us' in what seems to us, the universe's representatives, to be the universe's need to play a never-ending game of 'hide-and-seek with itself' (Spencer-Brown, 1969: 106). As an expression of continuous de-parture and continuation, the part now tells us that it seeks to re-present itself as an essential act of the 'productive receding of consciousness' (Bersani, 1986: 47).

Human agency is essentially a series of sentient acts in continuous process. The continuity of the act also tells us that the act is also primarily the movement of forms rather than their individual meanings. In other words, the act expresses the action of form rather than the forms themselves. This is another way of saying that parts are radically enfolded with each other so that every part has to be understood as an unfolding of an implicit reality. This implicit reality is another way of understanding 'tokens or expressions' as implying a version of reality which hides itself from conscious representation (Spencer-Brown, 1969: 104). The human agent unfolds this implicit reality in its continuous work of exchange with its environment. The human agent is thus an intrinsic part of this exchange in which it is itself enfolded in a continuous process of recursive work through which it continually reconstitutes itself: the body's organs and senses can only reflect themselves through the forms and objects by which the agent expresses itself. This is the essence of 'sentient continuity' in which the body's inside and outside generate each other in acts of mutual construction. Body and environment are recursions of each other in the processual sense that body and earth are extensions of each other. All this means that human agency is a continuous compositional process through which mental and physical acts of composition *ensure* the 'sentient continuity' of life as the body and its organs in continuous constructive interaction with its environment.

As the expression of the 'sentient continuity' of process, human agency has to be seen as a series of parts or 'participial acts' which reflect the 'shared alteration' between body and earth (Scarry, 1994: 49–90). It is as if the earth has to see itself but only as the partial and particular visibilities of a wholeness which forever recedes in the recursive play and process of hide-and-seek in which 'What is revealed will be concealed, but what is concealed will again be revealed' (Spencer-Brown, 1969: 106). The 'participial act' is thus a fundamental part of human creation and production; it comes before result or product as a finite form or object and demands to be understood as a primal existential force of human creation which reveals latency as the unfolding of a new world of possibilities. This serves to recreate human agency in its 'shared alteration' with the earth: 'what the human being has *made* is not object *x* or *y* but this excessive power' which remakes its human makers in their pursuit of 'sentient continuity' (Scarry, 1985: 318). This, significantly, is the essence of the relating of process. Human agency does not so much relate specific forms and objects but rather the mutable potential that the latent offers. 'Participial acts' are acts of composition before they are acts of representation. They relate the world as an infinite wholeness of mutability in which composition is the permutability of differences. As an invisible and infinite receptacle or container of differences, the latent 'cannot disappear but can only change its form or nature' (Kaplan, 1999: 59). In this respect, latency can be likened to the mutability of raw matter which is mute in the sense that it has no intrinsically specific characteristics and is thus amenable to infinite permutability. The human agent and its body has its source in the raw matter of mutability which, through the 'participial act', has to create and recreate itself as an identifiable part of the world from which it originally severed itself (Spencer-Brown, 1969: 105). The 'participial act' tells us that the world is the continuous movement of parts in pursuit of their missing forms. This means that the human world is not constituted by bounded objects or things but by the transitivity of relationships. Acts and action *between* forms and objects source the creative movement of the world rather than finite, bounded structures. This is process as *event* or the coming-to-appear of things rather than their taken-for-granted presences.

36.2 PARTICIPIAL PROCESS

The 'participial act' stresses the movement of process *between* identifiable terms. Betweenness reveals the otherness of things rather than their specific and particular features. Like the creative interaction between human agent and earth, the 'participial act' expresses the fundamental exchangeability between terms as well as their perpetual reversibility. The 'participial act' reveals the human world as a field of distinguishable forms and objects which, before the act of distinction and visibilization, do not come into form. Like the reversibility of figure and ground which constitute each other and are thus coterminous parts of each other, the 'participial act' is never simply itself but is part of a reversible process which reveals the latency intrinsic to the 'ground of things, the preoriginal ground of the ground' where thing and ground are 'both prior to the other and later than it, causer and caused, inside it and outside it at once' (Miller, 1995: 21). This is another version of 'constitutive negativity' where so-called positive terms are constituted by what they are *not* in a continuous process of deferral, just as seed, flower, and dust are transitional phases of each other (Bryson, 1988: 97). This is also another version of wholeness whose parts are always deferred in a field of enfolded relationships. Parts thus always supplement a deferred wholeness so that they are never more than steps 'in the supplemental movements of thought' (Bersani, 1986: 48).

The supplemental function of the part again stresses the 'participial act' as pure action and unfinished process. The act in this sense is always part of an infinite and continuous whole whose nature is forever to recede as if to remind the human agent that it acts in a world without end. The human agent is a part in the existential sense that it shares its life always with the raw matter of the world. This is the 'sentient continuity' which includes the 'shared alteration' between body and earth in which 'Man and world each act on the surface of the other' (Scarry, 1994: 84, 51). The 'participial act' reflects the reciprocal and recursive relationship between body and earth in its 'shared alteration'; it is the perpetual work of the human agent in trying to find and refind itself as an expression of the earth from which it severed itself. Human agent and earth are seemingly suspended in a 'sentient continuity' that never ends. The agent is thus a *part* that is always incomplete, always in search of its divided self. In this sense, the human agent is a part of the 'constitutive negativity' in which things are never themselves but are mutable reflections of each other in a process of 'shared alteration'. Process now begins to look like the reciprocity of cause and effect, of inside and outside, which are never themselves as individual terms but which always imply each other in an enfolded and mutual relationship. 'Participial acts' are thus acts of motion *between* terms and hence remind us that parts are essentially bearers and carriers of human agency and existential being. This is reality as the flux and flow of relationship and relating. It is also the double and reversible action of process and recess as recursions of each other. This is also how we can interpret the work of 'shared alteration' between body and earth.

Process is the ceaseless and suspended movement *between* differentiated, specific forms and things. Suspension is the continuously receding and undifferentiated ground of things which is intrinsically mute yet mutable in the sense that it is an infinite source of forms that can be made into the meaningful forms and objects of human agency. Like raw matter, the mute ground of things is like an unknown territory before it is mapped into specifiable, locatable forms. Process is also the 'shared alteration' or exchangeability of body and earth which mutually define each other; the earth is the mute, pre-original ground of things which has to be continuously made over into humanized forms and objects. This is also the *relating* of the latent. While relating in this sense is the communication of 'tokens' and 'expressions', it is more basically the translation and coming-to-presence of the mute and mutable ground of things. Here again we meet the covert source of parts rather than their explicit forms and objects. At this fundamental level of human agency, 'there are no objects, only parts, and...the configuration of parts at any moment of time is an interval of objecthood that is permutable, reassociable, and yet sensible as just-this-thing, in harmony and functional interrelation with itself throughout' (Fisher, 1991: 213). This means that objects are never discrete things but are essentially materialized *acts of participation* in the world through which the body extends and expands itself as a field of parts or provisional wholes in the 'constitutive negativity' of enfolded, deferred relationship. The spoon, for example, materializes the act of eating: its handle is a recursive representation of the clenched hand, while the bowl of the spoon is a recursion of the mouth; the tea cup similarly re-presents the hand in its handle as well as the lips of the mouth in its lip (Fisher, 1991: 243–4). The modern world expresses this fundamental feature of process in its increasing stress on the mass production of provisional parts instead of self-contained objects and bounded struc-tures which are now dispersed and deferred as fluid and fleeting parts. Hence there fol-lows a weakening of reality as a stable system since the production of provisional parts transfers 'the reality to the system as a whole and to the play of transformations and possibilities that it invites' (Fisher, 1991: 249). Modern production systems exemplify the flux and flow of process in their construction of a world of mutable parts rather than finite objects; objects now 'become restless and weak' and subservient to the mutability and infinity that parts forever imply (Fisher, 1991: 249).

Acts instead of things become central to this way of thinking process. This is the sig-nificance of the 'participial act' in which human agent and world are actively interlaced with each other in a permanent field of 'sentient continuity' and suspended action. Like the spoon and the tea cup, the object is also part of the 'participial act' since it 'is itself only a midpoint in a total action...of human creating' which 'includes both the creating of the object and the object's recreating of the human being' (Scarry, 1985: 310). Process in this sense is the unfolding of an expanding field of possibilities or opportunities that are yet to come rather than the making of specific objects for practical use: 'what the human being has *made* is not object x or y but this excessive power' by which human agents recreate themselves and their potential worlds in their pursuit of 'sentient conti-nuity' (Scarry, 1985: 318). 'Sentient continuity' is thus the 'participial act' that expresses this 'excessive power of reciprocation' or recursion by which creation recreates the crea-tors. Process becomes a compositional act which composes both actor and object in a mutually creative act of reciprocation.

Process as a series of compositional and 'participial' acts also implies a covert world of enfolded relationships from which parts are *unfolded*. Just as observer and observed constitute each other in a 'participial act' of mutual creation, enfoldment means that 'mind and matter are not separate substances. Rather, they are different aspects of one whole and unbroken movement' which 'interweave and inter-penetrate each other' (Bohm, 1980: 30, 185). The human agent is not an 'independent actuality' who simply 'interacts' with others; instead, the agent is a projection of a 'single totality' in which parts are projections of an enfolded wholeness (Bohm, 1980: 210). Process as movement is a primal force of enfoldment in which wholeness is 'an undivided flowing movement without borders' (Bohm, 1980: 172). Enfoldment reminds us of the *event* as a moving, unfinished part. The enfolded part is never itself but is a 'token or expression' of 'constitutive negativity'. This means that it is also an expression of a primal force that, like the negativity of wholeness, cannot be formally identified until it is *unfolded* and thus recognized as a specific form or term. The enfoldment of parts reveals their 'shared alteration' or *betweenness* rather than their specificities. Betweenness in this context means neither one part nor the other but both together; it also implies the movement between the parts rather than the parts as individualized terms. In this sense, betweenness is the movement that crosses the gaps or intervals between parts as specific and static terms. The crossing of intervals rather than the static location of their readable terms reminds us again of movement as the essential nature of process. Process as the crossing of intervals also returns us to the essential nature of 'sentient continuity' where 'continuity' implies 'the bridges among words that disguise the holes between them' (Bersani and Dutoit, 1993: 23).

The gaps and intervals between distinguishable terms now imply that betweenness is constituted by the holes between the knowable terms. The so-called holes are essentially the unmarked and hence invisible spaces that source the constitution of finite forms out of the undifferentiated infinity of negativity (Spencer-Brown, 1969). The undifferentiation of the unmarked is another version of wholeness as the invisible and infinite receptacle of parts. The process of 'sentient continuity' implies the unmarked and undifferentiated as the 'undivided wholeness' of modern physics which reveals that parts constitute wholeness as a totality of 'holes' in continuous movement or 'holomovement' (Bohm, 1980: 150–7). The negativity of 'undivided wholeness' is also the undifferentiation basic to the reversibility of cause and effect, inside and outside, where effect is as much a cause of cause as is cause of effect and where inside and outside reciprocate each other inasmuch as inside-out and outside-in are mutual expressions of each other and thus imply their undifferentiated origin. Betweenness thus implies an undifferentiated, placeless place that pre-exists the divisions and differentiations of human naming and knowing. Betweenness also implies neither one thing nor the other but the mobile enfoldment of parts that are always *de-parting*, always in *process*. The 'holes' of undivided wholeness are negative spaces that are mute and mutable; they indicate nothing that is specifically formed or meaningful to human agency. In this sense, undivided wholeness is an invisible and mutable source that has to be made visible by acts of division or differentiation; it can be likened to raw material that has yet to be made over into an endless variety of identifiable forms and objects. Here again we meet the essence of *relatability* whose latency is that invisible and mutable source that has to be *related* or expressed in a process of 'sentient continuity'.

To relate is to bridge or cross the gaps and intervals between the identifiable forms and objects of process. The gaps and intervals of betweenness imply the undifferentiated pre-original ground of forms and objects, a negative undivided wholeness which serves to contain and carry the divided parts in a process of continuous movement. The latent is this undifferentiated ground which sources the divided parts as the *nowhere* and *not yet* of infinity. This is the holomovement of modern physics as well as the 'constitutive negativity' that keeps events forever on the move. The latent is mute and mutable, a pre-original ground that invites us to fill it with forms and structures that reflect our human agency and being. The mute and mutable challenge us to express a world that is implicitly latent, that has yet to be made explicit. Undivided wholeness is the latent that supplements its divided parts as events that are always partial and thus are never more than transient steps in the movement of thought. This again re-minds the human mind that it is the expression of a suspended and continually deferred 'constitutive negativity' that motivates process as continuous withdrawal. To relate is thus the infinite re-presentation of a universe which '*must* expand to escape the telescopes through which we, who are it, are trying to capture it, which is us' (Spencer-Brown, 1969: 106).

To relate in its fundamental sense is basic to an understanding of process since it tells us that the latent is an ever-present reminder that presence itself is the result of a 'participial act' which is the *enfolded* movement *between* presence and absence, approach and withdrawal. Enfoldment also means that the 'participial act' implies the continuous crossing of the gaps and intervals that constitute the undivided wholeness of 'constitutive negativity' and which reveals the forever partial nature of human being in its continuous and infinite work of coming-to-presence. The human agent is never itself but is always a part that implies something other than itself; it is always *between* things and in this basic existential sense is neither one thing nor another and hence is a moving part of the 'participial act' that is always trying to locate and identify itself out of the undifferentiated, pre-original ground of things. The 'participial act' is the unfolding of parts that are intrinsically enfolded in each other and are thus 'tokens or expressions' of a pre-original ground that is destined to 'elude itself' in a perpetual withdrawal from conscious, and hence partial, representation (Spencer-Brown, 1969: 105).

The pre-original ground of things is the undivided wholeness that is the original source of things as divided parts. The act of division is grounded in the undivided or undifferentiated wholeness that supplements the continuous coming-to-presence of parts. Thing and ground, division and undivision, are counterchanges or mutual versions of each other: 'Each is both prior to the other and later than it, causer and caused, inside it and outside it at once' (Miller, 1995: 21). Parts are thus always enfolded parts of each other in an undifferentiated origin or ground which tells us that parts as divided forms are still also undivided: the causer not only causes the caused but the caused also causes the causer; likewise, inside and outside cause each other in a mutual relationship that is grounded in undivision and undifferentiation so that they are both simultaneously inside and outside each other in an inside-out that is also an outside-in. Parts in this sense again exemplify the enfolded and interactive nature of the 'participial act' before it is read as an act of unfoldment and division. The intrinsic mutuality of division and undivision is basic to the 'participial act' as an act of relating. The latent is the undifferentiated negativity of undivided wholeness that is also the 'constitutive negativity' of all relating as infinite movement. This means that we not only relate the world as a receptacle of readable forms and objects but also as an undivided, infinite latency from which we extract readily read-able forms: positive and negative, presence and absence, constitute each other in a 'sentient continuity' of unfoldment-enfoldment.

Process is the relating of the *event* as a coming-to-presence or unfolding of the latent. The latent in this sense is a suspended negative ground which, like undivision and undif-ferentiation, emerges out of acts of division and differentiation. Relating thus relates the latent as a coming-to-presence that never finally comes but is always deferred or postponed so that presence and absence supplement each other in a *holomovement* of crossings between the gaps and intervals of undivided wholeness. This is process as betweenness which means that individualized terms such as words are never indepen-dently meaningful but draw their significance from the 'constitutive negativity' that lies *between* and *beyond* them. Betweenness thus implies that interaction is basically neither one thing nor the other but an enfolded ambiguity that continually withdraws from dif-ferentiation and specific locatability. Some sense of betweenness as enfolded ambiguity appears in the relativity and quantum theories of modern science where, for example, the scientist can no longer be understood as an independent and thus differentiated observer of his or her subject matter: 'Rather, both observer and observed are merging and interpenetrating aspects of one whole reality, which is indivisible and unanalysable' (Bohm, 1980: 9).

Like the 'tokens or expressions' and 'existential precursors' of a universe that refuses to reveal itself, the scientist's findings are essentially transient indicators of a reality that 'will always partially elude itself' (Spencer-Brown, 1969: 104, 105). In this sense, science and its findings are constituted by what they are *not*, that is, by a 'constitutive negativity' that at best only implies itself in an enfolded ambi-guity which always withdraws from explicit unfoldment. Modern science such as quantum theory views reality as an implicit process that is ultimately unknow-able and unidentifiable, and which can make itself explicit only through 'tokens or expressions' (Bohm, 1980: 48–64). Implicit process reminds us of the 'participial act' which finds its source in the flux and flow of undivided wholeness and undif-ferentiation that resists conscious distinction. This, again, is how we may under-stand process as the work of relating parts and wholes and their implicit latency. Objects are never discrete things but unfolded versions of acts of participation or enfolded, deferred relationships between the body and its world such as we see in the example of the spoon whose handle is a converse of the clenched hand and whose bowl is a converse of the mouth (Fisher, 1991: 243–4). Objects now have to be interpreted as unfolded and enfolded conversions of each other in a continuous interweaving of betweenness and inter-action so that the object is a moving part of an undivided or implicit whole that resists explicit reification. As unfolded parts, objects constitute the flux and flow of holomovement in a process of projecting a 'higher-dimensional actuality' which always withdraws from direct, explicit representation (Bohm, 1980: 207–13). Process and reality as 'tokens or expres-sions' thus find their origins in a pre-original ground of undivided wholeness and undifferentiation.

36.3 PROCESS AND DIVISION

Enfoldment also means that the pre-original ground of undivided wholeness is revealed by its division into parts. In this sense, parts and wholes engender each other in a creative betweenness or enfoldment. In this context, division is the *di-vision* of dual perception such as we see in process as the continuous movement of approach and withdrawal and in the 'participial act' where the world cuts itself in two in order to see itself as part and whole (Spencer-Brown, 1969: 105). The two-ness or duality of di-vision is an act of severance which reveals the undivided wholeness of the world as a series of forever receding gaps or intervals that remind us of the enfolded, implicit nature of reality which forever withdraws from explicit expression. Di-vision now appears as a state of active suspension between approach and withdrawal, between the explicit and the implicit. Process is the continuous translation of the latent mutability of matter into the meaningful signs and symbols of human agency whose existential task is the continuous creation of a world that is constantly visible to us. But this visibility necessarily depends on its deferral of the invisible, so that process is the infinite suspension of the visible *and* the invisible in the continuous work of di-vision.

This is how the modern science of quantum physics interprets the scientist's relationship with the raw matter of the world as an implicit, enfolded order that defies explicit understanding. The implicit is also the undivided wholeness which exists independently of its division into parts and which serves as the negative 'pre-original ground' of the ground of things. The negative ground of things is the invisible and infinite receptacle that is forever ready to receive and to record all our impressions and interpretations of the world. In this sense, the implicit is a mutable field that is intrinsically unlocatable and which can only be approached indirectly through our various methods of representation. Mutability in this sense is the main message of quantum physics which tells us that the world of nature is intrinsically ungraspable and that what we observe as a so-called scientific fact is essentially a product of the experimental method and its techniques of observation: 'what answer we get depends on the question we put, the experiment we arrange, the registering device we choose. We are inescapably involved in bringing about that which appears to be happening' (Wheeler, 1983: 185). Observer and observed produce each other as a 'participial act' in which the scientific product is a form of catachresis, the attribution of a name, a word, to a condition that is essentially unnameable and inarticulable. This means that the undifferentiation of undivided wholeness is mute as well as mutable; it is intrinsically unknowable and invisible, serving as an implicit ground that 'can only change its form or nature' in the work of continuous mutability (Kaplan, 1999: 59).

Here again we note that reality is a mutable source which we reveal as 'tokens or expressions' of a primal force that forever recedes from our conscious attempts to *know* it. Process in this sense has no specific end but is the continuous regeneration of itself as pure action such as we see in the 'sentient continuity' and 'shared alteration' of the human body and its world. This is not so much a world of specific things or objects but the more general process of relating the world as an implicit or enfolded source in the 'participial acts' that keep human life forever on the move. The human act rather than the precise form of thing or object now has to be understood as the moving force of process. Division divides undivision into marked and unmarked spaces. The unmarked spaces serve as negative ground for the positive marks for which they also serve as crossings. Division in this context is also the betweenness that both connects and disconnects the specific parts of conscious being. The unmarked spaces between the letters and words of a sentence, for example, express division as the missing ground that sources all conscious movement. Here, the missing ground of positive things is the undifferentiation of undivided wholeness which is disclosed by the differentiation of division, just as sounds make mute silence emerge as a necessary missing ground of being. Division and undivision, sound and silence, create and reveal each other in a movement of existential crossing which both *crosses out* and *crosses over* the unmarked spaces of betweenness.

Division as a fundamental act of crossing invites us to interpret process as the crossing or bridging of forms so that the betweenness of division reminds us again that we relate and re-present the world as a series of 'participial acts' which imply that process is the continuous creating and revealing of the human world rather than its simple representation of objective forms and structures. This means that objects are no longer to be understood as independent objective forms but are materialized acts of participation in which body and earth construct each other. This is a way of defining the human world as a 'field of transformations' in which objects are no longer discrete forms but are active 'trans-forms' or crossings of each other (Bryson, 1988: 97). The trans-form is a recursive representation of the 'participial act' in which body and earth reflect each other just as the spoon reflects the bodily act of eating in its bowl and handle (Fisher, 1991: 243–4). Objects are thus constituted by what they are not in a mutable field of 'constitutive negativity' which recalls the covert latency of relating as a fundamental 'participial act' which divides the world into parts and infinite wholeness as well as the crossings and bridgings that this implies. Since parts are always and forever partial, they too reflect themselves as provisional contents of the invisible and infinite receptacle of wholeness as a 'constitutive negativity' which is always dispersed and deferred in a state of permanent suspension. Process in this sense is a suspended condition of being that is latent and thus always yet-to-come.

Process is also a condition of suspended division between the implicit and the explicit, between the latent and what has yet to be expressed in meaningful, specific terms. Parts are the basis of this suspended act of translation of wholeness as an invisible and infinite receptacle into the visible and explicit objects and structures that constitute the human world as a field of identifiable objects and forms. But the 'sentient continuity' of the 'participial act' reminds us that the reading of the world as a field of recognizable and familiar structures has its source in the physical and mental gestures that create the knowable forms of the world. This returns us to our original definition of process as a series of physical and mental gestures that underlie the constitution of readily meaningful, discrete structures. Process is primarily the expression of acts of movement rather than the constitution of specific things. Process reveals reality as the continuous unfolding of the latent and implicit in provisional acts of creating positive presences out of negative absences in the continuous work of approach and withdrawal. This is process as *event* or the basic act of creating forms as provisional appearances rather than objects and structures of an objective reality that is independent of its human participants. Process implies that reality is a humanly *realized* field of events that are continuously constructed and maintained as provisional expressions of an invisible and infinite source that constantly withdraws.

The double sense of di-vision means that division and undivision constitute each other in a primal act of otherness in which, like causer and caused, inside and outside, they are simultaneously before and after each other (Miller, 1995: 21). Division reveals undivision just as undivision reveals division; they constitute each other as mutual acts of creation. This is basic to the idea of process as an infinite series of acts which never complete themselves in the continuous work of approach and withdrawal and which are also simultaneously before and after each other and thus mutual. Mutuality implies that undivision inhabits division as ambiguity in which divided parts are neither one nor the other but imply an undivided wholeness at the root of partial forms. This again reminds us that the 'participial act' has to be understood as the basis of 'shared alteration' between man and his world which also tells us that the *inter-action* between forms is the continuous work of process, so that the *act* of knowing rather than the knowledge itself is what keeps human agency forever on the move (Scarry, 1994).

Di-vision in its primal sense implies that human agency originates in the primal severance of man and earth in which the relationship between the two is a 'shared continuity' and 'shared alteration'. This is inter-action in its most basic sense just as the modern physicist is a 'shared continuity' or interpenetrative part of their subject matter. Di-vision in this existential sense also means that forms and objects are *appearances* constructed out of an undifferentiated or undivided whole. The divisions of di-vision are essentially parts of an interpenetrative or enfolded whole in which they are mutual and mutable and thus constitute each other just as cause and effect, inside and outside, define each other in a fundamental relationship of undifferentiation that also coexists with the differentiation of divisions. In this most basic sense, di-vision is a severance that also implies that parts and wholes are intrinsically mutual and mutable so that mutability has to be considered as a definitive feature of process and human agency. The mutability of di-vision also implies that parts are essentially exchangeable forms which derive their meanings from each other in a dynamic process of crossings in which they supplement each other as mutual forms that are neither one nor the other. Mutability in this sense means that process is primarily the movement of suspension and deferral rather than the capturing of stable structures. Again, this reminds us of the processual significance of 'constitutive negativity' in its emphasis on withdrawal as a motivating force in the 'sentient continuity' of process in which approach and withdrawal, positive and negative, supplement each other.

This is how modern art theory, like quantum physics, interprets the composition of form. Both modern art and quantum theory displace our attention from their products to the mental and gestural acts that created them. The 'participial act' again reminds us that reality is a continuous process of human composition by which the forms and objects of the world are revealed as created products. Modern art theory interprets art as an exemplary 'participial act' in which the art work is never a specific, finite product but a generic expression of process as an act of composition and making. Like quantum theory, modern art reveals the latent as a source of hidden possibilities and hence is the continuous expansion of the world as an infinite potential. In this sense, modern art acknowledges the essential mutability of the world which it reveals as a mute and mutable source that is not so much an undifferentiated, empty space external to the human agent but more like an invisible and infinite receptacle that is ready to accommodate and absorb our varied and variable interpretations (Kaplan, 1999: 59). Modern art thus reveals the world as the negative ground of forms which forever invites us to view it and recreate it as a 'constitutive negativity' that refuses positive representation.

The artist Paul Klee defined the relationship between positive and negative form as two kinds of attention practised by the artist (Ehrenzweig, 1993: 21–31). Klee's analysis returns us to di-vision as a double way of seeing the world of forms. Positive attention focuses on the figure which it extracts from the negative ground; it thus sees the figure as a specific and finite form which has a singular identity. Klee then argues that positive attention neglects its complementary and mutually sourced relationship with the negative ground of positive forms. Positive and negative attention sustain and supplement each other just as cause and effect, inside and outside, are mutual and reciprocal versions or counterchanges of each other. Klee implies that the creative artist recognizes that their work is essentially a 'participial act' in which specific, finite objects and forms have to be understood as transient unfoldings of an implicit, multidimensional complex of which they are simply 'tokens or expressions'. This is process as *event* or the coming-to-presence of forms. This initiation and emergence of forms is exemplified in the paintings of Cézanne in which a landscape, for example, withdraws into the background brushwork and paint that constitute the material base of the represented scene. Klee returns us to a generic or pre-specific stage of human agency in which the composition of forms and objects is still uncertain and subject to ambiguity. Klee's counterchange exemplifies the intrinsic ambiguity of this initiation of form in its mutuality of positive and negative. In order to make this mutuality of form consciously perceptible, the creative artist must *scatter* their attention so as to include all aspects of the perceptual field 'in a single undivided act of attention' (Ehrenzweig, 1993: 24). Scattered attention is a version of process in the sense that it recognizes that the essence of human agency is the continuous work of crossing the gaps and intervals that constitute the betweenness of 'constitutive negativity' in which the *event* of process is a provisional act that never completes itself. Scattered attention also recognizes the intrinsic mutability of process in which forms emerge out of a negative background that both supplements and withdraws from positive identification. Again, we are reminded of the immanence of the mute and mutual as a complex enfolded process that recedes from conscious approach in a playing of 'hide-and-seek with itself' (Spencer-Brown, 1969: 106).

Scattered consciousness foregrounds movement as central to process and its intrinsic mutability. It views movement as the continuous mutation of parts in a flux and flow of division *and* undivision. Klee's view of artistic forms as counterchanges implies that di-vision as a double way of seeing is essentially ambiguous since it means that positive and negative are reciprocal parts of each other. Di-vision means that parts and wholes constitute each other just as cause and effect, inside and outside, imply that the primal act of division is also the primal act of undivision. Di-vision in this sense begins to look like process as the reciprocity of approach and withdrawal. Instead of clear, specific forms, scattered attention invites us to view reality as a 'blurred plasticity' of forms and objects (Ehrenzweig, 1993: 15). This, again, is Klee's counterchange which is ambiguous and 'blurred' because it is both divided and undivided at the same time. Di-vision in this sense is a primal and primitive act of distinction which simultaneously initiates division and undivision, part and whole, as reciprocal and recursive condensations of each other (Spencer-Brown, 1969: 84). This means that forms and objects are never themselves but are mutable reflections of each other in a process of holistic thinking 'in which elements are variable and exchangeable' (Ehrenzweig, 1993: 41). Scattered attention thus seeks to understand the intrinsic mutability that constitutes the essence of process as acts of movement rather than bounded, specific forms and objects.

36.4 THE ACT OF PROCESS

As previously defined, process is a series of acts and events. This means that the recognizable forms and objects of daily life are initially creations of human agency. Klee's scattered attention reminds us that the ready-made forms of life are provisional products of human agency as the continuous and unfinished work of coming-to-presence. Like approach and withdrawal, presence and absence constitute each other as recursive operations that are basic to the composition of reality. Reality is thus never external and independent of the human agent but is both a cause and an effect of the 'sentient continuity' that flows through all aspects of existence as an implicit, primal force. Cézanne's art works illustrate the idea of scattered attention when they remind us that their landscapes emerge out of the physical and mental gestures and the brushwork that constitute the act of painting as the implicit composition that results in our viewing of the landscape as a completed artistic object that is viewable as such. The act of process also reminds us that finite forms and objects are products of acts of work and in this sense are integral parts of human agency as the endless flow of composition. This means that the *product* is always also a *predict* that implies an *event* or a continuous coming-to-presence of forms such as we see in the continuous recursion of process as *approach* and *withdrawal*.

The act (from the Latin *agere*, to put in motion, to keep going) is thus basic to process as the 'sentient continuity' of life and human agency. Cézanne's art works express the *act* of painting rather than the objects depicted. The act of process is basic to the existential constitution of life in the sense that it constitutes the *acts of inter-action* that precede all finite, completed forms and objects. The act of process is the generic work of life that exceeds all specific structures. The act is always an *inter-action* between the human organism and its ground which are essentially parts of each other in a fundamentally enfolded relationship. The act as inter-action recalls the mutability of forms which inter-act with each other in a process of constant exchangeability so that forms and objects are never things in themselves but constitute each other as mutable structures forever on the move such as we see in the holomovement of quantum theory and the mutability of 'constitutive negativity'. This, again, is Klee's counterchange which stresses mutuality as the 'shared alteration' of things in a 'field of transformations' rather than their specificities. This is the essence of the *act* as *inter-act* in which the *inter* informs us that movement is always *between* things and not within the things themselves.

The act as inter-act again draws our attention away from singular, bounded forms and objects to the mutable relationships between them. The act in this context is a 'participial act' in which the human agent is never itself a singular, bounded entity but is always an ambiguous part of the material world with which it inter-acts (Scarry, 1994: 49–90). Human agent and world at this level are constitutive parts of each other so that the 'participial act' as inter-act is an 'interlacing of man and his materials' rather than bounded singularities in productive contact with each other (Scarry, 1994: 58). The act means that man and world merge with each other in an ambiguous mutuality 'so that there ceases to be a clear boundary separating them' (Scarry, 1994: 57). The act thus repeats the ambiguous mutuality of cause and effect and inside and outside which return us to the 'constitutive negativity' at the heart of 'undivided wholeness' and the enfoldment of parts. Again, the emphasis here is on the part that is never itself but always a vehicle for acts of movement in pursuit of an otherness which never fully arrives. The part, as we noted earlier, is the carrier and transmitter of a space that is forever *de-parting* from itself as if suspended in an unreachable limbo of counterchange. The 'participial act' of human agency means that the agent is actively suspended in a double and reversible inter-action between *you* and *me, now* and *then, today* and *tomorrow*. The part of the 'participial act' is thus never a full presence but is mutually defined by its absence. This is the essence of *pro-cess* as *approach* and *withdrawal* in a continuous coming-to-presence that is always on its way somewhere and hence never completes itself. Parts are thus never themselves but constitute a mutable field of 'sentient-intelligent-movable attachments' (Scarry, 1994: 85–6).

This is how process invites us to re-interpret bounded objects as constitutive parts of mutability that imply a presence that is yet to come. Objects may now be understood as 'participial acts' rather than specific forms. An object is now a materialized *act* of participation that is shared between human agent and world. The spoon, for example, materializes the act of eating in its handle which reflects the hand that holds it, while the bowl of the spoon reproduces the space of the mouth; the domestic chair reproduces the shape of the human body as well as a promised reversal of the state of bodily tiredness. Spoon and chair exemplify the reciprocal mutability and exchangeability at the heart of the 'sentient continuity' between man and world. Bounded objects thus lose their sense of structured specificity and become more like moving parts that are also permutable and thus capable of endless combinability and composition: 'objects become restless and weak' and are hence secondary to 'the system as a whole and to the play of transformations and possibilities that it invites (Fisher, 1991: 249). Mutability in this sense returns us to the interpretation of the world's matter as an invisible and infinite receptacle that 'can only change its form or nature' (Kaplan, 1999: 59). Reality now has to be seen as a 'plastic reality' that creatively withdraws from the objectivity of bounded forms and 'in which the elements are variable and exchangeable' (Ehrenzweig, 1993: 14, 41).

Acts of process simply act and as such do not lead to specific goals since, like parts, they fundamentally imply the continuous crossing of gaps and intervals. Objects as parts are to be understood as carriers and transmitters of human agency *between* things which also means that they imply a 'field of transformations' of which they are transitional and provisional 'trans-forms' rather than specifically defined terms. Reality as process now appears as a pliable and plastic field of mutable relations in which fluid and fleeting parts imply an enfolded, multidimensional universe which can only be approached through the 'tokens and expressions' of partial unfoldments. Reality is now interpretable as a permanent state of active suspension between approach and withdrawal. Its negative ground of mutability is like an invisible, infinite receptacle that eludes formal appropriation and can only be indirectly *approached*; it is thus a site of continuous *withdrawal* (Wheeler, 1973). Its mutability means that it defies formal division and analysis, and, like 'undivided wholeness', can only be named through an act of catachresis which makes explicit what is fundamentally implicit and thus covert. Implicit mutability is basic to human agency and its interlacing with the material world as 'sentient continuity'. The human agent has to reflect itself through the world from which it emerges (Spencer-Brown, 1969: 105–6). In other words, it is a partial being that has to make explicit what is implicit in the material world from which it severs itself. More simply, the human agent has to *relate* the negative ground of mutability as 'participial acts'.

Mutability is intrinsically mute in the sense that it has nothing specific to say to us; like an invisible and infinite receptacle, it is open to an infinity of variable interpretations. It is thus a latent source that can never be directly identified but only indirectly approached in a continuous flow of withdrawal. This returns us to the idea of *relating* process as a flow of 'tokens and expresssions' of a 'substratum' which, like the latency of mutability, can never be directly known (Spencer-Brown, 1969: 104). To relate ordinarily means to connect and to express or make explicit. Both these senses are implied by the 'sentient continuity' between the body and its environment. Objects as materialized acts of participation reflect this need of the partial body to know its severed and sentient self as an extension of earth's raw matter. In reaching out beyond itself, the body seeks to explore a generic power that exceeds the specific forms and objects of the practical world (Scarry, 1985). The body's sentience seeks to know itself through its acts of objectification which now remake the body and open it to a space of mutable possibilities. Everyday objects such as newspapers, televisions, radios, motor vehicles, telephones, and computers 'are taken back into the interior of human consciousness where they now reside as part of the mind or soul' (Scarry, 1985: 256). Objects in this sense become 'participial acts' that relate body and world in a 'shared alteration' of 'sentient continuity'. The body thus opens itself to a world that is essentially latent as a source of mutability and infinite possibilities. To relate in this sense is to reveal body and world not as a field of specific forms and objects but as shared parts of a generic field of 'constitutive negativity' which continually relates and remakes its human contents out of a latent source of creative withdrawal. Relating in this context is the expression of an invisible and infinite substratum that sources human agency in its continuous work of reconstructing reality as the generic and recursive alternation between approach and withdrawal.

Relating the latent also returns us to the essence of process as the coming-to-presence of forms that never complete themselves. The latent is thus always yet-to-be in a state of continuously suspended movement as if to keep human agency forever on the move. To relate thus means the continuous repetition of latency as 'constitutive negativity' or withdrawal. The human agent is a dispersed and provisional part of a whole whose mutability is destined to remain mute while also calling to us to relate it as the seemingly explicit 'tokens and expressions' of an implicit substratum or sub-reality that refuses explicit definition. Process in this context is the ever-active mutuality and reciprocation of approach and withdrawal, presence and absence, being and not-yet-being.

References

Bersani, L. (1986). *The Freudian Body: Psychoanalysis and Art* (New York: Columbia University Press).

—— and Dutoit, U. (1993). *Arts of Impoverishment: Beckett, Rothko, Resnais* (Cambridge, MA: Harvard University Press).

Bohm, D. (1980). *Wholeness and the Implicate Order* (London: Routledge & Kegan Paul).

Bryson, N. (1988). The Gaze in the Expanded Field', in H. Foster (ed.), *Vision and Visuality* (Seattle, WA: Bay Press): 87–108.

Ehrenzweig, A. (1993). *The Hidden Order of Art: a Study in the Psychology of Artistic Imagination* (London: Weidenfeld & Nicolson).

Fisher, P. (1991). *Making and Effacing Art: Modern American Art in a Culture of Museums* (New York: Oxford University Press).

Kaplan, R. (1999). *The Nothing That Is: A Natural History of Zero* (London: Allen Lane/ The Penguin Press).

Levinas, E. (1969). *Totality and Infinity: an Essay on Exteriority*, trans. A. Lingis (Pittsburgh, PA: Duquesne University Press).

Luhmann, N. (2000). *The Reality of the Mass Media* (Stanford: Stanford University Press).

Miller, J.H. (1992). *Illustration* (London: Reaktion Books).

——(1995). *Topographies* (Stanford, CA: Stanford University Press).

Scarry, E. (1985). *The Body in Pain: the Making and Unmaking of the World* (New York: Oxford University Press).

——(1994). *Resisting Representation* (New York: Oxford University Press).

Spencer-Brown, G. (1969). *Laws of Form* (London: Allen & Unwin).

Wheeler, J.A. (1973). From Relativity to Mutability, in J. Mehra (ed.), *The Physicist's Conception of Nature* (Dordrecht: Reidel): 202–47.

——(1983). Law without Law, in J.A. Wheeler and W.H. Zurek (eds), *Quantum Theory and Measurement* (Princeton, NJ: Princeton University Press): 182–213.

Whitehead, A.N. (1929). *Process and Reality: An Essay in Cosmology* (Cambridge: Cambridge University Press).

Index

Page references to footnotes will be followed by the letter 'n'.

Lightning Source UK Ltd.
Milton Keynes UK
UKOW05f1009300316

271165UK00002B/4/P